And So to Bed:
A Bibliography of Diaries Published in English

by
Patricia Pate Havlice

The Scarecrow Press, Inc.
Metuchen, N.J., & London
1987

Library of Congress Cataloging-in-Publication Data

Havlice, Patricia Pate.
   And so to bed.

   Bibliography: p.
   Includes indexes.
   1. Diaries--Bibliography. 2. Bibliography--
Bibliography--Diaries. 3. Diaries--Book reviews--
Bibliography. 4. Matthews, William, 1905-   .
American diaries in manuscript, 1580-1954--Indexes.
5. Matthews, William, 1905-   . British diaries--
Indexes. 6. Matthews, William, 1905-   .
Canadian diaries and autobiographies--Indexes.
I. Title.
Z5301.H38 **1987** [CT25]   016.92   86-13738
ISBN 0-8108-1923-6

Manufactured in the United States of America

CONTENTS

PREFACE

I began this bibliography out of frustration with William Matthews' diary compilations and hope it allays that feeling in others.

While working in libraries on my World Painting Index, it was my habit to stretch my legs by strolling the nearby stacks. I wandered one day into the American Civil War history section and noticed Brokenburn. Was this an obscure battle? I picked up the volume and from the preface learned that Brokenburn was a Louisiana plantation. The book was the diary of a young southern woman, written with grace and better plotted than many a novel. Having greatly enjoyed reading it, I sought other published Civil War diaries.

That brought me to William Matthews and his American Diaries. His bibliography ended when the Civil War began, his courage having flagged when confronted by a mountain of military and civilian publications. I studied his other bibliographies, British Diaries and Canadian Diaries and Autobiographies. Deciding to start where he stopped, I set about working out my own criteria for a bibliography of published diaries. And So to Bed is the result.

The majority of the diaries annotated here were written or translated into English and published as books, chapters in books, or journal articles. Also included are microform publications and dissertations because of their wide dissemination in today's world. There is no limitation on the nationality of the diarist or the time period covered. The material must only have been published in English. I did not repeat Matthews' listings except in a couple of instances when I felt he did not make the full import of the diary clear.

To simplify my task, I constructed an index to his three

v

volumes. In doing that I discovered some people appeared in more than one of the bibliographies. Others turned up, due to his criteria, in the "wrong" bibliography. I'd sought Alice James, sister of American novelist Henry, in American Diaries. She appeared instead in British Diaries because she was living in England at the time she wrote.

It seemed that this information would be helpful to readers of this book. I have indicated by a bracketted note after the diarist's name and dates where the user can find earlier editions of diaries not noted here. Thus, "[A213]" guides one to page 213 of American Diaries; a bracketted B stands for British Diaries; C for Canadian Diaries and Autobiographies.

Users of this volume can also learn if a diarist I omitted appears in one of Matthews' bibliographies. A separate index to all the diarists he annotated follows in one interfiled list the Index of Diarists in And So to Bed.

And So to Bed is arranged chronologically with all diaries begun in a given year alphabetized by the diarist's surname. Anonymous diaries, some with suggested attributions, precede those for which authorship is firmly established. I filed each diarist under the date of his/her first diary entry, noting also the closing date. When my dates do not coincide with the book or article title, it is because additional material, usually letters, appears. Omissions in the diarist's coverage are explained.

The inclusive dates for which the diary was kept are noted on a separate line below the diarist's name and before the annotation except where that information appears in the title of the diary.

Entries for those who kept several diaries covering different time periods are arranged with the earliest diary first, the editions and excerpts being numbered. Excerpts, most with no inclusive dates noted, are listed last. On occasion a news item turned up which I thought might be of interest. See, for example, the Thomas Merton or Che Guevara entries.

Reviews of some book-length diaries are noted after the annotation. The listing is by no means exhaustive but indicates what was found during the compilation of my working bibliography.

I examined each of the books or articles listed here. Because copies of some of the dissertations were unobtainable by deadline time, I wrote an annotation based on the material in volumes of <u>Dissertation Abstracts</u>. The abstract citations are noted for all dissertations.

I compiled the bibliography by searching title and subject entries in <u>American Book Publishing Record</u>, <u>Book Review Index</u>, <u>Book Review Digest</u>, <u>An Index to Book Reviews in the Humanities</u>, <u>America: History and Life</u>, <u>Historical Abstracts</u>, <u>Writings on American History</u>, <u>Cumulative Book Index</u>, <u>British National Bibliography</u>, <u>Readers' Guide to Periodical Literature</u>, <u>Social Sciences Index</u>, <u>Humanities Index</u>, <u>Writings on British History</u>, and several subject bibliographies. Though this turned up many duplicate titles, it also provided information on British and American editions of the same diary with different titles and on reprints and revisions.

The General Index (authors, editors, book titles, and subjects) is an attempt to guide the user to areas of interest when material about a particular diarist is not of prime importance. Diarists of a certain nationality, age group, religious persuasion, or occupation can be located by consulting the index; travel, political, letter, military, and literary diaries are subject headings; geographical entries are another large grouping.

I did not index every book title, only those which were unique. I omitted from the index those which began <u>Diary of ...</u> or <u>Journal of ...</u> followed by the person's name. Thus <u>Diary of Richard Cocks</u> can be found by consulting the Index of Diarists but <u>Chronicle of Colonial Lima</u> merits an entry in the General Index.

The annotations vary in length and are patterned on Matthews'. Notes on nationality, occupation, and place of residence seemed to me of greatest import to the user. I tried to make concrete remarks about the content while conveying something of the flavor of the diarist's style.

ACKNOWLEDGMENTS

I owe thanks to many people across the country whose names I don't even know. This bibliography could not have been completed without the help of interlibrary loan librarians and clerks who answered my requests for obscure titles and hot items. The Bracewell Branch of Houston Public Library and the University of Houston/Clear Lake handled hundreds of these requests and I am in their debt. I thank Patricia J. Garrett, Gay Carter, Deirdre Becker, Rebecca Christman, and Aimee Patterson for getting books, pointing out titles I might have missed, and keeping me afloat through some personally stormy times.

I did much of the work at the University of Houston/ University Park, Rice University, and the University of Texas at Austin. I am grateful to the libraries of these institutions for providing good collections and helpful staff which made my work more enjoyable.

BIBLIOGRAPHY OF BIBLIOGRAPHIES

1. BAGLEY, John Joseph. <u>Lancashire Diarists: Three Centuries of Lancashire Lives</u>. London: Phillimore, 1975.
Bagley includes those who wrote letters and autobiographies in his definition of diarists. He extracts the diaries of Nicholas Assheton, Henry Newcombe, two Roman Catholic squires, a weaver and a yeoman farmer from the seventeenth to the nineteenth centuries.

2. BEGOS, Jane DuPree. <u>Annotated Bibliography of Published Women's Diaries</u>. Pound Ridge, N.Y.: Begos, 1977.
This work is divided into eight types of material: anthologies, general works, fiction, poetry, calendars, almanacks and yearbooks, diaries and journals. Many of the entries are really memoirs. Some foreign language material is included. Annotations of one or two sentences accompany most entries. She lists "works that call themselves diaries and aren't; works that don't call themselves diaries and are."

3. BITTON, Davis. <u>Guide to Mormon Diaries and Autobiographies</u>. Provo, Utah: Brigham Young University Press, 1977.
This compilation includes published and unpublished material and was compiled by searching large collections of Mormon material. Each of the 2,894 entries is explained by an abstract or annotation of its contents.
> REVIEW: <u>Utah Historical Quarterly</u>, v. 46, pp. 322-24, Summer, 1978.

4. BOWRING, R. "Japanese Diaries and the Nature of Literature," <u>Comparative Literature Studies</u>, v. 18, pp. 167-74, June, 1981.
A general article on Japanese diaries.

5. DI SPALDO, Nick. "Prison Diarist's Coming of Age," <u>America</u>, v. 132, pp. 30-32, January 18, 1975.
The writer explains how he kept a diary while in prison and mentions other prison diaries.

6. D'OYLEY, Elizabeth. <u>English Diaries</u>. reprint London: Edward Arnold, 1930.
A bibliography of diary excerpts. See names of individual diarists.

7. FOLEY, Charles. "Those Phony Mussolini Diaries," <u>Atlas</u>, v. 15, pp. 46, 48, May, 1968.
Recounts the forging of the diaries by two Italian women.

8. FORBES, Harriette Merrifield. New England Diaries, 1602-1800:
    A Descriptive Catalogue of Diaries, Orderly Books and Sea Jour-
    nals. Topsfield, Mass.: 1923; reprinted New York: Russell
    and Russell, 1967.
       These diaries were "kept by a resident of New England at home
    or abroad, or by the stranger who comes ... and wrote his exper-
    iences and impressions." Diaries begun after 1800 are excluded.
    Manuscripts and published accounts are arranged alphabetically by
    diarist. Index of proper names.

9. FOTHERGILL, R.A. Private Chronicles: A Study of English
    Diaries. New York: Oxford, 1974.
       The writer considers the diary as literature and examines how a
    person's writings project a self-image. There is detailed criticism
    and descriptions of Pepys, Sir Walter Scott, Byron, Katherine Mans-
    field, Boswell, Benjamin Robert Haydon, Anaïs Nin and others.
       REVIEW: Book Review Digest 1975, p. 428.

10. FREIDEL, Frank. "Are There Too Many New Deal Diaries?"
    American Heritage, v. 6, pp. 109-12, April, 1955.
       The article considers more memoirs than diaries.

11. GREW, E. M. "Some Obscure English Diarists and Their Music,"
    Musical Quarterly, v. 16, pp. 314-21, July, 1930.
       Excerpts from the diaries of Sir Justinian Isham, Anthony Wood,
    James Woodforde, and Lt. Col. Peter Hawkes on the music they played
    and heard.

12. JONES, Katharine M., ed. Heroines of Dixie; Confederate
    Women Tell Their Story of the War. New York: Bobbs, Mer-
    rill, 1955.
       Excerpts from the diaries and letters of Southern women are ar-
    ranged in chronological order. Bibliography, index and photos.

13. KAGLE, Steven E. American Diary Literature 1620-1799. Bos-
    ton: Twayne, 1979.
       Kagle sees diaries as a form of autobiography; "a good diarist
    creates a distinct identity for his diary." He describes the diary
    tradition in America and divides the literature into five categories:
    spiritual journals, travel diaries, diaries of romance and courtship,
    war diaries, and life diaries.

14. LIFSHIN, Lyn. Ariadne's Thread: A Collection of Contemporary
    Women's Journals. New York: Harper and Row, 1982.
       Lifshin collected these excerpts from the writers themselves.
    Some had material on hand which she learned of through friends.
    Others kept diaries especially for this publication. Lifshin edited
    the material, trying to keep the spirit of the diarist's intent. Work,
    self, love and friendship, family, being somewhere else, society and
    nature are the themes. Over fifty women contributed. A biograph-
    ical sketch of each writer precedes her diary.

15. LOEHR, Rodney C. "Some Sources for Northwest History:
     Minnesota Farmers' Diaries," Minnesota History, v. 18, pp. 284-
     97, September, 1937.
     Loehr's bibliographic essay is limited to diaries of southern Min-
nesota. Weather, tools, prices, social life and politics are the chief
topics. Little mention is made of farmers' wives and/or their work.

16. MATTHEWS, William. "Diary: A Neglected Genre," Sewanee
     Review, v. 85, pp. 286-300, Spring, 1977.
     An essay in which the writer generalizes "upon human nature
and writing ... reflected in diaries" and lays down nine command-
ments of diary writing.

17. MICHIGAN. University, Ann Arbor. Michigan Historical Col-
     lections. Michigan Men in the Civil War by Ida C. Brown.
     Historical Collections Bulletin, no. 9, 1959, pp. 11-32. Sup-
     plement, 1960.
         A descriptive bibliography of manuscript diaries and letters
arranged by the name of the diarist.

18. O'BRIEN, Kate. "English Diaries and Journals," in: Walter J.
     Turner, ed. Romance of English Literature. New York: Hast-
     ings House, 1944; pp. 185-226.
     O'Brien believes "the best English diaries have been written by
bores" and defines a bore as "a person who mentions everything."

19. PIETTE, Charles, J. G., OFM. "The Diaries of Early California,
     1769-1784," Americas, v. 2, pp. 409-22, April, 1946.
     A bibliography of land and sea diaries in order of their opening
date.

20. PONSONBY, Arthur. British Diarists. reprint Folcroft Library
     Editions, 1974.
     Ponsonby has compiled a bibliographic essay on diaries classified
by type: historical, travel, sport, religious, social, and domestic.
There are chapters on diaries of women and children and a list of the
best diarists.

21. WEYGANDT, Ann M. "New England Colonial Diaries," Delaware
     Notes, v. 21, pp. 37-58, 1948.
     The writer covers the diaries of Sewall, Mather, Mary Rowland-
son and others. Short bibliography.

22. WILLIAMS, Ora G. "Muskets and Magnolias: Four Civil War
     Diaries by Louisiana Girls," Louisiana Studies, v. 4, no. 3,
     pp. 187-97, 1965.
     Williams discusses Kate Stone's Brokenburn, Sarah Morgan Daw-
son's A Confederate Girl's Diary, Julia Le Grand's Journal and the
manuscript diary of Coralie Buard, a native of Natchitoches.

23. WILLY, Margaret. Three Women Diarists: Celia Fiennes, Dorothy

Wordsworth, Katherine Mansfield. London: Longmans, 1964.
   A pamphlet of criticism which includes extracts from the three
diaries.

BIBLIOGRAPHY OF DIARIES

838

24. ENNIN (793/4-864)
    July 8, 838-January 23, 848
    Travel diary; Japanese Buddhist monk lived and traveled in
China; panoramic picture of ninth-century China; food, travel modes
and conditions, customs.
    • Ennin. Diary: The Record of a Pilgrimage to China in
    Search of the Law. Edwin O. Reischauer, trans. New York:
    Ronald Press, 1955; revision of Reischauer's 1939 Harvard dis-
    sertation, "Ennin's Diary of His Travels in Tang China 838-847."

900

25. SEI SHONAGON (963/67-1013?)
    Personal diary; undated excerpts; Japanese poet and novelist.
    • "Diary Excerpts," in: Mary Jane Moffat and Charlotte Painter,
    eds. Revelations: Diaries of Women. New York: Random House,
    1974.

935

26. KI, Tsurayuki (fl. 872-946)
    January 28-March 23, 935
    1. Travel diary; court nobleman traveled from Shikoku to his
home in Kyoto by boat; elegant style with touches of humor.
    • The Tosa Diary. William N. Porter, trans. New York: AMS
Press, 1976; reprint of 1912 London edition.

    2. Dunaway, Philip, and Mel Evans, eds. A Treasury of the
World's Great Diaries. New York: Doubleday, 1957; pp. 173-177.

1045

27. NASIR KHUSRAU (1003-72?)
    1045-1052
    Travel diary; Persian poet went from Balkh to Cairo via Jeru-
salem; returned through Mecca, Basra and Fars province.
    • "The Safar Namih (Travel Journal) of the Persian Nasir

Khusrau (A.D. 1003-1072?). Translated into English with an
Introduction and Notes." Mandana Nakhai, trans. Ph.D., University of Tennessee, 1979. (Dissertation Abstracts 40/09A p.
5065).

1405

28. ANONYMOUS
Public diary: a citizen of Paris, probably middle-class, perhaps
connected with the Sorbonne, recorded historic events; Anglo-French
conflict; siege of Orleans; Joan of Arc; material on prices, epidemics,
food, social and political history.
- A Parisian Journal, 1405-1449. Janet Shirley, trans. Oxford:
Clarendon Press, 1968.

1450

29. LANDUCCI, Luca (1436?-1516)
October 15, 1450-December 22, 1542
Personal and public diary; follower of Savonarola ran an apothe-
cary in Florence; noted events in his own and family's life; much
about public and daily life occurring in the city; continuation probably penned by a son; interesting portrait of everyday life in the
fifteenth and sixteenth centuries.
- A Florentine Diary from 1450 to 1516 ... Continued by an
Anonymous Writer Till 1542 with Notes by Iodoco del Badia.
Alice de Rosen Jervis, trans. New York: Dutton, 1927; reprinted New York: Arno Press, 1969.

1453

30. BARBARO, Nicolò
April 5-May 29, 1453
Personal diary; military and naval movements; little about the
common people involved.
- Nicolò Barbaro Diary of the Siege of Constantinople 1453.
J. R. Jones, trans. New York: Exposition Press, 1969.

1487

31. CH'OE, Pu (1454-1504)
October 3, 1487-1488
Personal diary; Korean official caught at sea in a storm reached
the coast of China and was arrested; Confucian of scholarly rank;
escorted to Peking where he won his release; life in fifteenth-century
China.
- Diary; A Record of Drifting Across the Sea. John Meskill,

trans. Tucson: University of Arizona Press for the Association
for Asian Studies, 1965.

1492

32. COLUMBUS, Christopher (1451-1506)
   1. August 3, 1492-February 15, 1493; Personal and travel diary;
sailing conditions, weather; deliberately misstated number of leagues
traveled in official log and gives the correct total in this record;
landing in Cuba; encounters with Indians; return to Spain; flora and
fauna observed; good reflection of his high expectations and barely
expressed fears.
   • Journal of First Voyage to America. Introduction by Van
   Wyck Brooks. Freeport, N.Y.: Books for Libraries, 1971; reprint of 1924 ed.
   • The Journal of Christopher Columbus. Cecil Jane, trans.
   Rev. and annotated by L.A. Vigneras. Appendix by R. A.
   Skelton. London: Blond, 1960. Based on the de Lollis
   and Paz 1892 transcription.
   • The Journal of Christopher Columbus (During His First Voy-
   age, 1492-93). Clements R. Markham, trans. London: Hakluyt
   Society, 1893; New York: Burt Franklin, 1970.

   2. August 3, 1492-March 15, 1493; May 30-August 31, 1498;
Exploration journal; discovery of the New World; third voyage and
discovery of South America; second and fourth voyages of Columbus
are in others' words and documents.
   • Journals and Other Documents on the Life and Voyages of
   Christopher Columbus. Samuel Eliot Morison, ed. and trans.
   New York: Heritage, 1963.

1497

33. ANONYMOUS
   July 8, 1497-April 25, 1499
   Travel diary; thought to have been written by either Alvaro
Velho or João da Sá; accompanied da Gama on his first voyage to
India; stops at African ports; simply written with much concern for
the religious faith of those met along the way.
   • A Journal of the First Voyage of Vasco da Gama, 1497-1499.
   E. G. Ravenstein, ed. and trans. London: Hakluyt Society,
   1898; reprinted New York: Burt Franklin, 1963.

34. GAMA, Vasco da (1469?-1524)
   July 8, 1497-April 25, 1499
   Exploration diary; from Lisbon around the Cape of Good Hope
to Calicut.
   • Journal of the First Voyage of Vasco da Gama 1497-1499. E.
   G. Ravenstein, trans. and ed. London: Hakluyt Society, 1898;
   New York: Burt Franklin, 1963.

1519

35. PIGAFETTA, Antonio (1480/91-1534?)
     August 10, 1519-September 18, 1522
     Exploration diary; Italian civilian accompanied Magellan on his
     circumnavigation of the world; this English version is translated from
     the 1525 Paris edition; very interesting.
     • The Voyage of Magellan: The Journal of Antonio Pigafetta.
     Paula Spurlin Paige, trans. Englewood Cliffs, N.J.: Prentice-
     Hall, 1969.

1520

36. DÜRER, Albrecht (1471-1528)
     July 12, 1520-July 15, 1521
     Travel diary; Dürer's trip to the Netherlands to obtain a pen-
     sion from Emperor Charles V; expenses, sale of his engravings; the
     art world of his time.
     • Diary of His Journey to the Netherlands, 1520-1521. William
     Conway, trans. Greenwich, Conn.: New York Graphic Society,
     1971.
         REVIEW: Book Review Digest 1972, p. 360.

1521

37. WRIOTHESLEY, Charles (1508-61)
     May 17, 1521-September 5, 1559
     Public diary; excerpts; Londoner who held the office of Windsor
     herald from the reigns of Henry VIII to Elizabeth I; notice of public
     events.
     • "The Chronicle of Charles Wriothesley," in: Elizabeth D'Oyley,
     ed. English Diaries. London: Edward Arnold, 1930; pp. 17-30.

1544

38. TORRE, Tomás de la
     January 12, 1544-March 12, 1545
     Sea diary; across the Atlantic to New Spain; Mayas at Campeche;
     detailed picture of travel conditions and life in the sixteenth century
     by a keen observer with a sense of humor.
     • "Travelling in 1544: From Salamanca, Spain, to Ciudad Real,
     Chiapas, Mexico: The Travels and Trials of Bishop Bartolomé
     de las Casas and his Dominican Fathers," F. Blom, ed. Sewanee
     Review, v. 81, pp. 429-569, September, 1973.

1549

39. GOUBERVILLE, Gilles, Sire de (1521-1578)

1549-1562
Household journal; births, marriages, deaths, accounts, invest-
ments in a Norman chateau; extracts of entries are bridged by edi-
tor's explanations.
  • Fedden, Katharine. Manor Life in Old France: From the
  Journal of the Sire de Gouberville for the Years 1549-1562. New
  York: Columbia University Press, 1933.

1551

40. MACHYN, Henry (1496?-1563?) [B2]
    July 6, 1551-February 18, 1559
    Public diary; London undertaker describes funerals and public
punishments.
  • "The Diary of Henry Machyn," in: Elizabeth D'Oyley, ed.
  English Diaries. London: Edward Arnold, 1930; pp. 31-42.

1590

41. CASTAÑO DE SOSA, Gaspar
    July 27, 1590-March 11, 1591
    Exploration diary; Portuguese led an expedition to colonize
present-day New Mexico; battle with Apaches; may have been written by Andres Pérez; from Rio Grande to Pecos Pueblo and return;
much about Indians and landscape along the way.
  • A Colony on the Move: Gaspar Castaño de Sosa's Journal,
  1590-1591. Annotations by Albert H. Schroeder. Dan S. Mat-
  son, trans. Santa Fe, N.M.: School of American Research, 1965.

1591

42. HENSLOWE, Philip (-1616) [B5]
    1. February, 1591-November 5, 1597; Business diary; daily re-
ceipts, expenditures, payments and miscellaneous notes dealing with
his theatres.
  • Henslowe's Diary. R. A. Foakes and R. T. Rickert, eds.
  Cambridge: Cambridge University Press, 1961.

    2. 1592-1603; not a transcription, but a guide and financial ac-
count of his life.
  • Chillington, Carol Anne. Philip Henslowe and His "Diary."
  Ph.D., University of Michigan, 1979. (Dissertation Abstracts
  40/02A p. 867)

1594

43. LASSOTA VON STEBLAU, Erich (1550?-1616)
    January 14-August 24, 1594

Diplomatic and travel diary; native of Upper Silesia visited the
Ukrainian Cossacks on a mission for Emperor Rudolf II; through Bo-
hemia, Moravia and Poland; detailed description of Kiev.
  • Habsburgs and Zaporozhian Cossacks: The Diary of Erich
  Lassota von Steblau 1594. Lubomyr R. Wynar, ed. Orest Sub-
  telny, trans. Littleton, Colo.: Ukrainian Academic Press, 1975.

1597

44. MAISSE, André Hurault, Sieur de (1539-1607)
    1. November 24, 1597-January 19, 1598 (Old Style); Diplomatic
    diary; ambassador from Henri IV of France to Elizabeth I of England
    during the war with Spain; some good description of England and the
    Queen.
      • The Journal of All That Was Accomplished by M. de Maisse.
      G. B. Harrison, trans. London: Nonesuch Press, 1931.

    2. "Diary Excerpts," in: Philip Dunaway and Mel Evans, eds.
    A Treasury of the World's Great Diaries. New York: Doubleday,
    1957; pp. 359-363.

1600

45. BRTNICKY Z VALDSSTEJNA, Zdenek (1581-1623)
    June 25-August 6, 1600
    Travel diary; written up from earlier notes; Czech nobleman's
    son toured Cambridge, Oxford, Windsor and London; audience with
    Queen Elizabeth I; stops at royal estates; extensive notes and illus-
    trations add to the interesting text.
      • The Diary of Baron Waldstein: A Traveller in Elizabethan
      England. G. W. Groos, trans. London: Thames & Hudson,
      1981.
      REVIEW: Book Review Index 1981, p. 577.

1602

46. MANNINGHAM, John (1575?-1622) [B7]
    March 29, 1602-April 14, 1603
    Social diary; witty, gossipy patchwork of notes and observations
    on people of the era; references to seeing Twelfth Night performed;
    Donne's poetry; sermons heard.
      • The Diary of John Manningham of the Middle Temple, 1602-
      1603: Newly Edited with an Introduction by Robert Parker Sor-
      lien. Hanover, N.H.: University Press of New England, 1976.
      REVIEWS: Book Review Index 1977, p. 287; 1978, p. 318.
      Book Review Digest 1977, p. 870.

1604

47. ESCOBAR, Fray Francisco de
     October, 1604-
     Exploration diary; undated; footnotes compare this account with
that of Zarates' diary of the trip along the California coast.
     • "Father Escobar's Relations of the Oñate Expedition to Cal-
     ifornia," Herbert E. Bolton, ed. and trans. Catholic Historical
     Review, v. 5, pp. 19-41, 1919-1920.

1613

48. SCOTT, Thomas (1566?-)
     1613-1633
     Personal diary; article based on manuscript diaries; concerned
with the intertwining of politics and religion.
     • Clark, Peter. "Thomas Scott and the Growth of Urban Op-
     position to the Early Stuart Regime," Historical Journal, v. 21,
     pp. 1-26, March, 1978.

1615

49. BONNER, Thomas (1580?-1616)
     January 24, 1615-June 18, 1616
     Sea diary; master of the vessel Red Dragon to the East; weather
and position; some longer entries.
     • "Journal," Michael Strachan and Boies Penrose, eds. The
     East India Company Journals of Captain William Keeling and Mas-
     ter Thomas Bonner, 1615-1617. Minneapolis: University of Min-
     nesota Press, 1971; pp. 171-217.

50. COCKS, Richard (-1624) [B8]
     June 1, 1615-January 14, 1619; December 5, 1620-March 24, 1622
     Personal diary; Englishman headed the trading company (factory)
in Japan; business dealings; Japanese customs and political life, personal relations with Portuguese traders.
     • Diary of Richard Cocks: A Cape-merchant in the English
     Factory in Japan, 1615-1622; with correspondence. Edward
     Maunde Thompson, ed. London: Hakluyt Society, 1883 (1st
     series, no. 66-67); New York: Burt Franklin, 1964?

51. KEELING, Captain William (1580?-1620)
     June 20, 1615-June 9, 1617
     Sea diary; leader of the fleet in the Red Dragon on a voyage
from Gravesend to Java, Sumatra and the East; health, discipline,
food; interesting.
     • "Journal," Michael Strachan and Boies Penrose, eds. The
     East India Company Journals of Captain William Keeling and

Master Thomas Bonner, 1615-1617. Minneapolis: University of
Minnesota Press, 1971; pp. 51-168.

1619

52. MUNK, Jens (1579-1628)
May 9, 1619-September 27, 1620
Exploration diary; widely experienced Danish seaman was chosen
by King Christian IV to search for the Northwest Passage; wintered
near Churchill, Manitoba and returned with only two of the 64 men
he sailed with from Copenhagen; scurvy, trichinosis and exposure
cost 62 lives.
• The Journal of Jens Munk 1619-1620. Edited with an intro.
by W. A. Kenyon. Toronto: Royal Ontario Museum, 1980.
REVIEW: Book Review Index 1981, p. 400.

1622

53. D'EWES, Sir Simonds, Bart. (1602-50)
1. January 1, 1622-April 20, 1624; Personal diary; member of
the Middle Temple; much on politics and plays of the period; details
of law cases; sermons heard.
• The Diary of Sir Simonds D'Ewes, 1622-1624. Paris: Didier,
1974.
REVIEW: Book Review Index 1979, p. 117.

2. Barber, Helen B. "The Journal of Sir Simonds D'Ewes from
the Abolition of the Star Chamber and High Commission Upon July 5,
1641 to the Adjournment of September 9, 1641," Ph.D., Cornell University, 1927.

3. October 12, 1641-January 10, 1642; Political diary; written
up like a secretary's minutes; very detailed.
• The Journal of Sir Simonds D'Ewes from the First Recess of
the Long Parliament to the Withdrawal of King Charles from London. Willson Havelock Coates, ed. New Haven: Yale University
Press, 1942; reprint Hamden, Conn.: Archon, 1970.

1631

54. EVELYN, John (1620-1706) [B16]
1. 1620-February 3, 1706; Personal diary; supporter of Charles
I; spent time abroad before and after 1649; Restoration; charter member of Royal Society; member of various government commissions; witnessed Great Fire of London; accession of William of Orange; friend
of Pepys (q.v.).
• The Diary of John Evelyn. E. S. de Beer, ed. 6 vols. Oxford: Clarendon Press, 1955.

- The Diary of John Evelyn. E. S. de Beer, ed. London: Oxford University Press, 1959; a one-volume condensation with additional material.
  REVIEWS: Book Review Digest 1956, pp. 300-01; 1960, pp. 429-30.

2. The Diary of John Evelyn. Selected and edited by John Bowle. New York: Oxford University Press, 1983; an edition for the general reader based on the 1955 Oxford edition.

3. "Diary Excerpts," Elizabeth D'Oyley, ed. English Diaries. London: Edward Arnold, 1930; pp. 108-35.

4. "Diary Excerpts," Philip Dunaway and Mel Evans, eds. A Treasury of the World's Great Diaries. New York: Doubleday, 1957; pp. 528-38.

1632

55. WOOD, Anthony à (1632-95) [B27]
    December 17, 1632-July 11, 1692
    Public diary; historian of the City of Oxford and the University.
    - "Diary Excerpts," in: Elizabeth D'Oyley, ed. English Diaries. London: Edward Arnold, 1930; pp. 43-60.

1633

56. MILDMAY, Sir Humphrey (1592-1666) [B14]
    - Ralph, Philip L. "A Portion of the Diary of Sir Humphrey Mildmay, 1633-1652," Ph.D., Yale University, 1935.

1634

57. HULL, John (1624-83) [A1]
    1634-March, 1682
    - "The Diaries of John Hull Mint-master and Treasurer of the Colony of Massachusetts Bay," Puritan Personal Writings: Diaries. New York: AMS Press, 1982; facsimile reprint of American Antiquarian Society Transactions, v. 3, 1857.

58. ROGERS, Samuel (-1643?)
    1634-1638
    Personal diary; excerpts; decision to emigrate to America.
    - Shipps, Kenneth W. "The Puritan Emigration to New England: A New Source on Motivation," New England Historical and Genealogical Register, v. 135, pp. 83-97, April, 1981.

59.   TROMP, Martin Harpertzoon (1597-1653)
      April 23-October 28, 1639
      Sea diary; captain of the Dutch ship Amelia in the armada of
1639; sea battles in the English Channel September 16 and 18; headings; details of the order of battle and life aboard.
      • Journal of Maarten Harpertszoon, anno 1639. C. R. Boxer,
      trans. and ed. Cambridge: University Press, 1930.
         REVIEW: Book Review Digest 1930, p. 1050.

                                    1640

60.   ANONYMOUS
      February 1-July 1, 1604; gaps
      Parliamentary diary; routine Lower House business; readings of
bills and petitions; complements D'Ewes (q.v.).
      • "Anonymous Diary," in: Maija Jansson. Two Diaries of the
      Long Parliament. New York: St. Martin's, 1984; pp. 81-141.

61.   MUGABURU, Josephe de (1607-86)
      September 1, 1640-October 31, 1696
      Military journal; Iberian-born professional soldier and his son
kept this diary; some mention of personal matters but most valuable
for its portrait of the life of Spanish and Creole people; public cere-
mony, religious life, fiestas; detailed social history.
      • Chronicle of Colonial Lima: The Diary of Josephe and Fran-
      cisco Mugaburu, 1640-1694. Robert Ryal Miller, trans. and ed.
      Norman: University of Oklahoma Press, 1975.

62.   SHEPARD, Thomas (1605-49) [A2]
      November 25, 1640-March 30, 1644
      Spiritual diary; article discusses the diary, the only one extant
of a first generation New England Puritan.
      • Tipson, Baird. "The Routinized Piety of Thomas Shepard's
      Diary," Early American Literature, v. 13, pp. 64-80, Spring,
      1978.

                                    1641

63.   DRAKE, William (1606-)
      January 23-May 28, 1641
      Parliamentary diary; notes on debates conducted in committees
unrecorded in Journal of the House of Commons; record of the Staf-
ford trial; important parliamentary history.
      • "William Drake's Parliamentary Notebook," in: Maija Jansson.
      Two Diaries of the Long Parliament. New York: St. Martin's,
      1984; pp. 1-73.

1642

64. TASMAN, Abel Janszoon (1603-59)
     August 14, 1642-June 15, 1643
     Exploration diary; sent by Governor General Anthony Van Die-
     men to explore the coast of Australia for the Dutch East India Com-
     pany; headings, weather.
     • The Journal of Abel Janszoon Tasman, 1642: With Documents
     Relating to His Exploration of Australia in 1644. C. H. Kenihan,
     ed. Adelaide: Australian Heritage Press, 1964; 500 copies.

1644

65. JOSSELIN, Ralph (1616-83) [B20]
     August 6, 1644-July 29, 1683
     Personal diary; clergyman, village schoolmaster and yeoman
     farmer in the village of Earls Colne, Essex; many details of farming
     and religious life of the period.
     • The Diary of Ralph Josselin, 1616-1683. Alan Macfarlane, ed.
     London: Oxford University Press, 1976.
        REVIEWS: Book Review Digest 1977, p. 692. Book Review
     Index 1977, p. 228; 1978, p. 254; 1980, p. 266.

1645

66. WINTHROP, John, Jr. (1606-76) [A3]
     November 11-December 5, 1645
     Travel diary; Boston via Springfield to Hartford, Saybrook and
     return.
     • "Overland to Connecticut in 1645: A Travel Diary of John
     Winthrop, Jr.," William R. Carlton, ed. and trans. New England
     Quarterly, v. 13, pp. 494-510, September, 1940.

1646

67. HARINGTON, John (1589-1654) [B21]
     March 31, 1646-November 29, 1653; gap from September, 1647
     to May, 1650
     Personal diary; Somerset landowner and lawyer was a member
     of Lincoln's Inn; service in the House of Commons as a Cromwell sup-
     porter.
     • The Diary of John Harington, M. P., 1646-53: With Notes
     for His Charges. Margaret F. Stieg, ed. Somerset: Somerset Rec-
     ord Society, 1977.
        REVIEW: Book Review Index 1979, p. 195.

1649

68.   BOWNE, John (1650-94) [A4]
      January 7, 1649-September 4, 1676; many gaps.
      Personal diary; business records; by ship to England and re-
turn to Flushing, New Amsterdam; Quaker whose nonviolent resistance
to the orders of Peter Stuyvesant (q.v.) and harboring of Quakers
brought them both before the board of the East India Company; good
description of shipboard life for the period.
      • The Journal of John Bowne 1650-1694. Herbert F. Ricard,
      ed. New Orleans: Polyanthos, 1975.
         REVIEW: Book Review Index 1980, p. 57.

1651

69.   BUCKERIDGE, Nicholas (-1688/89)
      July 15-September 11, 1651
      Personal diary; agent for East India Company in Africa; voyage
from India to Madagascar with several stops for trading.
      • Journal and Letter Book of Nicholas Buckeridge, 1651-1654.
      John R. Jenson, ed. Minneapolis: University of Minnesota
      Press, 1973.

1652

70.   PAUL OF ALEPPO, Archdeacon (fl. 1654-1666)
      July 8, 1652-November 21, 1660
      Travel diary; extracts and paraphrases; from Aleppo to Moscow;
life in Moscow; religious controversy and visits to monasteries and
convents.
      • The Travels of Macarius: Extracts from the Diary of the
      Travels of Macarius, Patriarch of Antioch, Written by His Son,
      Paul Archdeacon of Aleppo, 1652-1660. F. C. Balfour, trans.
      London: Oxford University Press, 1936.

1653

71.   WIGGLESWORTH, Michael (1631-1705) [A4]
      February, 1653-May, 1657
      Spiritual diary; Harvard instructor and Puritan; "a morbid, hu-
morless, selfish busybody"; sermons heard and given; some untranslated Latin passages.
      • The Diary of Michael Wigglesworth, 1653-1657: The Conscience
      of a Puritan. Edmund S. Morgan, ed. Gloucester, Mass.: Peter

Smith, 1966; reprint of Colonial Society of Massachusetts Publications, v. 35, pp. 311-444, 1946.

1654

72. WEALE, John (1630-)
August 3, 1554-April 12, 1656; gaps
Sea diary; junior officer with General Robert Blake on voyages in the Mediterranean; life on shipboard.
- "The Journal of John Weale, 1654-1656," Rev. J. R. Powell, ed. Naval Miscellany, v. 4, pp. 85-162, 1952.

1660

73. DERING, Sir Edward (1625-84) [B35]
April 25-August 15, 1660; March 29, 1673-September 24, 1675; April 13-June 5, 1675.
Parliamentary and personal diary; details of bills, speeches; actions on "poperie."
- The Diaries and Papers of Sir Edward Dering, Second Baronet, 1644 to 1684. Maurice F. Bond, ed. Lond: HMSO, 1976.
  REVIEWS: Book Review Index 1977, p. 111; 1978, p. 123.

74. PEPYS, Samuel (1633-1703) [B29]
1. January 1, 1660-May 31, 1669; Personal diary; probably the most famous diary written in English; official of the Royal Navy; voluminous information on the social history of London, the Navy and politics; the edition noted below is a tour de force; volume 10 is a "companion" to the transcription, a "detailed and extensive commentary" in dictionary form with articles on all aspects of Pepys' life and times; subjects discussed include scientific instruments, weather, travel, coffeehouses, music, domestic servants.
- The Diary of Samuel Pepys. Robert Latham and William Matthews, eds. 11 vols. London: G. Bell, 1970-83.
  REVIEWS: Book Review Digest 1970, p. 1103-04; 1972, p. 1020; 1973, p. 1014; 1975, pp. 984-85.
- The Illustrated Pepys: Extracts from the Diary. Selected and edited by Robert Latham. Berkeley: University of California Press, 1977.
- The Shorter Pepys. Robert Latham, ed. Berkeley: University of California Press, 1985.

2. "Diary Excerpts," Dunaway, Philip and Mel Evans, eds. A Treasury of the World's Great Diaries. New York: Doubleday, 1957; pp. 505-27.

3. "Diary Excerpts," Elizabeth D'Oyley, ed. English Diaries. London: Edward Arnold, 1930; pp. 61-94.

<u>1661</u>

75. GORDON OF AUCHLEUCHRIES, General Patrick (1635-99) [B26]
     July 25, 1661-December 31, 1699
     Personal diary; younger son of Scottish Roman Catholic gentry
     became a mercenary for the King of Sweden; service with the Czar
     as ambassador to England; excerpts with connecting narrative; Stre-
     litze Revolt.
        • Passages from the Diary of General Patrick Gordon of Auch-
        leuchries 1635-1699. Aberdeen: Spalding Club, 1859.

<u>1664</u>

76. YONGE, James (1647-1721) [B32]
     1664-1708
     Personal journal; not daily entries, long gaps; naval surgeon,
     prisoner of the Dutch in Amsterdam; lively, interesting; contemporary
     of Pepys (q.v.) and knew some of the same people.
        • The Journal of James Yonge, 1647-1721, Plymouth Surgeon.
        F. N. L. Poynter, ed. Hamden, Conn.: Archon Books, 1963.

<u>1669</u>

77. PENN, William (1644-1718) [B33]
     September 15, 1669-July 1, 1670
     Personal diary; founder of the American colony of Pennsylvania;
     sent by his father to settle matters with Irish tenants on the family
     estates; social life, business.
        • My Irish Journal, 1669-1670. Isabel Grubb, ed. London:
        Longmans, Green, 1952.

<u>1671</u>

78. ISHAM, Sir Thomas, Bart. (1657-81) [B34]
     November 1, 1671-September 30, 1673
     Personal diary; schoolboy and heir of Northamptonshire land-
     owner; family life, studies, racing, hunting; text in Latin and Eng-
     lish.
        • The Diary of Thomas Isham of Lamport (1658-81), Kept by
        Him in Latin from 1671 to 1673 at his Father's Command. Nor-
        man Marlow, trans. Farnborough: Gregg, 1971.

<u>1672</u>

79. NARBROUGH, John
     1. Sea diary; weather, positions, ship movements; fairly de-
     tailed.

- "Journal of John Narbrough, Lieutenant and Captain of the Prince January 7, 1671/2 to September 18, 1672," in: Journals and Narratives of the Third Dutch War. R. C. Anderson, ed. (Navy Records Society, v. 86) London: Navy Records Society, 1946; pp. 57-154.

2. "Journal of John Narbrough Captain of the Fairfax September 18, 1672 to July 1, 1673," op. cit.; pp. 187-296.

3. "Journal of John Narbrough Captain of the St. Michael July 1, 1673 to September 21, 1673," op. cit.; pp. 339-70.

80. SPRAGGE, Sir Edward (1673) [B34]
   1. Sea diary; weather, ship movements.
   - "Journal of Sir Edward Spragge Vice Admiral of the Red and Admiral of the Blue in the London May 2, 1672 to August 23, 1672," in: R. C. Anderson, ed. Journals and Narratives of the Third Dutch War. London: Navy Records Society, 1946; pp. 155-63.

   2. Sea diary; includes battle diagram.
   - "Journal of Sir Edward Spragge Admiral of the Blue in the Royal Prince May 1, 1673 to August 10, 1673," in: R. C. Anderson, ed. Journals and Narratives of the Third Dutch War. London: Navy Records Society, 1946; pp. 315-30.

1673

81. HADDOCK, Richard
   Sea diary; ship movements, weather.
   - "Journal of Richard Haddock Captain of the Royal Charles and the Sovereign May 11, 1673 to June 29, 1673," Journals and Narratives of the Third Dutch War. R. C. Anderson, ed. (Navy Records Society, v. 86) London: Navy Records Society, 1946; pp. 331-38.

82. LEGGE, George
   Sea diary; weather; ship movements
   - "Journal of George Legge Captain of Royal Katherine March 9, 1672/3 to September 14, 1673," Journals and Narratives of the Third Dutch War. R. C. Anderson, ed. (Navy Records Society, v. 86) London: Navy Records Society, 1946; pp. 297-314.

83. MARQUETTE, Jacques (1637-75)
   June-July, 1673
   Missionary diary; life in an Algonquin Indian village on Lake Michigan.
   - "Diary Excerpts," A Treasury of the World's Great Diaries. Philip Dunaway and Mel Evans, eds. New York: Doubleday, 1957; pp. 56-59.

84. SEWALL, Samuel (1652-1730) [A7]
     1. December 3, 1673-October 13, 1729; some lengthy gaps;
Harvard graduate and Overseer; held various offices in colonial government; merchant and printer; thrice married; worked and socialized
with the leading Bostonians of his day; one of the premier American
diaries providing an excellent portrait of the time; reticent on witchcraft.
     • The Diary of Samuel Sewall 1674-1729. M. Halsey Thomas,
     ed. 2 vols. New York: Farrar, Straus and Giroux, 1973.
          REVIEWS: Book Review Digest 1974, p. 1097; 1975, p. 1148.

     2. No note on Wish's reasons for choosing these particular en-
tries.
     • The Diary of Samuel Sewall. Abridged ed. Harvey Wish, ed.
     New York: Putnam, 1967.

     3. "Diary Excerpts," in: Philip Dunaway and Mel Evans, eds.
A Treasury of the World's Great Diaries. New York: Doubleday,
1957; pp. 459-64.

                              1675

85. LOCKE, John (1632-1704) [B26]
     November 12, 1675-May 10, 1679
     Travel diary; English philosopher studied and worked in France;
an outsider's view of the reign of Louis XIV and its effect on all
levels of society; social history, prices, etc.
     • Travels in France, 1675-1679, as Related in His Journal, Cor-
     respondence and Other Papers. John Lough, ed. Cambridge:
     Cambridge University Press, 1953.

86. TEONGE, Henry (1621-90) [B36]
     May 20, 1675-November 17, 1676
     Travel diary; by sea to the Mediterranean.
     • "Diary Excerpts," in: Elizabeth D'Oyley, ed. English Di-
     aries. London: Edward Arnold, 1930; pp. 95-107.

                              1676

87. WARCUP, Edmund (1627-1712?) [B36]
     February 20, 1676-December 3, 1684; gaps
     Public diary; notes on the Popish Plot.
     • "The Journals of Edmund Warcup 1676-1684," Keith Feiling
     and F. R. Needham, eds. in: Douglas G. Greene, comp. Diaries
     of the Popish Plot. Delmar, N.Y.: Scholars' Facsimiles and
     Reprints, 1977; pp. 91-120.

1678

88. SOUTHWELL, Sir Robert (1635-1702) [B38]
    October 7-19, 1678
    Public diary; investigations into the plot by the Secretary for
Ireland.
    • "Diary of What I Did About the Business in the Council
    Chamber, October, 1678," Patrick Melvin, ed. in: Douglas G.
    Greene, comp. Diaries of the Popish Plot. Delmar, N.Y.:
    Scholars' Fascimiles and Reprints, 1977; pp. 51-54.

89. TONGE, Israel (1621-80) [B38]
    June 13-September 28, 1678
    Personal diary; Titus Oates' ally in the plot.
    • "Journall [sic] of the Plot, 1678," Douglas G. Greene, ed.
    in: Douglas G. Greene, comp. Diaries of the Popish Plot. Del-
    mar, N.Y.: Scholars' Facsimiles and Reprints, 1977; pp. 1-49.

1679

90. CLOUGH, Jonas
    December 11, 1679-June 17, 1681
    Prison diary; English sailor captured by Spaniards and held for
violating terms of 1670 Treaty of Madrid.
    • Thornton, A. P. "The English at Campeachy, 1670-82,"
    Jamaican Historical Review, v. 2, pp. 27-38, December, 1953.

91. JOYNE, John
    November 24-December 22, 1679
    • "A Journal, 1679," R. E. Hughes, ed. in: Diaries of the
    Popish Plot, Douglas G. Greene, comp. Delmar, N.Y.: Scholars'
    Facsimiles and Reprints, 1977; 55-84.

92. THACHER, Peter (1651-1727) [A9]
    January 2, 1678/79-1686
    Personal diary; article based on the diary; mentioned in Samuel
Sewall's diary (q.v.)
    • Hamilton, Edward Pierce. "The Diary of a Colonial Clergy-
    man Peter Thacher of Milton," Massachusetts Historical Society
    Proceedings, v. 71, pp. 50-63, 1959; reprinted in: Puritan
    Personal Writings: Diaries. New York: AMS Press, 1982.

1681

93. HEDGES, Sir William (1632-1701)
    November 25, 1681-March 6, 1688
    Business diary; East India Company factor; voyage from England
to Hooghley Factory; charges of bribery against other merchants;

disputes over customs and duties on merchandise; relations with Dutch traders; return overland via Bagdad and Aleppo; by ship to Cyprus and Marseilles; valuable for early history of the John Company; all entries are in vol. 1.
- The Diary of William Hedges, Esq. (Hakluyt Society, 1st ser., no. 74-75, 78) 3 vols. New York: Burt Franklin, 1964.

1685

94. NAISH, Thomas (1669-1755)
     1685-1728
     Personal diary; family life and ecclesiastical politics; ambitious to become prebendary of Salisbury Cathedral; early entries are summaries; middle and later ones made on a daily basis.
- The Diary of Thomas Naish. Doreen Slatter, ed. Wiltshire: The Museum, 1965.

1686

95. REINA, Juan Jordán de
     January 3-March 4, 1686
     Exploration diary; log kept while searching for a nonexistent Bay of Espiritu Santo.
- "The Spanish Re-exploration of the Gulf Coast in 1686," Irving A. Leonard, ed. and trans. Mississippi Valley Historical Review, v. 22, pp. 547-57, 1935-36.

1689

96. ANONYMOUS
     March 23-May 1, 1689.
     Exploration diary; possibly written by De León; from Coahuila to Matagorda Bay to find a French settlement planted by La Salle in 1685; march to San Marcos River and return; found that the settlement had been sacked by Indians.
- "De León's Expedition of 1689," Elizabeth Howard West, ed. and trans. Quarterly of the Texas State Historical Association. 8:199-224, 1904-05.

1694

97. VARGAS, Don Diego de
     July 6-16, 1694
     Travel diary; north from Santa Fe to southern Colorado.
- "Journal of the Vargas Expedition to Colorado 1694," J. Manuel Espinosa, ed. Colorado Magazine, v. 16, pp. 81-90, May 1939.

1695

98. FIENNES, Celia [B49]
     1695
     Travel diary; Englishwoman touring her country; Hampton
Court and Windsor.
     • "Diary Excerpts," Philip Dunaway and Mel Evans, eds. A
     Treasury of the World's Great Diaries. New York: Doubleday,
     1957; pp. 178-80.

1697

99. BULLIVANT, Dr. Benjamin [A11]
     June 7, 1697-
     Travel diary; Boston to New York, New Jersey and Philadelphia;
on horseback, by coach and ship.
     • "A Glance at New York in 1697: The Travel Diary of Dr.
     Benjamin Bullivant," Wayne Andrews, ed. New-York Historical
     Society Quarterly, v. 40, pp. 55-73, January, 1956.

1698

100. LE MOYNE d'IBERVILLE, Pierre
     December 31, 1698-May 3, 1699
     Exploration journal; by ship from France to Louisiana; up the
Mississippi to the Red River and return through Lake Ponchartrain
to the Caribbean.
     • A Comparative View of French Louisiana, 1699 and 1762:
     The Journals of Pierre Le Moyne d'Iberville and Jean-Jacques
     Blaise d'Abbadie. Carl A. Brasseaux, trans. and ed. Lafay-
     ette: University of Southwestern Louisiana, 1979.
         REVIEWS: Journal of Mississippi History, v. 42, pp. 285-87,
     August, 1980. Louisiana History, v. 21, pp. 306-07, Sum-
     mer, 1980. Journal of Southern History, v. 46, p. 594,
     November, 1980.

101. KORB, Johann Georg
     January 11-September 27, 1698
     Travel diary; accompanied an embassy from the Holy Roman
Empire to Russia; through Poland to Moscow; details of travel; much
about "strange" Russian customs by an articulate observer; Strelitz
uprising.
     • Diary of an Austrian Secretary of Legation at the Court of
     Czar Peter the Great. Count MacDonnell, ed. and trans.
     London: Bradbury & Evans, 1863; New York; reprinted New
     York: Da Capo, 1968.

1700

102. GREEN, Rev. Joseph (1675-1715) [A15-16]
      March 4, 1700-July 18, 1715; gaps
      Personal diary; notes on weather, farm work; fracas with a
neighbor whose trespassing colt fell down Green's well.
      • "Biographical Sketch and Diary of Rev. Joseph Green, of
      Salem Village," facsimile reprint in: Puritan Personal Writings:
      Diaries. New York: AMS Press, 1982.

1704

103. KNIGHT, Sarah Kemble (1666-1727) [A17]
      October 7-December 6, 1704
      Travel diary; strongminded New Englander; visit to New Haven
and New York.
      • "The Private Journal on a Journey from Boston to New York,"
      in: Philip Dunaway and Mel Evans, eds. A Treasury of the
      World's Great Diaries. New York: Doubleday, 1957; pp. 52-
      55.

1705

104. TAS, Adam, 1668-1722
      June 14, 1705-February 27, 1706
      Personal diary; Dutchman came to the Cape Colony as a free
burgher; involved in a dispute with Governor van der Stel over the
policies of the Dutch East India Company which restricted farmers'
markets; portrays social relations among the Dutch colonists; breaks
off after his arrest for conspiring against the government; much on
everyday life as well as the "plot."
      • The Diary of Adam Tas (1705-1706). Leo Fouché, ed. A.
      C. Paterson, trans. New York: Longmans, Green, 1914.

1708

105. CLEGG, James (1679-1755) [B54]
      December 19, 1708-July 29, 1755
      Personal diary; dissenting minister, husband and father of a
large family; record of religious services, baptisms, etc.; had a medical practice and farmed; daily life, preparing sermons, treating patients; pious record of daily life.
      • The Diary of James Clegg of Chapel en le Frith, 1708-1755.
      Vanessa S. Doe, ed. Matlock: Derbyshire Record Society,
      1978-81.

1709

106. DUMMER, Jeremiah (1681-)
      July 15, 1709-August 24, 1711
      Travel diary; New England Calvinist in London; extracts; phi-
losophizing; Massachusetts representative to the Tory government.
      • Cohen, Sheldon S. "The Diary of Jeremiah Dummer," William
      and Mary Quarterly, v. 24, pp. 397-422, July, 1967.

107. HAMILTON, Sir David (1663-1721)
      December 9, 1709-July 29, 1714; gaps
      Medical and political diary; personal physician to Queen Anne
in her last years; his ministrations took in political matters and
Sarah, Duchess of Marlborough.
      • The Diary of Sir David Hamilton, 1709-1714. Philip Roberts,
      ed. Oxford: Clarendon Press, 1975.

1710

108. FONTAINE, John (1693-1767) [A22]
      September 16, 1710-December 5, 1719 (Old Style); gaps
      Travel diary; military service in Spain; voyage to Virginia; in
Williamsburg and New York State; visits with Indians in North Carolina; in Shenandoah Valley; factual reporting.
      • The Journal of John Fontaine: An Irish Huguenot Son in
      Spain and Virginia, 1710-1719. Edward Porter Alexander, ed.
      Williamsburg, Va.: Colonial Williamsburg Foundation, 1972.
          REVIEW: Book Review Digest 1973, p. 402

109. SWIFT, Jonathan (1667-1745) [B59, 62]
      November 24, 1710-December 11, 1711
      Personal diary; English writer and Whig turned Tory; extracts
from his Journal to Stella; life in London.
      • "Diary Excerpts," in: Philip Dunaway and Mel Evans. A
      Treasury of the World's Great Diaries. New York: Doubleday,
      1957; pp. 454-58.

1712

110. HEARNE, Thomas (1678-1735) [B57]
      March 30, 1712-June 7, 1731
      Personal diary; keeper of the Bodleian Library recorded the
foibles of his fellows.
      • "Diary Excerpts," in: Philip Dunaway and Mel Evans, eds.
      A Treasury of the World's Great Diaries. New York: Double-
      day, 1957; pp. 191-94.

111. MATHER, Cotton (1663-1728) [A9]
      February 12, 1712-March 14, 1713

Personal diary; Puritan busybody makes notes for improving
the spiritual lot of others and occasionally himself.
   • The Diary of Cotton Mather for the Year 1712. William R.
   Manierre, ed. Charlottesville: University Press of Virginia,
   1964.
        REVIEW: Book Review Digest 1965, p. 852.

                              1715

112. WANLEY, Humfrey (1672-1726) [B63]
      March 2, 1715-June 23, 1726; gap from August 22, 1715-January
      1, 1720
      Official diary; librarian to the 1st and 2nd Earls of Oxford;
daily record of buying books and those received as gifts; visiting
scholars; source for history of the Harleian Library.
   • The Diary of Humfrey Wanley, 1715-1726. C. E. Wright and
   Ruth C. Wright, eds. 2 vols. London: Bibliographical Society,
   1966.

                              1716

113. PEÑA, Diego
      August 4-October 2, 1716
      Military journal; notes the results of English-sponsored Indian
raids in Spanish Florida.
   • "Diego Peña's Expedition to Apalachee and Apalachicolo in
   1716," Mark F. Boyd, trans. Florida Historical Quarterly, v.
   28, pp. 1-27, July, 1949.

                              1717

114. BYRD, William (1674-1744) [A18]
      December 13, 1717-May 19, 1721
      Personal diary; Virginia plantation owner went to London to
settle his father-in-law's estate; his wife died while visiting him;
courting an heiress; colony business; his return to Virginia.
   • The London Diary, 1717-1721 and Other Writings. Louis B.
   Wright and Marion Tinling, eds. New York: Oxford University Press, 1958.

                              1718

115. CELIZ, Fray Francisco de
      April 9, 1718-February 10, 1719
      Exploration diary; chaplain of the expedition which founded
modern-day San Antonio, Texas; travel in East Texas.
   • Diary of the Alarcon Expedition into Texas, 1718-1719.

Fritz Leo Hoffmann, trans. Los Angeles: Quivira Society, 1935.

1719

116. PARKMAN, Ebenezer (1703-82) [A33-34]
     August 24, 1719-December, 1782
     Personal diary; Harvard graduate was a minister in Westborough,
Mass.; 16 children from two marriages; Great Awakening; much on
medical matters of the era; excellent, microscopic picture of eighteenth-
century life.
     • The Diary of Ebenezer Parkman, 1703-1782. Francis G.
     Walett, ed. Worcester, Mass.: American Antiquarian Society,
     1974.
          REVIEWS: Book Review Index 1976, p. 335.
          • Lockwood, Rose. "Birth, Illness and Death in Eighteenth
          Century New England," Journal of Social History, v. 12, pp.
          111-28, Fall, 1978. (Discusses epidemics, diseases and child-
          birth as noted in Parkman's diary.)

1721

117. LA HARPE, Bernard de
     December 16, 1721-April 30, 1722
     Exploration diary; set out to find the source of the Arkansas
River and survey nearby territory; description of countryside and
wildlife.
     • Smith, Ralph A., trans. "Exploration of the Arkansas River
     by Bernard de La Harpe, 1721-1722, Extracts from His Journal
     and Instructions," Arkansas Historical Quarterly, v. 10, pp.
     339-63, Autumn, 1951.

118. ROGGEVEEN, Jacob (1659-1729)
     July 26, 1721-July 18, 1722
     Exploration diary; voyage made under the auspices of the Dutch
East Indian Company; discovered Easter Island and charted parts of
the South Pacific.
     • The Journal of Jacob Roggeveen. Andrew Sharp, ed. and
     trans. Oxford: Clarendon Press, 1971.
          REVIEW: Book Review Digest 1971, p. 1161.

1722

119. KNATCHBULL, Sir Edward (-1730)
     October 9, 1722-March 17, 1730
     Parliamentary diary; politically involved country squire; admin-
istration supporter with an independent streak; only printed source
for many of the speakers of the period; valuable parliamentary history.

• The Parliamentary Diary of Sir Edward Knatchbull, 1722-1730.
A. N. Newman, ed. London: Royal Historical Society, 1963.

1724

120. BYROM, John (1691-1763) [B66]
      March 11, 1724-April 2, 1761; many gaps
      Personal diary; minor British literary figure and father of di-
arist Beppy Byrom (q.v.) [B79]; social and family notes; moved in
high circles in London; inventor and teacher of shorthand.
      • Selections from the Journals and Papers of John Byrom,
      Poet-Diarist-Shorthand Writer, 1691-1763. Henri Talon, ed.
      London: Rockliff, 1950.

121. RHENIUS, Johannes Tobias (fl. 1707-46)
      February 15-November 11, 1724
      Travel diary; from Fort of Good Hope to the area inhabited by
Amaqua Hottentots.
      • The Journals of Brik and Rhenius. E. E. Mossop, ed.
      Cape Town: Van Riebeeck Society, 1947.

1726

122. SHULTZE, David (1717-97)
      1726-97
      Public diary; surveyor of the Schwenkfelder sect lived in
Montgomery County, Pennsylvania; notes on world events, county
affairs, family life.
      • Journals and Papers. Andrew S. Berky, trans., and ed.
      2 vols. Pennsburg, Pa.: Schwenkfelder Library, 1952-53.

1727

123. RODENEY, Caesar (1707-45)
      May 30, 1727-November, 1729
      Personal diary; father of Declaration of Independence signer
Caesar Rodney; farmer and storekeeper; his marriage, social and
family life.
      • "'Fare Weather and Good Helth [sic]': The Journal of Caesar
      Rodeney, 1727-1729," Harold B. Hancock, ed. Delaware History,
      v. 10, pp. 33-70, April, 1962.

1729

124. JOHNSON, Samuel (1709-84) [B111]
      1729-December 5, 1784; many gaps
      Personal diaries; English lexicographer, friend and subject of

Boswell (q.v.); prayers; notes on his reading, expenditures; visits
to Wales and France; in Latin and English.
 • Diaries, Prayers and Annals. E. L. McAdam with Donald
  and Mary Hyde, eds. London: Oxford University Press, 1958.
  REVIEW: Book Review Digest 1958, pp. 580-81.

1731

125. WILSON, Thomas (1703-84)
     September 13, 1731-December 31, 1737; January 1-December
     28, 1750
     Personal diary; bishop's son living at Oxford knew the Wesley
brothers (q.v.); royal chaplain and prebendary; courting his widowed
cousin; quest for preferment; later parts are in the form of a journal.
 • The Diaries of Thomas Wilson, D.D., 1731-37 and 1750.
 C. L. S. Linnell, ed. London: S. P. C. K., 1964.

1732

126. EGMONT, John Percival, 1st Earl of (1683-1748) [B70]
     July 20, 1732-May 27, 1738
     Political diary; close associate of Oglethorpe, founder of the
Georgia colony; record of meetings; dry but with some verbatim transcripts of letters from the settlers on conditions.
 • The Journal of the Earl of Egmont: Abstract of the Trustees Proceedings for Establishing the Colony of Georgia, 1732-
 1738. Robert G. McPherson, ed. Athens: University of
 Georgia Press, 1962.

127. GORDON, Peter (1697-1740)
     November 17, 1732-October 31, 1734
     Personal diary; appointed a tithingman by the Georgia Colony
trustees, he went with the first group of settlers; life in the settlement; his return with letters of grievance from some "Malcontents."
 • Journal, 1732-1735. E. Merton Coulter, ed. Athens: University of Georgia Press, 1963.

128. GROVE, William Hugh
     April 17-July, 1732
     Travel diary; educated, scientific reporter on flora and fauna
of Virginia; impartial observer of planter class and its life style;
Williamsburg.
 • "Virginia in 1732: The Travel Journal of William Hugh
 Grove," Gregory A. Stiverson and Patrick H. Butler III, eds.
 Virginia Magazine of History and Biography, v. 85, pp. 18-44,
 January, 1977.

<u>1733</u>

129. SHEFTALL, Benjamin (1692-1765)
      July 25, 1733-August 20, 1808
      Official diary; record of births, deaths, marriages; arrivals of
emigrants; British occupation of the city; hurricane of September,
1804.
      • "The Sheftal Diaries: Vital Records of Savannah Jewry
      (1733-1808)," <u>American Jewish Historical Quarterly</u>, v. 54, pp.
      243-77, March, 1965.

<u>1736</u>

130. BOL(T)ZIUS, Johann (John) Martin [A32]
      1. February 7-May, 1736 (Old Style); Personal diary; pastor
of the emigrant Salzburgers to Georgia recorded the friction between
them and General Oglethorpe.
      • "The Secret Diary of Pastor Johann Martin Boltzius," George
      F. Jones, ed. <u>Georgia Historical Quarterly</u>, v. 53, pp. 78-110,
      March, 1969.

      2. October 12-29, 1742; Travel diary; went with Henry M.
Muhlenberg (q.v.) from Ebenezer to Charleston, S. Carolina; lengthy
descriptions of conditions and inhabitants.
      • "John Martin Boltzius' Trip to Charleston, October, 1742,"
      George Fenwick Jones, ed. <u>South Carolina Historical Magazine</u>,
      v. 82, pp. 87-110, April, 1981.

      3. August 2-September 30, 1748; Personal diary; much com-
ment on weather and crops.
      • "August, 1748 in Georgia, from the Diary of John Martin
      Bolzius," Lothar L. Tresp, ed. <u>Georgia Historical Quarterly</u>,
      v. 47, pp. 204-16, June, 1963; v. 47, pp. 320-32, September,
      1963.

131. RECK, Philipp Georg Friedrich von (-1798)
      February 27-October 12, 1736
      Personal diary; brought Salzburgers to Georgia to settle; coun-
tryside, flora, fauna.
      • "Von Reck's Second Report From Georgia," George F. Jones,
      ed. <u>William and Mary Quarterly</u>, v. 22, pp. 319-33, 1965.

132. STEPHENS, William (1671-1753) [A34]
      April 8-August 14, 1736; October 29, 1741-1745
      Official diary; secretary and president of the province of
Georgia; enjoined by the colony's trustees in England to keep them
informed; missions to South Carolina in 1736; official business and
many gossipy asides on colonial life.

- The Journal of William Stephens. E. Merton Coulter, ed.
2 vols. Athens: University of Georgia Press, 1958; 500
copies.

133. WESLEY, Charles (1707-88) [B73]
March 9, 1736-August 27, 1739
Personal diary; youngest brother of John Wesley, founder of
Methodism; arrival in Georgia as secretary to Governor Oglethorpe;
primitive conditions; disputes with several colonists; return to Eng-
land; preaching and proselytizing.
- "The Journal of the Rev. Charles Wesley, M.A.," Taylors,
S. Car.: Methodist Reprint Society, 1977.
REVIEW: Religious Studies Review, v. 7, p. 262, July,
1981.

1737

134. KAY, Richard (1716-51)
April 11, 1737-July 19, 1750
Personal and medical diary; Dissenter trained at Guy's Hospital,
London; many entries on sermons heard; prays for England's victory
over Spain; medical notes; worked with his father who was also a
doctor; visit to Oxford; news of the Scots rebellion of 1745.
- The Diary of Richard Kay, 1716-51, of Baldingstone, Near
Bury, a Lancashire Doctor. W. Brockbank and F. Kenworthy,
eds. Manchester: Manchester University Press, 1968.

135. WHITEFIELD, George (1714-70) [A35]
December 28, 1737-January 18, 1741; December 4, 1744-March,
1745
Spiritual diary; Oxonian converted to Methodism by the Wesleys
(q.v.); from London to the Georgia Colony and return; to Georgia
twice more; tour of New England; opened an orphanage in Georgia;
revival preaching; touring the British Isles.
- Journals. New Edition Containing Fuller Material Than Hith-
erto Published. London: Banner of Truth Trust, 1960.

1738

136. LA VERENDRYE (Pierre Gautier de Varennes) (1685-)
July 20, 1738-May 28, 1739
Travel diary; Canadian fur trader built Fort La Reine; travel
in North Dakota and Manitoba; much about Indians of the area.
- "The Journal of La Verendrye, 1738-39," Henry E. Haxo,
trans. North Dakota Historical Quarterly, v. 8, pp. 229-71,
July, 1941.

137. VITRY, Pierre, S. J. (1700-49) [C122]
     September 6, 1738-April 1, 1740
     Military journal; chaplain in the second campaign by the French
against the Chickasaw Indians.
     • "The Journal of Pierre Vitry, S. J., 1738-1740," Louisiana
     Studies, v. 3, pp. 247-313, Fall, 1964.

138. WESLEY, John (1703-91) [A33, B68]
     May 28, 1738-January 1, 1790
     Religious diary; extracts; founder of Methodism; preaching
throughout Britain.
     • "Diary Excerpts," in: Philip Dunaway and Mel Evans. A
     Treasury of the World's Great Diaries. New York: Doubleday,
     1957; pp. 227-36.

                                1741

139. BACKUS, Isaac (1724-1806) [A78]
     Fall, 1741-March 16, 1806
     Personal diary; Baptist minister, bookseller and agent for his
brother's ironworks; family and religious life; much travel throughout
New England; supported the American Revolution; active in religious
controversies; many publications.
     • The Diary of Isaac Backus. William G. McLoughlin, ed. 3
     vols. Providence, R.I.: Brown University Press, 1979.
        REVIEWS: Book Review Index 1980 p. 24; 1981, p. 35.
     William and Mary Quarterly, v. 40, p. 141, January, 1983.

                                1742

140. CLEAVELAND, John (1722-99) [A79]
     Religious diary; concerned with the Great Awakening at Yale;
introspective.
     • "The Diary of John Cleaveland January 15-May 11, 1742,"
     Ross W. Beales, Jr., ed. Essex Institute Historical Collections,
     v. 107, pp. 143-72, April, 1971.

141. MUHLENBERG, Henry Melchior (1711-87) [A130]
     1. January 2, 1742-September 29, 1787; gaps; Religious diary;
church business; official and personal.
     • The Journals of Henry Melchior Muhlenberg. Theodore G.
     Tappert and John W. Doberstein, eds. 3 vols. Philadelphia:
     Evangelical Lutheran Ministerium of Pennsylvania, 1942-58.

     2. September 22, 1742-September 29, 1787; An abridgement
containing about five percent of the three-volume edition of the journals.
     • The Notebook of a Colonial Clergyman. Philadelphia: Muhl-
     enberg Press, 1959.

1745

142. BYROM, Elizabeth (1722-1801) [B79]
      August 14, 1745-January 23, 1746
      Personal diary; Bonny Prince Charlie seen by an ardent Jacobite.
      • "Diary Excerpts," in: Elizabeth D'Oyley, ed. English Dia-
      ries. London: Edward Arnold, 1930; pp. 136-46.

1746

143. ROSE, Robert (1704-51)
      January 21, 1746-June 13, 1751
      Personal diary; active in parishes in Tidewater and Piedmont
      regions; very short entry; weather, parish activities.
      • The Diary of Robert Rose: A View of Virginia by a Scottish
      Colonial Parson, 1746-1751. Ralph Emmett Fall, ed. Verona,
      Va.: McClure Press, 1977.
         REVIEW: Virginia Magazine of History and Biography, v. 87,
      pp. 361-63, July, 1979.

1747

144. PRINCE, Nathan (1698-1748)
      June 12-July, 1747
      Travel diary; Harvard professor, alcoholic and "not much of a
      gentleman"; went to London to be ordained and obtain certificate as
      schoolmaster on ships of the Royal Navy; red tape and sightseeing.
      • "The Journal of Nathan Prince, 1747," William L. Sachse,
         ed. American Neptune, v. 16, pp. 81-97, April, 1956.

1748

145. Washington, George (1732-99) [A50]
         1. March 11, 1748-December 13, 1799; Personal diary; "Where
      and How My Time is Spent": majority of entries deal with weather,
      farm and plantation work; agricultural experiments; business, social
      and family life covered in cursory fashion; when coming on new sights
      in his travels he often describes them at length; interesting gems
      gleam among the pebbles.
         • The Diaries of George Washington. Donald Jackson and
         Dorothy Twohig, eds. 6 vols. Charlottesville: University Press
         of Virginia, 1976-79.
            REVIEWS: Book Review Digest 1977, pp. 1389-90; 1980, p.
         1273.

         2. October 31, 1753-January 11, 1754; Facsimile of the 1754
      edition.
         • The Journal of Major George Washington: An Account of

His First Official Mission, Made as Emissary From the Governor
of Virginia to the Commandant on the French Forces of the Ohio
October 1753-January 1754. Charlottesville: University Press
of Virginia, 1963.

3. "Diary Excerpts," in: Philip Dunaway and Mel Evans. A
Treasury of the World's Great Diaries. New York: Doubleday, 1957;
pp. 384-93.

1749

146. MELCOMBE, George Bubb Dodington, Baron (1691-1762) [B77]
     March 8, 1749-February 9, 1761
     Political diary; member of Parliament; written as his justifica-
tion to the world; political maneuvering and his fall from power.
     • The Political Journal of George Bubb Melcombe. John Cars-
     well, ed. New York: Oxford University Press, 1965.

147. SALUSBURY, John (1707-62) [C106]
     July 3, 1749-April 12, 1753
     Personal diary; impecunious father of Hester Thrale Piozzi was
a reluctant colonist in the settling of Nova Scotia; ran the land reg-
istry office; high in social standing but without much influence; Indian troubles.
     • Expeditions of Honour: The Journal of John Salusbury in
     Halifax, Nova Scotia, 1749-53. Ronald Rompkey, ed. Newark:
     University of Delaware Press, 1981.

1750

148. NEWTON, John (1725-1807)
     August 11, 1750-October 7, 1751; June 30, 1752-August 29,
     1753; October 21, 1753-August 7, 1754
     Travel diary; composer of hymn "Amazing Grace"; three voy-
ages as master on different vessels to the Windward Coast of Africa;
weather, headings, life aboard ship; some details of slaving.
     • The Journal of a Slave Trader, 1750-1754 Bernard Martin
     and Mark Spurrell, eds. London: Epworth, 1962.
     REVIEW: Book Review Digest 1966, p. 885.

1751

149. GAWTHERN, Abigail Frost (1757-1822)
     April 27, 1751-July 22, 1810
     Personal diary; some entries rewritten from earlier notes, some
original; well-to-do heiress, married a town lead manufacturer; widowed after eight years, she reared her two surviving children; active
social life; excursions to Bath; of local interest.

- The Diary of Abigail Gawthern of Nottingham 1751-1810.
Adrian Henstock, ed. Nottingham: Thoroton Society of Notting-
hamshire, 1980.

150. PICQUET, Abbé Francois (1708-   )
June 10, 1751-July 21, 1751
Missionary diary; Jesuit head of La Présentation Mission surveyed the Lake Ontario region for converts and to report on conditions; negotiations with Indians.
- "A 1751 Journal of Abbé Francois Picquet," John V. Jezierski,
ed. and trans. New York Historical Society Quarterly, v. 54,
pp. 361-81, October, 1970.

1752

151. CARTER, Landon (1710-78) [A97]
1752-September 2, 1778
Personal diary; son of Robert "King" Carter by his second
wife; wealthy planter of Richmond County, Va.; member of the House
of Burgesses; prolific writer on scientific and political subjects; introspective, upright man who felt he did not receive the recognition
from his peers his accomplishments deserved; appalled by the ingratitude and disrespect of his offspring; entries for 1752-55 chiefly concerned with political matters in the House of Burgesses; plantation
and family life, illnesses, social intercourse, crops, prices; treatment
of his slaves; occasionally tedious but usually interesting.
- The Diary of Colonel Landon Carter of Sabine Hall, 1752-
1778. Jack P. Greene, ed. 2 vols. Charlottesville: University
Press of Virginia, 1965.
REVIEW: Book Review Digest 1965, p. 208.

1753

152. ADAMS, John (1735-1826) [A61]
1. June 8, 1753-April, 1754; September 1758-January, 1759;
Personal diary; second American president; student days at Harvard;
notes on reading and lectures; flirtation with "Orlinda," Hannah
Quincy of Braintree; law work; a hodge podge which includes much
non-diary material.
- The Earliest Diary of John Adams. L. H. Butterfield, et
al., ed. Cambridge: Belknap Press, 1966.

2. November 17, 1755-1804; many gaps; Personal diary; va-
riety of subjects covered reveals the personality and times of the
writer; one of the outstanding American diaries.
- Diary and Autobiography. 4 vols. Cambridge: Belknap
Press, 1961.
REVIEWS: Book Review Digest 1961, p. 5; 1962, p. 7.

153. BOWEN, Ashley (1728-1813) [A78-79]
      November 20, 1753-September 23, 1804; gaps; entries previous
      to this beginning date were written later.
      Personal diary; from cabin boy to master and privateer; whaling;
in Royal Navy at the Siege of Quebec in 1759; later employed ashore;
three wives, numerous children; good account of colonial and Revolutionary eras; much on the town history of Marblehead.
      • The Journals of Ashley Bowen (1728-1813) of Marblehead.
      Philip Chadwick Foster Smith, ed. Boston: Colonial Society of
      Massachusetts, 1973.
            REVIEW: Book Review Digest 1974, pp. 123-24.

154. DAVIES, Samuel (1724-61) [A57]
      July 2, 1753-February 12, 1755
      Travel diary; Presbyterian leader in Virginia; sent on a mis-
sion to Britain to raise funds for the forerunner of Princeton University and secure books for the people of Hanover County; hampered
in his efforts by religious schism; "preached in a vacant church";
conditions of travel and longing for home.
      • The Reverend Samuel Davies Abroad: The Diary of a Jour-
      ney to England and Scotland, 1753-55. George William Pilcher,
      ed. Urbana: University of Illinois Press, 1967.

<hr>

1754

155. BURR, Esther Edwards (1732-58) [A37]
      1. October 1, 1754-September 2, 1757; Letter-diary; written
to Sarah Prince, a close friend; Burr was the daughter of Jonathan
Edwards, the wife of the president of what later became Princeton
University, and the mother of Aaron Burr; religious beliefs caused
mental conflict over her role as a submissive wife heavily burdened
with household duties.
      • The Journal of Esther Edwards Burr, 1754-1757. Carol F.
      Karlsen and Laurie Crumpacker, eds. New Haven: Yale Uni-
      versity Press, 1984.
            REVIEW: Publishers Weekly, v. 109, p. 63, March 23, 1984.

      2. October 1754-September 1757; Crumpacker, Laurie. "Esther
Edwards's Journal 1754-1757: A Document of Evangelical Sisterhood,"
Ph.D., Boston University, 1978. (Dissertation Abstracts 38/12A p.
7331)

156. TURNER, Thomas (1729-93) [B86]
      1. February 8, 1754-July 3, 1765; Personal diary; first a
poorly paid schoolteacher and then a prosperous tradesman in Sussex;
companionable, backsliding, convivial shopkeeper; recurring resolutions to mend his behavior; comments on the Seven Years War; his
reading; good picture of rural English life.
      • The Diary of a Georgian Shopkeeper: A Selection. R. W.
      Blencowe and M. A. Lower. 2nd ed. G. H. Jennings, ed.

Oxford: Oxford University Press, 1979. (Previous edition
titled The Diary of Thomas Turner of East Hoathly, 1754-1756.
Florence Maria Turner, ed. London: John Lane, 1925.)
    REVIEW: Punch, v. 277, p. 1154, December 12, 1979.

2. "Diary Excerpts," in: Philip Dunaway and Mel Evans, eds.
A Treasury of the World's Great Diaries. New York: Doubleday,
1957; pp. 465-67.

1755

157. ANONYMOUS
     June 10-July 8, 1755
     Military journal: British account of Braddock's defeat; note on
computer analysis made by the authors to determine if this diary and
Cholmley's batman's diary (q.v.) are forgeries; conclusion is they are
not.
     • "A British Officer's Journal of the Braddock Expedition--Et
     Cetera" Paul E. Kopperman and Michael J. Freiling. Western
     Pennsylvania Historical Magazine, v. 64, pp. 269-87, July, 1981.

158. ANONYMOUS
     June 19, 1755-1814
     Church diary: kept by various clergymen; congregation men-
tioned by name; Indian raids, Revolutionary War news.
     • "Extracts from the Diary of the Moravian Pastors of the
     Hebron Church, Lebanon, 1755-1814," John W. Heisey, ed. and
     trans. Pennsylvania History, v. 34, pp. 44-63, January, 1967.

159. ANONYMOUS
     January 8-August 8, 1755
     War diary; from Cork to Alexandria, Va.; marching, encounters
with Indians.
     • "The Journal of Captain Cholmley's Batman," in: Charles
     Hamilton, ed. Braddock's Defeat. Norman: University of
     Oklahoma Press, 1959; pp. 7-36.

160. TRUMBULL, Benjamin (1735-1820) [A122]
     September 8, 1755-March 4, 1756
     Personal diary; Congregational minister and historian; expelling
of a sophomore; earthquake; riot; sermons.
     • Cohen, Sheldon S. "The Yale College Journal of Benjamin
     Trumbull," History of Education Quarterly, v. 8, pp. 375-85,
     Fall, 1968.

1757

161. CELI, Francisco Maria
     April 10-May 10, 1757

Travel log; pilot of the Spanish fleet which surveyed Tampa Bay.
- "Tampa Bay in 1757: Francisco Maria Celi's Journal and Logbook," John D. Ware, ed. Florida Historical Quarterly, v. 50, pp. 158-79, October, 1971; pp. 262-77, January, 1972.

162. WOOLMAN, John (1720-72) [A24, B105]
    1. February 13, 1757-August 30, 1772; Personal diary; New Jersey-born Quaker; religious, social and family life.
    - The Journal and Major Essays of John Woolman. Phillips P. Moulton, ed. New York: Oxford University Press, 1971.
    REVIEW: Book Review Digest 1972, p. 1418.

    2. "Diary Excerpts," in: Philip Dunaway and Mel Evans, eds. A Treasury of the World's Great Diaries. New York: Doubleday, 1975; pp. 50-51.

1758

163. GLASIER, Benjamin (1734-74)
    March 28, 1758-June 14, 1760
    War diary; ship's carpenter fought at Oswego and Fort Edward in New York state; life on the march.
    - "French and Indian War Diary of Benjamin Glasier of Ipswich 1758-60," Essex Institute Historical Collections, v. 86, pp. 65-92, January, 1950.

164. SWEAT, William (1730-1808) (Swett)
    Personal diary; shipwright; life of a common soldier; food, marching.
    - "Captain William Sweat's Personal Diary of the Expedition Against Ticonderoga, May 2-November 7, 1758," Paul O. Blanchette, ed. Essex Institute Historical Collections, v. 93, pp. 36-57, January, 1957.

1759

165. BRIETZCKE, Charles (1738-95)
    April 23, 1759-December 31, 1760
    Personal diary; minor functionary in the British Secretary of State's Office; lived at Old Somerset House in the royal apartments with several family members; death of the king.
    - "The Brietzcke Diary, 1759-1765," Notes and Queries, v. 196, pp. 185-87, 357-61, 1951; v. 197, pp. 68-74, 141-42, 209-11, 543-44, 1952; v. 198, pp. 29-31, 203-05, 346-49, 1953; v. 199, pp. 60-63, 165-69, 205-08, 259-62, 297-99, 340-43, 1954.

166. KRASINSKA, Franciazka (1742-96)
    January 1, 1759-January 15, 1761

Personal diary; romance and secret marriage to Duke Charles
of Courland; his inconstancy.
* The Journal of Countess Francois Krasinka, Great Grand-
mother of Victor Emmanuel. Kasimir Dziekonska, trans. 7th
ed. Chicago: A. C. McClurg, 1896

167. WOODFORDE, James (1740-1803) [B91]
1. October 1, 1759-May 20, 1776; Personal diary; all the entries while he was at Oxford, in residence or on later visits; studies;
notes on companions; his health; prices; heavy drinking; good picture of university life.
* Woodforde at Oxford, 1759-1776. W. N. Hargreaves-Mawdsley,
ed. Oxford: Clarendon Press, 1969.

2. August 28, 1759-April 24, 1803; abridged edition includes
about one third of the five-volume work.
* The Diary of a Country Parson. John Beresford, ed. Lon-
don: Oxford University Press, 1935.
REVIEWS: Punch, v. 274, p. 1026, June 14, 1978. New
Yorker, v. 54, p. 151, October 2, 1978.

1760

168. HAYS, John (1730?-96) [A83]
May 5-June 30, 1760
Travel diary; accompanied Moravian missionary Christian F.
Post to the Indians of western Pennsylvania; invited them to a treaty
discussion in Philadelphia; Indian life; travel conditions.
* "John Hays' Diary and Journal of 1760," William A. Hunter,
ed. Pennsylvania Archaeologist, v. 24, p. 63-83, August, 1954.

1761

169. BRINK, Carel Frederik (fl. 1758-84)
July 16, 1761-April 27, 1762
Exploration journal; Brink accompanied Hendrik Hop into Great
Nansaqualand; surveying for minerals.
* The Journals of Brink and Rhenius. E. E. Mossop, ed.
Cape Town: Van Riebeeck Society, 1947.

1762

170. BEATTY, Charles (1715-72) [A65]
1762; August 12-October 15, 1766; 1769
Travel diaries; Presbyterian minister's visits to British Isles,
Ohio country and England; short entries; weather; recipes.
* Journals of Charles Beatty, 1762-1769. Guy Soulliard Klett,
ed. University Park: Pennsylvania State University Press, 1962.
REVIEW: Book Review Digest 1963, p. 64.

171. BOSWELL, James (1740-95) [B95]
1. November 15, 1762-August 4, 1763; Personal diary; member
of the Scottish nobility and biographer of Samuel Johnson (q.v.);
some entries made on a daily basis, others written up several days
later conveying the feel of a novel unfolding; living on an allowance,
young and unknown in London.
   • London Journal 1762-1763. Frederick A. Pottle, ed. New
   Haven: Yale University Press, 1950.

2. August 1, 1763-June 17, 1764; to Utrecht to study law.
   • Boswell in Holland 1763-1764. Frederick A. Pottle, ed. New
   York: McGraw-Hill, 1952.

3. June 18, 1764-January 1, 1765; Meetings with Voltaire and
Rousseau; in Utrecht, Berne, Geneva, Berlin and points between.
   • Boswell on the Grand Tour: Germany and Switzerland, 1764.
   Frederick A. Pottle, ed. New Haven: Yale Univ. Press, 1953.

4. January 1, 1765-February 23, 1766; Chiefly concerned with
sex, religion and politics; affairs with two Italian married women;
familiar with Jacobites in France and Rome.
   • Boswell on the Grand Tour: Italy, Corsica, and France
   1765-1766. Frederick A. Pottle, ed. New Haven: Yale University Press, 1955.

5. January 10, 1767-October 17, 1769; Diary entries begin in
1767; becoming a lawyer; married his first cousin Margaret Montgom-
erie; his widowed father remarries; publication of his Account of Corsica.
   • Boswell in Search of a Wife, 1766-1769. Frank Brady and
   Frederick A. Pottle, eds. New Haven: Yale University Press,
   1956.

6. March 14, 1772-September 24, 1774; gap in the journal to
this beginning date is filled in by several letters and the editors'
narrative.
   • Boswell for the Defence, 1769-1774. William K. Wimsatt, Jr.
   and Frederick A. Pottle, eds. New Haven: Yale University
   Press, 1959.

7. August 14-November 22, 1773; Interesting journal of a good
traveler not put off by petty annoyances; comments on scenery and
much about the people he met; with new material discovered since the
1936 edition was published.
   • Boswell's Journal of a Tour to the Hebrides with Samuel
   Johnson, LL.D., 1773. Frederick A. Pottle and Charles H.
   Bennett, ed. New ed. New York: McGraw-Hill, 1961.

8. September 24, 1774-May 15, 1776; in Edinburgh and London; Johnson figures extensively in these entries; threat of a duel.
   • Boswell: The Ominous Years 1774-1776. Charles Ryskamp
   and Frederick A. Pottle, eds. New York: McGraw-Hill, 1963.

9. June 12, 1776-May 28, 1778; Seesawing between bouts of sobriety and melancholy at the deaths of many around him (David Hume, relatives, etc.); thoughts on the early years of the American Revolution; in London and Edinburgh.
  • Boswell in Extremes 1776-1778. Charles McC. Weis and Frederick A. Pottle, eds. New York: McGraw-Hill, 1970.

10. August 19, 1778-September 4, 1782; On the death of his father Boswell became laird; problems of growing family and the decline of wife's health due to tuberculosis; rising literary reputation but the waning of his legal practice.
  • Boswell, Laird of Auchinleck, 1778-1782. Frederick A. Pottle, ed. New Haven: Yale Univ. Press, 1977.

11. August 30, 1782-September 28, 1785; Opens with his father's death; his wife's bouts with tuberculosis; periods of depression; living on his estates; death of Johnson and others.
  • Boswell: The Applause of the Jury 1782-1785. Irma S. Lustig and Frederick A. Pottle, eds. New York: McGraw-Hill, 1981.

12. November 15, 1762-September 21, 1774; Abridgement of the six-volume Yale edition.
  • Heart of Boswell: Six Journals in One Volume. Mark Harris, ed. New York: McGraw-Hill, 1981.

13. "Diary Excerpts," in: Philip Dunaway and Mel Evans. eds. A Treasury of the World's Great Diaries. New York: Doubleday, 1957; pp. 441-53.

14. "Diary Excerpts," in: Elizabeth D'Oyley, ed. English Diaries. London: Edward Arnold, 1930; pp. 147-60.

1763

172. ABBADIE, Jean-Jacques-Blaise d' (1726-   )
      June 21, 1763-December 20, 1764; many gaps
      Political diary; director-general of Louisiana; trip from France; relations with Indians and the English.
  • A Comparative View of French Louisiana, 1699 and 1762: The Journals Pierre La Moyne d'Iberville and Jean-Jacques-Blaise d'Abbadie. Lafayette: University of Southwest Louisiana, 1979.

173. MASON, Charles (1728-86)
      November 15, 1763-September 11, 1768
      Official diary; log of the survey of the Mason-Dixon Line; weather, measurements.
  • The Journal of Charles Mason and Jeremiah Dixon. (Memoirs of the American Philosophical Society, v. 76) Philadelphia: American Philosophical Society, 1969.

1764

174. BYRON, John (1723-86)
      June 21, 1764-May 7, 1766
      Exploration journal; sent by the British Admiralty to explore
South America and find a Northwest Passage; ignored his instructions in favor of a search to rediscover the Solomon Islands, which
he presumed to harbor riches; corrected previous reckonings of the
Falklands; interesting account by a minor explorer.
      • Byron's Journal of His Circumnavigation, 1764-1766. Robert
        E. Gallagher, ed. (Hakluyt Society Works 2nd series no. 122)
        Cambridge: Hakluyt Society, 1964.

175. KIRKLAND, Samuel (1741-1808) [A90]
      November 16, 1764-May 2, 1765; October 25-November 1, 1767-
      June 1, 1805
      Personal diary; Connecticut native and ordained minister; worked
with the Senecas in upstate New York; was chaplain to the American
forces in the Revolution; founded a school for the education of Indian
youth; active with the tribes of the Six Nations, especially the Onei-
das; sermons preached, texts; mission work; theological questions.
      • The Journals of Samuel Kirkland: 18th-century Missionary
        to the Iroquois, Government Agent, Father of Hamilton College.
        Walter Pilkington, ed. Clinton, N.Y.: Hamilton College, 1980.
        REVIEWS: Book Review Index 1981, p. 310; 1983, p. 299.

176. LOFTUS, Arthur
      February 27-March 10, 1764
      Military journal; retreated to New Orleans after an Indian attack.
      • Haffner, Gerald O., "Major Arthur Loftus' Journal of the
        Proceedings of His Majesty's Twenty-second Regiment up the
        River Mississippi in 1764," Louisiana History, v. 20, pp. 325-
        34, Summer, 1979.

177. WRANGEL, Rev. Carl Magnus (1727-86)
      October 7-16, 1764
      Travel diary; dean of the Swedish Lutheran churches in Amer-
ica, 1758-68; from Philadelphia across New Jersey and return; visiting,
preaching, church business.
      • "Pastor Wrangel's Trip to the Shore," Carl Magnus Anderson,
        ed. and trans. New Jersey History, v. 87, pp. 4-31, Spring,
        1969.

1765

178. BARTRAM, John (1699-1777) [A91]
      Travel diary; one of the charter members of the American
Philosophical Society and founder of the first botanical garden in the
U.S.; botanizing; description of Charleston, Savannah and St. Augus-
tine; geological features.

• Diary of a Journey Through the Carolinas, Georgia, and Florida, from July 1, 1765 to April 10, 1766. Annotated by Francis Harper. American Philosophical Society Transactions, new series, v. 33, part 1, 1942.

179. FUENTE, Pedro José de la
January 1-December, 1765
Military diary; camp life in a Spanish frontier fort at present-day El Paso, Texas.
• "Diary of Pedro José de la Fuente--Captain of the Presidio of El Paso del Norte January-July, 1765," James M. Daniel, trans. and ed. Southwestern Historical Quarterly, v. 60, pp. 260-81, October, 1956; v. 83, pp. 259-78, January, 1980.

180. MAWHOOD, William (1724-)
October 5, 1765-October 18, 1790
Personal diary; middle-class Catholic wrote a line or three a day concerning his family and business; getting his children started in the world; church visits; news of the Catholic community; orthography reflects the pronunciation of the times.
• The Mawhood Diary: Selections from the Diary Notebooks of William Mawhood, Woollen-draper of London, for the Years, 1764-1790. E. E. Reynolds, ed. Kent: Catholic Record Society, 1956.

1766

181. CARVER, Jonathan (1710-80)
May 20, 1766-August 29, 1767
Exploration diary; from Massachusetts to the Falls of St. Anthony; commissioned to map the area and find a Northwest Passage; fur trade with the Indians; basis for his book Travels; died leaving widows on each side of the Atlantic.
• The Journals of Jonathan Carver and Related Documents, 1766-1770. John Parker, ed. St. Paul, Minn.: Minnesota Historical Society Press, 1976.
REVIEWS: Book Review Index 1976, p. 73; 1977, p. 73. Book Review Digest 1977, p. 213.

182. LINCK, Wenceslaus (1736-)
February 20-April 18, 1766
Exploration diary; Bohemian Jesuit in the service of Spain's New World missionary efforts; set out to map the area and find sites for future missions.
• Wenceslaus Linck's Diary of His 1766 Expedition to Northern Baja California. Ernest J. Burrus, S. J., ed. and trans. Los Angeles: Dawson's, 1966.

183. PERKINS, Simeon (1735-1812) [A152]
May 29, 1766-December 31, 1789
Personal diary; Connecticut Yankee resided in Halifax, Nova

Scotia; merchant, prominent citizen and public official; time in Liver-
pool, England; privateering venture; excellent notes on political,
social and economic life of Nova Scotia.
- The Diary of Simeon Perkins. Harold Innis, ed. (Champlain
Society Publications, vols. 29, 36) Toronto: The Champlain
Society, 1948; New York: Greenwood Press, 1969.

184. ROBERTSON, George
      June 24, 1766-August 17, 1767
      Exploration diary; master of the Dolphin on a voyage commis-
sioned by the Admiralty to explore the South Pacific; from the Thames
estuary to Wallis Island; interesting account by a well-educated,
skilled seaman; rediscovery of Tahiti; native life.
- The Discovery of Tahiti: A Journal of the Second Voyage
of H. M. S. Dolphin Round the World ... in the Years 1766,
1767 and 1768. Hugh Carrington, ed. London: Hakluyt Society, 1948 (series 2, v. 98).

                              1767

185. BANKS, Sir Joseph (1743-1820) [B99]
      1. August 28, 1767-January 21, 1768; Travel diary; British
botanist and Fellow of the Royal Society; from Edinburgh to Downing;
visits to lead mines, herring fisheries, coal and salt mines, lime quar-
ries; Kay's flying shuttle; detailed descriptions of the workings with
his drawings; valuable.
- "British Industry in 1767: Extracts From a Travel Journal
of Joseph Banks," S. R. Broadbridge, ed. History of Tech-
nology [Great Britain] v. 5, pp. 119-42, 1980.

      2. August 25, 1768-July 12, 1771; Exploration journal; with
Captain Cook (q.v.) on the Endeavour; botanizing; through the South
Pacific; circling both islands of New Zealand; up the east coast of
Australia; at Cape Town on the return voyage; lengthy descriptions
of flora, fauna and people.
- The Endeavour Journal. J. G. Beaglehole, ed. 2nd ed.
Sydney: Angus and Robertson, 1963.

      3. August 15, 1769-March 30, 1770; Exploration journal; ex-
tracts; concerned with New Zealand; extended description of Maori
people.
- Sir Joseph Banks in New Zealand: From His Journal. W. P.
Morrell, ed. Wellington: Reed, 1958.

186. NEVILLE, Sylas (1741-1840)
      June 26, 1767-August 9, 1788; gaps
      Personal diary; impecunious doctor in Georgian Britain; his life,
loves; playgoing; medical training; his horse Pizarro and the "housekeeper" who kept his bed warm; sermons heard; entertaining and occasionally humorous.

• Diary, 1767-1788. Basil Cozens-Hardy, ed. London: Oxford University Press, 1950.

187. SOLIS, Fray Gaspar José de
November 15, 1767-October 13, 1768
Travel diary; near San Antonio and along the Gulf coast; comments on countryside, Indians.
• "Diary of a Visit of Inspection of the Texas Missions Made by Fray Gaspar José de Solís in the Year 1767-68," Margaret Kenney Kress, trans. Southwestern Historical Quarterly, v. 35, pp. 28-76, 1931-32.

1768

188. COOK, James (1728-79) [A144, B99]
May 27, 1768-July 13, 1771; November 28, 1771-July 19, 1775; February 10, 1776-January 17, 1779
Exploration diary; first circumnavigation aboard the Endeavour; second voyage aboard the Resolution; objective of the third voyage was to find a Northwest Passage; ended with Cook's death; lengthy descriptive passages; discoveries in the Pacific.
• The Journals of Captain James Cook on His Voyages of Discovery. J. C. Beaglehole, ed. Cambridge: Hakluyt Society, 1955-74.
REVIEW: Book Review Digest 1969, pp. 281-82.

1769

189. CAÑIZARES, José de
March 24-June 29, 1769
Exploration diary; overland from Velicata to San Diego; detailed descriptions of topography, flora and fauna.
• "Putting a Lid on California: An Unpublished Diary of the Portolá Expedition by José de Cañizares," Virginia E. Thickens and Margaret Mollins, trans. and eds. California Historical Society Quarterly, v. 31, pp. 109-24, June, 1952; pp. 261-70, September, 1952; pp. 343-54, December, 1952.

190. COSTANSÓ, Miguel
July 14, 1769-January 24, 1770
Exploration diary; engineer with the Portolá expedition; this diary is a different narrative from Costansó's Diario Histórico; Spanish and English texts on facing pages; details of terrain, flora, fauna and Indians.
• The Portolá Expedition of 1769-1770, Diary of Miguel Costansó. Frederick J. Teggert, ed. Manuel Carpio, trans. (Academy of Pacific Coast History Publications, v. 2 no. 4) Berkeley: University of California, 1911.

191. HERDER, Johann Gottfried (1744-1803)
    • "Journal of My Travels in the Year 1769," John F. Harrison,
    trans. Ph.D., Columbia University, 1952. (Dissertation Ab-
    stracts, 13/01, p. 93.) Not seen.

    LABÉ, Guillaume see SURVILLE, Jean de

192. MORISON, Daniel
    December 25, 1769-July 2, 1772
    Personal diary; British surgeon's mate at Fort Michilemackinac
    recounts his troubles with the officers in charge; good account of
    life endured by those not privileged to be officers; mostly a recital
    of the licentious conduct of Ensign Johnson in seducing enlisted men's
    wives and his drunkenness.
    • The Doctor's Secret Journal. George S. May, ed. Mackinac
    Island: Fort Mackinac Division Press, 1960.

193. PILMORE, Joseph (1734?-1825)
    Personal diary; one of the earliest British preachers to labor
    in America; covered territory from Savannah to New York and Phila-
    delphia; internal evidence suggests it was written for publication;
    almost daily entries; through repetition of his sermon texts and
    quotes the reader can gain a feeling for the flavor of the sect and
    its theology.
    • The Journal of Joseph Pilmore, Methodist Itinerant, for the
    Years August 1, 1769, to January 2, 1774. Frederick E. Maser
    and Howard T. Maag, eds. Philadelphia: Historical Society of
    the Philadelphia Annual Conference of the United Methodist
    Church, 1969.

194. SERRA, Junipero (1713-84)
    Travel diary; Spanish priest who established several California
    missions; a correlation of the three known texts and editions of the
    Diario; conditions of travel; stopping at missions; visits with pupils;
    friendly relations with Indians; a pleasant journey.
    • Diario: The Journal of Padre Serra, from Loreto, the Cap-
    ital of Baja California to San Diego ... March 28 to July 1,
    1769. Ben F. Dixon, trans. 2nd ed. San Diego, Don Diego's
    Libraria, 1967.

195. SURVILLE, Jean de (1717-70) and Guillaume LABÉ
    August 21, 1769-January 1, 1770
    Exploration diary; charting the Solomon Islands; from the
    Ganges in India to the Solomons, New Zealand and Peru; several
    encounters with natives and lengthy stays ashore.
    • The Expedition of the St. Jean Baptiste to the Pacific 1769-
    1770. John Dunmore, trans. and ed. London: Hakluyt Society,
    1981. (2nd ser., v. 158)

196. VILA, Vincente
    January 9-May 12, 1769; August 1-24, 1770

Sea diary; logbook of the San Carlos which carried troops and equipment from La Paz to San Diego; Spanish and English texts on facing pages.
- The Portolá Expedition of 1769-1770: Diary of Vincente Vila. Robert Selden Rose, ed. (Academy of Pacific Coast History. Publications v. 2, no. 1) Berkeley: University of California Press, 1911. (Western Americana: An Annotated Bibliography to the Microfiche Collection of 1012 Books and Documents of the 18th, 19th and Early 20th Century. Ann Arbor, Mich.: University Microfilms International, 1976.)

197. VIZCAINO, Juan
     February 15-April 7, 1769
     Sea diary; padre on the San Antonio which was to leave supplies along the California coast for land explorers establishing missions; weather; observations of Indians.
     - The Sea Diary of Fr. Juan Vizcaíno to Alta California, 1769. Arthur Woodward, trans. Los Angeles: G. Dawson, 1959; 225 copies.

1770

198. BURNEY, Charles (1726-1814) [B103]
     June 5-December 18, 1770
     Travel diary; brother of Fanny Burney, Oxford don and professional musician; from Dover to Paris, Geneva, and major Italian cities; vexations of travel, poor food and dishonest innkeepers; attended musical events; comments on libraries used in his research; very detailed, good social history and travelogue; interested in everything from women's fashions to the mismanagement of Italian post offices.
     - Music, Men and Manners in France and Italy, 1770: Being the Journal Written by Charles Burney During a Tour Through Those Countries Undertaken to Collect Material for a General History of Music. H. Edmund Poole, ed. London: Folio Society, 1969.

199. MORGAN, George (1743-1810) [A94]
     March 9-October 2, 1770
     Travel diary; British fur trader went to Illinois to salvage a business; difficulties made for him by military commandant of the area.
     - "George Morgan's 'Memorandums': A Journey to the Illinois Country, 1770," Robert F. Oaks, ed. Journal of the Illinois State Historical Society, v. 69, pp. 185-200, August, 1976.

1771

200. ASBURY, Francis (1745-1816) [A99]
     1771-1816
     Missionary journal; British-born Methodist circuit rider; began

his journal while on shipboard coming to America; this edition is
based on several previous ones, the original manuscripts having been
destroyed (see Introduction); traveled the East Coast logging a quarter of a million miles.
- _Journal and Letters_. Elmer E. Clark, ed. 3 vols. Nashville:
Abingdon Press, 1958.
    REVIEW: _Book Review Digest_ 1959, pp. 35-6.

201. FERSEN, Hans Axel von (1755-1810)
      1. October 17, 1771-November 19, 1778; January 1, 1792-
      November 18, 1793
      Personal diary; Swedish military man and confidante of Marie
Antoinette; accompanied Rochambeau in the American Revolution.
- _Diary and Correspondence of Count Axel Fersen, Grand-
Marshal of Sweden_. Katharine Prescott Wormeley, trans. Bos-
ton: Hardy, Pratt & Co., 1902. (Edition limited to 1250 copies.
Based on the 1878 Paris edition.)

      2. June 26, 1789-November, 1793; Personal diary; interspersed
with letters to and from Fersen; loved and was loved by Marie Antoinette; instrumental in the unsuccessful escape attempts of the
King, Queen and their retainers; entries end with the Queen's death;
moving account of his futile intrigues to free the royal family from
the revolutionaries. Based on the 1925 Swedish edition.
- _Rescue the Queen: A Diary of the French Revolution, 1789-
1793_. Anni Carlsson, comp. London: Bell, 1971.

202. HELFFERICH, Johann Heinrich (1739-1810) [A99]
      September 7, 1771-January 14, 1772
      Travel diary; from Amsterdam to New York with his half
brother.
- "The Journal of Reverend Johann Heinrich Helffrich: A
Diary of His Journey Across the Atlantic in 1771: A Literal
Rather Than a Free Translation of Same," _Pennsylvania Folklife_,
v. 28, pp. 17-24, Summer, 1979.

203. PARKER, Samuel (1744-1804)
      January 1-December 31, 1771
      Personal diary; Harvard graduate; law work; teaching school
in Greenland and Portsmouth, N.H.; line-a-day.
- Lacy, Harriet S. "An Eighteenth-Century Diarist Identified:
Samuel Parker's Journal for 1771," _Historical New Hampshire_,
v. 25, pp. 3-35, Summer, 1970.

204. ROBERTS, Ephraim (1756-1835)
      September 21, 1771-July 5, 1776; gaps
      Personal diary; eldest son settled in Alton, New Hampshire,
with his family; farm life.
- "Ephraim Roberts--Memorandum Book 1771-1776," _Historical
New Hampshire_, v. 24, no. 3, pp. 20-33, 1969.

<u>1772</u>

205. DAVIS, Moses (1743-1824) [A126]
      1772-1824
      Personal diary; article with excerpts; New Hampshire-born
housewright and farmer lived most of his adult life on Davis Island;
vivid picture of his life and times.
      • Chase, Virginia. "Moses Davis: Scribe of the Sheepscot,"
      <u>Down East</u>, v. 4, pp. 22-25, 42-44, June, 1958.

206. FORSTER, Johann Reinhold (1729-98)
      May 6, 1772-July 30, 1775
      Exploration journal; German-born immigrant to England accom-
panied Captain James Cook (q.v.) on his second and third voyages;
detailed scientific observations; interpersonal relations with Cook
and crew; problems and triumphs.
      • <u>The Resolution Journal of Johann Reinhold Forster, 1772-</u>
      <u>1775</u>. (Hakluyt Society, 2nd series, nos. 152-55) London:
      Hakluyt Society, 1982.

207. MORRIS, Robert (1743-93)
      May 15, 1772-July 5, 1774
      Personal diary; executor of the estate of 6th Lord Baltimore
and guardian to his natural daughter, Frances Mary Harford; an account of his elopement with her to the Continent; two marriage cere-
monies performed; finds her not to be quite the innocent he thought;
telegraphic style is sometimes difficult to follow.
      • <u>Radical Adventurer: The Diaries of Robert Morris, 1772-</u>
      <u>1774</u>. J. E. Ross, ed. Bath: Adams and Dart, 1971.

208. ROTH, Rev. Johannes (1725?-91)
      June 11-August, 1772
      Travel diary; descendant of Prussians lead Delaware Indians
to a Moravian settlement in Ohio; accomplished linguist; 380-mile
journey on land and water; deaths from measles; shooting bears,
deer and rattlesnakes; detailed; notes Delaware Indian names for
places.
      • "Diary of a Moravian Indian Mission Migration Across Penn-
      sylvania in 1772," August C. Mahr, ed. <u>Ohio State Archaeolog-</u>
      <u>ical and Historical Quarterly</u>, v. 62, pp. 247-90, July, 1953.

209. STEDMAN, John Gabriel (1744-97)
      October 29, 1772-December 24, 1776; January 31, 1778-June
      24, 1795
      Travel diary; Dutch-born son of an officer in the Scots Bri-
gade serving in Holland; joined an expedition to Surinam to protect
Dutch planters from their escaped slaves; voyage out; military life;
took a Negro slave as his mistress; return to England; marriage;
family life.
      • <u>The Journal of John Gabriel Stedman, 1744-1797, Soldier</u>
      <u>and Author</u>. Stanbury Thompson, ed. London: Mitre Press,
      1962.

210. SWEAT, Samuel (1744-92)
      September 9, 1772-August 25, 1774
      Travel diary; joiner of Kingston, New Hampshire, traveled to
Maine; life and work; prices; lumber bought; belonged to the Sons
of Freedom; forcing a tea merchant to burn his inventory.
      • Lacy, Harriet S. "Samuel Sweat's Diary, 1772-1774," Histor-
      ical New Hampshire, v. 30, pp. 221-30, Winter, 1975.

                                1773

211. FITHIAN, Philip Vickers (1747-76) [A103]
      July 1, 1773-October 25, 1774
      Personal diary; tutor to Carter children at Nomini Hall in tide-
water Virginia; details of plantation life viewed with a sympathetic
eye by an outsider who became one of the family; letters were written
to the family after his departure.
      • Journal and Letters of Philip Vickers Fithian, 1773-1774:
      A Plantation Tutor of the Old Dominion. Hunter Dickinson
      Farish. new ed. New York: Holt, 1964.
         REVIEW: Book Review Digest 1943 pp. 265-66.

212. HARDY, Mary (1733-1809) [B107]
      November 28, 1773-March 21, 1809
      Personal diary; daughter of yeoman married a man who rose
in Norfolk society; social and family life; daily chores; record of
weather; interest in crime news; prices; visit to London.
      • Mary Hardy's Diary. B. Cozens-Hardy, intro. Norfolk:
      Norfolk Record Society, 1968.

213. HARROWER, John (1733/34-77) [A104]
      December 6, 1773-July 28, 1776
      Personal diary; destitute Scotsman served an indenture as a
tutor to a wealthy Virginia planter near Fredericksburg; took in
other pupils to earn extra money to bring his family to Virginia;
good picture of colonial society and first reports of the impending
Revolution.
      • The Journal of John Harrower, an Indentured Servant in
      the Colony of Virginia, 1773-1776. Edward Miles Riley, ed.
      Williamsburg, Va.: Holt, Rinehart & Winston, 1963.
         REVIEW: Book Review Digest 1964, p. 534.

214. HECKEWELDER, John (1743-1823) [A181]
      April 13-May 5, 1773
      Travel diary; Moravian missionaries moved westward with their
Indian converts; to the Tuscarawas Valley.
      • "A Canoe Journey From the Big Beaver to the Tuscarawas
      in 1773: A Travel Diary of John Heckewelder," August C.
      Mahr, trans. and ed. Ohio State Archaeological and Historical
      Quarterly, v. 61, pp. 283-98, July, 1952.

1774

215. BELKNAP, Jeremy (1744-98) [A110]
      August 18-31, 1774
      Travel diary; Dartmouth graduate returned for a visit and to
attend a commencement.
      • Journey to Dartmouth in 1774. Edward C. Lathem, ed.
      Hanover, N.H.: Dartmouth Publications, 1950.

216. HARRISON, Jemima Condict (1755-79)
      August 24, 1774-Summer, 1778; many gaps
      Personal diary; woman living near Newark, New Jersey; family
life; being courted; watching militia training; epidemic of "bloody
flux."
      • "Diary August 24, 1774-Summer, 1778," in: Elizabeth Evans.
      Weathering the Storm: Women of the American Revolution.
      New York: Scribner's, 1975; pp. 33-51.

217. LITCHFIELD, Israel (1753-1840) [A107]
      November 4, 1774-August 25, 1775
      Personal diary; Scituate, Massachusetts native; sermons heard;
farm work; weather; neighborhood activities; drilling with the Minute
Men; capturing Tories.
      • "The Diary of Israel Litchfield," Richard Brigham Johnson,
      ed. New England Historical and Genealogical Register, v. 129,
      pp. 150-71, April, 1975; pp. 250-69, July, 1975; pp. 361-78,
      October, 1975.

218. PREVOST, Augustine (1744-1821)
      April 16-September 24, 1774
      Personal diary; from Kingston, Jamaica, to Baltimore; dealing
with Indian uprising at Fort Pitt.
      • "Turmoil at Pittsburgh: Diary of Augustine Prevost, 1774,"
      Pennsylvania Magazine of History and Biography, v. 85, pp.
      111-62, April, 1961.

219. RIVERA Y MONCADA, Don Fernando Javier
      November 23-December 13, 1774
      Exploration diary; first Spanish exploration of San Francisco
harbor; short but detailed.
      • "Rivera at San Francisco: A Journal of Exploration, 1774,"
      Alan K. Brown, trans. California Historical Society Quarterly,
      v. 41, pp. 325-41, December, 1962.

220. STORRS, Experience (1734-1801) [A120]
      November 21, 1774-June 28, 1775
      Military diary; second in command of the Connecticut troops at
Bunker Hill; account of daily life before the battle; drilling.
      • "Connecticut Farmers at Bunker Hill: The Diary of Colonel
      Experience Storrs," W. Hagelin and R. A. Brown, eds. New
      England Quarterly, v. 28, pp. 72-93, March, 1955.

<u>1775</u>

221. ADAIR, William
      May, 1775–October, 1783
      Personal diary; inhabitant of Sussex County, Delaware gives
glimpses of relations between Loyalists and rebels in his neighborhood.
      • "The Revolutionary War Diary of William Adair," Harold B.
      Hancock, ed. <u>Delaware History</u>, v. 13, pp. 154-65, October,
      1968.

222. BULL, Epaphras
      May 1–June 13, 1775
      Military journal; capture of the fort with Ethan Allen.
      • "Journal of Epaphras Bull From Stockbridge, Massachusetts,
      to Fort Ticonderoga and Return to Connecticut, May, 1775,"
      <u>Fort Ticonderoga Museum Bulletin</u>, v. 8, pp. 38-46, July,
      1948.

223. BUTLER, Richard (1743-91) [A158]
      August 22-September 20, 1775
      Military journal; Pittsburgh agent for Indian Commissioners;
tried to persuade Indians to remain neutral in the Revolution; visited
all the chiefs in the Ohio Territory.
      • "The Journal of Richard Butler, 1775: Continental Congress'
      Envoy to the Western Indians," <u>Western Pennsylvania Historical
      Magazine</u>, v. 46, pp. 381-95, October, 1963; v. 47, pp. 31-46,
      January, 1964; pp. 41-56, April, 1964.

224. CAMPA COS, Miguel de la
      March 16-November 20, 1775
      Exploration journal; Franciscan chaplain went on frigate San-
<u>tiago</u> to explore the west coast of America; from San Blas, Mexico,
to the Gulf of Alaska just shy of 58'; encounters with Indians at
several landfalls.
      • <u>A Journal of Explorations Northward Along the Coast from
      Monterey in the Year 1775</u>. John Galvin, ed. San Francisco:
      J. Howell-Books, 1964; 1000 copies.

225. CAMPBELL, Thomas (1733-95) [B110]
      February 23-August, 1775
      Travel diary; rural Irish curate and antiquary set out for
London; secured an introduction to the Thrale family and through
them met Dr. Samuel Johnson (q.v.) and James Boswell (q.v.); details of their conversations; playgoing; sightseeing; visits to galleries;
criticisms of sermons heard; opinionated and entertaining.
      • <u>Dr. Thomas Campbell's Diary of a Visit to England in 1775</u>.
      James L. Clifford, ed. Cambridge: Cambridge University
      Press, 1947.

226. CURWEN, Samuel (1715-1802) [A44, B110-11]
      April 24, 1775-September 25, 1784; some gaps

Personal diary; Tory of Salem, Massachusetts; fled to England during the Revolution; returned to find his business ruined by stay-at-home wife; back to England and eventual return to U.S.; life in London and other English cities; very detailed and interestingly written.
- The Journal of Samuel Curwen, Loyalist. Andrew Oliver, ed. Cambridge: Harvard University Press, 1972.
   REVIEW: Book Review Digest 1973, p. 280.

227. DEARBORN, Henry (1751-1829) [A112]
September 10, 1775-June 18, 1783
Military journal; probably the most complete journal kept by an American rebel; officer versed in tactics and knowledgeable about army's movements; Quebec expedition and his capture; at the Battle of Saratoga; Yorktown campaign; interesting details on food and transport.
- Revolutionary War Journals of Henry Dearborn, 1775-1783. Lloyd A. Brown and Howard H. Peckham, eds. Chicago: The Caxton Club, 1939.

228. GARCÉS, Francisco Tomás Hermenegildo (1738-81)
November 1, 1775-September 17, 1776
Travel diary; from Tubac, down the Gila River; to Yuma, San Gabriel; up and down the Colorado River; descriptions of Indians, countryside and rancherias.
- On the Trail of a Spanish Pioneer: The Diary and Itinerary of Francisco Garcés (Missionary Priest) ... 1775-1776. Elliott Coues, trans. and ed. New York: F. P. Harper, 1900; Western Americana: An Annotated Bibliography to the Microfiche Collection of 1012 Books and Documents of the 18th, 19th and Early 20th Century. Ann Arbor, Mich.: University Microfilms International, 1976.

229. GREENMAN, Jeremiah (1758-1828)
September 18, 1775-June, 1788
Military journal; expedition to capture Quebec originated in Kennebec, Maine; taken prisoner and later parolled; return to Rhode Island; in Delaware; at Valley Forge briefly; he sees only a small part of the scene and misunderstands some; comments give insight into the lot of the lower ranks.
- Diary of a Common Soldier in the American Revolution, 1775-1783: An Annotated Edition of the Military Journal of Jeremiah Greenman. Robert D. Bray and Paul E. Bushnell, eds. DeKalb: Northern Illinois University Press, 1978.
   REVIEWS: Book Review Index 1979, p. 182. Book Review Digest 1979, p. 500. Historical New Hampshire, v. 33, pp. 354-56, Winter, 1978. Journal of American History, v. 66, pp. 124-25, June, 1979. New Jersey History, v. 97, pp. 123-24, Summer, 1979.

230. HAWES, Samuel (-1780?)
April 19, 1775-February 10, 1776

Military journal; in the siege of Boston; mostly one-line entries, some longer; some humor.
- "The Journal of Samuel Hawes," Richard Brigham Johnson, ed. New England Historical and Genealogical Register, v. 130, pp. 208-19, July, 1976; pp. 273-83, October, 1976; v. 131, pp. 40-50, January, 1977.

231. PARRY, Edward
March 28, 1775-August 23, 1777
Personal diary; mast agent for the Royal Navy and Loyalist in the American Revolution; arrest, trial and imprisonment; released and returned to England.
- Maguire, James H. "A Critical Edition of 'Edward Parry's Journal,' March 28, 1775 to August 23, 1777," Ph.D., Indiana University, 1970. (Dissertation Abstracts, 31/09-A, p. 4724)

232. WILLIAMS, Rev. Stephen (1693-1782) [A35]
- Medlicott, Alexander G., Jr. "The Journals of Rev. Stephen Williams, 1775-1777," Ph.D., University of Washington, 1962. (Dissertation Abstracts 24/01, p. 285)

<u>1776</u>

233. ANONYMOUS
April 20, 1776-October 17, 1777
Military journal: probably written by a member of Brigadier-General Simon Fraser's brigade; relief of Quebec; arrival o. Burgoyne; early success and then disaster; impersonal.
- For Want of a Horse: Being a Journal of the Campaigns Against the Americans in 1776 and 1777 Conducted from Canada. Lt. Col. George F. Stanley, ed. Sackville, N.B.: Tribune Press, 1961.

234. BAURMEISTER, Carl Leopold (1734-1803)
September 2, 1776-April 23, 1784
Political/war diary; general staff officer who reported to the Landgrave of Hesse-Cassel; social and economic commentary.
- Revolution in America: Confidential Letters and Journals, 1776-1784, of Adjutant General Major Baurmeister of the Hessian Forces. Bernhard A. Uhlendorf, trans. and annotated. New Brunswick, N.J.: Rutgers University Press, 1957.

235. BENTLEY, Thomas (1730-80)
July 25-August 13, 1776
Travel diary; associate of Josiah Wedgwood ran the company's London showroom; went to France on business; reports an extended conversation with Jean-Jacques Rousseau; tourist notes.
- Journal of a Visit to Paris 1776. Brighton: University of Sussex Library, 1977.
  REVIEW: English Historical Review, v. 94, p. 201, January, 1979.

236. BLOOMFIELD, Joseph (1753-1823)
      February 8, 1776-February 12, 1782; some gaps
      War diary; lawyer-son of a prominent New Jersey family took
the Patriot side in the Revolution; officer in 3rd New Jersey Contin-
entals; one of the most detailed diaries kept by an American in the
war; aids in understanding of events and personalities which are
alluded to but not fully explained in other sources of the period;
wounded at the Battle of Brandywine; service in Mohawk Valley, N.Y.
      • Citizen Soldier: The Revolutionary War Journal of Joseph
      Bloomfield. Mark E. Lender and James Kirby Martin, eds.
      Newark: New Jersey Historical Society, 1982.

237. DODGE, Nathaniel Brown (-post-1818)
      March 23-August 5, 1776
      Military diary; service in Quebec; inoculated against smallpox;
fragmentary.
      • "Diary Kept by Nathaniel Brown Dodge, 1776," Vermont
      Quarterly, v. 21, pp. 29-35, January, 1953.

238. ENYS, John (1757-1818) [A171]
      February 15, 1776-April 20, 1788; some gaps
      Military journal; service with the 29th Regiment of Foot in Ver-
mont and New York; garrison duty in Ontario; visit to Niagara Falls;
returned home to Cornwall and toured Scotland; post-war sightseeing
in Maryland and Virginia; well-done account of conditions of life at
the time.
      • The American Journals of Lt. John Enys. Elizabeth Com-
      etti, ed. Syracuse, N.Y.: Syracuse University Press, 1976.

239. ESCALANTE, Fray Silvestre Veléz de
      1. July 29, 1776-January 3, 1777; Expedition journal; based
on the earliest known manuscript copy; failed in its objective to establish a trail from Santa Fe to the California missions; an important
journal in the history of Spanish America.
      • The Dominguez-Escalante Journal: Their Expedition Through
      Colorado, Utah, Arizona and New Mexico in 1776. Angelico
      Chavez, trans. Ted J. Warner, ed. Provo, Utah: Brigham
      Young University Press, 1976.

      2. August 1, 1776-January 3, 1777; Expedition journal; ex-
plored a mail and freight route from Santa Fe to Monterey and to
northern California missions; detailed entries on terrain, flora and
fauna.
      • Auerbach, Herbert S., ed. "Father Escalante's Journal
      1776-77," Utah Historical Quarterly, v. 11, pp. 1-132, 1943.

240. EWALD, Johann von (1744-1813) [A155]
      May 9, 1776-April, 1784
      Military journal; part of a jager company used in ambushes;
fought for the British throughout the colonies; leaving Hesse; in
Philadelphia and Charlestown, South Carolina; with Cornwallis in

Virginia; surrender at Yorktown; excellent picture of a dedicated soldier and tactician and a humane individual.
- Diary of the American War: A Hessian Journal. Joseph P. Tustin, trans. and ed. New Haven: Yale University Press, 1979.
     REVIEWS: Book Review Digest 1980, p. 368. Book Review Index 1979, p. 139; 1980, p. 156. Pennsylvania History, v. 47, pp. 274-75, July, 1980. Pennsylvania Magazine of History and Biography, v. 104, pp. 253-54, April, 1980. Virginia Magazine of History and Biography, v. 88, pp. 217-80, April, 1980.
- "A Hessian Visits the Victor: 1783," American Heritage, v. 30, pp. 97-103, August/September, 1979; excerpt of October 21-25, 1783 entries from Yale edition.

241. FISHER, Sarah Logan (-1796)
November 30, 1776-June 18, 1778
Personal diary; Philadelphia Quakeress and British sympathizer; husband was deported to Virginia by the rebels; period of British occupation; home life; details of war and civilian life; ends with the British evacuation of the city.
- "'A Diary of Trifling Occurrences' Philadelphia, 1776-1778," Pennsylvania Magazine of History and Biography, v. 82, pp. 411-69, October, 1958.

242. FITCH, Jabez (1737-1812) [A52]
August 22, 1776-December 15, 1777
Personal diary; prisoner on parole much of the time; his Bible reading; movements; eventual release; pedestrian.
- The New-York Diary of Lieutenant Jabez Fitch. W. H. W. Sabine, ed. New York: New York Times, 1954, 1971.

243. McCARTY, Thomas
August 23, 1776-February 16, 1777
Military diary; service in the 8th Virginia; troop movements throughout New Jersey, Delaware and Virginia; lost his possessions in a fire which destroyed his hut; several skirmishes.
- "The Revolutionary War Journal of Sergeant Thomas Mc-Carty," Jared C. Lobdell, ed. New Jersey History, v. 82, pp. 29-46, January, 1964.

244. MERRICK, Dr. Samuel Fisk (1751-1835/36) [A140]
May 11-September 16, 1776
Military diary; campaign in Quebec area; troop movements; inoculations.
- Davis, David B. "Medicine in the Canadian Campaign of the Revolutionary War: The Journal of Doctor Samuel Fisk Merrick," Bulletin of the History of Medicine, v. 44, pp. 461-73, September-October, 1970.

245. MORRIS, Margaret Hill (1737-1816) [A130]
1. December 6, 1776-June 14, 1777; Personal diary; Quaker

widow lived with her children in Burlington, N.J.; rumors and reports of the fighting; news of the Battle of Trenton; threats to her son who fought with the rebels; treating the wounded; conveys the uncertainty under which the noncombatants lived.
  • Margaret Morris, Her Journal. John W. Jackson, ed. Philadelphia: George S. MacManus, 1949. 350 copies.

  2. "Diary December 6, 1776-June 14, 1777," in: Elizabeth Evans. Weathering the Storm: Women of the American Revolution. New York: Scribner's, 1975; pp. 73-109.

246. PERRY, Joseph (1731-   )
  Personal diary; Harvard graduate and Congregational minister reports on the closing weeks of the siege of Boston from the vicinity of Roxbury.
  • "The Diary of Rev. Joseph Perry Written During the Siege of Boston February 16 to March 28, 1776," James S. Van Ness, ed. Bostonian Society Proceedings. January 15, 1963, pp. 19-56.

247. SNOW, Anne (1752-   )
  September, 1776-December 12, 1777
  Personal diary; undated extracts; London to Calais, Naples, Rome, Venice; acute observer.
  • "Anne Snow's Grand Tour, From Her 18th Century Diary," Trevor Allen, ed. Contemporary Review, v. 211, no. 1223, pp. 319-22, 1967.

248. STIRKE, Lt. Henry (fl. 1775-96)
  June 10, 1776-1777
  Military diary; junior officer in the 10th Regiment of Foot; New York City area; New Jersey.
  • "A British Officer's Revolutionary War Journal, 1776-1778," S. Sydney Bradford, ed. Maryland Historical Magazine, v. 56, pp. 150-75, June, 1961.

1777

249. BRIGHAM, Paul, 1747-1824
  Military diary; at Germantown, Monmouth and Fort Mifflin; very short entries.
  • "A Revolutionary Diary of Captain Paul Brigham: November 19, 1777-September 4, 1778," Edward A. Hoyt, ed. Vermont History, v. 34, pp. 2-30, 1966.

250. DRINKER, Elizabeth Sandwith (1735-1807) [A73]
  Personal diary; second wife of wealthy Philadelphia Quaker Henry Drinker; he was exiled to Virginia by the Pennsylvania Supreme Executive Council for remaining neutral; she stayed in the city with their children; many notes on injustices done to Quakers for their actions.

• "Diary September 2, 1777-December 31, 1780," in: Elizabeth Evans. Weathering the Storm: Women of the American Revolution. New York: Scribner's, 1975; pp. 152-84.

251. HASKINS, Dr. Jonathan (1755-1802)
     1776-1779
     "A Revolutionary Prison Diary: The Journal of Dr. Jonathan Haskins," New England Quarterly, v. 17, pp. 290-309, 424-42, 1944.
     • Alexander, John K. "Jonathan Haskins' Mill Prison 'Diary': Can It Be Accepted at Face Value?" New England Quarterly, v. 40, pp. 561-64, December, 1967. (Alexander believes Haskins plagiarized the diaries of Samuel Cutler and Charles Herbert.)

252. HAZARD, Ebenezer (1744/45-1817)
     May 22-December 17, 1777
     1. Travel diary; journey from Alexandria, Virginia; Williamsburg; description of countryside.
     • "The Journal of the Ebenezer Hazard in Virginia, 1777," Fred Shelley, ed. Virginia Magazine of History and Biography, v. 62, pp. 400-23, October, 1954.

     2. June 12-22, 1777; Suffolk, Virginia to Edenton; December 14, 1777-January 18, 1778; Williamsburg to Wilmington, North Carolina; weather, scenes, accommodations.
     • "The Journal of Ebenezer Hazard in North Carolina, 1777 and 1778," Hugh Buckner Johnston, ed. North Carolina Historical Review, v. 36, pp. 358-81, July, 1959.

     3. August 5-14, 1777; Travel diary; Rebel postmaster for the area from Falmouth, Maine to Philadelphia; from Philadelphia to Newark on an inspection trip; account of wartime conditions in New Jersey.
     • "Ebenezer Hazard's Diary: New Jersey During the Revolution," Fred Shelley, ed. New Jersey History, v. 90, pp. 169-80, Autumn, 1972.

     4. January 18-March 3, 1778; surveying for postal routes; good descriptions.
     • "A View of Coastal South Carolina in 1778: The Journal of Ebenezer Hazard," H. Roy Merrens, ed. South Carolina Historical Magazine, v. 73, pp. 177-93, October, 1972.

     5. February 16-25, 1778; Travel diary; kept while on post office business; mostly in Savannah.
     • "The Journal of Ebenezer Hazard in Georgia, 1778," Fred Shelley, ed. Georgia Historical Quarterly, v. 41, pp. 316-19, September, 1957.

253. HUGHES, Thomas (1759/60-90) [C59]
     September 18, 1777-July 23, 1789
     Military diary; British ensign in 53rd Regiment was sent to

Canada; captured by the Americans and lived under parole for a time;
visit to England and return to Canada; valuable for social history and
everyday life.
- A Journal by Thos. Hughes, For His Amusement and De-
signed Only for His Perusal by the Time He Attains the Age
of 50 If He Lives So Long. Cambridge: Cambridge University
Press, 1947.

254. NAPIER, Lord Francis (1758-1823)
May 6, 1777-June 31, 1778
Military diary; troop movements; fighting in the Hudson Valley;
surrender.
- "Lord Francis Napier's Journal of the Burgoyne Campaign,"
S. Sydney Bradford, ed. Maryland Historical Magazine, v. 57,
pp. 285-333, December, 1962.

255. TUCKER, St. George (1752-1827) [A161]
1. March 7-May 16, 1777; Travel journal; Bermuda-born American jurist; effusive account of unhappy love.
- "Journey to Charleston," Bermuda Historical Quarterly, v. 6,
pp. 135-43, July-September, 1949.

2. September 28-October 23, 1782; resident of the area and
more knowledgeable than some other participants.
- "St. George Tucker's Journal of the Siege of Yorktown,
1781," Edward M. Riley, ed. William and Mary Quarterly, v. 5,
pp. 375-95, July, 1948.

256. VAUGHAN, Zebulon (1744-1824)
August 4, 1777-January 10, 1780
Military diary; poorly spelled; 5th Massachusetts Regiment; in
New York under Col. Rufus Putnam; hard life, little food.
- "The Journal of Private Zebulon Vaughan Revolutionary
Soldier, 1777-1780," Virginia Steele Wood, ed. Daughters of the
American Revolution Magazine, v. 113, pp. 100-14, February,
1979; pp. 256-57, March, 1979; pp. 320-31, April, 1979; pp.
478-85, 87, May, 1979.

257. WISTER, Sarah (Sally) (1761-1804) [A143]
Personal diary; young girl living northeast of Valley Forge
witnessed General Howe's troops moving toward Philadelphia; American army troops quartered on her family's house and grounds; flirt-
ing with the soldiers; ends with Americans retaking Philadelphia.
- "Diary September 24, 1777-June 20, 1778," in: Elizabeth
Evans. Weathering the Storm: Women of the American Revolution. New York: Scribner's, 1975; pp. 110-51.

1778

258. ANONYMOUS
June 17, 1778-December 31, 1779

Military journal; written by either Capt. Lt. Stephen Adye
(d.1794) or Brig. Gen. James Pattison (1723-   ); both of the Royal
Artillery; evacuation of Philadelphia; Battle of Monmouth; siege of
Newport.
- "A New York Diary of the Revolutionary War" Dr. Carson
  I. A. Ritchie, ed. New York Historical Society Quarterly, v. 50,
  pp. 221-80, July, 1966; pp. 401-46, October, 1966.

259. ALMY, Mary Gould (1735-1808) [A143]
Personal diary; Loyalist of Newport, Rhode Island; her husband
was a rebel; reports on the Battle of Rhode Island.
- "Diary August 31-September 2, 1778," in: Elizabeth Evans.
  Weathering the Storm: Women of the American Revolution. New
  York: Scribner's, 1975; pp. 245-70.

260. FELL, John (1721-98) [A138]
November 29, 1778-November 23, 1779
Political diary; service with the Continental Congress; committee
work; dry.
- Delegate From New Jersey: The Journal of John Fell. Donald W. Whisenhunt, ed. Port Washington, N.Y.: Kennikat Press,
  1973.

261. GALLOWAY, Grace Growdon (-1782) [A144]
Personal diary; marriage to a Loyalist caused a Philadelphia
woman to lose her inherited property; account of her attempts to re-
gain it and the injustices done her by the Revolutionaries.
- "Diary July 9, 1778-September 28, 1779," in: Elizabeth
  Evans. Weathering the Storm: Women of the American Revolution. New York: Scribner's, 1975; pp. 185-244.

262. GILBERT, Benjamin, 1755-1828
January 1, 1778-July 11, 1780; January 27-March 22, 1782
Personal diary; Massachusetts native was present at Concord
on April 19, 1775; service in lower Hudson Valley, New York; camp
life, weather, illness.
- A Citizen-Soldier in the American Revolution: The Diary of
  Benjamin Gilbert in Massachusetts and New York. Rebecca D.
  Symmes, ed. Cooperstown: New York State Historical Asso-
  ciation, 1980.

263. HAMILTON, Henry (-1796) [A145]
1. August 6, 1778-June 16, 1779; Military journal; "Hair-
Buyer General" captured by George Rogers Clark at Vincennes and
imprisoned at Williamsburg; march from Detroit to Vincennes; much
detail about the march and Indians who accompanied the British.
- "Journal," in: John D. Barnhart, ed. Henry Hamilton and
  George Rogers Clark in the American Revolution. Crawfordsville, Ind.: R. E. Banta, 1951; pp. 102-205.

2. October 7-December 17, 1778; Military journal; from Detroit
to Vincennes.

• "A New Diary of Lt. Gov. Henry Hamilton," Missouri Historical Society Bulletin, v. 12, pp. 10-24, October, 1955.

264. McCREADY, Robert (1752?-)
November 4-December 8, 1778
Military journal; from Fort McIntosh to Fort Laurens, Northwest Territory.
    • "A Revolutionary Journal and Orderly Book of General Lachlan McIntosh's Expedition, 1778," Edward G. Williams, ed.
Western Pennsylvania Historical Magazine, v. 43, pp. 1-17, March, 1960; pp. 157-77, June, 1960; pp. 267-88, Sept., 1960.

265. MACLEOD, Normand (1731?-96) [A198]
September 25, 1778-January 22, 1779
Military journal; former British army officer, trader and merchant living in Detroit; escaped capture because he was on his way downriver to Vincennes; interesting details of the march.
    • Detroit to Fort Sackville, 1778-1779: The Journal of Normand MacLeod. Detroit: Wayne State University Press, 1977.
        REVIEW: Michigan History v. 63, p. 45, July-August, 1979.

266. SMITH, William (1728-93)
    1. Personal diary; New York Whig-Loyalist; sympathetic to the rebel cause but became an adviser to the British in New York City; chief justice of Quebec after independence; his hopes, fears and frustrations.
    • Acton, Arthur J. "The Diary of William Smith, August 26, 1778 to December 31, 1779," Ph.D., University of Michigan, 1970. (Dissertation Abstracts 31/08-A, p. 4074)

    2. January 24, 1784-October 5, 1785; Personal diary; in London to ask for compensation from the British government for losses in the American Revolution; tourist notes and fretting over slights he received.
    • Diary and Selected Papers of Chief Justice William Smith, 1784-1793. L.F.S. Upton, ed. Toronto: Champlain Society, 1963-65.

1779

267. MEYRONNET DE SAINT-MARC FAURIS, Joseph P.A., Chevalier, 1746-1813
September-October 3, 1779
Military journal; probably not an eyewitness.
    • "Meyronnet de Saint-Marc's Journal of the Operations of the French Army Under D'Estaing at the Siege of Savannah, September, 1779," Roberta Leighton, ed. New York Historical Society Quarterly v. 36, pp. 255-87, July, 1952.

268. NOURSE, James, Jr. (1758-99)
December 27, 1779-February 16, 1780

Travel diary; went with a party from Virginia to Kentucky to
obtain land; endured one of Kentucky's coldest winters.
- "The Journal of James, Nourse, Jr., 1779-1780," Neal O.
Hammon, ed. Filson Club Historical Quarterly, v. 47, pp. 258-
66, July, 1973.

269.   PELL, William
       1779-1794
       Personal diary; extracts with connecting narrative of farm
worker who enlisted in Grenadier Guards; in and around London.
- Adair, P.R. "Sergeant Pell in London," History Today,
v. 21, pp. 732-39, October, 1971.

270.   SPROULE, Moses (1749-1819)
       Military diary; American campaign against the Iroquois in Penn-
sylvania and New York.
- "The Western Campaign of 1779: The Diary of Quartermaster
Sergeant Moses Sproule of the 3rd New Jersey Regiment in the
Sullivan Expedition of the Revolutionary War, May 17-October
17, 1779," R.W.G. Vail, ed. New York Historical Society Quarterly, v. 41, pp. 34-69, January, 1957.

                                    1780

271.   BERTHIER, Louis-Alexander (1753-1815)
       October 4, 1780-June 22, 1781
       Letter journal; aide to Rochambeau; in and around Providence.
- "Alexander Berthier's Journal of the American Campaign:
The Rhode Island Sections," Marshall Morgan, trans. Rhode Is-
land History, v. 24, pp. 77-88, July, 1965.

272.   CLINTON, Sir Henry (1738?-95)
       April 3-May 30, 1780
       Military journal; Clinton's 2nd attack on Charleston succeeded;
5,000 Amer.can rebels captured.
- "Sir Henry Clinton's Journal fo the Siege of Charleston,
1780," William T. Bulger, ed. South Carolina Historical Magazine, v. 66, pp. 147-74, July, 1965.

273.   CLOSEN, Ludwig, Baron von (1752?-1830)
       April, 1780-June 30, 1783
       Personal diary; German aide-de-camp to Rochambeau; by ship
to America; battle preparations; Yorktown; return to New England;
the West Indies and return to France; some material added in later
years.
- Revolutionary Journal of Baron Ludwig von Closen, 1780-
1783. Evelyn M. Acomb, trans. and ed. Chapel Hill: University of North Carolina Press, 1958; selections appeared in
William and Mary Quarterly, April, 1953.

274. HERBERT, Henry, 10th Earl of Pembroke (1734-94) [B117]
     June 30, 1780-March 5, 1794
     More letters than diary entries.
     • Pembroke Papers (1780-1794) Letters and Diaries of Henry,
     10th Earl of Pembroke and His Circle. Lord Herbert, ed. Lon-
     don: Cape, 1950.

275. SAAVEDRA, Don Francisco de (1746-1819)
     • Perez-Alonso, Manuel I. "War Mission in the Caribbean:
     The Diary of Don Francisco de Saavedra, 1780-1783," Ph.D.,
     Georgetown University, 1954. (American Doctoral Dissertations
     W1954, p. 232)

276. SHERWOOD, Captain Justus (1747-98)
     May 7-25, 1781
     Military diary; meeting of diarist and Ethan Allen; negotiations.
     • "Journal. Miller's Bay 26 October, 1780," Vermont History,
     v. 24, pp. 101-09, April, 1956; pp. 211-20, July, 1956.

277. WILSON, John
     February 29-May 12, 1780
     Military journal; 71st British infantry, Corp of Engineers; the
     fall of Charleston.
     • "Lieutenant John Wilson's 'Journal of the Siege of Charles-
     ton,'" Joseph I. Waring, ed. South Carolina Historical Magazine,
     v. 66, pp. 175-82, July, 1965.

                              1781

278. ANONYMOUS
     March 22, 1781-June 17, 1783
     Naval journal; officer of the Foix Regiment; capture of Tobago;
     of Yorktown; return to West Indies; to France via Boston.
     • "Journal of the 1781, 1782, and 1783 Campaigns on the Royal
     Ship Hercule" Constance D. Sherman, ed. and trans. New York
     Historical Society Quarterly, v. 61, pp. 7-48, January-April,
     1977.

279. BYNG, John, 5th Viscount Torrington (1743-1813) [B120]
     May 31, 1781-September 28, 1794
     Travel diaries; to Sussex, Kent, Midlands and elsewhere with
     various companions, crusty, opinionated, entertaining.
     • The Torrington Diaries: A Selection from the Tours of the
     Hon. John Byng, 1781 and 1794. C. Bruyn Andrews, ed.
     Abridged ed. London: Eyre and Spottiswoode, 1954.

280. CLIFFORD, Anna Rawle (1757?-1828)
     Personal diary; Loyalist Philadelphia Quaker living with her
     sister; last days of the war; her house was attacked by victorious
     rebels after Cornwallis' surrender.

• "Diary February 24–October 25, 1781," in: Elizabeth Evans. Weathering the Storm: Women of the American Revolution. New York: Scribner's, 1975; pp. 283-302.

281. DENNY, Ebenezer (1761-1822) [A158]
     May 1, 1781-May 31, 1795; several gaps
     Military journal; fighting with Gen. Anthony Wayne; expedition to Presque Isle; campaign of 1790 in the Northwest Territory; troop movements, battle orders, weather.
     • Military Journal of Major Ebenezer Denny. New York: New York Times, 1971; reprint of 1859 ed.

282. FAGES, Pedro (fl. 1767-96)
     September 16, 1781-April 25, 1782
     Military diary; Spanish leader of an expedition against the Yuma Indians; from Pitic with stops at San Diego and San Juan Capistrano.
     • The Colorado River Campaign, 1781-1782: Diary of Pedro Fages. Herbert Ingram Priestley, ed. Berkeley: University of California Press, 1913; Western Americana: An Annotated Bibliography to Microfiche Collection of 1012 Books and Documents of the 18th, 19th and Early 20th Century. Ann Arbor, Mich.: University Microfilms International, 1976.

283. HONYMAN, Dr. Robert (1747-1824) [A115]
     Public diary; medical man living in Hanover County, Va.; accounts of the campaign gleaned from news reports, passing travelers, etc.
     • "News of the Yorktown Campaign: The Journal of Dr. Robert Honyman, April 17-November 25, 1781," Virginia Magazine of History and Biography, v. 79, pp. 387-426, October, 1971.

284. MIRANDA, Francisco de
     April 8-May 10, 1781
     Military diary; with Bernardo de Galvez besieging the British led by General Campbell.
     • "Miranda's Diary of the Siege of Pensacola, 1781," Donald E. Worcester, trans. Florida Historical Quarterly, v. 29, pp. 163-96, January, 1951.

285. MORRIS, Robert (1734-1806)
     June 8, 1781-April 23, 1784
     Diplomatic diary; extracts are coded indicating to whom Morris refers; concerned with financing the American Revolution.
     • Schappes, Morris U. "Excerpts from Robert Morris' Diaries in the Office of Finance, 1781-1784, Referring to Haym Salomon and Other Jews," American Jewish Historical Quarterly, v. 67, pp. 9-49, 140-61, September-December, 1977.

286. PIERSON, Abraham (1756-1822?)
     May 11, 1781-October 1786
     Personal diary; schoolteacher; birth of children; offices held; justice of the peace; of genealogical interest.

• "Autobiography of Abraham Pierson," <u>Connecticut Historical</u> <u>Society Bulletin</u>, v. 15, pp. 17-24, 31-32, July, 1951; v. 16, pp. 6-7, October, 1951.

1782

287. RIDLEY, Matthew (1749-   )
August 27-December 3, 1782
Diplomatic diary; agent for the state of Maryland; glimpses in Paris of Jay, Franklin and John Adams (q.v.); behind the scenes manuevers; social life.
• Klingelhofer, Herbert E. "Matthew Ridley's Diary During the Peace Negotiations of 1782," <u>William and Mary Quarterly</u>, v. 20, pp. 95-133, January, 1963.

1783

288. CHIPMAN, Ward (1754-1824)
September 21-October 6, 1783
Travel diary; New York to Boston, Marblehead and return.
• "Ward Chipman's Diary: A Loyalist's Return to New England in 1783," Joseph B. Berry, ed. <u>Essex Institute Historical Collections</u>, v. 87, pp. 211-41, July, 1951.

289. SNOWDEN, Gilbert Tennent (1766-97)
September 21, 1783-April 24, 1785
Personal diary; Princeton undergraduate; graduate work; spiritual troubles.
• "The Journal of Gilbert Tennent Snowden," J. Albert Robbins, ed. <u>Princeton University Library Chronicle</u>, v. 14, pp. 72-90, Winter, 1953.

290. WALPOLE, Horace (1717-97) [B84]
• Judd, Gerrit P., IV. "Horace Walpole's Journal, 1783-1791," Ph.D., Yale University, 1947. (American Doctoral Dissertations W1947, p. 72)

1784

291. ADAMS, Abigail Smith (1744-1818)
June 20-July 20, 1784; July 20-28, 1787; March 30-May 1, 1788
Travel diaries; wife of second U.S. president John Adams; tour of the west of England and a trip to America.
• Adams, John. <u>Diary and Autobiography</u>. Cambridge: Harvard University Press, 1960; v. 3, pp. 154-67, 203-08, 212-17.

292. BUTLER, Samuel Edward
February 20-May 12, 1784; March 12-20, 1786

Travel diary; from Hanover County, Virginia to Wilkes County, Georgia with two friends.
- "The Diary of Samuel Edward Butler, 1784-1786 and the Inventory and Aprpaisement of His Estate," G. Melvin Herndon, ed. Georgia Historical Quarterly, v. 52, pp. 203-20, June, 1968.

293. GREEN, John
February 22, 1784-January 12, 1785
Sea diary; master of the Empress of China which opened China to American merchants; from U.S. to Singapore; companion to Samuel Shaw's journal (Matthews A167).
- "Journal of the Ship Empress of China," William Bell Clark, ed. American Neptune, v. 10, pp. 83-107, April, 1950; pp. 220-29, July, 1950; pp. 288-97, October 1950; v. 11, pp. 59-71, January, 1951; pp. 134-44, April, 1951.

294. RUSH, Benjamin (1745?-1813) [A182]
April 2-7, 1784
Travel diary; American physician and signer of the Declaration of Independence; journey from Philadelphia to Carlisle for a meeting of the Dickinson College board of trustees.
- "Dr. Benjamin Rush's Journal of a Trip to Carlisle in 1784," Pennsylvania Magazine of History, v. 74, pp. 443-56, October, 1950.

295. SHERIDAN, Elizabeth (1758-1837)
September 30, 1784-September 16, 1786; July 21, 1788-March 28, 1790
Personal letter/diary; sister of British playwright Richard B. Sheridan; life in her father's house; with the Sheridans in London; Bath and Tunbridge Wells; courted by Henry LeFanu whom she married; gossip with a comic turn; good picture of Sheridan's circle, finances and theatrical life; entertaining.
- Betsy Sheridan's Journal: Letters from Sheridan's Sister, 1784-1786 and 1788-1790. William LeFanu, ed. London: Eyre & Spottiswoode, 1960.

296. WILKIN, James W. (1762-)
February 23-April 2, 1784
Personal diary; studies and food.
- "Princeton in 1784: The Diary of James W. Wilkin of the Class of 1785," Princeton University Library Chronicle, v. 12, pp. 55-66, Winter, 1951.

1785

297. CRANCH, Elizabeth (1743-)
October 5, 1785-March 3, 1786
Personal diary; niece of Abigail Adams (q.v.) visited relatives in Haverhill, Massachusetts; social and family life.

- "The Journal of Elizabeth Cranch," Essex Institute Historical Collections, v. 80, pp. 1-36, January, 1944.

298. ROGERS, Martha (Patty) (1761-1840)
January 1-November 16, 1785
Personal diary; life in Exeter, New Hampshire; caring for her ailing father; beaux; social life.
- "Diary," in: American Women's Diaries: New England Women. New Canaan, Conn.: Readex Microprint Corp., 1984; reel 1.

1786

299. CLARKE, Pitt (1763-1835)
Personal diary; extracts; Medfield, Massachusetts, native began study at Harvard at the age of 23; detailed record of required reading for course work; town and gown clashes; social activities.
- Knapton, Ernest John. "Pitt Clarke's Harvard Diary, 1786-1791," Harvard Library Bulletin, v. 21, pp. 167-86, April, 1973.

300. McCLEAN, Alexander
August 18-October 6, 1786
Exploration diary; from Sharon, Pennsylvania, north to shores of Lake Erie; hardships, weather and work of a survey party.
- "Alexander McClean's Journal of the 1786 Survey of the Western Boundary of Pennsylvania: Volume 2," James L. Murphy, ed. Western Pennsylvania Historical Magazine, v. 63, pp. 321-43, 1980.

1787

301. BECKFORD, William Thomas (1760-1844)
May 25, 1787-January 27, 1788
Travel journal; wealthy Englishman and author of Vathek, an Oriental tale, visited the Iberian Peninsula after the early death of his wife; persona non grata with the English community, he made friends with several titled Portuguese; sightseeing, court life; astute observer.
- The Journal of William Beckford in Portugal and Spain, 1787-1788. Boyd Alexander, ed. London: Hart-Davis, 1954.
  REVIEW: Book Review Digest 1955, p. 56.

302. DEWEES, Mary Coburn [A171]
1. February 27, 1787-January 29, 1788; Travel diary; journey with family party overland and by boat via York and Bedford to Maysville, Kentucky; on to Lexington; comments on modes of travel and fellow travelers.
- Journal of a Trip from Philadelphia to Lexington in Kentucky. Crawfordsville, Ind.: R.E. Banta, 1936; 75 copies.

2. September 27, 1788-February 11, 1789; Travel diary; via Pittsburgh and Wheeling; good description of conditions.
- "Mrs. Mary Dewees's Journal from Philadelphia to Kentucky," John L. Blair, ed. Kentucky Historical Society Register, v. 63, pp. 195-218, July, 1965.

303. LEDYARD, John (1751-89)
June 1, 1787-April 15, 1788
Travel diary; American who sailed with Captain Cook (q.v.) set out from London overland to Russia; planned to cross the American continent from west to east; arrested and deported from Siberia because of Russian protectiveness of their fur trading activities in their American colonies; interesting for its observations on Russian life.
- Journey Through Russia and Siberia, 1787-1788: The Journals and Selected Letters. Stephen D. Watrous, ed. Madison: University of Wisconsin Press, 1966.

304. VAUGHAN, Samuel (-1802)
June 18-July 13, 1787
Travel diary; by coach over the Forbes and Braddock Roads; in Bethlehem and Carlisle; to Washington, Pennsylvania; Cumberland, Maryland; a stop at Mt. Vernon.
- "Samuel Vaughan's Journal or 'Minutes Made by S. V., From Stage to Stage, On a Tour to Fort Pitt,'" Edward G. Williams, ed. Western Pennsylvania Historical Magazine, v. 44, pp. 51-65, March, 1961; pp. 159-73, June, 1961; pp. 261-85, September, 1961.

305. WHITE, John (1757/58-1832)
March 7, 1787-November 11, 1788
Personal diary; surgeon-general to the British expedition which set out for Botany Bay to establish a penal colony; voyage out; landing; exploring the nearby areas; collected flora and fauna for transport to London; pistol duel with his third assistant; medical matters; accompanied exploring parties to the interior.
- Journal of a Voyage to New South Wales. Alec C. Chisholm, ed. Sydney: Angus and Robertson, 1962.

1788

306. CONCHA, Don Fernando de la
August 22-October 6, 1788
Military diary; Spanish governor of New Mexico led an expedition against the Gila and Mimbres Apaches; skirmishes.
- "Colonel Don Fernando de la Concha diary, 1788," Adlai Feather, ed. New Mexico Historical Review, v. 34, pp. 285-304, 1959.

307. MAY, John (1748-1812) [A173]
April 14-September 3, 1788; April 23-December 16, 1789

Personal and business diary; agent of the Ohio Company made two trips to the Territory; merchandising; built a house in Marietta; extensive, detailed entries; well-rounded picture of pioneer Ohio.
- The Western Journals of John May, Ohio Company Agent and Business Adventurer. Dwight L. Smith, ed. Cincinnati: Historical and Philosophical Society of Ohio, 1961.

308. WESTON, James
Personal diary; extracts; farmer-shoemaker; weather, church and his work.
- "The Journal of James Weston, Cordwainer, of Reading, Massachusetts, 1788-1793," Essex Institute Historical Collections, v. 92, pp. 188-202, April, 1956.

1789

309. BASCOM, Ruth Henshaw (1772-1848)
1789-1846
Personal diary; twice married but childless; supplemented her husband's ministerial salary by doing millinery and cutting silhouettes.
- "Diary," in: American Women's Diaries: New England Women. New Canaan, Conn.: Readex Microprint Corp., 1984; reels 1-3.

310. MacKENZIE, Sir Alexander (1763-1820) [A174]
June 3-September 12, 1789; October 10, 1792-August 24, 1793
Exploration journal; by canoe from Lake Athabasca in search of a Northwest Passage to the Pacific; 2nd voyage from Fort Chipewyan to the Pacific.
- The Journals and Letters of Sir Alexander MacKenzie. W. Kaye Lamb, ed. Cambridge: University Press, 1970.

1790

311. FRANCIS, John (1763-96)
September 19-29, 1790
Travel diary; from Providence, Rhode Island via Boston to Dummerston, Vermont; business trip.
- "In Search of Cahoone, the 1790 Diary of John Francis," Old Time New England, v. 60, pp. 55-71, October-December, 1969.

312. INGRAHAM, Joseph (1762-1800) [A179]
September 16, 1790-November 6, 1792
Travel diary; "fullest and most vivid journal" of the times for the northwest coast of America and China; from Boston, around the Horn; in Hawaiian and Marquesas Islands; buying otterskins from Indians of the northwest coast; to China and Hawaii again; very well-written with digressions of narrative by a literate, forthright man.

• Journal of the Brigantine 'Hope' on a Voyage to the Northwest Coast of North America, 1790-92. Mark D. Kaplanoff, ed. Barre, Mass.: Imprint Society, 1971.

313. NILES, Elisha (1764-1845)
      1790-1845
      Personal diary; extracts with connecting narrative.
      • Cook, Doris E. "Living and Working in Central Connecticut, 1764-1845: The Journal of Elisha Niles," Connecticut Historical Society Bulletin, v. 35, pp. 114-21, October, 1970.

314. RODNEY, Thomas (1744-1811) [A132]
      June 1-16, 1790
      Travel diary; former member of the Continental Congress; much about accommodations, travel modes and the aftermath of the Revolution still visible in the landscape he passed through.
      • "Thomas Rodney's Diary of a Journey by Carriage From Delaware to New York City," M. M. Merwin, ed. Delaware History, v. 17, pp. 199-213, Spring-Summer, 1977.

                                    1791

315. SIMCOE, Elizabeth Posthuma Gwillim, 1766-1850 [C109, A180]
      September 17, 1791-October, 1796
      Personal diary; wife of the lieutenant-governor of Upper Canada accompanied her husband there with an infant and a toddler; meeting with George III; voyage to Canada; life at Quebec, Niagara and York; return to London; social life, politics; keen observer.
      • Diary. Mary Quayle Innis, ed. New York: St. Martin's, 1965.

316. SURÍA, Tomás de (1761-1835)
      February 16-August 13, 1791
      Sea diary; Mexican engraver accompanied a Spanish mapping expedition seeking a water passage across Central America; unromanticized view of the Indians and candid comments of a landlubber.
      • Journal of Tomás de Suría of His Voyage with Malaspina to the Northwest Coast of America in 1791. Donald C. Cutter, ed. Fairfield, Wash.: Ye Galleon Press, 1980; reprinted with additional material from: Pacific Historical Review, Henry R. Wagner, ed. and trans. v. 5, pp. 234-76, 1936.

317. ZEISBERGER, David (1721-1808) [A50]
      Official diary; Moravian missionary; an account of the Battle of Fallen Timbers.
      • Mueller, Paul E. "David Zeisberger's Official Diary, Fairfield 1791-1795," Ph.D., Columbia University, 1956. (Dissertation Abstracts 16/08, p. 1437)

1792

318. STEVENS, William Bagshaw (1756-1800)
      March 15, 1792-April 6, 1800
      Personal diary; English clergyman lived with his sister in Rep-
ton, Derbyshire; headmaster of a boys' school; in love with the daughter of the landed gentry and could not marry her; social life.
      • The Journal of the Rev. William Bagshaw Stevens. Georgina
      Galbraith, ed. Oxford: Clarendon Press, 1965.
         REVIEW: Book Review Digest 1967, pp. 1258-59.

319. UNDERWOOD, Thomas Taylor (-1844?)
      Military diary; many gaps; with Mad Anthony Wayne in Ohio;
adds nothing new to campaign accounts but helps corroborate others;
notes Wayne was a stickler for discipline; some unknown sidelights.
      • Journal Thomas Taylor Underwood, March 26, 1792 to March
      18, 1800; An Old Soldier in Wayne's Army. Cincinnati: Society
      of Colonial Wars in the State of Ohio, 1945; 500 copies.

1793

320. BADOLLET, John (1757-   )
      October 24, 1793-May 9, 1794
      Personal diary; Swiss immigrant and friend of Albert Gallatin;
employed as a road surveyor in Fayette and Bedford counties; describes countryside, travel, inhabitants.
      • "John Badollet's 'Journal of the Time I Spent in Stony Creeck
      [sic] Glades,' 1793-1794," William A. Hunter, ed. Pennsylvania
      Magazine of History and Biography, v. 104, pp. 162-99, 1980.

321. BUELL, John Hutchinson (1753-   ) [A154]
      March 25, 1793-February 14, 1795
      Military journal; major under General Anthony Wayne in the
Indian Wars; skirmishes and treaties with Indians.
      • The Diary of John Hutchinson Buell. Richard C. Knopf, ed.
      Columbus: Ohio State Museum, 1957.

322. FARINGTON, Joseph (1747-1821) [B129-30]
      July 13, 1793-December 30, 1821
      Personal diary; Norfolk-born landscape artist trained under
Richard Wilson; active in the Royal Academy; much information on
contemporary artists and their work; social, political and literary affairs of the era.
      • The Diary of Joseph Farington. Kenneth Garlick and Angus
      Macintyre, eds. 3 vols. New Haven: Yale University Press,
      1978-79.
         REVIEWS: Book Review Index 1979, p. 141; 1980, p. 158.

323. MACARTNEY, George (1737-1806)
      June 15, 1793-January 15, 1794

Diplomatic/travel diary; headed Britain's first effort to begin diplomatic relations with China; mission foundered because of each country's inability to understand the other; journey overland from Peking to Canton; observant; interesting.
- An Embassy to China, Being the Journal Kept by Lord Macartney During His Embassy to the Emperor Ch'ien-lung, 1793-1794. J. L. Cranmer-Byng, ed. London: Longmans, 1962.

324. NORMAN, Jeremiah (1771-1843)
1793-1801
Personal diary; undated extracts; well-educated; "revelation of his character and emotions"; organized the Methodist Episcopal circuit in Augusta, Georgia.
- Stokes, Durward T. "Jeremiah Norman, Pioneer Methodist Minister in Augusta, and His Diary," Richmond County [Ga.] History, v. 10, pp. 20-35, 1978.

325. TOULMIN, Harry (1767-1823)
July 19-August 7, 1793
Travel diary; British Unitarian minister made a voyage to America to ascertain whether his congregation should emigrate; dated entries constitute only a small portion and were written in Virginia; long essays on life, agriculture, weather in Kentucky; panoramic picture by keen observer.
- The Western Country in 1793: Reports on Kentucky and Virginia. Marion Tinling and Godfrey Davies, eds. San Marino, Cal.: Henry E. Huntington Library and Art Gallery, 1948.

1794

326. ANONYMOUS
Personal diary; detailed account by a ranking officer; construction of Fort Defiance; valuable for particulars of relations between General Wayne and subordinate James Wilkinson; "mine of information on the Wayne campaign."
- Smith, Dwight L., ed. "From Green Ville to Fallen Timbers: A Journal of the Wayne Campaign July 28-September 14, 1794," Indiana Historical Society Publications, v. 16, pp. 239-326, 1952.

327. ADAMS, John Quincy (1767-1848) [A170]
1. June 3, 1794-March 13, 1845; Personal diary; selections from Charles Francis Adams' edition of 1874-77; emphasizes "materials which throw light on the social background of the period"; for the general reader.
- The Diary of John Quincy Adams, 1794-1845. Allan Nevins, ed. New York: Scribner, 1951; New York: Ungar, 1969.

2. "Diary Excerpts," in: Philip Dunaway and Mel Evans, eds.

A Treasury of the World's Great Diaries. New York: Doubleday, 1957; pp. 195-208.

328. BISHOP, Charles
      October 17, 1794-March 31, 1796
      Travel diary; from Bristol to America to buy otter skins; trading with Indians; to Hawaii; landing at Rio de Janeiro; some interesting passages embedded in a stilted style.
      • *The Journal and Letters of Captain Charles Bishop on the North-west Coast of America, in the Pacific and in New South Wales, 1794-1799*. Michael Roe, ed. Cambridge: University Press, 1967.

329. CAZENOVE, Theophile (1740-1811) [A185-86]
      October 1-November 16, 1794
      Travel diary; Frenchman working for Dutch investors went to America with his valet to investigate possibilities for making money; detailed notes on travel, food, accommodations and sights.
      • *Cazenove Journal, 1794: A Record of the Journey Through New Jersey and Pennsylvania*. Rayner Wickersham, trans. and ed. Haverford, Pa.: Pennsylvania History Press, 1922.
      REVIEW: *Book Review Digest* 1922, p. 97.

330. DAVY, William (1757-1827) [B138]
      September 26-October 23, 1794
      Travel diary; Englishman with family and servants visited northern Pennsylvania with an eye to settling there; from Philadelphia west to Northumberland county; details of countryside, crops, prices.
      • "Mr. Davy's Diary 1794," Norman B. Wilkinson, ed. *Pennsylvania History*, v. 20, pp. 122-41, April, 1953; pp. 258-79, July, 1953.

331. EMLEN, James (1760-98)
      Personal diary; Quaker member of the commission; good description of the frontier, its inhabitants and the work of the treaty group.
      • "The Journal of James Emlen Kept on a Trip to Canandaigua, New York September 15 to October 30, 1794 to Attend the Treaty Between the U.S. and the Six Nations," William N. Fenton, ed. *Ethnohistory*, v. 12, pp. 279-342, Fall, 1965.

332. GRIERSON, William (1773-1852)
      January 1, 1794-January 24, 1811
      Personal diary; merchant in Dumfries, Scotland; acquaintance of Robert Burns; responsible for erecting a memorial to the poet; personal life; public happenings and current events; courtship, marriage and children; good social history.
      • *Apostle to Burns: The Diaries of William Grierson*. John Davies, ed. Edinburgh: Blackwood, 1981.

333. HAMBLY, John (1751-98)
      June 29-August 27, 1794

Travel diary; on a mission to the Indians for the Spanish governor.
* "Visit to the Indian Nations: The Diary of John Hambly," Daniel J. J. Ross and Bruce S. Chappell, eds. Florida Historical Quarterly, v. 55, pp. 60-73, July, 1976.

334. PARRY, Needham
May 21-June 15, 1794
Travel diary; down the Ohio River from Pittsburgh to sell saddles; return via Wilderness Road; keen observer.
* "John D. Shanes' Copy of Needham Parry's Diary of Trip Westward in 1794," Lucien Beckner, ed. Filson Club Historical Quarterly, v. 22, pp. 227-47, October, 1948.

335. RANDOLPH, ---
July 28-November 2, 1794
Military journal; self-consciously literary; aftermath of the Fort Recovery attack.
* "A Precise Journal of General Wayne's Last Campaign," Richard C. Knopf, ed. American Antiquarian Society Proceedings, v. 64, pp. 273-302, October, 1954.

336. THOMAS, Aaron (1762-   ) [B150]
April 15, 1794-February 4, 1795
Sea diary; letter journal kept for a friend; "rare account of life on a ship of the Royal Navy in 1794"; though listed as an able seaman he carried out errands such as a captain's steward would undertake; Boston guarded a convoy of traders on the Atlantic crossing during the war with France; well-written with much on life and customs of Newfoundland.
* The Newfoundland Journal of Aaron Thomas, Able Seaman in H. M. S. Boston. Jean M. Murray, ed. London: Longmans, 1968.

1795

337. ANDREWS, Joseph Gardner (1768?-   )
January 31-December 31, 1795
Personal diary; Harvard graduate stationed at Fort Defiance after General Wayne's defeat of the Indians at Fallen Timbers; visits from Indians suing for peace; weather notes; details of food and medicine; lucid.
A Surgeon's Mate at Fort Defiance: The Journal of Joseph Gardner Andrews for the Year 1795. Richard C. Knopf, ed. Columbus: Ohio Historical Society, 1957; reprinted from Ohio Historical Quarterly, v. 66, pp. 57-86, January, 1957; pp. 159-86, April, 1957; pp. 238-68, July, 1957.

338. BEETHOVEN, Ludwig van (1770-1827)
December, 1795-1818

Fragmentary diary entries interspersed with letters.
- Letters, Journals and Conversations. Michael Hamburger,
ed. and trans. London: Thames and Hudson, 1951.

339. LATROBE, Benjamin Henry (1764-1820) [A191]
1. November 25, 1795-November 30, 1798; some gaps; Personal
diary; English architect and engineer did his major work in the U.S.;
by ship from London to Norfolk, Virginia; lived chiefly in Richmond;
flora, fauna, social life and customs; his sketches are included here;
a scholarly and beautiful volume.
- The Virginia Journals of Benjamin Henry Latrobe 1795-1798.
Edward C. Carter II, ed. 2 vols. New Haven: Yale University Press, 1977.

2. September 17, 1799-September 21, 1801; July 28-December
11, 1806; December 21, 1818-September 3, 1820; Era of his greatest
professional success; work on the U.S. Capitol, canals, Roman Catholic Cathedral in Baltimore; written in Philadelphia, Washington, New
Orleans; not merely diaries but essays on natural history, Virginia
society, medicine; embellished by sketches and watercolors; excellent.
- The Journals of Benjamin Henry Latrobe 1799-1820: From
Philadelphia to New Orleans. (Vol. 3 of The Papers of Benjamin Henry Latrobe) Edward C. Carter II, John C. Van Horne,
and Lee W. Formwalt, eds. New Haven: Yale University Press,
1980.

3. December 21, 1818-August 14, 1820; Travel diary; by ship
from Baltimore to New Orleans; much on the lifestyle of the city's
varied population; sketches included.
- Impressions Respecting New Orleans ... Diaries and Sketches,
1818-1820. Samuel Wilson, Jr., ed. New York: Columbia University Press, 1951.

340. PEASE, John (1775-1808)
November 22, 1795-January 14, 1796
Travel diary; young man accompanied a businessman associated
with his family's firm; unconsciously humorous.
- "Journal of a Traveller in Scotland, 1795-1796," Peter Barber,
ed. Scottish Historical Review, v. 36, pp. 25-51, April, 1957.

341. SMITH, Elihu Hubbard (1771-98)
September 4, 1795-September 15, 1798
Personal diary; Connecticut doctor and Yale graduate; his prac-
tice, reading, social life; includes texts of letters to friends and pro-
fessional associates.
- The Diary of Elihu Hubbard Smith (1771-1798). James E.
Cronin, ed. Philadelphia: American Philosophical Society, 1973.
REVIEW: American Historical Review, v. 81, p. 654, June,
1976.

342. ZUÑIGA, José
April 9-May 29, 1795

Exploration journal; seeking a trade route between Sonora and Santa Fe; Spanish expedition with Apache scouts.
  • "The Zuñiga Journal, Tucson to Santa Fe: The Opening of a Spanish Trade Route, 1788-1795," New Mexico Historical Review, v. 6, pp. 40-65, January, 1931.

1796

343. ARRILLAGA, José Joaquin (1750-1814)
      June 14-November 21, 1796
      Exploration journal; expedition to find sites for Spanish missions and open a land route to the Sonora Mission in Baja, California; description of terrain; encounters with Indians.
        • José Joaquin Arrillaga: Diary of His Surveys of the Frontier, 1796. Fray Tiscareno, trans. John W. Robinson, ed. Los Angeles: Dawsons Book Shop, 1969.

344. DIMOCK, Joseph, 1768-1846
      October 13, 1796-December 15, 1844; infrequent entries.
      Personal diary; first Baptist minister born and ordained in Canada; preaching; church work; sermonizing.
        • The Diary and Related Writings of the Reverend Joseph Dimock (1768-1846). George E. Levy, ed. Hantsport, N.S.: Lancelot, 1979.
          REVIEW: Social History, v. 13, pp. 264-65, May, 1980.

345. GRANGER, Eli (-1823)
      October 13-November 2, 1796; March 14-August 11, 1797
      Personal diary; early settler in what became Rochester, New York; visit to Niagara Falls; daily life; surveying for a road.
        • Toth, Margaret. "The Diaries of Eli Granger," University of Rochester Library Bulletin, v. 6, pp. 49-57, Spring, 1951.

346. HUNTER, George (1755-1823)
      July 14-September 15, 1796; August 19-October 23, 1802; May 27-September 25, 1805
      Exploration diary; Edinburgh-born chemist and retail druggist went west probably to search for investments in land and to settle a friend's will; explored Louisiana at the request of President Thomas Jefferson; Natchez; one of the earliest accounts in English of the frontier of the time; later outshone by Lewis and Clark.
        • The Western Journals of Dr. George Hunter, 1796-1805. John Francis McDermott, ed. (American Philosophical Society Transactions, new series, v. 53, part 4, 1963) Philadelphia: American Philosophical Society, 1963.

347. JUVENAL, Father
      June 19-September 29, 1796
      Personal diary; Russian priest established a school; moved to another mission; stabbed by natives after telling a chief he had to give up all but one wife.

• "A Daily Journal Kept by the Rev. Father Juvenal, One of
the Earliest Missionaries to Alaska," Kroeber Anthropological
Society Papers, v. 6, pp. 26-59, June, 1952.

1797

348. CHABOILLEZ, Charles Jean Baptiste (1742-)
August 4, 1797-June 21, 1798
Personal diary; veteran fur trader worked in the area of pres-
ent day northern Minnesota and southern Manitoba; Chippewa Indians.
• "Journal of Charles Jean Baptiste Chaboillez, 1797-1798,"
Harold Hickerson, ed. Ethnohistory, v. 6, pp. 265-316, Sum-
mer, 1959; pp. 363-427, Fall, 1959.

349. HILL, Frances Baylor (-1799?)
January 1-December 31, 1797
Personal diary; young girl of indeterminate age lived at home
with her parents; family owned slaves; household work, knitting,
weaving, visiting, nursing.
• "The Diary of Frances Baylor Hill of 'Hillsborough' King and
Queen County Virginia, (1797)," William K. Bottorff and Roy C.
Flannagan, eds. Early American Literature, v. 2, pp. 4-53,
Winter, 1967. [entire issue]

350. LOUIS-PHILIPPE (1773-1850)
March 25-May 21, 1797
Travel diary; future king of France, two younger brothers and
a servant toured settled areas of U.S.; New York City, Buffalo, Up-
per South.
• Diary of My Travels in America. Stephen Becker, trans.
New York: Delacorte Press, 1977.
    REVIEW: Book Review Digest 1978, p. 817.

351. NIEMCEWICZ, Julian Ursyn (1758-1841)
    1. Budka, Metchie J. E. "The American Diaries of Julian
Ursyn Niemcewicz (1797-1799, 1805) with an Introduction and Notes,"
Ph.D., Harvard University, 1962.

    2. October 5-26, 1805; Travel diary; Polish poet journeyed
with friends from Elizabeth, New Jersey to Niagara Falls by carriage
and wagon; excellent portrait of travel conditions and scenery.
• "Journey to Niagara, 1805: From the Diary of Julian Ursyn
Niemcewicz," Metchie J. E. Budka, trans. New York Historical
Society Quarterly, v. 44, pp. 72-113, January, 1960.

352. THOMPSON, David (1770-1857) [A216]
    1. December 30, 1797-January 12, 1798; Exploration diary;
explorer and fur trader; explored areas of North Dakota; accurate
observations; weather.
• Wood, W. Raymond. "David Thompson at the Mandan-Hidatsa

Villages, 1797-1798: The Original Journals," <u>Ethnohistory</u>, v.
24, pp. 329-42, Fall, 1977.

2. April 20, 1808-March 13, 1812; gaps; Expedition diary; explored, surveyed and mapped Canada between Hudson Bay and the
Pacific coast; discovered the source of the Columbia River; in Montana and Oregon; on the Columbia and Fisher Rivers; at Clark Fork;
at Pend Oreille and Windermere Lakes; weather, distances, travel
notes in telegraphic style.
• <u>Journals Relating to Montana and Adjacent Regions, 1808-
1812</u>. M. Catherine White, ed. Missoula: Montana State University Press, 1950; 500 copies.

1798

353. WORDSWORTH, Dorothy (1771-1855) [B150]
    1. January 20-May 22, 1798; May 14, 1800-January 16, 1803;
Personal diary; sister of English poet William Wordsworth; a legacy
to him enabled the two to live together in the Lake District; rambles,
visits from friends; housekeeper and amanuensis to her brother;
poetic prose.
• <u>Journals of Dorothy Wordsworth: The Alfoxden Journal,
1798: The Grasmere Journals 1800-1803</u>. Helen Darbishire,
intro. Mary Moorman, ed. New ed. London: Oxford University
Press, 1971.

    2. Article with dated extracts.
• Brownstein, R. M. "Private Life: Dorothy Wordsworth's
Journals," <u>Modern Language Quarterly</u>, v. 24, pp. 48-63,
March, 1973.

    3. "Diary Excerpts," in: Philip Dunaway and Mel Evans.
<u>A Treasury of the World's Great Diaries</u>. New York: Doubleday,
1957; 115-21.

    4. "Diary Excerpts," in: Elizabeth D'Oyley, ed. <u>English Di-
aries</u>. London: Edward Arnold, 1930; pp. 195-210.

    5. "Diary Excerpts," in: Mary Jane Moffat and Charlotte
Painter, eds. <u>Revelations: Diaries of Women</u>. New York: Random
House, 1974; pp. 178-91.

1799

354. BULLEN, Joseph (1751-1825)
    March 26-June 27, 1799; July 3-November 3, 1800
    Missionary diary; Presbyterian missionary to the Choctaws in
Mississippi; life with Chickasaws near Tupelo; much on Indian culture
and their relations with whites.

- "Excerpts from the Journal of the Rev. Joseph Bullen, 1799 and 1800" Dawson A. Phelps, ed. Journal of Mississippi History, v. 17, pp. 254-81, October, 1955; reprinted from New York Missionary Magazine, v. 1, pp. 262-74, 365-75, 1800.

355. DREW, Abigail Gardner (1777-1868)
1799-1867; gaps
Personal diary; unhappily married scion of pioneer Nantucket family; con.ided in several women friends; poetry; family finances; social life.
- "Diary," in: American Women's Diaries: New England Women. New Canaan, Conn.: Readex Microprint Corp., 1984; reels 1-11.

356. MALTHUS, Thomas Robert (1766-1834)
May 25-August 3, 1799; June 4-July 21, 1825; June 17-July 19, 1826.
Travel diaries; English economist and population theorist; 1) throughout Scandinavia with friends; Cuxhaven, Copenhagen, by sea and land to Trondheim, south to Magnor; 2) Low Countries and Rhine from Calais east to Mainz and north to Alkmaar; 3) Scottish tour from Hertford to Aberfeldy, Edinburgh and Greenock; comments on scenery, people met and their mores, prices; first diary (Scandinavia) has the fullest entries and is the most interesting.
- The Travel Diaries of Thomas Robert Malthus. Patricia James, ed. London: Cambridge University Press, 1966.

357. RIPLEY, Sally (1785-   )
1799-1801; 1805-09
Personal diary; school days, family life; trips to Boston from native Greenfield, Massachusetts.
- "Diary," American Women's Diaries: New England Women. New Canaan, Conn.: Readex Microprint Corp., 1984; reel 1.

358. STURGIS, William (1782-1863)
February 13-May 17, 1799
Travel diary; Bostonian employed in the fur trade in the Pacific Northwest; journal begins with his arrival on the West Coast; details of trading and relations with Indians; valuable record.
- The Journal of William Sturgis. S. W. Jackman, ed. Victoria, B. C.: Sono Nis Press, 1978.
   REVIEWS: American Neptune, v. 39, p. 145, April, 1979. Alaska Journal, v. 8, pp. 378-79, Autumn, 1978. Alberta History, v. 27, p. 36, Winter, 1979. Choice, v. 15, p. 1421, December, 1978. Canadian Historical Review, v. 61, pp. 223-24, June, 1980.

1800

359. BAUDIN, NICOLAS (1750-1803)
October 18, 1800-August 5, 1803

Exploration journal; French naval officer with an interest in
natural history proposed and captained an expedition to Australia;
from Le Havre via Tenerife and the Cape of Good Hope; New Holland,
Van Dieman's Land, Timor; bad relations with some of the naturalists
aboard; problems with rations and illness; collecting specimens; very
detailed; Baudin was fictionalized as a character in Southern Cross
by Terry Coleman. (New York: Viking, 1979)
  • The Journal of Post Captain Nicolas Baudin Commander-in-
  Chief of the Corvettes "Geographe" and "Naturaliste." Chris-
  tine Cornell, trans. Adelaide: Library Board of South Australia, 1974.

360. CLEVELAND, William [A197]
     July 16-November 25, 1800
     Sea diary; from a family of Salem, Massachusetts, mariners;
anchored in Nagasaki harbor; unloading cargo; provisioning for the
next voyage; shore excursions; routine duties mixed with wonderment.
  • A Diary of William Cleveland, Captain's Clerk on Board the
  Massachusetts. Madoka Kanai, ed. Quezon City: Institute of
  Asian Studies, University of the Philippines, 1965.

361. COPE, Thomas Pym (1768-1854)
     1. July 3-16, 1800; Travel diary; trip to New Jersey and New
York to look into matters concerned with the waterworks project.
  • Maass, Eleanor A. "A Public Watchdog: Thomas Pym Cope
  and the Philadelphia Waterworks," American Philosophical Society Proceedings, v. 125, pp. 134-54, 1981.

     2. August 9, 1800-October 2, 1820; March 19, 1843-March 17,
1851; Personal diary; successful Quaker businessman who rose by his
own efforts to a place of respect in Philadelphia; family life, business
dealings; trips to New York, Washington; involvement in politics; at
times pompous but interesting for its comments on everyday affairs.
  • Philadelphia Merchant: The Diary of Thomas Pym Cope,
  1800-1851. Eliza Cope Harrison, ed. South Bend, Ind.: Gate-
  way Editions, 1978.
     REVIEW: Pennsylvania Magazine of History and Biography,
     v. 103, pp. 399-401, July, 1979.

362. KING, Reuben (1779-1867)
     February 13, 1800-October 30, 1806
     Personal diary; Connecticut tanner migrated to Darien, Georgia;
travel south; details of his work; relieved himself of colic by drinking whiskey and black pepper; good account of small town life for
the period.
  • "The Reuben King Journal 1800-1806," Virginia Steele Wood
  and Ralph Van Wood, eds. Georgia Historical Quarterly, v. 50,
  pp. 177-206, June, 1966; pp. 296-335, September, 1966; pp.
  421-58, December, 1966; v. 51, pp. 78-120, March, 1967.

363. PARK, Louisa Adams (1773-1813)
     1800-01

Personal diary; kept while her husband, a doctor with the U.S.
Navy, was away on a voyage; death of a son.
- "Diary," in: <u>American Women's Diaries: New England Women</u>.
New Canaan, Conn.: Readex Microprint Corp., 1984; reel 1.

364. POSTLETHWAITE, Samuel (1772-1825)
September 13, 1800-February 9, 1801
Travel diary; by flatboat down the Ohio and Mississippi Rivers;
good descriptions.
- "Journal of a Voyage from Louisville to Natchez-1800," <u>Mis-</u>
<u>souri Historical Society Bulletin</u>, v. 7, pp. 312-29, April, 1951.

365. SOUTHEY, Robert (1774-1843) [B187]
April 30, 1800-April 29, 1801; August 2-September 25, 1838
Travel diary; English Poet Laureate; arrival in Lisbon; excursions to Coimbra and the south; from home across the Channel and
in northern France.
- <u>Journal of a Residence in Portugal, 1800-1801, and a Visit</u>
<u>to France 1838</u>. Adolfo Cabral, ed. Oxford: Clarendon Press,
1960.

1801

366. LAMARTINE, Françoise-Alix de (-1829)
June 16, 1801-October 21, 1829; gaps due to loss of parts of
the manuscript
Personal diary; mother of French romantic poet Alphonse de Lamartine; "I am going to have much trouble with this child who is difficult to control"; pious, unreconstructed monarchist was a refugee
during the Napoleonic Wars; family matters; marriages of her daughters and birth of grandchildren; tried to aid those displaced by the
Revolution.
- <u>The Heart's Memory: Pages from the Diary of Mme. de La-</u>
<u>martine</u>. Eustace Hargreaves, ed. and trans. London: Dent,
1951.

367. "STENDHAL" (Marie Henri Beyle) (1783-1842)
1. April 18, 1801-July 4, 1814; Personal diary; French writer
and novelist; in Paris, Germany, Vienna and Italy; with Napoleon's
army in Italy; writing; his reading; enthusiastic and ebullient.
- <u>The Private Diaries of Stendhal</u>. Robert Sage, ed. and
trans. New York: Doubleday, 1954.

2. "Diary Excerpts," in: Philip Dunaway and Mel Evans, eds.
<u>A Treasury of the World's Great Diaries</u>. New York: Doubleday,
1957; pp. 36-41.

1802

368. GREATHEED, Bertie (1759-1826)

December 24, 1802-October 12, 1803
Travel diary; English squire went to Paris with his wife and
novice painter son; renewal of hostilities between France and England;
meetings with Napoleon and his mother; eventually paroled to visit
Germany; much on Parisian art life; pleasing.
- An Englishman in Paris, 1803. J. P. T. Bury and J. C.
Barry, eds. London: Bles, 1953.

369. HEMPHILL, James (1774-1833) [A183]
October 21-November 15, 1802
Travel diary; accompanied by a younger brother; by stage and
chaise through Delaware and Maryland; accommodations and travel con-
ditions.
- "James Hemphill's Account of a Visit to Maryland in 1802,"
John A. Munroe, ed. Delaware History. v. 3, pp. 61-78,
September, 1948.

370. SYMES, Michael
September 26, 1802-January 20, 1803
Diplomatic diary; sent by the governor-general of Fort William
to Burma to mediate a dispute; endless, fruitless negotiations; plagued
by his own and companions' illnesses; showing the flag.
- Michael Symes: Journal of His Second Embassy to the Court
of Ava in 1802. D. G. E. Hall, ed. London: Allen and Unwin,
1955.

1803

371. IRVING, Washington (1783-1859) [A203, B190]
1. July 30, 1803-January 17, 1806; August 17-November 18,
1820; April 25-May 5, 1821; August 1, 1822-February 8, 1826
Personal and travel diaries; American author and civil servant;
his first efforts in fiction; growing fame; political appointments abroad
and much traveling in Europe; notes on daily routine and trivia but
never fails to notice a good-looking woman; some entries are lengthy
essays, others are fragmentary.
- Journal and Notebooks. Nathalia Wright, et al., eds. 3
vols. Madison: University of Wisconsin Press, 1969-80.
REVIEWS: Book Review Digest 1970, p. 716. Book Review
Index 1981, p. 282.

2. August 2-September 1, 1832; Travel diary; the first published text of Journal Number 2 covering his travels from New York
to Cincinnati.
- Ross, Sue F. "New York to Cincinnati: A Critical Edition
of an 1832 Journal of Washington Irving," Ph.D., University
of North Carolina, 1976. (Dissertation Abstracts, 37/09-A p.
5832)

3. September 3-November 17, 1832; Travel diary; St. Louis

to Independence, Missouri; through southwestern Kansas; in Oklahoma at Canadian and Cimarron Rivers; accompanied by Charles Latrobe, son of Benjamin H. Latrobe (q.v.); and his charge, a Swiss count; became the basis of his book Tour on the Prairies; invaluable for fine detail of the period.
* The Western Journals of Washington Irving. Jon Francis Dermott, ed. Norman: University of Oklahoma Press, 1944.

372. MILLS, Robert (1781-1855) [A230]
1. July 2-12, 1803; Personal diary; architecture student of Benjamin H. Latrobe (q.v.); life in Georgetown; sketching, social life.
* "An Unpublished Diary by Robert Mills, 1803," South Carolina Historical and Genealogical Magazine, v. 51, pp. 187-94, October, 1950.

2. December 27, 1828-March 4, 1830; Personal diary; in South Carolina; notes on his architectural work; expenses.
* "The Journal of Robert Mills, 1828-1830," Hennig Cohen, ed. South Carolina Historical Magazine, v. 52, pp. 133-39, July, 1951; pp. 218-24, October, 1951; v. 53, pp. 31-36, January, 1952; pp. 90-100, April, 1952.

373. SELKIRK, Thomas Douglas, 5th Earl of (1771-1820) [A204, C107]
August 5, 1803-December 15, 1804
Travel diary; journey undertaken to learn more about the area for the purpose of planting colonies; in Massachusetts, Vermont, New York, Nova Scotia; detailed; comments on social, economic and political life.
* Lord Selkirk's Diary 1803-1804; A Journal of His Travels in British North America and the Northeastern U.S. Patrick C. T. White, ed. Toronto: Champlain Society, 1958; reprint New York: Greenwood Press, 1969.

374. SMITH, William (1769-1847)
November 3, 1803-February 7, 1804
Travel diary; son of a Canadian chief justice went to London to interview artists for work on a memorial.
* "London Diary of William Smith, 1803-1804: L. F. S. Upton, ed. Canadian Historical Review, v. 47, pp. 146-55, June, 1966.

375. SOLLY, Hannah (1771-1854)
June 25-August, 1803
Travel diary; extracts; London, Edinburgh, Glasgow and return; good picture of conditions.
* Anthony, R. M. "Diary of 1803," History Today, v. 16, pp. 476-83, July, 1966.

376. WERTMÜLLER, Adolf Ulric (1751-1811)
April 28-July 18, 1803
Personal diary; Swedish-born member of the French Academy;

after financial reverses due to the French Revolution he emigrated to
America; farming on the Delaware River.
  • "Wertmüller's Diary: The Transformation of Artist into
  Farmer," Franklin D. Scott, ed. and trans. Swedish Pioneer
  Historical Quarterly, v. 6, pp. 34-54, April, 1955.

1804

377. BIDDLE, Nicholas (1786-1844)
      Travel diary; undated excerpts; American financier who was
later head of the Bank of the United States; accompanied General
John Armstrong, U.S. Minister to France.
  • "Nicholas Biddle in Europe, 1804-1807," Pennsylvania Magazine of History and Biography, v. 103, pp. 3-33, January,
  1979.

      CLARK, William see LEWIS, Meriwether

378. HOPKINS, Gerard T. [A206]
      February 26-May 24, 1804
      Travel diary; Maryland Quaker journeyed to Fort Wayne, In-
diana Territory; travel, scenery; meeting with Indians.
  • "Plowshares and Pruning Hooks for the Miami and Potawa-
  tomi: The Journal of Gerard T. Hopkins, 1804," Joseph E.
  Walker, ed. Ohio History, v. 88, pp. 361-407, Autumn, 1979.

379. LEWIS, Meriwether (1774-1809) and William CLARK (1770-1838)
      [A206]
      May 14, 1804-September 26, 1806
      "An abridgement designed for the casual reader" based on the
Thwaites edition of 1904-05.
  • Journals of Lewis and Clark. Bernard De Voto, ed. Bos-
  ton: Houghton, Mifflin, 1953.
      REVIEW: Book Review Digest 1953, p. 564.

1805

380. BLAKE, Noah (1790-)
      March 25-December 24, 1805
      Personal diary; farmboy's listing of his activities are supple-
mented with the editor's extensive narrative; interesting.
  • Diary of an Early American Boy, 1805. Eric Sloane, ed.
  New York: Funk, 1962.
      REVIEW: Book Review Digest 1963, p. 936.

381. BREATHITT, John (1786-1834)
      March 28-July 29, 1805
      Travel diary; travel conditions and social life.

* "Commencement of a Journal from Kentucky to the State of
Pennsylvania--&c March 26, 1805," Kentucky Historical Society
Register, v. 52, pp. 5-24, January, 1954.

382. ISELIN, Isaac
September 5, 1805-April 4, 1808; gaps
Travel diary; Swiss emigrant and supercargo on the brig Mary-
land; New York; around Cape Horn; stops at Hawaii and Canton;
good descriptions of ports; well-written.
* "Journal of a Trading Voyage Around the World, 1805-1808,"
Jarvis Cromwell, ed. New York Historical Society Quarterly, v.
62, pp. 87-137, April, 1978.

383. NELSON, Horatio (1758-1805) [B153]
September 14-October 21, 1805
Sea diary; Britain's hero of Trafalgar; departure from Ports-
mouth; weather, headings, position; names of accompanying ships;
a last letter to Emma Hamilton and a prayer are included.
* Nelson's Last Diary: A Facsimile. Oliver Warner, ed. Kent,
OH: Kent State University Press, 1971.

384. PIKE, Zebulon Montgomery (1779-1813) [A210]
August 10, 1805-April, 1806; July 15, 1806-July 1, 1807
Exploration diary; American army officer; from St. Louis up-
river to explore the source of the Mississippi and return; Belle Fon-
taine, Louisiana Territory, east of the Sabine via San Antonio to
Chihuahua, Mexico and Santa Fe; Pike's Peak to St. Louis.
* Journals with Letters and Related Documents. Donald Jack-
son, ed. Norman: University of Oklahoma Press, 1966.
REVIEWS: Book Review Digest 1966, p. 957; 1967, p. 1037.

385. STEVENSON, Captain William (1774-1808)
June 1, 1805-[no closing date]
Personal journal; undated entries; Amsterdam, Lisbon, Java;
on the ship Erin; Muscat; observant and opinionated.
* "A Voyage to the East Indies, 1805," Frank F. White, Jr.,
ed. Maryland Historical Magazine, v. 59, pp. 182-98, 1964.

1806

386. BRIGHT, Jacob (-1807)
August 3-August 12, 1806
Travel journal; hoped to set up trading relationship with the
Indians; along the Arkansas River.
* "Jacob Bright's Journal of a Trip to the Osage Indians,"
Harold W. Ryan, ed. Journal of Southern History, v. 15, pp.
509-23, November, 1949.

387. SALTONSTALL, Leverett (1783-1845)
January 1, 1806-May 30, 1807

Personal diary; Harvard graduate opened his law practice; life
in Haverhill, Mass.; moved to Salem; weather, social notes.
- "Leverett Saltonstall: A Diary Beginning Jany. A.D. 1806,"
Robert E. Moody, ed. Massachusetts Historical Society Proceedings, v. 89, pp. 127-77, 1977.

1807

388. ANONYMOUS
October 30, 1807-January 23, 1808
Travel diary; Irishman went from Richmond to Charlottesville
and beyond; people, accommodations.
- "Trade and Travel In Post-Revolutionary Virginia: The Diary of an Itinerant Peddler, 1807-1808," Richard R. Beeman,
ed. Virginia Magazine of History and Biography, v. 84, pp.
174-88, April, 1976.

389. ALEXANDER, Henry
September 1, 1807-June 1, 1808
Meteorological diary; extracts from record of weather observa-
tions.
- "The Winter of 1807-1808 at Pembina, North Dakota," North
Dakota Historical Quarterly, v. 5, pp. 239-47, July, 1931.

390. WEETON, Nelly (1776-   ) [B166-67]
October 25, 1807-June 25, 1825
Personal diary; vicissitudes of life as a governess; family
troubles; contains a new introduction and epilogue with additional
information gathered since the publication of the first edition.
- Miss Weeton's Journal of a Governess. Edward Hall, ed.
New York: Oxford University Press, 1945; A. M. Kelley, 1969.

1808

391. FEW, Frances (1789-1885)
October 1, 1808-March 8, 1809
Personal diary; guest in the Albert Gallatin home in Washington,
D.C.; dined with Thomas Jefferson; social life; reading.
- "Diary of Frances Few, 1808-1809," Noble E. Cunningham,
Jr., ed. Journal of Southern History, v. 29, pp. 345-61, Au-
gust, 1963.

392. HAYDON, Benjamin Robert (1786-1846) [B198]
July 23, 1808-June 22, 1846
Personal diary; major British painter; personal life, work, relations with leading cultural figures of the first half of the century;
marriage, births and deaths of his children; financial troubles and
imprisonment for debt; last entry made just before his suicide; a revealing self-portrait.

• The Diary of Benjamin Robert Haydon. Willard Bissell Pope,
ed. 5 vols. Cambridge: Harvard University Press, 1960-63.
REVIEWS: Book Review Digest 1960, pp. 617-18; 1963, p.
448.

393. MORAGA, Gabriel (1767-   )
September 25-October 18, 1808
Exploration diary; Spanish officer looked for sites to plant missions; from Mission San Jose south to Merced River and thence north
of Sutter Buttes.
• The Diary of Ensign Gabriel Moraga's Expedition of Discovery in the Sacramento Valley, 1808. Donald C. Cutter, trans.
and ed. Los Angeles: G. Dawson, 1957.

394. TULLY, William (1785-1859)
September 15, 1808-January 3, 1809
Personal diary; three months medical education of a humorless
youth later in the forefront of his profession; good social history.
• The Journal of William Tully: Medical Student at Dartmouth
1808-1809. Oliver S. Hayward and Elizabeth H. Thomson, eds.
New York: Science History Publications, 1977.

395. WYNYARD, John Montague
July 24, 1808-January 16, 1809
Military diary; captain in the Coldstream Guards with Welling-
ton's staff; Battles of Rolica and Corunna.
• "From Vimeiro to Corunna, An Eye Witness Account," Royal
United Service Institute Journal, v. 114, no. 656, pp. 33-42,
1969.

1809

396. DARWIN, Charles Robert (1809-82) [B222-23]
1809-December 20, 1881; brief annual notes
Personal diary; family life; births of children; scientific work
and writing.
• Journal. Sir Gavin de Beer, ed. London: British Museum,
1959.

397. DOUGLAS, Neil (1779-1853)
July 15, 1809-October 15, 1810
Military journal; extracts; service in Portugal; wounded at
Busaco.
• "The Diary of Captain Neil Douglas, 79th Foot, 1809 to 1810,"
Antony Brett-James, ed. Journal of the Society for Army His-
torical Research, v. 41, pp. 101-07, 1963.

398. GILPIN, Joshua [A201]
September 14-October 22, 1809
Travel diary; with wife and eight-year-old son by carriage

from Philadelphia via York and Uniontown to Pittsburgh; return via
Johnstown, Harrisburg and Reading; man of wide interests; notes
on lodgings, land values, price, scenery. Fuller transcription of
material which appeared in the Pennsylvania Magazine of History and
Biography in 1926-28.
  • The Journal of Joshua Gilpin 1809: Pleasure and Business
  in Western Pennsylvania. Joseph G. Walker, ed. Harrisburg:
  Pennsylvania Historical and Museum Commission, 1975.

399. MARTIN, William Dickinson (1789-1833)
      April 30-May 25, 1809
      Travel diary; from Edgefield, South Carolina by sulky and mail
stage to study law; lengthy description of sights along the way.
  • Journal: A Journey from South Carolina to Connecticut in
  the Year 1809. Prepared by Anna D. Elmore. Charlotte, N.
  Car.: Heritage House, 1959.

1810

400. FLEMING, Marjory (1803-11) [B170]
      1. Summer, 1810; personal diary; Scottish girl living at home;
her tantrums; repeated adult conversation; "planty of gooseberys
which makes my teath watter."
  • "Diary Excerpts," in: Philip Dunaway and Mel Evans, eds.
  A Treasury of the World's Great Diaries. New York: Doubleday, 1957; pp. 181-85.

      2. Spring, 1811; poetic excerpt; in despair of ever mastering
her temper.
  • "Diary Excerpts," in: Moffat, Mary Jane and Charlotte
  Painter, eds. Revelations: Diaries of Women. New York:
  Random House, 1974; pp. 21-27.

1811

401. HEMPSTEAD, Stephen, Sr. (1754-1831)
      March 31, 1811-September 24, 1831
      Personal diary; Connecticut native settled on a farm near St.
Louis, Mo.; extracts; family, business and social life.
  • "I at Home: The Diary of a Yankee Farmer in Missouri,"
  Mrs. Dana O. Jensen, ed. Missouri Historical Society Bulletin,
  v. 13, pp. 30-56, October, 1956; pp. 284-317, April, 1957; v.
  14, pp. 59-96, October, 1957; pp. 272-88, April, 1958; v. 15,
  pp. 38-48, October, 1958; pp. 224-47, April, 1959; v. 22, pp.
  61-94, October, 1965; pp. 180-206, January, 1966; pp. 410-45,
  July, 1966.

402. LOSH, James (1763-) [B128]
      January 5, 1811-September 19, 1833

Personal diary; well-educated businessman of Tyneside; in law;
widely read; comments on his reading.
- The Diaries and Correspondence. Edward Hughes, ed. 2
vols. Durham: Andrews, 1962-63.

403. MILLER, Robert Johnstone (1758-1834)
     June 18-December 14, 1811; May 1-July 12, 1813
     Missionary journal; church work; preaching; circuit riding.
     - "The Journals of the Rev. Robert J. Miller, Lutheran Mis-
     sionary in Virginia, 1811 and 1813," Willard E. Wight, ed. Vir-
     ginia Magazine of History and Biography, v. 61, pp. 141-66,
     April, 1953.

404. ROBINSON, Henry Crabb (1775-1867) [B176]
     January 8, 1811-January 31, 1867
     Personal diary; minor 19th century British writer; close friend-
     ship with Wordsworth; acquainted with leading Georgian and Victorian
     writers; his reading, social life; thoughts on his contemporaries and
     their work; abridged from Henry Crabb Robinson on Books and Their
     Writers. Edith J. Morley, ed. London: Dent, 1938.
     - The Diary of Henry Crabb Robinson: An Abridgement.
     Derek Hudson, ed. New York: Oxford University Press, 1967.
     REVIEW: Book Review Digest 1967, p. 1106.

405. WATSON, John (1774-1864)
     April 29-August 1, 1811
     Travel diary; to Cincinnati and return by flatboat and horse-
back.
     - "The Journey of a Pennsylvania Quaker to Pioneer Ohio,"
     Dwight L. Smith and S. Winifred Smith, eds. Cincinnati Histor-
     ical Society Bulletin, v. 26, pp. 3-40, January, 1968; pp. 174-
     210, April, 1968.

                                   1812

406. BLACKMAN, Learner
     Personal diary; Methodist circuit rider accompanied Tennessee
Volunteers to Natchez; return to Nashville.
     - "The Diary of a Chaplain in Andrew Jackson's Army: The
     Journal of the Rev. Mr. Learner Blackman--December 28, 1812-
     April 4, 1813," Dawson A. Phelps, ed. Tennessee Historical
     Quarterly, v. 12, pp. 264-81, September, 1953.

407. JONES, Noah
     July 15-October 13, 1812; October 17, 1812-January 30, 1813
     Sea diary; 2 privateering cruises aboard a 168 ton brig cap-
tained by Oliver Wilson; 1st journal is a ship's log; 2nd is a private,
melodramatic narrative.
     - Journals of Two Cruises Aboard the "American Yankee," by
     a Wanderer. E. M. Eller, introduction. New York: Macmillan,
     1967.

408. UXKULL, Boris (1793-1870)
      March 17, 1812-September 30, 1819
      Personal diary; Estonian nobleman in Imperial Russian Cavalry
Guards Regiment; at Borodino and on to Paris; amorous interlude in
Vienna; lighthearted; entertaining.
      • Arms and the Woman: Intimate Journal of a Baltic Nobleman
      in the Napoleonic Wars. Estley von Uexkull, ed. Joel Carmi-
      chael, trans. New York: Macmillan, 1966.

409. WILSON, Sir Robert Thomas (1777-1849) [B154]
      July 17, 1812-January 6, 1814
      Military journal; British general with the 15th Light Dragoons;
opens at Constantinople; traveled north; with the Russian Army;
meeting the Czar; Battles of Borodino and Leipzig; Napoleon's great
losses and suffering of the French; brash, busy; on good terms with
all Britain's allies against Napoleon; interesting history and good
reading.
      • General Wilson's Journal, 1812-1814. Antony Brett-James,
      ed. London: Kimber, 1964.

                                  1813

410. ANONYMOUS (1787-   )
      November 15, 1813-June 2, 1814
      Travel diary; life aboard British man-o-war by captain's clerk;
vessel ordered to northwest coast of America to capture Astor's fur
trading post; stops in Rio, San Francisco, Hawaii and South American
ports; comments on people ("for we all know women are not at a loss
for scheming") and sights; lively writing by an operator who tries
all the angles.
      • Hussey, John A., ed. The Voyage of the Racoon: A "Se-
      cret" Journal of a Visit to Oregon, California and Hawaii, 1813-
      1814. San Francisco: Book Club of California, 1958.

411. WHEATLEY, Edmund (1793?-1841)
      August 9, 1813-May 9, 1814; June 21, 1814-May 2, 1817
      Military diary; kept by a headstrong English ensign in the
King's German Legion for his sweetheart; in southern France; siege
of Bayonne; brief return to England; from Ostend via circuitous
route to Waterloo; romantic, impetuous, wryly humorous account; enhanced by his sketches and watercolors.
      • The Wheatley Diary: A Journal and Sketch-book Kept Dur-
      ing the Peninsular War and the Waterloo Campaign. Christopher
      Hibbert, ed. London: Longmans, 1964.

                                  1814

412. ANDERSON, Richard Clough (1788-1826)
      May 17, 1814-July 12, 1826

Diplomatic and personal diary; Kentucky congressman and nephew
of George Rogers Clark; first American minister to Bolivar's La Gran
Colombia; family comings and goings; business; some description of
a sojourn in South America.
- Diary and Journal, 1814-1826. Alfred Tischendorf and E.
Taylor Parks, eds. Durham, N. Car.: Duke University Press,
1964.

413. BAKER, Isaac L.
July 15-August 21, 1814
Travel diary; from Nashville, Tennessee to Huntsville, Alabama.
- "The Journal of Captain Isaac L. Baker," C. F. Arrowood,
ed. Southwestern Historical Quarterly, v. 30, pp. 272-82, 1926-
27.

414. BRECK, Samuel (1771-1862)
January 1, 1814-December 31, 1840; some gaps
Personal diary; prosperous heir of a Philadelphia family active
in social, cultural and philanthropic life; entertains Lafayette; served
as state senator; death of daughter from typhus.
- "The Diary of Samuel Breck, 1814-1822," Pennsylvania Magazine of History and Biography, v. 102, pp. 469-508, October,
1978; v. 103, pp. 85-113, January, 1979; pp. 222-51, April,
1979; pp. 356-82, July, 1979; pp. 497-527, October, 1979.

415. CLAIRMONT, Claire (1798-1879)
August 14-November 9, 1814; January 28-April 20, 1818; March
7, 1819-August 1, 1820; August 5, 1820-September 20, 1822;
May 12, 1825-January 2, 1826; December 21, 1826-February 2,
1827.
Personal diary; mother of Lord Byron's (q.v.) daughter Allegra;
with Shelley and Mary Godwin when they eloped to Europe; life in
Italy and London; worked as a governess in Russia during the De-
cembrist Revolt; interesting counterpoint to letters and diaries of
others in her circle.
- The Journals of Claire Clairmont. Marion Kingston Stocking
and David MacKenzie Stocking, eds. Cambridge: Harvard
University Press, 1968.
REVIEW: Book Review Digest 1969, p. 252.
- Cores, Lucy. The Year of December. New York: McGraw-
Hill, 1974. (A novel based on the Stockings' edition of Clair-
mont's two Russian journals centers on the Decembrist Revolt
of 1825.)

416. DICKSON, Sir Alexander (1777-1840) [B184]
December 24, 1814-February 12, 1815
Military journal; commander of the British artillery in the Battle
of New Orleans; helped lose the battle through his conservatism in
command; his sketches are reproduced.
- "Journal of Operations in Louisiana," Louisiana Historical
Quarterly, v. 44, pp. 1-100, 140-46, July-October, 1961.

417. DUNCAN, Ennis, Jr.
      September 8, 1814–April 14, 1815
      Military journal; campaign in Upper Canada; from Newport,
Kentucky via Detroit; weather, miles marched and details of encamp-
ments and food; transcribes orders received and results of courts
martial; mentions many others in the company by name.
      • The Journal of Ennis Duncan, Jr., Orderly Sergeant, 16th
      Regiment, Kentucky Militia Detached. Richard C. Knopf, pref-
      ace. Columbus: Ohio State Museum, 1958.

418. FORMAN, Martha Browne Ogle (1785–1864)
      May 19, 1814–December 3, 1845
      Personal diary; plantation mistress of Cecil County, Maryland;
began her diary on the day of her marriage to a second husband;
trips to Washington, Philadelphia and New York City; kindhearted,
childless woman did a prodigious amount of work in supervising
slaves and extending hospitality to family, friends and strangers;
mentions crop yields, plantings, prices, medical practices; acquainted
with Sidney George Fisher (q.v.); terse entries provide a well-rounded
picture of plantation life.
      • Plantation Life at Rose Hill: The Diaries of Martha Ogle
      Forman 1814–1845. W. Emerson Wilson, ed. Wilmington: His-
      torical Society of Delaware, 1976.

419. FORREST, Charles Ramus
      1. November 25, 1814–January 7, 1815; Military journal; ex-
plains some of the causes of British defeat.
      • The Battle of New Orleans, a British View: The Journal of
      Major C. R. Forrest Asst. QM General, 34th Regiment of Foot.
      Hugh F. Rankin, ed. New Orleans: Hauser Press, 1961.

      2. November 25, 1814–February 12, 1815; Military journal;
description of company positions.
      • "Journal of the Operations Against New Orleans in 1814 and
      1815," Louisiana Historical Quarterly, v. 44, pp. 111–26, 146,
      July–October, 1961.

420. MICHELL, John
      December 11, 1814–February 12, 1815
      Military journal; responsible for gunnery at the Battle of New
Orleans.
      • "Diary," Louisiana Historical Quarterly, v. 44, pp. 127–30.
      July–October, 1961.

421. ROGERS, Samuel (1763–1855)
      August 20, 1814–May 6, 1815
      Travel diary; English poet who declined to be laureate after
Wordsworth's death; visits in France, Italy, Germany; breathless
style; crammed with tourist notes.
      • The Italian Journal of Samuel Rogers. J. R. Hale, ed.
      London: Faber and Faber, 1956.

422. SHELLEY, Mary Wollstonecraft (1797-1851) [B185]
      July 28, 1814-October, 1844
      Personal diary; author of Frankenstein; first transcriptions
of entire contents of the journals; 20 percent more material than in
F. L. Jones's Mary Shelley's Journals.
      • Feldman, Paula R. "The Journals of Mary Wollstonecraft
      Shelley: An Annotated Edition," Ph.D., Northwestern Univer-
      sity, 1974. (Dissertation Abstracts 35/10-A, p. 6663)

423. TODD, Matthew (1791?-1853) [B185]
      1. April 2, 1814-November 2, 1817; Yorkshireman valeted an
army captain on two Grand Tours from England to Naples with stops
in Paris, Geneva, Aix, Venice, Brussels and The Hague; much information on modes of travel, prices, lodgings; disputes with coachmen
and innkeepers; anecdotes and pranks heard of and perpetrated; interesting and entertaining.
      • Matthew Todd's Journal: A Gentleman's Gentleman in Europe,
      1814-1820. Geoffrey Trease, ed. London: Heinemann, 1968.

      2. January 1-June 17, 1815; Personal diary; extracts; New-
market, Breda, Paris, Geneva.
      • Hodge, Jane Aiken. "The Grand Tour 1814-1815," History
      Today, v. 15, pp. 99-107, February, 1965.

                                1815

424. BINGHAM, Hiram (1789-)
      May 6, 1815-November 31, 1816; many gaps
      Spiritual diary; in college and studying for the ministry.
      • "'Teach Me O My God': The Journal of Hiram Bingham
      (1815-1816)," Char Miller, ed. Vermont History, v. 18, pp.
      225-35, Fall, 1980.

425. IZARD, George (1776-1828)
      November 14, 1815-April 3, 1816
      Military journal; traveling home from Niagara frontier after dis-
charge.
      • "Diary of a Journey by George Izard, 1815-1816," Harold W.
      Ryan, ed. South Carolina Historical Magazine, v. 53, pp. 67-76,
      April, 1952; pp. 155-60, July, 1952; pp. 223-29, October, 1952.

426. LATROBE, Christian Ignatius (1758-1836)
      October 15, 1815-December 1, 1816
      Missionary journal; brother of architect Benjamin H. Latrobe
(q.v.) and Moravian minister; went to South Africa to reorganize
existing missions and founded another; scenery, flora, fauna; relations with Hottentots; dedicated amateur scientist; humorous, fair-
minded; very good.
      • Journal of a Visit to South Africa in 1815 and 1816 with
      Some Account of the Missionary Settlements. London: Seeley,

1818; Frank R. Bradlow, introduction. New York: Negro Universities Press, 1969.

427. LEWIS, Matthew Gregory (1775-1818)
November 8, 1815-May 2, 1818
Travel diary; English novelist, dramatist and poet; nicknamed "Monk"; journey to Jamaica to inspect inherited estates and slaves; poetry and letters included; written with intention of eventual publication but there is no evidence that entries were expanded afterward.
• Journal of a West India Proprietor, 1815-1817. Mona Wilson, ed. Boston: Houghton, Mifflin, 1929.

428. LOGAN, Deborah Norris (-1839)
1815-39
Personal diary; daughter of prominent Philadelphia Quakers; anecdotes; daily life; feminine interests.
• Barr, Marleen S. "The 'Worthy' and the 'Irrelevant': Deborah Norris Logan's Diary," Ph.D., State University of New York, Buffalo, 1980. (Dissertation Abstracts, 41/11A, p. 4702)

1816

429. ALLEN, George Wigram Dundas (1799-1877)
1816-May 25, 1841
Personal diary; British lad and his family arrived in New South Wales; law studies, founder of a prestigious firm; quoted and paraphrased entries.
• Early Georgian: Extracts from the Journal of George Allen (1800-1877). Sydney: Angus and Robertson, 1958.

430. CLERC, Laurent (1785-1869)
June 20-August 8, 1816
Travel diary; Frenchman who lost his hearing in a childhood accident attended and became a teacher at a Parisian school for the deaf; meeting with T. H. Gallaudet led to his coming to America; learning English and conversing with passing ships.
• The Diary of Laurent Clerc's Voyage from France to America in 1816. West Hartford, Conn.: American School for the Deaf, 1952.

431. DALHOUSIE, George Ramsay, 9th Earl of (1770-1838)
May 1816-June 7, 1820
Personal diary; Scottish-born lieutenant-governor of Nova Scotia; came with wife and youngest son to Canada; wide range of comments on people, climate, and conditions; interesting; pleasing style.
• The Dalhousie Journals. Marjory Whitelaw, ed. Ottawa: Oberon, 1978.
    REVIEWS: Queen's Quarterly, v. 86, pp. 325-27, Summer, 1979. Canadian Historical Review, v. 60, pp. 492-93, December, 1979. Social History, v. 13, pp. 267-68, May, 1980.

432.   LARCOM, Jonathan (1768-1834)
       December 21, 1816-November 6, 1817
       Personal diary; tollkeeper on Essex Bridge between Beverly
and Salem; weather; family deaths.
       • "Diary of Jonathan Larcom of Beverly, Massachusetts," Es-
       sex Institute Historical Collections, v. 87, pp. 65-95, January,
       1951.

433.   MILLER, John E. (1792-1847)
       October 23, 1816-May 11, 1817
       Travel diary; 2500 mile journey on horseback from Philadelphia,
through Virginia, the Carolinas, Tennessee and western Pennsylvania;
preaching and travel.
       • "John Miller's Missionary Journal--1816-1817: Religious Con-
       ditions in the South and Midwest," Jasper W. Cross, ed. Jour-
       nal of Presbyterian History, v. 47, pp. 226-61, September,
       1969.

                                  1817

434.   CHORIS, Louis (1795-1828)
       June 17-August 18, 1817
       Travel diary; Russian painter; from Kamchatza with a group
of Russians; Indian life; Aleuts; sealing; well-written.
       • "An Early 19th Century Artist in Alaska: Louis Choris and
       the First Kotzebue Expedition," James W. Vanstone, ed. Pacific
       Northwest Quarterly, v. 51, pp. 145-58, October, 1960.

435.   DOUGLASS, David Bates (1790-1849)
       1. May 5-August 13, 1817; Surveyor's journal; West Point fac-
ulty member and engineer; aboard a revenue cutter to chart Long
Island Sound.
       • "David Bates Douglass' Journal: An Account of the Survey
       of the Eastern Entrance to Long Island Sound in the Year 1817,"
       S. W. Jackman, ed. American Neptune, v. 24, pp. 280-94, Oc-
       tober, 1964.

       2. April 25-September 9, 1820; Exploration diary; with the
Cass Expedition to survey natural resources, contact Indians and
examine British fur trade in Upper Great Lakes and northern Mississippi Valley; to Detroit, Sault Ste. Marie, Prairie du Chien and
return; detailed; interesting.
       • A Voyageur: The Journal of David Bates Douglass. Syd-
       ney W. Jackman and John F. Freeman, eds. Marquette: North-
       ern Michigan University Press, 1969.

436.   GORREQUER, Gideon (1781-1841)
       June 3, 1817-December 21, 1823
       Personal diary; aide-de-camp to Sir Hudson Lowe during his
term as governor of St. Helena; an account of the closed society in
the British camp; sniping, backbiting, feuding.

• St. Helena During Napoleon's Exile: Gorrequer's Diary.
James Kemble, introduction. Hamden, Conn.: Archon Books,
1969.

437. GREENE, Welcome Arnold (1795-1870)
April 16, 1817-October 20, 1818; January 24, 1819-May 10,
1820; January 22-May 22, 1822; February 4-August 23, 1823;
January 27-June 24, 1824
Sea diary; voyages aboard the brig Perseverance to South
America, Norway and Gibraltar; three visits to southern U.S. to look
for business opportunities; also seeking an uncle who disappeared
mysteriously; good descriptions; astute character assessments of peo-
ple encountered.
• Journals. Howard Greene and Alice E. Smith, eds. Madison:
State Historical Society of Wisconsin, 1956.

438. KEEN, James (1781-1860)
November 27, 1817-April 5, 1818
Personal diary; Philadelphia ship joiner went to cut timber for
U.S. Navy ships; record of work and recreation.
• Wood, Virginia Steele. "James Keen's Journal of a Passage
from Philadelphia to Blackbeard Island, Georgia for Live Oak
Timber, 1817-1818," American Neptune, v. 35, pp. 227-47, Oc-
tober, 1975.

439. LONG, Stephen H. (1784-1864) [A232]
July 9-August 15, 1817; April 30-October 27, 1823
Exploration diaries; topographical engineer and pioneer in
mapping of the West; 1817 expedition from Belle Fontaine, Missouri
to the Falls of St. Anthony; up the Wisconsin River; in 1823 from
Philadelphia through Pennsylvania to Wisconsin and Minnesota; return
via Canada, the Great Lakes and the Erie Canal to Philadelphia; de-
tailed, well-done account of terrain, Indians, travel conditions.
• The Northern Expeditions of Stephen H. Long: The Jour-
nals of 1817 and 1823 and Related Documents. Lucile M. Kane,
et al., eds. St. Paul: Minnesota Historical Society, 1978.
REVIEWS: Canadian Historical Review, v. 60, pp. 357-58,
September, 1979. Mid-America, v. 61, pp. 153-54, April-
July, 1979. North Dakota History, v. 46, pp. 34-35, Spring,
1979. Ohio History, v. 88, pp. 94-95, Winter, 1979. South
Dakota History, v. 9, pp. 160-61, Spring, 1979. Western
Historical Quarterly, v. 10, pp. 505-06, October, 1979.
Minnesota History, v. 46, pp. 162-63, Winter, 1978.

440. MIX, Ebenezer Hooker (1776-1839)
July 1, 1817-April 25, 1818
Sea diary; excerpts of a log of a sealing voyage.
• Kihn, Phyllis. "The Sea Journal of Captain Ebenezer Hooker
Mix 1817-1818," Connecticut Historical Society Bulletin, v. 40,
pp. 8-18, January, 1975.

441. OXLEY, John Joseph William Molesworth (1781-1828)
      April 6-August 29, 1817; May 20-November 5, 1818
      Exploration diary; intrepid Briton set off across Australia on
horseback; meetings with natives; descriptions of terrain.
      • Journals of Two Expeditions into the Interior of New South
      Wales Undertaken by Order of the British Governor in the Years
      1817-18. London, 1820; facsimile reprint Adelaide: Library
      Board of South Australia, 1965.

442. PERKINS, Samuel Huntington (1797-1874)
      October 12, 1817-July 21, 1818
      Personal diary; Yale graduate spent a year on a plantation in
coastal Hyde county, North Carolina; observations on slavery and
poor whites.
      • "A Yankee Tutor in the Old South," Robert C. McLean, ed.
      North Carolina Historical Review, v. 47, pp. 51-85, Winter,
      1970.

                               1818

443. ABBOT, Abiel (1770-1828)
      November 9-December 9, 1818; November 2-14, 1827
      Travel diary; New England minister went to South Carolina for
his health; "a rich and copious journal."
      • "The Abiel Abbot Journals: A Yankee Preacher in Charles-
      ton Society, 1818-1827," South Carolina Historical Magazine,
      v. 68, pp. 51-73, April, 1967; pp. 115-39, July, 1967; pp.
      232-54, October, 1967.

444. BINGHAM, Henry Vest (-1823)
      May 9-July 9, 1818
      Travel diary; father of painter George Caleb Bingham; went
from western Virginia to Missouri looking for farm land; detailed account of conditions and sights.
      • "The Road West in 1818, The Diary of Henry Vest Bingham,"
      Missouri Historical Review, v. 40, pp. 21-54, October, 1944;
      pp. 174-204, January, 1945.

445. CAMPBELL, George Washington (1769-1848)
      1. July 22, 1818-August 23, 1820; Personal diary; appointed
by Pres. James Monroe; social and family life; travels; deaths of his
three children; description of Russian scenery, furniture, palaces.
      • "Diary of George Washington Campbell, American Minister to
      Russia, 1818-1820," Weymouth T. Jordan, ed. Tennessee His-
      torical Quarterly, v. 7, pp. 152-70, June, 1948; pp. 259-80,
      September, 1948.

      2. September 6, 1818-June 24, 1820; "only those portions of
the diary ... pertaining to ministerial duties [and] accounts of association with ... royal family."

• "Excerpts from the Diary of a Tennessean at the Court of the Czar, 1818-1820," Weymouth T. Jordan, ed. East Tennessee Historical Society Publications, v. 15, pp. 104-09, 1943.

446. ENGELBREHT, Jacob (1797-1878)
1818-January 5, 1878
Public diary; son of a Hessian soldier who stayed in the U.S.. after the American Revolution; tailor by trade; record of deaths, executions, sermons, visitors to Frederick; election returns, quotes from newspapers; very little personal information.
• The Diary of Jacob Engelbreht, 1818-1878. William R. Quynn, ed. 3 vols. Frederick, Md.: Historical Society of Frederick County, 1976.

447. MOORE, Thomas (1779-1852) [B193]
August 18, 1818- ; gap August, 1822-September, 1825 due to illegibility of the surviving manuscript
Personal diary; Irish expatriate poet; much information on Lord Byron's life (q.v.) in England and his first few years in Italy; friend of Byron, Lord John Russell and Richard Brinsley Sheridan; full, lengthy entries provide a record of daily activities but with little introspection; financial disaster; his wife Bessy stayed at Sloperton Cottage while he dined out in London and conducted his literary life; good reading.
• The Journal of Thomas Moore. Wilfred S. Dowden, ed. 2 vols. Newark: University of Delaware Press, 1983; 1984.

448. NEWTON, Ebenezer (1790-1859)
October 9-November 14, 1818
Travel diary; Georgia native journeyed to Shelbyville, Tennessee to visit relatives; describes countryside.
• Newton, Charlotte. "Ebenezer Newton's 1818 Diary," Georgia Historical Quarterly, v. 53, pp. 205-19, June, 1969.

1819

449. GALL, Ludwig (1791-1863)
August 2, 1819-August 30, 1820
Travel diary; German Socialist was an agent for a society promoting emigration to the U.S.; Philadelphia, Lancaster, Harrisburg; returned to Germany disillusioned.
• "Pennsylvania Through a German's Eyes: The Travels of Ludwig Gall, 1819-1820," Pennsylvania Magazine of History and Biography, v. 105, pp. 35-65, January, 1981.

450. HATHERTON, Edward John Littleton, Lord (1791-1863)
1. January 18, 1819-October 8, 1842; Personal diary; Member of Parliament for Staffordshire; details of parliamentary doings and notes on social life; detailed and interesting social history.

- Aspinall, A. "Extracts from Lord Hatherton's Diary," Parliamentary Affairs, v. 17, pp. 15-22, Winter, 1963-64; pp. 134-41, Spring, 1964; pp. 254-68, Summer, 1964.

2. June 28, 1831-August, 1833; Political diary; Whig.
- "Edward John Littleton's Diary," in: A. Aspinall. Three Early Nineteenth Century Diaries. London: Williams and Norgate, 1952; pp. 98-116, 147-65, 290-359.

451. HODGE, Charles (1797-1878)
October 20, 1819-1820
Personal diary; Philadelphian studying Hebrew; religious doubts; preaching.
- "The Pursuit of Piety: Charles Hodge's Diary, 1819-1820," Charles D. Cashdollar, ed. Journal of Presbyterian History, v. 55, pp. 267-83, Fall, 1977.

452. PEALE, Titian Ramsay (1799-1885)
1. May 3-August 1, 1829; Travel diary; son of American painter Charles Willson Peale; from Pittsburgh to Jackson County, Missouri with the Long Expedition (q.v.).
- "The Journal of Titian Ramsay Peale, Pioneer Naturalist," A. O. Weese, ed. Missouri Historical Review, v. 41, pp. 147-63, January, 1947; pp. 266-84, April, 1947.

2. August 1, 1838-February 19, 1842; Official diary; senior naturalist and collector sent by the U.S. government to explore the Pacific for trade and scientific purposes; shipwreck at the mouth of the Columbia River; well-written; a landmark in American exploration.
- Poesch, Jessie. Titian Ramsay Peale and His Journals of the Wilkes Expedition. Philadelphia: American Philosophical Society, 1961.

3. September 22-November 1, 1841; Exploration diary; accompanied an offshoot of the Wilkes Expedition under Lt. George F. Emmons; stops at Fort Sutter and three Roman Catholic missions; describes flora, fauna and terrain; includes his sketches.
- Dairy of Titian Ramsay Peale: Oregon to California, Overland Journey, September and October, 1841. Clifford M. Drury, ed. Los Angeles: G. Dawson, 1957; 300 copies.

453. PIGOT, Sophia (1804-81)
January 1, 1819-December 31, 1821
Travel diary; upper class father, stepmother and sister went with 58 retainers from England to settle in South Africa; voyage out; early days at Pigot Park; fragmentary recital of events.
- The Journals of Sophia Pigot, 1819-1821. Margaret Rainier, ed. Cape Town: Balkema, 1974.

454. SADLEIR, George Forster (1789-1859)
April 14-November 14, 1819

Travel diary; first European to cross Arabia from east to west; from Bombay to Jeddah on a diplomatic mission; excellent description of the hardships, people and countryside.
 • Diary of a Journey Across Arabia 1819. New York: Olean-der Press, 1977.
     REVIEW: Geographical Journal, v. 144, p. 349, July, 1978.

455. SMITH, Thomas, Jr.
       May 11-October 16, 1819
       Travel diary; excerpts; trip at the request of a parent to as-certain prospects for the family's immigration; in New York state, Kentucky and Cincinnati.
 • Appleton, Thomas H., Jr. "An Englishman's Perception of Antebellum Kentucky: The Journal of Thomas Smith, Jr., of Lincolnshire," Kentucky Historical Society Register, v. 79, pp. 57-62, Winter, 1981.

456. SPARKS, Jared (1789-1866) [A252]
       1. November 22, 1819-May 2, 1820; Travel diary; Harvard minister with a historical bent; attended an ordination.
 • "Jared Sparks Visits South Carolina," John Hammond Moore, ed. South Carolina Historical Magazine, v. 72, pp. 150-60, July, 1971.

       2. April 16-24, 1826; Travel diary; journey to Georgia to gather primary historical material on the American Revolution; Yankee comments on the South.
 • "Jared Sparks in Georgia--April, 1826," John Hammond Moore, ed. Georgia Historical Quarterly, v. 47, pp. 425-35, 1963.

       3. May 2-10, 1826; Travel diary; excerpts; journey to find and preserve documents, manuscripts and letters of American history; Raleigh, North Carolina; account of several papers and books he found.
 • Moore, John H. "Jared Sparks in North Carolina," North Carolina Historical Review, v. 40, pp. 285-94, July, 1963.

457. WINSTON, James (1773-   )
       October 5, 1819-July 2, 1827
       Personal diary; acting manager of Drury Lane; responsible for hiring, salaries and employment conditions of players; London the-atrical scene and leading literary luminaries of the period; Edmund Kean, William Charles Macready; dramatist Thomas Dibdin; impersonal tone.
 • Drury Lane Journal: Selections from James Winston's Dia-ries, 1819-1827. Alfred L. Nelson and Gilbert B. Cross, eds. London: Society for Theatre Research, 1974.

                                    1820

458. ADAMS, Charles Francis (1807-86)

January, 1820-June, 1836
Personal diary; son of Pres. John Quincy Adams; lengthy en-
tries of great detail; involved in business and politics in Massachu-
setts.
• Diary. Aida DiPace Donald, and David Donald, eds. 6 vols.
Cambridge: Harvard University Press, 1964-74.
    REVIEWS: Book Review Digest 1964, pp. 4-5; 1965, p. 5;
    1969, p. 7; 1975, p. 5.

459. BELL, John R. (1784/85-1825)
March-November, 1820
Exploration diary; 5300 mile journey from West Point, New York
through Pennsylvania, on the Ohio and Mississippi Rivers; through
Tennessee, Kentucky and Virginia to Washington, D.C.
• The Journal of Captain John R. Bell Official Journalist for
the Stephen H. Long Expedition to the Rocky Mountains, 1820.
Harlin M. Fuller and LeRoy R. Hafen, eds. Glendale, Cal.:
Arthur H. Clark, 1957.

460. BENTHAM, George
June 1, 1820-March 19, 1821
Personal diary; "only entries directly referring to John Stuart
Mill (q.v.) or having some bearing on the Journal or Notebook have
been included."
• "Excerpts from George Bentham's Manuscript Diary Journals,
1820-21," in: John Mill's Boyhood Visit to France. Anna J.
Mill, ed. Toronto: University of Toronto Press, 1960; pp. 116-
23.

461. CRUISE, Richard Alexander (1784?-1832)
February 16-December 5, 1820
Travel diary; commanding officer of store ship Dromedary was
in New Zealand to take a load of spars; Maori intertribal warfare;
trees felled by natives; searching for suitable timber; native women
living on board; straightforward writing.
• Journal of a Ten Months' Residence in New Zealand. Christ-
church: Pegasus Press, 1957; 650 copies.

462. FLETCHER, Calvin (1798-1866)
November 9, 1820-May 13, 1866
Personal diary; Ohioan settled in Indianapolis and built a suc-
cessful law practice; state senator from 1826-33; later a banker and
farmer; lengthy entries cover a variety of topics; details of business
and family life; widely traveled; reared eleven children to adulthood;
excellent, detailed.
• The Diary of Calvin Fletcher: Including Letter of Calvin
Fletcher and Diaries and Letters of His Wife Sarah Hill Fletcher.
Gayle Thornbrough, ed. 9 vols. Indianapolis: Indiana Historical
Society, 1972-83.
    REVIEWS: Book Review Digest 1976, p. 143; 1978, p. 160;
    1979, p. 149. Indiana Magazine of History, v. 80, pp. 166-
    72, 1984.

463. HOBHOUSE, Henry (1776-1854) [B169]
      January 31, 1820-November 6, 1827
      Diplomatic diary; old-fashioned Tory holding Civil Service
status under Sir Robert Peel; opens with the death of George III;
Queen Caroline contretemps; dry.
      • Diary, 1820-1827. Arthur Aspinall, ed. London: Home &
Van Thal, 1947.

464. MILL, John Stuart (1806-73) [B199]
      June 2, 1820-February 6, 1821
      Travel diary; trip to Paris with George Ensor; ten month stay
with Sir Samuel Bentham family near Toulouse; reading, study, sightseeing; in French and English.
      • John Mill's Boyhood Visit to France: Being a Journal and
Notebook Written by John Stuart Mill in France, 1820-21.
Anna Jean Mill, ed. Toronto: University of Toronto Press,
1960.

465. SHAW, William (1798-1872)
      February 3, 1820-January 17, 1822; December 27, 1826-October
18, 1829
      Personal diary; Methodist missionary went with his family to
South Africa; minister to white settlers and evangelized among the
natives; straightforward narrative.
      • The Journal of William Shaw. W. D. Hammond-Tooke, ed.
Cape Town: Balkema, 1972.

466. TROWBRIDGE, Charles C. (1800?-)
      May 24-September 13, 1820
      Exploration diary; appointed along with others by governor
Lewis Cass of the Michigan Territory to explore the interior of the
Northwest Territory; around Lake Michigan; up the Mississippi through
present-day Wisconsin and Minnesota by canoe.
      • "With Cass in the Northwest in 1820: The Journal of Charles
C. Trowbridge," Ralph H. Brown, ed. Minnesota History, v.
23, pp. 126-48, June, 1942; pp. 233-52, September, 1942; pp.
328-48, December, 1942.

467. WITTS, Francis Edward (1783-1854)
      January 3, 1820-May 1, 1852
      Personal diary; Tory rector of Upper Slaughter and vicar of
Stanway; served as a magistrate at Gloucester Quarter Sessions;
traveled throughout Gloucestershire; social life; the editor's occupation as an architectural historian shows in his highlighting of descriptions of monuments, churches, etc.; local interest.
      • The Diary of a Cotswold Parson. David Veerey, ed. Glou-
cester: Alan Sutton, 1978.
         REVIEWS: Books and Bookmen, v. 24, p. 48, June, 1979.
      Choice, v. 18, p. 578, December, 1980.

<u>1821</u>

468. AYLIFF, John (1797-1862)
      April 4, 1821-September 23, 1830; many gaps
      Official diary; silk weaver converted to Methodism went out to
South Africa with settlers in 1820; became an ordained pastor and
was obliged to keep a journal for the London headquarters; church
matters; preaching; sympathy for Hottentots and observations on
their witchcraft.
      • <u>The Journal of John Ayliff</u>. Peter Hinchliff, ed. Cape Town:
      Balkema, 1971.

469. BERTRAND, Henri Gratien (1773-1844)
      January-May 12, 1821
      Personal diary; an account of the last days of Napoleon by a
companion; written in the third person with much quoted conversation.
      • <u>Napoleon at St. Helena: The Journals of General Bertrand</u>
      <u>From January to May of 1821</u>. Francis Hume, trans. New York:
      Doubleday, 1952.
      For an interpretation of Napoleon's last days see: Ben Weider
and David Hapgood. <u>The Murder of Napoleon</u>. New York: Congdon
and Lattès, 1982.

470. CALLCOTT, Lady Maria Dundas Graham (1785/86-1842)
      1. July 31, 1821-December 18, 1823; Personal diary; daughter
of a British admiral; wife of British Foreign Service diplomat; tutored
the future Queen of Portugal in Rio; lengthy entries; much detail of
Brazilian life, customs, etc.; well done.
      • <u>Journal of a Voyage to Brazil, and Residence There During</u>
      <u>Part of the Years 1821, 1822, 1823</u>. A. C. Wilgus, ed. New
      York: Praeger, 1969; reprint of 1824 edition.

      2. April 28, 1822-March 1, 1823; Travel diary; death of her
husband early in this diary; lived at Valparaiso, Santiago and in
rural areas; details of native life; socializing; good observer.
      • <u>Journal of a Residence in Chile, During the Year 1822 and a</u>
      <u>Voyage From Chile to Brazil in 1823</u>. New York: Praeger, 1969.

471. CRAWFURD, John (1783-1868)
      November 23, 1821-December 29, 1822
      Diplomatic diary; sent by the British government to what is
now Thailand and Vietnam to negotiate political and trade treaties;
unsuccessful but paved the way for later efforts; detailed description
of land and people.
      • <u>Journal of an Embassy to the Courts of Siam and Cochin</u>
      <u>China</u>. David K. Wyatt, introduction. London: Oxford Uni-
      versity Press, 1968; reprint of 1828 edition.

472. FLETCHER, Sarah Hill (-1854)
      June 20, 1821-August 2, 1824; June 8-29, 1830; December 23,
      1837-February 14, 1838
      Travel diary; journey with her husband, Calvin (q.v.), to

Indianapolis; studies and reading; running a household; social life.
  • "Letters and Diary of Sarah Hill Fletcher June 20, 1821–
  August 2, 1824," in: The Diary of Calvin Fletcher. Indianapolis: Indiana Historical Society, 1972–83; v. 1, pp. 39–79;
  170–72, 474–78.

473. GREVILLE, Charles Cavendish Fulke (1794–1865) [B184]
     February 7, 1821–June 21, 1837
     Personal diary; moved in court circles in the reigns of George
IV and William IV; glimpse of Queen Victoria as a child; court intrigues.
     • "Diary Excerpts," in: Philip Dunaway and Mel Evans, eds.
     A Treasury of the World's Great Diaries. New York: Double-
     day, 1975; pp. 364–73.

474. PARSONS, Anna Quincy Thaxter
     May 6–27, 1821
     Personal diary; kept by the older half-sister of the bride;
wedding preparations, etc.; great detail.
     • "A Newburyport Wedding One Hundred and Thirty Years
     Ago: The Bride Elizabeth Margaret Carter," Essex Institute
     Historical Collections, v. 87, pp. 309–32, October, 1951.

475. STEELE, J. D.
     January 9–March 3, 1821
     Personal diary; kept on a business trip; long entries and good
picture of life; people, food, travel, climate.
     • "A New York 'Yankee' in Tennessee, 1821," Robert V. Re-
     mini, ed. Tennessee Historical Quarterly, v. 37, pp. 278–92,
     1978.

                                    1822

476. BIERCE, Lucius Verus (1801–76)
     October 10, 1822–October 19, 1823
     Travel diary; uncle of writer Ambrose Bierce; trip undertaken
after graduation from Ohio University; Charleston [West] Virginia,
the Carolinas, Alabama; encounters with Creeks and Choctaws; Southern mores and comments on slavery.
     • Travel in the Southland, 1822–1823; The Journal of Lucius
     Verus Bierce. George W. Knepper, ed. Columbus: Ohio State
     University Press, 1966.

477. BINGHAM, Abel (1786–1865)
     April 4, 1822–July 20, 1827
     Personal diary; mission at Tonawanda, New York; evangelizing
Red Jacket; travels to Buffalo.
     • "A Missionary Among the Senecas: The Journal of Abel
     Bingham, 1822–1828," John Cumming, ed. New York History,
     v. 60, pp. 157–93, April, 1979.

478. CANBY, Edmund (1804-48)
      February 13, 1822-June 8, 1848
      Personal diary; operated a family mill at Brandywine Bridge;
period of decline due to opening of the Erie Canal; converted to
Episcopalianism; family life; worked briefly as a banker.
      • "The Diaries of Edmund Canby, A Quaker Miller, 1822-1848,"
      Carol E. Hoffecker, ed. Delaware History, v. 16, pp. 79-131,
      October, 1974; pp. 184-243, Spring-Summer, 1975.

479. DELACROIX, Eugène (1798-1863)
      September 3, 1822-October 5, 1824; January 6-June 25, 1832;
      January 19-October 9, 1847; January 24, 1849-June 22, 1863.
      Personal diary; major French painter; social life, work, fellow
painters and their work; theory and practice of painting takes up
most of his thoughts.
      • The Journal of Eugene Delacroix. Walter Pach, trans. New
      York: Crown, 1948.
      • The Journal of Eugene Delacroix: A Selection. Hubert Wel-
      lington, ed. Lucy Norton, trans. New York: Phaidon, 1951;
      Ithaca: Cornell University Press, 1980; a more modern, less
      literary translation than the Pach edition.
      REVIEW: Book Review Index 1981, p. 145.

480. HAZLITT, Sarah Stoddart
      April 14-July 18, 1822
      Travel diary; Sarah went to Scotland to obtain a divorce from
English literary critic William; sightseeing while waiting out the term
of 40 days residence.
      • "Sarah Hazlitt's Journal of My Trip to Scotland," in The
      Journals of Sarah and William Hazlitt, 1822-1831. Willard Hal-
      lam Bonner, ed. (University of Buffalo Studies, v. 24, no. 3,
      February, 1959) Buffalo: University of Buffalo, 1959; pp. 185-
      252.

481. MORGAN, Youngs L. (1797-1888)
      May 30, 1822-August 25, 1823
      Business diary; Connecticut native grew up in Cleveland, Ohio;
trader for the American Fur Company on the Upper Great Lakes;
tending store; trapping for food and pelts.
      • "The Diary of an Early Fur Trader," Clarissa Headline and
      Milton N. Gallup, eds. Inland Seas, v. 18, pp. 300-05, Winter,
      1962; v. 19, pp. 30-46, Spring, 1963; pp. 113-22, Summer,
      1963; pp. 227-32, Fall, 1963; pp. 277-83, Winter, 1963.

482. PRINCE, Hezekiah (1800-43) [A184]
      June 1, 1822-October 5, 1828
      Personal diary; customs inspector at Thomaston, Maine; life in
a coastal town; much on shipping and his work; social life of a young
bachelor; comments on the town's residents.
      • Journals of Hezekiah Prince, Jr., 1822-1828. Walter Muir
      Whitehill, introduction. New York: Crown, 1965.
      REVIEW: Book Review Digest 1966, p. 976.

483. SHERMAN, Alpheus (1780-1866)
      September 28-October 23, 1822
      Travel diary; New York lawyer went with his wife and a friend
to look at land; notes on value of property, prices, scenery; interesting.
      • "By Horse and Waggon [sic]: The Diary of Alpheus Sher-
      man," New York History, v. 37, pp. 432-51, October, 1956.

484. TEAS, Thomas Scattergood (1794-1850) [A242]
      April 10-October 5, 1822
      Travel diary; down the Ohio River by boat; Louisville, Ken-
tucky, to the Mississippi River; prices, scenery and people; interesting.
      • "Trading Trip to Natchez and New Orleans, 1822: Diary of
      Thomas S. Teas," Julia Ideson and Sanford W. Higginbotham,
      eds. Journal of Southern History, v. 7, pp. 378-99, August,
      1941.

485. TOKETA, ---
      May-June, 1822
      Personal diary; work and social life.
      • "Tahitians in the Early History of Hawaiian Christianity:
      The Journal of Toketa," Hawaiian Journal of History, v. 13,
      pp. 19-35, 1979.

486. TYLER, Mary Palmer
      June 4, 1822-August 26, 1826
      Personal diary; extracts; wife of American novelist and play-
wright Royall Tyler; covers his bout with terminal cancer; business
failure; generosity and compassion of friends; taking in sewing to
make ends meet; "Industry can accomplish much."
      • Newbrough, George Floyd. "Mary Tyler's Journal," Ver-
      mont Quarterly, v. 20, pp. 19-31, January, 1952.

                              1823

487. COLHOUN, James Edward (1796-1889)
      July 1-29, 1823
      Exploration diary; on the Minnesota and Red Rivers with the
Long Expedition (q.v.).
      • "Up the Minnesota River with Long," in: Stephen H. Long.
      The Northern Expeditions of Stephen F. Long. St. Paul:
      Minnesota Historical Society, 1978; pp. 271-327.

488. DARRELL, John Harvey
      July 7-23, 1823
      Travel diary; from Bermuda to Washington, D.C.; stops in
Virginia; detailed descriptions.
      • "Diary of John Harvey Darrell: Voyage to America, 7th
      July 1823," Bermuda Historical Quarterly, v. 5, pp. 142-49,
      July-September, 1948.

489. ESTUDILLO, Don José María
      November 19, 1823-January 31, 1824
      Exploration diary; San Gabriel, California, to the Colorado
River.
      • "Diary of the Romero Expedition," in: Lowell J. Bean, ed.
      Diaries and Accounts of the Romero Expeditions in Arizona and
      California, 1823-26. Los Angeles: Ward Ritchie, 1962; pp.
      30-51.

490. HAZLITT, William (1778-1830)
      1823
      Personal diary; English essayist; after being divorced by his
first wife he took up with Sarah Walker; to insure himself of her fi-
delity to him he had a friend try to seduce her(!).
      • William Hazlitt's Journal of 1823. Willard Hallam Bonner, ed.
      (University of Buffalo Studies, v. 24, no. 3, February, 1959)
      Buffalo: University of Buffalo, 1959; pp. 265-77.

491. HEBER, Reginald (1783-1826) [B162]
      October 11, 1823-April 17, 1825
      Travel diary; English hymn writer; selections from the 1828
edition; about half of the original material printed here; concerned
with northern India from Calcutta to Bombay.
      • Bishop Heber in Northern India: Selections from Heber's
      Journal. M. A. Laird, ed. London: Cambridge University
      Press, 1971.

492. ROMERO, Captain Don José
      June 8-July 12, 1823
      Exploration diary; surveying the countryside for the locating
of a mail route to Tucson.
      • "Diary," in: Lowell J. Bean, ed. Diaries and Accounts of
      the Romero Expeditions in Arizona and California 1823-26. Los
      Angeles: Ward Ritchie, 1962; pp. 14-24.

493. WORDSWORTH, Mary (1770-   )
      May 16-June 1, 1823
      Travel diary; wife of poet laureate William; the first complete
transcription of the journal.
      • Abrams, Kenneth T. "Mary Wordsworth's Journal of a Tour
      of Belgium and Holland, 1823," Ph.D., Cornell University, 1965.
      (Dissertation Abstracts 26/06A, p. 3322)

                              1824

494. BLACK, Samuel (1780-1841)
      May 13-September 28, 1824
      Exploration diary; sent by the Hudson Bay Company to recon-
noiter territory in northern British Columbia; unusually severe weather
for summer with heavy rain, wind and frost.

• A Journal of a Voyage from Rocky Mountain Portage in Peace
River to the Sources of Finlays Branch and North West Ward in
Summer 1824. E. E. Rich, ed. London: Hudson's Bay Record
Society, 1955.

495. CLARE, John (1793-1864) [B207]
September 6, 1824-September 11, 1825
Personal diary; English "peasant poet"; his reading, dealings
with publishers; natural history.
• The Journals, Essays, and The Journey from Essex. Anne
Tibble, ed. Manchester: Carcanet New Press, 1980.
REVIEW: Book Review Index 1981, p. 111.

496. DELECLUZE, Etienne Jean
February 2, 1824-January 15, 1827
Personal diary; Delecluze's side of an amour with Amélie Cyvoct,
niece of Mme. Récamier; she eventually married another; a bittersweet
affair.
• Two Lovers in Rome: Being Extracts from the Journal and
Letters of Etienne Jean Delecluze. Louis Desterness, ed.
Gerard Hopkins, trans. London: Deutsch, 1958.

497. DOUGLAS, David (1799-1834) [A248]
July 24, 1824-August 28, 1827
Personal and travel diary; British naturalist; exploration and
plant collecting in present-day Washington, Oregon and British Co-
lumbia; edited and abridged from 1914 publication.
• Douglas of the Forest: The North American Journals of
David Douglas. John Davies, ed. Seattle: University of Wash-
ington Press, 1980.

498. MACDONALD, Donald (1791-1872)
October 2, 1824-August 6, 1825; October 1, 1825-June 1, 1826
Travel diary; accompanied Robert Owen to New Harmony, In-
diana; from Liverpool to Albany, New York; visits with Joseph Bona-
parte and Thomas Jefferson; return via New Orleans and Havana;
interesting descriptions.
• The Diaries of Donald Macdonald, 1824-1826. Caroline Dale
Snedeker, intro. Clifton, N.J.: A. M. Kelly, 1973; reprint of
Indiana Historical Society Publications, v. 14, no. 2, 1942.

499. MARSHALL, Adam (1785-1825)
December 4, 1824-August 10, 1825
Personal diary; chaplain to the USS North Carolina, the first
in the U.S. Navy; excerpts from his journal with account of his teach-
ing duties while the ship made an unsuccessful voyage to the Mediter-
ranean; visit to the Rock of Gibraltar; died at sea of consumption.
• Journal of Father Adam Marshall, 1824-1825. Joseph T.
Durkin, ed. Scranton: University of Scranton Press, 1943.

500. MOGG, William (1796-1875) [B176]
September 13, 1824-July 20, 1825

Exploration diary; with Edward Parry's third Arctic expedition as clerk on the Fury; looking for a Northwest Passage; excursions ashore to hunt game; "fancy dress ball" aboard for recreation; understated and occasionally humorous.
- "The Arctic Wintering of HMS Hecla and Fury in Prince Regent Inlet 1824-1825," Polar Record [Great Britain], v. 12, pp. 11-28, 1964.

501. NEWMAN, John Henry, Cardinal (1801-90) [B268]
1824-79; gap July 1826-March, 1828
Personal diary; Anglican theologian converted to Roman Catholicism; very short entries; visitors, travels.
- The Letters and Diaries of John Henry Newman. Charles Stephen Dessain, ed. 31 vols. London: Nelson, 1961-77.

502. OGDEN, Peter Skene (1794-   ) [A250]
1. December 10, 1824-July, 1826; September 19, 1826-March 12, 1827; September 7, 1827-July 6, 1829; Fur trade diary; the definitive edition of his journals; of premier importance in the history of the Northwest; fur trade; Anglo-American relations.
- Peter Skene Ogden's Snake Country Journals 1824-26, 1826-27, 1827-29. E. E. Rich, ed. (Hudson's Bay Record Society, vols. 13, 23, 28) London: Hudson's Bay Record Co., 1950, 1961, 1971.

2. April 26-June 1, 1825; reprint of pp. 40-56 in above entry.
- "Peter Skene Ogden's Journal of His Expedition to Utah, 1825," Utah Historical Quarterly, v. 20, pp. 159-86, 1952.

503. RIDOUT, Horatio (1769-1834)
September 15-October 6, 1824
Personal diary; shore excursions and fishing.
- "Journal of a Voyage Down the Chesapeake Bay on a Fishing Expedition, 1824," Maryland Historical Magazine, v. 51, pp. 140-53, June, 1956.

1825

504. ASHLEY, William H. (1778/85-1838) [B247]
1. Fur trade diary; key American figure in the Western fur trade; hazardous but successful trip bringing 9000 pounds of beaver pelts to market; through Great Divide Basin.
- "The Diary of William H. Ashley March 25-June 27, 1825: A Record of Exploration West Across the Continental Divide, Down the Green River and into the Great Basin," Dale L. Morgan, ed. Missouri Historical Society Bulletin, v. 11, pp. 9-40, October, 1954; pp. 158-86, January, 1955; pp. 279-302, April, 1955.

2. March 25-June 27, 1825

• The West of William H. Ashley, 1822-1838. Dale L. Morgan,
ed. Denver: Old West, 1964; pp. 104-17.

505. BROBSON, William P. (1786-1850)
January 18, 1825-August 1, 1828
Personal diary; Quaker lawyer, newspaper editor and customs
collector; supporter of Zachary Taylor.
• "William P. Brobson Diary, 1825-1828," George H. Gibson,
ed. Delaware History, v. 15, pp. 55-84, April, 1972; pp. 124-
55, October, 1972; pp. 195-217, April, 1973; pp. 295-311, October, 1973.

506. CLAPPERTON, Hugh (1788-1827)
December 7, 1825-March 11, 1827; Lander's portion November
20, 1826-November 28, 1827
Exploration diary; from the west coast inland to Soccatoo; death
and separation from some of the expedition members; Lander's return
to England; many details of natives.
• Journal of a 2nd Expedition into the Interior of Africa, from
the Bight of Benin to Soccatoo: to Which is Added the Journal
of Richard Lander from Kano to the Sea-coast, Partly by a More
Eastern Route. London: Cass, 1966; reprint of 1829 edition.

507. GLADSTONE, William Ewart (1809-98) [B212]
July 16, 1825-
Personal diary; British statesman and Liberal Party leader; re-
ligious, political and social life of his day with very brief entries for
the most part; usually only a listing of his day's activities with little
introspection.
• The Gladstone Diaries. M.R.D. Foot, ed. ? vols. Oxford:
Clarendon Press, 1966- .

508. KITTSON, William
April 26-May 31, 1825
Fur trade diary; trading in northern Utah; better description
than Ogden's journals (q.v.); portions dealing with Utah.
• "William Kittson's Journal Covering Peter Skene Ogden's
1824-1825 Snake Country Expedition," Utah Historical Quarterly,
v. 22, pp. 125-42, April, 1954.

509. LAURENS, Caroline Olivia
May 23-November 11, 1825
Travel diary; the journey, visiting; social life.
• "Journal of a Visit to Greenville from Charleston in the Sum-
mer of 1825," Louise C. King, ed. South Carolina Historical
Magazine, v. 72, pp. 164-73, July, 1971; pp. 220-33, October,
1971.

510. OWEN, Robert Dale (1801-77)
May 30, 1825-January 23, 1826
Travel diary; son of Welsh socialist Robert Owen; in the

Netherlands to observe co-operative communities; by ship to New
York; Philadelphia; icebound on a keelboat near Beaver, Pennsylvania;
some passages of the diary were reprinted verbatim as a series of
articles.
- To Holland and to New Harmony: Robert Dale Owen's Travel
  Journal, 1825-1826. Josephine M. Elliott, ed. (Indiana Histor-
  ical Society Publications, v. 23, no. 4) Indianapolis: Indiana
  Historical Society, 1969.

511. PEARD, George (1783-1837)
      May 29, 1825-May 27, 1828
      Exploration journal; 1st lieutenant on Blossom's voyage of sur-
vey and discovery; from England to the Bering Strait via Rio and
Acapulco; to Macao, Hawaiian and Society Islands and home; much
description of natives and their customs.
- To the Pacific and Arctic with Beechey: The Journal of
  Lieutenant George Peard of H.M.S. "Blossom," 1825-1828.
  Barry M. Gough, ed. London: Cambridge University Press,
  for the Hakluyt Society, 1973.

512. REEVES, Benjamin H.
      Travel diary; weather, scenery, mileage; encounter with In-
dians.
- "Diary of Benjamin H. Reeves on Return From the Boundary,
  October 8 to October 25, 1825," in Kate L. Gregg. The Road
  to Santa Fe. Albuquerque: University of New Mexico Press,
  1952; pp. 169-74.

513. SAVAGE, Pamela (1802-75)
      September 26, 1825-June 10, 1827
      Travel diary; New Yorker went to North Carolina by canalboat,
stage and frigate; taught at Oxford Female Academy; a visit to Virginia.
- "Pamela Savage of Champlain, Healthseeker in Oxford," Helen
  Harriet Salls, ed. North Carolina Historical Review, v. 29, pp.
  540-68, 1952.

514. SCOTT, Sir Walter (1771-1832) [B211]
      1. November 10, 1825-April 14, 1832; Personal diary; Scottish
poet, novelist and biographer; his writing; relations with publishers;
family visits; this edition corrects the bowdlerized, poorly done edition of 1890.
- The Journal of Sir Walter Scott: The Text Revised from a
  Photostat in the National Library of Scotland. John Guthrie
  Tait and W. M. Parker, eds. London: Oliver and Boyd, 1950;
  reprinted Westport, Conn.: Greenwood Press, 1978.

      2. November 10, 1825-April 15, 1832; Personal diary; "A
complete and accurate version of what Scott actually wrote"; intended
for publication and is not as free in his opinions as he is in his letters; begins with him at the height of his fame and rapidly declines

with the death of his wife, financial disaster and failing health; he
wrote to pay off his debts; at Abbotsford, in London; ends in Italy;
lengthy, detailed entries.
- The Journal of Sir Walter Scott, W.E.K. Anderson, ed.
New York: Oxford University Press, 1972.
    REVIEW: Book Review Digest 1974, p. 1087.

3. "Diary Excerpts," in: Elizabeth D'Oyley, ed. English Diaries. London: Edward Arnold, 1930; pp. 211-24.

4. "Diary Excerpts," in: Philip Dunaway and Mel Evans, eds.
A Treasury of the World's Great Diaries. New York: Doubleday,
1957; pp. 327-39.

515. SIBLEY, George Champlain (1782-1863) [A250]
    1. Exploration diary; weather, survey material.
    - "Diary of George C. Sibley From the Arkansas to Santa Fe,
    October 12 to December 31, 1825," in: Kate L. Gregg. Road
    to Santa Fe. Albuquerque: University of New Mexico Press,
    1952; pp. 120-36.

    2. Travel diary; weather, health, prices of items needed to
outfit the expedition.
    - "Diary of George C. Sibley, Santa Fe and Taos, January 1
    to March 31, 1826," in: Kate L. Gregg. ibid., pp. 137-61.

    3. Exploration diary; weather; travel notes.
    - "The Journal of George C. Sibley on an Expedition to Sur-
    vey and Mark a Road from the Missouri Frontier to the Settle-
    ments of Mexico, St. Louis, June 22, to Santa Fe, November
    30, 1826," in: Kate L. Gregg. ibid., pp. 49-119.

    4. Travel diary; health, weather, survey notes.
    - "Journal of George C. Sibley on Correction of the Survey
    and Making of Report May 12 to October 27, 1827," in: Kate
    L. Gregg. ibid., pp. 175-95.

516. TAYLOE, Edward Thornton (1803-76)
    May 5, 1825-April 16, 1828; gaps
    Travel diary; accompanied J. R. Poinsett to Mexico as its first
minister from the U.S.; three year sojourn enabled him to revisit
different areas more than once; balanced, observant, well done.
    - Mexico, 1825-1828; The Journal and Correspondence of Ed-
    ward Thornton Tayloe. C. Harvey Gardiner, ed. Chapel Hill:
    University of North Carolina Press, 1959.

517. TEMPLE, Edmund
    October 23, 1825-May 19, 1826
    Travel diary; extracts; by ship to Buenos Aires; overland to
Potosi, Peru.
    - "Diary Excerpts," in: Philip Dunaway and Mel Evans. A

Treasury of the World's Great Diaries. New York: Doubleday,
1957; pp. 81-90.

1826

518. AUDUBON, John James (1772-1851) [A238]
June 30, 1826-May 1, 1827
Travel diary; American ornithologist and artist; trip to England
to make his fortune and reputation.
- "Diary Excerpts," in: Dunaway, Philip and Mel Evans, eds.
A Treasury of the World's Great Diaries. New York: Double-
day, 1957; pp. 300-07.

519. CLARK, William (1770-1838) [A186]
May 1, 1826-February 28, 1831
Official diary; brother of George Rogers Clark (q.v.) and
supervisor of Indian affairs in St. Louis; some entries were made
by clerks in his office; weather, river data; Indian visits.
- "William Clark's Diary," Louise Barry, ed. Kansas Historical Quarterly, v. 16, pp. 1-36, February, 1948; pp. 136-74,
May, 1948; pp. 274-305, August, 1948; pp. 384-410, November,
1948.

520. GLOVER, John
October 2, 1826-November 10, 1826
Travel diary; from Kentucky to Missouri overland; costs of
travel and lodging.
- "Westward Along the Boone's Lick Trail in 1826, The Diary
of Colonel John Glover," Missouri Historical Review, v. 39, pp.
184-99, 1945.

521. HUTCHISON, Susan Nye (1790-   )
October 7, 1826-November 16, 1833
Personal diary; Duchess County, New Yorker; conducted a fe-
male seminary; classes for blacks; several destructive fires in the
town.
- "Extracts From the Journal of Susan Nye Hutchison While
She Was Living at Augusta, Ga.," Virginia E. deTreville, ed.
Richmond County [Ga.] History, v. 11, pp. 26-33, 1979.

522. JENKINS, Thomas (1813-71)
September 14, 1826-December 2, 1870
Personal diary; line-a-day type with much information on cab-
inetmaker of the Towy Valley in West Wales; fine craftsman interested
in spelunking, astronomy, fossils; gives the reader some glimpses of
his life with some maddening omissions.
- The Diary of Thomas Jenkins of Llandilo, 1826-1870. D.C.
Jenkins, ed. Bala: Dragon Books, 1976.

523. NIKITENKO, Aleksandr (1804-77)
January 1, 1826-July 19, 1877

Personal diary; born a serf in the Ukraine; close friend of an
executed Decembrist; became secretary to the head of the St. Petersburg school district; member of the censorship department of the
czarist government; censored Gogol's and Pushkin's work; this translation is based on the three volume Soviet edition of 1955-56; picture
of 19th century censorship and ponderous bureaucracy replicated by
the Soviets in the 20th century; excellent.

* Diary of a Russian Censor. Helen Saltz Jacobson, ed. and
trans. Abridged ed. Amherst: University of Massachusetts,
1975.
REVIEWS: Book Review Digest 1976, p. 883. Book Review
Index 1977, p. 323; 1979, p. 339.

524. POCOCK, John Thomas (1814-76)
October 29, 1826-January 11, 1830
Personal diary; son of a London merchant who suffered business
reverses in the panic of 1825; sinking family fortunes; left school and
worked for his father who was imprisoned for debt for a time; ends
with his last sight of England from a ship bound for Australia;
straightforward style.

* The Diary of a London Schoolboy: 1826-1830. Marjorie
Holder and Christina Gee, eds. London: Camden History So-
ciety, 1980.
REVIEW: Book Review Index 1981, p. 445.

525. RICE, Shadrach
March 25, 1826-August 6, 1862; gaps
Personal diary; Peedee River country of South Carolina; Lau-
derdale County, Tenn.

* "The Shadrach Rice Diary," R. E. Rice, ed. West Tennessee Historical Society Papers, v. 15, pp. 105-16, 1961.

526. SCHIRMER, Jacob Sass (1803-80)
Public diary; record of births, marriages and deaths; civic and
social life of Charleston, South Carolina; of genealogical interest.

* "The Schirmer Diary," South Carolina Historical Magazine,
v. 61, p. 163, July, 1960; p. 232, October, 1960; v. 62, p.
54, January, 1961; pp. 113-14, April, 1961; p. 182, July,
1961; p. 237, October, 1961; v. 67, pp. 229-33, October, 1966;
v. 68, pp. 97-100, April, 1967; pp. 37-41, January, 1967; v.
69, pp. 139-44, April, 1968; pp. 59-65, January, 1968; pp.
204-08, July, 1968; pp. 262-66, October, 1968; v. 70, pp. 122-
25, April, 1969; pp. 59-63, January, 1969; pp. 196-99, July,
1969; v. 72, pp. 115-18, April, 1971; pp. 236-37, October,
1971; v. 73, pp. 97-98, April, 1972; pp. 156-58, July, 1972; v.
v. 73, pp. 220-21, October, 1972; v. 74, pp. 103-04, April,
1973; pp. 39-40, January, 1973; v. 75, pp. 249-51, October,
1974; v. 76, pp. 35-37, January, 1975; pp. 87-88, April, 1975;
pp. 171-73, July, 1975; pp. 250-52, October, 1975; v. 77, pp.
49-51, January, 1976; pp. 127-29, April, 1976; pp. 171-73,
July, 1976; pp. 194-95, October, 1976; v. 78, pp. 71-73, January, 1977.

<u>1827</u>

527. CLOPPER, Edward Nicholas
      November 10, 1827-March 14, 1828
      Travel diary; down the Ohio and Mississippi Rivers; arrival
in Harrisburg and Houston, Texas; good description of passing scenery.
      • "Journal of a Voyage from Cincinnati to the Province of
      Texas in 1827," in: An American Family: Its Ups and Downs
      Through Eight Generations in New Amsterdam, New York,
      Pennsylvania, Maryland, Ohio and Texas, from 1650 to 1880.
      Cincinnati: The Author, 1950; pp. 156-69.

528. CORCORAN, John
      June 25-September 12, 1827
      Travel journal; journey from the Red River Colony in Hudson's
Bay Territory to St. Louis; accompanied by his wife and three daughters; herds of buffalo sighted; bad weather.
      • "The Diary of John Corcoran," Charles Van Ravenswaay,
      ed. Missouri Historical Society Bulletin, v. 13, pp. 264-74,
      April, 1957.

529. LAPHAM, Increase Allen (1811-75) [A263]
      October 6, 1827-July 1, 1830
      Personal diary; budding geologist and experienced canalman
employed on Louisville project; botanizing; fossils; study; well done
and interesting.
      • "The Falls of the Ohio River and Its Environs: The Journals
      of Increase Allen Lapham for 1827-1830," Samuel W. Thomas and
      Eugene H. Conner, eds. Filson Club Historical Quarterly, v. 45,
      pp. 5-34, January, 1971; pp. 199-226, April, 1971; pp. 381-
      403, October, 1971; pp. 315-41, July, 1971.

530. O'SULLIVAN, Humphrey (1780-1838) [B214]
      January, 1827-July 31, 1835; many gaps
      Personal diary; Irish schoolmaster of Kilkenny noted weather
and natural phenomena; food riots; comments on English treatment
of the Irish; prices, the state of agriculture; excellent picture of
all classes of people.
      • The Diary of Humphrey O'Sullivan: 1827-1835. Tomas de
      Bhaldraithe, trans. Dublin: Mercier, 1979.

531. SALISBURY, Frances Mary Gascoyne-Cecil (1802-39)
      March 25, 1827-August 8, 1839
      Personal diary; 2nd Marchioness of Salisbury; politics and
social life.
      • Oman, Carola. The Gascoyne Heiress: The Life and Di-
      aries of Frances Mary Gascoyne-Cecil, 1802-39. London: Hod-
      der and Stoughton, 1968.

532. VINTON, John R. (1801-47)
      February 8-March 28, 1827

Travel diary; excerpts; journal kept on a mission for the Secretary of War to the governor of Georgia and others; low opinion of
the people he met.
- Bonner, James C. "Journal of a Mission to Georgia in 1827,"
Georgia Historical Quarterly, v. 44, pp. 74-85, March, 1960.

1828

533. BONAR, Andrew Alexander (1810-92) [B215]
August 21, 1828-December 6, 1892
Spiritual diary; Scottish churchman worked in a parish near
the Glasgow dockyards; his reading, especially the Bible.
- Diary and Life. Marjory Bonar, ed. London: Banner of
Truth Trust, 1960.

534. COLE, Thomas (1801-48) [A262]
October 2-9, 1828
Personal diary; poetry in paint and on paper.
- "Two's Company: The Diaries of Thomas Cole and Henry
Cheever Pratt on Their Walk Through Crawford Notch, 1828,"
Catherine H. Campbell, abridger. Historical New Hampshire,
v. 33, pp. 309-33, Winter, 1978.

535. COOPER, James Fenimore (1789-1851) [A254]
May 29, 1828-September 5, 1833; January 1-May 14, 1848
Travel diary; American novelist went to Holland, Switzerland,
France and Italy; Paris; notes made in preparation for writing his
travel books; the diary has more immediacy than the narratives.
- The Letters and Journals of James Fenimore Cooper. James
Franklin Beard, ed. 6 vols. Cambridge: Harvard University
Press, 1960-68.

536. HENDERSON, James Patterson (1803-189?)
May 6-June 1, 1828
Travel diary; amorous young man journeyed on horseback;
stops in Harrisburg and York; low opinion of the Germans he meets;
many references to medicine; detailed descriptions of countryside,
women encountered and relatives visited; indiscreet.
- Journal of a Tour to Lancaster County, Pennsylvania, in
the Spring of 1828. Raymond Martin Bell, ed. Washington, Pa.:
Washington and Jefferson College, 1973.

537. POTTS, William S. (1802-52)
March 20-April 22, 1828
Missionary diary; minister commissioned by the board of edu-
cation in Philadelphia to solicit funds for the education of Presbyter-
ian clergy.
- "An Account of Alabama Indian Missions and Presbyterian
Churches in 1828 From the Travel Diary of William S. Potts,"
Alabama Review, v. 18, pp. 134-52, April, 1965.

538. PRATT, Henry Cheever
      October 2-8, 1828
      Personal diary; sketching and walking; more factual than Cole
(q.v.).
      • "Two's Company: The Diaries of Thomas Cole and Henry
      Cheever Pratt on Their Walk Through Crawford Notch, 1828,"
      Catherine H. Campbell, abridger. Historical New Hampshire,
      v. 33, pp. 309-33, Winter, 1978.

539. VAN DER LYN, Henry (1784-1865)
      February 2, 1828-November 13, 1856
      Personal diary; upstate New York lawyer who wrote copiously
on law, education and politics; staunch Whig, later a Democrat; excerpts printed here deal with his political beliefs.
      • "The Diary of Henry Van Der Lyn," Thomas J. Curran, ed.
      New York Historical Society Quarterly, v. 55, pp. 119-52,
      April, 1971.

540. WORK, John (1792-1861) [A246, C127]
      1. May 20-August 15, 1828; Fur trade diary; important figure
in the Northwest fur trade along with Peter Skene Ogden (q.v.).
      • "Journal of John Work," T. C. Elliott, ed. Washington His-
      torical Quarterly, v. 11, pp. 104-14, 1920.

      2. August 22, 1830-July 20, 1831; Fur trade diary.
      • "Journal of John Work, 1830-31," Francis D. Haines, Jr.,
      ed. Ph.D., State College of Washington, 1955. (Dissertation
      Abstracts v. 16, p. 737)

      3. August 17, 1832-October 31, 1833; Exploration diary; from
Vancouver to look for the source of the Sacramento River.
      • "Fur Brigade to the Bonaventura: John Work's California
      Expedition of 1832-33 for the Hudson's Bay Company," Alice B.
      Maloney, ed. California Historical Society Quarterly, v. 22, pp.
      193-222, September, 1943; pp. 323-48, December, 1943; v. 23,
      pp. 19-40, March, 1944, pp. 123-46, June, 1944.

      4. An article on his life and work with a bibliography of his
journals in manuscript and printed form.
      • "An Irishman in the Fur Trade: The Life and Journals of
      John Work," Henry Drummond Dee, ed. British Columbia His-
      torical Quarterly, v. 7, pp. 229-70, 1943.

                              1829

541. ARMIJO, Antonio
      November 6/7, 1829-April 25, 1830
      Exploration diary; very brief entry; from Santa Fe to Los An-
geles.
      • "Armijo's Journal of 1829-30: The Beginning of Trade

Between New Mexico and California," LeRoy R. Hafen, ed.
Huntington Library Quarterly, November, 1947; reprinted in
Colorado Magazine, v. 27, pp. 120-31, April, 1950; reprinted
in Old Spanish Trail. LeRoy R. Hafen, ed. Glendale, Cal.:
Arthur H. Clark, 1954; pp. 159-65.

542. CROSS, Joseph
      June 26, 1829-November 7, 1821; gaps
      Exploration journals; mileage, description of countryside,
weather, geologic notes.
      • Journals of Several Expeditions Made in Western Australia
      During the Years 1829, 1830, 1831 and 1832. Facsimile of
      1833 London ed. Nedlands, Australia: University of Western
      Australia Press, 1980.
           REVIEW: Journal of Historical Geography, v. 7, p. 434,
           October, 1981.

543. GREEN, Thomas (1798-1883)
      Personal diary; Richmond lawyer who was a spectator at the
convention; notes on his practice and social life.
      • "Richmond During the Virginia Constitutional Convention of
      1829-1830: An Extract From the Diary of Thomas Green, Oc-
      tober 1, 1829, to January 31, 1830," Joanne L. Gatewood, ed.
      Virginia Magazine of History and Biography, v. 84, pp. 287-
      332, July, 1976.

544. MOFFAT, Robert (1795-1883)
      November 9, 1839-January, 1830; May 13-August 12, 1835;
      May 31-November 27, 1854; July 29, 1857-January 2, 1958;
      August 7, 1859-January 2, 1860
      Missionary diary; Scottish minister under the direction of the
London Missionary Society spent most of his life in South Africa; diary is in the form of journal-letters to his wife; chiefly concerned with
with Moselekatse, the chief of Bahurutse; the two men hit it off and
Moffat was able to persuade the chief to modify some of his ideas of
retribution; interesting account by a religious sympathetic to and re-
spectful of native African people.
      • The Matabele Journals of Robert Moffat, 1829-60. J. P. R.
      Wallis, ed. London: Chatto and Windus, 1945; Salisbury: Na-
      tional Archives of Rhodesia, 1976.

545. WAILES, Benjamin, L. C. (1797-1862) [A345]
      1. December 24-December 30, 1829; Travel diary; on the Chesa-
peake and Delaware Canal; visit to Peale's Museum and the U.S. Mint.
      • "A View of Philadelphia in 1829: Selections From the Journal
      of B. L. C. Wailes of Natchez," John Hebron Moore, ed. Penn-
      sylvania Magazine of History and Biography, v. 78, pp. 353-
      60, July, 1954.

      2. August 9-September 5, 1852; Travel diary; trip for the
purpose of making an agricultural and geological survey.

• "South Mississippi in 1852: Some Selections from the Journal of Benjamin L. C. Wailes," John Hebron Moore, ed. Journal of Mississippi History, v. 18, pp. 18-32, January, 1956.

1830

546. BARROW, Bennet H. (1811-54)
   1. Davis, Edwin A. "Social and Economic Life in West Feliciana Parish, Louisiana, 1830-1850, as Reflected in the Plantation Diary of Bennet H. Barrow," Ph.D., Louisiana State University, 1936. (American Doctoral Dissertations W1936, p. 74)

   2. February 1, 1836-March 10, 1846; Plantation diary; weather; listing of work done for different crops, yields, etc.; information about his slaves, their health and behavior; financial concerns; generally unemotional picture of life on a Louisiana cotton plantation.
   • Davis, Edwin Adams. Plantation Life in the Florida Parishes of Louisiana, 1836-46, As Reflected in the Diary of Bennet H. Barrow. New York: Columbia University Press, 1943.

547. ELLENBOROUGH, Edward Law, 1st Earl of (1790-1871) [B215]
   November 18, 1830-July 25, 1833
   Political diary; Lord Privy Seal under Wellington.
   • "Lord Ellenborough," in: Aspinall, A. Three Early Nineteenth Century Diaries. London: Williams and Norgate, 1952; pp. 19-277, 290-353.

548. FITCH, Asa (1809-79)
   December 1, 1830-February 20, 1831
   Personal diary; excerpts; tried a practice in Bond county; unsuccessful and returned to New York; illness; crude conditions in Illinois.
   • "Diary of a New York Doctor in Illinois--1830-1831," Samuel Rezneck, ed. Illinois State Historical Society Journal, v. 54, pp. 25-50, Spring, 1961.

549. HONE, Philip (1780-1851) [A255]
   November 27, 1830-April 30, 1851
   Personal diary; American businessman; life in New York City where "living ... is exorbitantly dear"; a glimpse of Audubon (q.v.) and his birds.
   • "Diary Excerpts," in: Philip Dunaway and Mel Evans, eds. A Treasury of the World's Great Diaries. New York: Doubleday, 1957; pp. 539-51.

LANDER, John (1807-39) see LANDER, Richard L.

550. LANDER, Richard Lemon (1804-34)
   March 22, 1830-June 10, 1831

Exploration diary; two Cornish working class brothers volunteered for an expedition to Africa; interleaved journals detail the
search for the mouth of the Niger River; rousing adventure.
  • The Niger Journal of Richard and John Lander. Robin Hal-
  lett, ed. Abridgement of 1832 ed. New York: Praeger, 1965.

551. LE MARCHANT, Denis
     November, 1830-June, 1834
     Political diary; principal secretary to Lord Brougham.
       • "Le Marchant's Diary," in: Aspinall, A. Three Early Nine-
       teenth Century Diaries. London: Williams and Norgate, 1952;
       pp. 1-18, 278-89, 360-82.

552. MOORE, George Fletcher
     June 4, 1830-July 11, 1841
     Personal diary; member of the Irish Bar immigrated to Australia
     to take advantage of the British government's offer of land; voyage
     out; obtained land and became prominent in the colony; wide range
     of topics: agriculture, travel, kangaroo hunts, natives; excellent
     picture of pioneer life.
       • Diary of Ten Years Eventful Life of an Early Settler in West-
       ern Australia, and Also A Descriptive Vocabulary of the Lan-
       guage of the Aborigines. C. T. Stannage, intro. London:
       M. Wallbrook, 1884; Fascimile ed. Nedlands, W. A.: University
       of Western Australia Press, 1978.

553. RANDALL, Alexander (1803-81)
     May 22, 1830-May 17, 1831
     Travel journal; extracts; ship and train travel; Delaware canal
boats.
       • "Travel Extracts From the Journal of Alexander Randall,
       1830-1831," Richard H. Randall, ed. Maryland Historical Maga-
       zine, v. 49, pp. 251-56, September, 1954.

                              1831

554. BROWNING, Elizabeth Barrett (1806-61)
     June 4, 1831-April 22, 1832
     Personal diary; English poet's life before her marriage to Robert
     Browning; daily routine at Hope End, her father's Herefordshire es-
     tate, which the family lost shortly after this diary ended; her reading,
     study and writing; family affairs; much worry about the impending
     loss of Hope End.
       • Diary by E. B. B.: The Unpublished Diary of Elizabeth
       Barrett Browning, 1831-1832. Philip Kelley and Ronald Hudson,
       eds. Psychoanalytical observations by Robert Coles. Athens:
       Ohio University Press, 1969.
         REVIEWS: Book Review Digest 1969, p. 180. Book Review
         Index 1979, p. 61.

555. BUSBY, James (1801-71)
      September 26-December 22, 1831
      Travel diary; Briton exploring sources for vines for settlers
to New South Wales, Australia, toured wine-producing areas on the
Continent; a gold mine of information on viticulture for the time.
      • Journal of a Tour Through Some of the Vineyards of Spain
      and France. Philadelphia: Jacob Snider, 1838; Gladesville,
      N.S.W.: David Ell Press, 1979.

556. CLARKSON, Clara (1811-89)
      October 10, 1831-December 31, 1876; several long gaps
      Personal diary; young Victorian of Yorkshire ages into a crusty
spinster over the course of these entries; family life, sermons heard;
her investments and the disposition of her effects; hypochondria;
Jacques' commentary and footnotes add much to the transcription;
interesting social history.
      • Jacques, Ann K. Merrie Wakefield: Based on Some of the
      Diaries of Clara Clarkson, 1811-89, of Alverthorpe Hall, Wake-
      field. Wakefield: West Yorkshire Printing Co., 1971.

557. EMERSON, Edward Bliss (1805-34)
      April 6, 1831-June 9, 1832
      Personal diary; extracts; younger brother of Ralph Waldo Emer-
son; sent to the island for his health; tourist notes.
      • "Puerto Rico in the 1830's: The Journal of Edward Bliss
      Emerson," Americas, v. 16, pp. 63-75, July, 1959.

558. HOLLAND, Henry Richard Vassall Fox, 3rd Baron (1773-1840)
      July 15, 1831-October 21, 1840
      Personal and political diary; Whig politician and noble; host
to one of the world's last salons in Holland House; important source,
well written.
      • The Holland House Diaries, 1830-1840: The Diary of Henry
      Richard Vassall Fox, 3rd Lord Holland, with Extracts from the
      Diary of John Allen. Abraham D. Kriegel, ed. London: Rout-
      ledge and Kegan Paul, 1977.

      LITTLETON, Edward John (1791-1863) see No. 450

559- SHELBY, Major Thomas Hart
560. April 20-August 4, 1831
      Travel diary; in Washington, New York and Baltimore.
      • "Journal of Travels East in 1831: The Same Being the Jour-
      nal of Major Thomas Hart Shelby of Fayette County Kentucky,"
      William Campbell Scott, ed. Kentucky Historical Society Register,
      v. 65, pp. 163-86, July, 1967.

561. SILSBEE, Francis Henry (1811-48)
      August 8-31, 1831
      Travel diary; the White Mountains; lower New Hampshire and
Massachusetts; scenery, travel arrangements.

• Booth, Alan R. "Francis Silsbee's August Odyssey, 1831,"
Essex Institute Historical Collections, v. 100, pp. 59-69, January, 1964.

562. STRANG, James Jesse (1813-56) [A263]
      May 29, 1831-May 29, 1836
      Personal diary; Mormon convert from the "burned over" area
of New York state; leader of a splinter group on Beaver Island,
Michigan; reveals his character; dreams of glory and flights of fancy;
improbable future plans; teaching school; national politics.
      • Diary. Mark A. Strang, ed. East Lansing: Michigan State
University Press, 1961.

                              1832

563. BRADFORD, Phoebe George (1794-1840)
      January 16, 1832-April 15, 1839
      Personal diary; Whig supporter and member of Wilmington's up-
per class; chiefly concerned with religion, gardening, family and
town news; travel to Pennsylvania and Maryland; sons' college graduation and a new home.
      • "Phoebe George Bradford Diaries," W. Emerson Wilson, ed.
Delaware History, v. 16, pp. 1-21, April, 1974; pp. 132-51,
October, 1974; pp. 244-67, Spring-Summer, 1975; pp. 337-57,
Fall-Winter, 1975; reprinted as Diaries of Phoebe George Bradford 1832-1839. Wilmington: Historical Society of Delaware,
1976.

      BROWN, Pamela (1816-) see BROWN, Sally

564. BROWN, Sally (1807-)
      January 22, 1832-March 11, 1838
      Personal diary; separate diaries kept by two sisters of Plymouth
Notch, Vermont; daily life; housework, reading.
      • The Diaries of Sally and Pamela Brown, 1832-1838. Blanche
Brown Bryant and Gertrude Elaine Baker, eds. Springfield, Vt.:
William L. Bryant Foundation, 1970.

565. FOX, Barclay (1817-55)
      January 1, 1832-December 31, 1844
      Personal diary; brother of diarist Caroline Fox (B232) and
scion of a wealthy Quaker family in Falmouth, Cornwall; friend of
John Sterling, John Stuart Mill and Thomas Carlyle; travel in Britain
and Italy with notes on modes of transportation; energetic, high-
spirited but thoughtful individual; social and family life; interested
in political and commercial affairs.
      • Barclay Fox's Journal R. L. Brett, ed. Totowa, N.J.: Row-
man and Littlefield, 1979.

566. GRAY, Mildred Richards Stone (1800-51)

December 1, 1832-February 12, 1840; November 20, 1838-January 26, 1839

Personal diary; life in Fredericksburg, Virginia; visits, family life; business reversals of her husband William (q.v.); gave music lessons to supplement the family income; much sickness and death; dull.

- The Diary of Millie Gray, 1832-1840 Recording Her Family Life Before, During and After Col. William F. Gray's Journey to Texas in 1835 and the Small Journal Giving Particulars of All That Occurred During the Family's Voyage to Texas in 1838. Houston, Tx.: Fletcher Young Publishing Co., 1967.

567. GUERIN, Maurice de (1810-39)

July 10, 1832-October 13, 1835; many gaps

Personal diary; minor French poet; over-wrought posturing.

- Journal of Maurice de Guerin. G. S. Trebutien, ed. Edward Thornton Fisher, trans. New York: Leypoldt and Holt, 1867.

568. MACREADY, William Charles (1793-1873) [B229]

April 12, 1832-December 31, 1851

Personal diary; leading English actor of his day; dissections of his performances and criticism of others'; theatre business; touring America.

- The Journal of William Charles Macready, 1832-1851. J. C. Trewin, ed. Abridged ed. Carbondale: Southern Illinois University Press, 1967.

569. MUNK, Christoph Jacob (-1870)

Travel diary; prosperous Pietist vintner emigrated with his reluctant wife and four children by water and wagon; one of the most complete accounts for a trip of this length.

- "Down the Rhine to the Ohio: The Travel Diary of Christoph Jacob Munk April 21-August 17, 1832," Ohio State Archaeological and Historical Quarterly, v. 57, pp. 266-310, July, 1948.

570. ROMILLY, Joseph (1791-1864) [B199]

February 7, 1832-March 18, 1842

Personal diary; cultured clergyman lived with two unmarried sisters in Cambridge; academic politics, town and gown disputes, boisterous undergraduates; social life.

- Cambridge Diary, 1832-42: Selected Passages from the Diary of The Rev. Joseph Romilly, Fellow of Trinity College and Registrary of the University of Cambridge. J.P.T. Bury, ed. London: Cambridge University Press, 1967.

571. SCOTT, Jacob Richardson (1815-61)

October 7, 1832-September 2, 1860; gaps

Personal diary; one of the most popular Baptist preachers of his time in Virginia; undergraduate work at Brown University; trips to Boston; church work.

• Roscoe, Elizabeth Hayward and Roscoe, Ellis Scott. To Thee This Temple: The Life, Diary and Friends of Jacob Richardson Scott, 1815-1861. Chester, Pa.: American Baptist Historical Society, 1955.

572. SMYTHE, Georgina (-1867)
May 17, 1832-July 4, 1833
Personal diary; from debut in society to her marriage; a London season, courtships and a love match; lively.
• The Prettiest Girl in England: The Love Story of Mrs. Fitzherbert's Niece. Richard Buckle, ed. London: John Murray, 1958.

1833

573. BENTON, Colbee Chamberlain (1805-80)
July 12-August 29, 1833
Travel diary; from Windsor, Vermont, to La Salle County, Illinois via Buffalo, Cleveland and Detroit; jaunt to see the Indians in southern Wisconsin; lengthy description of Chicago; well done.
• A Visitor to Chicago in Indian Days: "Journal to the Far-Off West." Paul M. Angle and James R. Getz, eds. Chicago: Caxton Club, 1957.

574. CAMPBELL, Robert (1804-79)
September 21-December 31, 1833
Fur trade diary; partner with William Sublette [A295] in St. Louis-based trading company; in competition with Astor's American Fur Company; building Fort William; being spied on by Astor's operatives.
• "The Private Journal of Robert Campbell," George R. Brooks, ed. Missouri Historical Society Bulletin, v. 21, pp. 3-24, October, 1963; pp. 107-18, January, 1964.

575. DAVIDSON, Margaret Miller (1823-38)
May 31-July 31, 1833
Travel diary; precocious and sentimental poet kept a journal on a visit to Canada; a visit from Washington Irving (q.v.).
• "Sentimental Journey: The Diary of Margaret Miller Davidson," Walter Harding, ed. Rutgers University Library Journal, v. 13, pp. 19-24, December, 1949.

576. FLOY, Michael (1808-37)
October 1, 1833-January 31, 1837
Personal diary; strict Methodist, horticulturist and amateur mathematician operated a nursery with his father in The Bowery; a record of his book purchases and reading; tree planting in Washington Square; interesting life of a small businessman with a keen mind.
• The Diary of Michael Floy, Jr., Bowery Village, 1833-1837. Richard Albert Edward Brooks, ed. New Haven: Yale University Press, 1941.

577. HAWTHORNE, Sophia Peabody (1809-71)
Personal diary; wife of writer Nathaniel Hawthorne; letter-
journal written while on a trip to Cuba for her health; stayed on
a Cuban sugar plantation.
 • Badaracco, Claire M. "'The Cuba Journal' of Sophia Peabody
   Hawthorne, Volume 1 Edited From the Manuscript with an Introduction," Ph.D., Rutgers University, 1978 (Dissertation Abstracts 39/07A, p. 4252).

578. HERSCHEL, Sir John (1792-1871)
January 9, 1833-December 23, 1838
Scientific and personal diary; son of astronomer Sir William
Herschel; astronomical observations at the Cape of Good Hope; sci-
ence, politics, literature and reading; includes correspondence with
his wife; a motley collection.
 • Herschel at the Cape: Diaries and Correspondence of Sir
   John Herschel, 1834-1838. David S. Evans, et al., eds. Aus-
   tin: University of Texas Press, 1969.

579. LONGFELLOW, Frances Appleton (1817-61)
February 7, 1833-February 17, 1861
Personal diary; begins with the death of her mother; trip to
Europe and meeting American poet Longfellow; their courtship and
marriage; life together and birth of children; pleasing.
 • Mrs. Longfellow: Selected Letters and Journals. Edward
   Wagenknecht, ed. New York: Longmans, Green, 1956.

580. SWAN, William (1813-80)
June, 1833-March, 1880; gaps
Personal diary; son of William Thomas Swan (q.v.) worked as
a baker; involved with a Baptist sect; frequently unemployed and in
debt; retains faith in God's goodness through numerous sorrows.
 • "Journal," in: The Journals of Two Poor Dissenters, 1786-
   1880. London: Routledge and Kegan Paul, 1970; pp. 42-102.

581. TRAVIS, William Barret (1809-36)
Personal diary; South Carolinian who died at the Alamo; social
life in Austin; business dealings; law office; gambling; expenses.
 • Diary, August 30, 1833-June 26, 1834. Robert E. Davis,
   ed. Waco, Tx.: Texian Press, 1966.

581a. WALKER, Mary Richardson (1811-97) [A269]
 1. January 12, 1833-December 31, 1847; Personal diary; sam-
ple extracts from the entire period; decision to marry Elkanah Walker
(q.v.); immediately pregnant; set off for Oregon as a missionary
couple; birth of several children and their life to the time of the
Whitman (q.v.) massacre.
 • "Diary," in: Cathy Luchetti and Carol Olwell. Women of
   the West. St. George, Utah: Antelope Island Press, 1982;
   pp. 60-75.

2. Personal diary.
*   "Diary April to September, 1838," in: Clifford Merrill Drury,
ed. First White Women Over the Rockies. Glendale, Cal.:
Arthur H. Clark, 1963; v. 2, pp. 70-118.

3. Personal diary; life at the mission with the Whitmans and
others in crowded conditions; hard life; evangelizing; ending in Whit-
man massacre by Indians; births of six children.
*   "Diary September, 1838 to July, 1848," in: Clifford Merrill
Drury, ed. First White Women Over the Rockies. Glendale,
Cal.: Arthur H. Clark, 1963; v. 2, pp. 125-343.

1834

582. ANDERSON, William Marshall (1807-81) [A270]
1. March 13-September 29, 1834; Fur trade diary; first daily
record of a rendezvous; accompanied Sublette's party [A295] to the
Rockies.
*   The Rocky Mountain Journals of William Marshall Anderson:
The West in 1834. Dale L. Morgan and Eleanor Towles Harris,
eds. San Marino, Cal.: Huntington Library, 1967.

2. March 29, 1865-June 6, 1866; Personal diary; Unionist with
Southern sympathies; went to Mexico to survey the situation and find
a place for defeated Confederates to colonize; empathy with Mexicans;
interesting.
*   An American in Maximilian's Mexico: 1865-1866: The Diaries of William Marshall Anderson. Ramón Eduardo Ruiz, ed.
San Marino, Cal.: Huntington Library, 1959.

583. CLARK, C. H.
April 14-August 23, 1834
Travel diary; young gentleman's Grand Tour took him westward
instead of to Europe; landed at Quebec; on the Erie Canal; Philadelphia to Washington, New York and return to Liverpool; constant comparisons with life in England to America's detriment.
*   "American Journey 1834," in: R. C. Bell, ed. Diaries From
the Days of Sail. New York: Holt, Rinehart, and Winston,
1974; pp. 11-70.

584. DANA, Richard Henry, Jr. (1815-82) [B282]
1. August 14, 1834-September 21, 1836; Sea diary; American
sailor, author and lawyer; journal on which he based his American
classic Two Years Before the Mast; fragmentary notes.
*   "Journal of a Voyage From Boston to the Coast of California,"
James Allison, ed. American Neptune, v. 12, pp. 177-85, July,
1952.

2. December 7, 1841-September 27, 1860; gaps; Personal diary;
begun after the publication of Two Years Before the Mast; upper

class Boston social world; an eye for revealing detail; political forays; death of Daniel Webster; the 1853 constitutional convention; a trip around the world; work as a lawyer throughout; interesting.
• The Journal of Richard Henry Dana. Robert F. Lucid, ed. Cambridge: Belknap Press, 1968.
REVIEW: Book Review Digest 1968, p. 305.

585. FISHER, Sidney George (1809-71)
1. August 6, 1834-July 22, 1871; Personal diary; gentleman farmer, sometime lawyer and Philadelphia native; anonymous poet was widely read; very satisfied with his own superiority; comments on politics; caustic, opinionated procrastinator; excellent social history; among the best of the nineteenth century diaries.
• A Philadelphia Perspective: The Diary of Sidney George Fisher Covering the Years, 1834-1871. Nicholas B. Wainwright, ed. Philadelphia: Historical Society of Pennsylvania, 1967; contains about 20% more material than was printed in the Pennsylvania Magazine of History and Biography installments (v. 76, 77, 79, 86-89, 1952-65).

2. May 30, 1837-June 1, 1850; Personal diary; inherited the Cecil County, Maryland, plantation and lived there in the spring and fall of each year; these entries were omitted from A Philadelphia Perspective; much on farming practices; planted a variety of crops while also raising sheep and cattle; excellent social history on antebellum Maryland.
• Mount Harmon Diaries of Sidney George Fisher 1837-1850. W. Emerson Wilson, ed. Wilmington: Historical Society of Delaware, 1976.

586. GUÉRIN, Eugénie de (1805-48)
November 15, 1834-December 31, 1840
Personal diary; letter journal; French poet made introspective entries.
• Journal of Eugénie de Guérin. G. S. Trebutien, ed. New York: A. Strahan, 1865; New York: Dodd, Mead, 1893.

587. MELVILLE, Gansevoort (1816?-46)
1. January 4-March 24, 1834; Personal diary; American novelist Herman Melville's older brother; work in the family's fur and cap business; reading and theatre-going.
• "An Albany Journal by Gansevoort Melville," Jay Leyda, ed. Boston Public Library Quarterly, v. 2, pp. 327-47, October, 1950.

2. January 1-April 4, 1846; Personal diary; employed as secretary of the American Legation in London; publication of Herman's Typee; comments on English social life and American visitors.
• 1846 London Journal and Letters from England. Hershel Parker, ed. Reprinted from Bulletin of the New York Public Library, December, 1965 and January, 1966, issues. New York: New York Public Library, 1966.

588. POPE, William (1811-1902) [C97]
      March 23, 1834-December 11, 1846
      Personal diary; son of the English gentry and keen sportsman
traveled to Upper Canada to paint; rural life; shooting and sketching;
editor quotes and summarizes journal entries; sketches and watercolors
reproduced.
      • The 19th Century Journals and Paintings of William Pope.
      Harry B. Barrett, ed. Toronto: Feheley, 1976.
          REVIEW: Canadian Historical Review, v. 59, pp. 232-34,
          June, 1978.

589. "SAND, George" (Amandine Aurore Lucie Dupin, Baronne Dude-
      vant) (1804-76)
      1. French writer who led a liberated life for her time. "Di-
ary Excerpts," in: Mary Jane Moffat and Charlotte Painter, eds.
Revelations: Diaries of Women. New York: Random House, 1974;
pp. 79-85.

      2. "Diary Excerpts," in Philip Dunaway and Mel Evans, eds.
A Treasury of the World's Great Diaries. New York: Doubleday,
1957; pp. 143-46.

590. SIMS, Edward Dromgoole (1805-45)
      Personal diary; professor at Randolph-Macon College went to
Massachusetts to study with a tutor of Hebrew; interesting for his
comments on travel, people and sights.
      • "The Diary of Edward Dromgoole Sims June 17-August 2,
      1834," John P. Branch Historical Papers, new ser. v. 3, pp.
      5-6, 9-26, December, 1954.

591. STEPHENS, Alexander Hamilton (1812-83)
      April 19, 1834-January 8, 1837
      Personal diary; vice-president of the Confederacy in later life;
his law studies.
      • "Alexander H. Stephens's Diary, 1834-1837," James Z. Ra-
      bun, ed. Georgia Historical Quarterly, v. 36, pp. 71-96, March,
      1952; pp. 163-89, June, 1952.

592. WHEELOCK, Lt. Thompson B. (1801-36) [A273]
      June 21-August 24, 1834
      Military diary; with Col. Henry Dodge from Fort Gibson to the
Pawnees to invite them for a formal conference; killing heat disabled
more than half the men and horses.
      • "Peace on the Plains," George H. Shirk, ed. Chronicles of
      Oklahoma, v. 28, pp. 8-41, Spring, 1950.

                                   1835

593. BARNARD, Joseph Henry (1804-60/61)
      Military journal; service in the Texas War for Independence;

journey to Texas; a northern on the way to Victoria; fighting; long, full entries.
  • Journal: A Composite of Known Versions of the Journal of Dr. Joseph H. Barnard, One of the Surgeons of Fannin's Regiment Covering the Period from December 1835 to June 5, 1836. Hobart Huson, ed. Refugio, Tx.?: The Author, 1949; 333 copies.

594. CHAMPION, George (1810-41)
      December 22, 1835-March 1, 1839
      Missionary diary; Yale graduate sent by Foreign Mission Board with his wife and others to South Africa; opened a mission; built a house and started a school; forced to leave because of intertribal warfare and Boer attacks.
        • Journal of the Rev. George Champion, American Missionary in Zululand, 1835-9. Alan R. Booth, ed. Cape Town: Struik, 1967.

595. COBDEN, Richard (1804-65)
      May 25-August 16, 1835; February 21-June 28, 1859
      Travel diaries; British statesman urged English neutrality during the American Civil War; comparison of British and American labor conditions; comments on social conditions.
        • American Diaries. Elizabeth Hoon Cawley, ed. Princeton: Princeton University Press, 1952; reprinted Westport, Conn.: Greenwood Press, 1969.

596. CROWNINSHIELD, Clara (1811-1907)
      May 25, 1835-September 26, 1836
      Personal diary; friend of Longfellow's first wife; accompanied the couple on a European tour aimed at the improvement of Longfellow's German; death of Mrs. L. after a miscarriage; London, Stockholm, Rotterdam; social life, scenery, foreign customs, interesting.
        • The Diary of Clara Crowninshield: A European Tour with Longfellow, 1835-36. Andrew Hilen, ed. Seattle: University of Washington Press, 1956.

597. FOLGER, William C. (1806-91)
      May 8, 1835-March 29, 1837
      Personal diary; Nantucket native worked as a surveyor; farm work; prices; social notes.
        • "Diary of William C. Folger," Nancy S. Adams, ed. Historic Nantucket, v. 8, pp. 141-44, October, 1960; pp. 30-35, January, 1961; pp. 70-74, April, 1961; v. 9, pp. 110-17, July, 1961; pp. 152-58, October, 1961; pp. 30-34, January, 1962; pp. 72-74, April, 1962.

598. FOUNTAIN, Sarah Jane Lide
      November 18-December 26, 1835
      Travel diary; trip from Springville, South Carolina, to Carlowville, Alabama; immigrating with a large family party.

• The Lides Go South ... and West: The Record of a Planter Migration in 1835. Fletcher Melvin Green, ed.: University of South Carolina Press, 1952; pp. 1-8.

599. FRANCIS, Convers (1795-1863)
      August 11, 1835-January 3, 1863
      Personal diary; extracts; minister taught at Harvard Divinity School; Transcendentalist.
      • Myerson, Joel. "Convers Francis and Emerson," American Literature, v. 50, pp. 17-36, March, 1978.

600. GANTT, Daniel (1814-   )
      January 3, 1835-November 28, 1871
      Personal diary; excerpts on politics, investments and his personal life; journeys between his native Pennsylvania and Nebraska.
      • "Chief Justice Daniel Gantt of the Nebraska State Supreme Court, Letters and Excerpts from His Journal 1835-1878," Mary Cochran Grimes, ed. Nebraska History, v. 61, pp. 281-309, Fall, 1980.

601. GILES, Chauncey (1813-93)
      October 22, 1835-May 12, 1893
      Personal diary; excerpts interspersed with family letters; schoolteacher and minister of New-Church Union; genealogical and religious interest.
      • The Life of Chauncey Giles as Told in His Diary and Correspondence. Carrie Giles Carter, ed. Boston: New-Church Union, 1920.

602. GORDON, John Montgomery (1810-84)
      March 18-October 7, 1835
      Personal diary; social and family life.
      • "A Virginian and His Baltimore Diary," Douglas Gordon, ed. Maryland Historical Magazine, v. 49, pp. 196-213, September, 1954; v. 50, pp. 109-19, June, 1955; v. 51, pp. 224-36, September, 1956; v. 56, pp. 198-203, June, 1961.

603. GRAY, William Fairfax (1787-1841)
      October 6, 1835-July 12, 1838
      Travel diary; accommodations; people and scenery encountered; much material on Texas.
      • Diary of Col. William Fairfax Gray: Giving Details of His Journey to Texas and Return in 1835-36 and Second Journey to Texas in 1837. Houston: Fletcher Young Publishing Co., 1965; reprint of 1909 ed.

604. GUSTORF, Frederick Julius (1800-45)
      May 9, 1835-September 9, 1836
      Travel diary; immigrant to German colonies in Illinois and Missouri with an idea of possible settlement; interesting view of East Coast and Midwest for the period by a well-educated German.

• The Uncorrupted Heart: Journal and Letters of Frederick
Julius Gustorf, 1800-1845. Fred Gustorf, ed. Fred and Gisela
Gustorf, trans. Columbia: University of Missouri Press, 1969.

605. HOLGATE, William C. (1814-88)
    May 16-June 24, 1835
    Travel diary; from Utica, New York, to Toledo, Ohio, via the
Erie canal; by steamer to Detroit; stops in Defiance and Fort Wayne;
interludes of fishing.
    • Maumee River 1835: William C. Holgate Journal. Louis A.
Simonis, ed. Defiance, Ohio: Defiance County Historical Society, 1979.

606. HOLLEY, Mary Austin (1784-1846)
    April 30, 1835-June 22, 1838
    Travel diary; Connecticut native and first cousin to Texas
pioneer Stephen F. Austin; trips to the Anglo colony to gather material for her writing; met leaders of the settlements; visited Houston
and the Gulf Coast area; weather, visiting; sketches reproduced.
    • "Texas Diary, 1835-38," James Perry Bryan. Texas Quar-
terly, v. 8, pp. 7-119, Summer, 1965.
    • Mary Austin Holley: The Texas Diary, 1835-38. James
Perry Bryan, ed. Austin: University of Texas Press, 1965.

607. JOHNSON, William (1809-51)
    October 12, 1835-June 14, 1851
    Personal diary; freedman and slaveholder operated a barber
shop catering to whites; short daily entries; life of black and white
communities in Natchez; business dealings; acquired land and farmed;
records a great deal of violence; interesting picture of a free black
in the ante-bellum South.
    • William Johnson's Natchez; The Ante-bellum Diary of a Free
Negro. William Ransom Hogan and Edwin Adams Davis, eds.
Baton Rouge, La.: Louisiana State University Press, 1951.

608. KIERKEGAARD, Søren (1813-55)
    1. July 29, 1835-October 27, 1855; Personal diary; Danish
philosopher and writer; introspective, melancholic man; philosophizing;
tidbits of his personal life.
    • The Journals of Soren Kierkegaard: A Selection. Alexander
Dru, ed. and trans. London: Oxford University Press, 1938.

    2. July 29, 1835-1854; Personal diary; meditations, philosophi-
cal ponderings.
    • Journals. Alexander Dru, trans. abridged ed. New York:
Harper, 1959.

    3. 1836-1854; Entries dated by year and numbered; arranged
by topic.
    • Diary. Gerda M. Andersen, trans. Peter P. Ronde, ed.
New York: Philosophical Library, 1960.

4. March 1, 1854-September 25, 1855; Personal diary; most
of these entries have never before been published in English; musings on life, thoughts on suicide; Arthur Schopenhauer; marriage;
Martin Luther; Christianity.
  • The Last Years: Journals 1853-1855. Ronald Gregor Smith,
  ed. and trans. New York: Harper and Row, 1965.

609. LAMAR, Mirabeau Buonaparte (1798-1859)
      June 15-October, 1835
      Travel diary; Georgian became second president of the Republic
of Texas; trip from Columbus, Georgia, to Brazoria County, Texas.
  • "Mirabeau B. Lamar's Texas Journal," Nancy Boothe Parker,
  ed. Southwestern Historical Quarterly, v. 84, pp. 197-220,
  October, 1980; pp. 309-30, January, 1981.

610. LINCECUM, Gideon (1793-1874)
      January 9-March 8, 1835
      Travel diary; came with a party looking for a place to settle;
flora, fauna; situation of the Indians.
  • "Journal of Lincecum's Travels in Texas, 1835," A. L. Bradford and T. N. Campbell, eds. Southwestern Historical Quarterly, v. 53, pp. 180-201, October, 1949.

611. MAVERICK, Samuel (1803-70)
      March 16, 1835-January 1, 1836; September 11, 1842-April, 1843;
      August 27-December 10, 1848
      Personal diary; South Carolinian came to Texas in 1835 and be-
came one of its leading citizens; trip to Texas from Alabama; siege of
San Antonio by the Mexicans; imprisoned at Perote and released by
Santa Ana; expedition to Chihuahua to find a trading route.
  • Samuel Maverick, Texan: 1803-1870 A Collection of Letters,
  Journals and Memoir. Mary Rowena Maverick Green, ed. San
  Antonio: Pvt. ptd., 1952.

612. RUSKIN, John (1819-1900)
      June 2, 1835-May 12, 1889
      Personal diary; English art critic; travels with his parents on
the Continent for health; work on Modern Painters; schooling at Oxford; marriage to Euphemia Gray; meeting with Millais; annulment;
mental depression; lecturing; attacks of insanity; "I don't know what
is going to become of me"; did no work the last twelve years of his
life.
  • The Diaries of John Ruskin. Joan Evans and John Howard
  Whitehouse, eds. 3 vols. Oxford: Clarendon Press, 1956-59.

613. STRONG, George Templeton (1820-75)
      1. 1835-1875; Personal diary; upper class New Yorker and
lawyer; family life, work; interest in politics; a humorous and fair
man produced one of the premier nineteenth-century American diaries;
40 years of New York City social history; excellent.
  • The Diary of George Templeton Strong. Allan Nevins and

Milton Halsey Thomas, eds. 4 vols. New York: Macmillan, 1952.

2. 1860-1865; the Civil War years.
• Diary of the Civil War 1860-1865. Allan Nevins, ed. New York: Macmillan, 1962; reprint of volume 3 of the above.

614. WILLIAMSON, John Gustavus Adolphus (1793-1840)
    1. May 3, 1835-May 7, 1840; Diplomatic diary; North Carolinian appointed by Andrew Jackson; social life in a small Anglo-American diplomatic community; a revolution; trials with his wife who, on the whole, would rather have been in Philadelphia; interesting.
    • Caracas Diary, 1835-1840: The Journal of John G. A. Williamson First Diplomatic Representative of the United States to Venezuela. Jane Lucas De Grummond, ed. Baton Rouge, La.: Camellia Publishing Co., 1954.

    2. Lucas, Nancy J. "The Annotated Diary of John Gustavus Adolphus Williamson of Person County North Carolina, First Diplomatic Representative of the United States to Venezuela, 1835-1840," Ph.D., Louisiana State University, 1946. (American Doctoral Dissertations W1946, p. 51)

1836

615. ALCOTT, Bronson (1799-1888) [A251]
    1. January 3-December 31, 1836; Personal diary; American Transcendentalist and father of novelist Louisa May; spoke with Harriet Martineau; heard lectures by Emerson (q.v.) and Orestes A. Brownson; running his Temple School; his reading and literary work.
    • Myerson, Joel. "Bronson Alcott's 'Journal for 1836,'" Studies in the American Renaissance, pp. 17-104, 1978.

    2. Carlson, Larry A. "Bronson Alcott's Journal for 1837: An Edition with Notes and an Introduction," Ph.D., Pennsylvania State University, 1979 (Dissertation Abstracts 40/09A, p. 5053).

616. ALMONTE, Juan Nepomuceno (1804-69)
    Military diary; follower of Mexican General Santa Ana; with him throughout the Texas campaign.
    • "The Private Journal of Juan Nepomuceno Almonte, February 1-April 16, 1836," Samuel E. Aubury, ed. Southwestern Historical Quarterly, v. 48, pp. 10-32, 1944.

617. ATHERTON, Faxon Dean (1815-77)
    March 26, 1836-December 28, 1839
    Personal diary; Massachusetts native was a successful merchant in Chile and Hawaii before his arrival in California; sailing on business up and down the California Coast; stops in Los Angeles, San Francisco; voyages to Oahu, Boston and Valparaiso; full, very descriptive entries with comments on people and customs.

    • California Diary, 1836–1839. Doyce B. Nunis, Jr., ed. San Francisco: California Historical Society, 1964.

618. BROCKWAY, George W. (–1837)
January 7–April 28, 1836
Travel diary; extracts; Vermont drummer for the Fairbanks Scale Company; in the Illinois River Valley.
    • Cornet, Florence Doll. "The Experiences of a Midwest Salesman in 1836," Missouri Historical Society Bulletin, v. 29, pp. 227–35, July, 1973.

619. CATHER, Thomas (fl. 1836)
February 16, 1836–January 5, 1837
Travel diary; with a Londonderry neighbor and schoolmate undertook a 12,000 mile journey to America; stops in New York, Philadelphia and Cuba; up the Mississippi by steamer and northward to Canada; letters of introduction enabled them to meet Andrew Jackson, Henry Clay; well done.
    • Voyage to America, The Journals of Thomas Cather. Thomas Yoseloff, ed. New York: T. Yoseloff, 1961; Westport, Conn.: Greenwood Press, 1973; also published under the title Journal of a Voyage to America in 1836. Emmaus, Pa.: Rodale, 1955.

620. CROCKETT, Davy (1786–1836)
February 19–March, 1836
Military diary; the last days of the Alamo; spurious?
    • "Diary Excerpts," in: Dunaway, Philip and Mel Evans, eds. A Treasury of the World's Great Diaries. New York: Doubleday, 1957; pp. 60–64.

621. DAVIS, Mary Elizabeth Moragne (1815?–1903)
January 16, 1836–March 12, 1842; several long gaps
Personal diary; romantic novelist of French Huguenot ancestry lived in rural Abbeville District of South Carolina; wrote for Southern literary magazines; gave up fiction at the time of her marriage to a minister but continued to write poetry and articles; reading, family affairs and visits to town cousins; courtship; lively writing with a gift for the pleasing or sarcastic turn of phrase.
    • The Neglected Thread: A Journal from the Calhoun Community, 1836–1842. Delle Mullen Craven, ed. Columbia: University of South Carolina Press, 1951.
    • Craven, Delle M. "Mary E. Moragne: Her Journal and Its Environment, A Study in Upper South Carolina Culture," Ph.D., University of Tennessee, 1952. (American Doctoral Dissertations W1952, p. 230)

622. HENTZ, Caroline Lee (1800–56)
Personal diary; excerpts; novelist of sentimental romances about plantation aristocrats and the Northern rich led a poverty-stricken life in Florence, Alabama, before her books became bestsellers; comparisons between what is reported in the diary and later episodes and characters in the novels; entertaining.

• Ellison, Rhoda Coleman. "Caroline Lee Hentz's Alabama Diary, 1836," Alabama Review, v. 4, pp. 254-69, October, 1951.

623. HOLMAN, Richard Henry (1817-41)
May 30, 1836-August 9, 1837
Personal diary; his junior and senior years at the forerunner of Indiana University; social life and studies.
• "An Indiana College Boy in 1836: The Diary of Richard Henry Holman," Holman Hamilton, ed. Indiana Magazine of History, v. 49, pp. 281-306, September, 1953.

624. LONDONDERRY, Frances Anne Vane-Tempest-Stewart, Marchioness of (1800-65)
August 3, 1836-April 15, 1837
Travel diary; second wife of 3rd Marquis of Londonderry; six weeks journey overland from Calais to Sweden; by yacht to St. Petersburg; social life there and in Moscow; many details of travel and sights; return overland through Riga, Warsaw, Berlin, and Paris; good descriptions.
• Russian Journal of Lady Londonderry, 1836-7. W. A. L. Seaman and J. R. Sewell, eds. London: John Murray, 1973.

625. MEEK, Alexander Beaufort (1814-65)
February 21-April 29, 1836
Personal diary; South Carolinian and lawyer enlisted to save Florida from the Seminoles; sentimentality brought low by diarrhea.
• "The Journal of A. B. Meek and the Second Seminole War, 1836," John K. Mahon, ed. Florida Historical Quarterly, v. 38, pp. 302-18, April, 1960.

626. NICOLLET, Joseph Nicolas (1786-1843)
July 29-September 21, 1836; August 2-11, 1837
Exploration diary; Frenchman fled his country after financial reverses; first diary is an account of his expedition to find the source of the Mississippi; corrected earlier cartographer's mistakes; good descriptions of topography, Indians; second expedition on St. Croix River.
• The Journals of Joseph N. Nicollet: A Scientist on the Mississippi Headwaters, with Notes on Indian Life, 1836-37. Andre Fertey, trans. Martha Coleman Bray, ed. St. Paul: Minnesota Historical Society, 1970.

627. PICKELL, John
July 16-August 1, 1836; November 8-December 16, 1837
Military journal; scouting Seminoles near Jacksonville, Florida; flora, fauna.
• "The Journals of Lieutenant John Pickell, 1836-1837," Frank L. White, Jr., ed. Florida Historical Quarterly, v. 38, pp. 142-71, October, 1959.

628. SMIT, Erasmus (1778-   )
November 14, 1836-January 31, 1839

Personal diary; mission worker in the Dutch Reformed Church trekked with his wife and her relatives along the Vet and Sand Rivers of South Africa; endured depredations by Kaffirs and wild animals; arrival at Durban area; death of his eldest son on the Trek; simply written by a pious man suffering great hardships; internal evidence suggests parts were rewritten after the events described.
- The Diary of Erasmus Smith. H. F. Schoon, ed. W. G. A. Mears, trans. Cape Town: C. Struik, 1972.

629. SPALDING, Eliza Hart (1807-51)
February 1, 1836-July 28, 1840; gaps
Travel diary; with her missionary husband (q.v.) to Oregon.
- "Diary," in: Clifford Merrill Drury, ed. First White Women Over the Rockies. Glendale, Cal.: Arthur H. Clark, 1963; v. 1, pp. 183-208.

630. THOMAS, Mary Harris (1787-1875)
July 1-December 31, 1836
Travel diary; Australian pioneer made the voyage out from England with her husband and children; around the Cape of Good Hope; details of life aboard ship; mention of steerage passengers; living in tents at Holdfast Bay on arrival.
- The Diary and Letters of Mary Thomas (1836-1866). Evan Kyffin Thomas, ed. 2nd ed. Adelaide: W. K. Thomas and Co., 1915.

631. THOMPSON, Philo E. (1811-)
March 28-April 23, 1836
Travel diary; 2,200 miles from Ellington, Connecticut, to Quincy, Illinois; by canal, steamboat and railroad; many technical details.
- "Philo E. Thompson's Diary of a Journey on the Main Line Canal," Joel A. Tarr, ed. Pennsylvania History, v. 32, pp. 295-304, July, 1965.

632. WHITMAN, Narcissa Prentiss (1808-47) [A277-78]
1. March, 1836-March, 1837; Travel diary; with her minister-husband and a party to establish Protestant missions to the Indians of the Oregon Territory; by steamboat and overland; lengthy entries by an observant traveler.
- "Diary," in: Clifford Merrill Drury, ed. First White Women Over the Rockies. Glendale, Cal.: Arthur H. Clark, 1963; v. 1, pp. 39-60, 71-128.

2. July 18-November 1, 1836.
- My Journal, 1836. Lawrence Dodd, ed. Fairfield, Wash.: Ye Galleon Press, 1982.

633. WILEY, Oren (1805?-89)
August 28, 1836-March 1, 1842
Personal diary; extracts; worked in a tin shop near Cleveland; a trip to Detroit.

- "The Journal of a Vermont Man in Ohio, 1836-1842," LeRoy
P. Graf, ed. Ohio State Archaeological and Historical Quarterly,
v. 60, pp. 175-99, April, 1951.

1837

634. BUCHANAN, Robert Christie (1811-   )
      November 23, 1837-January 7, 1838
      Military journal; bridge-building; Battle of Okeechobee.
      - "A Journal of Lt. Robert C. Buchanan During the Seminole
      War," Frank F. White, Jr., ed. Florida Historical Quarterly, v.
      29, pp. 132-51, October, 1950.

635. CHAMBERS, Thomas Jefferson (1802-65)
      January 1-December 31, 1837
      Personal diary; return from Kentucky recruiting trip; dealings
      with Sam Houston; prices, weather.
      - "Major General Thomas Jefferson Chambers Texas Army of
      the Reserves, 1837," James M. Day, ed. Military History of
      Texas and the Southwest, v. 4, pp. 223-63, Winter, 1964.

636. CREE, Edward Hodges (1814-1901)
      June 8, 1837-February 19, 1856; gaps
      Personal diary; Englishman was a graduate of the Edinburgh
      medical school; surgeon in the Royal Navy; service in the Far East,
      Borneo, Hong Kong, Singapore; in the Crimean War; some exciting
      times; text is greatly enhanced by Cree's sketches and watercolors;
      interesting diary beautifully presented.
      - Naval Surgeon: The Voyages of Dr. Edward H. Cree, Royal
      Navy as Related in His Private Journals, 1837-1856. Michael
      Levien, ed. New York: Dutton, 1981.

637. GALE, Hannah Anna (1818-51)
      1837-38
      Personal diary; schoolgirl records the happenings at Green[e]
      Street School in Providence, Rhode Island; Transcendentalist Margaret
      Fuller (q.v.) was one of the teachers.
      - "Diary," in: American Women's Diaries: New England
      Women. New Canaan, Conn.: Readex Microprint Corp., 1984;
      reel 1.

638. GREY, Sir George (1812-98)
      July 20, 1837-February 15, 1839
      Exploration diary; diarist later became colonial governor of
      Australia and prime minister of New Zealand; charted the area be-
      tween Swan River and Sharks Bay; aboard the Beagle [not clear if
      this was Darwin's ship]; copious observations perhaps rewritten
      from notes; informative.
      - Journals of Two Expeditions of Discovery in North-west and
      Western Australia, 1837-39. Facsimile reprint of 1841 ed.
      Adelaide: Library Board of South Australia, 1964.

639. LAWRENCE, Honoria (1808-54)
      April 3, 1837-November 19, 1853
      Journal-diary; pair of Protestant Northern Irish Victorians mar-
ried in India and came to feel more at home there than in England;
service at various posts; trips to Nepal and Kashmir; long, detailed
descriptions of Indian life; informative and thoughtful with a touch
of fun.
      • The Journals of Honoria Lawrence: India Observed 1837-
      1854. John Lawrence and Audrey Woodiwiss, eds. London:
      Hodder and Stoughton, 1980.
        REVIEWS: Book Review Index 1980, p. 298; 1981, p. 328.

640. LEIGH, John Studdy (1815?-)
      1. August 2-September 1837; June 24-August 18, 1838; October
13-26, 1838; March 15-May 31, 1839; Travel diary; arrival in Zanzibar;
on Pemba Island; descriptions of interior areas rarely visited by whites.
      • "Zanzibar Diary of John Studdy Leigh," J. S. Kirkman, ed.
      International Journal of African Historical Studies, v. 13, pp.
      281-312; pp. 492-507, 1980.

      2. December 11-24, 1838; January 15-28, 1839; March 9-13,
1839; Travel diary.
      • "John Studdy Leigh in Somalia," James Kirkman, ed. In-
      ternational Journal of African Historical Studies, v. 8, pp. 441-
      56, 1975.

641. MICKLE, Isaac (1822-55)
      April 7, 1837-May 30, 1845; gaps
      Personal diary; New Jersey lawyer and politician wrote for
newspapers in Camden in his teens; became editor of the Camden
Eagle; suffered financial reverses and poor health; comments on local
and national politics; his reading; family life; slightly conceited man
but interesting picture of small town life; effusive style.
      • A Gentleman of Much Promise: The Diary of Isaac Mickle,
      1837-1849. Philip English Mackey, ed. Philadelphia: Univer-
      sity of Pennsylvania Press, 1977.
        REVIEWS: Journal of American History, v. 65, pp. 154-55,
      June, 1978. Pennsylvania Magazine of History and Biography,
      v. 102, pp. 127-28, January, 1978.

642. TAYLER, William (1807-92)
      1. January 1-December 31, 1837; Personal diary; son of an
Oxfordshire farmer was in the service of a wealthy widow in St.
Marylebone; much family visiting; excellent social history and a good
account of life upstairs and down; gossipy; tattletale with his own
unique orthography.
      • Diary of William Tayler, Footman, 1837. Dorothy Wise, ed.
      London: Strathmore Bookshop, 1962.

      2. January 1-December 31, 1837; Article with extracts.
      • Cox-Johnson, Ann. "Gentleman's Servant's Journal," His-
      tory Today, v. 13, pp. 102-07, February, 1963.

643. THOREAU, Henry David (1817-62) [A282]
    1. October 22, 1837- ; Personal diary; American writer and
occasional recluse; "The complete journal as Thoreau originally wrote
it"; introspective daily entries and much on his writings; aphorisms;
in the style of his Walden and at greater length.
    • Journal. John C. Broderick, ed. Princeton, N.J.: Prince-
    ton Univeristy Press, 1981-

    2. March 7, 1838-November 3, 1861; Selections from the 1906
edition of his journals The Writings of Henry David Thoreau edited
by Torrey and Sanborn which are concerned with his writing.
    • H. D. Thoreau: A Writer's Journal. Laurence Stapleton,
    ed. New York: Dover, 1960.

    3. "Diary Excerpts," in: Philip Dunaway and Mel Evans, eds.
A Treasury of the World's Great Diaries. New York: Doubleday,
1957; pp. 293-99.

                                1838

644. ALLEN, William Y. (1805-85) [A283]
    March 28-October 14, 1838
    Travel diary; clergyman's arrival at Galveston; life in Houston.
    • "Extracts from the Diary of W. Y. Allen, 1836," William S.
    Red, ed. Southwestern Historical Quarterly, v. 17, pp. 43-60,
    1913-14; Reprinted from the Texas Presbyterian.

645. BAKER, John W.
    June 27-August 4, 1838
    Travel diary; from Philadelphia by rail, canal boat, stage and
steamboat to Cincinnati, St. Louis and Chicago; return via the Great
Lakes; interesting comments on food, accommodations.
    • "Western Travels," Harry R. Stevens, ed. Bulletin of the
    Historical and Philosophical Society of Ohio, v. 6, pp. 127-55,
    October, 1948.

646. BLACKFORD, John (1780?-1839)
    Plantation diary; Maryland plantation grew a variety of grains
and bred livestock for home consumption and sale; manned by slaves
and hired labor; social life; interesting account of life on a small plantation.
    • Ferry Hill Plantation Journal, January 4, 1838-January 15,
    1839. Fletcher M. Green, ed. Chapel Hill: University of
    North Carolina Press, 1961.

647. DUCHARME, Leandre (1816?-) [C36]
    November, 1838-January 15, 1845
    Prison diary; French Canadian took part in a rebellion against
British rule in Lower Canada; transported to Australia; daily entries
for the voyage out; dreary days at Longbottom and return home;
period of servitude is summarized; evenhanded, unembittered account.

• Journal of a Political Exile in Australia. George Mackaness, trans. (Australian Historical Monographs, v. 2, new series) Sydney: New South Wales Teachers' College, 1944.

648. DURHAM, Louisa Grey Lambton, Countess of [B242]
April 23-December 1, 1838
Personal diary; wife of the first Earl of Durham, radical Whig; sent to Canada to deal with the rebellion of 1837; interspersed with letters to her sister; loyal, self-effacing wife; scenic descriptions; sympathetic to Canadians.
• Letters and Diaries of Lady Durham. Patricia Godsell, ed. Ottawa: Oberon, 1979.
REVIEWS: Canadian Historical Review, v. 61, pp. 375-76, September, 1980. Queen's Quarterly, v. 87, pp. 505-06, Autumn, 1980.

649. DUYCKINCK, George Long (1823-63)
June-September 2, 1838
Travel diary; New York City to Boston.
• "A Boy's Journal of a Trip into New England in 1838," Leland Schubert, ed. Essex Institute Historical Collections, v. 86, pp. 97-105, April, 1950.

650. EELLS, Myra Fairbanks (1838-78) [A284]
Travel diary; drudgery of the westward march from Westport, Missouri to Oregon.
• "Diary, [intertwined with Mary Walker's] (q.v.) April to September, 1838," in: Clifford Merrill Drury, ed. First White Women Over the Rockies: Diaries, Letters and Biographical Sketches of the Six Women of the Oregon Mission Who Made the Overland Journey in 1836 and 1838. Glendale, Cal.: Arthur H. Clark, 1963; v. 2, pp. 70-118.

651. ELLICE, Jane [C38]
April 24-December 26, 1838
Personal diary; wife of Edward, private secretary to Lord Durham, Governor General of British North America (see above, Durham, Countess of); voyage to Canada; social life in Quebec and Montreal; trip to Washington, D.C.; "Americans are very inquisitive people"; held hostage for a week by French Canadian rebels; sprightly, opinionated, thoroughly British.
• The Diary of Jane Ellice. Patricia Godsell, ed. Ottawa: Oberon Press, 1975.
REVIEW: Canadian Forum, v. 56, p. 57, June, 1976.

652. EVANS, Mary Peacock (1821-1912)
January 1, 1838-January 1, 1839
Personal diary; excitement over the Canadian war and threats to burn Buffalo; life at boarding school and at home in Mayville, New York.
• The Journal of Mary Peacock: Life, a Century Ago, as Seen

in Buffalo and Chautauqua County by a Seventeen Year Old
Girl in Boarding School and Elsewhere. Buffalo, N.Y.: Pvt.
ptd., 1938.

653. FRÉMONT, John Charles (1813-90) [A292]
October 22-26, 1838
Exploration diary; U.S. Army officer and member of Nicollet's
(q.v.) expedition; a stay at Lake Pepin.
  • The Expeditions of John Charles Frémont. Donald Jackson
  and Mary Lee Spence, eds. Urbana: University of Illinois
  Press, 1970; v. 1, pp. 25-28.
     REVIEW: North Dakota History, v. 45, pp. 36-37, Summer,
     1978.

654. GRAY, William Henry (1810-89) [A276]
May 24-July 10, 1838
Travel diary; from Westport, Maine, to the Black Hills.
  • "Gray's Journal of 1838," in: Clifford Merrill Drury, ed.
  First White Women Over the Rockies: Diaries, Letters and
  Biographical Sketches of the Six Women of the Oregon Mission
  Who Made the Overland Journey in 1836 and 1838. Glendale,
  Cal.: Arthur H. Clark, 1963; v. 3, pp. 240-45.

655. HAPPOLDT, Christopher (1823-78)
June 5-December 27, 1838
Travel diary; accompanied John Bachman, Audubon's collabora-
tor, to Europe; touring the Continent.
  • The Christopher Happoldt Journal: His European Tour with
  John Bachman (June-December, 1838). Claude Henry Neuffer,
  ed. Charleston, S. Car.: Charleston Museum, 1960.

656. HERNDON, John Hunter (1813-78)
January 15-May 5, 1838
Personal diary; visiting; a trip to Galveston; law practice.
  • "Diary of a Young Man in Houston, 1838," Andrew Forest
  Muir, ed. Southwestern Historical Quarterly, v. 53, pp. 276-
  307, January, 1950.

657. KASHEVAROV, Aleksandr Filippovich (1809-)
July 5-September 5, 1838
Exploration journal; sent by the Russian government to survey
the Alaskan coast; weather, terrain and notes on native people.
  • A. F. Kashevarov's Coastal Explorations in Northwest Alaska,
  1838. James W. VanStone, ed. David H. Kraus, trans. Chicago: Field Museum of Natural History, 1977.
     REVIEWS: Pacific Northwest Quarterly, v. 70, p. 182, Oc-
     tober, 1979. Alaska Journal, v. 8, pp. 377-78, Autumn,
     1978.

658. KRAUSS, Ferdinand (1812-90)
February 15, 1838-April 22, 1840

Travel diary; German with a summa cum laude degree from Heidelberg was hired by Baron von Ludwig as an assistant; the Republic of Natal was formed at this time; collected botanical and zoological specimens; dry, fact-filled descriptions of countryside and people; valuable.
- Travel Journal/Cape to Zululand: Observations by a Collector and Naturalist, 1838-40. Dr. O. H. Spohr, ed. Cape Town: A. A. Balkema, 1973.

659. McCRAE, Georgiana Huntly Gordon (1804-91)
September 5, 1838-November 1, 1848
Personal diary; skilled portraitist and student of John Varley immigrated to New South Wales to join her lawyer husband in 1841; family and social life in town; transplanted Victorian managed to be at the center of things.
- Georgiana's Journal: Melbourne 1841-1865. Hugh McCrae, ed. 2nd ed. London: Angus and Robertson, 1967.

660. SIMPSON, Sir George (1792-1860) [A240, C110]
August 27-September 16, 1838
Travel diary; with the governor of the Hudson Bay Company to negotiate the Stikine Affair with the Russian American Company; notes of a wide-eyed tourist.
- "Simpson in Russia," Beaver, [Canada] v. 33, pp. 14-23, Autumn, 1980.

661. SMITH, Sarah White (1813/14-55)
Personal diary; call to missionary life; journey to Oregon.
- "Diary of Sarah White Smith: March 16, 1838 to September 14, 1838," in: Clifford Merrill Drury, ed. First White Women Over the Rockies. Glendale, Cal.: Arthur H. Clark, 1963; v. 3, pp. 61-128.

662. SPALDING, Henry Harmon (1803-74)
November 26, 1838-March 7, 1843
Missionary diary; missionary to the Oregon Indians; work; family life; coming of whites in increasing numbers; important for its chronicle of relations among the missionaries.
- The Diaries and Letters of Henry H. Spalding and Asa Bowen Smith Relating to the Nez Perce Mission, 1838-1842. Clifford M. Drury, ed. Glendale, Cal.: Arthur H. Clark, 1958.

663. STEELE, John Hardy (1789-1865)
November-December, 1838
Travel diary; New Hampshire governor and successful in the textile industry; visit to his birthplace; Jacksonian Democrat interpolates political comments into his travel narrative.
- "Journal Kept by John H. Steele on a Journey From Peterborough, N.H. to Salisbury, North Carolina in the Months of November & December 1838," John Lindenbusch, ed. Historical New Hampshire, v. 18, pp. 3-41, December, 1963.

664. WALKER, Elkanah (1805-77)
    1. Travel diary; missionary to the Oregon Indians; Portland,
Maine to Oregon; ceases before his arrival.
    • "Diary of Elkanah Walker: March 7 to May 15, 1838," in:
    Clifford M. Drury, ed. First White Women Over the Rockies.
    Glendale, Cal.: Arthur H. Clark, 1963; v. 3, pp. 251-65.

    2. Background information on the couple without diary ex-
tracts.
    • Drury, Clifford M. "Wilderness Diaries: A Missionary
    Couple in the Pacific Northwest 1839-48," American West, v.
    13, pp. 4-9, 62-63, November/December, 1976.

                                1839

665. BACHE, Søren (1814-90)
      June 10, 1839-1847
      Personal diary; one of the founders of the Norwegian colony
at Muskego, Wisconsin; journey to America and life there; travel to
other Norwegian settlements and the American frontier; religious controversies.
    • A Chronicle of Old Muskego, The Diary of Soren Bache,
    1839-1847. Clarence A. Clausen and Andreas Elviken, eds. and
    trans. Northfield, Minn.: Norwegian-American Historical Asso-
    ciation, 1951.

666. BELKNAP, Kitturah Penton (1820-1913)
    1. October 17, 1839-April 10, 1848; gaps; Personal diary;
from Ohio to a cabin on the Des Moines River; farm work; birth and
death of children; decision to go to Oregon.
    • "Family Life on the Frontier: The Diary of Kitturah Penton
    Belknap," Glenda Riley, ed. Annals of Iowa, v. 44, pp. 31-51,
    Summer, 1977.

    2. October 17, 1839-July, 1848; Personal commentary; journal
with later additions; from Allen County, Ohio, with her new husband
to Illinois; farming there and in Iowa; births of children; detailed
description of preparations for emigration to Oregon; tale of the threat
by another woman in the wagon train to leave her husband with a
crying baby while she returned home.
    • "The Commentaries of Keturah Belknap," in: Kenneth L.
    Holmes, ed. and comp. Covered Wagon Women: Diaries and
    Letters From the Western Trails 1840-1890. Glendale, Cal.:
    Arthur H. Clark, 1983- ; v. 1, pp. 189-229.

    3. August 20, 1841-April 22, 1848; Personal diary; extracts;
several moves with husband and family to better land farther west.
    • "Journal," in: Cathy Luchetti and Carol Olwell. Women of
    the West. St. George, Utah: Antelope Island Press, 1982;
    pp. 127-50.

667. CALDERÓN DE LA BARCA, Fanny (Frances Erskine Inglis)
      (1804-82)
      October 27, 1839-April 29, 1842
      Personal diary; Scottish wife of Spain's envoy to Mexico; lively
writing by a keen and sympathetic observer of Mexican life.
      • Life in Mexico: The Letters of Fanny Calderón de la Barca
      with New Material from the Author's Private Journals. Howard
      T. Fisher and Marion Hall Fisher, eds. New York: Doubleday,
      1966.

668. CUSTINE, Astolphe Louis (1790-1857)
      June 5-September 26, 1839
      Personal diary; Frenchman went to Russia "in search of argu-
ments against representative government"; Ems to St. Petersburg;
Moscow; observations on the life of the people; reactions to the
despotism of czar's rule; ends by professing disillusionment with
Russian life.
      • Journey for Our Time: The Journals of the Marquis de
      Custine. Phyllis Penn Kohler, ed. and trans. Chicago:
      Regnery, 1951.

669. FREEMAN, Thomas Birch (1809-90)
      January 31-April 23, 1839; November 6, 1841-February 9, 1842;
      September 29, 1842-March 28, 1843.
      Missionary diary; Methodist missionary to West Africa; son of
African (West Indian?) father and English mother; developing attitudes
toward the Africans; more extroverted than most missionaries and a
good observer.
      • Journals of Various Visits to the Kingdoms of Ashanti, Aku,
      and Dahomi in Western Africa. 3rd ed. with a new intro. by
      Harrison M. Wright. London: Cass, 1968.

670. FULLER, Margaret (1810-50) [A316]
      July 31-August 10, 1839
      Personal diary; visit to the De Wolfe family in Rhode Island;
reflecting differences between Fuller and the host family, their
wealth and position.
      • "Margaret Fuller's 1839 Journal: Trip to Bristol," Harvard
      Library Bulletin, v. 27, pp. 445-70, 1979.

671. GRANT, Hugh Fraser (-1873)
      March 11, 1839-December 28, 1858
      Plantation diary; details of planting, slaves, crops harvested
and general upkeep of a rice plantation on the Georgia coast; intro-
ductory material and financial account book makes a well-rounded
picture of the production and marketing of rice.
      • Planter Management and Capitalism in Ante-bellum Georgia:
      The Journal of Hugh Fraser Grant, Ricegrower. Albert Virgil
      House, ed. New York: Columbia University Press, 1954.

672. GREEN, Ezra (-1862)
      Sea diary; article based on the journal of a yeoman of the

Relief which was part of the Wilkes Expedition; escaped shipwreck at Tierra del Fuego.
 • Bradford, Gershom. "On a Lee Shore," American Neptune, v. 12, pp. 282-87, October, 1952.

673. ISENBERG, Karl Wilhelm (1806-64)
     April 2, 1839-May 4, 1842
     Travel diary; joint journal; missionaries sent out by the Church Missionary Society; conflict with the Catholic Church in Ethiopia; matters of doctrine.
 • The Journals of C. W. Isenberg and J. L. Krapf Detailing Their Proceedings in the Kingdom of Shoa and Journeys in Other Parts of Abyssinia in the Years 1839, 1840, 1841 and 1842. London: Seeley, Burnside and Seeley, 1843; London: Cass, 1968.

674. KEMBLE, Frances Anne (1809-93) [A265, B223]
     January, 1839
     Letter-journal; English actress and wife of American plantation owner Pierce Butler; thoughts on slavery.
 • "Diary Excerpts," in: Mary Jane Moffat and Charlotte Painter, eds. Revelations: Diaries of Women. New York: Random House, 1974; pp. 255-69.

     KRAPF, J. L. see ISENBERG, Karl W.

674a. MORGAN, William (1780-1857)
     April, 1839-July 10, 1857
     Personal diary; physician lost money in the "silk mania"; a joiner; Sons of Temperance meetings; justice of the peace; political rallies; death of a town miser; colorful style.
 • "William Morgan's Autobiography and Diary: Life in Sussex County, 1780-1857," Delaware History, v. 19, pp. 39-52; pp. 106-26, 1980.

675. NICHOLS, Thomas Low (1815-1901)
     June 18-October 15, 1839
     Prison diary; New York journalist accused of libel was incarcerated; prison life; philosophizing; poetry; over-wrought.
 • Journal in Jail Kept During Four Months' Imprisonment for Libel in the Jail of Erie County. Reprint of 1840 ed. New York: Arno, 1970.

676. OAKLEY, Obadiah (1815-50)
     May-August, 1839
     Travel diary; Peoria, Illinois resident traveled the Santa Fe Trail to Bent's Fort thence to Brown's Hole; turned back to Illinois after deciding he could not reach Oregon before winter.
 • "Obadiah Oakley Journal," in: LeRoy R. Hafen and Ann W. Hafen. To the Rockies and Oregon 1839-42. Glendale, Cal.: Arthur H. Clark, 1955; pp. 25-64.

677. SHERIDAN, Francis Cynric (1812/13-43)
      December 29, 1839-February 3, 1840
      Travel diary; grandson of playwright Richard Brinsley Sheri-
dan; in the diplomatic service; sent by the governor of the Windward
Islands to observe the Texas Republic; by ship via Jamaica; landed
at Galveston; stays in Houston, Austin and Velasco; humorous and
well done.
      • Galveston Island. Willis W. Pratt, ed. Austin: Univ. of
      Texas Press, 1954.

678. SMITH, Rev. Asa Bowen (1809-86)
      November 11, 1839-January 31, 1940; October 13-December 5, 1840
      Personal diary; missionary work in Oregon.
      • "Diary," in: Clifford Drury, ed. The Diaries and Letters
      of Henry H. Spalding and Asa Bowen Smith. Glendale, Cal.:
      Arthur H. Clark, 1958; pp. 121-24, 195-98.

679. SMITH, Elias Willard (1814/16-   )
      1. August 6, 1839-June 24, 1840; Fur trade diary; from Inde-
pendence, Missouri with Sublette's party; well-educated young man
later an engineer; first record of a voyage along the South Platte to
the Mississippi River; by wagon and horseback; detailed.
      • "With Fur Traders in Colorado, 1839-40: The Journal of E.
      Willard Smith," LeRoy R. Hafen, ed. Colorado Magazine, v. 27,
      pp. 161-88, July, 1950.

      2. August, 1839-June 1840; from Independence, Missouri;
notes wildlife, scenery; arrival at Brown's Hole.
      • "The E. Willard Smith Journal," in: LeRoy R. and Ann W.
      Hafen. To the Rockies and Oregon 1839-1842. Glendale, Cal.:
      Arthur H. Clark, 1955; pp. 154-95.

      3. August 6, 1839-July 3, 1840; excerpt from Oregon Historical
Quarterly, v. 14, pp. 250-79, September, 1913; party of 36 led by
Vaquez and Sublette left Independence, Missouri to buy pelts; meet-
ing with Kit Carson.
      • "An Excerpt From the Journal of E. Willard Smith, 1839-1840,"
      J. Nielson Barry, ed. Annals of Wyoming, v. 15, pp. 287-97, 1943.

680. SMITH, Larratt William Violett (1820-1905) [C112]
      September 12, 1839-September 24, 1857
      Personal diary; lawyer in Toronto; notes on his studies and
practice; marriage, family life; good picture of upper class life for
the period.
      • Young Mr. Smith in Upper Canada. Mary Larratt Smith, ed.
      Toronto: University of Toronto Press, 1980.

681. SMITH, Sidney (1809-80)
      June, 1839-October, 1839
      Travel diary; member of the Peoria group who went to Oregon
(see Obadiah Oakley); diary begins eight days after the party left
Independence, Missouri; reached the area of Mt. Hood.

• "Sidney Smith Diary," in LeRoy R. and Ann W. Hafen. To the Rockies and Oregon 1839-42. Glendale, Cal.: Arthur H. Clark, 1955; pp. 67-93.

682. YOUNG, Brigham (1801-77)
    1. February 14, 1839-July 31, 1847; Personal diary; Mormon leader; move to Quincy, Illinois, from Missouri; journey East and to England; return to the U.S.; persecutions at Nauvoo; death of Joseph Smith; arming of the Mormons; discussions on settling in another part of the country; building a temple at Nauvoo; decision to go West after repeated persecutions; encamped at Winter Quarters; arrival in the Salt Lake Valley; laying out Temple Square; straightforward account.
    • The Journal of Brigham: Brigham Young's Own Story in His Own Words. Leland R. Nelson, comp. Provo, Utah: Council Press, 1980.

    2. May 27-September 21, 1857; Official diary; in the handwriting of his scribes; church business; relations with Indians; events leading to the Utah War.
    • Diary of Brigham Young, 1857. Everett L. Cooley, ed. Salt Lake City: University of Utah Library, 1980; 1250 copies.
        REVIEW: AB Bookman's Weekly, v. 68, p. 2480, October 12, 1981.

1840

683. BALLARD, Addison Montague (1799-1879)
    August 23, 1840-January 24, 1841
    Travel diary; from Henry County, Kentucky, to Spotsylvania County, Virginia, to visit his father; weather and mileage.
    • "Diary 1840-1841," Kentucky Historical Society Register, v. 52, pp. 125-33, April, 1954.

684. BREWSTER, Edward (1793-1886)
    February 20-May 21, 1840
    Travel diary; New York schoolteacher went to farm in Illinois; by canalboat and steamer; another trip to the Upper Peninsula of Michigan and Lake Superior.
    • "From New York to Illinois by Water in 1840," Lewis Beeson, ed. Michigan History, v. 32, pp. 270-89, September, 1948.

685. CAMPBELL, Jessie
    August 25-December 27, 1840
    Sea diary; mother of five with her children on a passage from London to Wellington, New Zealand; death of an infant; account of living conditions aboard.
    • "Journal Kept on Board the Ship Blenheim August-December, 1840," in: Basil Greenhill. Women Under Sail. Newton Abbott: David and Charles, 1970; pp. 49-74.

686. DOYLE, Richard (1824-83)
      January 1-December 2, 1840
      Personal diary; facsimile edition; schoolboy who three years
later became an illustrator for Punch; life in London; seeing the
Queen and Prince Albert; early artistic efforts; going to the theatre;
legible penmanship enhanced by his sketches.
      • Richard Doyle's Journal, 1840. Edinburgh: Bartholomew,
      1980.

687. GARDINER, Margaret (1822-57)
      May 5-July 16, 1840
      Travel diary; sister-in-law of President John Tyler; touring
with her parents and sister in Italy, Switzerland, Germany and England; sightseeing and gallery-going; young woman of decided opinions.
      • Leaves from a Young Girl's Diary: The Journal of Margaret
      Gardiner, 1840. New Haven: Tuttle, Morehouse and Taylor,
      1925.

688. GRAY, Mary Augusta Dix (1810-81)
      May 10, 1840-September 21, 1842
      Personal diary; woman's everyday duties at the mission; fric-
tion with Narcissa Whitman (q.v.); family life and mission activities.
      • "Diary," in: Clifford Merrill Drury, ed. First White Women
      Over the Rockies. Glendale, Cal.: Arthur H. Clark, 1963;
      v. 1, pp. 248-65.

689. HOBBS, Thomas Hubbard (1836-62)
      November 2, 1840-February 9, 1862; some gaps
      Personal diary; ten years in Limestone County, Alabama; stu-
dent days at the University of Virginia; wide travel; moderate interest.
      • The Journals of Thomas Hubbard Hobbs: A Contemporary
      Record of an Aristocrat from Athens, Alabama, Written Between
      1840 ... 1862. Faye Acton Axford, ed. University: Univer-
      sity of Alabama Press, 1976.
      REVIEW: Book Review Index 1977, p. 203.

690. LEPAILLEUR, François-Maurice (1806-91)
      March 11, 1840-January 14, 1842
      Prison diary; French Canadian tried for treason for his part
in the 1837 rebellion in Upper Canada; transported to New South
Wales; only daily account by a convict; from arrival in Sydney to
the time of receiving his ticket of leave; life in the penal colony;
relations with other convicts; longing for home and hopeful of eventual
pardon; forebearance; disgust with the faults of others.
      • Land of a Thousand Sorrows: The Australian Prison Journal,
      1840-1842 of the Exiled Canadien Patriote Francois-Maurice Le-
      pailleur. F. Murray, trans. and ed. Vancouver: University
      of British Columbia Press, 1980.

691. MOTT, Lucretia Coffin (1793-1880) [A288, B243]
      May 27-August 26, 1840

Personal diary; American suffragette; women were denied seats
on the convention floor because of their sex; politics and sightseeing;
full social life; telegraphic style.
   • Slavery and "The Woman Question": Lucretia Mott's Diary
   of Her Visit to Great Britain to Attend the World's Anti-Slavery
   Convention of 1840. Frederick Tolles, ed. Haverford, Pa.:
   Friends Historical Association, 1952; Friends Historical Society
   Journal Supplement #33.

692. PARKER, Theodore (1810-60)
   Personal diary; Massachusetts native and Unitarian minister;
daily life; thoughts on Margaret Fuller (q.v.) and Ralph Waldo Emerson (q.v.); notes on projected works; "an unmodernized, genetic-
text edition."
   • Johnston, Carol E. "The Journals of Theodore Parker:
   July-December, 1840," Ph.D., University of South Carolina,
   1980. (Dissertation Abstracts 41/07A, p. 3108)

693. PENNY, Charles W. (1812-92)
   May 23-July 31, 1840
   Exploration diary; New Yorker immigrated to Detroit and pros-
pered; accompanied Douglas Houghton's expedition to Michigan's
Upper Peninsula; survey of the south shore of Lake Sueprior and
Keweenaw Peninsula; lengthy entries on geology and terrain.
   • North to Lake Superior, The Journal of Charles W. Penny,
   1840. 3rd ed. James L. Carter and Ernest H. Rankin, eds.
   Marquette, Mich.: Marquette County Historical Society, 1970.

694. SMITH, Elizabeth Grant (1797-1885)
   January 1, 1840-December 8, 1850
   Personal diary; lived on estates inherited by her husband;
time of famine and other Irish troubles; impatient and unsympathetic
to the Irish; a product of her class and upbringing.
   • The Irish Journals of Elizabeth Smith, 1840-1850: A Selection. David Thomson, ed. Oxford: Clarendon Press, 1980.

695. STERNE, Adolphus (1801-52) [A285]
   September 28, 1840-April 4, 1844; February 2-November 18,
   1851
   Personal diary; German-Jewish immigrant and supporter of
Texas independence; friend of Sam Houston; businessman; service in
the Texas House of Representatives; business, social and family life.
   • Hurrah for Texas!: The Diary of Adolphus Sterne 1838-
   1851. Archie P. McDonald, ed. Waco, Tx.: Texian Press,
   1969.

1841

696. BRACKENBRIDGE, William Dunlop (1810-93) [A289]
   October 1-28, 1841

Travel diary; Scottish botanist with the Wilkes Expedition of
1838-42; notes on specimens.
   • "A Botanist on the Road to Yerba Buena," California Historical Society Quarterly, v. 24, pp. 321-36, December, 1945.

697. EYRE, Sir Vincent (1811-81)
      November 3, 1841-June 19, 1842
      Prison diary; lieutenant in the Bengal Artillery was captured
with his wife and child on the retreat from Jellalabad; detailed account with notes on politics and troop deployment.
   • Journal of an Afghanistan Prisoner. Reprint of 1843 ed.
   titled The Military Operations at Cabul. Boston: Routledge
   and Kegan Paul, 1976.
      REVIEWS: Book Review Index 1976, p. 135; 1977, p. 135.

698. FORBES, Susan E. Parsons Brown (1824-1910)
      1841-1908
      Personal diary; begun when New Hampshire native was teaching
school; early entries are fragmentary; lengthier in later years; marriage; changing financial situation; husband's infidelity; DAR member.
   • "Diary," in: American Women's Diaries: New England
   Women. New Canaan, Conn.: Readex Microprint Corp., 1984;
   reels 1-11.

699. GLEASON, James Henry
      August 15, 1841-June 14, 1856
      Letter diary; by ship from Massachusetts to Hawaii; to Mon-
terey, California; involved in the Mexican War; life in San Francisco.
   • "James Henry Gleason: Pioneer Journal and Letters, 1841-
   1856," Historical Society of Southern California Quarterly, v.
   31, pp. 9-52, 1949.

700. GREGG, Josiah (1806-50) [A287]
      Travel diary; extracts; from Jackson County, Missouri, via
Arkansas to Texas; present at the inauguration of Sam Houston as
president of the Republic of Texas.
   • Horgan, Paul. "The Lost Journals of a Southwestern Fron-
   tiersman," Southwestern Historical Quarterly, v. 44, pp. 1-15,
   1940.

701. HUNT, Sarah Morey (1797-1889)
      Spiritual diary; widowed Quakeress of Saratoga County, New
York and minister of the gospel; attending Friends' meetings in New
York and Pennsylvania; opened a school with her daughters; married
a second time; record of her travels and faith in God and the good-
ness of people.
   • Journal of the Life and Religious Labors of Sarah Hunt.
   Philadelphia: Friends' Book Association, 1892.

702. JOHNSON, Daniel Noble (1822-63)
      April 24, 1841-June 19, 1844

Sea diary; aboard the warship Delaware as a clerk; on the
schooner Enterprise; life afloat and ashore at several South American
ports; keen, thoughtful observer.
* The Journals of Daniel Noble Johnson United States Navy.
Mendel L. Peterson, ed. Washington, D.C.: Smithsonian Institution, 1959; (Smithsonian Miscellaneous Collections, v. 136,
no. 2).

703. MEYERS, William H. (1815-   )
November 1, 1841-October 1, 1844
Sea diary; warrant officer and gunner, experienced hand; from
Norfolk around the coast of South America; on to California with the
suspicion that the British were bent on occupying the territory; three
months in Hawaii; found a girl in every port and VD in one; candid,
humorous, entertaining; watercolors by the diarist.
* Journal of a Cruise to California and the Sandwich Island in
the U.S. Sloop-of-war "Cyane," 1841-1844. John Haskell Kemble, ed. San Francisco: Book Club of California, 1955; 400
copies.

704. PARKMAN, Francis (1823-93)
July 19-August 13, 1841; July 15-August 14, 1842; November
16, 1843-August 18, 1845; March 29-October 1, 1846; September
1-October 7, 1870; notebooks for 1871-73, 1878-79, 1885, 1889-
92, all with scanty entries.
Personal and work diary; American historian; mainly a record
of his fieldwork for the writing of his histories; New England vaca-
tion trips during his Harvard years; European grand tour; along the
Oregon Trail; two trips to Paris; upstate New York, Canada and
Florida; shows his developing literary style.
* The Journals of Francis Parkman. Mason Wade, ed. New
York: Harper, 1947.
REVIEW: Book Review Digest 1947, pp. 697-98.

705. SALE, Lady Florentia Wynch (1787-1853)
October 9, 1841-September 19, 1842
Personal diary; "The Grenadier in petticoats" married to the
second in command at Kabul at the outbreak of the war; the garrison
at Kabul; disastrous retreat to Jellalabad; captured by Afghans and
taken back to Kabul; earthquakes; spirited, sardonic and above all,
BRITISH.
* The First Afghan War. Patrick Macrory, ed. Hamden,
Conn.: Shoe String Press, 1969; reprint of 1843 edition A
Journal of the First Afghan War.

706. SWAN, William Thomas (1786-1854)
July 31, 1841-August 24, 1853; large gaps
Personal diary; East London laborer and Baptist convert; his
life was dogged by a frequent lack of work and semi-invalidism; marriage, birth of children; plodding, unimaginative life.
* "Journal," in: The Journals of Two Poor Dissenters, 1786-
1880. London: Routledge and Kegan Paul, 1970; pp. 1-41.

707. TOMLINSON, Ruffin Wirt (-1844)
      June 19, 1841-June 8, 1842
      Personal diary; college and social life; studies.
      • "The Journal of Ruffin Wirt Tomlinson: The University of
      North Carolina, 1841-1842," John L. Sanders, ed. North Caro-
      lina Historical Review, v. 30, pp. 86-114, January, 1953; pp.
      233-60, April, 1953.

708. WOLLASTON, John Ramsden (1791-1856)
      1841-March 17, 1856
      Personal diary; minister in southwest Australia with his wife
      and sons; church work; several tours as archdeacon.
      • Journals and Diaries, 1841-1856. Percy U. Henn, ed. 2
      vols. Perth: Paterson Brokensha, 1954?

                              1842

709. ANONYMOUS
      January 9, 1842-November 6, 1844
      Travel diary; voyage from Virginia with stops at Rio, Hawaii
      and California; mostly descriptions of landfalls.
      • Anderson, Charles Roberts, ed. Journal of a Cruise to the
      Pacific Ocean, 1842-1844 in the Frigate United States with Notes
      on Herman Melville. Durham, N.C.: Duke University Press,
      1937.
            REVIEWS: Books, p. 17, January 9, 1938. New York Times,
      p. 20, November 21, 1937.

710. BROWNE, John Ross (1821-75)
      July 2, 1842-June 2, 1843; February 4-25, 1849
      Travel diary; American traveler and writer; whaling cruise;
      by ship around the Horn to California; letters to his wife supplement
      the journal; well done.
      • John Ross Browne: His Letters, Journals and Writings.
      Lina Fergusson Browne, ed. Albuquerque: University of New
      Mexico Press, 1969.

711. CAPELL, Eli J. (1814-88)
      Plantation diary; article about the diarist with some extracts;
      progressive agricultural practices; manuscript held by the Louisiana
      State University Library.
      • Stephenson, Wendell Holmes. "A Quarter-Century of a Mis-
      sissippi Plantation: Eli J. Capell of 'Pleasant Hill,'" Mississippi
      Valley Historical Review, v. 23, pp. 355-74, 1936.

712. GLASSCOCK, James Abner (1816-76)
      December 24, 1842-September 12, 1844
      Prison diary; Texan captured by Mexicans and imprisoned at
      Perote Castle.
      • "Diary of James A. Glasscock, Mier Man," James M. Day, ed.

Texana, v. 1, pp. 85-119, Spring, 1963; pp. 225-38, Summer, 1963.

713. KOHN, Abraham (-1871)
June 15, 1842-June 19, 1843
Travel diary; from Bavaria to Bremen on foot; by ship to New York; unable to find a job, he took to peddling throughout New England; contacts with other peddlers; much religious lamentation.
   • "A Jewish Peddler's Diary: 1842-1843," Abram Vossen Goodman, ed. American Jewish Archives, v. 3, pp. 81-111, June, 1951.

714. M'COY, John (1782-1859)
January 1, 1842-December 31, 1844; July 17, 1847-March 30, 1852; January 1, 1856-February 23, 1859
Personal diary; Baptist and founder of Franklin College and the American Indian Mission Association; preaching in southern Indiana; college business.
   • John M'Coy: His Life and His Diaries. Elizabeth McCoy Hayward, ed. New York: American History Co., 1948.

715. PFEIFFER, Ida Laura (1797-1858)
March 23-December 6, 1842
Travel diary; woman with grown children fulfilled her childhood dream of visiting Palestine; by steamer down the Danube to the Black Sea; Constantinople; Scutari; a slave market; good descriptions.
   • Journey of a Viennese Lady to the Holy Land. H. W. Dulcken, trans. London: Ingram, Cooke, 1852.

716. PREUSS, Charles (1803-54)
June 4-October 2, 1842; May 30, 1843-July 15, 1844; December 15, 1848-February 12, 1849
Exploration diary; German topographical engineer employed by Frémont (q.v.); Choteau's Landing to the Wind River Mountains and back; Far West; Sangre de Cristo Mountains and Taos; excellent maps were produced but the diarist was totally unsuited to endure the hardships and shows it.
   • Exploring with Frémont: The Private Diaries of Charles Preuss, Cartographer for John C. Frémont on his First, Second, and Fourth Expeditions to the Far West. Edwin G. and Elisabeth K. Gudde, eds. and trans. Norman: University of Oklahoma Press, 1958.

717. TAYLOR, James Wickes (1819-93)
August 2, 1842-September 24, 1844
Personal diary; New Yorker settled in Cincinnati after studying law with his father; descriptions of the bustling Queen City, its German and Irish populations; reports on legal cases; account of Salmon P. Chase's (q.v.) defense of the accused in a civil suit for damages in a runaway slave case.
   • A Choice Nook of Memory: The Diary of A Cincinnati Law

Clerk.   James Taylor Dunn, ed.   Columbus: Ohio State Archaeological and Historical Society, 1950.

718.   VICTORIA, Queen of England (1819-1901) [B227]
   1.   August 29, 1842-September 19, 1842; other visits usually
in August or September to 1900; Personal diary; building of Balmoral;
holidays with Prince Albert and their children; excursions with the
family after his death; many photos and sketches; excerpts with connecting narrative.
   • Queen Victoria's Highland Journals.   New and rev. ed.
   Exeter: Webb and Bower, 1980; previous ed. titled Victoria in
   the Highlands.   London: Muller, 1980.

   2.   April 13-May 2, 1855; August 18-28, 1855; Personal diary;
details of the two visits in literate yet personal style.
   • Leaves from a Journal: A Record of the Visit of the Emperor and Empress of the French to the Queen and of the Visit
   of the Queen and H. R. H. the Prince Consort to the Emperor
   of the French: 1855.   New York: Farrar, Straus and Cudahy,
   1961.

   3.   "Diary Excerpts," in: Philip Dunaway and Mel Evans, eds.
A Treasury of the World's Great Diaries.   New York: Doubleday,
1957; pp. 104-14.

719.   WALKER, Samuel H. (1815?-47)
   March 6, 1842-September 3, 1843
   Military diary; Texan in the Mexican War; Walker's diary was
the basis for Thomas J. Green's pirated account Texian Expedition
Against Mier; imprisoned near Mexico City and escaped back to Texas.
   • Samuel H. Walker's Account of the Mier Expedition.   Marilyn
   McAdams Sibley, ed.   Austin: Texas State Historical Association,
   1978.
      REVIEWS: Arizona and the West, v. 21, pp. 300-01, Au-
      tumn, 1979.   Journal of Southern History, v. 45, pp. 607-
      08, November, 1979.   Western Historical Quarterly, v. 11,
      p. 89, January, 1980.

                              1843

720.   ALCOTT, Louisa May (1832-88) [A292]
   1.   September 1-December 10, 1843; Personal diary; American
novelist and daughter of Bronson Alcott (q.v.); lessons and daily
life at Fruitlands.
   • "Diary Excerpts," in: Philip Dunaway and Mel Evans, eds.
   A Treasury of the World's Great Diaries.   New York: Doubleday, 1957; pp. 416-18.

   2.   September 1, 1843-March, 1846; Personal diary; lessons
and family life at Fruitlands; later comments are appended to entries.

• "Diary Excerpts," in: Mary Jane Moffat and Charlotte
Painter, eds. Revelations: Diaries of Women. New York:
Random House, 1974; pp. 28-33.

721. BOSWELL, Annabella Innes (1826-1916)
      March 4, 1843-May 4, 1848
      Personal diary; amalgamation of original entries and later addi-
tions; life at Lake Innes, New South Wales, with her mother and
sister; upper class life; visitors.
      • Journal. Morton Herman, ed. Sydney: Angus and Robert-
son, 1965.

722. COOKE, George
      May 28-October 25, 1843
      Military diary; with a company of U.S. Dragoons from Fort
Leavenworth; encounter with Texans 150 miles from Santa Fe.
      • "A Journal of the Santa Fe Trail," Mississippi Valley Histor-
ical Review, v. 12, pp. 227-98, 1925-26.

723. HADLEY, James (1821-72)
      February 24, 1843-October 28, 1852
      Personal diary; student days; hearing Fanny Kemble's (q.v.)
readings; study, reading; dull.
      • Diary (1843-1852) of James Hadley, Tutor and Professor of
Greek in Yale College, 1845-1872. Laura Hadley Moseley, ed.
New Haven: Yale University Press, 1951.

724. HARRIS, Edward (1799-1863)
      March 13-December 21, 1843
      Travel diary; amateur ornithologist and prosperous businessman
accompanied Audubon (q.v.); from Philadelphia to the Rockies; hunting and fur trading; buffalo hunts and encounters with Indians punc-
tuate the search for birdlife; includes a list of skins and specimens;
well done.
      • Up the Missouri with Audubon: The Journal of Edward Har-
ris. John Francis McDermott, ed. Norman: University of
Oklahoma Press, 1951.

725. KINSMAN, Rebecca Chase
      June 10-November 2, 1843
      Letter journal; on the ship Probus with her husband and fam-
ily; domestic life aboard; Macao.
      • "Journal of Rebecca Chase Kinsman Kept on Her Voyage to
China in 1843," Essex Institute Historical Collections, v. 90,
pp. 289-308, July, 1954; pp. 389-409, October, 1954.

726. McLANE, Louis T. (1819-1905)
      November 11, 1843-March 1, 1848; gaps
      Sea diary; outspoken American naval officer in Rio, Hawaii and
California; joins the Pacific Squadron's land force; marches to Santa
Barbara with Frémont (q.v.); end of the Mexican War.

- The Private Journal of Louis T. McLane, 1844-1848. Jay
Monaghan, ed. Los Angeles: Dawson's, 1971.

727. MALLORY, James (1807-77)
      1843-77
      Personal diary; earlier entries not on a daily basis but narra-
tive summaries; farm life; American Civil War and its aftermath.
      - "The Journal of James Mallory, 1834-1877," Edgar A. Stewart,
      ed. Alabama Review, v. 14, pp. 219-32, July, 1961.

728. MAXWELL, James Darwin (1815-92)
      October 17-25, 1843
      Travel diary; from Bloomington, Indiana, to Philadelphia to
study medicine; via Buffalo and Albany; wide-eyed Hoosier going
East.
      - "Journal of James Darwin Maxwell," Doris M. Reed, ed.
      Indiana Magazine of History, v. 46, pp. 73-81, March, 1950.

729. PATTON, William (1796-1856)
      April 24-May 21, 1843
      Travel diary; accompanied two other ministers to missions; saw
schools; observations on Indian customs.
      - "Journal of a Visit to the Indian Missions, Missouri Confer-
      ence," Missouri Historical Society Bulletin, v. 10, pp. 167-80,
      January, 1954.

                                  1844

730. ANDERSON, Edward Clifford (1815-83)
      May 16-December 31, 1844
      Sea diary; sailing master of the General Taylor, a coastal
steamer patrolling the Florida Territory; after his retirement from
the Navy he was mayor of Savannah, Georgia.
      - Florida Territory in 1844: The Diary of Master Edward
      Clifford Anderson USN. W. Stanley Hoole, ed. University:
      University of Alabama Press, 1977.

731. HEWITT, S. C.
      July 25-August 24, 1844
      Personal diary; intermittent entries; wanderings in New England;
giving speeches and organizing; discusses conditions and advocates a
ten hour day.
      - Foner, Philip S. "Journal of an Early Labor Organizer,"
      Labor History, v. 10, pp. 205-27, Spring, 1969.

732. JACOBS, Zina Diantha Huntington (1821-1901)
      June 5, 1844-September 21, 1845
      Personal diary; murders of Mormons at Carthage, Illinois; later
a wife of Brigham Young; much about other prominent Mormons in
the area.

- "All Things Move in Order in the City: The Nauvoo Diary of Zina Diantha Huntington Jacobs," Maureen Ursenbach Beecher, ed. Brigham Young University Studies, v. 19, pp. 285-320, 1979.

733. LEICHHARDT, Friedrich Wilhelm Ludwig (1813-48?)
     October 1, 1844-December 17, 1845
     Exploration diary; with several companions by bullock cart across Australia; notes on flora, fauna, geologic formations; detailed.
     - Journal of an Overland Expedition in Australia from Moreton Bay to Port Essington, 1844-5. Fascimile reprint of 1847 London ed. Adelaide: Library of South Australia, 1964.

734. McCUTCHAN, Joseph D. (1823-53)
     June 1, 1844-November 10, 1844
     Prison diary; member of the Mier Expedition in the Mexican War; record of incarceration at Perote Castle, Mexico.
     - Mier Expedition Diary: A Texas Prisoner's Account. Joseph Milton Nance, ed. Austin: University of Texas Press, 1978. REVIEWS: Journal of the West, v. 18, p. 121, October, 1979. Southwestern Historical Quarterly, v. 83, pp. 81-82, July, 1979. Journal of Southern History, v. 45, pp. 607-08, November, 1979. Western Historical Quarterly, v. 11, p. 89, January, 1980.

735. PREUS, Caroline Dorothea Keyser (1829-80)
     August 19, 1844-May 27, 1864; many gaps in later years
     Personal diary; daughter of Norwegian minister lived at home with her sisters and widowed father; at his death the girls went to live with their grandmother; marriage to her minister-cousin; immigration to Wisconsin; birth of a son; her husband's ministry; much about family and church matters.
     - Lina's Diary, on Land and Sea, 1845-1864. Johan Carl Keyser Preus and Diderikke Margrethe Brandt Preus, trans. and eds. Minneapolis: Augsburg Publishing House, 1952.

736. STOUT, Hosea (1810-89)
     October 4, 1844-July 10, 1861; sporadic entries to 1869
     Personal diary; Mormon convert and member of the hierarchy; police chief in Nauvoo, Illinois; trek west to Salt Lake City; in Winter Quarters 1846-47; missionary trip to China; trouble with the U.S. government; Mormon Battalion; one of the best Mormon diaries for the period; comprehensive picture of the sect's social, economic and legislative life.
     - On the Mormon Frontier: The Diary of Hosea Stout, 1844-1861. Juanita Brooks, ed. 2 vols. Salt Lake City: University of Utah Press, 1964.

1845

737. ANONYMOUS

May 29-August 28, 1845
Military diary; from Fort Des Moines and return; weather,
marching, making camp; sighted large buffalo herds; encountered
Indians.
* "The Dragoons in the Iowa Territory, 1845," Robert Rut-
land, ed. Iowa Journal of History, v. 51, pp. 156-82, April, 1953.

738. BARCLAY, Alexander (1810-55)
November 11, 1845-February 22, 1850
Personal diary; British-born fur trader at Bent's Fort and on
his own in northern New Mexico; life on a farm at Hardscrabble;
notes on Santa Fe Trail users.
* The Adventures of Alexander Barclay, Mountain Man: Narrative of His Career, 1810 to 1855, His Memorandum Diary, 1845-
1850. Denver: Old West, 1976.
REVIEWS: Pacific Historical Review, v. 48, pp. 296-97,
May, 1979. Annals of Wyoming, v. 49, pp. 142-43, Spring,
1977. Arizona and the West, v. 19, pp. 383-85, Winter,
1977.

739. FRANKLIN, William B. (1823?-1903)
May 24-August 24, 1845
Exploration diary; West Point graduate and topographer was to
map terrain from Fort Laramie to Bent's Fort; very well-written description of 2000 mile ride in 99 days.
* March to South Pass: Lieutenant William B. Franklin's Journal of the Kearny Expedition of 1845. Frank N. Schubert, ed.
Washington, D.C.: Army Corps of Engineers, Historical Division, 1979.

740. GAULDIN, Martin Austin
November 27-December 25, 1845
Travel diary; scenery; traveling; map.
* "From Missouri to Texas in 1845: Martin Austin Gauldin's
Journal," Jackie McElhaney, ed. Southwestern Historical Quar-
terly, v. 83, pp. 151-65, October, 1979.

741. KERN, Edward M. [A298]
November 5, 1845-February 15, 1846
Exploration diary; expedition under the command of Captain
John C. Frémont (q.v.); topography, Indians, flora and fauna.
* "Journal of Edward M. Kern of an Exploration of the Mary's
or Humboldt River, Carson Lake, and Owens River and Lake,
in 1845," in: John Charles Frémont. The Expeditions of John
Charles Frémont. Urbana: University of Illinois Press, 1970;
pp. 48-63.

742. LAUB, George
January 1, 1845-June 6, 1846
Personal diary; carpenter; details of the Nauvoo exodus from a
little-known member of the congregation.

- "George Laub's Nauvoo Journal," Eugene England, ed.
Brigham Young University Studies, v. 18, pp. 151-78, Winter,
1978.

743. MONTGOMERY, John Berrien (1794-1873)
      September 28, 1845-July 10, 1846
      Sea diary; blockade of Mazatlan; dealings with Captain Frémont
(q.v.).
      - "The Navy on the Pacific Coast, 1845-47," Journal of the
      Military Service Institution of the United States, v. 30, pp.
      708-20, 1902.

744. MOORE, Nathaniel Fish (1782-1872)
      July 31-September 20, 1845
      Travel diary; recently resigned Columbia College president; by
boat, train and stage; gleaned much information from conversation
with his fellow passengers.
      - Diary: A Trip from New York to the Falls of St. Anthony
      in 1845. Stanley Pargellis and Ruth Lapham Butler, eds. Chi-
      cago: University of Chicago Press, 1946.
         REVIEW: Book Review Digest 1946, p. 585.

745. PEABODY, Charles (1816-)
      October 4, 1845-May 19, 1846
      Travel diary; Congregational minister and district secretary
for the American Tract Society in Ohio; Toledo, Dayton and "Pork-
opolis"; observant and occasionally humorous.
      - "The Diary of Charles Peabody," William E. and Ophia D.
      Smith, eds. Historical and Philosophical Society of Ohio Bulletin,
      v. 11, pp. 274-92, October, 1953; v. 12, pp. 119-39, April, 1954.

746. WARD, Henry Dana
      September 1, 1845-May 9, 1847
      Personal diary; minister of a Charleston parish in Virginia,
1845-48; extracts.
      - "Henry Dana Ward: Early Diary Keeper of the Kanawha
      Valley," Charles Carpenter, ed. West Virginia History, v. 37,
      pp. 34-48, October, 1975.

                                  1846

747. ABERT, James W. (1820-97) [A297]
      June 27, 1846-March 16, 1847
      Travel diary; from Fort Leavenworth to survey New Mexico;
fell ill and recuperated at Bent's Fort; observed flora and fauna;
harrowing return in winter.
      - Western American in 1846-1847: The Original Travel Diary
      of Lieutenant J. W. Abert. John Galvin, ed. San Francisco:
      John Howell Books, 1966.

748. BIGLER, Henry William (1815-1900) [A300]
     1. June 30, 1846-September 23, 1848; Expedition diary; ori-
ginal member of the Mormon Battalion; detailed account of the trip
across the West and life in California; religious notes.
     • "Extracts from the Journal of Henry W. Bigler," Utah His-
torical Quarterly, v. 5, pp. 35-64, April 1932; pp. 87-112,
July, 1932; pp. 134-60, October, 1932.

     2. January 10, 1847-July 30, 1848; Personal diary; crossing
the Colorado River to Los Angeles; San Diego; discovery of gold at
Sutter's Mill.
     • "Diary of H. W. Bigler in 1847 and 1848," Overland Monthly
Magazine, v. 10, pp. 233-45, 1887.

     3. October 8, 1849-January 18, 1850; Travel diary; from Salt
Lake City to California.
     • "The Henry W. Bigler Journal," in: LeRoy R. and Ann W.
Hafen. Journals of Forty-niners: Salt Lake to Los Angeles.
Glendale, Cal.: Arthur H. Clark, 1954; pp. 142-80.
     • Chronicle of the West: The Conquest of California, Discov-
ery of Gold and Mormon Settlement, as Reflected in Henry William Bigler's Diaries. Erwin G. Gudde, ed. Berkeley: University of California Press, 1962.

749. BLISS, Robert S. (1805-51) [A300]
     August 18, 1846-May 2, 1848
     Military journal; Mormon marched to California; back to the
Missouri River and return to Utah; focuses on his own personal concerns; discovery of the remains of the Donner Party.
     • "Journal of Robert S. Bliss, with the Mormon Battalion,"
Everett L. Cooley, ed. Utah Historical Quarterly, v. 4, pp.
67-96, July, 1931, pp. 110-28, October, 1931; v. 27, pp. 380-
404, October, 1959.

750. BREEN, Patrick (1792?-1868) [A300]
     November 10, 1846-March 1, 1847
     Travel diary; daily account of the Donner Party.
     • "Diary," in: Dale Morgan, ed. Overland in 1846: Diaries
and Letters of the California Oregon Trail. Georgetown, Cal.:
Talisman Press, 1963; pp. 310-22.

751. BRYANT, Edwin (1805-69) [A300]
     Travel diary; from Fort Bridger by Hastings Cutoff to Evans-
ton, Wyoming; detailed, well-presented account; basis for his best-
seller What I Saw in California.
     • "The Journal of Edwin Bryant: July 17-August 8, 1846,"
Utah Historical Quarterly, v. 21, pp. 50-107, 1951.

752. CARRIGER, Nicholas (1816-85)
     April 27-September 26, 1846
     Travel diary; early account of Old Fort Kearny Road by wagon.

● "Diary," in: Dale Morgan, ed. Overland in 1846: Diaries and Letters of the California Oregon Trail. Georgetown, Cal.: Talisman Press, 1963; pp. 150-58.

753. CLYMAN, James [A296]
Travel diary; from Elko, Nevada, to Evanston, Wyoming.
● "The Journal of James Clyman: May 21-June 7, 1846," Utah Historical Quarterly, v. 19, p. 21-42, 1951.

754. COOLEY, Elizabeth Ann (1825-48)
March 15, 1846-
Personal diary; Carroll County, Virginia, woman; marriage and emigration to Texas then on to Missouri; some entries by her husband; died of typhoid; some good description.
● "From Virginia to Missouri in 1846: The Journal of Elizabeth Ann Cooley," Missouri Historical Review, v. 60, pp. 162-206, January, 1966.

755. CORNISH, John Hamilton (1815-78)
November 16, 1846-December 31, 1860
Church diary; minister of Aiken, South Carolina, congregation comments on parish affairs and members.
● "The Diary of John Hamilton Cornish, 1846-1860," R. Conover Bartram, ed. South Carolina Historical Magazine, v. 64, pp. 73-85, April, 1963; pp. 145-58, July, 1963.

756. CRAVEN, Tunis Augustus (1813-63)
July 6, 1846-August 19, 1849
Sea diary; service in the Mexican War aboard the warship Dale; Bear Flag incident; comments on battles and the officers under whom he served.
● "Notes from the Journal of Lt. T. A. M. Craven, U.S.N., U.S.S. Dale, Pacific Squadron, 1846-49," Charles Belknap, ed. United States Naval Institute Proceedings, v. 14, pp. 119-48, pp. 301-36, 1888.

757. DU PONT, Samuel Francis (1803-65)
July 18, 1846-October 18, 1848
Sea diary; on shipboard and in Mexico.
● From Private Journal-letters of Captain S. F. Du Pont While in Command of the "Cyane" During the War with Mexico, 1846-1848. Wilmington, Del.: Ferris Bros., 1885; Western Americana: An Annotated Bibliography to the Microfiche Collection of 1012 Books and Documents of the 18th, 19th and Early 20th Century. Ann Arbor, Mich.: University Microfilm International, 1976; WA 06005.

758. DUVALL, Marius (1818-91)
April 1846-May 13, 1847
Sea diary; surgeon aboard the Portsmouth; frequent shore excursions; material about Captain John C. Frémont (q.v.); much on

the politics of the period in California; little medical material.
- A Navy Surgeon in California, 1846-1847: The Journal of Marius Duvall. Fred Blackburn Rogers, ed. San Francisco: J. Howell, 1957.

759. EMORY, William Hemsley (1811-87) [A301]
June 23, 1846-December 29, 1846
Personal diary; excerpt from entry for August 30 of a journey from Fort Leavenworth, Kansas to San Diego; describes Santa Fe; prices, people and scenery.
- "New Mexico Diary-1846," New Mexico Magazine, v. 26, pp. 24, 47, October, 1948.

760. GAINES, John Pollard (1795-1857)
June 12-October 20, 1846
Military diary; from Memphis to Mexico with the Kentucky Volunteer Cavalry.
- "Diary of Major John Pollard Gaines," Texana, v. 1, pp. 20-41, Winter, 1963.

761. GRIFFIN, John Strother (1816-98)
September 26, 1846-August 14, 1847
Military journal; one of the few accounts of the Santa Fe-Gila River Trail; surgeon with Kearny's march to California; when Kit Carson brought news of the American victory in California, Kearny split his company; diarist was among those who went on to California; at the Battle of San Pascual; medical notes; thoughtful; chafed under "Frémont's thirst for glory."
- "A Doctor Comes to California, The Diary of John S. Griffin, Assistant Surgeon with Kearny's Dragoons, 1846-1847," California Historical Society Quarterly, v. 21, pp. 193-224, September, 1942; pp. 333-57, December, 1942; v. 22, pp. 41-66, March, 1943; reprinted San Francisco: California Historical Society, 1948; reprinted The United States Conquest of California. New York: Arno Press, 1976.

762. HOLLAND, James K. (1822-98)
May 24, 1846-February 6, 1847
Military diary; belonged to the 17th Rangers, Mounted Company of Texas Volunteers; Battle of Monterrey; comments on Mexican people and towns.
- "Diary of a Texan Volunteer in the Mexican War," Southwestern Historical Quarterly, v. 30, pp. 1-33, July, 1926.

763. HOLT, Thomas (1815?-96)
December 4, 1846-January 21, 1847
Expedition diary; part of a Mormon rescue party giving relief to immigrants on the Applegate Road.
- "Diary," Dale Morgan, ed. Overland in 1846: Diaries and Letters of the California Oregon Trail. Georgetown, Cal.: Talisman Press, 1963; pp. 191-98.

764. LANE, Henry S. (1811-)
      June 11, 1846-June 5, 1847
      Military journal; lieutenant colonel in the Indiana Volunteers;
shipwreck; fighting and monotony in Mexico.
      • "The Mexican War Journal of Henry S. Lane," Indiana Maga-
      zine of History, v. 53, pp. 383-434, December, 1957.

765. LATTIE, Alexander (1802-49)
      February 25-July 25, 1846
      Fur trade journal; Scotsman with the Hudson's Bay Company
as a pilot and second mate; relations with Americans in the area.
      • "Alexander Lattie's Fort George Journal, 1846," Oregon
      Historical Quarterly, v. 64, pp. 197-245, September, 1963.

766. LEE, John Doyle (1812-77) [A303]
      1. August 30-November 19, 1846; Travel diary; Mormon con-
vert and adopted son of Brigham Young; trip from the Missouri River
to Santa Fe and return; weather, camp life.
      • "Diary of the Mormon Battalion Mission: John D. Lee,"
      Juanita Brooks, ed. New Mexico Historical Review, v. 42,
      pp. 165-209, July, 1967; pp. 281-332, October, 1967.

      2. February 29, 1848-August 17, 1849; December 27, 1857-
June 12, 1861; December 29, 1861-April 8, 1874; August 9, 1875-
April 18, 1876; Personal diary; organized and led a wagon train of
1848; "sealed" to 19 wives and fathered 65 children; pioneer life in
Utah; arrest and imprisonment; much on Mormon life of the period
and clashes with "Gentiles"; executed for his participation in the
Mount Meadows Massacre of 1857.
      • A Mormon Chronicle: The Diaries of John D. Lee, 1848-
      1876. Robert Glass Cleland and Juanita Brooks, eds. San
      Marino, Cal.: Huntington Library, 1955.

      3. Personal diary; Mormon company sent to southern Utah
made the first iron manufactured west of the Mississippi; lengthy,
detailed entries on the work of the colony.
      • "Journal of the Iron Country Mission: John D. Lee, Clerk:
      December 10, 1850-March 1, 1851," Gustive O. Larson, ed.
      Utah Historical Quarterly, v. 20, pp. 109-34, April, 1952; pp.
      253-82, July, 1952; pp. 353-83, October, 1952.

767. LIENHARD, Heinrich (1822-1903)
      Travel diary; Swiss immigrant to America; from Fort Bridger
via Hastings Cutoff; very good.
      • "The Journal of Heinrich Lienhard: July 26-September 8,
      1846," Utah Historical Quarterly, v. 19, pp. 108-76, 1951.

768. McCLINTOCK, William A. (-1874)
      September 1, 1846-January 10, 1847
      Letter journal; served in the 2nd Kentucky Regiment; from Ken-
tucky to Monterrey; much on flora, fauna and terrain; killed at Buena
Vista.

• "Journal of a Trip Through Texas and Northern Mexico in 1846-1847," Southwestern Historical Quarterly, v. 34, pp. 20-37; pp. 141-58, 1930; v. 34, pp. 231-56, 1931.

769. McKINSTRY, George (1810?-90?) [A304]
May 12-November 6, 1846; gaps
Travel diary; on the Hastings Cutoff to California.
• "Diary," in: Dale Morgan, ed. Overland in 1846: Diaries and Letters of the California Oregon Trail. Georgetown, Cal.: Talisman Press, 1963; pp. 203-18.

770. MACNAB, Sophia Mary (1832-1917)
January 20-July 8, 1846
Personal diary; daughter of a Hamilton, Ontario, representative to the Canadian Parliament; life at Dundurn Castle on Burlington Bay; lessons, family life; the slow decline and death of her mother; ends with hopes of a visit to Boston; holds nothing back in expressing her feelings.
• The Diary of Sophia Macnab. Charles Ambrose Carter and Thomas Melville Bailey, eds. Hamilton, Ont.: W. L. Griffin, 1968.

771. MATHERS, James (1790-1870)
July 4-September 7, 1846
Travel diary; from Fort Laramie across the San Joaquin River.
• "Diary," in: Dale Morgan, ed. Overland in 1846: Diaries and Letters of the California Oregon Trail. Georgetown, Cal.: Talisman Press, 1963; pp. 225-36.

772. MILLER, Hiram O. (1818-67)
1. April 26-October 4, 1846; Travel diary; from Independence, Missouri to California.
• "Diary," in: Dale Morgan, ed. Overland in 1846: Diaries and Letters of the California Oregon Trail. Georgetown, Cal.: Talisman Press, 1963; pp. 256-59.

2. April 26-October 4, 1846; Travel diary; jointly written with James F. Reed.
• "Miller-Reed Diary," in Carroll Douglas Hall, ed. Donner Miscellany: 41 Diaries and Documents. San Francisco: Book Club of California, 1947; pp. 11-27.

773. PATTERSON, Giles J. (1829-91)
October 14, 1846-April 10, 1847
Personal diary; son of an up-country plantation family; attended South Carolina College in Columbia; taught by Frances Lieber; thoughtful entries by a serious student somewhat shocked by others' shenanigans.
• Journal of a Southern Student, 1846-48: With Letters of a Later Period. Henry Nelson Croom Beatty, ed. Nashville: Vanderbilt University Press, 1944.
REVIEW: Book Review Digest 1945, p. 551.

774. PRINGLE, Virgil (1804-   ) [A304]
      April 15-November 30, 1846
      Travel diary; via Applegate Cutoff to Oregon.
      • "Diary," in: Dale Morgan, ed. Overland in 1846: Diaries
      and Letters of the California Oregon Trail. Georgetown, Cal.:
      Talisman Press, 1963; pp. 159-88.

775. REED, James Frazier (1800-74) [A309]
         1. Travel diary; with the Donner Party from Fort Bridger to
      the banks of the Humboldt River.
      • "The Journal of James Frazier Reed July 31-October 4, 1846,"
      Utah Historical Quarterly, v. 19, pp. 186-201, 1951.

         2. February 7-March 6, 1847; 2nd Donner Relief party.
      • "Diary," in: Dale Morgan, ed. Overland in 1846: Diaries
      and Letters of the California Oregon Trail. Georgetown, Cal.:
      Talisman Press, 1963; pp. 259-68, 342-50.

         3. February 7-May 6, 1847; Travel diary; banished from the
      Donner Party because he killed a man; returned to Donner Lake to
      rescue his family.
      • "Diary," in: Carroll D. Hall, ed. Donner Miscellany: 41
      Diaries and Documents. San Francisco: Book Club of Califor-
      nia, 1947; pp. 60-75.

776. RICHARDSON, William H. [A305]
      August 4, 1846-July 10, 1847
      Military diary; enlisted man from Anne Arundel County, Mary-
      land; Battles of Bracito and Sacramento; the only existing record of
      the march to Santa Fe.
      • "Journal of William H. Richardson, A Private Soldier in Col.
      Doniphan's Command," Missouri Historical Review, v. 22, pp.
      193-236; 331-60; 511-42, 1928.

777. TARBUCK, Edward Lance (1828-   )
      January 2-December 10, 1846
      Personal diary; architect and silver medalist of the British Insti-
      tute of Architects; his work; a visit to the Royal Academy; J. M. W.
      Turner's picture "a daub here and there."
      • "Diary of Edward Lance Tarbuck, for 1846," Notes and Quer-
      ies, v. 118, pp. 256-61; pp. 309-10, 1953.

778. TAYLOR, William E. (1820-1905)
      April 20-September 13, 1846
      Travel diary; from Missouri to California.
      • "Diary," in: Dale Morgan, ed. Overland in 1846: Diaries
      and Letters of the California Oregon Trail. Georgetown, Cal.:
      Talisman Press, 1963; pp. 123-30.

779. TENNERY, Thomas Douthit (1819-91)
      June 29, 1846-July 1, 1847

Military diary; enlistment in the 4th Illinois Infantry; to Mexico; wounded; some sentimentality but good description on the whole.
- The Mexican War Diary of Thomas D. Tennery. D. E. Livingston-Little, ed. Norman: University of Oklahoma Press, 1970.

780. TOLSTOY, Leo N., Count (1828-1910)
    1. March 17, 1846-December 31, 1852; Personal diary; Russian novelist, philosopher and mystic; in Moscow and on his estates; setting tasks for himself; detailed criticism of his reading; sojourn in the Caucasus; military service as a gunner; introspective.
- Diaries. New York: Dutton, 1918.
  REVIEW: Book Review Digest 1917.

    2. June 1, 1853-December 31, 1857; Personal diary; introspection; life in the army; beginning to write; service at various posts; visits outside Russia.
- The Private Diary of Leo Tolstoy 1853-1857. Aylmer Maude, ed. Louise and Aylmer Maude, trans. London: Heinemann, 1927.

    3. October 28, 1895-December 20, 1899; Personal and spiritual diary; his life and writings; speculative; thoughts on his followers; life at Yasnaya Polyana; the sublime and the mundane.
- Journal. Rose Strunsky, trans. New York: Knopf, 1917.
  REVIEW: Book Review Digest 1917, p. 562.

    4. January 1-November 3, 1910; An amalgam of two diaries; one similar to the diaries he kept all his life and another "Diary For Myself Alone"; contretemps with his wife Sonia over his followers; her efforts to preserve a heritage for herself and their children.
- Last Diaries. Lydia Weston-Kesich, trans. Leon Stilman, ed. New York: Capricorn Books, 1960.

781. TURNER, Henry Smith (1811-81)
    July 30-December 4, 1846; May 31-August 22, 1847
    Military diary; West Pointer and captain in the First Dragoons; service in the Mexican War; 1847 journal recounts a horseback trip from Monterey, California, to Fort Leavenworth, Kansas; the 1846 journal has much fuller, more human entries.
- The Original Journals of Henry Smith Turner, With Stephen Watts Kearny to New Mexico and California 1846-1847. Dwight L. Clarke, ed. Norman: University of Oklahoma Press, 1966.

1847

782. AMIEL, Henri Frédéric (1821-81)
    1. December 16, 1847-April 29, 1881; Literary/personal diary; Swiss poet and philosopher; many long entries; fragments of poems; essays ranging over a wide variety of topics.

• The Private Journal of Henri Frederic Amiel. Van Wyck
Brooks and Charles Van Wyck Brooks, trans. enl. and rev. ed.
New York: Macmillan, 1935.

2. July 16, 1848-April 29, 1881; Personal/literary diary; philosophizing; comments on his reading.
• Amiel's Journal: The Journal Intime of Henri Frederic Amiel.
Mrs. Humphrey Ward, trans. 2nd ed. New York: Macmillan,
1889.

3. "Diary Excerpts," in: Philip Dunaway and Mel Evans, eds.
A Treasury of the World's Great Diaries. New York: Doubleday,
1957; pp. 139-42.

783. BLANCHET, Augustine Magloire Alexander (1797-1887) [A307]
Travel diary; down the Ohio River to St. Louis; via the Oregon
Trail to Fort Walla Walla; the party arrived three months before the
Whitman Massacre; part travelogue and part report on the condition
of Catholics along the way; lucid presentation by a strong-minded
cleric.
• Journal of a Catholic Bishop on the Oregon Trail: The Over-
land Crossing, from Montreal to Oregon Territory March 23,
1847 to January 12, 1851. Edward J. Kowrach, ed. Fairfield,
Wash.: Ye Galleon Press, 1978.
REVIEWS: Book Review Digest 1979, p. 44; 1981, p. 62.

784. BROWN, Ford Madox (1821-93) [B247-48]
September 4, 1847-December 27, 1866; gaps
Personal diary; English historical painter; mostly notes on his
work listing the number of hours devoted to canvasses; occasional
lines on the Rossettis (q.v.) and their circle.
• The Diary of Ford Madox Brown. Virginia Surtees, ed.
New Haven: Yale University Press, 1981.
REVIEWS: Book Review Digest 1982, p. 174. Book Review
Index 1981, p. 81.

785. BURGE, Dolly Sumner Lunt (1817-91)
1. February 6, 1847-September 29, 1876; large gaps in later
years; Personal diary; thrice widowed Maine native spent most of
her life in Georgia; taught school; married a plantation owner; mother
to her own children and stepchildren; wide range of topics; social
and family life; plantation work; neighbors; interesting account of
Southern life.
• "The Diary of Dolly Lunt Burge," James I. Robertson, Jr.
ed. Georgia Historical Quarterly, v. 44, pp. 202-19, June,
1960; pp. 321-38, September, 1960; pp. 434-55, December,
1960; v. 45, pp. 57-73, March, 1961; pp. 155-70, June, 1961;
pp. 257-75, September, 1961; pp. 367-84, December, 1961; v.
46, pp. 59-78, March, 1962.

2. February 6, 1847-September 29, 1879; gaps in later years;

Personal diary; reprint of <u>Georgia Historical Quarterly</u> entries with an index of names.
* <u>Diary</u>. James I. Robertson, Jr. ed. Athens: University of Georgia Press, 1962.

3. January 1, 1864-December 25, 1865; many gaps; Personal diary; Civil War as experienced by the diarist and its aftermath and effects on her family.
* <u>A Woman's Wartime Journal: An Account of the Passage Over a Georgia Plantation of Sherman's Army on the March to the Sea, As Recorded in the Diary of Dolly Sumner Lunt (Mrs. Thomas Burge)</u>. Julian Street, intro. Macon, Ga.: J. W. Burke Co., 1927.

4. November 19, 1864; single entry.
* "Diary Excerpt," in: Philip Dunaway and Mel Evans, eds. <u>A Treasury of the World's Great Diaries</u>. New York: Doubleday, 1957; pp. 283-84.

786. COX, Leander M. (1812-   )
November 1, 1847-April 19, 1848
Military diary; captain in the 3rd Kentucky Regiment; part of the occupation force in Mexico City at the end of the Mexican War; march from Vera Cruz; very full entries; undisciplined style.
* "Mexican War Journal of Leander M. Cox," Charles F. Hinds, ed. <u>Register of the Kentucky Historical Society</u>, v. 55, pp. 29-52; pp. 213-36, 1957; v. 56, pp. 47-69, 1958.

787. DONNER RELIEF PARTY
February 18-March 4, 1847
Official diary; found the Donner Party and conducted them to safety.
* "Donner Relief Party Diary," in: Carroll D. Hall, ed. <u>Donner Miscellany: 41 Diaries and Documents</u>. San Francisco: Book Club of California, 1947; pp. 52-55.

788. DUYCKINCK, Evert Augustus (1816-78)
Personal diary; editor, critic and co-author with his brother of the <u>Cyclopedia of American Literature</u> (1855); had just been fired from position as editor of <u>Literary World</u>; family life; work; art exhibits; visiting in New York City.
* "Diary: May 29-November 8, 1847," <u>Studies in the American Renaissance</u>, pp. 207-58, 1978.

789. EMPEY, William A. (1808-90)
Work diary; ran the ferry at the upper crossing of the North Platte to aid California and Oregon immigrants; supplemented by the journal of Appleton M. Harmon.
* "The Mormon Ferry of the North Platte: the Journal of William A. Empey, May 7-August 4, 1847," Dale L. Morgan, ed. <u>Annals of Wyoming</u>, v. 21, pp. 110-67, July-October, 1949.

790. FOSTER, Benjamin Browne (1831-1903)
      May 20, 1847-November 13, 1853
      Personal diary; Orono, Maine, native; apprenticed as a grocery
clerk; widely read; life in Massachusetts towns and as a student at
Bowdoin College; entertaining.
      • Down East Diary. Charles H. Foster, ed. Orono: Univer-
      sity of Maine Press, 1975.
      REVIEW: American Studies, v. 19, p. 114, Fall, 1978.

791. GUE, Benjamin F. (1828-1904)
      March 6, 1847-December 25, 1856; gaps
      Personal diary; farmer, newspaper editor and briefly an Iowa
legislator; much information on farming practices; social life; prices.
      • Diary of Benjamin F. Gue in Rural New York and Pioneer
      Iowa, 1847-1856. Earle D. Ross, ed. Ames: Iowa State Uni-
      versity Press, 1962.

792. HALLECK, Henry Wager (-1872)
      October 25, 1847-April 9, 1848
      Military diary; excerpts, mostly undated; lieutenant on Shu-
brick's flagship; Mazatlán and surrounding area.
      • "Insurgents on the Baja Peninsula: Henry Halleck's Journal
      of the War in Lower California, 1847-1848," John D. Yates, ed.
      California Historical Quarterly. v. 54, pp. 221-44, Fall, 1975.

793. HURLEY, Kealing
      July 15, 1847-September 8, 1848
      Travel diary; from Galway to Boston; enlisted for the Mexican
War.
      • "Kealing Hurley's Scrip Book: An Irish Immigrant in
      America, 1847-48," Lucille O'Connell, ed. Eire-Ireland, v. 15,
      pp. 105-12, Summer, 1980.

794. JOHNSON, William S. (-1880)
      January 27, 1847-July 10, 1848
      Military diary; private in the Palmetto Regiment; from Mobile
to Mexico and return to South Carolina.
      • "Private Johnson Fights the Mexicans, 1847-1848," John Ham-
      mond Moore, ed. South Carolina Historical Magazine. v. 67,
      pp. 203-28, 1966.

795. KEMPER, James Lawson (1823-95)
      January 5-March 10, 1847
      Personal diary; enlistment in the Virginia Regiment of Volun-
teers; life at Fort Monroe; social life in Washington, D.C.; by ship
to Gulf of Mexico; anchorage at the Brazos River, Texas.
      • "The Mexican War Diary of James Lawson Kemper," Robert
      R. Jones, ed. Virginia Magazine of History and Biography,
      v. 74, pp. 387-428, October, 1966.

796. LEAR, Edward (1812-88) [B250]

1.   July 25–October 4, 1847; Travel diary; English landscape
painter and writer of nonsensical verse; travel notes.
   • Edward Lear in Southern Italy: Journals of a Landscape
   Painter in Southern Calabria and in the Kingdom of Naples.
   London: Kimber, 1964.

2.   September 9, 1848–June 9, 1849; Travel diary.
   • Journals of a Landscape Painter in Greece and Albania: Edward Lear in Greece. London: Richard Bentley, 1851.

3.   September 9–November 4, 1848; July 25–September 5, 1847;
April 8–May 5, 1848. Travel diary; in Greece, Albania, Southern
Calabria and Corsica.
   • Journals: A Selection. Herbert Van Thal, ed. New York:
   Coward-McCann, 1952.
      REVIEW: Book Review Digest 1953, p. 550.

4.   November 22, 1873–January 9, 1875; Travel diary; detailed
entries, as graphic as his drawings, of his last tour; dogged by illness but managed to paint 2,000 watercolors.
   • Indian Journal: Watercolours and Extracts From the Diary
   of Edward Lear, 1873–1875. Ray Murphy, ed. London: Jar-
   rolds, 1953.

797. McWILLIAMS, William Joseph (1817–1902)
      January 1, 1847–July 17, 1848
      Military diary; carpenter from Murrysville, Pa.; service in the
2nd Regiment of Pennsylvania Volunteers; mustered in; a norther in
the Gulf; Mexico City; return home.
   • "A Westmoreland Guard in Mexico, 1847–1848: The Journal
   of William Joseph McWilliams," John W. Larner, ed. Western
   Pennsylvania Historical Magazine, v. 52, pp. 213–40, July,
   1969; pp. 387–413, October 1969.

798. PRESTON, William (1816–87)
      Military diary; Harvard Law School graduate; by ship from
New Orleans to Vera Cruz; siege of the city; at Perote Castle; march
to Mexico City; notes on people, prices and sights.
   • Journal in Mexico, By Lieutenant Colonel William Preston of
   the Fourth Kentucky Regiment of Volunteers, Dating from November 1, 1847, to May 25, 1848. Paris, Ky.: n.p., 192?

799. ROBERTS, George B. (1816–83)
      August 23, 1847–February 17, 1851
      Official journal; Hudson's Bay Company employee who became
an American citizen; agent for a large-scale farm; details of weather,
farming and livestock operation.
   • "The Round Hand of George B. Roberts: The Cowlitz Farm
   Journal, 1847–51," Oregon Historical Quarterly, v. 63, pp. 101–
   74, June–September, 1962.

800. SESSIONS, Patty (1795-1892)
      June 21-September 26, 1847
      Travel diary; Mormon midwife and developer of the Session
plum tree; from Winter Quarters near Omaha to Salt Lake City; delivered five babies on the journey.
      • "A Pioneer Mormon Diary Patty Sessions," in Kenneth L.
      Holmes, ed. and comp. Covered Wagon Women: Diaries and
      Letters From the Western Trails 1840-1890. Glendale, Cal.:
      Arthur H. Clark, 1983- ; v. 1, pp. 158-87.

801. SKELLY, James (1823-.)
      January 2-December 19, 1847
      Military diary; enlistment in the 2nd Regiment of Pennsylvania
Volunteers; siege and capture of Mexico City; details of camp life.
      • "Diary of a Pennsylvania Volunteer in the Mexican War,"
      James K. Greer, ed. Western Pennsylvania Historical Maga-
      zine, v. 12, pp. 147-54, 1929.

802. SMITH, Elizabeth Dixon (1808/09-55) [A310]
      April 21, 1847-February 24, 1848
      Travel diary; from La Porte, Indiana, to Oregon; via Fort
Laramie; tale of poet Edwin Markham's mother, who did not want to
go west (September 15 entry); widowed and left with seven children
on her arrival in Oregon.
      • "The Diary of Elizabeth Dixon Smith," in: Kenneth L.
      Holmes, ed. and comp. Covered Wagon Women: Diaries and
      Letters From the Western Trails 1840-1890. Glendale, Cal.:
      Arthur H. Clark, 1983- ; v. 1, pp. 111-52.

803. SMITH, Levi Lathrop (-1848)
      May 17, 1847-August 29, 1848
      Personal diary; pioneer settler of Olympia, Washington; farm
work, health, weather.
      • "The Journal of Levi Lathrop Smith, 1847-1848," James Rob-
      ert Tanis, ed. Pacific Northwest Quarterly, v. 43, pp. 277-
      301, October, 1952.

804. SNOW, Erastus (1818-)
      April 6-August 26, 1847
      Personal diary; with the first party of Mormons to enter Salt
Lake Valley; from Winter Quarters to the founding of Salt Lake City;
detailed.
      • "Journey to Zion," Western Humanities Review, v. 2, pp.
      107-28, April, 1948, pp. 264-84, July, 1948.

                                   1848

805. ANONYMOUS
      June 28-July 8, 1848
      Personal diary; good description of the land.

• Harlan, Edgar R., ed. "The Upper Des Moines Valley--
1848," <u>Annals of Iowa</u>, v. 9, pp. 94-104, 1909-11.

806. CONGDON, John
September 12-20, 1848
Sea diary; went down in a hurricane 300 miles off Nantucket;
made away in a boat after rescuing some provisions; picked up by a
packet; exciting.
• "The Wreck of the Bark Montgomery," Rebecca C. Skillin,
intro. <u>Rhode Island History</u>, v. 24, pp. 97-116, October, 1965.

807. COUTS, Cave Johnson (1821-74) [A314]
January 10, 1848-January 8, 1849
Travel diary; member of the 1st U.S. Dragoons and West Point
graduate; missed the fighting in the Mexican War; shows incompetence
of some of his superiors; relieved his frustrations by writing; interesting observations on Indians and Mexicans encountered.
• <u>Hepah, California! The Journal of Cave Johnson Couts From
Monterey, Nuevo Leon, Mexico to Los Angeles, California During
the Years 1848-1849</u>. Henry F. Dobyns, ed. Tucson: Arizona
Pioneers' Historical Society, 1961.

808. FORBES, Captain Cleveland (-1857)
October 6, 1848-February 7, 1849
Sea diary; New York City via Rio de Janeiro, Valparaiso and
Lima to San Francisco; fuller entries at landfalls.
• "Log Book of Capt. Cleveland Forbes of the Steamer Cali-
fornia," in: John E. Pomfret, ed. <u>California Gold Rush Voy-
ages, 1848-1849</u>. San Marino, Cal.: Huntington Library, 1954;
pp. 177-232.
• "Journal of a Voyage from San Francisco to Panama Via
Monterey, Santa Barbara, San Diego, Mazatlan, San Blas and
Acapulco-1849," in: Pomfret, <u>ibid</u>.; pp. 233-42.

809. GARFIELD, James Abram (1831-81)
1. 1848-July 1, 1881; many gaps; entire Civil War omitted;
Personal diary; 20th U.S. president; last entry written the day before his assassination by Charles Guiteau; wide range of topics; candid and opinionated.
• <u>The Diary of James A. Garfield</u>. Harry James Brown and
Frederick D. Williams, eds. 4 vols. East Lansing: Michigan
State University Press, 1967-81.
REVIEW: <u>Book Review Digest</u> 1968, p. 475.

2. August 8-September 11, 1872; Travel diary; excerpts; from
Fort Leavenworth; accompanied a commission to persuade the Flathead
Indians to move to the Jocko Reservation.
• "Peregrinations of a Politician: James A. Garfield's Diary
of a Trip to Montana in 1872," Oliver W. Holmes, ed. <u>Montana</u>,
v. 6, pp. 34-45, Autumn, 1956.

810. HASSLOCK, Thekla Dombois (1824-   )
      November 6, 1848-February 2, 1849
      Travel diary; German family from Nassau came via Cologne and
Paris to New Orleans; lengthy entries; good descriptions.
      • "The Diary of a German Immigrant," George R. Mayfield,
      trans. and ed. Tennessee Historical Quarterly, v. 10, pp. 249-
      81, September, 1951.

811. HUTCHINGS, James Mason (1820-1902)
      May 29, 1848-October 10, 1849
      Travel diary; British immigrant came to New York; on to Cal-
ifornia for the Gold Rush; brief stint as an army wheelwright; much
detail, very well-written.
      • Seeking the Elephant, 1849, James Mason Hutchings' Journal
      of His Overland Trek to California. Shirley Sargent, ed. Glen-
      dale, Cal.: Arthur H. Clark, 1980.

812. KERN, Benjamin (1818-   )
      October 20, 1848-January 7, 1849
      Exploration diary; with Frémont's expedition in the San Juan
Mountains to survey a railroad route to the Pacific; see the diary of
Richard Kern for a continuation (813).
      • "Diary of Benjamin Kern 1848-1849," in: LeRoy R. and Ann
      W. Hafen. Frémont's Fourth Expedition: A Documentary Ac-
      count of the Disaster of 1848-1849. Glendale, Cal.: Arthur
      H. Clark, 1960; pp. 79-108.

813. KERN, Richard (1821-53)
      October 12, 1848-January 10, 1849
      Exploration diary; parallels Benjamin Kern diary (see above)
and three weeks later; four pages of manuscript sketches.
      • "Diary of Richard Kern," LeRoy R. and Ann W. Hafen.
      Frémont's Fourth Expedition: A Documentary Account of the
      Disaster of 1848-1849. Glendale, Cal.: Arthur H. Clark,
      1960; pp. 109-34.

814. LONG, John Davis (1838-1915) [A312]
      February 14-August 29, 1848
      Personal diary; Buckfield, Maine schoolboy; includes comments
by his father on his penmanship which is "not good"; later became
governor of Massachusetts and Secretary of the Navy.
      • "The America That Used to Be: From the Diary of John
      Davis Long," Lawrence Shaw Mayo, ed. Atlantic, v. 130, pp.
      721-30, December, 1922.

815. McGAVOCK, Randal W. (1826-63)
      January 2-December 28, 1848; March 20-December 31, 1851;
      January 1, 1855-September 30, 1860; February 4-October 8,
      1862.
      Personal diary; student at Harvard Law School; travel in
Europe, North Africa and the Middle East; mayor of Nashville;

delegate to the Democratic National Convention at the time of the
secession movement; fall of Forts Henry and Donelson; European
section has very full entries; well done.
* **Pen and Sword: The Life and Journals of Randal W. McGa-**
  vock. Herschel Gower and Jack Allen, eds. Nashville: Tennessee Historical Commission, 1959.

816. PERKINS, Arozina (1826-54)
      Personal diary; Vermont native and youngest of twelve children
taught in New Haven, Connecticut; applied to the National Popular
Education Board and was sent to Iowa to teach; romanticized early
passages; disappointment in a broken love affair with a young minister who dropped her because her brother was in jail; yearning to
belong despite being a Yankee outsider; difficulties encountered by
a woman on her own; not self-pitying but inspires sympathy in the
reader.
      * "Diary of Arozina Perkins: November 13, 1848, to June 5,
      1851 (With a Letter from Fairfield, Iowa, August 30, 1851),"
      in: Polly Welts Kaufman. Women Teachers on the Frontier.
      New Haven: Yale University Press, 1984; pp. 51-152.
            REVIEW: Publishers Weekly v. 225, p. 71, January 27,
            1984.

817. PRATT, Addison (1802-72)
      1. October 2-December 1, 1848; Travel diary; journey from
Salt Lake City to Cucamonga, California.
      * "Addison Pratt's Diary," in: LeRoy R. and Ann W. Hafen.
      Journals of the Forty-niners: Salt Lake to Los Angeles. Glen-
      dale, Cal.: Arthur H. Clark, 1954; pp. 66-112.

      2. October 9-December 22, 1849; Travel diary; with a party
of Mormon immigrants from Nephi, Utah, to California.
      * "Journal," in: Margaret Long. The Shadow of the Arrow.
      rev. and enl. ed. Caldwell, Id.: Caxton, 1950; pp. 152-62.

818. PRATT, Orville C. (1819-91)
      August 27-October 25, 1848
      Travel diary; journey on the Old Spanish Trail from Santa Fe
to Los Angeles.
      * "The Journal," in: LeRoy R. and Ann W. Hafen. Old Span-
      ish Trail: Santa Fe to Los Angeles. Glendale, Cal.: Arthur
      H. Clark, 1954; pp. 341-58.

819. ROOT, Riley [A312]
      April 3, 1848-December 31, 1849
      Travel diary; a collection of diary entries and advice to emi-
grants; comments on the Whitman massacre; travel notes.
      * Journal of Travels From St. Josephs to Oregon with Obser-
      vations of That Country, Together with a Description of Cal-
      ifornia ... and Its Goldmines. Oakland, Cal.: Biobooks, 1955.

820. STOKES, John
      1848-1849
      Travel diary; article with extracts; English emigrant to the
U.S.; work in the mills and life in America; return to England.
      • "John Stokes's American Diary," F. A. Rice. National Re-
      view, [Britain] v. 110, pp. 78-86, January, 1938.

821. TORBERT, James Monroe
      1. January 1-December 31, 1848; Personal diary; life on a
Macon County, Alabama, farm; weather and work.
      • "James M. Torbert's 1848 Day Book," Peter A. Brannon, ed.
      Alabama Review, v. 1, pp. 226-35, July, 1948.

      2. January 1-December 31, 1856; Personal diary; weather and
work.
      • "James M. Torbert's Journal for 1856," Alabama Historical
      Quarterly, v. 18, pp. 218-80, Summer, 1956.

      3. January 1-December 31, 1857; 1858-1874; Personal diary;
day-by-day account for 1857; summaries for 1858-74.
      • "James M. Torbert's Journal for 1857-1874," Alabama Histor-
      ical Quarterly, v. 22, pp. 1-76, Spring and Summer, 1960.

822. WINNER, Septimus (1827-1902)
      January 8, 1848-November 22, 1902
      Personal diary; excerpts; American composer of sentimental,
popular ballads; family and social notes; receipts and expenditures;
earnings from the sale of his music.
      • Claghorn, Charles Eugene. The Mocking Bird: The Life
      and Diary of Its Author, Septimus Winner. Philadelphia: Ma-
      gee Press, 1937; 300 copies.

                                1849

823. ALDRICH, Lorenzo D. (1818/19-51) [A313]
      April 18, 1849-December 23, 1850; gap
      Travel diary; goldseeker's journey from Troy, New York via
Cincinnati; on the Santa Fe Trail to San Diego; return via Panama;
no entries for the time spent in the mines.
      • A Journal of the Overland Route to California & the Gold
      Mines. Glen Dawson, notes. Los Angeles: Dawson's Book
      Shop, 1950.

824. ARMSTRONG, J. Elza (1826/27-1905)
      April, 1849-June, 1852
      Travel diary; see John Banks annotation [1849]; Armstrong
made laconic entries about distance and weather which are interleaved with Banks'.
      • The Buckeye Rovers in the Gold Rush: An Edition of Two
      Diaries. Howard Lee Scamehorn, ed. Athens: Ohio University
      Press, 1965.

825. BACHMAN, Jacob Henry (1815-79)
      November 21, 1849-January 1, 1878; sporadic entries
      Personal diary; related to John Woodhouse Audubon's wife;
began on shipboard in San Francisco Bay; to the mines with a party
of other miners; digging in Calaveras County.
      • "The Diary of a 'Used-up' Miner: Jacob Henry Bachman,"
      Jeanne Skinner Van Nostrand, ed. California Historical So-
      ciety Quarterly, v. 22, pp. 67-83, March, 1943.

826. BANKS, John Edwin (1818?-95?)
      April 24, 1849-June 8, 1852
      Travel diary; went with a group from Athens County, Ohio,
to St. Joseph, Missouri, Fort Kearny; through South Pass, north
of Salt Lake to Vernon, California; mined in several locations; returned to Ohio on a steamer from San Francisco via Panama to New
York; notes on conditions but also tells much about himself; interesting.
      • The Buckeye Rovers in the Gold Rush: An Edition of Two
      Diaries. Howard L. Scamehorn, ed. Athens: Ohio University
      Press, 1965.

      BARNES, Julius (1815-1906) see BARNES, Laura A.

827. BARNES, Laura Augusta (1825-52)
      June 25-October 19, 1849
      Travel diary; kept jointly by husband and wife; Bureau County,
Illinois, to the Platte River.
      • "Journals of Trek of Barnes Family," Joe H. Bailey, ed.
      Annals of Iowa, v. 32, pp. 576-601, April, 1955.

828. BENNETT, James Augustus (1831-1909) [A324]
      November 22, 1849-August 15, 1856; gaps
      Personal diary; enlisted in the U.S. Army in Rochester, New
York; journey west; life in forts of New Mexico with visits to Santa
Fe, Las Vegas; met Kit Carson; rough frontier justice.
      • "James A. Bennett: A Dragoon in New Mexico, 1850-1856,"
      Clinton E. Brooks and Frank D. Reeve, eds. New Mexico His-
      torical Review, v. 22, pp. 51-97, January, 1947; pp. 140-76,
      April, 1947; Reprinted with title Forts and Forays ... A Dra-
      goon in New Mexico, 1850-1856. Albuquerque: University of
      New Mexico Press, 1948.

      BRYARLY, Wakeman see GEIGER, Vincent

829. CHAMBERLIN, William H.
      February 26-September 25, 1849

Travel diary; to California via Fort Smith and on to Santa Fe; escorted by Major Marcy part of the way to Choteau's Trading House; keen observer; well-written.
- "From Lewisburg (Pa.) to California in 1849: (Notes from the Diary of William H. Chamberlin)," Lansing B. Bloom, ed. New Mexico Historical Review, v. 20, pp. 14-57, January, 1945; pp. 144-80, April, 1945; pp. 239-68, July, 1945; pp. 336-57, October, 1945.

830. COGSWELL, Moses Pearson (1822-50)
March 1-August 26, 1849
Travel diary; by ship from Boston to California gold fields; description of San Francisco.
- "The Gold Rush Diary of Moses Cogswell of New Hampshire," Elmer Munson Hunt, Ed. Historical New Hampshire, pp. 1-59, 1949.

831. DAVENPORT, Sarah (1838-)
May 1, 1849-May 16, 1852
Personal diary; Connecticut schoolgirl; lessons; family life; father leaves for the gold rush; a circus; death of her brother, "... and I alone remain"; a new baby after her father's return.
- "The Journal of Sarah Davenport," New Canaan Historical Society Annual, v. 2, no. 4, pp. 25-89, 108, 1950.

832. DECKER, Peter (1822-88)
1. April 4, 1849-May 30, 1851; Travel diary; Ohio native set out for the gold fields; trip across the plains; prospecting; one of the best '49er diaries.
- The Diaries of Peter Decker: Overland to California in 1849 and Life in the Mines. Helen S. Giffen, ed. Georgetown, Cal.: Talisman Press, 1966.
   REVIEW: Book Review Digest 1967, p. 332.

2. April 4-August 10, 1849; Travel diary; from Cincinnati to California; very well-done.
- "A Journal of 'Items' on a Trip to California Overland," Society of California Pioneers Publications, pp. 13-34, 1953.

833. DOTEN, Alfred (1829-1903)
March 18, 1849-
Personal diary; Plymouth, Massachusetts, native sailed to California for a two-year stint in the diggings and stayed the rest of his life; in Mother Lode country; a variety of jobs; became a correspondent for his hometown newspaper; met Mark Twain; in Virginia City; his financial rise and fall; becomes an alcoholic; works in journalism most of his life; tour de force.
- The Journals of Alfred Doten 1849-1903. Walter Van Tilburg Clark, ed. Reno: University of Nevada Press, 1973.
   REVIEWS: Book Review Index 1976, p. 119; 1979, p. 122.

834. DOUGLAS, William H. (1822-95)
      April 7-November 21, 1849
      Travel diary; Connecticut native who did some of the engrav-
ings in the five volume publication on the Wilkes Expedition; sea voyage from the East Coast around South America to San Francisco;
weather, temperature; shore stops; supplemented by letters home.
      • Off for California The Letters, Log and Sketches of William
      H. Douglas, Gold Rush Artist. Frank M. Stanger, ed. Oak-
      land, Cal.: Biobooks, 1949.

835. DWINELLE, John W. (1816-81)
      August 27-October 31, 1849
      Travel diary; good description of Panama and the overland
journey; San Diego and San Francisco.
      • "Diary of John W. Dwinelle from New York to Panama in
      1849," Quarterly of the Society of California Pioneers, v. 8,
      pp. 99-129, June, 1931; pp. 141-83, September, 1931.

836. ECCLESTON, Robert (1830-1911/14)
      1. April 3-December, 1849; Travel diary; by ship from New
York to Galveston, Texas; overland to the Nueces and Pecos Rivers; El Paso; ends before destination is reached; lengthy entries
with many details of terrain and the people in the party; excellent.
      • Overland to California on the Southwestern Trail, 1849:
      Diary of Robert Eccleston. George P. Hammond and Edward
      H. Howes, eds. Berkeley: University of California Press,
      1950.

      2. October 20, 1850-June 3, 1851; Military journal; '49er joined
with others in a campaign against Indians who wanted whites off
their lands; few skirmishes but many observations on the countryside; return to mining.
      • The Mariposa Indian War, 1850-1851, Diaries of Robert Ec-
      cleston: The California Gold Rush, Yosemite and the High
      Sierra. C. Gregory Crampton, ed. Salt Lake City: Univer-
      sity of Utah Press, 1957.

837. EGAN, Howard (1815-78) [A307]
      November 18, 1849-January 8, 1850
      Travel diary; scattered notes.
      • "Howard Egan's Diry from Fort Utah to California," in:
      LeRoy R. and Ann W. Hafen. Journals of Forty-niners: Salt
      Lake to Los Angeles. Glendale, Cal.: Arthur H. Clark, 1954;
      pp. 308-19.

838. ELLIS, Charles H. (-1850)
      January 16-July 9, 1849
      Travel diary; Boston to San Francisco; weather; sightings of
other ships; brief.

• "Journal of Charles H. Ellis, Passenger on the North Bend," in: John E. Pomfret, ed. California Gold Rush Voyages, 1848- 1849. San Marino, Cal.: Huntington Library, 1954; pp. 8-96.

839. EVANS, George W. B. (1819-50)
February 23, 1849-November 6, 1850
Travel diary; took a little-traveled path through northern Mex- ico; from Defiance, Ohio, down the Mississippi to New Orleans; by ship to Matagorda Bay, Texas; thence overland; in the Mariposa dig- gings; one of the better diaries for the time.
• Mexican Gold Trail: The Journal of a Forty-niner. Glenn S. Dumke, ed. San Marino, Cal.: Huntington Library, 1945.

840. EVERSHED, Thomas (1817-90)
May 21-August 16, 1849
Letter/diary; successful civil engineer supervised construction of Erie Canal locks; to California via Fort Laramie; on the Mormon Ferry at Green River; tarried in Salt Lake City; arrival in Sacra- mento; lengthy descriptions.
• "The Gold Rush Journal of Thomas Evershed: Engineer, Artist and Rochesterian," Joseph W. Barnes, ed. Rochester History, v. 39, pp. 1-44, January and April, 1977.

841. FARNHAM, Elijah Bryan (1825-98)
April 19-September 23, 1849
Travel diary; from Independence, Missouri, via the Green River to San Francisco; lengthy entries with good description.
• "From Ohio to California in 1849: The Gold Rush Journal of Elijah Bryan Farnham," Merrill J. Mattes and Esley J. Kirk, eds. Indiana Magazine of History, v. 46, pp. 297-318, Septem- ber, 1950; pp. 403-20, December, 1950.

842. FARRER, William (1821-1906)
October 11-December 9, 1849
Travel diary; scattered notes.
• "William Farrer Diary," in: LeRoy R. and Ann W. Hafen, eds. Journals of Forty-niners: Salt Lake to Los Angeles. Glendale, Cal.: Arthur H. Clark, 1954; pp. 193-218.

FINN, Elizabeth Anne McCaul (1825-1921) see FINN, James

843. FINN, James (1806?-72)
July 2, 1849-November 21, 1858
Personal diary; entries by British government representative and his wife are interleaved; both jealous of their position; constant battles with the disparate population of Jerusalem; footnotes are es- sential to understanding the cryptic entries.
• A View from Jerusalem, 1849-1858: The Consular Diary of James and Elizabeth Anne McCaul Finn. Arnold Blumberg, ed. Cranbury, N.J.: Fairleigh Dickinson University Press, 1980.

844. FLINT, Isaac A. (1816-92)
      November 28, 1849-January 7, 1850
      Travel diary; from San Francisco by ship.
      • "Golden Gate to Columbia River on the Bark Keoka: Isaac
      A. Flint's Journal," Ted Van Arsdol, ed. Oregon Historical
      Quarterly, v. 63, pp. 41-54, March, 1962.

845. FOSTER, Rev. Isaac
      March 26, 1849-March 14, 1850
      Travel diary; from Plainfield, Illinois; laconic entries with mile-
      age noted interspersed with lengthy letters to family left behind; de-
      tails of arrival in California; wintering over in a tent.
      • "A Journal of the Route to Alta, California," in: Lucy Ann
      Sexton, ed. The Foster Family, California Pioneers. Santa
      Barbara, Cal.: Schauer Printing, 1925; pp. 14-76.

846. GARRETT, Thomas Miles (1830-64)
      June 13, 1849-November 16, 1850
      Personal diary; long, full entries detailing university life in an
      era when the student body numbered 200.
      • "Diary of Thomas Miles Garrett at the University of North
      Carolina, 1849," John Bowen Hamilton, ed. North Carolina His-
      torical Review, v. 38, pp. 63-93, January, 1961; pp. 241-62,
      April, 1961; pp. 380-410, July, 1961; pp. 534-63, October,
      1961.

847. GEIGER, Vincent (1823/24-69)
      May 10-June 23, 1849, by Geiger; June 24-August 30, 1849, by
      Bryarly.
      Travel diary; kept consecutively by two men who were part of
      one of the best organized companies of gold seekers; from St. Joseph
      via Laramie, Fort Hall and the Humboldt Sink to Sacramento; one of
      the best '49er diaries.
      • The Trail to California: The Overland Journal of Vincent
      Geiger and Wakeman Bryarly. New Haven: Yale University
      Press, 1945.

848. GORDON, Andrew
      April 30-September 24, 1849
      Travel diary; hardships endured in going west by wagon; "Are
      we crazy?"
      • "Diary Excerpt," in: Philip Dunaway and Mel Evans, eds.
      A Treasury of the World's Great Diaries. New York: Double-
      day, 1957; pp. 65-68.

849. GRAY, Charles Glass (1820-   )
      May 1-November 19, 1849
      Travel diary; to the diggings with the Newark, New Jersey
      overland company of General John Stevens Darcy; detailed descrip-
      tion of conditions.
      • Off at Sunrise: The Overland Journal of Charles Glass Gray.

Thomas D. Clark, ed. San Marino, Cal.: Huntington Library, 1976.

850. GREEN, Robert B. (1821-49)
      February 26-September 26, 1849
      Travel diary; one of the few diaries of the southern route to the gold fields; via Fort Smith, Albuquerque; along the Gila River to Los Angeles; of the same party as William H. Chamberlin (q.v.); supplements his tale with humor and comments which most writers would have omitted; died of dysentery shortly after his arrival.
      • On the Arkansas Route to California in 1849: The Journal of Robert B. Green of Lewisburg, Pennsylvania. J. Orin Oliphant, ed. Lewisburg, Pa.: Bucknell University Press, 1955.

851. HALL, William Henry Harrison (1823-1907)
      April 15, 1849-October 22, 1881; gaps
      Personal diary; Vermonter went three times to Oregon; in search of his fortune; involved through his brother in the Pennsylvania oil rush at Pithold; well-illustrated with pictures and facsimiles.
      • The Private Letters and Diaries of Captain Hall. Eric Schneirsohn, ed. Glendale, Cal.: London Book Co., 1974; 1450 copies.

852. HESTER, Sallie (1835-   )
      March 20, 1849-June 3, 1850
      Travel diary; from Bloomington, Indiana, by train, steamboat and wagon to San Jose, California.
      • "The Diary of a Pioneer Girl: Sallie Hester," in: Kenneth L. Holmes, ed. and comp. Covered Wagon Women: Diaries and Letters From the Western Trails 1840-1890. Glendale, Cal.: Arthur H. Clark, 1983-   ; v. 1, pp. 231-46.

853. JENKINS, F. H.
      November 12, 1849-May 6, 1850
      Travel diary; facsimile edition; on the bark Orion from Boston; notes the ship's position at the end of each day's entry; ashore at Rio de Janeiro; occasionally interesting.
      • Journal of a Voyage to San Francisco 1849. Northridge: California State University, 1975.

854. JOSSELYN, Amos Piatt (1820-85)
      Travel diary; Ohioan's trip to the diggings via the Ohio and Mississippi Rivers; overland via Fort Laramie, South Pass and Salt Lake City to Sacramento; reports on weather, mileage and terrain.
      • The Overland Journal of Amos Piatt Josselyn: Zanesville, Ohio to the Sacramento Valley, April 2, 1849 to September 11, 1849. J. William Barrett II, ed. Baltimore: Gateway Press, 1978.
           REVIEW: Nebraska History, v. 60, pp. 119-20, Spring, 1979.

855. KAMEHAMEHA IV, King of the Hawaiian Islands (Alexander
Liholiho) (1834-63)
September 18, 1849-June 29, 1850
Travel diary; from Hawaii to San Francisco; on to New York
via Panama; London, Paris; nephew of Kamehameha III accompanied
his minister of finance on a treaty mission; Hawaiian view of the
Anglo world.
   • The Journal of Prince Alexander Liholiho: The Voyages
   Made to the U.S., England and France in 1849-1850. Jacob
   Adler, ed. Honolulu: University of Hawaii Press, 1967.
      REVIEWS: Library Journal, v. 93, p. 2240, June 1, 1968.
      Saturday Review, v. 51, p. 71, June 22, 1968.

856. KELLAM, Robert F. (1825-   )
June 23-September 14, 1849
Travel diary; Camden, Arkansas, store clerk went to Rusk
County, Texas, to visit his parents; travel conditions; expenses.
   • "Journal of a Trip From Camden to Texas," Orville W. Tay-
   lor, ed. Arkansas Historical Quarterly, v. 10, pp. 285-94,
   1951.

857. McDOUGAL, Jane (-1862)
May 1-June 20, 1849
Travel diary; wife of the second governor of California; down
the coast by ship; overland to Chagres; detailed; shorter version of
this same journal appeared in Overland Monthly, 2nd series, v. 16,
pp. 273-80, September, 1890.
   • "A Diary Kept by Mrs. Jane McDougal When Returning from
   San Francisco to Her Home in Indianapolis in May, 1849 on the
   Steamer California," in: Sandra L. Myres, ed. Ho for California! San Marino, Cal.: Huntington Library, 1980; pp. 9-
   33.

858. MELVILLE, Herman (1819-91) [A320, B255]
   1. October 11, 1849-January 30, 1850; Travel diary; American
novelist went to London to find a publisher for White Jacket; New
York to London; sightseeing; social life; homesickness.
   • Journal of a Visit to London and the Continent 1849-1850.
   Eleanor Melville Metcalf, ed. Cambridge: Harvard University
   press, 1948.

   2. Travel diary; England, Scotland; Liverpool to Constantinople by ship; to Jaffa; up the Italian boot; mostly description of
people and places.
   • Journal of a Visit to Europe and the Levant, October 11,
   1856-May 6, 1857. Howard C. Horsford, ed. Princeton:
   Princeton University Press, 1955; originally a dissertation
   (Dissertation Abstracts 15/01, p. 584).

   3. "Diary Excerpts," in: Philip Dunaway and Mel Evans, eds.
A Treasury of the World's Great Diaries. New York: Doubleday,
1957; pp. 409-15.

859. MORISON, James (1818-82)
      November 15, 1849-June, 1850
      Travel diary; went to California to set up a medical practice;
accompanied by his sister-in-law; stops in Rio, Valparaiso, Lima, and
Acapulco are described at length.
      • By Sea to San Francisco, 1849-50: The Journal of Doctor
      James Morison. Lonnie J. White and William R. Gillaspie, eds.
      Memphis: Memphis State University Press, 1976.

860. OSBUN, Albert Gallatin (1807-62)
      April 9, 1849-January 21, 1851
      Personal diary; Ohioan went with a party financed by a rela-
tive to the California diggings; the party dissolved after a poor season of mining; by ship to the Samoan Islands to obtain goods to sell
in San Francisco; not a financial success; generally full entries.
      • To California and the South Seas: The Diary of Albert Gal-
      latin Osbun, 1849-1851. John Haskell Kemble, ed. San Marino,
      Cal.: Huntington Library, 1966.

861. PERKINS, Elisha Douglass, 1823-52
      May 9, 1849-February 28, 1850
      Travel diary; goldseeker with a company of men from Marietta,
Ohio; followed the usual '49er route; after a late start the party was
inclined to dawdle providing Perkins with time to make long, full entries; one of the better '49er diaries.
      • Gold Rush Diary, Being the Journal of Elisha Douglass Per-
      kins on the Overland Trail in the Spring and Summer of 1849.
      Thomas D. Clark, ed. Lexington: University of Kentucky
      Press, 1967.
           REVIEW: Saturday Review, v. 50, pp. 27-28, May 27, 1967.

862. POWNALL, Joseph
      June 10-September 7, 1849
      Travel diary; New Jersey physician contracted gold fever; from
El Paso to Los Angeles and up to San Jose; sights and situations en
route.
      • "From Los Angeles to Mariposa," Robert Glass Cleland, ed.
      Pacific Historical Review, v. 18, pp. 24-32, February, 1949.

863. PRITCHARD, James Avery (1816-62) [A321]
      April 15-August 13, 1849
      Travel diary; left early in the season; one of the few describ-
ing the trip from St. Louis to Independence, Missouri; at Forts
Kearny, Laramie and Hall; keen observer; many details of the arrival
in Sacramento.
      • The Overland Diary of James A. Pritchard from Kentucky to
      California in 1849. Dale L. Morgan, ed. Denver: Old West,
      1959.

864. RAMSAY, Alexander (1810-1901)
      May 4-October 14, 1849

Travel diary; from Park County, Indiana, on the Oregon-California Trail in an entirely male company; weather, mileage; illness, etc.
- "Alexander Ramsay's Gold Rush Diary of 1849," Pacific Historical Review, v. 18, pp. 437-68, November, 1949.

865. REID, Bernard Joseph (1823-)
May 24-October 7, 1849
Travel diary; son of Irish immigrants was born near Pittsburgh; well-educated and working as a surveyor in St. Louis at the time of the California gold discovery; passenger on the Pioneer Line, a wagon train which ran from Independence, Missouri, to San Francisco; via Fort Laramie, Hudspeth's Cutoff and Humboldt Sink to Sacramento; supplemented with excerpts from other diarists on the same train; detailed and very well done; one of the better gold rush diaries.
- Overland to California with the Pioneer Line: The Gold Rush Diary of Bernard J. Reid. Mary McDougall Gordon, ed. Stanford: Stanford University Press, 1983.
  REVIEW: Library Journal, v. 108, p. 2328-29, December 15, 1983.

866. RICH, Charles Coulson (1809?-)
October 8-December 15, 1849; Travel diary.
- "Charles C. Rich Diary," in: LeRoy R. and Ann W. Hafen. Journals of Forty-niners: Salt Lake to Los Angeles. Glendale, Cal.: Arthur H. Clark Co., 1954; pp. 181-92.

867. ROSSETTI, William Michael (1829-1919) [B256]
1. May 15, 1849-January 29, 1853; Personal/literary diary; English art critic; brother of Dante Gabriel and Christina; first printing of the complete journal including the personal references which were excised from the 1900 edition; day-to-day activities of the members of the Pre-Raphaelite Brotherhood.
- The P. R. B. Journal: William Michael Rossetti's Diary of the Pre-Raphaelite Brotherhood 1849-1853 Together with Other Pre-Raphaelite Documents. William E. Fredeman, ed. Oxford: Clarendon Press, 1975.

2. April 25, 1870-August 6, 1873; Personal diary; visits to Germany and Italy; social and working life of the Pre-Raphaelites; interesting account by a busy man.
- The Diary of W. M. Rossetti 1870-1873. Odette Bornand, ed. Oxford: Clarendon Press, 1977.
  REVIEWS: Book Review Index 1978, p. 414; 1979, p. 394. Book Review Digest 1978, 1122.

868. STAPLES, David Jackson (1824-1900)
April 16-September 1, 1849
Travel diary; from Boston to California by train, steamboat and wagon; to the Humboldt River.
- "The Journal of David Jackson Staples," Harold F. Taggart,

ed. California Historical Society Quarterly, v. 22, pp. 119-50,
March, 1943.

869. STONE, John N.
February 6-August 28, 1849
Travel diary; New York City to San Francisco; stops at Rio
de Janeiro and Callao, Peru.
• "Journal of John N. Stone, Passenger on the Robert Bowne,"
in: John E. Pomfret, ed. California Gold Rush Voyages, 1848-
1849. San Marino, Cal.: Huntington Library, 1954; pp. 97-
176.

870. STOWELL, Levi (1820-55)
January 1-December 31, 1849
Travel diary; attracted by opportunities in California; set out
with friends before hearing news of the gold discovery; overland
journey across Panama; by ship to San Francisco; arrival at the
mines; in the construction business in San Francisco; pithy, vivid.
• "Bound for the Land of Canaan, Ho! The Diary of Levi
Stowell," California Historical Society Quarterly, v. 27, pp. 33-
50, March, 1948; pp. 157-64, June, 1948; pp. 259-66, September, 1948; pp. 361-70, December, 1948; v. 28, pp. 57-68,
March, 1949.

871. SWAIN, William (1821-1904)
April 11, 1849-January 31, 1851
Travel diary; Niagara County, New York, native went to the
diggings; diary interspersed with letters home to his family; detailed
and well written.
• Holliday, J. S. The World Rushed In: The California Gold
Rush Experience. New York: Simon and Schuster, 1981.

872. SWEENY, Thomas William (1820-92)
1849; June 6, 1851-December 11, 1853
Military diary; Irish immigrant saw service with the 1st New
York Volunteers in the Mexican War where he lost an arm; at Fort
Yuma; by ship to California; chafed under the command of Major
Samuel Heintzelman; much material on Apache and Yuma Indians.
• Journal of Lt. Thomas W. Sweeny 1849-1853. Arthur Wood-
ward, ed. Los Angeles: Westernlore Press, 1956.

873. TAPPAN, Henry (1820?-   )
April 27-September 8, 1849
Travel diary; New Yorker joined a Jerseyville, Illinois, group,
one of the first of those going to California after the discovery of
gold; helps establish the date that Hudspeth's Cutoff began to be
used.
• "The Gold Rush Diary of Henry Tappan," Everett Walters
and George B. Strother, eds. Annals of Wyoming, v. 25, pp.
113-39, July, 1953.

874.   TATE, James A. (1795-   )
       April 5-May 10, 1849
       Travel diary; from Virginia to Missouri.
       • "One Who Went West," Missouri Historical Review, v. 57, pp.
       369-78, 1963.

874a. THOMASON, Jackson (1816-84)
       April 1, 1849-July 31, 1850
       Travel diary; merchant of Pontotoc County, Mississippi, traveled
with a company on the Oregon Trail; joined a new company in Salt
Lake City; arrived at Weaverville, California; later entries are summaries of several days' events; interesting weather diary of a rainy
California winter (pp. 109-111).
       • From Mississippi to California: Jackson Thomason's 1849
       Overland Journal. Michael D. Heaston, ed. Austin, Tx:
       Jenkins, 1978.

875.   TINKER, Charles (1821-1908)
       May 20-August 17, 1849
       Travel diary; gold rusher from Ashtabula, Ohio, with the
Kingsville Company to California; had good luck on the trail.
       • "Charles Tinker's Journal: A Trip to California in 1849,"
       Eugene H. Roseboom, ed. Ohio State Archaeological and His-
       torical Quarterly, v. 61, pp. 64-85, January, 1952.

876.   TRASK, Sarah E. (1828?-92)
       January 15-August 15, 1849
       Personal diary; article with extracts; her work and her friends;
longing for her beau away at sea.
       • Blewett, Mary E. "I Am Doom to Disapointment (sic): The
       Diaries of a Beverly, Massachusetts, Shoebinder, Sarah E.
       Trask, 1849-51," Essex Institute Historical Collections, v. 117,
       pp. 192-212, July, 1981.

877.   WHIPPLE, Amiel Weeks (1817/18-63) [A338]
       1. Exploration diary; official government report by the leader
of a corps of topographical engineers; much interest in the Indians
met.
       • The Whipple Report: Journal of an Expedition From San
       Diego, California, to the Rio Colorado, From September 11 to
       December 11, 1849. E. I. Edwards, intro. Los Angeles:
       Westernlore Press, 1961.

       2. May 30-September 7, 1853; Exploration diary; commissioned
by Secretary of War Jefferson Davis to survey a southern route for
a transcontinental railroad; field notes; westward along the 35th parallel from Fort Smith.
       • "The Journal of Lieutenant A. W. Whipple," Muriel H. Wright
       and George H. Shirk, eds. Chronicles of Oklahoma, v. 28,
       pp. 235-83, Autumn, 1950.

878. WHITE, Caroline Barrett (1828-1915)
      1849-1915
      Personal diary; financially comfortable wife and mother; active
and large extended family; travel abroad and through much of the
U.S.; good social history.
      • "Diary," in: American Women's Diaries: New England
      Women. New Canaan, Conn.: Readex Microprint Corp., 1984;
      reels 1-6.

879. WILKINS, James F. (1808?-88)
      May 6-October 16, 1849
      Travel diary; British-born artist went by ox wagon to Califor-
nia making sketches of the scenery; on his return to St. Louis he
exhibited his work in a panorama; lengthy entries in an elegant style;
sketches reproduced.
      • An Artist on the Overland Trail: The 1849 Diary and
      Sketches of James F. Wilkins. John Francis McDermott, ed.
      San Marino, Cal.: Huntington Library, 1968.

880. WINDELER, Adolphus
      December 6, 1849-October 28, 1853
      Personal diary; intelligent and technologically adept German
went to the diggings with several shipmates; at Marysville, Ophir
City, on the Feather River; detailed entries over a long period in
the diggings make it historically important; illustrations done by a
companion.
      • The California Gold Rush Diary of a German Sailor. W. Tur-
      rentine Jackson, ed. Berkeley, Cal.: Howell-North Books,
      1969.

881. YOUNG, Sheldon (1815-92)
      1. March 18, 1849-February 5, 1850; Travel diary; from Joliet,
Illinois, to California; short entries.
      • "Log," in: Margaret Long. The Shadow of the Arrow. rev.
      and enl. ed. Caldwell, Ida.: Caxton, 1950; pp. 259-80.

      2. July 25, 1849-October 23, 1849; Travel diary; one of the
best accounts of the Death Valley route.
      • "Sheldon Young's Log," in LeRoy and Ann W. Hafen, eds.
      Journals of the Forty-niners, Salt Lake to Los Angeles. Glen-
      dale, Cal.: Arthur H. Clark, 1955; pp. 60-130.
      REVIEW: Book Review Digest 1955, p. 382.

1850

882. ALEMANY, José Sadoc (-1888)
      June 11, 1850-July 14, 1853; gaps
      Official diary; Spanish archbishop of San Francisco; official
visits; diocesan business.
      • "The Long Lost Ecclesiastical Diary of Archbishop Alemany,"

Francis J. Weber, ed. and trans. California Historical Society Quarterly, v. 43, pp. 319-30, December, 1964.

883. ANDREWS, William (1835-1914)
      August 18, 1850-December 31, 1866
      Personal diary; resident of Coventry, England, who worked
as a silk weaver; interested in astronomy; daily work; humorless,
taciturn.
      • "Diary," in: Valerie Edith Chancellor, ed. Master and Art-
isan in Victorian England: The Diary of William Andrews and
the Autobiography of Joseph Gutteridge. New York: Augustus
M. Kelley, 1969.

884. ARMSTRONG, Benjamin John (1817-90) [B257]
      1850-January 6, 1887
      Personal diary; vicar of East Dereham; family life; visit to Lon-
don; church business; comments on national events, e.g., the Crimean War and Miss Nightingale; losing a manservant who enlisted;
visit to Ireland; high and low church politics; enjoyable; good picture of a clergyman's beliefs and prejudices.
      • Armstrong's Norfolk Diary. Herbert B. J. Armstrong, ed.
London: Hodder and Stoughton, 1963.

885. BELL, William H.
      September 17, 1850-September 12, 1851
      Personal diary; New York City patrolman; details of his duties;
gangs, beggars, political graft.
      • "Crime, Poverty and the Streets of New York City: The
Diary of William H. Bell, 1850-51," Sean Wilentz, ed. History
Workshop [Great Britain] v. 7, pp. 126-55, 1979.

886. BROWN, Adam Mercer (1826-1910)
      April 25-September 9, 1850
      Travel diary; from St. Joseph, Missouri, via Fort Laramie;
weather and hardships.
      • "Over Barren Plains and Rock-bound Mountains," David M.
Kiefer, ed. Montana Magazine of Western History, v. 22, pp.
16-29, October, 1972.

887. BURRELL, Clarissa Wright (1805-57)
      February 28, 1850-August 17, 1856
      Letter-diary; also some letters from her son Birney (1840-   );
home activities while her husband went to California; she later joined
him; ranch life in Santa Clara County, California; good account of
family activity in Gold Rush era.
      • The Burrell Letters. Reginald R. Stuart, ed. Oakland,
Cal.: n.p., 1950; reprinted from California Historical Society
Quarterly, v. 18-19, 1949-50.

888. BYERS, William N.
      May 7, 1850-December 31, 1853

Personal diary; founder and editor of the Rocky Mountain News;
extracts; in Ohio, Iowa and Oregon; in California mines; surveying.
- "The Early Diaries of William N. Byers (1850-1853)," Levette
  J. Davidson, ed. Colorado Magazine, v. 22, pp. 146-57, July,
  1945.

889. CHALMERS, Robert (1820-91)
     April 17-September 2, 1850
     Travel diary; Canadian set off for the diggings in California;
lost his belongings in a Missouri River steamboat fire but continued
on; via the Salt Desert route.
- "The Journal of Robert Chalmers: April 17-September 1,
  1850," Utah Historical Quarterly, v. 20, pp. 31-55, 1952.

890. CHURCHILL, Joseph Fleetwood (1827-80)
     November 1, 1850-November 13, 1852
     Personal diary; Englishman went to South Africa for his health;
worked as a trader; trips to outlying areas.
- A Merchant Family in Early Natal: Diaries and Letters of
  Joseph and Marianne Churchill, 1850 to 1880. Daphne Child,
  ed. Cape Town: A. A. Balkema, 1979; pp. 5-51.

891. CHURCHILL, Marianne
     October 31, 1857-March 23, 1858
     Travel diary; accompanied her brother; pp. 101-18 of above
title.

892. COLLINSON, Richard (1811-83) [C26]
     April 16, 1850-May 5, 1855
     Exploration diary; commissioned by the Admiralty to search for
Franklin; spent three years in the arctic; unsuccessful but came
through with little loss of life under trying conditions.
- Journal of HMS Enterprise, on the Expedition in Search of
  Sir John Franklin's Ships by Behring Strait 1850-55. T. B.
  Collinson, ed. Reprint of 1889 London ed. New York: AMS
  Press, 1976.

893. CULBERTSON, Thaddeus Ainsworth (1823-) [A324]
     March 21-July 6, 1850
     Fur trade journal; based on four sources (see Preface for ex-
planation); the only account of the Missouri River fur trade for the
year 1850; botanizing and fossil collecting; interesting.
- Journal of an Expedition to the Mauvaises Terres and the
  Upper Missouri in 1850. John Francis McDermott, ed. (U.S.
  Bureau of American Ethnology Bulletin no. 147) Washington,
  D.C.: U.S. Government Printing Office, 1952.

894. DAVIS, Sarah Green (1826-1906)
     May 21-October 19, 1850
     Travel diary; mother and her infant daughter went with her
brother-in-law to meet her husband; family party traveled from St.
Joseph to Nevada City by ox wagon.

• "Diary from Missouri to California, 1850: Sara Davis," in: Kenneth L. Holmes, ed. and comp. <u>Covered Wagon Women: Diaries and Letters From the Western Trails 1840-1890</u>. Glendale, Cal.: Arthur H. Clark, 1983- ; v. 2, pp. 171-206.

895. DAVIS, Stephen Chapin (1833-56)
June 1, 1850-May 26, 1854
Travel diary; Massachusetts native shipped for San Francisco with 500 copies of New York City newspapers which he sold to men in Panama and California at double his purchase price; worked in the gold fields as a merchant and able seaman; trips home; engaging.
• <u>California Gold Rush Merchant: The Journal of Stephen Chapin Davis</u>. Benjamin B. Richards, ed. San Marino, Cal.: Huntington Library, 1956.

896. DENVER, James W. (1817-92)
May 20-September 5, 1850
Travel diary; by carriage with mail for California; had pleasanter trip than others on the same route.
• "The Denver Diary: Overland to California in 1850," Richard E. Meyer, ed. <u>Arizona and the West</u>, v. 17, pp. 35-62, Spring, 1975.

897. ELY, Edward (1827-58)
1. December 11, 1850--Travel diary; Bucks County, Pennsylvania, native and doctor abandoned his practice for health reasons; ship's doctor on a voyage from New York to India; around Cape Horn; several stops in California; Honolulu; later U.S. Consul in Bombay; rambling style.
• <u>The Wanderings of Edward Ely: A Mid-19th Century Seafarer's Diary</u>. Anthony and Allison Sirna, eds. New York: Hastings House, 1954.

2. "Diary Excerpts," in: Philip Dunaway and Mel Evans, eds. <u>A Treasury of the World's Great Diaries</u>. New York: Doubleday, 1957; pp. 69-71.

898. FAIRBANK, Nathaniel Kellogg (1829-1903)
February 16, 1850-June 2, 1852; gaps
Personal diary; young blade of Rochester, New York; death of his father and sister; sowing wild oats; recurring resolutions to mend his ways and be a financial success.
• "Extracts From the Journal of Nathaniel K. Fairbank 1850-52," Joseph W. Barnes, ed. <u>Rochester History</u>, v. 40, pp. 1-24, July, 1978.

899. FLEETWOOD, Joshua C.
September 11, 1850-January 25, 1851
Travel diary; pleasant journey.
• "Joshua C. Fleetwood's Diary Made During a Journey on Horseback from North Carolina to Fayette County, Tennessee

in 1850," West Tennessee Historical Society Papers, v. 10, pp. 5-19, 1956.

900. FRENCH, John
January 31-October 17, 1850
Travel diary; Michigan native in the gold rush; by ship from New York to San Francisco; map shows zigzag route of the Hindoo from French's daily sightings.
  • "California Diary of John French, 1850-51," Rev. Victor L. Dowdell and Helen C. Everett, eds. Michigan History, v. 38, pp. 33-44, March, 1954.

901. FRINK, Margaret Ann (1818-93) [A325]
March 31-September 21, 1850
Travel diary; from Morgan County, Indiana, with her store-keeper husband and relatives to California; across the plains on a sidesaddle; provisions to protect themselves against scurvy; arrival in Sacramento; opened a hotel; enjoyable, well-done narrative.
  • "Adventures of a Party of Gold-seekers: Margaret A. Frink," in: Kenneth L. Holmes, ed. and comp. Covered Wagon Women: Diaries and Letters from the Western Trails 1840-1890. Glendale, Cal.: Arthur H. Clark, 1983- ; v. 2, pp. 55-169.

902. GOODRIDGE, Sophia Lois (1826-1903)
June 7-October 14, 1850
Travel diary; from Kanesville, Iowa, to Salt Lake City, with her parents and siblings; several births and deaths; a dance on the banks of the Sweetwater River; mileage, several severe storms.
  • "The Mormon Trail, 1850: Sophia Lois Goodridge," in: Kenneth L. Holmes, ed. and comp. Covered Wagon Women: Diaries and Letters From the Western Trails 1840-1890. Glendale, Cal.: Arthur H. Clark, 1983-; v. 2, pp. 207-35.

903. HEYWOOD, Martha Spence (-1873)
January 1, 1850-August 24, 1856
Personal diary; plural wife of Joseph lived in Salt Lake City; after her conversion in the East came to Utah; birth of a child; life in polygamous household; hints of disaffection among wives.
  • Not By Bread Alone: The Journal of Martha Spence Heywood, 1850-56. Juanita Brooks, ed. Salt Lake City: Utah Historical Society, 1978.
      REVIEWS: Western Historical Quarterly, v. 10, pp. 239-40, April, 1979. American West, v. 16, pp. 52-53, March/April, 1979. Montana, v. 28, pp. 60-61, Autumn, 1978. Colorado Magazine, v. 56, pp. 94-96, Winter/Spring, 1979. Pacific Historical Review, v. 49, pp. 659-60, November, 1980.

904. HOUGH, Dr. Warren (-1901)
March 21-July 12, 1850
Travel diary; Illinois native's trip to California.
  • "The 1850 Overland Diary of Dr. Warren Hough," Annals of Wyoming, v. 46, pp. 207-16, Fall, 1974.

905. HUSE, Charles Enoch (1825-98)
      June 14, 1850-September 19, 1857
      Personal diary; New Englander came to California to make his
fortune and practice law; original written in Spanish as a practice
exercise; active in municipal life, especially in the clearing of land
titles; interesting picture of the town's transformation from a placid
Spanish pueblo to a bustling American city.
      • The Huse Journal, Santa Barbara in the 1850's. Edith B.
      Conkey, ed. Francis Price, trans. Santa Barbara, Cal.:
      Santa Barbara Historical Society, 1977.
         REVIEWS: Western Historical Quarterly, v. 10, p. 383,
         July, 1979. Southern California Quarterly, v. 60, pp.
         445-48, Winter, 1978.

906. JAMISON, Samuel M. (-1890)
      April 1-September 18, 1850
      Travel diary; from Independence, Missouri; wagon journey;
mileage; prices of items bought and traded for; arrival at Georgetown.
      • "Diary of Samuel M. Jamison 1850," Nevada Historical Society
      Quarterly, v. 10, pp. 4-26, Winter, 1967.

907. KILGORE, William H. (1817/18-)
      April 10-August 5, 1850
      Travel diary; from Lee County, Iowa, to Hangtown, Cal.
      • The Kilgore Journal of an Overland Journey to California in
      the Year 1850. Joyce Rockwood Muench, ed. New York:
      Hastings House, 1949.

908. LANDER, Samuel, Jr.
      November 7, 1850-March 19, 1851
      Personal diary; serious student; studies.
      • "Private Journal of Samuel Lander, Jr.: Randolph-Macon
      College, 1850-1851," John P. Branch Historical Papers, new
      series, v. 3, pp. 6-8, 29-47, December, 1954.

909. McKINSTRY, Byron Nathan (1818-94)
      March 18, 1850-August 10, 1852
      Travel diary; Vermonter went from his Illinois farm to California;
observant and interested in a variety of subjects; many details of life
in the mines; one of the better Gold Rush diaries.
      • The California Gold Rush Overland Diary of Byron N. Mc-
      Kinstry, 1850-52. Glendale, Cal.: Arthur H. Clark, 1975.

910. MASON, James
      April 8, 1850-August 4, 1851; few entries after September,
      1850
      Travel diary; Irish-born emigrant joined a company from Cam-
bridge, Ohio.
      • "The Diary of James Mason, Ohio to California, 1850," Ne-
      braska History Magazine, v. 33, pp. 103-21, March, 1952.

911. MIERTSCHING, Johann August (1817-   )
      January 18, 1850-November 10, 1854
      Personal diary; Moravian missionary went as interpreter with
the group sent to find Sir John Franklin; unsuccessful; entries to
April 15, 1853 were reconstructed because the original was left on
the abandoned ship.
      • Frozen Ships: The Arctic Diary of Johann Miertsching, 1850-
      1854. L. H. Neatby, trans. New York: St. Martin's, 1967.

912. MOORMAN, Madison Berryman (1824-1915)
      April 27, 1850-February 4, 1851
      Travel diary; Member of the Havilah Company; one of the few
diarists to use the Hastings Cutoff; well-written.
      • The Journal of Madison Berryman Moorman, 1850-1851. Irene
      Dakin Paden, ed. San Francisco: California Historical Society,
      1948.

913. MORRIS, Anna Maria De Camp (1813-61)
      May 2-July 17, 1850
      Travel diary; wife of Major Gouverneur Morris, commander of
the 3rd Infantry; from Fort Leavenworth to Santa Fe; an easy journey
for her with a maid; rode in the company's ambulance; found Santa
Fe "squalid."
      • "A Military Wife on the Santa Fe Trail: Anna Maria Morris,"
      in: Kenneth L. Holmes, ed. and comp. Covered Wagon Women:
      Diaries and Letters From the Western Trails 1840-1890.   Glen-
      dale, Cal.: Arthur H. Clark, 1983-; v. 2, pp. 15-43.

914. PARSONS, Lucena Pfuffer (1821-1905)
      June 13, 1850-June 17, 1851; gaps
      Travel diary; young couple left Wisconsin the day after their
wedding for California; in a party of 50 wagons; notes on graves
passed; winter layover in Salt Lake City; acid comments on Mormon-
ism, "Womens [sic] rights are trampled under foot"; arrival in Carson Valley, California; a strongminded woman.
      • "An Overland Honeymoon: Lucena Parsons," in: Kenneth
      L. Holmes, ed. and comp. Covered Wagon Women: Diaries and
      Letters From the Western Trails 1840-1890. Glendale, Cal.:
      Arthur H. Clark, 1983-; v. 2, pp. 238-94.

915. PAYNE, James A.
      August 3, 1850-April, 1853
      Travel diary; interesting account of life on a steamboat.
      • "St. Louis to San Francisco: Being an Account of a Journey
      Across the Plains in 1850, Together with His Experiences in
      Steamboating on the California Rivers Until the Fall of 1853,"
      Pacific Historical Review, v. 9, pp. 448-59, 1940.

916. PETERSON, Andrew (1818-98)
      1. May 19-July 30, 1850; Travel diary; from Goteborg to Wa-
conia, Minnesota, by ship, rail and canal boat.

- "Andrew Peterson's Emigrant Voyage of 1850," Roger Mc-
Knight, ed. and trans. <u>Swedish Pioneer Historical Quarterly</u>,
v. 31, pp. 3-11, 1980.

2. 1855-1898; Personal diary; extracts from diaries which were
used by Swedish novelist Vilhelm Moberg for his trilogy on immigrant
life.
- "Diary of a Swedish Immigrant Horticulturist, 1855-1898,"
Carlton C. Qualey. <u>Minnesota History</u>, v. 43, pp. 63-69, Summer, 1972.

917. PIGMAN, Walter Griffith (1818-92)
April 1, 1850-March 2, 1851
Travel diary; to the Hangtown, California, diggings from Felicity,
Ohio, via steamboat and wagon; Forts Kearny and Laramie; wound
up burning a coal pit; return home via Panama; fair amount of detail
on life in the diggings.
- <u>The Journal of Walter Griffith Pigman</u>. Ulla Staley Fawkes,
ed. Mexico, Mo.: W. G. Staley, 1942.

918. RHODES, Joseph (1823-53)
May 5-August, 1850
Travel diary; Indiana native went with a group to the California
diggings; mileage, weather, prices and hardships.
- "Joseph Rhodes and the Gold Rush of 1850," Merril J. Mat-
tes, ed. <u>Annals of Wyoming</u>, v. 23, pp. 52-71, January, 1951.

919. TAYLOR, Calvin
July 3-September 30, 1850
Travel diary; from the Black Hills via Salt Lake with a long
description of the city; arrival at Georgetown, California; very well
written.
- "Overland to California in 1850: The Journal of Calvin Taylor," Burton J. Williams, ed. <u>Utah Historical Quarterly</u>, v. 38,
pp. 312-49, Fall, 1970.

920. TENNYSON, Emily Sellwood, Baroness (1813-96)
Summer, 1850-September, 1874
Personal diary; wife of the poet laureate; family life; brief
record of events; much about her husband, his reading, work and
movements.
- <u>Lady Tennyson's Journal</u>. James O. Hoge, ed. Charlottesville: University Press of Virginia, 1981.

921. WHITMORE, Ellen Rebecca (1828-61)
October 3, 1850-April 9, 1852; gaps
Travel diary; Mount Holyoke student set out with a friend to
teach at the Cherokee National Female Seminary in the Indian Territory; from Philadelphia via Cincinnati and Cairo, Illinois; of slight
interest.
- <u>Journal of Ellen Whitmore</u>. Lola Garrett Bowers and Kathleen

Garrett, eds. Tahlequah, Ok.: Northeastern State College,
1953.

922. WILLIAMS, Thomazene (1823-1912)
      July 24-September 2, 1850
      Travel diary; accompanied her husband who was captain of the
barque; knowledgeable about navigation having grown up in a seafar-
ing family.
      • "Sea Log Written on a Passage From Newport to Quebec in
        1850," in: Basil Greenhill. Women Under Sail. Newton Ab-
        bott: David and Charles, 1970; pp. 103-09.

923. WOODRUFF, Lt. Israel C. (-1878)
      July 14-September 5, 1850
      Personal diary; West Point graduate conducted a survey of
boundaries between the Creek and Cherokee Nations; well-done account of work and conditions.
      • "An Account of a Creek Boundary Survey, 1850," Carl Coke
        Rister and Bryan W. Loveland, eds. Chronicles of Oklahoma,
        v. 27, pp. 268-302, Autumn, 1949.

                              1851

924. BAKER, Jean Rio Griffiths (1810-83)
      June 4, 1851-March 22, 1852
      Travel diary; widowed Scottish woman and Mormon convert
emigrated with her children; by ship from Liverpool to New Orleans;
by steamboat up the Mississippi; from Iowa to Salt Lake City by
wagon; strife on shipboard caused by "levity of behavior" of three
Mormon women with the ship's officers; lengthy descriptions of New
Orleans layover and steamboating; one of the best of the women's
diaries of westward migration.
      • "By Windjammer and Prairie Schooner London to Salt Lake
        City: Jean Rio Baker," in: Kenneth L. Holmes, ed. and
        comp. Covered Wagon Women: Diaries and Letters From the
        Western Trails 1840-1890. Glendale, Cal.: Arthur H. Clark,
        1983-; v. 3. pp. 203-81.

925. BOGGS, Mary Jane (1833-)
      June 10-30, 1851
      Travel diary; trip with her father and four relatives; food,
travel, scenery; lively.
      • "Rambles Among the Virginia Mountains: The Journal of
        Mary Jane Boggs, June, 1851," Virginia Magazine of History
        and Biography, v. 77, pp. 78-111, January, 1969.

926. BOYCE, George Price (1826-97)
      May 1, 1851-August 31, 1875; many gaps
      Personal diary; English watercolorist and friend of Dante Gab-
riel Rossetti; social life among the Pre-Raphaelites; comments on his
work and that of others.

• The Diaries of George Price Boyce. Virginia Surtees, ed.
(Old Water-colour Society Club Annual, v. 19, 1941) Norwich:
Real World, 1980.

927. BUCKINGHAM, Harriet Talcott (Clarke) (1832-90)
      May 4-September 26, 1851
      Travel diary; to Oregon from Norwalk, Ohio, with her brother,
aunt and uncle Hiram Smith; the last named had made the journey in
1846; Council Bluffs, across the Black Hills; Fort Bridger; several
different Indian tribes encountered; arrival in Portland; two versions
intertwined, rough notes and a more polished account written later.
      • "Crossing the Plains in 1851: Harriet Talcott Buckingham,"
      in: Kenneth L. Holmes, ed. and comp. Covered Wagon Women:
      Diaries and Letters From the Western Trails 1840-1890. Glen-
      dale, Cal.: Arthur H. Clark, 1983- ; v. 3, pp. 16-52.

928. CARPENTER, Zacheus
      July 22-August 29, 1851
      Travel diary; from Shelby County, Kentucky, to Richmond,
Virginia, to collect an inheritance.
      • Carpenter, J. R. "Diary and Letter," Kentucky Historical
      Society Register, v. 50, pp. 358-69, October, 1952.

929. COLLES, James (1828-98)
      September 12-23, 1851
      Personal diary; ornately written, humorous account.
      • Journal of a Hunting Excursion to Louis Lake, 1851. Blue
      Mount Lake, N.Y.: Adirondack Museum, 1961.

930. CRANSTON, Susan Amelia Marsh (1829-57)
      May 8-August 27, 1851
      Travel diary; Ohioan traveled to Oregon with her husband in
a company of 14 wagons; from St. Joseph to Fort Kearny, Chimney
Rock; notes graves passed; mileage; straightforward description.
      • "An Ohio Lady Crosses the Plains: Susan Amelia Cranston,"
      in: Kenneth L. Holmes, ed. and comp. Covered Wagon Women:
      Diaries and Letters From the Western Trails 1840-1890. Glen-
      dale, Cal.: Arthur H. Clark, 1983- ; v. 3, pp. 96-126.

930a. DOBLE, John (1828-66)
      October 27, 1851-February 11, 1854
      Personal diary; Indiana native and Mexican War veteran; by
sea from New York to Nicaragua; worked in the southern part of the
California diggings; detailed record kept throughout his stay; mining
methods, living conditions, social life; prices.
      • Journal and Letters From the Mines: Mokelumne Hill, Jack-
      son, Volcano and San Francisco, 1851-1865. Charles L. Camp,
      ed. Denver: Old West, 1962.

930b. FOWLER, Matthew Van Benschoten (1814-81)
      February 21-May 6, 1851

Travel diary; begun aboard a schooner in San Francisco Bay; customs inspector in San Francisco; tour of the Santa Clara Valley; by ship to Acapulco and overland across Panama; detailed; ornate style.
- "The 1851 California Journal of M. V. B. Fowler," Mary Joan Elliott, ed. Southern California Quarterly, v. 50, pp. 113-60, July, 1968; pp. 227-65, September, 1968.

GONCOURT, Edmond (1822-96) see GONCOURT, Jules

930c. GONCOURT, Jules (1830-70)
1. December, 1851-July 3, 1896; Personal diary; kept jointly by the brothers to the death of Jules; thereafter by Edmond; classic picture of life in Paris among the literary and artistic worlds; high life and low; gossipy.
- Pages from the Goncourt Journal. Robert Baldick, ed. and trans. London: Oxford University Press, 1962.

2. December 2, 1851-June 22, 1870; "A translation of the most informing and agreeable pages of the best years of the diaries."
- The Goncourt Journals, 1851-1870. Lewis Galantiere, ed. and trans. Garden City, N.Y.: Doubleday Doran, 1937.

3. June 20, 1870-June 20, 1871; Personal diary; the Prussian siege and occupation; begins with Jules' death and ends with the first anniversary of his passing.
- Paris Under Siege, 1870-1871: From the Goncourt "Journal." George J. Becker, ed. and trans. Ithaca: Cornell University Press, 1969.

4. "Diary Excerpts," in: Philip Dunaway and Mel Evans, eds. A Treasury of the World's Great Diaries. New York: Doubleday, 1957; pp. 552-60.

930d. HADLEY, Amelia Hammond (1825-86)
May 5-August 23, 1851
Travel diary; from Galesburg, Illinois, on their honeymoon accompanied by the groom's brother; wagon pulled by horses rather than an ox team afforded them a speedier trip than most Oregon immigrants; passed the Mormon Winter Quarters, Loup Fork, Fort Loring; Portland.
- "Journal of Travails [sic] to Oregon: Amelia Hadley," in: Kenneth L. Holmes, ed. and comp. Covered Wagon Women: Diaries and Letters From the Western Trails 1840-1890. Glendale, Cal.: Arthur H. Clark, 1983- ; v. 3, pp. 53-96.

931. LIVINGSTONE, David (1813-73)
1. April, 1851-May 16, 1852; June 8, 1852-November 8, 1853; Exploration journal; Scottish-born African explorer; journeys in Bechuanaland, Barotseland and Upper Zambesi; much on flora, fauna; relations with the natives and immigrant Europeans; very interested in the different languages.

• Private Journals, 1851-1853. I. Schapera, ed. Berkeley:
University of California Press, 1960.

2. November 11, 1853-May 20, 1856; Much geographic and
ethnographic information about Africa; contains much material not
found in his published Travels; "for commerce and Christianity."
• African Journal, 1853-1856. I. Schapera, ed. Berkeley:
University of California Press, 1963.

932. MIDGLEY, Sarah (1831-93)
September 10, 1851-September 14, 1862; gap from 1852-September
4, 1855
Personal diary; Englishwoman emigrated to Victoria, Australia,
with her family for reasons not made clear in the text; "proper"
Victorian and staunch Methodist; entertaining narrative of family
farm, visiting and news from relatives left behind; ends a few days
before her marriage to Richard Skilbeck (q.v., 1858).
• The Diaries of Sarah Midgley and Richard Skilbeck, A Story
of Australian Settlers, 1851-1864. H. A. McCorkell, ed. Melbourne: Cassell, 1967; pp. 11-115.

933. NORELIUS, Eric (1833-1916) [A327]
August 5, 1851-October 1, 1856; October 1, 1885-May 9, 1886
Personal diary; Lutheran immigrant ministered to settlements
of Swedes in Illinois; student life at Capitol University in Columbus,
Ohio; stays in New York and Chicago; extended journey to the West
Coast inspecting work underway by the Augustana Synod.
• The Journals of Eric Norelius, A Swedish Missionary on the
American Frontier. G. Everett Arden, trans. and ed. Phila-
delphia: Fortress, 1967.

934. TOWNSEND, Edward Davis (1817-93)
November 17, 1851-February 21, 1856
Travel diary; West Point graduate and Massachusetts native;
by ship from New York City to California via Havana and Chagres;
stationed in Benicia and San Francisco; active in the Episcopal Church;
extensive descriptions of sights and some military matters.
• The California Diary of E. D. Townsend. Malcolm Edwards,
ed. Los Angeles: Ward Ritchie Press, 1970.

935. WILLIAMS, Lucia Loraine Bigelow (1816-74)
May 31-September 27, 1851
Travel letter/diary; second wife to an Oregon emigrant; with
his grown children and their own; death of son who fell from the
wagon when the oxen bolted; notes on life in Oregon, "It is a great
place to make money."
• "A Letter to Mother: Lucia Loraine Williams," in: Kenneth
L. Holmes, ed. and comp. Covered Wagon Women: Diaries and
Letters From the Western Trails 1840-1890. Glendale, Cal.:
Arthur H. Clark, 1983- ; v. 3, pp. 127-59.

936. WOOD, Elizabeth (Morse) (1828-1913) [A331]
       June 29-September 15, 1851
       Travel diary; young single woman of Tazewell County, Illinois,
emigrated in a company of 25 wagons; a "fuss" with Indians; some
lengthy description.
       • "Journal of a Trip to Oregon: Elizabeth Wood," in: Ken-
       neth L. Holmes, ed. and comp. Covered Wagon Women: Di-
       aries and Letters From the Western Trails 1840-1890. Glendale,
       Cal.: Arthur H. Clark, 1983- ; v. 3, pp. 161-78.

937. WURTS, George, 1829-1923
       July 3-15, 1851
       Travel diary; Pennsylvania newspaper printer and later New
Jersey secretary of state; visit to New York State Lunatic Asylum
and state prison; tourist notes and poetry.
       • "Journal of a Tour to Niagara Falls, Montreal, Lake Cham-
       plain, &c," New Jersey Historical Society Proceedings, v. 69,
       pp. 342-62, October, 1951.

938. ZIEBER, Eugenia (Bush) (1833-63)
       April 27-October 26, 1851
       Travel diary; daughter of an Illinois newspaper publisher emi-
grated to Oregon in a family party; from near Birmingham, Iowa;
snowstorm in May; much on other members of the wagon train.
       • "Journal of a Trip to Oregon: Eugenia Zieber," in: Kenneth
       L. Holmes, ed. and comp. Covered Wagon Women: Diaries and
       Letters From the Western Trails 1840-1890. Glendale, Cal.:
       Arthur H. Clark, 1983- ; v. 3, pp. 179-201.

                              1852

939. ANONYMOUS
       May 1, 1852-December, 1857
       Travel diary; McGuirk was the finder of the diary in Virginia
City, Nevada; diary of an unnamed scout traveling with a covered
wagon train from St. Joseph, Missouri, to Placerville, California; editor's paraphrase.
       • Hutcheson, Austin E., ed. "Overland in 1852: The Mc-
       Guirk Diary," Pacific Historical Review v. 13, pp. 426-32,
       1944.

940. BAILEY, Mary Stuart (1830-99)
       April 13-November 8, 1852
       Travel diary; with her physician husband from Sylvania, Ohio,
to Amador County, California by canal boat, train and wagon; via
Chicago, St. Joseph and Salt Lake City; uneventful journey pleasantly
written up.
       • "A Journal of Mary Stuart Bailey," in: Sandra L. Myres, ed.
       Ho for California! San Marino, Cal.: Huntington Library, 1980;
       pp. 49-91.

941. BLACK, Elizabeth G. Dale (1823-1902)
      January 1-May 17, 1852
      Personal diary; businessman's wife lived in Springfield, Illinois;
death of her son; churchgoing; social life.
      • "Took Tea at Mrs. Lincoln's: The Diary of Mrs. William M.
      Black," Illinois State Historical Society Journal, v. 48, pp. 59-
      64, Spring, 1955.

942. BRIGHT, Henry Arthur (1830-84)
      1. May 1-October 15, 1852; Travel diary; English traveler in
the U.S. who met many prominent Americans of the day; from the
East Coast to Virginia and through the Upper Midwest; keen observer;
interesting.
      • Happy Country This America: The Travel Diary of Henry
      Arthur Bright. Anne Henry Ehrenpreis, ed. Columbus: Ohio
      State University Press, 1978.

      2. June 8-23, 1852; Travel diary; stops at Washington, Rich-
mond, Charlottesville and White Sulphur Springs.
      • "A Victorian Englishman on Tour: Henry Arthur Bright's
      Southern Journal, 1852," Anne Henry Ehrenpreis, ed. Virginia
      Magazine of History and Biography, v. 84, pp. 333-61, July,
      1976.

943. BUSH, Edwin Welsh (-1898)
      Travel diary; excerpts; Tennessee native visited Texas twice.
      • Nall, C. T. "The Texas Diary of Edwin Welsh Bush, 1852-
      54," East Texas Historical Journal, v. 5, pp. 94-100, October,
      1967.

944. CLARK, John Hawkins (1813-1900)
      April 22-September 4, 1852
      Travel diary; from Cincinnati to Sacramento to prospect; via
Salt Lake City; good descriptions.
      • "Overland to the Gold Fields of California in 1852: The
      Journal of John Hawkins Clark, Expanded and Revised from
      Notes Made During the Journey," Kansas Historical Quarterly,
      v. 11, pp. 227-96, 1942.

945. CORNELL, William (1802?-91)
      May 4-September 29, 1852
      Travel diary; from Ohio to Oregon; deaths from cholera.
      • "William Cornell's Journal, 1852, with His Overland Guide to
      Oregon," Karen M. Offen and David C. Duniway, eds. Oregon
      Historical Quarterly, v. 79, pp. 359-93, Winter, 1978; v. 80,
      pp. 66-100, Spring, 1979.

946. CUMMINGS, Marett (Mariett) Foster (1827-   )
      1. April 13-August 14, 1852; Travel diary; from Illinois with
her family; daughter of Isaac Foster (q.v.); wore a bloomer costume
to avoid the mud; lengthy description of Salt Lake City and Mormons.

● "Second Trip Across Continent," in: Lucy Ann Sexton, ed. The Foster Family, California Pioneers. Santa Barbara, Cal.: Schauer Printing, 1925; pp. 115-42.

2. April 13-August 14, 1852; "A Trip Across the Continent," in: Kenneth L. Holmes, ed. and comp. Covered Wagon Women. Glendale, Cal.: Arthur H. Clark, 1983- ; v. 4, pp. 117-68.

947. DAVIS, John Shedden
February 8-April 25, 1852
Sea diary; from San Francisco to Hawaii; stops at several islands in the chain.
● "A Scotsman Views Hawaii: An 1852 Log of a Cruise of the Emily Bourne," D. E. Livingston-Little, ed. Journal of the West, v. 9, pp. 196-221, April, 1970.

948. DODSON, John F.
April 13-September 14, 1852
Travel diary; from Buffalo Grove, Illinois, to Bitteroot Valley, Montana Territory; laconic entries; one of the earliest records of the route; "scalped by Blackfeet in sight of the fort."
● "Dodson's Death: The Diary of John F. Dodson: His Journey from Illinois to His Death at Fort Owen in 1852," Montana Magazine of History, v. 3, pp. 24-33, Spring, 1953.

949. GREEN, Jay
May 1-July 27, 1852
Travel diary; by mule-drawn covered wagon from Missouri to Hangtown, now Placerville, California; notes on mileage and terrain.
● Diary of Jay Green. Merrell Kitchen, ed. Stockton, Cal.: San Joaquin Pioneer and Historical Society, 1955.

950. HAMPTON, William H.
March 14, 1852-August 16, 1855; notes on 1856-59
Travel diary; from Illinois by train and wagon; in the diggings of California; mining less than $10 worth of gold per day; price conscious.
● Diary of William H. Hampton, 1852: An Account of His Trip to California in 1852. Sacramento: California Department of Natural Resources, 1958.

951. LUCAS, George A. (1824-1909)
November 7, 1852-November 12, 1908
Personal and business diary; went to Europe in 1857 to travel and remained there till his death; commissioned by fellow Americans to buy art, he gradually developed into a paid dealer; colleague of Samuel P. Avery (q.v.), another American art dealer.
● The Diary of George A. Lucas: An American Art Agent in Paris 1857-1909. Lilian M. C. Randall, transcriber. Princeton: Princeton University Press, 1979.
    REVIEWS: Book Review Index 1980, p. 318; 1981, p. 349. Book Review Digest 1981, pp. 880-81.

202 And So to Bed

951a. McAULEY, Eliza Ann (1835-1919)
     April 7-September 19, 1852
     Travel diary; by wagon with a family party to meet their father
in northern California; across the Des Moines River to Scottsbluff
and Fort Laramie; safe arrival and the pleasure of again having vege-
tables to eat.
     • "Iowa to the 'Land of Gold,'" in: Kenneth L. Holmes, ed.
     and comp. Covered Wagon Women. Glendale, Cal.: Arthur H.
     Clark, 1983- ; v. 4, pp. 33-81.

952. MAGOON, George D. (1825?-)
     February 9, 1852-February 15, 1854
     Travel diary; Muscatine, Iowa, to California via New York City;
by boat to Nicaragua and on to San Francisco; gold seeking and
working in Sacramento; details of mining.
     • "The California Journey of George D. Magoon 1852-1854,"
     Iowa Journal of History and Politics, v. 54, pp. 131-68, April,
     1956.

953. MELROSE, Robert (1828?-98)
     August 11, 1852-July 31, 1857
     Personal diary; Scotsman worked as a laborer for a subsidiary
of the Hudson's Bay Company on Vancouver Island; much on living
and working conditions at Craigflower Farm; itineraries of ships and
coasting vessels calling at the island; line-a-day but with telling detail.
     • "The Diary of Robert Melrose," British Columbia Historical
     Quarterly, v. 7, pp. 119-34, 199-218, 283-95, 1943.

954. PAGE, Charlotte Augusta (1836-1907)
     May 1-October 30, 1852
     Travel diary; sent by her parents to Europe for her health;
daughter of the ship's captain was a companion and pupil; to Mobile
and Liverpool; return; uneventful.
     • Under Sail and in Port in the Glorious 1850's. Salem: Pea-
     body Museum, 1950.

955. PERRY, Matthew Calbraith (1794-1858)
     November, 1852-June 28, 1854
     Diplomatic diary; American naval officer signed a treaty with
Japan opening the country to trade with Westerners; dictated to a
yeoman; Navy Department political machinations; includes some correspondence omitted from the official Narrative; details of life in Macao; passage around the Cape of Good Hope; Singapore, Hong Kong;
treaty negotiations in Japan; coast surveys, sailing instructions; interesting but sometimes stilted.
     • The Japan Expedition, 1852-1854: The Personal Journal of
     Commodore Matthew C. Perry. Roger Pineau, ed. Washington,
     D.C.: Smithsonian Institution Press, 1968.

955a. PRATT, Sarah (1832?-)
     Travel diary; started from Liberty, Michigan, with her father

and siblings; via Iowa City, Des Moines and the Mormon Corridor to San Bernardino, California; ten day layover in Salt Lake City; informative early entries shorten to a line or two.

- "The Daily Notes of Sarah Pratt," in: Kenneth L. Holmes, ed. and comp. Covered Wagon Women. Glendale, Cal.: Arthur H. Clark, 1983- ; v. 4, pp. 169-207.

956. RUDD, Lydia Allen
     May 6-October 27, 1852
     Travel diary; from the Missouri River overland to Oregon; beset by sickness; across the Columbia River in an Indian canoe.
- "Notes by the Wayside En Route to Oregon, 1852," in: Lillian Schlissel. Women's Diaries of the Westward Journey. New York: Schocken, 1982; pp. 187-98.

956a. SAWYER, Francis
      May 9-August 17, 1852
      Travel diary; wife with masculine spelling of her name and husband went west with a one-horse carriage; via St. Joseph, the Black Hills; decided to change their destination from Oregon to California; arrived at Sacramento.
- "Kentucky to California by Carriage and Feather Bed," in: Kenneth L. Holmes, ed. and comp. Covered Wagon Women. Glendale, Cal.: Arthur H. Clark, 1983- ; v. 4, pp. 83-115.

957. SMITH, Jesse Nathaniel (1834-1906)
     May 13, 1852-April 25, 1906
     Personal diary; native New Yorker and youngest cousin of LDS leader Joseph Smith; vitally involved in the Mormon Church's early life; revealing details of practice of polygamy with his five wives; by covered wagon in 1846-47 to Utah; in several settlements there and in Arizona; two missions to Europe.
- Six Decades in the Early West: The Journal of Jesse Nathaniel Smith. Oliver R. Smith, ed. 3rd ed. Provo, Utah: Jesse N. Smith Family Assn., 1970.

958. WARD, John
     October 1, 1852-October 1, 1853
     Office diary; worked in the office of Indian affairs in Santa Fe; dealings with several tribes.
- "Indian Affairs in New Mexico Under the Administration of William Carr Lane: From the Journal of John Ward," Annie Heloise Abel, ed. New Mexico Historical Review, v. 16, pp. 206-32, April, 1941, pp. 328-58, July, 1941.

959. WAYMAN, John Hudson (1820-67)
     March 25, 1852-March 25, 1853
     Travel diary; graduate of the Cincinnati Medical College left his Indiana practice for the diggings; via St. Louis, Forts Kearny and Laramie, Soda Springs to Sonora; lengthy descriptions of the cross country journey deteriorate to weather reports when he begins working a claim.

• A Doctor on the California Trail: The Diary of Dr. John
Hudson Wayman From Cambridge City, Indiana to the Gold
Fields in 1852. Edgeley Woodman Todd, ed. Denver: Old
West Publishing Co., 1971.

960. WENDELL, George Blunt (1831-81)
      September 30, 1852-July 2, 1863; gaps
      Sea diary; letters and diary entries for three voyages; Ports-
mouth, New Hampshire, native shipped as a cabin boy first; two others as a clipper ship master; for salt water historians.
      • George Blunt Wendell: Clipper Ship Master. Mystic, Conn.:
      Marine Historical Association, 1949.

961. WOODHAMS, William H. (1829-91)
      October 24, 1852-March 5, 1855
      Travel diary; by ship from New York around Cape Horn to
California and return through Nicaragua; overland to California and
return by sea; animated by a sense of humor and the diarist's illustrations.
      • "The Diary of William H. Woodhams, 1852-1854: The Great
      Deserts or Around and Across," Charles W. Martin, ed. Ne-
      braska History, v. 61, pp. 1-101, Spring, 1980.

                                1853

962. ANONYMOUS
      19th day of the 1st month--13th day of the 3rd month, 7th
      year of the Kayei Era
      Personal diary; Japanese view of Perry's visit to Japan.
      • "Diary of an Official of the Bakufu," Asiatic Society of Ja-
      pan. Transactions. Series 2, v. 7, pp. 98-119, December,
      1930.

963. ARTHUR, Malvina (1832-1916)
      1853; 1869
      Personal diary; younger sister of U.S. President Chester Alan
Arthur; excerpts from 1853 and 1869 diaries; unhappy family life.
      • "The Diaries of Malvina Arthur: Windows into the Past of
      Our 21st President," Vermont History, v. 38, pp. 177-88, Sum-
      mer, 1970.

964. CLEAVER, Joseph (1833-1909)
      August 31, 1853-November 21, 1854
      Personal diary; pranks, dorm life, studies, the debating and
literary societies by an average student of the times.
      • Diary of a Student at Delaware College, August, 1853, to
      November 1854. William Ditto Lewis, ed. Baltimore: J. H.
      Furst, 1951; reprinted from Delaware Notes, v. 24, pp. 1-87.

965. CUSHMAN, Margery (1836?-68)
      May 7, 1853-May 9, 1859

Personal diary; eldest daughter of Avoyelles Parish, Louisiana, planter; family life; visits to Alexandria; very close to her father; parents died two months apart in 1855 and she taught to support her siblings; somewhat melodramatic but occasionally revealing.
  • Farewell to Youth: The Diary of Margery Cushman. Lafayette, La.: University of Southern Louisiana, 1982.

966. EUBANK, Mary James (1832-   )
      October 6, 1853-January 4, 1854
      Travel diary; by wagon from Glasgow, Kentucky, to Williamson County, Texas; via Memphis and Little Rock.
        • "A Journal of Our Trip to Texas October 6, 1853," W. C. Nunn, ed. Texana, v. 10, pp. 30-44, 1972.

967. EVELYN, George Palmer (1823-89)
      December 13, 1853-June 25, 1855
      Military diary; descendant of diarist John Evelyn; energetic second son and excellent horseman was at Constantinople, and on the Danube; staff appointment to the Turkish Army; missed seeing the charge of the Light Brigade; a fast-paced, critical account of tactics and British mismanagement.
        • Diary of the Crimea. Cyril Falls, ed. London: Duckworth, 1954.

968. GRAVES, Ebenezer
      March 21-August 29, 1853
      Travel diary; Stoddard, New Hampshire, and travels in Maine; sold piece goods; attended a Catholic Mass, "such horrid ceremonies"; paid 42 cents for bed and breakfast and gave the landlady a piece of his mind for her high prices; inhibited by the "Peddlars Law"; valuable for many comments on towns visited, their industries and the textile trade in general.
        • "Journal of a Peddling Trip Kept by Ebenezer Graves of Ashfield, Massachusetts," Old Time New England, v. 56, pp. 81-90, January-March, 1966; pp. 108-16, April-June, 1966.

969. GREGG, David Lawrence (1814?-68)
      October 7, 1853-December 6, 1858
      Personal diary; a rising star in Illinois Democratic politics, he was defeated in his attempt to gain the gubernatorial nomination; his loyalty was rewarded with a post as commissioner to the Hawaiian Kingdom; active in political and social life of the Islands; he and his wife enjoyed a close personal friendship with King Kamehameha IV (q.v.) and Queen Emma; very readable.
        • The Diaries of David Lawrence Gregg: An American Diplomat in Hawaii 1853-1858. Pauline King, ed. Honolulu: Hawaiian Historical Society, 1982.

970. HEAP, Gwinn Harris (1817-87) [A337]
      May-August, 1853
      Travel diary; reprint of A337 together with a letter of Senator

of Thomas H. Benton; speeches supporting a railroad route to the
West Coast; correspondence of Jefferson Davis, Kit Carson and Ed-
ward F. Beale.
- "Central Route to the Pacific," in: LeRoy R. and Ann W.
  Hafen, eds. Central Route to the Pacific with Related Material.
  Glendale, Cal.: Arthur H. Clark, 1957.

971. KETCHAM, Rebecca
     May 22-September 13, 1853
     Travel diary; party of 15 commanded by William H. Gray went
from Independence to Oregon; prim Victorian lady; quarrels within
the party; very detailed, lengthy entries; one of the best overland
diaries.
- "From Ithaca to Clatsop Plains: Miss Ketcham's Journal of
  Travel," Leo M. Kaiser and Priscilla Knuth, eds. Oregon Historical Quarterly, v. 62, pp. 237-87, September, 1961; pp.
  337-402, December, 1961.

972. KNIGHT, Amelia Stewart [A337]
     April 9-September 17, 1853
     Travel diary; mother of seven journeyed with her husband
from Monroe County, Iowa, to Oregon; birth of her eighth child by
a roadside; continues on by canoe and flatboat; straightforward.
- "Diary of Mrs. Amelia Stewart Knight," in: Lillian Schlissel. Women's Diaries of the Westward Journey. New York:
  Schocken, 1982; pp. 199-216.

973. KOREN, Else Elisabeth Hysing (1832-1918)
     September 16, 1853-December 3, 1854
     Travel diary; cultured wife of a Lutheran minister left her na-
tive Norway for Decorah, Iowa; Atlantic voyage; overland journey
and first year of life on the prairie; well-done descriptions of sights
along the way; forced to live with others till their cabin was finished;
much on the life of other Norwegian immigrants in the area.
- The Diary of Elizabeth Koren, 1853-1855. David T. Nelson,
  trans. and ed. New York: Arno Press, 1979; reprint of
  Norwegian-American Historical Association 1955 edition.

974. LANE, William Carr (1789-1862) [A334]
     February 28-December 25, 1853
     Personal diary; Territorial governor of New Mexico; life in
Santa Fe; journey to Washington, D.C.; social life, scenery.
- "William Carr Lane, Diary," G. B. Carson, ed. New Mexico
  Historical Review, v. 39, pp. 181-234, 274-332, 1964.

975. LAW, Rosanna Stuart Glenn (1813-65)
     Personal diary; doctor's widow and mother of two adolescents;
comfortable financially with a "rockaway" and slaves; family visits,
churchgoing; of local and genealogical interest.
- Diary of Rosanna Stuart, January 1-November 5, 1853, Greenwood, South Carolina. Louise M. Watson, intro. Greenwood,
  S. Car.: Greenwood County Historical Society, 1963.

976. LEWIS, John R. C. (1834-98)
February 25, 1853-June 26, 1854
Travel diary; shipped with his twin brother aboard the Macedonian as masters mates; journal and log entries are interspersed with
those of William B. Allen; "Memorandum" written aboard the Vandalia;
a view of Perry (q.v.) and the expedition from two young men of the
ranks; their lives aboard ship, a near mutiny; some grousing; several
seamen's deaths; alien customs and startling scenery in Japan; exuberant and sober by turns.
   • Bluejackets with Perry in Japan. Henry Franklin Graff, ed.
New York: New York Public Library, 1952; reprinted from
New York Public Library Bulletin, v. 55, pp. 3-22, 66-85, 133-
47, 162-80, 255-40, 276-87, 339-50, 1950.

977. MACAULEY, Edward Yorke (1827-94)
February 13, 1853-June 9, 1854
Travel diary; scion of American naval family; with Perry (q.v.)
on the second cruise of the East India squadron to Japan; attitude
of superiority toward things Japanese; life aboard ship and observations ashore.
   • With Perry in Japan: The Diary of Edward Yorke Macauley.
Allan B. Cole, ed. Princeton: Princeton University Press,
1942.

978. MOORE, Charles B. (1822-1901)
December 1, 1853-January 11, 1854
Travel diary; millwright was in Cincinnati on business; Bedini
riot; social life.
   • "A Tennessean Visits Cincinnati in 1853-1854," Larry G.
Bowman and Jack B. Scroggs, eds. Cincinnati Historical So-
ciety Bulletin, v. 36, pp. 151-72, Fall, 1978.

979. MYER, Nathaniel (1786-1870)
March 21-October 4, 1853
Travel diary; overland from Van Buren County, Iowa, to Ore-
gon; via Fort Laramie and Sublette Cutoff; bad weather; a murder.
   • "Journey into Southern Oregon: Diary of a Pennsylvania
Dutchman," Edward B. Ham, ed. Oregon Historical Quarterly,
v. 60, pp. 375-407, September, 1959.

980. PREBLE, George Henry (1816-85) [A292]
April 10, 1853-August 15, 1856
Sea diary; career naval officer on the Macedonia under Commodore Perry (q.v.); ostensibly written for his wife but in defiance of
Perry's order forbidding anyone to tell friends in America of the
movements of the expedition; sailed throughout the Far East, touch-
ing at China and Formosa; well-read, observant individual; very good
diary.
   • The Opening of Japan: A Diary of Discovery in the Far
East, 1853-1856. Boleslaw Szczesniak, ed. Norman: University of Oklahoma Press, 1962.

981. PULSIPHER, John (1827-   )
    1. May 27, 1853-July 4, 1858; a summary of his life to this
point; a mission to the Indians; the Utah War.
    • "From the Journal of John Pulsipher," Western Humanities
    Review, v. 3, pp. 38-55, January, 1949.

    2. 1855-1857; Personal diary; extracts; a mission to the Sho-
shone Indians.
    • "From the Journal of John Pulsipher," Western Humanities
    Review, v. 2, pp. 351-79, October, 1948.

    3. May 1857-May, 1858; Military diary; a Mormon account of
the events in Utah after Brigham Young forbad the entry of U.S.
troops into the Territory; daily life; siege preparations.
    • "Diary of John Pulsipher," in: LeRoy R. and Ann W. Hafen,
    eds. The Utah Expedition 1857-1858. Glendale, Cal.: Arthur
    H. Clark, 1958; pp. 198-219.

982. SCHREIBER, Lady Charlotte Elizabeth (Guest) (1812-95) [B279]
    1. January 18, 1853-February 24, 1891; Personal diary; daugh-
ter of the Earl of Lindsay whose first marriage to a "tradesman"
brought an unfavorable reception from her peers and much happiness;
three years after his death she married her eldest son's tutor; collector of English china; good picture of upper class life; children
growing up, her mother's death; trips abroad.
    • Lady Charlotte Schreiber: Extracts From Her Journal, 1853-
    1891. Earl of Bessborough, ed. London: John Murray, 1952.

    2. Article based on the diary.
    • Earl of Bessborough. "Early Victorian Diary," Quarterly
    Review, v. 283, pp. 44-56, January, 1945.

    3. "Diary Excerpts," in: Philip Dunaway and Mel Evans, eds.
A Treasury of the World's Great Diaries. New York: Doubleday,
1957; pp. 468-76.

983. STEWART, Helen Marnie (1835-73)
    April 1-August 3, 1853
    Travel diary; daughter of Scottish immigrants travelled from
Pennsylvania to the Willamette Valley of Oregon; via Fort Boise; member of the "Lost Wagon Train of 1853."
    • Diary of Helen Stewart 1853. Eugene, Ore.: Lane County
    Pioneer-Historical Society, 1961.

984. SWETT, John (1830?-1913)
    Travel diary; a voyage to San Francisco; fruitless work at the
diggings.
    • "John Swett's Diary: January 25 to November 16, 1853,"
    Will S. Cluff, Jr., ed. California Historical Society Quarterly,
    v. 33, pp. 289-308, December, 1954.

985. TROWBRIDGE, William Petit (-1892)
      July 27-August 15, 1853
      Travel diary; encounters with various tribes and the excava-
tion of a burial mound.
      • "Journal of a Voyage on Puget Sound in 1853 by William
      Petit Trowbridge," Lancaster Pollard, ed. Pacific Northwest
      Quarterly, v. 33, pp. 391-407, 1942.

986. VAN HORNE, George W. (1833-95)
      May 30, 1853-May 11, 1855
      Personal diary; in a law office in Chicopee, Massachusetts;
study; notes on recreational reading; to Akron, Ohio, to study and
return home; long intervals between entries.
      • "The Diary of a Law Student, 1853-1855," Mildred Throne,
      ed. Iowa Journal of History and Politics, v. 55, pp. 167-86,
      April, 1957.

987. WARD, Harriet Sherrill (1803-65)
      April 20-October 9, 1853
      Travel diary; with her husband and children by wagon from
Dartford, Wisconsin, to Plumas County, California; journey unremark-
able but for usual hardships.
      • DeWitt, Ward G. and Florence Stark DeWitt. Prairie Schooner
      Lady: The Journal of Harriet Sherrill Ward, 1853. Los Angeles:
      Westernlore Press, 1959.

                                  1854

988. ANONYMOUS
      September 28-October 2, 1854
      Travel diary; Philadelphian (?), college student or lawyer;
mock-heroic style; contrast between Pennsylvania and Virginia in
slavery, speech, pronunciation, farming, etc.
      • "From Paoli to Frederick in 1854: An Anonymous Travel
      Account," Don Yoder, ed. Pennsylvania Folklife, v. 17, no.
      3, pp. 14-19, 1968.

989. ANDERSON, Nicholas Longworth (1838-92)
      September 1, 1854-July 4, 1857; January 1, 1862-January 13,
      1864
      Personal diary; father of American diplomat Lars Anderson;
first three years at Harvard; studies, visits to and from family; enlistment in the 6th Ohio Volunteer Infantry during the Civil War; on
duty at a court-martial; much drilling and some fighting; Harvard
years are fuller, more interesting entries.
      • The Letters and Journal of General Nicholas Longworth An-
      derson: Harvard, Civil War, Washington, 1854-1892. Isabel
      Anderson, ed. New York: Revell, 1942.

990. BROWN, Thomas Dunlop (1807-74)
      April 10, 1854-January, 1857
      Official diary; sent by Brigham Young with his family and oth-
ers to civilize the Indians; record of farming and mission work.
      • Journal of the Southern Indian Mission: Diary of Thomas D.
      Brown. Juanita Brooks, ed. Logan: Utah State University
      Press, 1972.

991. DAVIDSON, Greenlee (1834-63) [A346]
      November, 1854-March 29, 1863
      Personal diary; native of Rockbridge County, Virginia; student
life at Washington College; enlistment; more letters than diary entries.
      • Captain Greenlee Davidson, C. S. A.: Diary and Letters,
      1851-1863. Charles W. Turner, comp. Verona, Va.: McClure
      Press, 1975.

992. EASTLACK, John Cawman (1808-88)
      March 1, 1854-May 16, 1887
      Personal diary; shipbuilder and manufacturer of pumps in Man-
tua, New Jersey; line or two a day; listing of sales, births, deaths,
marriages; weather; of genealogical interest.
      • Gloucester County in the Eighteen-fifties: Being the Diary
      of John Cawman Eastlack. Woodbury, N.J.: Gloucester County
      Historical Society, 1952.

993. ERSKINE, Michael Henry (1794-1862)
      1. April 23-November 10, 1854; Travel diary; extracts; cattle-
man hoping to sell his herd at a high price to miners in California;
set out from central Texas; hardships of the trail; fewer calamities
than befell other drives.
      • "A Cattle Drive from Texas to California: The Diary of M.
      H. Erskine, 1854," Walter S. Sanderlin, ed. Southwestern His-
      torical Quarterly, v. 67, pp. 397-412, January, 1964.

      2. May 24-November 10, 1854; Trail diary.
      • The Diary of Michael Erskine: Describing His Cattle Drive
      from Texas to California Together with Correspondence from
      the Gold Fields, 1854-1859. J. Evetts Haley, ed. Midland,
      Tx.: Nita Stewart Haley Memorial Library, 1979.

994. FORTEN, Charlotte L. (1838?-1914)
      1. May 24, 1854-May 15, 1864; gap from January, 1860-June
22, 1862; Personal diary; daughter of free black family active in the
Philadelphia abolitionist movement; life as a teacher in Salem, Massachusetts; involved in the Port Royal, South Carolina, "experiment"
wherein 10,000 slaves freed by Union troops early in the Civil War
were recruited in the Army and taught to read and write; reading,
study, abolitionist work; introspective; modest.
      • Journal Ray Allen Billington, intro. New York: Dryden
      Press, 1953.
         REVIEW: Book Review Index 1981, p. 192.

2. October 28, 1862-February 7, 1863; Personal diary; extracts; her own experiences; repeats what others have said to her of life on the Sea Islands.

* "A Social Experiment: The Port Royal Journal of Charlotte L. Forten, 1862-1863," Journal of Negro History, v. 35, pp. 233-64, July, 1950.

995. GREGORY, Hugh McCulloch (1834-1903)
February 24, 1854-February 16, 1855
Sea diary; written by a ship's "boy" who probably got the position through the influence of his father; much description of everyday chores, food, fellow seamen; docked in San Francisco and the Orient; straightforward style.

* The Sea Serpent Journal: Hugh McCulloch Gregory's Voyage Around the World in a Clipper Ship, 1854-55. Robert H. Burgess, ed. (Mariner's Museum Publications, no. 32) Charlottesville: University Press of Virginia, 1975.

996. HODGE, Edward Cooper (1810-94)
January 16, 1854-June 30, 1856
Military diary; served with the 4th Dragoon Guards; went off to war reluctantly; saw major battles; reiterates appalling conditions of weather and poor supply.

* "Little Hodge": Being Extracts from the Diaries and Letters of Colonel Edward Cooper Hodge Written During the Crimean War, 1854-1856. Marquess of Anglesey, ed. London: Cooper, 1971.

997. JEMISON, Robert Seaborn (1824-68)
April 1-May 24, 1854
Travel diary; from Alabama to Austin, San Antonio and Galveston; illness; description of terrain.

* "Journey to Texas, 1854: The Diary of Robert Seaborn Jemison," Hugh Reagan, ed. Alabama Historical Quarterly, v. 33, pp. 190-209, Fall-Winter, 1971.

998. JOLLY, John (1823-99)
April 12, 1854-July 27, 1855
Personal diary; Englishman immigrated to the California diggings; laconic entries on work but no mention of his take; weather unusually cold and rainy.

* Gold Spring Diary: The Diary of John Jolly. Carlo M. De Ferri, ed. Sonora, Cal.: Tuolumne County Historical Society, 1966; 500 copies.

999. LAWRIE, Arthur (1832-   )
December 5, 1854-January 20, 1855
Travel diary; Indiana farmer went to Texas to obtain land for a French colony at Reunion.

* "Lawrie's Trip to Northeast Texas, 1854-1855," Southwestern Historical Quarterly, v. 48, pp. 238-53, 1944.

1000.   LOMAX, Elizabeth Lindsay (1796-   )
        January 1, 1854-February 2, 1863
        Personal diary; Virginia planter's widow supported herself by
giving music lessons; in Washington much of the time but with little
sense of the place; social life; comments on the visit of the Prince of
Wales; moved to Charlottesville early in the war; early years are less
interesting than wartime.
        • Leaves from an Old Washington Diary, 1854-1863. · Lindsay
        Lomax Wood, ed. New York: Books, Inc., 1943.

1001.   LYON, Alanson Forman (1798-1901)
        September 4-28, 1854
        Travel diary; boat trip upriver with his son to look over tim-
ber; scenery, hunting.
        • "A Trip Up the Menominee River in 1854: Alanson Forman
        Lyon," Michigan History, v. 47, pp. 301-11, December, 1963.

1002.   MILLWARD, Benjamin (-1904)
        March 4-April 21, 1854
        Travel diary; by packet from Liverpool to New York.
        • "The Voyage of an Iowa Immigrant," Timothy Walch, ed.
Annals of Iowa, v. 44, pp. 137-45, Fall, 1977.

1003.   REES, William (-1858)
        1854
        Travel diary; extracts; at Philadelphia: "We went up 5 or 6
stories high, and saw the city in every direction"; visits to Quaker
meetings along the way.
        • "From Indiana to North Carolina in 1854: The Diary of
        William Rees," Opal Thornburg, ed. Quaker History, v. 59,
        pp. 67-80, Autumn, 1970.

1004.   SITWELL, Lady Louisa Lucy Hely (1830-1911)
        October 8, 1854-December 25, 1855
        Personal diary; social doings, family births and news of the
Crimea.
        • "English Scenes During the Crimean War: Excerpts From
        the Journal of Louisa Lucy Hely Hutchinson, Afterwards Lady
        Sitwell, 1852-8," Osbert Sitwell, ed. Life and Letters To-day,
        v. 29, pp. 208-24, June, 1941.

1005.   SPROSTON, John Glendy (1828-62)
        March 8-August 10, 1854
        Personal diary; naval career man and officer on the frigate
Macedonian with Perry's (q.v.) fleet to Japan; at Yedo Bay and Si-
moda; good descriptions.
        • A Private Journal of John Glendy Sproston, U.S.N. Shio
        Sakanishi, ed. Tokyo: Sophia University, 1940.

1006.   STARLEY, James (1817?-1914)
        April 14, 1854-January 15, 1858

Travel diary; Mormon and his family left England shortly after their conversion for Americâ; notes on life in Utah.
- "Journal of James Starley," Utah Historical Quarterly, v. 9, pp. 169-78, July/October, 1941.

1007. WALKER, Charles L. (1832-1904)
November 4, 1854-February 11, 1899
Personal diary; English immigrant and Mormon convert went to Salt Lake City; well-read book lover and versifier; marriage and a calling to the Cotton Mission in St. George where he spent the remainder of his life; persecution for polygamy by the U.S. government; active in church affairs; plain-spoken, revealing record.
- The Diary of Charles L. Walker. A. Karl Larson and Katharine Miles Larson, eds. 2 vols. Logan: Utah State University Press, 1980.

1855

1008. ARTEM'YEV, Aleksandr Ivanovich (1820-   )
June 1, 1855-May 31, 1857
Personal diary; extracts; statistician for the Ministry of Interior under Alexander II; a progressive bureaucrat.
- Lincoln, W. Bruce. "Marginalia: Russia on the Eve of Reform: A Chinovnik's View," Slavonic and East European Review [Great Britain], v. 59, pp. 264-71, 1981.

1009. BARKER, Jane Sophia Harden (1807-76)
1855-1857
Personal diary; extracts; daughter of Anglo-Irish-Scots gentry married a Liverpool clergyman who became Bishop of Sydney, Australia; their Evangelical fervor put them at odds with their peers in Australia.
- "Mrs. Barker and Her Diary," K. J. Cable, ed. Journal of the Royal Australian Historical Society, v. 54, pp. 67-105, 1968.

1010. BEAN, George W.
April 6, 1855-February 28, 1857
Personal diary; Mormon missionary lived at Las Vegas Springs, New Mexico Territory; family life; farm and religious work.
- "The Journal of George W. Bean," Harry C. Dees, ed. Nevada Historical Society Quarterly, v. 15, pp. 3-30, Fall, 1972.

1011. CARROLL, Lewis (Charles Lutwidge Dodgson) (1832-98) [B 261]
1. January 1, 1855-December 23, 1897; gap May, 1858-May, 1862; Personal diary; English mathematician and children's writer; opens with reception of degree from Oxford; reading, writing, family life, work; knew many prominent people in London in his day.
- The Diaries: Now First Edited and Supplemented by Roger Lancelyn Green. London: Cassell, 1953.

REVIEW: <u>Book Review Digest</u> 1954, pp. 155-56.

2. "Diary Excerpts," in: Philip Dunaway and Mel Evans, eds. <u>A Treasury of the World's Great Diaries</u>. New York: Doubleday, 1957; pp. 95-103.

1012. DOTY, James (1779-1865) [A239]
February 13-December 29, 1855
Official diary; secretary for Indian treaties to Governor Isaac I. Stevens of the Washington Territory; negotiations transcribed.
   • <u>Journal of Operations of Governor Isaac Ingalls Stevens of Washington Territory in 1855</u>. Edward J. Kowrach, ed. Fairfield, Wash.: Ye Galleon Press, 1978; 442 copies.
      REVIEW: <u>Pacific Northwest Quarterly</u>, v. 71, p. 140, July, 1980.

1013. HALLIDAY, John (1815-1906)
August 28-September 16, 1855
Travel diary; Scottish shoemaker and his family on a voyage to America.
   • "Diary Excerpts," in: Philip Dunaway and Mel Evans, eds. <u>A Treasury of the World's Great Diaries</u>. New York: Doubleday, 1957; pp. 43-49.

1014. HARRIS, Townsend (1804-78) [A342]
May 21, 1855-June 9, 1858
Personal diary; American diplomat and consul to Japan; revised portion includes the first printing of Harris' mission to Siam; the Japanese portion is presented without abridgement; from diplomacy to his incubating canary; very readable.
   • <u>The Complete Journal of Townsend Harris</u>. Mario E. Cosenza, intro. Douglas MacArthur II, preface. 2nd ed. rev. Rutland, Vt.: Tuttle, 1959.

1015. HEUSKEN, Henry C. J. (1832-61)
October 25, 1855-June 8, 1858; January 1-8, 1861
Personal/diplomatic diary; first secretary of the American legation and interpreter under Townsend Harris (q.v.); by steam frigate from New York to Japan via Cape Town; much concerned with Harris' diplomatic mission; sympathetic to Japanese; earlier entries more in the style of a travel book.
   • <u>Japan Journal 1855-61</u>. Jeannette C. van der Corput and Robert A. Wilson, trans. and eds. New Brunswick: Rutgers University Press, 1964.

1016. JOHNSTON, Eliza Griffin
1. Article based on the diary of the wife of Brigadier General Albert Sidney Johnston; she got him a job as paymaster to frontier forts in Texas; journey there and life on the post.
   • Shaw, Arthur Marvin. "Regimental Pilgrimage: Diary of Mrs. Albert Sidney Johnston, October, 1855-May, 1856,"

Kentucky Historical Society Register, v. 50, pp. 293-306,
October, 1952.

2. October 29, 1855-May 7, 1856; Personal diary; weather,
scenery and observations on others in the group traveling from St.
Louis to San Antonio; party included Robert E. Lee and other figures
prominent in the Civil War.
- "The Diary of Eliza (Mrs. Albert Sidney) Johnston: The Second Cavalry Comes to Texas," Charles P. Roland and Richard C. Robbins, eds. Southwestern Historical Quarterly, v. 60, pp. 463-500, April, 1957.

1017. KELLY, Plympton J. (1828?-1906)
November 22, 1855-May 3, 1856
Military diary; Kentucky native worked donation lands; in the
1st Regiment of Oregon Mounted Volunteers; service from The Dalles
to Forts Henrietta and Walla Walla; from the Blue Mountains to the
Simcoe Mountains; life on the march.
- We Were Not Summer Soldiers: The Indian War Diary of Plympton J. Kelly, 1855-1856. William N. Bischoff, ed. Tacoma: Washington State Historical Society, 1976.

1018. MILLER, Henry W.
July 5, 1855-November 9, 1856
Personal diary; Mormon mission to the Cherokees and Creek
Indians.
- "Missionaries of the Latter Day Saints Church in Indian Territory," Chronicles of Oklahoma, v. 13, pp. 196-213, 1935.

1019. SIMS, Mary Ann Owen (1830-   )
July 21, 1855-April 24, 1861; many gaps
Personal diary; Arkansas widow's life after the death of her
doctor husband; family life; much sadness.
- "Private Journal of Mary Ann Owen Sims," Clifford Dale Whitman, ed. Arkansas Historical Quarterly, v. 35, pp. 142-87, Summer, 1976; pp. 261-91, Autumn, 1976.

1020. SNEDAKER, Morris Jackson (1818-82)
September 11, 1855-November 8, 1856
Missionary diary; Mormon on a proselytizing in Texas; Salt
Lake City to Frankfort, Kentucky; to Houston; beaten by a mob for
being a Mormon.
- "The Diary of Morris Jackson Snedaker, 1855-1856," Norman B. Ferris, ed. Southwestern Historical Quarterly, v. 66, pp. 516-46, April, 1963.

1021. STEWART, James Green (1820?-81)
February 6-November 5, 1855
Travel diary; Overland from Fort Resolution to seek survivors
of Franklin's Arctic expedition.
- Holmgren, Eric J. "The Diary of J. G. Stewart, 1855," Beaver [Canada], v. 311, pp. 12-17, Spring, 1980.

1022.   STEWART, James R. (1829-68)
        April 19, 1855-November, 1860
        Personal diary; came to Kansas from Pennsylvania with a party
of anti-slavery and temperance settlers; saddler by trade who read
law; early entries have information on the settlement of the county.
        •   "The Diary of James R. Stewart, Pioneer of Osage County,"
        Kansas Historical Quarterly, v. 17, pp. 1-36, February, 1949,
        pp. 122-75, May, 1949, pp. 254-95, August, 1949; pp. 360-
        97, November, 1949.

1023.   TODD, John B. S. (1814-72)
        May 28-December 2, 1855
        Expedition diary; from Fort Laramie to Fort Pierre via Fort
Kearny; good description of a battle with Indians.
        •   "The Harney Expedition Against the Sioux: The Journal
        of Capt. John B. S. Todd," Ray H. Mattison, ed. Nebraska
        History, v. 43, pp. 89-130, June, 1962.

1024.   "TWAIN, Mark" (Samuel Langhorne Clemens) (1835-1910)
        1. June, 1855- ; many gaps; Personal diary; American jour-
nalist and novelist some entries cryptic, some extremely detailed;
range from steamboating days to life in the gold camps to trips
abroad.
        •   Mark Twain's Notebooks and Journals, Frederick Anderson,
        ed. 3 vols. Berkeley: University of California Press, 1975.

        2. "Diary Excerpts," in: Philip Dunaway and Mel Evans,
        eds. A Treasury of the World's Great Diaries. New York: Double-
        day, 1957; pp. 91-94.

1025.   WEIR, Robert (1836?-1905)
        August 19, 1855-January 1, 1858
        Personal diary; son of the painter Robert Walter Weir; "in
debt and disgraced" boarded the Clara at New Bedford, Massachusetts;
seasick and heartsick; sailed around the Cape of Good Hope to the
Indian Ocean; saw Napoleon's tomb on St. Helen's; quilted to pass
the time; his sketches are reproduced.
        •   Harevan, Tamarra K. "The Adventures of a Haunted Whal-
        ing Man," American Heritage, v. 28, pp. 46-65, August, 1977.

                                    1856

1026.   ANONYMOUS
        October-November, 1856
        Rescue diary; laconic notes on the effort to rescue the hand-
cart immigrants from death in an early snowstorm 300 miles from civi-
lization.
        •   "Journal of the First Rescue Party," Hafen, LeRoy R. and
        Ann W. Hafen. Handcarts to Zion: The Story of a Unique
        Western Migration 1856-1860. Glendale, Cal.: Arthur H.
        Clark, 1960; pp. 222-26.

1027.   BEALE, Joseph Bogg (1841-1926)
        January 1, 1856-October 15, 1826; gaps
        Personal diary; Philadelphia native encouraged in artistic en-
deavors by his family; during the Civil War did sketches for Harper's and Frank Leslie's Illustrated Magazine; family life, school, coming war; artistic work.
        • "Education of an Artist: The Diary of Joseph Boggs Beale,
        1856-1862," Pennsylvania Magazine of History and Biography,
        v. 97, pp. 485-510, October, 1973.

1028.   COLT, Miriam Davis (1817-   ) [A344]
        January 5-July 16, 1856
        Travel diary; American daughter of a poor tanner married an
English peer and went with him, his siblings and other Britons to
settle a vegetarian colony in Kansas; by railroad, steamer and wagon
from Montreal to Kansas; disappointments with conditions on arrival.
        • "Diary," in: Cathy Luchetti and Carol Olwell, eds. Women
        of the West. St. George, Utah: Antelope Island Press, 1982;
        pp. 79-87.

1029.   DE LACY, Walter W.
        June 12-August 29, 1856
        Military diary; battle of Grande Ronda.
        • "The Last Campaign of the Yakima Indian War," Yale Uni-
versity Library Gazette, v. 26, pp. 53-72, October, 1951.

        EBEY, Emily Palmer (-1863) see No. 1030

1030-   EBEY, Isaac Neff (1818-57)
  31.   October 13, 1856-January 6, 1857; entries after December 9
        made by Mrs. Ebey
        Personal diary; life on a farm on Whidbey Island; interesting
account of work, prices.
        • "Diary of Colonel Isaac N. and Mrs. Emily Ebey, 1856-1857,"
        Kibbe, L. A., ed. Pacific Northwest Quarterly, v. 33, pp. 297-
        323, 1942.

1032.   GALLOWAY, Andrew [A344]
        June-September, 1856
        Travel diary; short entries, notes of weather, distances cov-
ered, deaths; Iowa City to Salt Lake City.
        • "Official Journal of the First Handcart Company," in: LeRoy
        R. and Ann W. Hafen. Handcarts to Zion: The Story of a
        Unique Western Migration 1856-1860. Glendale, Cal.: Arthur H.
        Clark, 1960; pp. 199-213; reprinted from Utah Genealogical and
        Historical Magazine, v. 17, pp. 247-49; v. 18, pp. 17-21, 49-56.

1033.   JACOBS, Victoria (1838-61)
        June 13, 1856-February 20, 1857
        Personal diary; British-born girl of Polish-Jewish lineage kept
a diary for her fiancé; scenes of early San Diego; "Steamer day"
when boats arrived with mail; social life; ephemeral.

• <u>Diary of a San Diego Girl, 1856.</u> Sylvia Arden, ed. Santa
Monica, Cal.: N. B. Stern, 1974; 500 copies.

1034. LAWRENCE, Mary Chipman (1827-1906)
        November 25, 1856-June 13, 1860
        Sea diary; captain's wife and five-year-old daughter accom-
panied him on a voyage from New Bedford; touched at Hawaii, the
Marquesas, Arctic Ocean, New Zealand and return; feminine view of
a whaler's work with flashes of wit.
        • <u>The Captain's Best Mate; The Journal of Mary Chipman</u>
        <u>Lawrence on the Whaler "Addison," 1856-1860.</u> Stanton Gar-
        ner, ed. Providence: Brown University Press, 1966.

1035. LEEDS, George (1816-85)
        June 20, 1856-July 27, 1857
        Personal diary; church work; family life.
        • "Diary of Reverend George Leeds, D.D., Rector of St.
        Peter's Episcopal Church, Salem, 1855-60," <u>Essex Institute</u>
        <u>Historical Collections</u>, v. 90, pp. 154-66, April, 1954.

1036. MILLER, Jacob (1835-1911)
        April 21, 1856-May 24, 1904; a few entries each year
        Personal diary; Mormon convert and immigrant to Utah; active
in church work; missions to Arizona and Australia; school teaching;
civic affairs; work on the Denver and Rio Grande Railroad.
        • <u>Journal.</u> Joseph Royal Miller and Elna Miller, comp. Salt
        Lake City: Mercury Publishing, 1967.

1037. PAGE, Alvin R., Jr. (1840-58)
        September 20, 1856-January 30, 1857
        Sea diary; voyage from the U.S. to England and Wales.
        • "Extracts from Journal of Alvin R. Page, Jr.," in: Char-
        lotte A. Page. <u>Under Sail and in Port in the Glorious 1850's.</u>
        Salem: Peabody Museum, 1950; pp. 64-79.

1038. POWELL, William Henry (1827-95)
        November 15-21, 1856
        Military diary; account of an assault on the Barrier Forts near
Canton, China.
        • "Our First 'War' in China: The Diary of William Henry
        Powell, 1856," Julius W. Pratt, ed. <u>American Historical Re-</u>
        <u>view</u>, v. 53, pp. 776-86, July, 1948.

1039. POWERS, Mary Rockwood (-1858)
        April 7-October, 1856
        Travel diary; from Palmyra, Wisconsin, overland by rail and
wagon; with her husband and three children; many hardships.
        • "A Woman's Overland Journal to California, 1856," <u>The</u>
        <u>Amateur Book Collector</u>, v. 1, nos. 1-5, September, 1950-
        January, 1951.

1040. RUFFIN, Edmund (1794-1865) [A347]
       October, 1856-June, 1863
       Personal diary; vehement defender of slavery and ardent se-
cessionist; participant in the major events of the pre-war and war
years; leading Tidewater planter and advocate of scientific agriculture;
committed suicide rather than live under Reconstruction; serious, wide-
ranging; good picture of his class in the South but atypical; excellent.
       • The Diary of Edmund Ruffin. William Kauffman Scarborough,
       ed. 2 vols. Baton Rouge: Louisiana State University Press,
       1972-76.
           REVIEWS: Book Review Digest 1973, p. 1132. Book Re-
           view Index 1978, p. 418.

1041. SPYKER, Leonidas Pendleton (1818-67)
       Weather diary; extracts; plantation owner in Bossier and More-
house Parishes, Louisiana; "earliest known continuous instrumental
meteorological data points for northeastern Louisiana."
       • Weather Extractions From the Diary of Leonidas Pendleton
       Spyker July 1, 1856 to October 31, 1860. Michael R. Helfert,
       ed. (Occasional Publications of the Northern Louisiana Cli-
       matic Research Center, No. 2, May, 1978) Monroe, La.: North-
       eastern Louisiana University, Climatic Research Center, 1978.

1042. WESLEY, John (1819-1900)
       July 28, 1856-
       Travel diary; Methodist preacher went from Birmingham to
New York City with his wife and children; on to Adrian, Michigan.
       • "From England to the United States in 1856: The Diary of
       John Wesley," Lewis Beeson, ed. Michigan History, v. 48,
       pp. 47-65, March, 1964.

                                  1857

1043. BODICHON, Barbara Leigh Smith (1827-91)
       December 6, 1857-June 12, 1858
       Travel diary; English feminist and founder of Girton College;
interested in education; on a wedding journey with her husband;
down the Mississippi by steamboat; in New Orleans; great interest in
slaves; good description of life in the South just prior to the Civil
War.
       • An American Diary, 1857-8. Joseph W. Reed, Jr., ed.
       London: Routledge and Kegan Paul, 1972.

1044. BOZEMAN, Henry I.
       January 1-December 31, 1857
       Plantation diary; weather, work; laconic.
       • "A Clark County Plantation Journal for 1857," Farrar New-
       berry, ed. Arkansas Historical Quarterly, v. 18, pp. 401-
       09, Winter, 1959.

1045.   CARPENTER, Helen (1838?-1917)
        May 26-October 22, 1857
        Travel diary; young bride with husband and relatives left
Kansas for Grass Valley, California; excellent account of the crossing complete with Indian raids on the stock and family squabbles.
        • "A Trip Across the Plains in an Ox Wagon, 1857," in:
        Sandra L. Myres, ed. Ho for California! San Marino, Cal.:
        Huntington Library, 1980; pp. 93-188.

1046.   DU BOIS, John Van Deusen (1843?-79)
        1.   April 19, 1857-March 30, 1861; Military diary; West Point
graduate and native New Yorker; in three campaigns: Gila-Apache
of 1857, Utah War of 1858 and Navajo actions of 1859; well-written;
good description of conditions and occasionally sympathetic to the Indians he fought.
        • Campaigns in the West, 1856-1861: The Journal and Letters
        of Colonel John Van Deusen Du Bois. George P. Hammond,
        ed. Tucson: Arizona Pioneers Historical Society, 1949.

        2.   Military diary; competent but often tactless and opinionated
officer; at the Battle of Wilson's Creek; well-versed in military tactics.
        • "The Civil War Journal and Letters of Colonel John Van
        Deusen DuBois, April 12, 1861, to October 16, 1862," Jared
        C. Lobdell, ed. Missouri Historical Review, v. 60, pp. 436-
        59, July, 1966; v. 61, pp. 21-50, October, 1967.

1047.   EBEY, Winfield Scott
        1.   August 14, 1857-April 5, 1860; Personal diary; brother of
the colonel (q.v.) recounts his murder by Indians.
        • "The Death of Colonel Isaac N. Ebey, 1857," Harry N. M.
Winton, ed. Pacific Northwest Quarterly, v. 33, pp. 325-47, 1942.

        2.   June 4-November, 1862; Personal diary; details of work
and prices; good description of living conditions and landscape.
        • "The Powder River and John Day Mines in 1862; Diary of
        Winfield Scott Ebey," Pacific Northwest Quarterly, v. 33, pp.
        409-37, 1942; v. 34, pp. 39-86, 1943.

1048.   "ELIOT, George" (Mary Ann Evans) (1819-80) [B265]
        December 6, 1857-March 5, 1858
        Personal diary; British novelist; excerpts from the expurgated
remainder of her diary; happiness at the favorable reviews of Scenes
of Clerical Life and an essay on "How I Came to Write Fiction."
        • "Diary Excerpts," in: Mary Jane Moffat and Charlotte
        Painter, eds. Revelations: Diaries of Women. New York:
        Random House, 1974; pp. 218-24.

1049.   LAZELLE, Henry M. (1832-1917)
        April 21-June 13, 1857
        Personal diary; Massachusetts native and West Point graduate;

participated in the Bonneville campaign against the Apaches; well-
read and a critical observer with a Puritanical view of people and
customs of the Southwest; entertaining writing at the expense of his
fellows.
   • "Puritan and Apache: A Diary," Frank D. Reeve, ed.
   New Mexico Historical Review, v. 23, pp. 269-301, October,
   1948; v. 24, pp. 12-53, January, 1949.

1050. LOWE, Percival G. (1828-)
       May-September, 1857
       Military diary; in charge of transportation for the Cheyenne
expedition from Fort Kearny and return.
   • "Percival G. Lowe's Journal of the Sumner Wagon Train,"
   in: LeRoy R. and Ann W. Hafen. Relations with the Indians
   of the Plains, 1857-1861. Glendale, Cal.: Arthur H. Clark,
   1959; pp. 49-96.

1051. MARSDEN, William (1814-90)
       June 4, 1857-December 24, 1871; many gaps
       Personal diary; Mormon convert immigrated to Utah; life in
Provo; church work; employed as Recorder of Consecration deeds;
planted the first cotton in Deseret.
   • "Journal and Diary of William Marsden," Hearth Throbs of
   the West, v. 12, pp. 141-80, 1951.

1052. MORAN, Benjamin (1820-86) [B259]
       January 26, 1857-May 31, 1865
       Personal diary; secretary to the U.S. Legation in London un-
der George M. Dallas and Charles Francis Adams (q.v.); life in London through American eyes; English diplomacy in the period before
and during the Civil War; interesting, well-written.
   • The Journal of Benjamin Moran, 1857-1865. Sarah Agnes
   Wallace and Frances Elma Gillespie, eds. Chicago: University
   of Chicago Press, 1948.

1053. PHELPS, John Wolcott (1813-85)
       June-September, 1857
       Military diary; West Point graduate; U.S. expedition against
the Mormons; commenced at Fort Leavenworth; fought Indians; to
Fort Kearny; arrival at Ham's Fork.
   • "Diary of Captain Phelps," in: LeRoy R. and Ann W.
   Hafen. The Utah Expedition 1857-1858. Glendale, Cal.:
   Arthur H. Clark, 1958; pp. 90-138.

1054. REMMONDS, Martha Jane Roundy (1818-1907)
       1857-1895
       Personal diary; extracts; family life; nine years of marriage
to a sea captain; church work and charity.
   • Lovett, Robert W. "The Many Sides of Martha Jane,"
   Essex Institute Historical Quarterly, v. 97, pp. 277-91, October, 1961.

1055. SANFORD, Mollie Dorsey (1839-1915)
       March 23, 1857-January 15, 1866; gaps
       Personal diary; eldest daughter of an Indiana family accom-
panied her parents and seven siblings west; homesteading in Nebraska; a move to Denver; teaching school; courtship, marriage and
the birth of a son; very well done.
       • Mollie: The Journal of Mollie Dorsey Sanford in Nebraska
       and Colorado Territories, 1857-1866. Donald F. Danker, ed.
       Lincoln: University of Nebraska Press, 1959.

1056. SCOTT, Charles A. (1830-   )
       March 28, 1857-October 22, 1861
       Personal diary; with Federal troops to Utah in the "Utah
War"; from Fort Leavenworth to Salt Lake City; occupation.
       • "Charles A. Scott's Diary of the Utah Expedition, 1857-
       1861," Robert E. Stowers and John M. Ellis, eds. Utah His-
       torical Quarterly, v. 28, pp. 154-76, April, 1960; pp. 388-
       402, October, 1960.

1057. SEARS, Captain Joshua
       April 6, 1857-December 16, 1859
       Sea diary; New England clipper ship captain; weather, dis-
tances and philosophizing.
       • "Diary Excerpts," in: Philip Dunaway and Mel Evans. A
       Treasury of the World's Great Diaries. New York: Doubleday,
       1957; pp. 77-80.

1058. SWIFT, Elijah (1831-   )
       October 19-November 1, 1857
       Travel diary; from Boston to Tallahassee by rail, steamboat,
wagon and stage; daunting.
       • "Elijah Swift's Travel Journal from Massachusetts to Florida,
       1857," Virginia Steele Wood, ed. Florida Historical Quarterly,
       v. 55, pp. 181-88, October, 1976.

1059. TUTTLE, Newton (1825-1907)
       August 8-December 5, 1857
       Military journal; Mormon from Bountiful; mobilized by Brigham
Young's order.
       • "A Territorial Militiaman in the Utah War: Journal of New-
       ton Tuttle," Hamilton Gardner, ed. Utah Historical Quarterly,
       v. 22, pp. 297-320, October, 1954.

1060. WHITEHEAD, Alexander (1840?-76)
       June 14, 1857-May 23, 1858
       Sea diary; teen-aged cabin boy sailed from England to Shang-
hai; very short entries but much about the crew's life and work
aboard a sailing vessel.
       • "China and Back 1857," in: R. C. Bell, ed. Diaries from
       the Days of Sail. New York: Holt,.Rinehart and Winston,
       1974; pp. 70-110.

<u>1858</u>

1061. ACKLEY, Richard Thomas (1832-81)
        June 21, 1858-January 1, 1859
        Travel diary; From Fremont County, Iowa, with three friends;
carried trade goods to Salt Lake City; Mormon State Fair; Camp Floyd;
Col. Albert Sidney Johnston and U.S. troops.
        • "Across the Plains in 1858," <u>Utah Historical Quarterly</u>, v.
        9, pp. 190-228, 1941.

1062. BARKER, Anselm Holcomb (1822-95)
        September 20, 1858-
        Travel diary; on the Ox Bow Trail; up the Platte River and
on the Emigrant Trail to present-day Denver.
        • <u>Anselm Holcomb Barker Pioneer Building and Early Settler</u>
        <u>of Auraria: His Diary of 1858</u>. Nolie Mumey, ed. Denver:
        Golden Bell Press, 1959.

1063. BOLLER, Henry A.
        September 1-December 31, 1858
        Fur trade diary; Missouri trader in the Fort Atkinson, North
Dakota, area; dealings with Indians of several tribes.
        • "Journal of a Trip to, and Residence in, the Indian Coun-
        try," Ray H. Mattison, intro. <u>North Dakota History</u>, v. 33,
        pp. 260-315, Summer, 1966.

1064. BRIGGS, Charles Edward (1833-94)
        January 6-March 29, 1858
        Travel diary; Harvard medical school graduate went as a
surgeon on a brig to the Azores and return; sightseeing in the islands.
        • <u>Civil War Surgeon in a Colored Regiment</u>. Walter De Blois
        Briggs, ed. Berkeley, Cal.: The Editor, 1960; pp. 29-56.

1065. CALDER, William Cormack (1825-1905)
        May 22-October 10, 1858
        Personal diary; life aboard the <u>Bee</u> and in Adelaide.
        • "Jottings by the Way or Journal of a Trip From Edinburgh
        to Adelaide, South Australia, with a Few Weeks' Residence
        There by William Cormack Calder, 1858," C. G. Kerr, ed.
        <u>South Australiana</u>, v. 8, pp. 43-83, 1969.

        CORMANY, Rachel Bowman (1836-99) <u>see</u> No. 1066

1066. CORMANY, Samuel Eckerman (1838-1921)
        October 30, 1858-August 27, 1865; Rachel
        April, 1859-September 1, 1865; Samuel
        Personal diaries; students met and married at Ohio's Otterbein
College just prior to the Civil War; their diaries are presented in al-
ternate chapters; both were from rural Midwestern families active in
United Brethren Churches; family and conjugal life; he served in the

16th Pennsylvania Volunteer Cavalry; she remained in Pennsylvania
with their baby in a town twice overrun by Rebels; excellent social
history.
> • The Cormany Diaries: A Northern Family in the Civil War.
> James C. Mohr, ed. Pittsburgh: University of Pittsburgh
> Press, 1982.
> > REVIEW: Library Journal, v. 107, p. 1981, October 15,
> > 1982.

1067. GILLESPIE, Emily Hawley (1838?-)
       1. 1858-1888; Personal diary; Iowa farmwife recorded her
harvest of produce; finances; teaching; her marriage.
> • "'My Only Confidant'--The Life and Diary of Emily Hawley
> Gillespie," Judy Nollte Lensink, et al., eds. Annals of Iowa,
> v. 45, pp. 288-312, Spring, 1980.

> 2. Article with extracts describing one-room schools in Iowa.
> • Smith, L. Glen. "The Gillespie/Huftalen Diaries--A Window
> on American Education," Vitae Scholasticae, v. 2, pp. 243-66,
> Spring, 1983.

1068. GRIMBALL, John Berkley (1800-93)
       April 1, 1858-June 17, 1865
       Personal diary; Princeton graduate; owned a plantation in
Charleston County, South Carolina; social and family life; many actions at law; finances; large investments in Confederate bonds which
were worthless at the war's end.
> • "Diary of John Berkley Grimball, 1858-1865," South Caro-
> lina Historical Magazine, v. 56, pp. 8-30, January, 1955;
> pp. 92-114, April, 1955, pp. 157-77, July, 1955, pp. 205-25,
> October, 1955; v. 57, pp. 28-50, January, 1956, pp. 88-102,
> April, 1956.

1069. HAWTHORNE, Nathaniel (1804-64) [A280, B261]
       January-December, 1858
       Personal diary; article based American novelist's newly dis-
covered diary; family life; begins work on The Marble Faun.
> • Hart, James D. "Hawthorne's Italian Diary," American
> Literature, v. 34, pp. 562-67, January, 1963.

1070. KIRK, Dr. John (1832-)
       March 3, 1858-December 13, 1863
       Exploration diary; went with David Livingstone (q.v.) to ex-
plore the Zambesi; notes on flora, fauna, weather, natives; relations
with others in the party.
> • The Zambesi Journal and Letters of Dr. John Kirk 1858-63.
> Reginald Foskett, ed. Edinburgh: Oliver and Boyd, 1965.

1071. LINDSEY, Sarah Crosland (-1876)
       1. March 18-April 19, 1858; Travel diary; couple with injunc-
tion to visit isolated Friends came to Kansas; appalled but not deterred
by frontier conditions; from St. Louis to Kansas City.

• "English Quakers Tour Kansas 1858: From the Journal of Sarah Lindsey," Kansas Historical Quarterly, v. 13, pp. 36-52, 1944.

2. November 19, 1859-January 3, 1860; Travel diary; visits to Salem and Eugene, Oregon; prison visit.
• "Willamette Valley in 1859: The Diary of a Tour," Oregon Historical Quarterly, v. 46, pp. 235-54, September, 1945.

3. June 10, 1859-August 18, 1860; Travel diary; transcription omits personal and religious material; mining area, San Francisco; lengthy entries by observant individual.
• "An English Quaker Tours California: The Journal of Sarah Lindsey 1859-1860," Sheldon G. Jackson, ed. Southern California Quarterly, v. 51, pp. 1-33, March, 1969, pp. 153-75, June, 1969, pp. 221-46, September, 1969.

1072. MANLY, Dr. Basil (1798-1868)
December 11, 1858-March 14, 1867
Personal diary; former president of the University of Alabama and Baptist pastor; the Civil War and its aftermath; social notes; much on the home life of non-combatants.
• "The Diary of Dr. Basil Manly, 1858-1867," W. Stanley Hoole, ed. Alabama Review, v. 4, pp. 127-49, April, 1951, pp. 221-36, July, 1951, pp. 270-89, October, 1951; v. 5, pp. 61-74, January, 1952, pp. 142-55, April, 1952.

1073. MENDENHALL, Abby Grant (1832-1900)
May 31, 1858-January 5, 1900; gaps
Personal diary; Massachusetts native lived in Minneapolis her entire married life; line-a-day entries; pious thoughts and lamentations.
• Some Extracts from the Personal Diary of Mrs. R. J. Mendenhall. Minneapolis: 1900?

1074. MORSE, Bliss (1837-1923)
January 1, 1858-November 12, 1866; gaps
Personal diary; Lake County, Ohio, native served in the 105th Ohio Volunteer Infantry; early entries are one line; later ones are of greater length; farm life; teaching; camp life.
• Civil War Diaries Loren J. Morse, ed. Pittsburgh, Kan.: Pittcraft, 1964.

1075. RUSSELL, Sir William Howard (1820-1907) [B280]
1. January 29, 1858-March 2, 1859; Military diary; intrepid British correspondent covered the aftermath of the Indian Mutiny for the London Times; present at the retaking of Lucknow; sifted truth from exaggeration for his editor; vivid writing.
• My Indian Mutiny Diary. Michael Edwardes, ed. London: Cassell, 1957.

2. March 3, 1861-March 19, 1862; reporting for the Times

on the American Civil War; saw many Federal officials and military
men; had less intercourse with Southern higher-ups; valuable for
portraits of people who became prominent in later years; generally
fair and usually correct; enjoyable reading.
> • My Diary North and South. London: Bradbury and Evans,
> 1863; reprinted with the title My Civil War Diary. Fletcher
> Pratt, ed. London: Hamish Hamilton, 1954.
> • Crawford, Martin. "William Howard Russell and the Con-
> federacy," Journal of American Studies [Great Britain], v. 15,
> pp. 191-210, August, 1981. (Article discusses the portion of
> Russell's diary dealing with the South.)

1076. ST. JOHN, Mary (1838?-69)
       March 31-December 31, 1858
       Travel diary; with contributions by her sister Esther; domes-
tic life in Decorah, Iowa.
> • "A Prairie Diary," Glenda Riley, ed. Annals of Iowa, v.
> 44, pp. 103-17, 1977.

1077. SCAMMON, Charles Melville (1825-1911)
       November 12, 1858-April 24, 1859
       Sea diary; whaling captain and expert on the California gray
whale; from San Francisco to Baja California; weather, headings;
record of whales taken.
> • Journal Aboard the Bark Ocean Bird on a Whaling Voyage
> to Scammon's Lagoon, Winter of 1858-1859. David A. Hender-
> son, ed. Los Angeles: Dawson's Book Shop, 1970.

1078. SEWARD, Frances Adeline (1844-66)
       December 25, 1858-October 7, 1866
       Personal diary; daughter of Lincoln's Secretary of State, Wil-
liam H. Seward; family life in Auburn, New York, and in Washington;
neophyte writer was very good at description; better educated and
read than most of her sex at the time; interest in politics; reflects
her father's opinions; died of tuberculosis.
> • Johnson, Patricia C. "Sensitivity and Civil War: The Se-
> lected Diaries and Papers, 1858-1866 of Frances Adeline Se-
> ward," Ph.D., University of Rochester, 1964. (Dissertation
> Abstracts 26/03A, p. 1613)

1079. SKILBECK, Richard (1838-1924)
       February 16, 1858-November 8, 1863
       Personal diary; Englishman went Down Under to the Colony of
Victoria; the voyage out; clearing land and house building; farming;
married his cousin Sarah Midgley (q.v.); amusing account of their
wedding day.
> • The Diaries of Sarah Midgley and Richard Skilbeck: A
> Story of Australian Settlers 1851-1864. H. A. McCorkell, ed.
> Melbourne: Cassell, 1967.

1080. TRACY, Albert (1818-93)
       1. March 24, 1858-April 30, 1860; Military diary; veteran of

the Mexican War; under the command of Col. Albert Sidney Johnston;
at Camp Scott before moving into the Salt Lake Valley; duty in Provo;
marches in the area; sarcasm toward Johnston; return East through
St. Louis to Washington; long, full entries; well done.
  • "The Utah War: Journal of Albert Tracy 1858-1860," Utah
  Historical Quarterly, v. 13, pp. 1-128, 1945.

  2. February 4-November 26, 1861; Military diary; army service in St. Louis; commanded the magazine near Jefferson Barracks;
campaigning with Frémont in southeast Missouri; good account.
  • "Missouri in Crisis: The Journal of Captain Albert Tracy,
  1861," Ray W. Irwin, ed. Missouri Historical Review, v. 51,
  pp. 8-21, October, 1956; pp. 151-64, January, 1957; pp.
  270-83, April, 1957.

  3. March 23-July 4, 1862; Military diary; pursuing the Confederates under Stonewall Jackson; full entries of an acute observer
in camp, on the march and in battle; includes the text of two letters
from Pres. Lincoln.
  • "Frémont's Pursuit of Jackson in the Shenandoah Valley:
  The Journal of Colonel Albert Tracy, May-July, 1862," Francis
  F. Wayland, ed. Virginia Magazine of History and Biography,
  v. 70, pp. 165-93, pp. 332-54, 1962.

1081. UDELL, John (1795-1872) [A328]
  March 28, 1858-June 30, 1859
  Travel diary; settler with itchy feet looking for new pastures
immigrated to California over the Santa Fe Trail; an Indian attack
forced a retreat to Albuquerque.
  • John Udell Journal, Kept During a Trip Across the Plains
  ... in 1859. Los Angeles: N. A. Kovach, 1946.

1082. UPSON, Theodore Frelinghuysen (1845-1919)
  1. September 28, 1858-May 20, 1865; Personal diary; begins
with a visit by slaveholding relatives to Indiana; service with the
100th Regiment of Indiana Volunteers; much detail on everyday life
in the army not found in other diaries; observant individual.
  • With Sherman to the Sea: The Civil War Letters, Diaries
  and Reminiscences of Theodore F. Upson. Oscar O. Winther,
  ed. Baton Rouge: Louisiana State University Press, 1943.

  2. "Diary Excerpts," in: Philip Dunaway and Mel Evans,
eds. A Treasury of the World's Great Diaries. New York: Doubleday, 1957; pp. 258-59.

1083. WAY, Phocion R. (1827?-98) [A349]
  May 11-October 17, 1858
  Travel diary; Driver on the San Antonio, Texas, to San Diego
mail line; interesting diary by an opinionated observer.
  • "Overland Via 'Jackass Mail' in 1858: The Diary of Phocion
  R. Way," William A. Duffen, ed. Arizona and the West, v. 2,

pp. 35-53, Spring, 1960; pp. 147-64, Summer, 1960; pp. 279-
92, Fall, 1960; pp. 353-70, Winter, 1960.

1084. WEBSTER, John Brown (1822-64)
       Plantation diary; cotton plantation in Harrison County, Texas;
records work done by slaves and weather.
         • "The Plantation Journal of John B. Webster, February 17,
         1858-November 5, 1859," Max S. Lale and Randolph B. Camp-
         bell, ed. Southwestern Historical Quarterly, v. 84, pp. 49-79,
         July, 1980.

1085. WILLIAMS, Eliza Azelia Griswold
       September 7, 1858-October 13, 1861
       Sea diary; the captain's wife; from New Zealand to the Sea
of Japan; return to the U.S.; visits ashore and to passing whalers;
fair picture of the whaling life.
         • "Journal of a Whaleing [sic] voyage to the Indian and Pa-
         cific Oceans, Kept on Board the Ship Florida, T. W. Williams,
         Master, Commencing September 7, 1858," in: Harold Williams,
         ed. One Whaling Family. Boston: Houghton Mifflin, 1964;
         pp. 3-204.

1086. WILSON, Charles William (1836-   )
       July 12, 1858-July 14, 1862
       Exploration diary; member of the Royal Engineers; secretary
to the British Boundary Commission charged with surveying the U.S.-
Canadian border as determined by the Oregon Treaty of 1846; intended for the amusement of his sister; humorous, instructive.
         • Mapping the Frontier: Charles Wilson's Diary of the Sur-
         vey of the 49th Parallel, 1858-1862. George F. G. Stanley,
         ed. Seattle: University of Washington Press, 1960.

                              1859

1087. ALDRICH, Owen (1795?-   )
       Personal diary; extracts; sheriff of Milwaukee County; prices;
terse notes on rebuilding a house.
         • Aldrich, Ruth L. "An 1859 Milwaukee Diary," Milwaukee
         History, v. 3, pp. 80-83, 1980.

1088. ALLEN, Young John (1836-1907)
       November 21, 1859-July 26, 1860
       Sea diary; Georgia-born Methodist Episcopal missionary;
weather, sickness, poor food; some land excursions.
         • Diary of a Voyage to China, 1859-1860. Arva Colbert
         Floyd, ed. Atlanta, Ga.: Emory University Library, 1943.

1089. ALMADA, Bartolomé Eligio (1817-72)
       September 1, 1859-August 17, 1863
       Personal diary; scion of wealthy Mexican mining family of

Alamos, Sonora; allied with the Liberals in the War of Reform; period
before Emperor Maximilian and Carlota's stay; deputy to the National
Congress; his efforts to free an uncle from a political prison; much
on the fluctuating political situation.
* Almada of Alamos: The Diary of Don Bartolomé. Carlota
Miles, trans. Tucson: Arizona Silhouettes, 1962.

1090. BOWEN, Edwin A. (-1900)
       February 23-October 2, 1859
       Travel diary; from La Salle, Illinois, to Colorado; mileage,
conditions; hard labor of working a claim.
* "Pikes Peak Fifty-niner: The Diary of E. A. Bowen," Smith,
Duane A. ed. Colorado Magazine, v. 47, pp. 269-311, Fall, 1970.

1091. BROWN, James Berry (1837-)
       May 14, 1859-
       Travel diary; by ox wagon from Nebraska City to Fort Lara-
mie; via Lander Cut-off to Inskip, California; one of the few later
accounts.
* Journal of a Journey Across the Plains in 1859. George R.
Stewart, ed. San Francisco: Book Club of California, 1970.

1092. CAMP, Joseph (1834-1914/16)
       May 21-September 23, 1859
       Travel diary; from Iowa to Omaha.
* "The Journal of Joseph Camp, 1859," Nebraska History, v.
46, pp. 29-38, March, 1965.

1093. DOEDERLEIN, Ferdinand (1835-1915)
       Travel diary; minister went with a group to do mission work
among the Crow Indians near Fort Laramie.
* "The Doederlein Diary 17 May 1859-February 1860," Roger
Moldenhauer, ed. Concordia Historical Institute Quarterly,
v. 51, pp. 99-136, 1978.

1094. DONNELLY, Ignatius (1831-1901)
       Personal diary; Philadelphian, author and editor.
       Nydahl, Theodore L. "The Diary of Ignatius Donnelly, 1859-
1884," Ph.D., University of Minnesota, 1942 (American Doctoral Dissertations, W1942, p. 93).

1095. EDWARDS, David Fay (1834-60)
       May 15, 1859-December 1, 1860
       Travel diary; overland to Colorado for his health; of genea-
logical interest.
* Valiant-for-Truth: Life, Letters and Diaries of David Fay
Edwards, 1834-60. Richard Henry Edwards, ed. Lisle, N.Y.:
n. p., 1952; pp. 73-104.

1096. HASKELL, Thales H. (1834-1909)
       October 4, 1859-March 27, 1860

Missionary diary; part of a party of Mormon missionaries to the Hopis in northern Arizona; life among the Indians.
- "Journal of Thales H. Haskell," Juanita Brooks, ed. <u>Utah Historical Quarterly</u>, v. 12, pp. 69-98, January/April, 1944.

1097. HUNT, Ellen Elizabeth Kellogg (1835-80)
April 25-September 15, 1859
Travel diary; from Kansas City with her husband to Pike's Peak for the gold rush; took in boarders upon arrival to earn money; did prodigious amount of work despite ill health.
- "Diary of Mrs. A. C. Hunt, September, 1859," Hafen, LeRoy R., ed. <u>Colorado Magazine</u> v. 21, pp. 161-70, 1944.

1098. KINGMAN, Romanzo S. (1829-   )
March 21-July 28, 1859
Travel diary; by wagon from Sparta, Wisconsin, to Pike's Peak for gold; weather; decided his claim was no good and returned home.
- "Romanzo Kingman's Pike's Peak Journal, 1859," <u>Iowa Journal of History and Politics</u>, v. 48, pp. 55-85, 1950.

1099. MANWARING, Joshua (1824-1903)
June 16-October 2, 1859
Travel diary; from Fort Laramie to Colorado; unsuccessful mining venture; return home.
- "Journal of a Fifty-niner," Robert M. Warner, ed. <u>Colorado Magazine</u>, v. 36, pp. 161-73, July, 1959.

1100. MARSH, Elias J. (1835-1908)
May 31-August 16, 1859
Travel diary; from St. Louis via Florence, Nebraska, and Fort Pierre to Fort Benton; reaching farther up the Missouri than any steamboat had ever gone; excellent, detailed descriptions of sights, fellow passengers and activity.
- "Journal of Dr. Elias J. Marsh: Account of a Steamboat Trip on the Missouri River, May-August, 1859," <u>South Dakota Historical Review</u>, v. 1, pp. 79-125, 1935-36.

1101. MORGAN, Lewis Henry (1818-81)
1. May 17-June 23, 1859; May 23-June 15, 1860; July 7-August 7, 1861; May 1-July 7, 1862; American ethnologist and lawyer; strong interest in Indian kinship patterns and languages; trips from his home in upstate New York to Kansas, Nebraska and the Rockies to do research; contemporary and colleague of Bandelier (q.v.).
- <u>The Indian Journals, 1859-1862</u>. Leslie A. White, ed. Ann Arbor: University of Michigan Press, 1959.

2. July 9, 1870-August 11, 1871; Travel diary; less a diary than essays on the sights; little personal detail.
- <u>Extracts of Lewis Henry Morgan's European Travel Journal</u>. Leslie A. White, ed. Rochester, N.Y.: 1937; reprint of <u>Rochester Historical Society Publications</u>, v. 16, 1937.

1102. MUNBY, Arthur Joseph (1828-1910)
       January, 1859-December, 1903
       Personal diary; lengthy excerpts bridged by Hudson's narra-
tive; minor English poet, barrister and friend of prominent British
writers and artists; secretly married a housemaid, Hannah Cullwick,
who kept her position and insisted on being his servant.
       • Hudson, Derek. Munby: Man of Two Worlds: The Life
       and Diaries of A. J. Munby, 1828-1910. London: John Mur-
       ray, 1972.

1103. PRINCE, Eliza (1832-99)
       July 13-November 17, 1859
       Travel diary; two voyages: from Massachusetts to Brazil and
return to New York, from New York to Glasgow and return; unmarried woman in poor health undertook visits; some sightseeing on land.
       • Journals, 1859-1860 (With Letters to Christopher Prince
       1855-1865). Middletown, N.Y.: Whitlock Press, 1969; pp.
       173-215.

1104. PUTNAM, Theodore L. (1834?-   )
       March 16-April 20, 1859
       Travel diary; pilot of one of the largest rafts ever to go down
the Allegheny River; wind, weather and difficulty of handling the
raft caused many problems.
       • "Down the Rivers: A Rafting Journal of 1859-From War-
       ren, Pa., to Louisville, Ky." Ernest C. Miller, ed. Western
       Pennsylvania Historical Magazine, v. 40, pp. 149-62, Fall, 1957.

1105. RAVENEL, Henry William (1814-87)
       Personal diary; South Carolina planter and botanist of national
repute; fairly prosperous before the Civil War, he and his family fell
on hard times during Reconstruction; visits to Saratoga, New York,
before the war; secession; selling his botanic specimens supplemented
his meagre income after the war; upright man scolded his publishers
for putting the title "doctor" before his name.
       • The Private Journal of Henry William Ravenel, 1859-1887.
       Arney Robinson Childs, ed. Columbia: University of South
       Carolina Press, 1947.

1106. SALISBURY, William W. (1838?-1920)
       April 4-September 11, 1859
       Travel diary; from Cleveland, Ohio to California.
       • "The Journal of a Pike's Peak Gold Seeker," David Lindsey,
       ed. Kansas Historical Quarterly, v. 22, pp. 321-41, Winter,
       1956.

1107. SCUDDER, Horace Elisha (1838-1902)
       January 7-September, 1859
       Travel diary; extracts; from New York by ship; to San Antonio;
sidetrips.
       • Ballou, Ellen Bartlett, "Scudder's Journey to Texas, 1859,"

<u>Southwestern Historical Quarterly</u>, v. 63, pp. 1-14, July, 1959.

1108.   SEARS, Mary E. (1838-63)
        January 1, 1859-August 26, 1860
        Personal diary; her trials as a teacher; life with her family
in Illinois and Ohio.
        • "A Young Woman in the Midwest: The Journal of Mary
        Sears, 1859-1860," Daryl E. Jones and James H. Pickering,
        eds. <u>Ohio History</u>, v. 82, pp. 215-34, Summer-Autumn, 1973.

1109.   SMITH, Elias (1804-88)
        Personal diary; editor of the <u>Deseret News</u> in Salt Lake City;
covers an important period in the city's history when Gentile and
Mormon aims were often in conflict.
        • "Elias Smith: Journal of a Pioneer Editor, May 6, 1859-
        September 23, 1863," A. R. Mortesen, ed. <u>Utah Historical</u>
        <u>Quarterly</u>, v. 21, pp. 1-24, January, 1953; pp. 137-68, April,
        1953; pp. 237-66, July, 1953; pp. 333-60, October, 1953.

1110.   SPAIN, David F.
        March 8-July 27, 1859
        Travel diary; with a party from South Bend, Indiana; found
gold after much hard labor.
        • "The Diary of David F. Spain: Gregory's Grubstakers at
        the Diggings," John D. Morrison, ed. <u>Colorado Magazine</u>, v.
        35, pp. 11-34, January, 1958.

1111.   STEELE, Edward Dunsha (or Dunsha Edward) (1829-65)
        May 17-August 31, 1859
        Travel diary; by wagon with a family party; via Dubuque,
Des Moines, Fort Kearny and Julesburg.
        • "In the Pike's Peak Gold Rush of 1859," <u>Colorado Magazine</u>,
        v. 29, pp. 299-309, October, 1952.
        • <u>Edward Dunsha Steele, 1829-1865 ... Diary of His Journey</u>
        <u>From Lodi Wisconsin, to Boulder, Colorado ... in 1859</u>. Nolie
        Mumey, ed. Boulder, Col.: Johnson Publishing Co., 1960;
        500 copies.

1112.   SUCKLEY, George (1830?-69)
        July 14-August 12, 1859
        Military diary; medical doctor went with army recruits to the
Utah Territory; from Fort Leavenworth via the Oregon Trail to west
of the Continental Divide.
        • "The 1859 Overland Journal of Naturalist George Suckley,"
        Richard G. Beidleman, ed. <u>Annals of Wyoming</u>, v. 28, pp.
        68-79, 1956.

1113.   YOUNGER, Williamson (1817-76)
        December 28, 1859-June 19, 1876; many gaps
        Personal diary; "accounts kept and charges made against my
children"; war news, illness.

- "The Diary of Williamson Younger (1817-1876)," Marshall Wingfield, ed. Tennessee Historical Society Papers, v. 13, pp. 55-77, 1959.

1860

1114. ANONYMOUS, 1837-
April 20, 1860-December 22, 1864
Personal diary; teaching at various schools; visits home; suffers from migraine; spiritual matters; little concrete detail except for comments on wartime inflation.
- Diary of a Virginia Schoolmistress, 1860-65. Glenn Curtiss Smith, ed. Harrisonburg, Va.: Madison College, 1949; reprinted from Madison Quarterly, v. 9, pp. 25-58, March, 1949.

1115. ANONYMOUS
December 7, 1860-January 2, 1861
Travel diary; sickly seventeen-year old New Englander went South for his health.
- "New Orleans in December 1860," Charles R. Schultz, ed. Louisiana History, v. 9, pp. 53-61, Winter, 1968.

1116. ABBA, Giuseppe Cesare
May 3-November 9, 1860
Military diary; common soldier wrote on the march from Genoa to Sicily; some notes were added later; hurry up and wait; observant.
- The Diary of One of Garibaldi's Thousand. E. R. Vincent, trans. London: Oxford University Press, 1962.
  REVIEW: Book Review Digest 1963, p. 1.

1117. BANCROFT, Albert Little (1841-1914)
January 1, 1860-July 26, 1861
Personal diary; brother of historian Hubert Howe Bancroft; his stationery store business; church-going.
- "Albert Little Bancroft: His Diaries, Account Books, Card String of Events and Other Papers," Henry R. Wagner, ed. California Historical Society Quarterly, v. 29, pp. 97-128, June, 1950, pp. 217-27, September, 1950, pp. 357-67, December, 1950.

1118. BARRY, James Buckner (1821-1906)
January 1, 1860-May 30, 1862
Personal diary; daily life in Bosque County, Texas.
- "The Diary of James Buckner Barry, 1860-1862," James K. Greer, ed. Southwestern Historical Quarterly, v. 36, pp. 144-62, October, 1932.

1119. BROOKE, Samuel Roebuck (1844-98?)
February 1, 1860-September 15, 1865
Personal diary; shy, unathletic boy was mature for his age;

studies at a grammar school and Corpus Christi College, Oxford;
stilted style.
- Journal: The Diary of a Lancing Schoolboy, 1860-65. N.p.:
Friends of Lancing Chapel, 1953.

1120. BURGES, Samuel Edward (1832-1916)
        January 1, 1860-February 18, 1862
        Personal diary; newspaper collection agent; travel conditions
on his rounds; joins his company after Fort Sumter's fall.
- "The Diary of Samuel Edward Burges, 1860-1862," Thomas
W. Chadwick, ed. South Carolina Historical and Genealogical
Magazine, v. 48, pp. 63-75, April, 1947; pp. 141-63, July,
1947; v. 48, pp. 206-18, October, 1947.

1121. BUXTON, Elizabeth Ellen (1848-   )
        January 17, 1860-November 18, 1864
        Personal diary; daughter of a large, prosperous middle class
family living near Epping Forest; birth of siblings; visits to grandparents; gay, lighthearted; enhanced by her sketches.
- Ellen Buxton's Journal 1860-1864. London: Bles, 1967.

1122. CISNE, Jonah Girard (1834-77)
        April 4, 1860-October 6, 1863
        Travel diary; from Hannibal, Missouri; buying and selling
claims.
- "Across the Plains and in Nevada City: Journal of Jonah
Girard Cisne," A. T. Cisne, ed. Colorado Magazine, v. 27,
pp. 49-57, January, 1950.

1123. CURD, Mary Samuella Hart (1835-1919)
        May 3, 1860-June 15, 1863
        Personal diary; Virginian married and moved to Fulton, Mis-
souri; honeymoon included a stop at the Woman's Rights Convention--
"The proceedings were contemptable" [sic]; early married life, birth
of a daughter; widowhood; tries to feel as she thinks other people
want her to.
- Sam Curd's Diary: The Diary of a True Woman. Susan S.
Arpad, ed. Athens, Ohio: Ohio University Press, 1984.
    REVIEW: Library Journal, v. 109, p. 1124, June 1, 1984.

1124. EDMONDSTON, Catherine Ann Devereux (1823-75)
        1. June 1, 1860-January 4, 1866; Personal diary; childless
plantation mistress of Halifax County, North Carolina; relations with an
an extended family; husband active in state politics; her health;
gardening; war news, rumors; daily life; verbose but not especially
revealing.
- Journal of a Secesh Lady. Beth G. Crabtree and James
W. Patton, eds. Raleigh, N. Car.: Division of Archives and
History, 1979.
    REVIEWS: Book Review Index 1979, p. 130; 1980, p. 146.
    Civil War Times Illustrated, v. 18, p. 49, June, 1979.

2. Journal, 1860-1866 Margaret Mackay Jones, ed. n.p., Pvt. ptd., 1954; 500 copies.

3. September 5, 1860-December 31, 1865; Excerpts; believed Lincoln would not be elected; prices; against the Confederate Conscription Act.
- "Diary of a Soldier's Wife on Looking Glass Plantation," in: Clarence Poe, ed. True Tales of the South at War. Chapel Hill: University of North Carolina Press, 1961; pp. 101-40.

1125. FERRIS, Anna M. (1815-90)
November 2, 1860-December 31, 1865
Personal diary; excerpts; Quaker of Wilmington, Delaware; Lincoln supporter; family affairs and war news.
- "The Civil War Diaries of A. M. Ferris," Harold B. Hancock, ed. Delaware History, v. 9, pp. 221-64, April, 1961.

1126. FIELDS, Annie Adams (1834-1915)
1. September 21, 1860-September 13, 1898; Personal diary; prominent Boston hostess and second wife of James T. Fields of the publishing firm Ticknor and Fields; life in Boston; visit with Dickens; knew Sarah Orne Jewett and other writers of the era.
- Memories of a Hostess: A Chronicle of Eminent Friendships Drawn Chiefly from the Diary of Mrs. James T. Fields, 1834-1915. Mark Antony de Wolfe Howe, ed. Boston: Atlantic Monthly Press, 1922.

2. March 10, 1871-May 1, 1876; Excerpts relating to Mark Twain (q.v.) and Bret Harte.
- "Bret Harte and Mark Twain in the 'Seventies: Passages from the Diaries of Mrs. James T. Fields," M. A. de Wolfe Howe, ed. Atlantic, v. 130, pp. 341-48, September, 1922.

1127. FLEET, Benjamin Robert (1846-64)
January 9, 1860-April 4, 1864
Personal diary; boy in his teens lived on a plantation 30 miles northeast of Richmond; school life at Aberdeen Academy; brother's enlistment; Sheridan bivouacs on the front lawn; interesting.
- Green Mount: A Virginia Plantation Family During the Civil War; Being the Journal of Benjamin Robert Fleet and Letters of His Family. Betsy Fleet and John D. P. Fuller, eds. Lexington: University of Kentucky Press, 1962.

FOWLER, Anna Kate (1838-1909) see HUME, Walter C.

1128. HAWLEY, H. J. (1839-1923) [A352]
May 21-December 31, 1860
Travel diary; Wisconsin native went with his uncle to the Colorado diggings; in Golden; hard work and little play.
- "H. J. Hawley's Diary, Russell Gulch in 1860," Lynn I. Perrigo, ed. Colorado Magazine, v. 30, pp. 133-49, 1953.

1129. HOLMAN, James Hardy (1836-1910)
        Military diary; commissioned by Robert E. Lee to escort a
party looking for a site for a military post on the Rio Grande near
San Carlos; mileage, terrain, hardships.
        • "A Tennessean, Texas and Camels: The Diary of James H.
        Holman, June 11 to August 25, 1860," Beatrice Milhus Rees and
        William T. Alderson, eds. Tennessee Historical Magazine, v.
        16, pp. 250-61, September, 1957.

1130. HUME, Walter Cunningham (1840-1921)
        January 28, 1860-September 28, 1866
        Personal diary; Extracts from the two diaries interleaved;
courtship; her journey to Australia to marry him; lighthearted, delightful.
        • A Victorian Engagement: Letters and Journals of Walter
        Hume and Anna Kate Fowler During the 1860's. Bertram Hume,
        ed. St. Lucia: University of Queensland Press, 1975.

1131. KAUTZ, August V. (1828-95) [A337]
        May 1-September 15, 1860
        Personal diary; West Point graduate; with Major George Blake
to the headwaters of the Missouri over the Mullan Road.
        • "From Missouri to Oregon in 1860: The Diary of August V.
        Kautz," Martin F. Schmitt, ed. Pacific Northwest Quarterly,
        v. 37, pp. 193-230, July, 1946.

1132. LAW, John G.
        November 6, 1860-September 8, 1862
        Military diary; minister wounded at Shiloh; very full entries.
        • "Diary of a Confederate Soldier," Southern Historical So-
        ciety Papers, v. 10, pp. 378-81, 564-59, 1882; v. 11, pp. 175-
        81, 297-303, 460-65, 1883; v. 12, pp. 22-28, 215-19, 390-95,
        538-43, 1884.

1133. McBETH, Sue L.
        1. April 17, 1860-June 18, 1861; gaps; Personal diary; grad-
uate of Steubenville (Ohio) Female Seminary with an interest in Indians; journey to Indian Territory to teach; weather reports to the
Smithsonian; interesting and unprejudiced account of life at a mission
school; well done.
        • "Diary of a Missionary to the Choctaws: 1860-61," Anna
        Lewis, ed. Chronicles of Oklahoma, v. 17, pp. 428-47, 1939.

        2. April 16, 1860-June 17, 1861; Covers the same time period
as the above but with different entries.
        • "The Diary of Sue McBeth, A Missionary to the Choctaws
        1860-1861," Anna Lewis, ed. Chronicles of Oklahoma, v. 21,
        pp. 186-95, June, 1943.

1134. McCAIN, G. S. (1836-85)
        September 10-November 29, 1860

Travel diary; mileage and weather.
* "A Trip from Atchison, Kansas, to Laurette, Colorado,"
Colorado Magazine, v. 27, pp. 95-102, April, 1950.

1135. ONAHAN, William J. (1836-1919)
May 16, 1860-May 20, 1872
Personal diary; extracts; Chicago Catholic made notes on national and city events; loss of the Lady Elgin; active in civic and church affairs; florid style.
* "The Diaries of William J. Onahan," Mid-America, v. 14,
pp. 64-72, 152-77, July, 1931.

1136. OVERTON, Walter Alexander (1830-   )
January 1, 1860-May 24, 1861
Personal diary; worked as a brickmason and teacher; in the
2nd Regiment of Mississippi Volunteers.
* "Excerpts from the Diary of Walter Alexander Overton, 1860-
1862," Beulah M. D'Olive Price, ed. Journal of Mississippi
History, v. 17, pp. 191-204, July, 1955.

1137. PIPER, Alexander
July-September, 1860
Military diary; facsimile reproduction; in the company of the
3rd Artillery; from Fort Umpqua to guard the emigrant trail into
Oregon from Indians.
* "Alexander Piper's Reports and Journal," Oregon Historical
Quarterly, v. 69, pp. 223-55, September, 1968.

1138. PROCTER, Lovell James (1833-1910)
October 1, 1860-March 11, 1864
Personal diary; Yorkshire priest went with a party of clerics
to establish a mission in the Zambesi River area explored by Livingston (q.v.); met his future wife on the outward voyage; mission work;
not a forceful personality; many details of daily life of the natives;
vivid picture of mission life.
* The Central African Journal of Lovell J. Procter, 1860-1864.
Norman Robert Bennett and Marguerite Ylvisaker, eds. Boston: Boston University, 1971.

1139. RIDGLEY, Anna (Mrs. James L. Hudson) (1841-1926)
January 1, 1860-June 4, 1865; many gaps
Personal diary; daughter of a prominent Springfield, Illinois,
family; social life; mentions Lincoln; trips to New York and Washington.
* "A Girl in the Sixties: Excerpts from the Journal of Anna
Ridgley," Octavia Roberts Corneau and Georgia L. Osborne,
eds. Illinois State Historical Society Journal, v. 22, pp. 401-
46, October, 1929.

1140. STUART, James Ewell Brown (1833-64)
1. May 15-August 15, 1860; gaps; Military diary; from Fort

Riley under the command of Major John Sedgwick; a year of drought;
weather, distances and routes traveled; skirmish with Kiowas.
- "The Kiowa and Comanche Campaign of 1860 as Recorded
in the Personal Diary of Lt. J. E. B. Stuart," W. Stitt Robinson, ed. Kansas Historical Quarterly, v. 23, pp. 832-400,
Winter, 1957.

2.   "Lt. J. E. B. Stuart's Journal May 15, to August 11,"
in: LeRoy R. and Ann W. Hafen, eds. Relations with the Indians
of the Plains, 1857-1861.   Glendale, Cal.: Arthur H. Clark, 1959;
pp. 217-44.

1141. TALLMAN, Augusta
Personal diary; excerpts; upper class life in Janesville, Wisconsin, through the eyes of a 22-year-old woman.
- Salisbury, Rachel. "1860--The Last Year of Peace: Augusta Tallman's Diary," Wisconsin Magazine of History, v. 44, pp.
pp. 85-94, Winter, 1961.

1142. TOLSTOY, Countess Sophia (1844-1919)
1.   June 14-15, 1860; October 8, 1862-January 23, 1891;
Personal diary; wife of Russian novelist Leo (q.v.); daily life with
him and their children; copying his writings; his health; often rails
against him for his kindnesses to hangers-on; visits from prominent
Russians.
- The Diary of Tolstoy's Wife, 1860-1891.   Alexander Werth,
trans. London: Gollancz, 1928.

2.   1862; excerpts.
- "Diary Excerpts," in: Mary Jane Moffat and Charlotte
Painter, eds. Revelations: Diaries of Women.   New York:
Random House, 1974; pp. 138-47.

3.   January 25, 1891-November 19, 1897; Personal diary; con-
tinued rows with her husband.
- Later Diary 1891-1897.   Alexander Werth, trans. London:
Gollancz, 1929.

4.   January 2,-December 31, 1910; Personal diary; her diary
is matched with entries from her husband's for the same day; relations with each other, family and numerous visitors; notes on his
health; dissension caused by V. G. Chertkov; her husband's death
at Astapovo in November.
- The Final Struggle: Being Countess Tolstoy's Diary for
1910 With Extracts From Leo Tolstoy's Diary of the Same Period. Aylmer Maude, trans. New York: Oxford University
Press, 1936.

5.   "Diary Excerpts," in: Philip Dunaway and Mel Evans,
eds. A Treasury of the World's Great Diaries.   New York: Doubleday, 1957; pp. 122-29.

1143. TUTTLE, John W. (1837-1927)
       June 1, 1860-December 31, 1866; gaps
       Personal diary; native of Wayne County, Kentucky, enlisted
in the 3rd Kentucky Infantry on the Union side; begins with his law
practice; social and family life; at Shiloh, Chickamauga; battle for
Atlanta; very well-written; entertaining, humorous.
       • The Union, The Civil War, and John W. Tuttle, A Kentucky
       Captain's Account. Hambleton Tapp and James C. Klotter, eds.
       Frankfort: Kentucky Historical Society, 1980.

1144. WARD, Lester Frank (1841-1913) [A353]
       July 8, 1860-August 14, 1862
       Personal diary; extracts; pioneering American sociologist wrote
in French to practice his language skills; farm life; courting his wife.
       • "Diary Excerpts," in: Philip Dunaway and Mel Evans. A
       Treasury of the World's Great Diaries. New York: Doubleday,
       1957; pp. 21-29.

1145. WHEELER, Mattie
       1860-October 21, 1865
       Personal diary; social life and war news.
       • "Journal of Mattie Wheeler: A Blue Grass Belle Reports on
       the Civil War," Frances L. S. Dugan, ed. Filson Club His-
       torical Quarterly, v. 29, pp. 118-44, April, 1955.

1146. WILLIAMSON, John Coffee (1833-98)
       1. November 6, 1860-January 30, 1861; Personal diary; teach-
ing school; reading law; shows his gradual swing to the Southern
cause.
       • "The Education of a Southern Mind: Extracts From the
       Diary of John Coffee Williamson, 1860-1861," Ben Harris Mc-
       Clary, ed. East Tennessee Historical Society Publications, v.
       32, pp. 94-105, 1960.

       2. August 11-October 31, 1864; Military diary; commissary
sergeant of the 5th Tennessee Cavalry looking for food and forage.
       • "The Civil War Diary of John Coffee Williamson," J. C.
       Williamson, ed. Tennessee Historical Quarterly, v. 15, pp.
       61-74, March, 1956.

1147. YANAGAWA, Masakiyo K.
       January 18-September 29, 1860
       Travel diary; head of the embassy of 93 men sent to ratify a
commercial treaty; rough voyage to San Francisco; his first train ride;
visits to the White House; Baltimore, Philadelphia and New York;
"We did not see even one beggar."
       • The First Japanese Mission to America (1860): Being a
       Diary Kept by a Member of the Embassy. Junichi Fukuyama
       and Roderick H. Jackson, trans. M. G. Mori, ed. Kobe:
       J. L. Thompson, 1937.

<u>1861</u>

1148. ALISON, Joseph Dill (1828-1905)
       May 9, 1861-July 4, 1863
       Personal diary; hospital life; the siege of Vicksburg.
       • "War Diary of Dr. Joseph Dill Alison of Carlowville, Ala-
       bama," <u>Alabama Historical Quarterly</u>, v. 9, pp. 385-98, Fall,
       1947.

1149. ALLEN, Michael M. (1830-)
       September 4-25, 1861
       Military diary; first Jew to serve as a chaplain in the U.S.
       Army; at Camp Stoneman, Washington, D.C.; weather; conducting
       services.
       • "The Diary of Chaplain Michael M. Allen, September, 1861,"
       D. de Sola Pool, ed. <u>American Jewish Historical Society Pub-
       lications</u>, v. 39, pp. 177-82, December, 1949.

1150. ALLEY, Charles
       October 9, 1861-March 17, 1862
       Military diary; Irish immigrant from the Nebraska Territory;
       enlistment; religiously inclined; at Fort Henry, Tennessee.
       • "Excerpts from the Civil War Diary of Lieutenant Charles
       Alley, Company 'C,' Fifth Iowa Cavalry," John S. Ezell, ed.
       <u>Iowa Journal of History</u>, v. 49, pp. 241-56, July, 1951.

1151. BARNES, John Sanford (1836-1911)
       Sea diary; Naval Academy graduate; aboard the steam frigate
       <u>Wabash</u>; service at Savannah and in Florida.
       • "The Battle of Port Royal: From the Journal of John San-
       ford Barnes, October 8 to November 9, 1861," John D. Hayes,
       ed. <u>New York Historical Society Quarterly</u>, v. 45, pp. 365-
       95, October, 1961.

1152. BARROW, Willie Micajah (1843-63)
       September 24, 1861-July 13, 1862
       Personal diary; service in Louisiana; captured and imprisoned
       at Camp Douglas; much about his reading, food and leisure in camp.
       • "The Civil War Diary of Willie Micajah Barrow, September
       23, 1861-July 13, 1862," Wendell H. Stephenson and Edwin A.
       Davis, eds. <u>Louisiana Historical Quarterly</u>, v. 17, pp. 436-
       51, 712-31, 1934.

1153. BEATTY, John (1828-1914)
       1. June 22, 1861-January 1, 1864; Military diary; 3rd Ohio
       Volunteer Infantry; little about his own actions in fighting; interest-
       ing with full, running commentary; humorous; a likeable person.
       • <u>Memoirs of a Volunteer, 1861-1863</u>. Harvey S. Ford, ed.
       New York: Norton, 1946; reprint of 1879 ed.
       REVIEW: <u>Book Review Digest</u> 1946, p. 48.

2. January 1-June 26, 1884; Personal diary; active in Ohio politics; Republican Convention in Chicago; much about political personalities of Ohio and the nation.
  • "The Diary of John Beatty," Harvey S. Ford, ed. Ohio State Archaeological and Historical Quarterly, v. 58, pp. 119-51, April, 1949; pp. 390-427, October, 1949; v. 59, pp. 58-91, January, 1950; pp. 165-95, April, 1950.

3. "Diary Excerpts," in: Philip Dunaway and Mel Evans, eds.; A Treasury of the World's Great Diaries. New York: Doubleday, 1957; pp. 272-74.

1154. BERKELEY, Henry Robinson (1840-1918)
May 16, 1861-June 24, 1865
Military diary; private in the Hanover Artillery; at Fredericksburg, Gettysburg; Yankee prisoner for a time.
  • Four Years in the Confederate Artillery: The Diary of Henry Robinson Berkeley. William H. Runge, ed. Chapel Hill: University of North Carolina Press, 1961.

1155. BIRCHER, William (1846-)
August 1, 1861-June 15, 1865
Personal diary; siege of Atlanta; hospital duty.
  • A Drummer-boy's Diary: Comprising Four Years of Service with the Second Regiment Minnesota Veteran Volunteers, 1861 to 1865. St. Paul, Minn.: St. Paul Book and Stationery Co., 1889.

1156. BOYD, Cyrus F.
October 15, 1861-March 14, 1863
Military diary; written up afterward from fragmentary notes jotted in the field; joined at Indianola, Iowa; at Shiloh, Corinth and Memphis, Tennessee; Vicksburg; opinionated, frank and humorous; one of the better diaries of the period.
  • "The Civil War Diary of Cyrus F. Boyd, Fifteenth Iowa Infantry," Mildred Throne, ed. Iowa Journal of History, v. 50, pp. 47-82, January, 1952; pp. 155-84, April, 1952; pp. 239-70, July, 1952; pp. 345-78, October, 1952; reprinted New York: Kraus, 1977.

1157. BRADFORD, Ruth
September 16, 1861-April 23, 1864
Travel diary; sea captain's daughter went to China and Hong Kong with him; life in China and return voyage; no-nonsense woman comments on the ship's crew and passengers; 'Maskee' means 'what the hell': enjoyable.
  • Maskee! The Journal and Letters of Ruth Bradford, 1861-1872. Hartford: The Prospect Press, 1938; 350 copies.

1158. BROWN, John Henry
1. September 11-December 31, 1861; Military diary; Confederate

officer; journey from area of the Red River in Texas to Fayetteville, Arkansas.
- "War-time Diary in Northwest Arkansas," W. J. Lemke, ed. Flashback [Washington County (Arkansas) Historical Society] v. 6, pp. 3-11, November, 1956.

2. November 29, 1861-April 10, 1862; Military diary; on Brigadier General Ben McCulloch's staff; accompanied a body to Austin, Texas.
- "'The Paths of Glory' (The War-time Diary of Major John Henry Brown, C. S. A.)," W. J. Lemke, ed. Arkansas Historical Quarterly, v. 15, pp. 344-59, Winter, 1956.

1159.   BROWN, John Mason (1837-90)
May 1-November 4, 1861
Travel diary; from St. Louis through Dakota, Washington and Oregon Territories; to San Francisco and return through Salt Lake City; Indians; buffalo hunt; scenery; well-done.
- "A Trip to the Northwest in 1861," Filson Club Historical Quarterly, v. 24, pp. 103-35, April, 1950; pp. 246-75, July, 1950.

1160.   BUCK, Lucy Rebecca (1842-1918)
December 25, 1861-April 15, 1865
Personal diary; eldest daughter of Front Royal, Virginia family; had Yankees quartered on them; taking in refugees; family news; ornate style.
- Sad Earth, Sweet Heaven: The Diary of Lucy Rebecca Buck During the War Between the States. Birmingham, Ala.: Cornerstone, 1973; 1940 edition titled Diary of Lucy Rebecca Buck.

1161.   BURGE, Louisiana (1843?-63)
January, 1861-March 4, 1863
Personal diary; stepdaughter of Dolly Sumner Lunt Burge (q.v.); illness forced her to leave Macon College; home life.
- "Louisiana Burge: The Diary of a Confederate College Girl," Richard B. Harwell, ed. Georgia Historical Quarterly, v. 36, pp. 144-63, June, 1952.

1162.   CAMPBELL, Andrew Jackson (1834-63)
November 25, 1861-March 10, 1863
Military diary; captained a company of the 48th Regiment of Tennessee Volunteers raised in Maury County; taken prisoner at Fort Donelson.
- Civil War Diary. Jill Knight Garrett, ed. Columbia, Tenn.: n.p., 1965.

1163.   CARTER, Robert Goldthwaite
July 16, 1861-August, 1865
Military diary; intertwined diaries and letters of the four

Carter brothers, John H., Eugene, Robert Goldthwaite, and Walter; covers the entire war; Bull Run, Fredericksburg, Chancellorsville, Gettysburg and the aftermath; life in camp and on the march; some incidents in Benet's poem John Brown's Body were inspired by this book.

 • Four Brothers in Blue, or Sunshine and Shadows of the War
   of the Rebellion: A Story of the Great Civil War, From Bull
   Run to Appomattox. Austin: University of Texas Press, 1978;
   reprint of 1913 ed.

1164. CHASE, Charles Monroe (1829-1902)
      July 21-October 10, 1861
      Personal diary; 13th Illinois Infantry; interesting, very de-
tailed account of camp life from an unusual perspective.
 • "A Union Band Director Views Camp Rolla: 1861," Donald
   H. Welsh, ed. Missouri Historical Review, v. 55, pp. 307-43,
   July, 1961.

1165. CHASE, Salmon Portland (1808-73)
      1. December 9, 1861-May 1, 1865; gaps; Political diary; Lin-
coln's treasury secretary; cabinet meetings; treasury business; conduct of the war; presidential candidate for a short time; his resignation; becomes Chief Justice of the Supreme Court after Roger B.
Taney's death; Lincoln assassination; interesting portrait of war time
conditions as seen from Washington.
 • Inside Lincoln's Cabinet: The Civil War Diaries of Salmon
   P. Chase. David Donald, ed. New York: Longmans, Green,
   1954.

      2. July 21-October 12, 1862; Personal diary; wartime duties.
 • Diary and Correspondence of Salmon P. Chase. American
   Historical Association Annual Report for 1902, pp. 45-106; re-
   printed New York: Da Capo Press, 1971.

1166. CHEAVENS, Henry Martyn (1830-1920)
      1. June 22-August 5, 1861; Military diary; Battle of Carthage,
Missouri.
 • "Journal of the Civil War in Missouri: 1861, Henry Martyn
   Cheavens," Virginia Easley, ed. Missouri Historical Review,
   v. 56, pp. 12-25, October, 1961.

      2. August 3-December 13, 1862; Military diary; imprisoned;
at Vicksburg.
 • "A Missouri Confederate in the Civil War: The Journal of
   Henry Martyn Cheavens, 1862-1863," James E. Moss, ed.
   Missouri Historical Review, v. 57, pp. 16-52, October, 1962.

1167. CHESNUT, Mary Boykin Miller (1823-86)
      1. November 8, 1860-August 2, 1865; Personal diary; con-
densed and revised for publication.
 • A Diary from Dixie. Isabella D. Martin and Myrta Lockett
   Avery, eds. New York: Appleton, 1905.

• A Diary from Dixie. Ben Ames Williams, ed. New York: Houghton, Mifflin, 1949.
   REVIEW: Book Review Digest 1949, p. 160.

2. February 18, 1861–July 26, 1865; Personal diary; this definitive edition is primarily a combination of two versions of the diary; the introduction and statement of editorial policies explains Woodward's method; childless wife of Confederate government official; wealthy, planter class; opinionated, lively, excellent.
   • Mary Chesnut's Civil War. C. Vann Woodward, ed. New Haven: Yale University Press, 1981.

3. February 18, 1861–December 8, 1861; January–June 26, 1865; Personal diary; life on her in-laws' Alabama plantation; in Camden and Charleston, South Carolina; in Virginia; with her husband at the Confederate Provisional Congress; friendship with Varina Davis; early postwar days.
   • The Private Mary Chesnut: The Unpublished Civil War Diaries. C. Vann Woodward and Elisabeth Muhlenfeld, eds. New York: Oxford University Press, 1984.
   REVIEW: Choice, v. 22, p. 1398, May, 1985.

4. "Diary Excerpts," in: Philip Dunaway and Mel Evans, eds. A Treasury of the World's Great Diaries. New York: Doubleday, 1957; pp. 239–57.

5. "Diary Excerpts," in: Mary Jane Moffat and Charlotte Painter, eds. Revelations: Diaries of Women. New York: Random House, 1974; pp. 270–87.

1168. CHITTENDEN, Lucius Eugene (1824–1900)
   Personal diary; Vermonter was Register of the Treasury under Salmon P. Chase (q.v.); later a lawyer and state senator; life in wartime Washington; department business.
   • Invisible Siege: The Journal of Lucius E. Chittenden, April 15, 1861–July 14, 1861 John R. Adams, ed. San Diego, Cal.: American Exchange Press, 1969; 1500 copies.

1169. CLARKE, Miss ---
   December 24, 1861–January 1, 1863
   Personal diary; work as a nurse in a Charlottesville, Virginia, hospital; duties; letters from home.
   • "Midway Hospital: 1861–1863: The Diary of Miss Clarke of South Carolina," Magazine of Albemarle County History, v. 22, pp. 161–90, 1963–64.

1170. COOK, Anna Maria Green (1844–1936)
   January 1, 1861–December 31, 1867; gaps
   Personal diary; social life and beaus; Yankees in Milledgeville; melodramatic posturing.
   • The Journal of a Milledgeville Girl, 1861–1867 James C. Bonner, ed. Athens: University of Georgia Press, 1964.

1171. CRACROFT, Sophia (1816-92)
       April 22-June 25, 1861
       Travel diary; niece of the widow of Sir John Franklin accom-
panied her aunt to Hawaii; entertaining account of their visit.
       • Korn, Alfons L. The Victorian Visitors: An Account of
       the Hawaiian Kingdom, 1861-1866. Honolulu: University of
       Hawaii Press, 1968.

1172. CRAIG, Samuel Alfred (1839-1920)
       May, 1861-December 25, 1866
       Personal diary; enlisted from Jefferson College in Pennsylvania;
wounded at the Battle of Fair Oaks; at Chancellorsville and Fredericksburg; invalided and sent to Camp Morton, a Federal prison camp, as
a guard; after the war went to Freedman's Bureau in Galveston,
Texas; mixture of diary entries and memoir written later.
       • "Captain Samuel A. Craig's Memoirs of Civil War and Re-
       construction," Western Pennsylvania Historical Magazine, v.
       13, pp. 215-35, October, 1930; v. 14, pp. 43-60, January,
       1931; pp. 115-37, April, 1931; pp. 191-206, July, 1931; pp.
       258-779, October, 1931.

1173. CRENSHAW, Edward (1842-1911)
       July 4, 1861-June 19, 1865
       Military diary; in the 17th Alabama; wounded at Chickamauga;
later a marine lieutenant under Admiral Semmes (q.v.); service on
and sea; one of the most complete Civil War diaries for the length
of time covered.
       • "Diary of Captain Edward Crenshaw of the Confederate
       States Army," Alabama Historical Quarterly, v. 1, pp. 261-70,
       Fall, 1940; pp. 438-52, Winter, 1940; v. 2, pp. 52-71, Spring,
       1940; pp. 221-38, Summer, 1940; pp. 365-85, Fall, 1940, pp.
       465-82, Winter, 1940.

1174. CRIPPEN, Edward W. (-1863)
       Military diary; Cairo, Illinois; Stone's River, Tennessee; died
at Chattanooga; good battle descriptions.
       • "The Diary of Edward W. Crippen, Private 27th Illinois
       Volunteers, War of the Rebellion, August 7, 1861, to Septem-
       ber 19, 1863," Robert J. Kerner, ed. Transactions of the Illi-
       nois State Historical Society for the Year 1909, v. 10, pp.
       220-82.

1175. CROSSLEY, William J.
       July 22, 1861-May 31, 1862
       Military diary; lengthy descriptions; some humor and irony.
       • Extracts from My Diary, and from Experiences While Board-
       ing with Jefferson Davis, in Some of His Notorious Hotels.
       Providence: The Rhode Island Soldiers and Sailors Historical
       Society, 1903; 250 copies.

1176. DALY, Maria Lydig (1824-94)
       January 31, 1861-December 30, 1865

Personal diary; wartime experiences of a New York City judge's
wife; staunch Unionist of Irish-American upper class; effect of the
war on New Yorkers; 1863 Draft Riots; gossipy, insightful, catty,
generous; one of the better non-combatant diaries.
- _Diary of a Union Lady, 1861-65_. Harold Earl Hammond, ed.
New York: Funk & Wagnalls, 1962.
REVIEWS: Book Review Digest 1962, p. 273. Book Review
Index 1979, p. 107.

1177. DAVIS, Charles E.
August 1-9, 1862
Military diary; life on the march.
- "Diary Excerpts," in: Philip Dunaway and Mel Evans,
eds.; A Treasury of the World's Great Diaries. New York:
Doubleday, 1957; pp. 260-63.

1178. DAY, David L.
September 6, 1861-November 2, 1864
Military diary; comments on countryside, people, mores, food;
transcribed dialog; very detailed; one of the better Civil War diaries.
- My Diary of Rambles with the 25th Mass. Volunteer Infantry,
With Burnside's Coast Division. Milford, Mass.: King & Bill-
ings Printers, 1884.

1179. DODD, James McKee (1840-62)
July 11, 1861-February 7, 1862
Military diary; life on the march.
- "Civil War Diary of James M. Dodd of the 'Cooper Guards,'"
Register of the Kentucky Historical Society, v. 59, pp. 343-
49, October, 1961.

1180. DOWNING, Alexander G. (1842-   )
Military diary; service in Tennessee with the 11th Iowa Infantry; siege and surrender of Vicksburg; through Georgia with Sherman; Grand Review in Washington, D.C.; covers the whole war but
is not especially illuminating.
- Downing's Civil War Diary ... August 15, 1861-July 31,
1865. Olynthus B. Clark, ed. Des Moines: The History Department of Iowa, 1916.

1181. EAGLETON, Ethie M. Foute (1835-   )
December 25, 1861-December 31, 1867; gaps
Personal diary; Tennessee native; wife of a Confederate sol-
dier; anxieties for her husband during the war; marauding Yankees.
- "'Stray Thoughts': The Civil War Diary of Ethie M. Foute
Eagleton," Elvie Eagleton Skipper, ed. East Tennessee His-
torical Society Publications, v. 40, pp. 128-37, 1968; v. 41,
pp. 116-28, 1969.

1182. EAGLETON, George
1861

Personal diary; extracts; article based on the diaries of a married couple in Tennessee; see above entry for wife.
* Pearson, Alden B., Jr. "Middle-Class, Border-State Family During the Civil War," Civil War History, v. 22, pp. 318-36, December, 1976.

1183. ELY, Alfred (1815-92)
July 24-November 29, 1861
Prison diary; civilian New York congressman observing the 1st Battle of Bull Run was taken prisoner; parolled in Richmond for part of the time; well-treated; contradicts Yankee newspaper accounts of conditions in Richmond; lengthy entries; as chivalrous as the Southerners.
* Journal of Alfred Ely, A Prisoner of War in Richmond. Charles Lanman, ed. New York: D. Appleton & Co., 1862.

1184. ELY, Ralph (1819-83)
August 12, 1861-April 1, 1864
Personal diary; line or two a day with some longer entries.
* With the Wandering Regiment: The Diary of Captain Ralph Ely of the Eighth Michigan Infantry. George M. Blackburn, ed. Mt. Pleasant: Central Michigan University Press, 1965.

1185. FARRINGTON, Josiah (1827-95)
July 27, 1861-January 17, 1863; gaps
Letter journal; service in Kentucky and Tennessee with the 14th Ohio Infantry.
* "Josiah Farrington's Civil War Diary and Letters," Myron Bradley, ed. Northwest Ohio Quarterly, v. 49, pp. 87-97, Summer, 1977.

1186. FAVILL, Josiah Marshall
April 16, 1861-May 11, 1864
Military diary; life on the march with the 71st New York Regiment.
* The Diary of a Young Officer Serving With the Armies of the United States During the War of the Rebellion. Chicago: R. R. Donnelley & Sons Co., 1909.

1187. FLETCHER, William B. (1837-1907)
June 6-27, 1861
Personal diary; medical man in West Virginia; includes his sketches.
* "The Civil War Journal of William B. Fletcher," Loriman S. Brigham, ed. Indiana Magazine of History, v. 57, pp. 41-76, March, 1961.

1188. FROST, Griffin
August 1, 1861-April 12, 1865
Military diary; enlisted in the Missouri State Guards, Co. A in Marion County; service in Arkasas; captured; in Gratiot Street

Prison; released and later in Alton Military Prison; details on prison
life; well written.
- Camp and Prison Journal, Embracing Scenes in Camp, on
  the March, and in Prisons. Quincy, Ill.: Quincy Herald
  Book and Job Office, 1867.

1189. GEER, Allen Morgan (1840-1926)
       June 8, 1861-July 14, 1865
       Military diary; at Vicksburg; with Sherman to the sea; briefly
imprisoned and exchanged; short entries for the entire period; good.
- The Civil War Diary of Allen Morgan Geer, 20th Regiment
  Illinois Volunteers. Mary Ann Andersen, ed. Denver: R. C.
  Appleman, 1977.

1190. GIESECKE, Julius
       October 23, 1861-March 12, 1865
       Military diary; German immigrant to Austin County, Texas;
recruited for the invasion of northern Mexico; battle at Glorieta Pass;
Louisiana campaigns.
- "The Diary of Julius Giesecke, 1861-1865," Oscar Haas,
  trans. Military History of Texas and the Southwest, v. 3, pp.
  228-42, Winter, 1963; v. 4, pp. 27-54, Spring, 1964.

1191. GLENN, William Wilkins (1824-76)
       January 1, 1861-October 28, 1869
       Personal diary; successful businessman owned a controlling
interest in the Baltimore Daily Exchange; the pro-Southern bias of
the paper caused his imprisonment early in the war; spent a year in
Europe; extensive comments along with a report of facts provide
background to the social life of his time at home and abroad; one of
the better non-combatant diaries.
- Between North and South: A Maryland Journalist Views
  the Civil War: The Narrative of William Wilkins Glenn, 1861-
  1869. Bayly Ellen Marks and Mark Norton Schatz, eds. Rutherford, N.J.: Fairleigh Dickinson University Press, 1976.

1192. GULICK, William O. (1843-63)
       September 15, 1861-November 12, 1862
       Personal diary; letters interspersed with diary entries; camp
life; food; ends with a letter to his sister from a friend telling of
Gulick's death.
- "The Journal and Letters of Corporal William O. Gulick,"
  Max H. Guyer, ed. Iowa Journal of History, v. 28, pp. 194-
  267, April, 1930; pp. 390-455, July, 1930; pp. 543-603, October, 1930.

1193. GUROWSKI, Adam (1805-66)
       March 4, 1861-1865
       Personal diary; Polish expatriate; reports and comments on
the war; its conduct by both sides; knew many Union officials.
- Diary. 3 vols. New York: Burt Franklin, 1963.

1194. HALL, James Edmond (1841-1915)
        May, 1861-April 28, 1865
        Military diary; native of Barbour County, Virginia; captured
after the Battle of Gettysburg; imprisoned at Fort Delaware; eventual
release.
        • The Diary of a Confederate Soldier, James E. Hall. Ruth
        Woods Dayton, ed. Charleston, W. Va.: Education Founda-
        tion, 1961.

1195. HAMILTON, James Allen (1842-64)
        October 4, 1861-1864
        Military diary; service with the 15th Texas Infantry in the
Trans-Mississippi Department and Louisiana; very short entries.
        • "The Civil War Diary of James Allen Hamilton, 1861-1864,"
        Alwyn Barr, ed. Texana, v. 2, pp. 132-45, 1964.

1196. HANCOCK, Richard Ramsey (1840-1906)
        June 26, 1861-October 29, 1864
        Military diary; service in Kentucky and Tennessee; short,
daily entries.
        • Hancock's Diary: Or, A History of the Second Tennessee
        Confederate Cavalry. Nashville, Tenn.: Brandon Printing
        Co., 1887.

1197. HARRISON, Dr. Samuel A. (1822-   )
        July 17, 1861-May 31, 1865
        Personal diary; extracts from a manuscript in the Maryland
Historical Society; good picture of life in Baltimore during the war.
        • "The Civil War Journal of Dr. Samuel A. Harrison," Charles
        L. Wagandt, ed. Civil War History, v. 13, pp. 131-46, June,
        1967.

1198. HAY, John Milton (1838-1905)
        1. April 18, 1861-December 12, 1870; Personal diary; private
secretary to President Lincoln during the war; secretary of the American Legation in Paris; diplomatic service in Vienna and Madrid;
friendly with prominent Americans throughout the decade; very full
entries for the war years, shorter, less informative as time wears
on; good picture of Lincoln and those near him.
        • Lincoln and the Civil War in the Diaries and Letters of John
        Hay. Tyler Dennett, ed. New York: Dodd, Mead, 1939.

        2. April 18, 1861-October 6, 1869; extracts appear in volume
1.
        • Letters of John Hay and Extracts from Diary. New York:
        Gordian Press, 1969.

        3. "Diary Excerpts," in: Philip Dunaway and Mel Evans,
eds. A Treasury of the World's Great Diaries. New York: Doubleday, 1957; pp. 278-80.

1199.   HEARTSILL, William Williston (1839-1916)
        1.   April 19, 1861-May 20, 1865; Military diary; service with
the 2nd Texas Cavalry, Lane Rangers, in Texas; imprisoned at Camp
Butler, Illinois; exchanged; guard duty at Camp Ford, Tyler, Texas;
humorous; three versions printed here, original and two revisions.
        •   Fourteen Hundred and Ninety-One Days in the Confederate
        Army. Jackson, Tenn.: McCowat-Mercer Press, 1954; pp.
        269-92.

        2.   November 9, 1862-January, 1863; excerpt.
        •   "A Texas Ranger Company at the Battle of Arkansas Post,"
        Arthur Marvin Shaw, ed. Arkansas Historical Quarterly, v.
        9, pp. 270-77, Winter, 1950.

1200.   HENRY, James
        January 1-December 31, 1861
        Personal diary; farm chores and war news.
        •   "A Washington County Diary of 1861," W. J. Lemke, ed.
        Flashback [Washington County (Arkansas) Historical Society],
        v. 7, pp. 11-17, August, 1957.

1201.   HOLMES, Emma Edwards (1838-1910)
        1.   February 13, 1861-April 7, 1866; Personal diary; daughter
of prominent South Carolina family; in Charleston during the fall of
Fort Sumter; home destroyed by fire in December, 1861; subsequent
periods spent on plantations in the area and in Camden, South Carolina; encountered Sherman's army; life under Reconstruction; intelligent but often poorly informed on the war's progress; conscious of
society's strictures on women; often ill; "her own enemy in her dic-
tatorial character & prejudiced views"; "What a bundle of contradic-
tions I am"; excellent.
        •   The Diary of Miss Emma Holmes, 1861-1866. John F. Mars-
        zalek, ed. Baton Rouge: Louisiana State University Press,
        1979.
            REVIEWS: Book Review Digest 1980, p. 571. Book Review
            Index 1980, p. 240; 1981, p. 266. America: History and
            Life 18B:696.

        2.   December 16, 1861; describes fire which occurred Decem-
ber 11-12 and its aftermath.
        •   "The Charleston Fire of 1861 as Described in the Emma E.
        Holmes Diary," John F. Marszalek, Jr., ed. South Carolina
        Historical Magazine v. 76, pp. 60-67, April, 1975.

        3.   December 7, 1862; sermon preached by Rev. John H.
Elliott.
        •   "A Civil War Sermon as Recounted in the Emma E. Holmes
        Diary," John F. Marszalek, ed. Historical Magazine of the
        Protestant Episcopal Church, v. 46, pp. 57-62, March, 1977.

1202.   HOLMES, Oliver Wendell (1841-1935)
        1.   May 1, 1861-July 8, 1864; Personal diary; intermixed with

letters home; in later life a judge of the U.S. Supreme Court; camp
life; fighting; wounded.
  • Touched with Fire; Civil War Letters and Diary of Oliver
  Wendell Holmes, 1861-1864. Mark De Wolfe Howe, ed. New
  York: Da Capo Press, 1969; reprint of 1946 ed.

     2. "Diary Excerpts," in: Philip Dunaway and Mel Evans,
eds. A Treasury of the World's Great Diaries. New York: Doubleday, 1957; pp. 268-71.

1203. HOTCHKISS, Jedediah (1828-99)
     1861-1865
     Military diary; staff aide to General Stonewall Jackson.
       • McDonald, Archie P. "The Journal of Jedediah Hotchkiss,
       1861-1865," Ph.D., Louisiana State University, 1965. (Disser-
       tation Abstracts, 25/12, p. 7227)

1204. HOWE, Henry Warren (1841-)
     May 14, 1861-April 28, 1865
     Military diary; served in the 30th Massachusetts Infantry;
early entries are sometimes lengthy and colorful; those after January,
1863, are only a few words in length.
       • Passages from the Life of Henry Warren Howe, Consisting
       of Diary and Letters Written During the Civil War 1861-65.
       Lowell, Mass.: Courier-Citizen Co., 1899.

1205. HUDSON, James G.
     May 1-September 18, 1861
     Military diary; service in Virginia.
       • "A Story of Company D, 4th Alabama Infantry Regiment,
       C. S. A.: Alma H. Pate, ed. Alabama Historical Quarterly,
       v. 23, pp. 139-79, Spring, 1961.

1206. ICKIS, Alonzo, Ferdinand (1836-1917)
     October 27, 1861-June 7, 1863
     Personal diary; Ohioan who went to the Colorado gold rush
joined the Union Army; Battle of Valverde; marching; observations
on people and sights in New Mexico by a wide-eyed Midwesterner.
       • Bloody Trails Along the Rio Grande: A Day-by-day Diary
       of Alonzo Ferdinand Ickis, 1836-1917, A Soldier and His Ac-
       tivities Company B. Denver: Old West, 1958; 500 copies.

1207. ILLARION, Father (1818-)
     June 20, 1861-August 21, 1868
     Missionary diary; extracts; chiefly concerned with priest's at-
titudes toward native peoples; church work.
       • "Eskimos and Indians of Western Alaska 1861-1868: Ex-
       tracts from the Diary of Father Illarion," Wendell H. Oswalt,
       ed. University of Alaska Anthropological Papers, v. 8, pp.
       100-18, May, 1960.

1208.   JAMES, Westwood Wallace (-1868)
        July 26, 1861-January 19, 1862
        Military diary; civilian doctor enlisted in the 16th Alabama
Volunteer Infantry after the first Battle of Manassas; service in Kentucky and Tennessee.
        • "'This is War--Glorious War': The Diary of Corproal West-
        wood James," Michael Musick, ed. Civil War Times Illustrated,
        v. 17, pp. 34-42, October, 1978.

1209.   JONES, Andrew J.
        July 1-7, 1861
        Military diary; account of Confederate defeat at Beverly, Vir-
ginia, which made possible McClellan's victory at Rich Mountain.
        • Miller, William D. "What Happened at Beverly?: The Ac-
        count of Andrew J. Jones," West Virginia History, v. 36,
        pp. 225-28, 1975.

1210.   JONES, John Beauchamp (1810-66)
        1. April 12, 1861-April 19, 1865; Personal diary; achieved
some fame with books about his youth published before the war;
served under five Confederate secretaries of war; petty office squabbles; news of the war received in Richmond; takes great delight in
being right at others' expense; gossipy; an outstanding non-combatant
diary of the time.
        • A Rebel War Clerk's Diary at the Confederate States Cap-
        ital. Philadelphia: J. B. Lippincott, 1866; several other edi-
        tions.

        2. "Diary Excerpts," in: Philip Dunaway and Mel Evans,
        eds. A Treasury of the World's Great Diaries. New York: Double-
day, 1957; pp. 275-77.

1211.   JOSSELYN, Francis
        April 14, 1861-May, 1864
        Personal diary; extracts; served on the steamer Reliance of
the Potomac Flotilla; rescued survivors from the collision of two troop
transports.
        • Taylor, John M. "Francis Josselyn: A Gunboat Captain's
        Diary," Manuscripts, v. 33, pp. 113-22, Spring, 1981.

1212.   KEAN, Robert Garlick Hill (1828-98)
        September 15, 1861-October 23, 1865; gaps
        Personal diary; Virginian and lawyer; appointed to a bureau
of the Confederate War Department which co-ordinated much work;
service in the 11th Virginia Infantry in the early days of the war;
good picture of life in higher echelons of government.
        • Inside the Confederate Government: The Diary of Robert
        Garlick Hill Kean, Head of the Bureau of War. Edward
        Younger, ed. New York: Oxford University Press, 1957.

1213.   KIENE, Francis A. (1839-1924)
        August 19, 1861-May 29, 1865

Personal diary; German emigrant settled in Ohio with his family at the age of 14; enlisted in the 49th Ohio Volunteers; at the battles of Shiloah, Murfreesboro, Chickamauga, Chattanooga and Atlanta; daily entries for almost the entire period.

• A Civil War Diary: The Journal of Francis A. Kiene, 1861-1864: A Family History. Ralph E. Kiene, Jr., comp. Shawnee Mission, Kan.: The Author, 1974.

1214. KITTINGER, Joseph (1839-)
November 25, 1861-July 14, 1865
Personal diary; Volunteer Light Artillery of Niagara County, N.Y.; 23rd New York Independent Battery; served almost exclusively in North Carolina; stationed outside Washington, D.C., early in his enlistment; hospitalized with fevers; his battery supposedly fired the last shots of the war; rose from private to first lieutenant.

• Diary of Joseph Kittinger, 1861-1865. Buffalo, N.Y.: Buffalo and Erie County Historical Society, 1963?

1215. LANDSBOROUGH, William (-1886)
November 18, 1861-June 5, 1862
Exploration diary; expedition set out from Brisbane before Howitt's letter on the "melancholy fate" of Burke and Wills reached Melbourne; details of terrain.

• Journal of Landsborough's Expedition from Carpentaria in Search of Burke and Wills. New York: Baillere Bros., 1862; reprinted Adelaide: Libraries Board of South Australia, 1963.

1216. LA TOUCHE, Rose (1848-)
March 7-April 1, 1861; January 1-February 24, 1867
Travel diaries; journey with her family in France and Italy; autobiographical notes; caring for a dying uncle; courted by Ruskin and refused him.

• John Ruskin and Rose La Touche: Her Unpublished Diaries of 1861 and 1867. Van Akin Burd, ed. Oxford: Clarendon Press, 1979.

1217. LITTLE, Lewis Henry (1817-62)
May 2, 1861-September 19, 1862
Military journal; troop movements; an account of his death.
• "The Diary of General Henry Little, C.S.A." Albert Castel, ed. Civil War Times Illustrated, v. 11, pp. 4-11, 41-47, October, 1972.

1218. LURIA, Albert Moses (1843-62)
August 19, 1861-January, 1862
Personal diary; served in the 23rd Regiment of North Carolina Volunteers; at the first Battle of Bull Run; thoughts on his sweetheart; died of a head wound received in the Battle of Seven Pines.

• "Albert Moses Luria, Gallant Young Confederate," American Jewish Archives, v. 7, pp. 90-103, January, 1955.

1219. McGUIRE, Judith White Brockenbrough
       1. May 4, 1861–May 4, 1865; Personal diary; Virginian forced
by the war to leave her home; spent time in Richmond; her husband
was in the Confederate government then became a chaplain; worked
in the Commisary Department; details of how non-combatants coped;
very "genteel" manner and acid comments on the "infallibility" of
Southern generals.
       • Diary of a Southern Refugee, During the War New York:
       E. J. Hale & Son, 1867; New York: Arno, 1972.

       2. May 4, 1861–May 4, 1865; excerpts.
       • "Diary of a Refugee in Richmond," in: Clarence Poe, ed.
       True Tales of the South at War.   Chapel Hill: University of
       North Carolina Press, 1961; pp. 149-84.

1220. McKINLEY, William (1843-1901)
       June 15–November 3, 1861
       Personal diary; became 25th president of the United States,
assassinated in office; service in 23rd Ohio Volunteers; boot camp at
Camp Chase, Ohio; in Virginia; reveals something of his character.
       • "A Civil War Diary of William McKinley," H. Wayne Morgan,
          ed.   Ohio Historical Quarterly, v. 69, pp. 272-90, 1960.

1221. MACKLEY, John
       April 18, 1861–March 20, 1862
       Military diary; served with Company A, 2nd Iowa Volunteer
Infantry; early entries read like a secretary's meeting minutes; from
Keokuk to St. Joseph, Missouri; short entry, mostly troop movements.
       • "The Civil War Diary of John Mackley," Mildred Throne, ed.
       Iowa Journal of History, v. 48, pp. 141-68, April, 1950.

1222. MALONE, Bartlett Yancey (1838-90)
       January 1, 1861–March 4, 1865; gaps
       Military diary; service with Company H, 6th North Carolina
Regiment; phonetically spelled account of battles in Virginia, Maryland and Pennsylvania; imprisoned at Point Lookout, Maryland; mostly
weather.
       • Whipt 'em Every Time: The Diary of Bartlett Yancey Ma-
       lone. William Whatley Pierson, Jr., ed. in: James Sprunt
       Historical Publications, v. 16, pp. 3-59, 1919; reprinted Jack-
       son, Tenn.:   McCowat-Mercer Press, 1960.

1223. MAURY, Betty Herndon
       June 3, 1861–February 18, 1863
       Personal diary; life in Fredericksburg, Virginia, by a young
wife with her small daughter; visits and news of the war; much second hand information about the progress of the war.
       • The Confederate Diary of Betty Herndon Maury, daughter
       of Lieut. Commander M. F. Maury ... 1861-1863.   Alice Maury
       Parmelee, ed.   Washington, D.C.:   Pvt. ptd., 1938.

1224. MAYFIELD, Leroy S. (1841-)
       July 17, 1861-June 30, 1864; gaps
       Letter journal; service with the 22nd Indiana Volunteers; Chat-
tanooga campaign; with Sherman through Georgia; very good descriptions of camp life.
       • "A Hoosier Invades the Confederacy: Letters and Diaries
       of Leroy S. Mayfield," John D. Barnhart, ed. Indiana Maga-
       zine of History, v. 39, pp. 144-91, March, 1943.

1225. MEANS, Alexander (1801-83)
       January 1-December 31, 1861
       Personal diary; medical doctor taught and practiced in Atlanta;
research experiments; the coming war.
       • Diary for 1861. Ross H. McLean, ed. Atlanta: Emory
       University Library, 1949.

1226. MOORE, Nancy (1807-89)
       Official journal; a record of society business; caught between
Union and rebels by reason of their location and reputation for generosity; much on war news and the activities of Shakers; rail line
passed the community; interesting, well-written noncombatant account.
       • The Journal of Eldress Nancy, Kept at the South Union Ken-
       tucky, Shaker Colony, August 15, 1861-September 4, 1864.
       Mary Julia Neal, ed. Nashville: Parthenon Press, 1963.

1227. MOORE, Robert Augustus (1838-63)
       May 27, 1861-September 19, 1863; gaps
       Personal diary; well-educated private with the 17th Mississippi
from Holly Springs; died at Chickamauga the day after the last entry;
sometimes humorous.
       • "Robert A. Moore, The Diary of a Confederate Private,"
       James W. Silver, ed. Louisiana Historical Quarterly, v. 39,
       pp. 235-374, July, 1956; reprinted as A Life for the Confed-
       eracy, As Recorded in the Pocket Diaries of Pvt. Robert A.
       Moore, Company G, 17th Mississippi Regiment, Confederate
       Guards, Holly Springs, Mississippi. Jackson, Tenn.: McCowat-
       Mercer Press, 1959.

1228. MORGAN, George P. (1820-61)
       July 8-September 15, 1861
       Personal diary; died at Camp Chase, Ohio.
       • "A Confederate Journal," George E. Moore, ed. West Vir-
       ginia History, v. 22, pp. 210-06, July, 1961.

1229. MORGAN, Stephen A. (1835-1911)
       October 3-December 26, 1861
       Personal diary; nephew of George P. Morgan (q.v.).
       • "A Confederate Journal," George E. Moore, ed. West Vir-
       ginia History, v. 22, pp. 207-16, July, 1961.

1230. ONDERDONK, James H. (1845-63)
       1861-July 28, 1863

Personal diary; undated excerpts from a lad who died of dysentery.

- Fabris, Dino. "A Civil War Diary," New York History, v. 49, pp. 76-89, 1968.

1231. PATTERSON, Edmund DeWitt (1842-)
July 9, 1861-April 9, 1865
Military diary; Ohioan working in Alabama at the war's opening believed in the Southern Cause; joined the 9th Alabama Infantry; well-read; captured at Gettysburg and imprisoned on Johnson's Island for almost two years; well done.
- Yankee Rebel: The Civil War Journal of Edmund DeWitt Patterson. John G. Barrett, ed. Chapel Hill: University of North Carolina Press, 1966.

1232. PEARL, Louisa Brown (1810-86)
September 1, 1861-March 22, 1862
Personal diary; ran a boarding house in Nashville; her husband joined the Union, her son the 1st Tennessee Infantry.
- "The Civil War Diary of Louisa Brown Pearl," James A. Hoobler, ed. Tennessee Historical Quarterly, v. 38, pp. 308-21, 1979.

1233. POE, James T. (1829-1913)
August 22, 1861-September 1, 1862
Personal diary; second cousin of Edgar Allan Poe; imprisoned on Johnson's Island, Ohio.
- The Raving Foe: The Civil War Diary of Major James T. Poe, C. S. A., and the 11th Arkansas Volunteers, and a Complete List of Prisoners. J. C. Poe, comp. and ed. Eastland, Tx.: Longhorn Press, 1967.

1234. PORTER, William Clendenin (1832-67)
July 3, 1861-July 4, 1863
Personal diary; siege of Port Hudson.
- "War Diary of W. C. Porter," J. V. Frederick, ed. Arkansas Historical Quarterly, v. 11, pp. 286-314, Winter, 1952.

1235. RICKETTS, Fanny
July-December 13, 1861
Personal diary; article based on the diary kept by the wife of a Federal officer wounded at the First Manassas.
- Naisawald, L. VanLoan. "Fanny Ricketts: Nurse, Diarist, Devoted Wife," Virginia Cavalcade, v. 21, pp. 14-21, Winter, 1972.

1236. ROBERTSON, Martha Wayles (1812-67)
January 27, 1861-May 26, 1866
Spiritual diary; extracts; life on a plantation in Chesterfield County, Virginia; war news intrudes; concern for family.
- Helmreich, Jonathan E. "A Prayer for the Spirit of

Acceptance: The Journal of Martha Wayles Robertson, 1860-66," Historical Magazine of the Protestant Episcopal Church, v. 46, pp. 397-408, 1977.

1237. ROBINSON, Oliver S. (1839-63)
    October 21, 1861-May 11, 1863
    Military diary; life on the march with the 11th Wisconsin Volunteers; siege of Vicksburg; died of lockjaw resulting from a hip wound.
    • The Diary and Letters of Oliver S. Robinson. Opal Hanson, comp. and ed. Kensington, Md.: Village Press, 1968.

1238. ROSS, Charles (1838-   )
    1. 1861; Military diary.
    • "Diary of Charles Ross 1861," Vermont History, v. 29, pp. 65-78, April, 1961.

    2. January 1, 1862-December 31, 1862; Military diary; 11th Vermont Infantry; civilian and soldier life.
    • "Diary of Charles Ross, 1862," Vermont History, v. 30, pp. 85-148, 1962.

    3. "Diary of Charles Ross for 1863," Vermont History, v. 31, no. 1, pp. 4-64, 1963.

    4. June 23, 1864-November 23, 1864; Prison diary; many deaths, hardships; exchanged.
    • "A Vermonter in Andersonville: Diary of Charles Ross, 1864," C. M. Destler ed. Vermont History, v. 25, pp. 229-45, July 1957.

1239. RUDISILL, James Jefferson (1811-99)
    July 20, 1861-April 14, 1886; fullest entries are for the war years.
    Military diary; camp life; letters to and from his family; of historical interest.
    • The Day of Our Abraham, 1811-1899. York, Pa.: York Printing Co., 1936.

1240. SALISBURY, De Witt Clinton (1844?-1915)
    January 27, 1861-
    Personal diary; farm boy of Dane County, Wisconsin; school days, student life at the University of Wisconsin; marriage and family life; extracts connected by the editor's summaries; fair account of nineteenth century rural life.
    • Pages from the Diaries of De Witt Clinton Salisbury, 19th Century Wisconsin Citizen, and Civil War Soldier. Mildred Hansen Osgood, ed. Wauwatosa, Wis.: M. H. Osgood, 1974.

1241. SANDERS, Lorenzo Jackson (1838-1925)
    Military diary; extracts; army career from his enlistment in

the 30th Tennessee Infantry in September, 1861 to his return home;
in several Yankee prison camps.
> • Harrison, Lowell H. "The Diary of an 'Average' Confederate
> Soldier," Tennessee Historical Quarterly, v. 29, pp. 256-71,
> Fall, 1970.

1242. SANFORD, Mrs. Byron (-1915)
December 1, 1861-March 15, 1862
Personal diary; travel conditions between the two forts; the
life of a cavalry wife.
> • "Life at Camp Weld and Fort Lyon in 1861-62: An Extract
> From the Diary of Mrs. Byron N. Sanford," Colorado Magazine,
> v. 7, pp. 132-39, July, 1930.

1243. SCATES, James Madison (1837-84)
June 4, 1861-July, 1964
Military diary; rose to captain of the 40th Virginia Infantry;
at the Second Battle of Manassas; Antietam; Fredericksburg; captured
and sent to Johnson's Island.
> • "The Civil War Journal of James Madison Scates," W. Har-
> rison Daniel, ed. Virginia Social Science Journal, v. 2, pp.
> 3-20, April, 1967.

1244. SEATON, Benjamin M. (1831?-   )
November 5, 1861-April 24, 1865
Military diary; with the 10th Texas Volunteer Infantry; nothing
written while imprisoned at Camp Douglas; in the Atlanta campaign;
pedestrian.
> • The Bugle Softly Blows: The Confederate Diary of Benja-
> min M. Seaton. Harold B. Simpson, ed. Waco, Tx.: Texian
> Press, 1965.

1245. SHILLICH, John (1843-73)
September 12, 1861-March 31, 1864
Military diary; drummer boy of Company A, 51st Regiment of
Pennsylvania Volunteers; at Bull Run, Vicksburg, and Petersburg;
illustrated with contemporary prints and a picture of his drum.
> • Parsons, Phyllis Vibbard. "Diary," Pennsylvania Folklife,
> v. 28, pp. 27-37, 1979.

1246. SILL, Edward Rowland (1841-87)
Sea diary; Yale graduate; poet and professor of English at the
University of California, Berkeley; introspective; descriptions of fish
and birds sighted.
> • Around the Horn: A Journal, December 10, 1861 to March
> 25, 1862. Stanley T. Williams and Barbara A. Simison, eds.
> New Haven: Yale University Press, 1944.

1247. SMITH, Benjamin T. (1844-1908)
October 8, 1861-November 8, 1865
Military diary; Kankakee citizen with the 51st Illinois Regiment;

2 enlistments in the Army of the Cumberland; at Chickamauga; on to
Atlanta and return to Tennessee; orderly and scout; well done.
- Private Smith's Journal: Recollections of the Late War.
Clyde C. Walton, ed. Chicago: R. R. Donnelley, 1963.

1248. SMITH, Elizabeth Oakes (1806-93)
        October 25-November 18, 1861
        Personal diary; poet, novelist, lecturer and feminist married
to humorist Seba Smith; life at their Long Island home; seeing troops
off to war.
- "Excerpts from the Diary of Elizabeth Oakes Smith," Joy
Wiltenberg, ed. Signs, v. 9, pp. 534-48, Spring, 1984.

1249. SMITH, Isaac Noyes (1831-   )
        September 15-November 30, 1861
        Military diary; 27th Regiment of Virginia Volunteers; resigned
his commission to be with his family which was divided in loyalty between North and South.
- "A Virginian's Dilemma," William C. Childers, ed. West Virginia History, v. 27, pp. 173-200, April, 1966.

1250. SOUTHWICK, Thomas Paine (1837-92)
        May 27, 1861-May 14, 1863; gaps
        Military diary; orphaned New Yorker was at both battles of
Bull Run; service in Virginia with the 5th New York Volunteers;
lengthy account of the attack on Fredericksburg; probably includes
later additions.
- A Duryee Zouave. Washington, D.C.: Acme Printing Co.,
1930.

1251. STONE, E. Wyman (1831-   )
        July 19, 1861-April 6, 1862
        Military diary; extracts and commentary; his service with the
21st Massachusetts ended with the amputation of a foot.
- "From the Civil War Diary and Letters of Corporal E. W.
Stone, 21st Massachusetts," Paul Mariani, ed. Massachusetts
Review, v. 16, pp. 759-80, August, 1975.

1252. STONE, Sarah Katherine (Holmes) (1841-1907)
        May 15, 1861-September 28, 1868
        Personal diary; life on a Louisiana cotton plantation with a
widowed mother, siblings and slaves; fled to Texas when the Yankees
came and stayed until the war's end; death of her brothers in the
fighting; intelligent, well-read, thoughtful young woman; excellent.
- Brokenburn: The Journal of Kate Stone, 1861-1868. John
Q. Anderson, ed. Baton Rouge: Louisiana State University
Press, 1955.

1253. STORY, James Osgood Andrew (-1862)
        January 11-December 29, 1861
        Personal diary; student life at Southern University, Greens-
boro, Alabama.

- "Pocket Diary for 1861," Dr. Llerena Friend, ed. Alabama Historical Quarterly, v. 28, p. 51-121, Spring and Summer, 1966.

1254.   TEAL, John W. (1828?-80)
September 24, 1861-November 12, 1864
Military diary; service in California, New Mexico and Arizona with the California Volunteers, Company B; return to his Canadian home via the Isthmus of Panama; weather and life on the march; some longer entries reveal his personality.
- "Soldier in the California Column: The Diary of John W. Teal," Henry P. Walker, ed. Arizona and the West, v. 13, pp. 33-82, Spring, 1971.

1255.   TENNEY, Luman Harris (1841-80)
September 9, 1861-July 11, 1865
Military diary; Oberlin college student enlisted in the 2nd Ohio Cavalry; at Camp Wade; in the 1863 East Tennessee campaign and 1864 Virginia campaign; rose to brevetted major; staccato style conveys the disjointedness of life on the march.
- War Diary of Luman Harris Tenney, 1861-1865. Cleveland: Evangelical Publishing House, 1914.
- For an interesting comment on his diary and family see: Elizabeth Hampsten. Read This Only to Yourself. Bloomington: Indiana University Press, 1982; pp. 134-43.

1256.   TORRENCE, Leonidas (-1863)
June 4-July 4, 1863
Military diary; in the Gettysburg campaign with the 13th North Carolina Regiment; died of wounds.
- "The Road to Gettysburg: The Diary and Letters of Leonidas Torrence of the Gaston Guards," Haskell Monroe, ed. North Carolina Historical Review, v. 36, pp. 476-517, 1959.

1257.   VEDDER, Charles Stuart (1826-1917)
May 10-July 2, 1861
Military diary; New Yorker and minister; stationed in Monticello, Georgia; displays Southern sympathies.
- "The Diary of the Rev. Charles S. Vedder, May-July, 1861," Willard E. Wight, ed. Georgia Historical Quarterly, v. 39, pp. 68-90, March, 1955.

1258.   WAINWRIGHT, Charles Shiels (1826-1907)
December 25, 1861-May 23, 1865
Military diary; well-to-do Albany citizen with the 1st New York Artillery; officer with the Army of the Potomac; at Chancellorsville, Antietam and Gettysburg; comments on military, social and political aspects of the war; detailed and well-balanced.
- A Diary of Battle: The Personal Journals of Col. Charles Shiels Wainright, 1861-1865. Allan Nevins, ed. New York: Harcourt, Brace and World, 1962.
  REVIEW: Book Review Digest 1963, p. 1035.

1259. WAITZ, Julia Ellen LeGrand (1829-81)
       December 1, 1861-April 8, 1863
          Personal diary; lived with her sister on Prytania Street;
   brother in the Confederate Army; fall of the city and Federal occupation; social life and friends; rumors of troop movements; victories
   and disasters; one of the best written women's diaries of the war.
          • The Journal of Julia Le Grand, New Orleans, 1862-1863.
       Kate Mason Rowland and Mrs. Morris L. Croxall, eds. Rich-
       mond: Everett Waddey Co., 1911.

1260. WALDEN, James A. (1843-95)
       July 1, 1861-February 12, 1864; July 7, 1870-April 15, 1890
          Personal diary; two phases of an Arkansas native's life; en-
   listment and service in the Confederate Army; the siege of Port Hudson; capture and imprisonment at Johnson's Island; life as a Methodist circuit rider in Arkansas; family life with a wife and six children;
   farm chores and preaching.
          • The Journals of James A. Walden. W. J. Lemke, ed. (Bul-
       letin Series nos. 4-5) Fayetteville, Ark.: Washington County
       Historical Society, 1954.

1261. WELD, Stephen Minot (1842-   )
       October 6, 1861-May 26, 1865
          Military diary; Harvard graduate; with the 56th Massachusetts
   Volunteers in almost all the campaigns of the Army of the Potomac;
   involved in the General Fitz John Porter court-martial; on the staff
   of General Horatio G. Wright; briefly in Libby Prison; very full entries; one of the most comprehensive of those diaries which cover the
   entire war period.
          • War Diary and Letters of Stephen Minot Weld, 1861-1865.
       2nd ed. Boston: Massachusetts Historical Society, 1979; 850
       copies.

1262. WELLES, Gideon (1802-78)
          1. 1861-June 6, 1869; Political diary; Connecticut native and
   former Democrat became a charter member of the Republican Party;
   from the Civil War and Reconstruction to the end of Andrew Johnson's
   term; fair-minded and sensible.
          • Diary of Gideon Welles: Secretary of the Navy Under Lin-
       coln and Johnson. Howard K. Beale and Alan W. Brownsword,
       eds. 3 vols. New York: Norton, 1960.

          2. "Diary Excerpts," in: Philip Dunaway and Mel Evans,
   eds. A Treasury of the World's Great Diaries. New York: Doubleday, 1957; pp. 289-91.

1263. WHITE, Thomas Benton (1843-1922)
       November 3, 1861-December 31, 1862
          Military diary; life on the march in Kentucky with the 42nd
   Ohio Infantry.
          • "Down the Rivers: Civil War Diary of Thomas Benton White,"

Charles G. Williams, ed. Register of the Kentucky Historical Society, v. 67, pp. 134-74, April, 1969.

1264. WILLS, Charles Wright (1840-83)
April 28, 1861-May 19, 1865; gaps
Military diary; service with the 8th Illinois Infantry in Mississippi, Alabama and Tennessee; with Sherman through Georgia and South Carolina; "I like soldier ways much the best."; lengthy, detailed entries.
• Army Life of an Illinois Soldier, Including a Day by Day Record of Sherman's March to the Sea: Letters and Diary of the Late Charles W. Wills. Mary E. Kellogg, comp. Washington, D.C.: Globe Printing Co., 1906.

1265. WISTER, Sarah Butler (1835-)
1. April 15-September 4, 1861; Personal diary; daughter of American Pierce Butler and English actress Fanny Kemble (q.v.); mother of writer Owen Wister (q.v.); Northern sympathizer in contrast to her slave-owning father; visited by her mother; national and personal news.
• Wister, Fanny Kemble. "Sarah Butler Wister's Civil War Diary," Pennsylvania Magazine of History and Biography, v. 102, pp. 271-327, July, 1978.

2. April 15-September 8, 1861; Personal diary.
• "Sarah B. Wister's Civil War Journal," in: Fanny Kemble Wister, ed. That I May Tell You: Journals and Letters of the Owen Wister Family. Wayne, Pa.: Haverford House, 1979; pp. 23-57.

1266. WOMACK, James J. (1834-1922)
May 16, 1861-December 31, 1863
Military diary; short entries on weather and camp life.
• The Civil War Diary of Captain J. J. Womack, Co. E, Sixteenth Regiment, Tennessee Volunteers (Confederate). McMinnville, Tenn.: Womack Printing Co., 1961.

1267. WOOLWINE, Rufus James (1840-1908)
July 24, 1861-June 11, 1865
Military diary; service with the 51st Regiment of Virginia Infantry in southwestern and western Virginia; some entries written up from earlier notes.
• "The Civil War Diary of Rufus J. Woolwine," Louis H. Manarin, ed. Virginia Magazine of History and Biography, v. 71, pp. 416-48, 1963.

1268. WRIGHT, Marcus Joseph (1831-1922)
Military diary; life on the march with the 154th Senior Regiment of Tennessee Infantry; march from Chattanooga to Kentucky; battle of Perryville; wounded at Shiloh; impersonal notes.

• "Diary of Brigadier-General Marcus Joseph Wright, C. S. A., From April 23, 1861, to February 26, 1863," William and Mary College Quarterly, 2nd ser., v. 15, pp. 89-95, 1935; reprinted 193?

1269. YANCEY, William Lowndes (-1863)
March 15-June 18, 1861
Travel diary; commissioned by President Jefferson Davis to win diplomatic recognition for the Confederacy.
• "William L. Yancey's European Diary, March-June, 1861," W. Stanley Hoole, ed. Alabama Review, v. 25, pp. 134-42, April, 1972.

1862

1270. ANONYMOUS
April, 1862-January, 1867; many long gaps
Personal diary; mother of Louisiana plantation family chronicles travels in Mexico and abroad to escape Yankees; gushy style reeking of sentimentality; fiction?
• Fearn, Frances Hewitt, ed. Diary of a Refugee. New York: Moffat, York and Co., 1910.
REVIEW: Book Review Digest 1911, pp. 149-50.

1271. ANONYMOUS
September 5-December 7, 1862
Personal diary; 19th Iowa; found on the battlefield at Prairie Grove, Arkansas; service in Benton Barracks, Missouri; battle at Elkorn Tavern; observant, sarcastic; well-done.
• The Diary of an Unknown Soldier, September 5, 1862 to December 7, 1862, Found on a Battlefield. Elsa Vaught, ed. Van Buren, Ark.: Press-Argus Printing Co., 1959; reprinted from Arkansas Historical Quarterly, v. 18, pp. 50-89, Spring, 1959.

1272. ADAMS, Jacob (1842-)
February 15, 1862-July 31, 1865
Military diary; from Findlay, Ohio; in Alabama and Tennessee; Chickamauga; in the Atlanta campaign.
• "Diary of Jacob Adams, Private in Company F, 21st O. V. V. I," Ohio Archaeological and Historical Quarterly, v. 38, pp. 627-721, October, 1929.

1273. ALEXANDER, Richard Henry (1844-1915)
April 29-November 14, 1862
Travel diary; one of a party which traveled by Red River carts from Ontario to the gold diggings in British Columbia; arrived dead broke to find the mines closed for the winter.
• The Diary and Narrative of Richard Henry Alexander in a Journey Across the Rocky Mountains. Neil Brearley, ed. Richmond, B. C.: Alcuin Society, 1973; 500 copies.

1274.   BAER, Charles A. (1831-63)
         July 3, 1862-August 26, 1863
         Personal diary; pastor of Trinity Lutheran Church; church
work; trips to Washington and to Gettysburg shortly after the battle.
         • "The Diary of Charles A. Baer, Norristown, 1862-1863,"
         Kirke Bryan, ed. Historical Society of Montgomery County
         [Pa.] Bulletin, v. 7, pp. 101-26, April, 1950, pp. 197-212,
         October, 1950.

1275.   BARDEEN, Charles William (1847-1924)
         September 1, 1862-May 28, 1864
         Personal diary; a problem son in his mother's second marriage,
the diarist enlisted as a drummer and switched to a fife; 1st Massachusetts Infantry; at Fredericksburg and Gettysburg; hospital work;
original diary entries are distinguished by typeface from hindsight
comments; together they make a well-rounded portrait.
         • A Little Fifer's War Diary, with 17 Maps, 60 Portraits, and
         246 Other Illustrations. Nicholas Murray Butler, intro. Syra-
         cuse, N.Y.: C. W. Bardeen, 1910.

1276.   BELL, George (1821?-69)
         April 11-August 7, 1862
         Prison diary; Irish immigrant imprisoned after the fall of Fort
Pulaski on Governor's Island, New York.
         • "Diary of George Bell: A Record of Captivity in a Federal
         Military Prison, 1862," Whitfield J. Bell, Jr., ed. Georgia
         Historical Quarterly, v. 22, pp. 169-84, June, 1938.

1277.   BENSELL, Royal Augustus (1838-1921)
         March 20, 1862-October 16, 1864
         Military diary; former printer's devil saw monotonous service
in Oregon with the 4th California Infantry; good account in a theatre
of war little written of; humorous with an eye for detail.
         • All Quiet on the Yamhill, The Civil War in Oregon: The
         Journal of Corporal Royal A. Bensell. Gunter Barth, ed.
         (University of Oregon Monographs. Studies in History, no. 2)
         Eugene: University of Oregon Books, 1959.

1278.   BERRY, John Green, Jr. (1840-1924)
         1. December 1, 1861-September 16, 1862; Travel diary; from
San Francisco to Idaho by steamboat and on foot with a fifty-pound
pack.
         • "A Prospecting Trip to Idaho: The 1862 Diary of John
         Green Berry, Jr." Charles R. Berry, ed. Idaho Yesterdays,
         v. 24, pp. 2-22, Fall, 1980.

         2. March 18-September 23, 1864; Travel diary; from Santa
Clara, California, to central Nevada; weather, mileage; staccato notes.
         • "Prospecting in the Reese River Mines of Nevada in 1864:
         The Diary of John Green Berry, Jr." Charles R. Berry, ed.
         Nevada Historical Society Quarterly, v. 24, pp. 51-78, 1981.

1279. BIGGERT, Florence C. (-1900)
       September 16-26, 1862; June 16-27, 1863; July 13-August 14,
       1863
       Military diary; service with the 15th Pennsylvania Militia; An-
       tietam; garrison duty in Pittsburgh.
       • "Some Leaves from a Civil War Diary," Harry R. Beck, ed.
       Western Pennsylvania Historical Magazine, v. 42, pp. 363-82,
       December, 1959.

1280. BIRD, George (fl. 1862-83)
       January 3, 1862-November 18, 1883
       Personal diary; begun in his schooldays; lived at Corby,
       southeast of Leicester, England; employed as a wheelwright in his
       father's shop; details of village life, garden work, prices; glossary of
       unfamiliar words used by Bird; linguistic interest.
       • The Diary of George Bird Johan A. Liddie, ed. Notting-
       ham: University of Nottingham, 1980.

1281. BOYER, Samuel Pellman (1839-70)
       June 24, 1862-October 4, 1866; February 8, 1868-December
       31, 1869
       Sea diary; v. 1: on shipboard off the Carolinas and Georgia;
       notes on medical treatment; shore excursions; well-done; v. 2: serv-
       ice with the American Navy in Japan; visited throughout the country;
       keen observer of the dispute between the Shogun and the emperor.
       • Naval Surgeon: The Diary of Dr. Samuel Pellman Boyer.
       Elinor Barnes and James A. Barnes, eds. Bloomington: In-
       diana University Press, 1963.

1282. BRECKINRIDGE, Lucy G. (1843?-65)
       1. August 11, 1862-December 25, 1864; Personal diary; like-
       able young woman of Botetourt County, Virginia; social life, family;
       the effects of the war; thoughts on the lot of women; courtship; in-
       trospective, engaging.
           • Lucy Breckinridge of Grove Hill: The Journal of a Vir-
           ginian Girl, 1862-1864. Mary D. Robertson, ed. Kent, Ohio:
           Kent State University Press, 1980.
           REVIEWS: Library Journal, v. 105, p. 195, January 15,
           1980. North Carolina Historical Review, v. 57, pp. 469-
           70, Autumn, 1980. Register of the Kentucky Historical
           Society, v. 78, pp. 283-84, Summer, 1980.

       2. August 12, 1862-July 23, 1864; several extracts.
       • Robertson, Mary D. "Dusky Wings of War: The Journal of
       Lucy G. Breckinridge, 1862-1864," Civil War History, v. 23,
       pp. 26-51, March, 1977.

1283. BROWN, John, Sr.
       June 11-July, 1860
       Travel diary; from San Bernardino to Fort Mojave and return;
       mileage and weather.

- "The Diary of John Brown, 1862," Southern California Historical Publications, v. 13, pp. 360-64, 1927.

1284. CAMPBELL, Henry (-1915)
Military diary; service with 18th Indiana Artillery Battery; with the Army of the Cumberland; at Chickamauga.
- "The War in Kentucky and Tennessee as Seen By a Teen-aged Bugler," Civil War Times, v. 2, pp. 26-29, November, 1963; pp. 42-45, January, 1964; v. 3, pp. 34-37, May, 1964; pp. 46-48, August, 1964; pp. 46-48, October, 1964; pp. 36-39, January, 1965.

1285. CARY, Harriet
May 6-July 23, 1862
Personal diary; in Williamsburg, Virginia.
- "Diary of Miss Harriet Cary, Kept by Her From May 6, 1862, to July 24, 1862," Tyler's Quarterly Historical and Genealogical Magazine, v. 9, pp. 104-15, 1928; v. 12, pp. 160-73, 1928.

1286. CLEVELAND, Edmund J.
1. August 24, 1862-June 5, 1863; Military diary; life on the march.
- "The Early Campaigns in North Carolina as Seen Through the Eyes of a New Jersey Soldier," New Jersey Historical Society Proceedings, v. 68, pp. 119-62, April, 1950; pp. 221-66, July, 1950.

2. June 1-September 19, 1864; Military diary; based at Bermuda Hundred, Virginia.
- "The Second Battle of Cold Harbor, as Seen Through the Eyes of a New Jersey Soldier (Private Edmund J. Cleveland, Co. K, Ninth New Jersey Volunteers, 1st Brigade, 2nd Division, 18th Corps): June 1 to June 14, 1864," Edmund J. Cleveland, Jr., ed. Proceedings of the New Jersey Historical Society, v. 66, pp. 25-37, January, 1948; "The Siege of Petersburg ... June 14-September 19, 1804 [sic]," v. 66, pp. 76-96, April, 1948; "The Siege of Petersburg ... July 30-September 19, 1804 [sic]," v. 66, pp. 176-96, July, 1948; "The Campaign of Promise and Disappointment ... March 17-May 27, 1864," v. 67, pp. 218-40, July, 1949; pp. 308-28, October, 1949.

1287. COE, Hamlin Alexander (1840-99)
September 14, 1862-
Military diary; wagonmaker joined the 19th Michigan Volunteer Infantry; confined in Libby Prison; parolled and worked as a carpenter; provost marshall's clerk.
- Mine Eyes Have Seen the Glory: Combat Diaries of Union Sergeant Hamlin Alexander Coe. David Coe, ed. Rutherford, N.J.: Fairleigh Dickinson University Press, 1975.

1288. COGSHALL, Israel
       October 24, 1862-September 9, 1863
       Military diary; Methodist minister was chaplain to the 19th
Michigan Infantry; illness; marching.
       • "Journal of Israel Cogshall, 1862-1863," Cecil K. Byrd, ed.
       Indiana Magazine of History, v. 42, pp. 69-87, March, 1946.

1289. COLTON, Matthias Baldwin (1839-1915)
       August 20, 1862-February 17, 1863
       Military diary; served with the 15th Pennsylvania Cavalry;
captured in Tennessee; in Libby Prison; exchanged.
       • The Civil War Journal and Correspondence of Matthias Bald-
       win Colton. Jessie Sellers Conton, ed. Philadelphia: Macrae-
       Smith, 1931; diary on pp. 3-49.

1290. CONNOLLY, James Austin (1840-1914)
       1. August 19, 1862-March 21, 1865; Letter journal; addressed
to his fiancée and later wife; with the 123rd Illinois Infantry at Chickamauga, Missionary Ridge and Lookout Mountain; with Sherman to the
sea and through the Carolinas; well-written entries brimming with
color and sympathy for sufferers on both sides.
       • Three Years in the Army of the Cumberland: The Letters
       and Diary of Major James A. Connolly. Paul M. Angle, ed.
       Bloomington: Indiana University Press, 1959.

       2. February 24, 1862-December 21, 1864.
       • "Major James Austin Connolly," Illinois State Historical So-
       ciety Proceedings, pp. 215-438, 1928.

1291. CORT, Charles Edwin (1841-1903)
       August 27, 1862-July 7, 1865
       Personal diary; more letters than diary entries; service with
the 92nd Illinois Volunteer Infantry in Kentucky, Tennessee, Alabama
and Georgia; Atlanta campaign.
       • Dear Friends: The Civil War Letters and Diary of Charles
       Edwin Cort. Helyn W. Tomlinson, ed. and comp. Minneapo-
       lis, Minn.: The Author, 1962.

1292. CRARY, Jerry (1842-1936)
       October 10, 1862-February 1, 1865
       Military diary; with the 143rd Regiment of New York Volun-
teers; line-a-day diary.
       • Jerry Crary, 1842-1936: Teacher, Soldier, Industrialist.
       Warren, Pa.: Newell Press, 1960; pp. 31-62.

1293. CUMMING, Kate (1835-1909)
       April 7, 1862-May 29, 1865
       Personal diary; born in Edinburgh, Scotland; came to Mobile,
Alabama, as a child; service as a hospital matron with the Army of
Tennessee in Georgia, Tennessee and Alabama.
       • A Journal of Hospital Life in the Confederate Army of

Tennessee, From the Battle of Shiloh to the End of the War.
Louisville: J. P. Morgan & Co., 1866; reprinted as Kate:
The Journal of a Confederate Nurse.   Richard Barksdale Harwell, ed.   Baton Rouge: Louisiana State University Press,
1959.

1294.   CUNNINGHAM, David (1837-1917)
January 1-December 31, 1862
Personal diary; at Antietam with the 30th Ohio Regiment; in
southern West Virginia.
  • "Major Cunningham's Journal, 1862," Elizabeth Cometti, ed.
West Virginia History, v. 34, pp. 187-211, January, 1973.

1295.   DAWSON, Sarah Morgan (1842-1909)
    1.   March 9, 1862-June 15, 1865; Personal diary; daughter of
wealthy Louisiana family; Baton Rouge home destroyed by Union
troops; moved several times, settling in New Orleans at war's end;
injured early in the war and spent much time bed-ridden; good picture of life in war-time Louisiana; exclamatory, gushy style in some
entries.
  • A Confederate Girl's Diary.   Warrington Dawson, ed.   Boston: Houghton, Mifflin, 1913; reprinted with same title, James
D. Robertson, Jr., ed. (Civil War Centennial Series) Bloomington: Indiana University Press, 1960.

    2.   "Diary Excerpts," in: Philip Dunaway and Mel Evans, eds.
A Treasury of the World's Great Diaries.   New York: Doubleday,
1947; pp. 264-67.

1296.   DELANY, John O'Fallon (-1930)
May 15-October 13, 1862
Travel diary; well-to-do St. Louisan went by steamer; accompanied Father De Smet; from Fort Benton overland; much bad weather;
hunting.
  • "Up the Missouri to the Montana Mines: John O'Fallon Delany's 'Pocket Diary for 1862,'" John E. Sunder, ed.   Missouri
Historical Society Bulletin, v. 19, pp. 3-22, October, 1962,
pp. 127-49, January, 1963.

1297.   DeWOLF, Charles Wesley (1834-1927)
December 12, 1862-January 1, 1863
Military diary; with the 7th Regiment of Cavalry of Missouri
Volunteers; in camp at Prairie Grove before the battle.
  • "The Capture of Van Buren, Arkansas, During the Civil
War: From the Diary of a Union Horse Soldier," Thomas E.
Wright, ed.   Arkansas Historical Quarterly, v. 38, pp. 72-89,
Spring, 1979.

1298.   DICKSON, James (1836-78)
February 21-March 31, 1862; gaps
Sea diary; Southern blockade runner; lengthy, detailed entries.

* "Voyage of Fear and Profit," <u>Civil War Times Illustrated</u>,
  v. 18, pp. 14-19, November, 1979; pp. 30-36, December,
  1979.

1299. DIMON, Theodore (1816-89)
      September 15-18, 1862
      Military diary; with the 19th New York Infantry; very good
account of the battle and its aftermath.
      * "A Federal Surgeon at Sharpsburg," James I. Robertson,
      Jr., ed. <u>Civil War History</u>, v. 6, pp. 134-51, 1960.

1300. DODD, Ephraim Shelby (-1864)
      Personal diary; service in Tennessee; shot as a spy on evi-
dence of the diary which was in his possession.
      * <u>Diary of Ephraim Shelby Dodd, Member of Company D,</u>
      <u>Terry's Texas Rangers, December 4, 1862-January 1, 1864</u>.
      Austin, Tx.: E. L. Steck Press, 1914.

1301. DOOLEY, John Edward (1842-73)
      August 27, 1862-May 6, 1865
      Military diary; Virginia-born son of Irish immigrants; with the
1st Virginia Regiment; at Fredericksburg and Gettysburg; imprisoned
at Johnson's Island.
      * <u>John Dooley, Confederate Soldier: His War Journal</u>. Joseph
      T. Durkin, S. J., ed. n. p.: Georgetown University Press,
      1945; Notre Dame, Ind.: University of Notre Dame, 1963.

1302. DORITY, Orin G.
      August 5, 1862-June 2, 1865; gaps
      Military diary; service with the 1st Ohio Light Infantry at
Gettysburg and Chancellorsville; battle of Fredericksburg; in Virginia;
very descriptive.
      * "The Civil War Diary of Orin G. Dority," <u>Northwest Ohio</u>
      <u>Quarterly</u>, v. 37, pp. 7-26, Winter, 1964-65; pp. 104-17,
      Summer, 1965.

1303. DYE, Henry L. (-1880)
      August, 1862-1865
      Personal diary; Plano, Texas, physician and graduate of Jef-
ferson Medical College; undated extracts; sketches of patients; details
of treatment; comments of poor health habits of rebels; effects of
soldiers innoculating themselves for smallpox; very interesting.
      * Elsas, Frederick J. "The Journal of Henry L. Dye Con-
      federate Surgeon," <u>Surgery</u>, 63, pp. 352-62, February, 1968.

1304. ELDER, William Henry (1819-1904)
      October 26, 1862-March 27, 1865
      Personal diary; Catholic bishop ministered to his diocese in
the midst of war; sermon themes; visits to parishioners; dispute with
the occupying Federal troops over a Prayer for the Authorities; of
local interest.

- Civil War Diary (1862-1865) of Bishop William Henry Elder, Bishop of Natchez. Natchez? Miss.: R. O. Gerow, 1960?

1305. FAUNTLEROY, James Henry (1842-64)
       April 21-24, 1862
       Military diary; life on the march with the 1st Missouri Volunteer Cavalry.
       - Calkin, Homer L. "Elkhorn to Vicksburg," Civil War History, v. 2, pp. 7-43, March, 1956.

1306. FLETCHER, Stephen Keyes (1840-97)
       March 3-October 12, 1862
       Military diary; ordnance sergeant with the 33rd Indiana Infantry; life in camp and his duties; very detailed.
       - "The Civil War Journal of Stephen Keyes Fletcher," Maxwell Keyes Fletcher III, contributor. Perry McCandless, ed. Indiana Magazine of History, v. 54, pp. 141-90, 1958.

1307. FOREMAN, Susan E.
       April 7, 1862-December 6, 1863; gaps
       Personal diary; teacher at the Cherokee Nation School at Webber's Falls, Oklahoma; pupil attendance; fleeing the Yankees.
       - Finley, Linda. "Notes From the Diary of Susan E. Foreman," Chronicles of Oklahoma, v. 47, pp. 388-97, 1969-70.

1308. FOSTER, Samuel Thompson (1829-1919)
       September 19, 1862-June 15, 1865
       Military journal; with the Army of Tennessee; siege of Atlanta; prisoner at Camp Chase, Ohio; exchanged; Confederate surrender; journey home; good.
       - One of Cleburne's Command: The Civil War Reminiscences and Diary of Capt. Samuel T. Foster, Granbury's Texas Brigade, CSA. Norman D. Brown, ed. Austin: University of Texas Press, 1980.

1309. FULLAM, George Townley (1841-79)
       July 29, 1862-June 14, 1864
       Sea diary; British-born Confederate responsible for prize cargoes and captured seamen taken by the Alabama; final entry ends before the vessel's defeat by the Union Kearsarge; ship's log.
       - The Journal of George Townley Fullam, Boarding Officer of the Confederate Sea Raider Alabama. Charles G. Summersell, ed. University: University of Alabama Press, 1973.

1310. GAILOR, Frank M. (1833-62)
       September 20-October 4, 1862
       Military diary; with the 7th Regiment Tennessee Infantry in Kentucky; died at the Battle of Perryville; troop movements.
       - "The Diary of a Confederate Quartermaster," Charlotte Cleveland and Robert Daniel, eds. Tennessee Historical Quarterly, v. 11, pp. 78-85, March, 1952.

1311. GARDNER, Henry Rufus (1842-1913)
       November 18, 1863-1866
       Military diary; with the 18th New York Independent Battery
Light Artillery; occupying New Orleans and Baton Rouge; New Orleans riot of 1866; well-written.
       • "A Yankee in Louisiana: Selections From the Diary and
         Correspondence of Henry R. Gardner, 1862-1866," Kenneth
         E. Shewmaker and Andrew K. Prinz, eds. Louisiana History,
         v. 5, pp. 271-95, Summer, 1964.

1312. GORGAS, Josiah (1818-83)
       June 12, 1862-May 14, 1865
       Military diary; Chief of Ordnance for Confederates; great deal
of second hand war news; life in Richmond, Virginia; hard-working
man could not overcome the material scarcities the rebels faced.
       • The Civil War Diary of General Josiah Gorgas. Frank E.
         Vandiver, ed. University: University of Alabama Press,
         1947.

1313. GOULD, Jane Holbrook (later Tourtillott) (1833-   )
       1. April 27-October 8, 1862; Travel diary; journeyed with
her husband, two sons and other relatives from Mitchell County,
Iowa; to the Oregon Territory and on to Stockton, California; Indian
attacks; observant individual; informative entries.
       • "Iowa to California in 1862," Philip K. Lack, ed. Annals
         of Iowa, v. 37, pp. 460-76, Fall, 1964; pp. 544-59, Winter,
         1965; pp. 623-40, Spring, 1965; v. 38, pp. 68-75, Summer,
         1965.

       2. April 27-October 8, 1862; Travel diary.
       • "Touring from Mitchell, Iowa, to California, in 1862," in:
         Lillian Schlissel. Women's Diaries of the Westward Journey.
         New York: Schocken, 1982; pp. 217-31.

1314. GRAYSON, William John (1788-   )
       May 10-November 18, 1862
       Personal diary; plantation owner served in the U.S. and state
legislatures; war news; much personal commentary on the state of
affairs; lengthy entries; well done.
       • "The Confederate Diary of William John Grayson," Elmer L.
         Puryear, ed. South Carolina Historical Magazine, v. 63, pp.
         137-49, July, 1962; pp. 214-26, October, 1962.

1315. GREER, George H. T.
       November 7-December 25, 1862
       Military diary; on General Jubal Early's staff; Battle of Fred-
ericksburg, Virginia.
       • "'All Thoughts are Absorbed in the War,'" Civil War Times
         Illustrated, v. 17, pp. 30-35, December, 1978.

1316. GUY, John Henry
       April 21-May 10, 1862

Military diary; captured at Fort Donelson; imprisoned at Camp Chase and Johnson's Island.
* "A Virginian at Fort Donelson: Excerpts From the Prison Journal of John Henry Guy," B. Franklin Cooling, ed. Tennessee Historical Quarterly, v. 27, pp. 176-90, Summer, 1968.

1317. HANEY, John Hancock (1835?-)
August 20-October 26, 1862
Military diary; Ohioan enlisted with the New Orleans Artillery Company.
* "Bragg's Kentucky Campaign: A Confederate Soldier's Account," Will Frank Steely and Orville W. Taylor, eds. Kentucky Historical Society Register, v. 57, pp. 49-55, January, 1959.

1318. HANNA, Ebenezer (1844-62)
February 10-March 27, 1862
Military journal; historian with Sibley's Brigade in the New Mexico campaign; had a horse shot out from under him; much hardship.
* Hall, Martin H. "The Journal of Ebenezer Hanna," Password, v. 3, pp. 14-29, January, 1958.

1319. HARDING, George A. (1843-1926)
May 6-October 16, 1862
Personal diary; from Oregon City by steamer and horseback to the diggings at Elk City; panning and paperhanging.
* "A Journal Kept by George A. Harding," Steven Tanasoca and Susan Sudduth, eds. Oregon Historical Quarterly, v. 79, pp. 172-202, Summer, 1978.

1320. HARRIS, John H. (1827-64)
March 4, 1826-March 1, 1863
Military diary; service in Virginia with the 44th Regiment Georgia Volunteers.
* "Diary of Captain John H. Harris," in: Raynor Hubbel, ed. Confederate Stamps, Old Letters and History. n.p., 1959; Appendix pp. 2-13.

1321. HAVILAND, Thomas P.
August 30-September 23, 1862
Military diary; member of the 12th Massachusetts Volunteers; captured at Manassas; prison life.
* Haviland, Thomas P. "A Brief Diary of Imprisonment," Virginia Magazine of History and Biography, v. 50, pp. 230-37, 1942.

1322. HAYNES, Draughton Stith (1837-79)
May 28-August 7, 1862
Military diary; service with the 49th Georgia Volunteer Infantry; very short entries.

• The Field Diary of a Confederate Soldier, Draughton Stith
Haynes, While Serving with the Army of Northern Virginia,
C. S. A. Darien, Ga.: Ashantilly Press, 1963.

1323. HELMAN, Howard (1845?-86)
August 6-November 30, 1862
Military diary; life on the march with the 131st Pennsylvania
Volunteers.
• "A Young Soldier in the Army of the Potomac: Diary of
Howard Nelman, 1862," Arthur W. Thurner, ed. Pennsylvania
Magazine of History and Biography, v. 87, pp. 139-55, April,
1963.

1324. HIGGINSON, Thomas Wentworth (1823-1911) [A318]
November 24, 1862-January 21, 1863
Military diary; Unitarian minister, abolitionist and biographer;
raised a company of mostly ex-slaves which became the 1st South
Carolina Volunteers; excessively "literary" style; condescending toward his men.
• "Camp Diary," in: Army Life in a Black Regiment. 1869;
reprinted East Lansing: Michigan State University Press, 1960;
pp. 5-47; reprinted Boston: Beacon Press, 1962, pp. 6-61.

1325. HOLLISTER, Ovando James (1834-92)
March 1-September 7, 1862
Military journal with the 1st Colorado Volunteers in a campaign
against Texans bent on taking New Mexico for the Confederacy; il-
luminating account of little-known incident in Civil War; well-done.
• Boldly They Rode. 1863; reprinted Lakewood, Col.:
Golden Press, 1949.

1326. HOLMES, Robert Masten (1844-64)
November 11, 1862-May 13, 1863
Military diary; life in camp with the 24th Regiment Mississippi
Volunteers; "more mud than glory."
• Kemper County Rebel: The Civil War Diary of Robert Mas-
ten Holmes. C. S. A. Frank Allen Dennis, ed. Jackson:
University and College Press of Mississippi, 1973.

1327. HOLTON, William C.
January 28, 1862-August 10, 1863; gaps
Sea diary; the ship was captained by Admiral Farragut; into
New Orleans; up the Mississippi to Baton Rouge; off the mouth of the
Red River; shelling Port Hudson; return to New York harbor.
• Cruise of the U.S. Flag-ship "Hartford," 1862-1863. New
York: L. W. Paine, 1863; reprinted Magazine of History,
extra no. 87, pp. 14-97, 1922.

1328. HUBBELL, Finley L.
June 24, 1862-May 5, 1863
Military diary; Battle of Corinth, Mississippi.

• "Diary of Lieut. Col. Hubbell, of 3d Regiment Missouri Infantry, C. S. A.," The Land We Love, v. 6, pp. 97-105, December, 1868.

1329. HUGHES, Frank (-1864)
May 4-July 9, 1862
Prison diary; member of the 37th Indian Volunteers imprisoned
at Macon, Georgia; food, illness.
    • "Diary of Lieutenant Frank Hughes," Norman Niccum, ed.
    Indiana Magazine of History, v. 45, pp. 275-84, September,
    1949.

1330. IBBETSON, William H. H. (-1883)
October 8, 1862-August 8, 1864
Military diary; from Camp Palmer, Illinois; service in Tennes-
see and Mississippi.
    • "William H. H. Ibbeston, Co. D, 122 Reg. Ill." Publications
    of the Illinois State Historical Library, no. 37, pp. 236-73,
    1930.

1331. INZER, John Washington (1834-1928)
March 18, 1862-July 18, 1865
Military diary; St. Clair County lawyer served at Mobile with
the 9th Alabama Battalion; captured at the Battle of Missionary Ridge;
imprisoned on Johnson's Island, Ohio.
    • The Diary of a Confederate Soldier: John Washington Inzer,
    1834-1928. Mattie Lou Teague Crow, ed. Huntsville, Ala.:
    Strode, 1977.

1332. JACKSON, Luther (-1862)
April 6-June 1, 1862
Prison diary; member of 12th Iowa Infantry captured at Shiloh;
imprisoned in a cotton shed in Montgomery, Alabama; journey to Macon,
Georgia; died of dysentery before he could be exchanged; good ac-
count of prison life.
    • "A Prisoner of War," Annals of Iowa, 3rd ser., v. 19, pp.
    23-41, July, 1933.

1333. JACKSON, Samuel McCartney (1833-1906)
January 1-31, 1862
Military diary; service with the 11th Pennsylvania Reserves and
the 40th Pennsylvania Infantry; at Camp Pierpoint, Virginia; visit
home to Pittsburgh; in Washington, D.C.; weather.
    • Diary of General S. M. Jackson for the Year 1862.   Apollo,
    Pa.: Pvt. ptd. 1925.

1334. JONES, Jenkin Lloyd (1843-1918)
August 14, 1862-July 3, 1865
Military diary; with the 6th Wisconsin Battery.
    • An Artilleryman's Diary. Madison, Wis.: History Commis-
    sion, 1914.

1335. KITTS, John Howard (1842-70)
        August 23-December 7, 1862; October 12-16, 1864
        Military diary; enlistment with the 11th Kansas; service in
Arkansas; several skirmishes with the Rebels; tracking Confederate
General Sterling Price in Missouri and Arkansas; Kansas newspaper-
man writes literate entries.
        • "The Civil War Diary of John Howard Kitts," Transactions
        of the Kansas Historical Society, v. 14, pp. 318-32, 1918.

1336. LACEY, Edward
        May 28-August 25, 1862
        Sea diary; London to Port Adelaide, Australia; a visit from
Neptune at the Equator; rough voyage.
        • "Clipper to Adelaide 1862," in: R. C. Bell, ed. Diaries
        From the Days of Sail. New York: Holt, Rinehart and Wins-
        ton, 1974; pp. 111-47.

1337. LANE, David
        August 31, 1862-June 8, 1865
        Military diary; with the 17th Michigan Volunteers chiefly in
Kentucky, Tennessee and Virginia; fairly good picture of soldier life;
yearning for home and family.
        • A Soldier's Diary: The Story of a Volunteer, 1862-1865.
        Jackson? Mich.: n. p., 1905.

1338. LEE, Mary Charlton Greenhow (1819-)
        Personal diary; extract from entries written at the time of the
occupation and evacuation of the city by Stonewall Jackson; detailed.
        • "An Extract From the Journal of Mrs. Hugh H. Lee of Win-
        chester, Va., May 23-31, 1862," C. A. Porter Hopkins, ed.
        Maryland Historical Magazine, v. 53, pp. 380-93, December,
        1958.

1339. LEON, Louis
        May 31, 1862-April 1, 1865
        Military diary; life on the march with the 53rd North Carolina
Regiment; boredom; imprisonment.
        • Diary of a Tar Heel Confederate Soldier. Charlotte, N.
        Car.: Stone Publishing Co., 1913.

1340. LYNCH, Charles H.
        August 17, 1862-July 7, 1865
        Military diary; service in Maryland and Virginia; rarely missed
a daily entry, making each a good summary of events; no heroics,
just march and fight; often short of rations; footsore and weary;
well-done.
        • The Civil War Diary, 1862-1865, of Charles H. Lynch, 18th
        Connecticut Vol's. Hartfort, Conn.: Case, Lockwood & Brain-
        ard, 1915.

1341. McCOMAS, Evans Smith (1839-1911)

May 14, 1862-November 18, 1867; gaps in later years
Travel diary; from Iowa City to Oregon; probably immigrated
to avoid military service; well-educated; sketches of mining life
around Auburn City.
- A Journal of Travel. Portland, Ore.: Champoeg Press,
1954; 500 copies.

1342. McCREARY, James Bennett (1838-1918)
August 30, 1862-November 29, 1862
Military diary; Confederate cavalry major captured in Morgan's
raid; effusive style.
- "The Journal of My Soldier Life," Kentucky Historical So-
ciety Register, v. 33, pp. 97-117, 191-211, April, 1935.

1343. McDONALD, Cornelia Peake (1822-1909)
March, 1862-October, 1865
Personal diary; Virginia mother cared for her children during
her husband's service in the Confederate Army; well-told tale of pri-
vations and Yankee occupation; some material may have been added
later.
- A Diary with Reminiscences of the War and Refugee Life in
the Shenandoah Valley, 1860-1865. Nashville: Cullom &
Ghertner, 1935.

1344. McINTYRE, Benjamin Franklin (1827-   )
September 4, 1862-August 14, 1864
Military diary; service with the Iowa Infantry in the Trans-
Mississippi area, especially Texas; service in the Ozarks and Browns-
ville, Texas.
- Federals on the Frontier: The Diary of Benjamin F. Mc-
Intyre, 1862-1864. Nannie M. Tilley, ed. Austin: University
of Texas Press, 1963.

1345. MALLORY, Mary Alice Shutes (1849-1939)
May 4-June 12, 1862
Travel diary; lively, observant 13 year-old and her family
left Wyandott County, Ohio, to homestead in Carroll County, Iowa;
diary of the wagon journey was kept at the request of her parents;
full account of her impressions and adults' speech; delightful.
- Diary: Eight Hundred Miles in 36 Days by Covered Wagon-
1862. Bloomington, Ill.: L. L. Shutes, 1967; reprinted as
"Pioneer Migration: The Diary of Mary Alice Shutes," Glenda
Riley, ed. Annals of Iowa, v. 43, pp. 487-514, Winter, 1977;
pp. 566-92, Spring, 1977.

1346. MARKELL, Catherine Susannah Thomas (1828-1900)
Personal diary; Frederick was the provisional capital of the
Confederacy; days before the Battle of Sharpsburg; Barbara Frietzsche
incident mentioned.
- "Frederick Diary: September 5-14, 1862," Virginia O.
Bardsley, ed. Maryland Historical Magazine, v. 60, pp. 132-
38, June, 1965.

1347. MILLINGTON, Ada (later Jones) (1849-1930)
       April 29-September 16, 1862
       Travel diary; first account of the trail through central Nevada;
with a family party from Van Buren County, Iowa; to Fort Laramie,
Salt Lake City, Carson City; ending in Santa Rosa, California; nicely
done account with some humor.
       • "Journal Kept While Crossing the Plains," Charles G. Clarke,
       ed. Southern California Quarterly, v. 59, pp. 13-48, Spring,
       1977; pp. 139-84, Summer, 1977; pp. 251-69, Fall, 1977;
       Journal Kept While Crossing the Plains From Keosauqua, Iowa,
       to Santa Rosa, Cal., During April 29th to September 16th,
       1862. Tacoma, Wash.: n. p. 194-

1348. MOSMAN, Chesley A.
       January 24-December 25, 1862
       Military diary; service in Missouri and Arkansas; in camp and
on several marches; mileage, weather; skirmishes.
       • "Mosman's Diary. The Following is From a Diary Kept By
       C. A. Mosman, Late Lieutenant Company D, Fifty-ninth Illi-
       nois Infantry," in: George Washington Herr. Episodes of the
       Civil War. San Francisco: Bancroft Co., 1890; pp. 361-97.

1349. NICHOLS, Norman K. (1835?-1915)
       January 1-December 31, 1862
       Military diary; very short entries by an "operator" in the
101st New York Regiment; AWOL episode; captured by Confederates;
ambulance driver.
       • "The Reluctant Warrior: The Diary of Norman K. Nichols,"
       T. Harry Williams, ed. Civil War History, v. 3, pp. 17-39,
       March, 1957.

1350. NIXON, Liberty Independence
       March 9-April 6, 1862
       Military diary; enlistment in the 26th Alabama Infantry; Battle
of Shiloh.
       • "An Alabamian at Shiloh: The Diary of Liberty Independ-
       ence Nixon," Hugh C. Bailey, ed. Alabama Review, v. 11,
       pp. 144-55, April, 1958.

1351. PATON, James E.
       July 1-August 4, 1862
       Prison diary; at Camp Morton, Indiana; long report of Fort
Donelson, Kentucky.
       • "Civil War Journal of James E. Paton," Kentucky Historical
       Society Register, v. 61, pp. 220-31, July, 1963.

1352. PATRICK, Marsena Rudolph (1811-88)
       January 1, 1862-June 15, 1865
       Military diary; military governor of Federal-occupied Virginia;
lenient with civilians and harsh with his own troops; day by day account of the duties of the military staff; generally short entry; for
the specialist.

And So to Bed

- Inside Lincoln's Army: The Diary of Marsena Rudolph Patrick, Provost Marshal General, Army of the Potomac. David S. Sparks, ed. New York: Yoseloff, 1964.

1353. PATRICK, Robert (1835-66)
October 21, 1862-January 30, 1865
Military diary; service with the 4th Louisiana Infantry; clerk in the Confederate Commissary and Quartermaster departments; upper middle class background; reader and drinker; romantic interlude; humorous, telling details.
- Reluctant Rebel, The Secret Diary of Robert Patrick, 1861-1865. F. Jay Taylor, ed. Baton Rouge: Louisiana State University Press, 1959.

1354. PEARSON, Benjamin Franklin
1. July 22, 1862-May 20, 1865; Military diary; service with the 36th Iowa Infantry; lengthy entries; good observer.
- "Benjamin Franklin Pearson's War Diary," Annals of Iowa, v. 15, pp. 83-129, October, 1925; pp. 194-222, January, 1926; pp. 281-305, April, 1926; pp. 377-389, July, 1926; pp. 433-63, October, 1926; pp. 507-35, January, 1927.

2. Travel diary; notes on mode of travel and weather.
- "A Trip to Kansas and Return May 20, 1872 to June 27, 1872," Annals of Iowa, v. 20, pp. 207-18, January, 1936.

1355. PETTIT, Ira (1841-)
January 1, 1862-October 20, 1863
Personal diary; Niagara County, New Yorker enlisted in the 11th Regiment of the U.S. Army; entries of 2 or 3 lines per day are amply supplemented by lengthy letters to his family; captured in Virginia and sent to Andersonville where he contracted scurvy.
- The Diary of a Dead Man. Jean P. Ray, comp. Priv. ptd., 1976.
  REVIEW: Civil War Times Illustrated, v. 16, pp. 49-50, August, 1977.

1356. PITTS, Florison D.
November 8, 1862-June 25, 1865; gap from July 1-December 31, 1864
Military diary; bugler with the Chicago Mercantile Battery; at Vicksburg; in Louisiana and Matagorda Bay, Texas; life on the march; condition of the countryside.
- "The Civil War Diary of Florison D. Pitts," Mid-America, v. 40, pp. 22-63, 1958

1357. PITTS, Joseph J. (1834?-)
December 1, 1862-November 31, 1864; many gaps
Personal diary; Tennessee clergyman in an area that frequently changed hands; difficulties with transport, food; impediments to his ministry.

- "A Methodist Circuit Rider Between the Lines: The Private Journal of Joseph J. Pitts, 1862-1864," John M. Martin, ed. <u>Tennessee Historical Quarterly</u>, v. 19, pp. 252-59, September, 1960.

1358. POLIGNAC, Camille A. J. M. (1832-1913)
April 17-October 31, 1862
Military diary; French colonel with the 18th Louisiana; at Corinth, Mississippi; sarcastic, opinionated, egotistical comments on American mores and military tactics.
- "Polignac's Diary," <u>Civil War Times Illustrated</u>, v. 19, pp. 14-18, August, 1980; pp. 34-39, 41, October, 1980.

1359. PRESSLEY, John G.
July 22, 1862-July 18, 1863
Military diary; interesting account (pp. 55-56) of a member of Beauregard's staff duping a Yankee into teaching him Federal signals; full entry; well-done.
- "Extracts From the Diary of Lieutenant-Colonel John G. Pressley, of the Twenty-fifth South Carolina Volunteers," <u>Southern Historical Society Papers</u>, v. 14, pp. 35-62, 1886.

1360. RATHBUN, Isaac R.
Military diary; wounded at Bull Run; hospitalized in Washington and New York City.
- "A Civil War Diary: The Diary of Isaac R. Rathbun, Co. D, 86th N.Y. Volunteers, August 23, 1862-January 30, 1863," Lawrence R. Cavanaugh, ed. <u>New York History</u>, v. 36, pp. 336-45, July, 1955.

1361. RHODES, Samuel (1841-64)
May 12, 1862-April 3, 1864
Personal diary; Mennonite who fled service in the Confederate Army; journal of his escape from Virginia to Pennsylvania and Iowa.
- "The Journal of a Refugee," Samuel L. Horst, ed. and trans. <u>Mennonite Quarterly Review</u>, v. 54, pp. 280-304, October, 1980.

1362. RICHARDS, Louis (1842-   )
September 13-24, 1862
Military diary; joined the Reading, Pennsylvania, militia in a hastily organized effort to defend the state from General Lee's advance; entries bear evidence of hindsight; detailed.
- <u>Eleven Days in the Militia During the War of the Rebellion: Being a Journal of the "Emergency" Campaign of 1862</u>. Philadelphia: Collins, 1883.

1363. ROPES, Hannah Anderson (1809-63)
October 1-December 27, 1862
Personal diary; matron of the Union Hotel Hospital in Georgetown, D.C.; nursing, trying to get better treatment for "her boys"; superior of Louisa May Alcott (q.v.); died of typhoid.

• Brumgardt, John R. <u>Civil War Nurse: The Diary and</u>
<u>Letters of Hannah Ropes</u>. Knoxville: University of Tennessee
Press, 1980.

1364. ROWE, George Henry Clay (1830–78)
        August 13–September 14, 1862
        Prison diary; arrested by the Federals in retaliation for Con-
federate arrests of Northerners; meeting with Belle Boyd; full entries; parolled.
        • "Fredericksburg's Political Hostages: The Old Capitol Jour-
        nal of George Henry Clay Rowe," Lucille Griffith, ed. <u>Vir-</u>
        <u>ginia Magazine of History and Biography</u>, v. 72, pp. 395–429,
        October, 1964.

1365. RUMLEY, Charles (1824–97)
        May 14, 1862–April 26, 1863
        Travel diary; by sidewheeler to Fort Benton; on horseback;
hunting along the way; paused for a bit of prospecting.
        • <u>Diary of Charles Rumley from St. Louis to Portland, 1862</u>.
        Helen Addison Howard, ed. Missoula: Montana State Univer-
        sity Press, 1939; reprinted from <u>Frontier and Midland</u>, v. 19,
        no. 3, 1939.

1366. RUMPEL, John W. (–1910)
        June 1, 1862–May 27, 1865
        Military diary; letters to parents and excerpts from his diary;
with the 55th Ohio Infantry at Gettysburg; Chattanooga campaign;
with Sherman to Savannah.
        • "Ohiowa Soldier," H. E. Rosenberger, ed. <u>Annals of Iowa</u>,
        3rd ser., v. 36, pp. 111–48, Fall, 1961.

1367. SEXTON, Franklin Barlow (1828–   )
        July 23, 1862–May 2, 1863
        Travel diary; journey from Texas to Richmond, Virginia; con-
gressional business.
        • "Diary of a Confederate Congressman, 1862–1863," Mary S.
        Estill, ed. <u>Southwestern Historical Quarterly</u>, v. 38, pp.
        270–301, 1934–35, v. 39, pp. 33–65, 1935–36.

1368. SHEERAN, James B. (1819–81)
        August 2, 1862–April 24, 1865
        Military diary; Irish-born Catholic Redemptorist priest stationed
at a parish in New Orleans volunteered for chaplain duty with the
Confederate Army; always willing to think the worst of Yankees;
somewhat stiffnecked but respected by his men.
        • <u>Confederate Chaplain: A War Journal of Rev. James B.</u>
        <u>Sheeran, 14th Louisiana, C. S. A</u>. Rev. Joseph T. Durkin,
        ed. Milwaukee: Bruce Publishing Co., 1960.

1369. SMITH, George Gilbert (1825–   )
        March 17, 1862–July 24, 1865; gaps

Military diary; capture and occupation of New Orleans; siege of Port Hudson; at Shreveport; full entries.
* Leaves from a Soldier's Diary: The Personal Record of Lt. George G. Smith, Co. C., 1st Louisiana Regiment Infantry Volunteers [White] During the War of Rebellion. Putnam, Conn.: G. G. Smith, 1906.

1370. SMITH, Thomas Crutcher (1843-1913)
Military diary; life on the march.
* Here's Yer Mule: The Diary of Thomas C. Smith, 3rd Sergeant, Company "G," Wood's Regiment, 32nd Texas Cavalry, C. S. A., March 30, 1862-December 31, 1862. Waco: Little Texan Press, 1958.

1371. SPEER, William Henry Asbury
May 28-August 27, 1862
Prison diary; of the 28th North Carolina Volunteers; prisoner on a Lake Erie island; exchanged; not subject to the harsh conditions which prevailed later in the war.
* "A Confederate Soldier's View of Johnson's Island Prison," James B. Murphy, ed. Ohio History, v. 79, pp. 101-11, 1970.

1372. STAMPER, Isaac J.
August 4, 1862-December 19, 1863
Military diary; with the 43rd Tennessee Infantry in the sieges of Vicksburg and Knoxville; harrassed by Yankees while home on leave in Cleveland.
* The Civil War Diary of Isaac J. Stamper of Bradley County, Tennessee, Enlisted December 26, 1861 at Sweetwater, Tennessee: His Regiment Surrendered May 9, 1865. Cleveland, Tenn.: Cleveland Public Library, 1970.

1373. STEWART, James (1831-1905)
February 1, 1862-April 30, 1863
Travel diary; Scottish minister and admirer of Dr. Livingstone (q.v.) went to Africa to open a mission and develop the region as a cotton producing area; beset by difficulties, ill health and misunderstanding of his aims and others' intentions; lengthy descriptions of natives, their customs and habits.
* The Zambesi Journal of James Stewart: 1862-1863. J. P. R. Wallis, ed. London: Chatto and Windus, 1952.

1374. STONER, George W. (1830-1912)
January 1-December 31, 1862
Personal diary; life in Madison, Wisconsin; weather, social life; war news; work of the state legislature.
* "Diary of George W. Stoner, 1862," L. P. Kellogg, ed. Wisconsin Magazine of History, v. 21, pp. 194-212, December, 1937; pp. 322-36, March, 1938; pp. 420-31, June, 1938; v. 22, pp. 74-89, September, 1938.

1375. STROTHER, David Hunter (1816-88)
       1. February 27, 1862-August 9, 1864; free lance writer and
artist for Harper's in the 1850's; in the Army of the Potomac; Second
Battle of Bull Run; Antietam; in New Orleans and up the Mississippi
to the Red River; Gettysburg; ends with his resignation from the
service; one of the better war diaries.
       • A Virginia Yankee in the Civil War: The Diaries of David
       Hunter Strother. Cecil D. Eby, Jr., ed. Chapel Hill: Uni-
       versity of North Carolina, 1961.

       2. May 1-16, 1864; with the 3rd West Virginia Cavalry; a
Union account of the battle.
       • "With Sigel at New Market: The Diary of Col. David H.
       Strother," Cecil D. Eby, Jr., ed. Civil War History, v. 6,
       pp. 73-83, March, 1960.

1376. TAYLOR, Isaac Lyman (1837-   )
       January 1, 1862-July 2, 1863
       Military diary; camp life and marching; killed at Gettysburg
in the charge of the 1st Minnesota.
       • "Campaigning with the First Minnesota: A Civil War Diary,"
       Hazel C. Wolf, ed. Minnesota History, v. 25, pp. 11-39,
       March, 1944, pp. 117-52, June, 1944, pp. 224-57, September,
       1944, pp. 342-61, December, 1944.

1377. TAYLOR, Robert Belt (1831-88)
       October 1-12, 1862
       Military diary; lengthy, florid account of the battle.
       • "The Battle of Perryville, October 8, 1862, as Described
       in the Diary of Captain Robert B. Taylor," Hambleton Tapp,
       ed. Register of the Kentucky Historical Society, v. 60, pp.
       255-92, October, 1962.

1378. TAYLOR, Thomas Jones (1829-94)
       July, 1862-January 1, 1865; gaps
       Prison diary; member of the 49th Alabama Regiment imprisoned
on Johnson's Island; entries summarize the events of several days.
       • "'A Extraordinary Perseverance,' The Journal of Captain
       Thomas J. Taylor, C. S. A." Lillian Taylor Wall and Robert
       M. McBride, eds. Tennessee Historical Quarterly, v. 31, pp.
       328-59, 1972.

1379. THOMPSON, Joseph Dimmitt (1825-   )
       1. April 5-10, 1862; Military diary; with the 38th Tennessee
Regiment; lengthy description with hourly notes.
       • "The Battle of Shiloh: From the Letters and Diary of
       Joseph Dimmit Thompson," John G. Biel, ed. Tennessee His-
       torical Quarterly, v. 17, pp. 250-74, September, 1958.

       2. May 25-June 1, 1862; Military diary; "very weary march."
       • "The Evacuation of Corinth, From the Diary and a Letter

of Joseph Dimmitt Thompson," John G. Biel, ed. Journal of
Mississippi History, v. 24, pp. 40-56, January, 1962.

1380. TORREY, Rodney Webster (1836-)
       October 31, 1862-February 10, 1863
       Military diary; with the 49th Massachusetts Volunteers at Port
Hudson.
          • War Diary of Rodney W. Torrey, 1862-1863. N.p.: 19--.

1381. TOWNE, Laura Matilda (1825-1901)
       April 8, 1862-July 2, 1884
       Personal diary; daughter of an abolitionist went to St. Helena
Island, South Carolina, to teach slaves freed by Federal troops; entries fullest and most numerous in the 1860's; busy with teaching;
cf. Charlotte Forten's diary for the same area and time period.
          • Letters and Diary of Laura M. Towne: Written from the
          Sea Islands of South Carolina, 1862-1884. Rupert Sargent
          Holland, ed. Cambridge: Riverside Press, 1912; reprinted
          New York: Negro Universities Press, 1969.

1382. TRIMBLE, Isaac Ridgeway (1802-88)
       July 14, 1862-April 22, 1864
       Military diary; in the Chancellorsville and Gettysburg cam-
paigns; wounded; a Union prisoner.
          • "The Civil War Diary of General Isaac Ridgeway Trimble,"
          William Starr Myers, ed. Maryland Historical Magazine, v. 17,
          pp. 1-20, 1922.

1383. TRIPLETT, J. F. (-1921)
       May 1, 1862-June 27, 1862
       Trail diary; cattle roundup from Carson City, Nevada, gath-
ered 1300 head; comments on cowboys, ranchers, terrain, weather;
"Hell is an ice house to some of the places they'll see before a week
passes."; engaging personality.
          • "The Scouts Story From the Journal of a Cattle Man,"
          Atlantic Monthly, v. 135, pp. 493-500, April, 1925.

1384. TUCKER, John S. (1834-)
       March 23, 1862-February 28, 1865; gaps
       Personal diary; monotony behind the lines with the 5th Ala-
bama Regiment.
          • "The Diary of J. S. Tucker: Confederate Soldier From
          Alabama," Gary Wilson, ed. Alabama Historical Quarterly, v.
          43, pp. 5-33, Spring, 1981.

1385. VAN ALSTYNE, Lawrence (1839-)
          1. August 19, 1862-June 15, 1864; Military diary; action in
       Louisiana; in the Red River campaign; lengthy, detailed entries; well
       written.
          • Diary of an Enlisted Man. New Haven, Conn.: Tuttle,
          Morehouse and Taylor, Co., 1910.

2. "Diary Excerpts," in: Philip Dunaway and Mel Evans, eds.
A Treasury of the World's Great Diaries. New York: Doubleday,
1957; pp. 285-88.

1386. WALKER, Georgiana Freeman Gholson (1833-1904)
November 18, 1862-February 12, 1876; many gaps in later
years.
Personal diary; wife and daughter of Confederate blockade
runners lived in Virginia, Bermuda and England during the war;
social and family life; view of Confederate life outside the Southern
states.
• Private Journal, 1862-1865, With Selections From the Post-
war Years, 1865-1876. Dwight Franklin Henderson, ed. Tus-
caloosa, Ala.: Confederate Publishing Co., 1963.

1387. WALLACE, Mary Austin (1837/38-1921)
August 25-December 1, 1862
Personal diary; energetic and resourceful farmer's wife of
Calhoun County, Michigan, with a toddler and a nursing infant; ran
a farm and was neighborhood nurse while her husband served in the
19th Michigan Volunteer Infantry; notes on prices, crop yields, farm
chores and social life.
• Mary Austin Wallace: Her Diary, 1862: Michigan Soldier's
Wife Runs Their Farm. Julia McCune, ed. Lansing: Michigan
Civil War Centennial Observance Commission, 1963.

1388. WELLS, Seth James (1842-64)
November 3, 1862-July 22, 1863
Military diary; with the 8th and 17th Illinois; detailed entries
of the siege.
• The Siege of Vicksburg From the Diary of Seth J. Wells.
Detroit: W. H. Rowe, 1915.

1389. WHETTEN, Harriet Douglas
July 15-August 28, 1862
Nursing diary; life of a Sanitary Commission (Union) nurse in
Virginia aboard a hospital ship; dedicated, sensible woman who did
not suffer fools.
• "A Volunteer Nurse in the Civil War: the Diary of Harriet
Douglas Whetten," Paul H. Hass, ed. Wisconsin Magazine of
History, v. 48, pp. 205-21, Spring, 1965.

1390. WILCOX, Charles Edwards (1839-1931)
1. July 25, 1862-October 13, 1862; Military diary; with the
33rd Illinois Infantry confiscating cotton from Southern planters; return to Cairo, Illinois.
• "Hunting for Cotton in Dixie: From the Civil War Diary of
Captain Charles E. Wilcox," Edgar L. Erickson, ed. Journal
of Southern History, v. 4, pp. 493-513, 1938.

2. March 14-July 17, 1863; Military diary; full entries give

a comprehensive picture of the siege from the Union lines.
- "With Grant at Vicksburg: From the Civil War Diary of Captain Charles E. Wilcox," Edgar L. Erickson, ed. Journal of the Illinois Historical Society, v. 30, pp. 440-503, January, 1938.

1391. WILKINS, William Duncan (1826-82)
    1. Prison diary; Michigan native and Mexican War veteran; captured at Cedar Mountain; his sickness and sufferings and those of fellow prisoners; parolled.
- "My Libby Prison Diary August 12 to September 26, 1862," Detroit in Perspective, v. 3, pp. 77-113, Winter, 1979.

    2. August 12, 1862-September 25, 1862; Prison diary.
- "Forgotten in the 'Black Hole': A Diary From Libby Prison," Civil War Times Illustrated, v. 15, pp. 36-44, June, 1976.

1392. WILSON, John (-1910)
    Military diary; with the 56th Illinois Volunteer Infantry at the battle of Corinth, Mississippi.
- "An Illinois Soldier in North Mississippi: Diary of John Wilson, February 15-December 30, 1862," J. V. Frederick, ed. Journal of Mississippi History, v. 1, pp. 182-94, January, 1939.

1393. WILSON, William Lyne (1843-1900)
    1. May 1, 1862-April 9, 1865; Military diary; with the 12th Virginia Cavalry in campaigns in the Shenandoah Valley, Spotsylvania Courthouse and Appomattox; fighting, camp life; briefly imprisoned.
- A Borderland Confederate. Festus P. Summers, ed. Pittsburgh: University of Pittsburgh Press, 1962.

    2. January 1, 1896-March 6, 1897; Political diary; Grover Cleveland's Postmaster General and confidante; Free Silver; mostly cabinet matters; McKinley's election.
- The Cabinet Diary of William L. Wilson, 1896-1897. Festus P. Summers, ed. Chapel Hill: University of North Carolina Press, 1957.

1394. WINGFIELD, Henry Wyatt (1829-1902)
    May 1, 1862-September 17, 1864
    Military diary; life on the march.
- "Diary of Capt. H. W. Wingfield, 58th Va. Reg. 4th Brigade, Early's Division, Ewell's Corps," W. W. Scott, ed. Bulletin of the Virginia State Library, v. 15, pp. 7-47, July, 1927.

1395. WYETH, John Jasper (1841/41-)
    August 11, 1862-June 18, 1863
    Military diary; enlistment; to New Berne, North Carolina; siege of Washington, North Carolina; lengthy entries in formal, stilted prose.

- Leaves from a Diary Written While Serving in Co. E, 44th Mass. Dept. of North Carolina From September, 1862 to June, 1863. Boston: L. F. Lawrence and Co., 1878.

1863

1395a. ANONYMOUS [Dora Richards Miller?]
January 7-July 23, 1863
Personal diary; while the city was under siege a native New Orleanian bride nursed her husband, a victim of typhoid; rented a cave in which to live; beset by worries about her husband who was avoiding conscription because of opposition to the war; exceptional account of cave life.
- "A Woman's Diary of the Siege of Vicksburg," George Washington Cable, ed. The Century Illustrated Monthly Magazine, v. 30, pp. 767-75, 1885.

1395b. AFFELD, Charles E.
May 24-July 4, 1863
Military diary; with the 1st Illinois Light Artillery; "one of the best ... accounts" of Vicksburg in the editor's opinion; long, detailed entries.
- "Pvt. Charles E. Affeld Describes the Mechanicsburg Expeditions," Edwin C. Bearss, ed. Illinois State Historical Society Journal, v. 56, pp. 233-56, Summer, 1963; "Pvt. Charles E. Affeld Reports Action West of the Mississippi," Edwin C. Bearss, ed. Illinois State Historical Society Journal, v. 60, pp. 267-96, Autumn, 1967.

1396. ATKINS, Mary (1819-82)
November 10, 1863-February, 1864
Travel diary; Ohioan who taught for many years in Benicia, California, went on the brig Advance from San Francisco to Shanghai; ashore in Honolulu; pleasant interlude.
- The Diary of Mary Atkins: A Sabbatical in the Eighteen Sixties. Mills College, Cal.: Eucalyptus Press, 1937; 500 copies.

1397. ATWOOD, Evans (1836-)
April 29, 1863-January 1, 1865; many gaps
Prison/letter diary; captured in Mississippi; moved to St. Louis, then Johnson's Island and Point Lookout, Maryland; much reminiscing about better days.
- "Prisoner-of-war Diary," W. J. Lemke, ed. Arkansas Historical Quarterly, v. 12, pp. 340-69, Winter, 1953.

1398. AYERS, James T. (1805-65)
December 25, 1863-May 15, 1865
Personal diary; part-time minister was paid for each recruit he signed up; chaplain duty to a regiment of Colored Troops; conditions in the South; thoughts on blacks; interesting.

* The Diary of James T. Ayers, Civil War Recruiter. John
Hope Franklin, ed. Springfield: Printed by Authority of
the State of Illinois, 1947.

1399. BELL, John N.
April 2-July 4, 1863
Military diary; siege of Vicksburg; well done.
* "Diary of Captain John N. Bell of Co. E, 25th Iowa Infantry,
at Vicksburg," Iowa Journal of History, v. 59, pp. 181-221,
April, 1961.

1400. BIGELOW, Edwin B. (1838-1916)
January 1, 1863-June 14, 1864
Military diary; with the 5th Michigan Cavalry in camp near
Washington, D.C.; imprisoned at Belle Isle, Virginia, and escaped;
recaptured and escaped again.
* "Edwin B. Bigelow, A Michigan Sergeant in the Civil War,"
Frank L. Klement, ed. Michigan History, v. 38, pp. 193-
252, September, 1954.

1401. BLAIR, John Insley (1802-99)
June 15-July, 1863
Survey diary; undated entries; much about Mormons encoun-
tered in the course of the survey.
* "Surveying the First Railroad Across Iowa," Anthony L.
Cassen, ed. Annals of Iowa, v. 35, pp. 321-62, Summer,
1960.

1402. BOSWELL, James Keith
January 1-April 18, 1863
Military diary; on Stonewall Jackson's staff; died with him at
Chancellorsville.
* "The Diary of a Confederate Staff Officer," Civil War Times
Illustrated, v. 15, pp. 30-38, April, 1976.

1403. BRINKERHOFF, Arch M.
May 26-July 4, 1863
Military diary; the siege of Vicksburg.
* "Diary of Private Arch M. Brinkerhoff, Co. H, 4th Iowa
Infantry, at Vicksburg," Edwin C. Bearss, ed. Iowa Journal
of History, v. 59, pp. 222-37, April, 1961.

1404. BRINTON, Daniel Garrison (-1899)
April 24-July 17, 1863
Personal diary; Yale graduate studied medicine in Paris and
Germany; monotony alternated with furious action.
* "From Chancellorsville to Gettysburg, A Doctor's Diary,"
D. G. Brinton Thompson, ed. Pennsylvania Magazine of His-
tory and Biography, v. 89, pp. 292-315, July, 1965.

1405. BURTON, Anthony B.
May 16-July 4, 1863

Military diary; one of the better Vicksburg siege accounts.
• "Lt. Anthony B. Burton's Account of the Activities of the
5th Battery, Ohio Light Artillery, at Vicksburg," Edwin C.
Bearss, ed. Louisiana Studies, v. 10, pp. 274-330, Winter,
1971.

1406.   CAMPBELL, John Q. A.
        May 19-June 22, 1863
        Military diary; service in and around Vicksburg.
        • "The Civil War Diary of Lt. John Q. A. Campbell, Co. B,
        5th Iowa Infantry," Edwin C. Bearss, ed. Annals of Iowa,
        3rd ser., v. 39, pp. 519-33, Winter, 1969.

1407.   CHAPIN, James W. (1825?-1906)
        1.   June 24-November 3, 1863; Military diary; camp routine
and marches; laconic.
        • "With the Army of the Cumberland in the Chickamauga
        Campaign: The Diary of James W. Chapin, Thirty-ninth In-
        diana Volunteers," Donald E. Reynolds and Max H. Kele, eds.
        Georgia Historical Quarterly, v. 59, pp. 223-42, Summer,
        1975.

        2.   January 28-March 25, 1865; Military diary; very short en-
tries.
        • "A Yank in the Carolinas Campaign: The Diary of James
        W. Chapin, Eighth Indiana Cavalry," Donald E. Reynolds and
        Max H. Kele, eds. North Carolina Historical Review, v. 46,
        pp. 42-57, 1969.

1408.   CLANDENING, William H. (1834-1914)
        May 23, 1863-January 29, 1865
        Travel journal; via Fort Benton to the mines in Nevada; re-
turn to Canada.
        • "Across the Plains in 1863-1865, Being a Journal Kept by
        William H. Clandening of Walkerton, Upper Canada, Now On-
        tario, Canada," North Dakota Historical Quarterly, v. 2, pp.
        247-72, 1927-28.

        CLEMSON, Floride see LEE, Floride C.

1409.   COIT, Joseph Howland (1831-1906)
        June 14-July 1, 1863
        Personal diary; clergyman at the College of St. James near
Hagerstown, Maryland; prep school life during wartime.
        • "The Civil War Diary of Joseph H. Coit," James McLachlan,
        ed. Maryland Historical Magazine, v. 60, pp. 245-60, Septem-
        ber, 1965.

1410.   COOKE, Mrs. George
        January 2, 1863-December 27, 1864
        Personal diary; rural life in Corinth, New Hampshire; hard
work; war news.

• "Mrs. Cooke's Civil War Diary for 1863 and 1864," Vermont History, v. 25, pp. 56-65, January, 1957.

1411. CORBIN, Henry
April 20, 1863-September 14, 1864
Military diary; marching and fighting with the 18th Virginia Cavalry around Lynchburg; mileage; poor speller.
• "Diary of a Virginian Cavalry Man, 1863-4, From the Original Manuscript," Historical Magazine, 3rd ser., v. 2, pp. 210-15, 1873.

1412. DOUGHERTY, Michael (1846-)
October 10, 1863-December 10, 1864
Prison diary; Irish immigrant and recipient of the Congressional Medal of Honor; in Libby Prison, Andersonville and others; vaccinated and immediately washed it out; deaths of fellow prisoners from vaccinations; details of rations; tearing down a stockade for firewood; visit by Captain Henry Wirz looking for escape tunnels, "... he passed over two that I know of"; left for home aboard the riverboat Sultana with other parolled soldiers; a boiler explosion killed many but the diarist survived; excellent.
• Prison Diary, of Michael Dougherty, Late Co. B, 13th Pennsylvania Cavalry ... Sole Survivor of 127 of His Regiment. Bristol, Pa.: C. A. Dougherty, 1908; reprinted New York: Pyramid Books, 1960.

1413. ELLIS, E. John (1841-)
1863-June 13, 1865
Prison diary; excerpts; Johnson's Island was a prison for officers.
• Buck, Martina. "A Louisiana Prisoner-of-war on Johnson's Island, 1863-65," Louisiana History, v. 4, pp. 233-42, Summer, 1963.

1414. EVERETT, Eben
August 5-28, 1863
Military journal; probable author served with Company B, 1st New Mexico Volunteers under Kit Carson; scorched earth policy against the Indians; well written.
• "A Diary of Kit Carson's Navaho Campaign," Raymond E. Lindgren, ed. New Mexico Historical Review, v. 21, pp. 226-46, 1946.

1415. FERGUSON, Leonard C. (1839-73)
May 25, 1863-April 15, 1865
Military diary; guard duty with the 57th Pennsylvania Volunteer Infantry; captured at Petersburg; imprisoned at Andersonville and Florence, South Carolina; served as a camp policeman for extra rations.
• "The Civil War Diaries of Leonard C. Ferguson," William A. Hunter, notes. Pennsylvania History, v. 14, pp. 196-224, July, 1947; pp. 289-313, October, 1947.

1416.   FORREST, Douglas French (1837-1902)
        1. May 27, 1863-June 25, 1865; Sea diary; officer and pay-
master on the Confederate ship Rappahannock; blockade running;
tours ashore in Europe; a last effort to continue the war in Texas
and final surrender; well-written and one of the few naval diaries.
        • Odyssey in Gray: A Diary of Confederate Service, 1863-
        1865. William N. Still, Jr., ed. Richmond: Virginia State
        Library, 1979.
            REVIEWS: Civil War Times Illustrated, v. 19, p. 6, Jan-
            uary, 1981. Journal of Southern History, v. 46, pp. 610-
            11, November, 1980. Virginia Magazine of History and Bi-
            ography, v. 88, pp. 502-03, October, 1980.

        2. Article with excerpts and photos.
        • "An Odyssey in Gray: Selections from a Diary of Confed-
        erate Naval Life with the C. S. S. Rappahannock." Virginia
        Cavalcade, v. 29, pp. 124-29, Winter, 1980.

1417.   FREMANTLE, Sir Arthur James Lyon (1835-1901)
        March 2-July 14, 1863
        Personal diary; Briton sympathetic to the Southern cause on
a busman's holiday; across Texas, Louisiana, Mississippi and Georgia;
with Lee on the way to Gettysburg; meetings with Jefferson Davis;
opinions of Confederate generals; how Texas females take their snuff;
rescued by an Irishman; New York draft riots; exuberant; strong interest in military matters.
        • The Fremantle Diary: Being the Journal of Lieutenant Colo-
        nel Arthur James Lyon Fremantle, Coldstream Guards, on His
        Three Months in the Southern States. Walter Lord, ed. Bos-
        ton: Little, Brown, 1954; 1863 ed. titled Three Months in the
        Southern States.

1418.   HABERSHAM, Josephine Clay (1821-93)
        June 17-November 1, 1863
        Personal diary; wife and mother of a large family on a Georgia
plantation; musical, well-read; much war news but the fighting does
not touch them in this period.
        • Ebb Tide: As Seen Through the Diary of Josephine Clay
        Habersham, 1863. Spencer Bidwell King, Jr., ed. Athens:
        University of Georgia Press, 1958.

1419.   HAGADORN, Henry J. (1832-1903)
        January 11-August 31, 1863
        Military diary; with the 7th Minnesota on the Sioux expedition;
marching and pursuing Indians.
        • "On the March with Sibley in 1863: The Diary of Private
        Henry J. Hagadorn," John Perry Pritchett, ed. North Dakota
        Historical Quarterly, v. 5, pp. 103-29, January, 1931.

1420.   HANDER, Christian Wilhelm (1834-1912)
        May 13-July 18, 1863

Personal diary; Danish immigrant settled in Texas; service in the Vicksburg, Mississippi, area.
- "Excerpts From the Hander Diary," Leonard B. Plummer, ed. and trans. Journal of Mississippi History, v. 26, pp. 141-49, May, 1964.

1421. HARRISON, Mary Douglass Waring (1845-)
July 26-August 12, 1863; March 27-April 16, 1865
Personal diary; first part is a picture of everyday life during the war; second is an account of the fall of Mobile to the Yankees.
- Miss Waring's Journal: 1863 and 1865, Being the Diary of Miss Mary Waring of Mobile, During the Final Days of the War Between the States. Thad Holt, Jr., ed. Chicago: Wyvern Press of S. F. E., 1964.

1422. HEGEMAN, George (1845-)
October 8, 1863-January 15, 1865
Prison diary; captured at Auburn, Virginia; poor food and living conditions; by train from one prison to another.
- "The Diary of a Union Soldier in Confederate Prisons," James J. Heslin, ed. New York Historical Society Quarterly, v. 41, pp. 233-78, July, 1957.

1423. HOAG, Levi L. (1831-)
April 1-July 3, 1863
Military diary; with the 24th Iowa on the march to Vicksburg; foraging; weather.
- "The Civil War Diary of Sgt. Levi L. Hoag," Edwin C. Bearss, ed. Annals of Iowa, 3rd ser., v. 39, pp. 168-93, Winter, 1968.

1424. HOPKINS, Owen Johnston (1844-1902)
April 29, 1863-July 10, 1865
Military diary; with the 42nd Ohio Regiment in the Vicksburg campaign; the letters are more notable than the diary entries.
- Under the Flag of the Nation: Diaries and Letters of a Yankee Volunteer in the Civil War. Otto F. Bond, ed. Columbus: Ohio State University Press, for the Ohio Historical Society, 1961.

1425. HOWARD, Harlan Smith
September 19-December 27, 1863
Military diary; with the 3rd Wisconsin Light Artillery; escape from Danville Prison.
- "Prisoner of the Confederacy: Diary of a Union Artilleryman," Warren A. Jennings, ed. West Virginia History, v. 36, pp. 309-23, 1975.

1426. INGRAHAM, Elizabeth Mary Meade (1806-)
Personal diary; sister of Union General George G. Meade; lived in Grand Gulf when Union and Rebel forces overran the area.

• "The Vicksburg Diary of Mrs. Alfred Ingraham (May 2-
June 13, 1863)," W. Maury Darst, ed. Journal of Mississippi
History, v. 44, pp. 148-79, May, 1982.

1427.   IRWIN, Samuel S.
        Military diary; Douglas County, Illinois, school superintendent;
with the 2nd Illinois Cavalry following the fall of Vicksburg.
        • "Excerpts from the Diary of Samuel S. Irwin, July 5, 1863
to July 17, 1863," James Monahan, ed. Journal of Mississippi
History, v. 27, pp. 390-94, November, 1965.

1428.   KEY, Thomas J. (1831-   )
        December 7, 1863-May 7, 1865
        Military diary; newspaper publisher joined the 15th Arkansas
Infantry; at the Battle of Chickamauga; siege of Atlanta; battle of
Nashville; well done.
        • Two Soldiers: The Campaign Diaries of Thomas J. Key,
C. S. A., December 7, 1863-May 17, 1865, and Robert J.
Campbell, U.S.A., January 1, 1864-July 21, 1864.   Wirt Arm-
istead Cate, ed.   Chapel Hill: University of North Carolina
Press, 1938.

1429.   KILLGORE, Gabriel M. (1825-63)
        February 13-July 20, 1863
        Military diary; service with the Claiborne "Invincibles" (Louis-
iana); siege and surrender; died a week after the final entry.
        • "Vicksburg Diary: The Journal of Gabriel M. Killgore,"
Douglas Maynard, ed.   Civil War History, v. 10, pp. 33-53,
1964.

1430.   LABADIE, Cecilia (1839?-   )
        January 29-February 5, 1863
        Personal diary; a Federal blockade and a norther.
        • "Cecilia Labadie: Diary Fragment," Marjorie Logan Williams,
ed.   Texana, v. 10, pp. 273-83, 1972.

1431.   LEE, Florida Clemson (1842-71)
        1.   January 1, 1863-October 24, 1866; Personal diary; South-
ern woman's life in Bladensburg, Maryland, and Pendleton, South
Carolina; social and family life; Yankee scares.
        • A Rebel Came Home: The Diary of Floride Clemson Tells
Her Wartime Adventures in Yankeeland, 1863-64, Her Trip
Home to South Carolina and Life in the South During the Last
Few Months of the Civil War and the Year Following.   Charles
M. McGee, Jr. and Ernest M. Lander, Jr., eds.   Columbia:
University of South Carolina Press, 1961.

        2.   July 29-September 3, 1863; Letter journal; a visit to
Pennsylvania relatives by a Southern sympathizer; of Pittsburgh,
"This place is by far the dirtiest I ever saw."
        • "A Confederate Girl Visits Pennsylvania, July-September,

1863," Ernest M. Lander, Jr., ed. Western Pennsylvania Historical Magazine, v. 49, pp. 111-26, April, 1966; pp. 197-211, July, 1966.

1432. McKELL, William J. (-1864)
September 20, 1863-May 26, 1864
Military diary; with the 89th Ohio Volunteer Regiment; imprisoned at Andersonville; escape and recapture; some undated, long entries.
• "The Journal of Sergt. Wm. J. McKell," Watt P. Marchman, ed. Civil War History, v. 3, pp. 315-40, 1957.

1433. MACY, William Madison (1833-1926)
January 1, 1863-August 1, 1865; gaps
Military diary; with the 94th Illinois Volunteers in Missouri, Mississippi and Brownsville, Texas.
• "The Civil War Diary of William M. Macy," Indiana Magazine of History, v. 30, pp. 181-97, June, 1934.

1434. MINOR, Hubbard Taylor, Jr. (1845-74)
August 7, 1863-April 14, 1865; gaps
Sea diary; training on the CSS Patrick Henry; duty aboard the Savannah; captured the USS Water Witch; visits to a sweetheart.
• "'I Am Getting a Good Education ...': An Unpublished Diary by a Cadet at the Confederate Naval Academy," Civil War Times Illustrated, v. 13, pp. 25-32, November, 1974; "Diary of a Confederate Naval Cadet: Conclusion," Civil War Times Illustrated, v. 13, pp. 24-26, December, 1974.

1435. MORGAN, John S. (1841-74)
February 24-December 31, 1863
Military diary; weather, marching.
• "Diary of John S. Morgan, Company G, Thirty-third Iowa Infantry," Annals of Iowa, 3rd ser., v. 13, pp. 483-508, 1923.

1436. MORROW, Henry A. (-1891)
January 21, 1863-February 7, 1865; gaps
Military diary; with the 24th Michigan Infantry in the Army of the Potomac; material on the army's commanders; at Chancellorsville and Petersburg; wounded.
• "To Chancellorsville with the Iron Brigade: The Diary of Colonel Henry A. Morrow, Part I," Civil War Times Illustrated, v. 14, pp. 12-22, January, 1976; "The Last of the Iron Brigade: The H. A. Morrow Diary: Conclusion," Civil War Times Illustrated, v. 14, pp. 10-21, February, 1976.

1437. NUTT, Laetitia Lafon Ashmore (1835-)
October 12, 1863-August 28, 1864
Personal diary; wife of a captain in the Red River Rangers, Louisiana Cavalry, followed her husband with three daughters in tow; filled with laments on past and present trials.

• Courageous Journey: The Civil War Journal of Laetitia
Lafon Ashmore Nutt.   Florence Ashmore C. H. Martin, ed.;
Miami, Fla.:   E. A. Seemann, 1975.

1438.   O'BRIEN, George W. (1833-1909)
        May 9-December 29, 1863
        Military diary; with the 11th Battalion Texas Volunteers at
the Battle of Fordoche; service in Texas and Louisiana.
        • "The Diary of Captain George W. O'Brien, 1863," Cooper
        W. Ragan, ed.   Southwestern Historical Quarterly, v. 67, pp.
        26-54, July, 1963; pp. 235-46, October, 1963; pp. 413-33,
        January, 1964.

1439.   ODEN, John Piney (1823-   )
        April 6-June 29, 1863
        Military diary; prominent Selma, Alabama, native served in
the 10th Alabama Infantry; observer at the Battle of Chancellorsville.
        • "The End of Oden's War: A Confederate Captain's Diary,"
        Michael Barton, ed.   Alabama Historical Quarterly, v. 43,
        pp. 73-98, Summer, 1981.

1440.   O'HAGAN, Joseph B. (1826-78)
        February 1-19, 1863
        Military diary; Irish-born Jesuit; at Falmouth, Virginia.
        • "The Diary of Joseph B. O'Hagan, S. J., Chaplain of the
        Excelsior Brigade," Rev. William L. Lucey, ed.   Civil War His-
        tory, v. 6, pp. 402-09, December, 1960.

1441.   PARK, Robert Emory
        1.   "War Diary of Capt. Robert Emory Park, Twelfth Alabama
Regiment, January 28th, 1863-January 27th, 1864.   Accounts of the
Battles of Chancellorsville, Gettysburg, Jeffersonton, Bristow Station,
Locust Grove, Mine Run, the March into Maryland and Pennsylvania,
with Reminiscences of the Battle of Seven Pines," Southern Historical
Society Papers, v. 26, pp. 1-31, 1898.

        2.   June 6-August 17, 1864; Military diary; life on the march
in Winchester, Virginia, and Martinsburg, West Virginia.
        • "Diary of Robert E. Park, Macon, Georgia, Late Captain
        Twelfth Alabama Regiment, Confederate States Army," Southern
        Historical Society Papers, v. 1, pp. 370-86, May, 1876.

1442.   PATTISON, John J.
        July 17-November 29, 1863; March 7, 1865-May 21, 1866
        Military diary; fragmentary notes on service with the 7th Iowa
Cavalry.
        • "With the U.S. Army Along the Oregon Trail, 1863-66:
        Diary by Jno. J. Pattison," Nebraska History Magazine, v. 15,
        pp. 79-93, 1934.

1443.   PIERCE, Nathan Frank (1825-   )
        June 18, 1863-July 25, 1864

Military diary; service with the 1st Regiment U.S. Sanitary
Service at Antietam; took in other soldiers' washing.
- "A Michigan Soldier's Diary, 1863," Russell Kirk, ed.
Michigan Historical Magazine, v. 28, pp. 231-45, 1944.

1444. POCHÉ, Felix Pierre
       July 11, 1863-May 12, 1865
       Personal diary; bilingual Creole on the staff of Brigadier Gen-
eral Henry Gray in the Trans-Mississippi Department; permitted to
travel about Louisiana when not on official duty; devout Catholic
and devoted husband gives a good overview of military and civilian
life in the state.
       - A Louisiana Confederate: Diary of Felix Pierre Poché.
       Edwin C. Bearss, ed. Eugenie Watson Somdal, trans. Natchi-
       toches: Louisiana Studies Institute Northwestern State Univer-
       sity, 1972.

1445. RANSOM, John L. (1843-1919)
       November 22, 1863-December 25, 1864
       Prison diary; brigade quartermaster of the 9th Michigan Cav-
alry; captured at Rogersville, Tennessee; at Belle Isle, Virginia;
"Digging a tunnel to get out of this place."; full entries give a comprehensive view of life in Andersonville; scribe for other prisoners;
escaped, recaptured, escaped again; well done.
       - Andersonville Diary: Escape and List of Dead, With Name,
       Company, Regiment, Date of Death and Number of Grave in
       Cemetery. Auburn, N.Y.: The Author, 1881; new ed. New
       York: Paul S. Eriksson, 1963.

1446. RAYNOR, William H. (1834-1912)
       April 16, 1863-July 3, 1864
       Military diary; with Grant from Milliken's Bend to capture
Vicksburg; detailed, well written.
       - "The Civil War Experiences of an Ohio Officer at Vicksburg:
       Diary of Colonel William H. Raynor, 56th Ohio Infantry," Ed-
       win C. Bearss, ed. Louisiana Studies, v. 9, pp. 243-300,
       Winter, 1970.

1447. ROGERS, Lucien Payne (1838-1914)
       April 16, 1863-January 3, 1865
       Military diary; service with the 92nd Illinois Volunteers in
Tennessee and Georgia.
       - "Excerpts From the Civil-War Diary of Lucien Payne Rog-
       ers," P. Burwell Rogers, ed. Bucknell University Studies,
       v. 4, p. 1-28, March, 1953.

1448. ROOT, William H. (1842-   )
       April 1-June 14, 1863
       Military diary; with the 75th New York Volunteers; from Mor-
gan City, Louisiana, to Port Hudson; long entries with description of
countryside.

• "The Experiences of a Federal Soldier in Louisiana in 1863,"
Walter Prichard, intro. Louisiana Historical Quarterly, v. 19,
pp. 635-67, 1936.

1449. SCHREEL, Charles (1842-1912)
        January 7-May 9, 1863
        Military diary; with the 71st Ohio Infantry at Forts Henry and
Donelson; short entries showing the tedium of his duty.
        • "Charley Schreel's Book: Diary of a Union Soldier on Gar-
rison Duty in Tennessee," Edward F. Keuchel and James P.
Jones, eds. Tennessee Historical Quarterly, v. 36, pp. 197-
207, Summer, 1977.

1450. SHAFFNER, Dr. J. F., Sr.
        Military/medical diary; surgeon in the 4th North Carolina
Regiment; involved in a court-martial by a martinet of a commanding
officer; acquitted; on leave in Virginia; a few details about the
wounded and their treatment.
        • Diary of Dr. J. F. Shaffner, Sr., Commencing September
13, 1863, Ending February 5, 1865. C. L. Shaffner, ed.
Priv. ptd., 1936.

1451. SHULTZ, John A. (1839-)
        Military diary; Illinois farmer in the 73rd Illinois; in campaigns
in Kentucky, Georgia and Tennessee; ill in various hospitals several
times.
        • One Year at War: The Diary of Private John A. Shultz,
August 1, 1863-August 1, 1864. Hobart L. Morris, Jr., ed.
New York: Vantage, 1968.

1452. SIMONS, Maurice Kavanaugh (1824-67)
        April 14, 1863-July 11, 1863
        Military diary; with the 2nd Texas Infantry at the siege of
Vicksburg; parolled to Alabama.
        • "The Vicksburg Diary of M. K. Simons, 1863," Walter H.
Mays, ed. Military History of Texas and the Southwest, v.
5, Spring, 1965; entire issue.

1453. SMITH, James West (1830?-63)
        May 29-July 12, 1863
        Military diary; siege of Vicksburg; defeat and its aftermath;
long entries, observant.
        • "A Confederate Soldier's Diary: Vicksburg in 1863,"
Southwest Review, v. 28, pp. 293-327, Spring, 1943.

1454. SPOONER, John (1845-)
        November 15, 1863-April 14, 1864
        Sea diary; fragmentary notes of a sailor.
        • "More Concerning the Life of J. Spooner," Sarah Scribner,
ed. Pacific Historian, v. 14, pp. 86-89, Fall, 1970.

1455. STEARNS, Amos Edward (1833-1912)
       May 4, 1863-January 16, 1865
       Prison diary; with the 25th Massachusetts Volunteer Infantry
in Libby Prison; prisons at Charleston and Florence; short entries;
weather, food, conditions.
       • The Civil War Diary of Amos E. Stearns, A Prisoner at
       Andersonville. Leon Basile, ed. Rutherford, N.J.: Fair-
       leigh Dickinson University Press, 1980.

1456. STEVENSON, William Grafton (-1910)
       August 23, 1863-April 26, 1864
       Military diary; service in the Carolinas.
       • "Diary of William Grafton Stevenson, Captain, C. S. A."
       Carl Rush Stevenson, ed. Alabama Historical Quarterly, v.
       23, pp. 45-72, Spring, 1961.

1457. SWAN, Samuel Alexander Ramsey (1826-1913)
       April 29-July 9, 1863
       Military diary; former teacher in General Stephen D. Lee's
brigade; well-done, detailed account of the siege from the inside.
       • "A Tennessean at the Siege of Vicksburg: The Diary of
       Samuel Alexander Ramsey Swan, May-July, 1863," George C.
       Osborn, ed. Tennessee Historical Quarterly, v. 14, pp. 353-
       72, December, 1955.

1458. TALBOT, Joseph Cruickshank (1816-83)
       May 25-December 9, 1863
       Travel diary; visit to parts of his diocese in Colorado, New
Mexico, Utah and Nevada.
       • "Journal of the 1st Bishop of the North West, Joseph Cru-
       ickshank Talbot," Thomas Jenkins, ed. Historical Magazine
       of the Protestant Episcopal Church, v. 17, pp. 60-105, March,
       1948.

1459. THOMPSON, Henry Yates (1838-1928)
       July 10-December 13, 1863
       Travel diary; wealthy Briton with American connections toured
the U.S.; Boston, New York, Philadelphia, Washington, Philadelphia;
saw the Battle of Chattonooga; his sketches and letters home; incisive
comments.
       • An Englishman in the American Civil War: The Diaries of
       Henry Yates Thompson 1863. Sir Christopher Chancellor, ed.
       New York: New York University Press, 1971.

1460. TOURGÉE, Albion Winegar (1838-1905)
       May 14-November 10, 1863
       Military diary; American politician, writer, and judge; with
the 105th Ohio Volunteer Infantry; his marriage at Columbus, Ohio;
stationed at Nashville.
       • "A Civil War Diary of Albion W. Tourgée," Dean H. Keller,
       ed. Ohio History, v. 74, pp. 99-131, 1965.

1461. TURCHIN, Nadine Lvova (-1904)
       May 26, 1863-April 26, 1864
       Personal diary; Russian emigre and wife of a Union officer;
rambling, self-pitying; some good description of conditions; spiteful
to those who disagree with her husband; rails against men in general.
       • "'A Monotony Full of Sadness': The Diary of Nadine Tur-
         chin, May, 1863-April, 1864," Mary Ellen McElligott, ed. Illi-
         nois State Historical Society Journal, v. 70, pp. 27-89, Fall,
         1977.

1462. TURNER, William H. (-1900)
       March 3-May 3, 1863
       Medical diary; doctor on the City of Memphis, a hospital boat
on the Mississippi during the siege of Vicksburg; from Corinth; comments on nurses, wounded, and the way the war is being run.
       • "Diary of W. H. Turner, M.D., 1863," Mildred Throne,
         comp. Iowa Journal of History and Politics, v. 48, pp. 267-
         82, July, 1950.

1463. VAUGHAN, Turner
       Military diary; life on the march; at Gettysburg.
       • "Diary of Turner Vaughan, Co. 'C.' 4th Alabama Regiment,
         C. S. A., Commenced March 4th, 1863 and Ending February
         12th, 1864," Alabama Historical Quarterly, v. 18, pp. 573-604,
         Winter, 1956.

1464. WALLACE, Elizabeth Curtis (1816-66)
       April 1, 1863-December 31, 1864
       Personal diary; plantation mistress of Norfolk County, Virginia;
journalist under the pseudonym "Allie Zandt"; husband imprisoned by
Yankees; hired free blacks; problems with a jealous neighbor tale-
bearing to Yankees.
       • Glencoe Diary; The War-time Journal of Elizabeth Curtis
         Wallace. Eleanor P. Cross and Charles B. Cross, Jr., eds.
         Chesapeake, Va.: Norfolk County Historical Society, 1968.

1465. WARMOTH, Henry Clay (1842-)
       Personal diary; with the 32nd Missouri Infantry; Illinois car-
petbagger who became governor of Louisiana in 1868; sometimes lighthearted and humorous.
       • "The Vicksburg Diary of Henry Clay Warmoth: Part I
         (April 3, 1863-April 27, 1863," Journal of Mississippi History,
         v. 31, pp. 334-47, November, 1969; Part II (April 28, 1863-
         May 26, 1863), Paul H. Hass, ed. Journal of Mississippi His-
         tory, v. 32, pp. 60-74, February, 1970.

1466. WESCOAT, Arthur Brailsford (1848-1941)
       January 1, 1863-August 24, 1864
       Personal diary; plantation life in Pinopolis, South Carolina;
school; glimpses of the war.

• "Journal of Arthur Brailsford Wescoat, 1863, 1864," South Carolina Historical Magazine, v. 55, pp. 71-102, April, 1954.

1467.   WESCOAT, Joseph Julius (1842-1908)
        September 8, 1863-April 30, 1865
        Military diary; service in Florida, Virginia and North Carolina
with the 11th South Carolina Volunteers; imprisoned at Fort Delaware.
        • "Diary of Captain Joseph Julius Wescoat, 1836-1865," Anne
        King Gregorie, ed. South Carolina Historical Magazine, v. 59,
        pp. 11-23, January, 1958; pp. 84-95, April, 1958.

1468.   WEST, John Camden (1834-1927)
        April 12, 1863-April 18, 1864
        Military diary; with the 4th Texas Infantry at Gettysburg
and Chickamauga; sometimes barefoot and often ragged but still
found occasions of humor.
        • A Texan in Search of a Fight, Being the Diary and Letters
        of a Private Soldier in Hood's Texas Brigade. Waco, Tx.:
        Press of J. S. Hill and Co., 1901; reprinted Waco, Tx: Texian
        Press, 1969.

1469.   WINNE, Peter (-1916)
        April 9-June 13, 1863
        Travel diary; expanded from a jotted diary to a diary-memoir;
left from Waukeska County, Wisconsin; by covered wagon; originally
bound for California but settled near Greeley, Colorado; comments
on others' poor grammar; weather; passing scenery.
        • "Across the Plains in 1863: The Diary of Peter Winne,"
        Iowa Journal of History and Politics, v. 49, pp. 221-40, July,
        1951.

1470.   WRIGHT, John P.
        January 1, 1863-April 12, 1864
        Military diary; excerpts; homesick Iowa farmboy in Arkansas
with the 29th Iowa Infantry.
        • "Diary of Private John P. Wright, U.S.A., 1864-1865,"
        Ralph R. Rea, ed. Arkansas Historical Quarterly, v. 16, pp.
        304-18, Autumn, 1957.

                              1864

1471.   ABBOTT, Lemuel Abijah (1842-)
        January 1-December 31, 1864
        Military diary; service with the 10th Vermont Volunteer Infan-
try in Grant's Rapidal River and Sheridan's Shenandoah campaigns;
well done.
        • Personal Recollections and Civil War Diary, 1864. Burling-
        ton: Free Press Printing Co., 1908.

1472.   AMES, Amos W. (1840-1913)
        August 31, 1864-April 28, 1865

Military diary; service with the 4th Regiment of Iowa Infantry;
spent some time in Andersonville.
- "A Diary of Prison Life in Southern Prisons," Annals of
Iowa, 3rd ser. v. 40, pp. 1-19, Summer, 1969.

1473. ANDERSON, James W.
December 11, 1864-January 19, 1865
Letter/diary; service at Camp Chase, Columbus, Ohio.
- "Writings of a Confederate Prisoner of War," George C. Os-
born, ed. Tennessee Historical Quarterly, v. 10, pp. 74-90,
March, 1951; pp. 161-84, June, 1951.

1474. ANDREWS, Eliza Francis
December 19, 1864-August 29, 1865
Personal diary; introduction by the diarist quite interesting;
her father sympathized with the Union; staying with her sister on
a plantation near Albany, Georgia; long entries; one of the better
non-combatant diaries.
- The Wartime Journal of a Georgia Girl, 1864-1865. New
York: D. Appleton and Co., 1908.

1475. ARNOLD, Joseph Warren (1841-1903)
March 2, 1864-July 28, 1866
Travel diary; from Galena, Illinois, to Montana; prospecting;
worked as a hotel clerk in Nevada City; returned to Illinois by steam-
boat.
- "Joseph Warren Arnold's Journal of His Trip to and From
Montana, 1864-1866," Charles W. Martin, ed. Nebraska His-
tory, v. 55, pp. 463-552, Winter, 1974.

1476- BENSON, William C. (-1865)
  77. January 1, 1864-March 9, 1865
Military diary; life on the march with the 120th Indiana Volunteers.
- "Civil War Diary of William C. Benson," Indiana Magazine
of History, v. 23, pp. 333-64, September, 1927.

BERRY, John Green, Jr. see No. 1278

1478. BOYLE, Francis Atherton (1838-1907)
May 4, 1864-May 21, 1865
Prison diary; captured at the Battle of the Wilderness; impris-
oned at Fort Delaware; full entries describing daily life.
- "The Prison Diary of Adjutant Francis Atherton Boyle,
C. S. A." May Lindsay Thornton, ed. North Carolina Histor-
ical Review, v. 39, pp. 58-84, Winter, 1962.

1479. BRAWLEY, William H. (1841-1916)
June 8, 1864-March 27, 1865
Travel diary; discharged Confederate veteran visited England
on unspecified business for the South; in Paris and environs; pleasant travelogue.

• The Journal of William H. Brawley, 1864-1865. Francis Poe Brawley, ed. Charlottesville, Va.: n.p., 1970; 300 copies.

1480. BROTHER, Charles (1844-1917)
March 14-August 5, 1864
Sea diary; Marine private aboard Admiral Farragut's flagship, USS Hartford; life aboard; Battle of Mobile Bay; valuable for a view of shipboard routine and Farragut's battle preparations.
• Two Naval Journals, 1864, at the Battle of Mobile Bay. C. Carter Smith, ed. Chicago: Wyvern Press, 1964.
• "Journal," in: Civil War Naval Chronology: 1861-1865. Part 6, re-edited [editor not named]. Washington, D.C.: U.S. Naval History Division Navy Department, 1971; v. 6, pp. 47-83.

1481. BROWN, Augustus C.
May 10, 1864
Personal diary; account of one day's activities in a Civil War field hospital.
• "Diary Excerpts," in: Philip Dunaway and Mel Evans, eds. A Treasury of the World's Great Diaries. New York: Doubleday, 1957; pp. 281-82.

1482. BURDICK, John M. (-1865)
June 20-October 24, 1864
Prison diary; captured at Lynchburg and sent to Andersonville; the editor's footnotes have more information than the diary itself.
• "The Andersonville Journal of Sergeant M. M. Burdick," Ovid L. Futch, ed. Georgia Historical Quarterly, v. 45, pp. 287-95, 1961.

1483. BURTON, Elijah P.
March 7, 1864-June 22, 1865
Personal diary; service in Alabama and the Carolinas; many bouts of illness and hospitals stays.
• Diary of E. P. Burton, Surgeon, 7th Reg. Ill. 3rd Brig., 2nd Div. 16 A. C. Des Moines: Iowa Historical Records Survey, 1939.

1484. CAMPBELL, Robert J. (1837-1927)
January 1-July 22, 1864
Military diary; in winter quarters with the 3rd Iowa Infantry; at Vicksburg; with Sherman to Atlanta where he was captured.
• Two Soldiers. Wirt Armistead Cate, ed. Chapel Hill: University of North Carolina Press, 1938.

1485. CARY, Clarence Fairfax (1845-)
September 24, 1864-March 18, 1865
Sea diary; service on the CSS Chickamauga; running the Federal blockade; in Bermuda.

• "The War Journal of Midshipman Cary," Brooks Thompson and Frank L. Owsley, Jr., eds. Civil War History, v. 9, pp. 187-202, 1963.

1486.   CHURCH, Frank L. (1842-1910)
        February 19-May 5, 1864
        Sea diary; lieutenant commanded the Marine Guard aboard the tinclad Black Hawk; from Cairo, Illinois, to the Red River in Louisiana; the campaign was a failure.
        • Civil War Marine: A Diary of the Red River Expedition, 1864. James P. Jones and Edward F. Keuchel, eds. Washington, D.C.: U.S. Marine Corps, History and Museums Division, 1975. [SuDoc no. D 214.13:L49]

1487.   CLARKE, John T.
        May 1-August 30, 1864
        Military diary; destroying Georgia with the 31st Missouri Infantry.
        • "The Diary of a Civil War Soldier with Sherman in Georgia," Bulletin of the Missouri Historical Society, v. 8, pp. 356-70, July, 1952.

1488.   COHEN, Fanny (1840-1938)
        December 21, 1864-January 3, 1865
        Personal diary; daughter of a well-to-do merchant; two Yankee officers were billeted with the family.
        • "Fanny Cohen's Journal of Sherman's Occupation of Savannah," Spencer B. King, Jr., ed. Georgia Historical Quarterly, v. 41, pp. 407-16, December, 1957.

1489.   COOK, F. A.
        June 2-August 19, 1864
        Military journal; expedition against the Indians in the territory between the Little Colorado and Gila Rivers.
        • "War and Peace: Two Arizona Diaries," Frank D. Reeve, ed. New Mexico Historical Review, v. 24, pp. 95-129, 1949.

1490.   COOKE, Giles Buckner (1838-1937)
        June 15-August 21, 1864; March 29-April 11, 1865
        Military diary; excerpts.
        • "Rev.-Maj. Giles Buckner Cooke," Tyler's Quarterly, v. 19, pp. 1-10, July 1937; pp. 87-94, October 1937.

1491.   COX, Jabez Thomas
        May 12-August 29, 1864
        Military diary; enlisted for 100 days service; marching and foraging in Kentucky.
        • "Civil War Diary of Jabez Thomas Cox," Indiana Magazine of History, v. 28, pp. 40-54, March, 1932.

1492.   CRAIG, J. M.
        September 1, 1864-February 3, 1865

Personal diary; minimal information.
- "The Diary of Surgeon Craig, Fourth Louisiana Regiment, C. S. A., 1864-65," John S. Kendall, ed. Louisiana Historical Quarterly, v. 8, pp. 53-70, 1925.

1493. DANA, Gustavus Sullivan
February 4-April 5, 1864
Military diary; Union officer at the Battle of Olustee, Florida; observant.
- "Captain Dana in Florida: A Narrative of the Seymour Expedition," Lester L. Swift, ed. Civil War History, v. 11, pp. 245-56, 1965.

1494. DELOACH, Olivia Hill
Travel diary; vicissitudes of war-time travel.
- "Journey of a Confederate Mother June 7-September 12, 1864," John A. Holden, ed. West Tennessee Historical Society Papers, v. 19, pp. 36-57, 1965.

1495. DICKINSON, Henry Clay (1830-71)
September 13, 1864-May 23, 1865
Prison diary; captured near Richmond in May, 1864; hardships, illness; resistance and finally capitulation to taking oath to U.S. Government.
- Diary of Capt. Henry C. Dickinson, C. S. A. Morris Island 1864-1865. Denver: Press of Williamson-Haffner Co., 191- ; 225 copies.

1496. DOUGHERTY, William Thompson
January 1-December 31, 1864
Personal diary; Greentown schoolteacher with the 104th Ohio Volunteer Infantry; duty in Tennessee.
- "Civil War Diary of an Ohio Volunteer," Donald J. Coan, ed. Western Pennsylvania Historical Magazine, v. 50, pp. 171-86, 1967.

1497. DOYLE, James M. (1839-1909)
August 1, 1864-April 9, 1865
Military diary; service in Virginia with the 23rd Illinois Volunteers.
- "The Diary of James M. Doyle," Mid-America, v. 20, pp. 273-83, 1938.

1498. DOZER, Jesse L.
February 14, 1864-April 29, 1865
Military diary; enlistment in the 26th Illinois Infantry; foraging in Tennessee.
- "Marching with Sherman Through Georgia and the Carolinas: Civil War Diary of Jesse L. Dozer," Wilfred W. Black, ed. Georgia Historical Quarterly, v. 52, pp. 308-36, September, 1968; pp. 451-79, December, 1968.

1499. DRAKE, John M. (1830-1913)
       April 20-October 10, 1864
       Military journal; detailed, well-written account of a journey
from Fort Dalles through eastern Oregon; actions against the Snake
Indians.
       • "Cavalry in the Indian Country, 1864," Priscilla Knuth, ed.
       Oregon Historical Quarterly, v. 65, pp. 5-118, March, 1964.

1500. EBERHART, James W.
       August 18, 1864-March 18, 1865
       Prison diary; in Libby and Salisbury Prisons; parolled at Wil-
mington, N. Car.; poor food, monotony and death all around.
       • "Diary of Sailsbury [sic] Prison by James W. Eberhart,
       Sergt. Co. 'G' 8th Pa. Res. Vol. Cor(ps) Also Co. "G" 191st
       Pa. Vet. Volunteer," Florence C. McLaughlin, ed. Western
       Pennsylvania Historical Magazine, v. 56, pp. 211-51, July,
       1973.

1501. EGGLESTON, Edmund T.
       February 7-December 31, 1864
       Military diary; in the Atlanta campaign with the 1st Mississippi
Artillery; defeat at Nashville.
       • "Excerpts From the Civil War Diary of Edmund T. Eggles-
       ton," Edward Noyes, ed. Tennessee Historical Quarterly, v.
       17, pp. 336-58, December, 1958.

1502. FORBES, Eugene (-1865)
       May 1, 1864-February 5, 1865
       Prison diary; with the 4th Regiment New Jersey Volunteers;
food, work details; discovery of escape tunnels by Southern guards
and loss of rations in consequence.
       • Diary of a Soldier and Prisoner of War in the Rebel Pris-
       ons. Trenton, N.J.: Murphy & Bechtel, 1865.

1503. GALLAHER, DeWitt Clinton (1845-1926)
       June 8, 1864-April 8, 1865
       Military diary; Company E of the 1st Virginia Cavalry; at the
Battle of the Wilderness; some notes written up later.
       • A Diary Depicting the Experiences of DeWitt Clinton Gal-
       laher in the War Between the States While Serving in the Con-
       federate Army. Charleston, W. Va.: n. p., 1945.

1504. GARNETT, James Mercer
       Military diary; long, thoughtful entries.
       • "Diary of Captain James M. Garnett, Ordnance Officer of
       Rodes's Division, 2d Corps, Army of Northern Virginia, From
       August 5th to November 30th, 1864, Covering Part of General
       Early's Campaign in the Shenandoah Valley," Southern Histor-
       ical Society Papers, v. 27, pp. 1-16, 1899; v. 28, pp. 58-71,
       1900.

1505. GILLET, Orville
       May 14, 1864-October 26, 1865
       Military diary; on duty in Arkansas with the 3rd Michigan
Cavalry.
       • "Diary of Lieutenant Orville Gillet, U.S.A., 1864-1865,"
       Ted R. Worley, ed. Arkansas Historical Quarterly, v. 17, pp.
       164-204, Summer, 1958.

1506. HABERSHAM, Anna Wylly
       August 20-October 16, 1864
       Personal diary; the adolescent loves of a 15-year-old girl on
a Georgia plantation; no mention of the Civil War; ephemeral.
       • Journal. new ed. Darien, Ga.: Ashantilly Press, 1961.

1507. HEINEMANN, Captain F.
       April 18-26, 1864
       Personal diary; lengthy descriptions.
       • "The Federal Occupation of Camden as Set Forth in the
       Diary of a Union Officer," Arkansas Historical Quarterly, v.
       9, pp. 214-19, Autumn, 1950.

1508. HILLEARY, William M. (1840-1917)
       November 16, 1864-July 21, 1866
       Military diary; Iowan went to Oregon and joined the 1st Ore-
gon Infantry; protected immigrants from the Indians; service in
Oregon, Washington and Idaho territories; life in camp and on the
march.
       • A Webfoot Volunteer: The Diary of William M. Hilleary,
       1864-1866. Herbert Nelson and Preston Onstad, eds. Cor-
       vallis: Oregon State University Press, 1965.

1509. HINSON, William Godber (1838-1919)
       April 6, 1864-April 30, 1865
       Military diary; extracts; service with the 7th South Carolina
Cavalry.
       • "The Diary of William G. Hinson During the War of Seces-
       sion," Joseph Ioor Waring, ed. South Carolina Historical Mag-
       azine, v. 75, pp. 14-23, 111-20, 1974.

1510. HITCHCOCK, Henry (1829-1902)
       October 31, 1864-February 7, 1865
       Military diary; St. Louis lawyer on Sherman's staff in Georgia
and Carolinas campaigns; lengthy entries with many details of troop
life and civilian experiences.
       • Marching with Sherman: Passages from the Letters and
       Campaign Diaries of Henry Hitchcock ... November, 1864-May,
       1865. M. A. DeWolfe Howe, ed. New Haven: Yale Univer-
       sity Press, 1927.

1511. HOWE, Henry (1811-68)
       January 1, 1864-May 11, 1868

Personal diary; missionary traveled by horse and buggy
preaching and baptizing; died of pneumonia two weeks after the
last entry; bald record of farm work, amount of collections and payments in kind.
    • The Diary of a Circuit Rider: Excerpts From the Notes of
    Henry Howe, Made While Traveling in Southern Wisconsin Be-
    tween the Years 1864 & 1868 as a Missionary of the Disciples
    of Christ. Jessie Howe Nebelthau, ed. Minneapolis, Minn.:
    Voyageur Press, 1933.

1512.   HULL, Lewis Byram (1841-1902)
        February 2, 1864-July 14, 1866
        Personal diary with the 11th Ohio Cavalry at Fort Laramie;
soldiering on the Oregon Trail; Indian attacks; social life; "Must be
going to have a cold winter as weddings are all the rage."
    • "Soldiering on the High Plains: The Diary of Lewis Byram
    Hull, 1864-1866," Myra E. Hull, ed. Kansas Historical Quar-
    terly, v. 7, pp. 3-53, February, 1938.

1513.   JAMES, Frederic Augustus (1832-64)
        February 20-August 27, 1864
        Military diary; Navy man captured in the attack on Fort Sum-
ter in 1863; prison experiences.
    • Frederic Augustus James's Civil War Diary: Sumter to An-
    dersonville. Jefferson J. Hammer, ed. Rutherford, N.J.:
    Fairleigh Dickinson University Press, 1973.

1514.   JONES, Mary Sharpe (1808-69)
        December 13, 1864-January 27, 1865
        Personal diary; mother and daughter who were the widow and
wife of Presbyterian ministers; beset by troops of both sides; "We
are prisoners in our own home."
    • Yankees A'coming: One Month's Experience During the In-
    vasion of Liberty County, Georgia, 1864-1865. With Mary
    Jones Mallard. Tuscaloosa, Ala.: Confederate Publishing Co.,
    1959.

1515.   JONSSON, Jonas (John Johnson) (1814-97)
        1864-1895
        Personal diary; Swedish farmer; his family life near Orrefors;
deaths of two of his children; farm bankruptcy and auction; working
as a bookbinder; emigration to Minnesota; on to Tacoma.
    • Emeroy, Johnson, "Jonas Jonsson-John Johnson: Pages
    From a Diary, 1864-1895," Swedish Pioneer Historical Quarterly,
    v. 28, pp. 7-26, January, 1977.

1516.   KELLY, Seth (1836-68)
        January 1-December 30, 1864
        Military diary; service in Missouri and Arkansas with the 9th
Kansas Volunteer Cavalry.
    • "The 1864 Diary of Cpl. Seth Kelly," Anne E. Hemphill, ed.
    Kansas History, v. 1, pp. 189-210, Autumn, 1978.

1517. KOEMPEL, Philip (1840-)
       March 19, 1864-February 13, 1865
       Personal diary; German immigrant worked as a wood carver in
New Haven; joined the 1st Connecticut Cavalry; with Frémont in the
Shenandoah campaign; at the 2nd Battle of Bull Run; captured June
29, 1864 and imprisoned at Andersonville and Florence, South Carolina;
3 or 4 lines per day.
       • Phil Koempel's Diary, 1861-1865. Prv. ptd, n.d.

1518. LADD, James Royal (1836?-)
       November 13-December 12, 1864
       Military diary; captain in the 113th Ohio Volunteers marching
with Sherman to Savannah; past Kennesaw Mountain; burning of Atlanta; foraging and destroying what they couldn't eat or carry; har-
assed by shreds of Rebel cavalry; "We have had a gay time."
       • "From Atlanta to the Sea," American Heritage, v. 30, pp.
       4-11, December, 1978.

1519. LARNED, William L. (1817-)
       June 29, 1864-January 31, 1866
       Travel diary; wagon train going from Minnesota to the Mon-
tana gold fields beset by Indians; Civil War veteran hoped to sell
supplies to miners; sketch of breastworks constructed by the party
which held off Sioux for 14 days.
       • "The Fisk Expedition of 1864: The Diary of William L.
       Larned," Ray H. Mattison, ed. North Dakota History, v. 36,
       pp. 209-74, Summer, 1969.

1520. LeCONTE, Emma (1847?-) see also #2113
       December 31, 1864-August 10, 1865
       Personal diary; daughter of Joseph LeConte (q.v.) living in
Columbia, South Carolina; a Soldiers' Bazaar; on a college campus;
shelling by Yankees; burning of Columbia; war's end and occupation
by Federals; sometimes melodramatic but with much background information.
       • When the World Ended: The Diary of Emma LeConte. Earl
       S. Miers, ed. New York: Oxford University Press, 1957.

1521. LeCONTE, Joseph (1823-1901)
       1. December 9, 1864-February 24, 1865; Personal diary; pro-
fessor at South Carolina College in Columbia; journey from Columbia
to a plantation 35 miles south of Savannah; crossing a swamp; hiding
from Yankees; good.
       • 'Ware Sherman, A Journal of Three Months' Personal Ex-
       perience in the Last Days of the Confederacy. Berkeley: Uni-
       versity of California Press, 1937.
       REVIEWS: American Historical Review, v. 44, p. 219, 1938.
       Journal of Southern History, v. 4, pp. 396-97, 1938. Mis-
       sissippi Valley Historical Review, v. 25, pp. 283-84, 1938.

       2. July 21-August 26, 1870; Travel diary; University of

California professor went with a party of his students to study the
geology of the Sierras and Yosemite; lighthearted.
* A Journal of Ramblings Through the High Sierra of California, by the University Excursion Party. San Francisco:
Sierra Club, 1875; 1960.

1522. LEE, Charles G. (-1865)
January 1-December 31, 1864
Prison diary; excerpts; member of the 16th Connecticut Volun-
teers; well-educated Guildford native.
* "The Diary of Charles G. Lee in the Andersonville and
Florence Prison Camps, 1864," Paul C. Helmreich, ed. Con-
necticut Historical Society Bulletin, v. 41, pp. 12-28, 1976.

1523. LETTEER, Alfred W.
July 29-September 14, 1864
Prison diary; short entries.
* "Andersonville, Diary of a Prisoner, from the Original
Manuscript, Now First Printed," Historical Magazine, 2nd ser.,
v. 9, pp. 1-7, 1871.

1524. McCLATCHEY, Minerva Leah Rowles (1820-80)
January, 1864-September, 1865
Personal diary; wife and mother living on Georgia plantation;
in Marietta; dealing with Yankee and Confederate troops in the neigh-
borhood.
* "A Georgia Woman's Civil War Diary; The Journal of Min-
erva Leah Rowles McClatchey, 1864-65,' T. Conn Bryan, ed.
Georgia Historical Quarterly, v. 51, pp. 197-216, June, 1967.

1525. McDONALD, David (1803-69)
January 7, 1864-August 31, 1868
Personal diary; lawyer and later U.S. District judge; legal
and political life in Indiana; doubted the legality of Lincoln's assas-
sins' death sentences; acid comments.
* "Hoosier Justice: The Journal of David McDonald, 1864-
1868," Donald O. Dewey, ed. Indiana Magazine of History,
v. 62, pp. 175-232, September, 1966.

1526. MACKALL, Thomas Bennett (1840-)
May 14-June 4, 1864
Military diary; article on the journal and its five versions
published as Part 3 of v. 38 War of the Rebellion (USGPO, 1891);
with the Army of Tennessee in the Atlanta campaign.
* McMurry, Richard M. "Mackall Journal and Its Antecedents,"
Civil War History, v. 20, pp. 311-28, December, 1974.

1527. MACKEY, James F.
January 1, 1864-March 14, 1865
Military diary; service in North Carolina; imprisoned at Macon,
Georgia; on parole at Annapolis, Maryland.

● "Diary of Maj. James F. Mackey," in: Luther S. Dickey.
History of the 103d Pennsylvania Volunteer Infantry, 1861-65.
Chicago: L. S. Dickey, 1910; pp. 314-40.

1528. MATTHEWS, James Louis (1839-1924)
December 8, 1864-July 23, 1865
Military diary; life on the march with the 12th Indiana Infantry.
● "Civil War Diary of Sergeant James Louis Matthews," Roger
C. Hackett, ed. Indiana Magazine of History, v 24, pp. 306-
16, December, 1928.

1529. MECHLING, William Thompson (-1898)
Military diary; West Point graduate in Monett's Ferry operation;
Red River campaign.
● "William T. Mechling's Journal of the Red River Campaign,
April 7-May 10, 1864," Alwyn Barr, ed. Texana, v. 1, pp.
363-79, Fall, 1963.

1530. MEDFORD, Harvey C. (1831-1902)
January 19, 1864-April 14, 1864
Military diary; with Lane's Texas Cavalry; battles at Sabine
and Pleasant Hill; visit to Galveston; food, reading, camp life; phi-
losophizing.
● "The Diary of H. C. Medford, Confederate Soldier, 1864,"
Rebecca W. Smith and Marion Mullins, eds. Southwestern His-
torical Quarterly, v. 34, pp. 106-40, 203-30, 1930.

1531. MILLER, James Knox Polk (1845-91)
August 10, 1864-June 21, 1867; gaps
Personal diary; young New Yorker out west; extended stays
in Salt Lake and Virginia City; revealing descriptions of hell-raising
and sober citizens; one of the few diaries for this time and place.
● The Road to Virginia City: The Diary of James Knox Polk
Miller. Andrew F. Rolle, ed. Norman: University of Okla-
homa Press, 1960.

1532. MOCKETT, Richard H. (1838-1935)
November 3, 1864-January 17, 1865
Military diary; shoemaker in the 43rd Wisconsin Volunteers;
comments on Southerners, white and black; marching and camp life.
● "The Richard H. Mockett Diary," James L. Sellers, ed.
Mississippi Valley Historical Review, v. 26, pp. 233-40, 1939.

1533. NEWCOMB, Sam P.
February 1-April 3, 1864
Travel diary; trip with six companions through central Texas;
hunting; good description of frontier Texas.
● "A Journal of a Trip from the Clear Fork in Stephens
County to the San Saba River," in: Sallie Reynolds Matthews.
Interwoven: A Pioneer Chronicle. 4th ed. College Station:
Texas A & M University Press, 1982; pp. 195-209.

1534. NICHOLS, George Ward (1837-85)
       September 16, 1864-May 24, 1865
       Military diary; aide-de-camp to General Sherman; burning of
Atlanta; campaigning in the Carolinas; detailed account with much
transcribed conversation with civilians and slaves met.
       • The Story of the Great March: From the Diary of a Staff
       Officer. London: Sampson Low, Son & Marston, 1865.

1535. O'CONNELL, John Charles (1837-   )
       May 17, 1864-March 2, 1865
       Sea diary; 2nd assistant engineer on the Tennessee; battle of
Mobile Bay; captured and imprisoned at Ship Island.
       • Two Naval Journals, 1864, at the Battle of Mobile Bay. C.
       Carter Smith, ed. Chicago: Wyvern Press, 1964.

1536. PAGE, Richard C. M. (1841-   )
       October 7, 1864-April 12, 1865
       Military diary; marching; camp life.
       • "Diary of Major R. C. M. Page, Chief of Confederate States
       Artillery, Department of Southwest Virginia and East Tennessee,
       from October, 1864 to May, 1865," Southern Historical Society
       Papers, v. 16, pp. 58-68, 1888.

1537. PATTEN, James Comfort (1826-1903)
       July 4-December 30, 1864
       Military diary; assistant surgeon with the 58th Indiana Volun-
teers; good descriptions of civilians and scenery of Georgia.
       • "An Indiana Doctor Marches with Sherman: The Diary of
       James Comfort Patten," Robert G. Athearn, ed. Indiana Mag-
       azine of History, v. 49, pp. 405-22, December, 1953.

1538. PHILLIPS, John Wilson (1837-96)
       February 28-December 9, 1864
       Military diary; fighting with the 18th Pennsylvania Cavalry in
the Shenandoah Valley; captured; in Libby Prison.
       • "The Civil War Diary of John Wilson Phillips," Robert G.
       Athearn, ed. Virginia Magazine of History and Biography,
       v. 62, pp. 95-123, 1954.

1539. PIERSON, Marshall Samuel (1838-1909)
       April 1-December 13, 1864
       Military diary; fighting near Mansfield, Texas.
       • Delaney, Norman C. "The Diary and Memoirs of Marshall
       Samuel Pierson Company C, 17th Reg., Texas Cavalry 1862-
       1865," Military History of Texas and the Southwest, v. 13, pp.
       23-38, 1976.

1540. POWERS, Elvira J.
       April 1, 1864-June 18, 1865
       Personal diary; intrepid, outspoken New Englander; nursed
soldiers and small pox victims in the South; quoted conversation;
lively, opinionated; one of the better nursing diaries.

• Hospital Pencillings: Being a Diary While in Jefferson General Hospital, Jeffersonville, Indiana and Others at Nashville, Tennessee, as Matron and Visitor. Boston: E. L. Mitchell, 1866.

1541. RATHBONE, Thomas W.
Military diary; service with the 153rd Ohio Volunteer Infantry; captured at Paw Paw Station; in Roper Hospital at Charleston, South Carolina; escape.
• "Captain T. W. Rathbone's 'Brief Diary of Imprisonment' July 1-November 21, 1864," Louis Bartlett, ed. Ohio History, v. 71, pp. 33-56, January, 1962.

1542. RICHARDS, David Allen (1820-93)
September 2, 1864-July 1, 1865
Military diary; sober, religious man dismayed by the wickedness of army life; with the 13th Michigan Battery; nursing duty at Forts Sumner and Reno camp hospitals; sightseeing in Washington, D.C.
• "The Civil War Diary of David Allen Richards," Frederick D. Williams, ed. Michigan History, v. 39, pp. 183-220, June, 1955.

1543. RIDGWAY, Frank (1840-1911)
January 12-July 31, 1864
Military diary; article based on the diary; more concerned with military matters than his hospital work.
• Heslin, James J. "From the Wilderness to Petersburg: The Diary of Surgeon Frank Ridgway," New York Historical Society Quarterly, v. 45, pp. 112-40, April, 1961.

1544. ROBERTSON, Melville Cox (1840-65)
March 30, 1864-March 14, 1865
Military diary; with the 93rd Indiana Volunteers; captured and imprisoned in Mississippi; died of typhoid.
• "Journal of Melville Cox Robertson," Indiana Magazine of History, v. 28, pp. 116-37, June 1932.

1545. RYAN, Benjamin Williams (1826-98)
April 13-December 31, 1864
Travel diary; from Bureau County, Illinois; mileage, weather; prices paid for goods; Platte River, up the Yellowstone; gold panning.
• "The Bozeman Trail to Virginia City, Montana in 1864: A Diary," Annals of Wyoming, v. 19, pp. 77-104, July, 1947.

1546. RZIHA, John
November 15-December 1, 1864
Military diary; Austrian immigrant and topographical engineer; from Atlanta to Louisville, Georgia.
• "With Sherman Through Georgia: A Journal," David J. de Laubenfels, ed. Georgia Historical Quarterly, v. 41, pp. 288-300, September, 1957.

1547. SEDGWICK, Arthur G. (1844-1914)
       July 28-September 12, 1864
       Prison diary; extracts; member of the 20th Massachusetts In-
fantry mistook Confederates for his own men and was captured; food,
prison life.
       • Armstrong, William M. "Libby Prison: The Civil War Diary
       of Arthur G. Sedgwick," Virginia Magazine of History and
       Biography, v. 71, pp. 449-60, 1963.

1548. SHATZEL, Albert Harry (-1908)
       Prison diary; hardships, food.
       • "Imprisoned at Andersonville: The Diary of Albert Harry
       Shatzel, May 5, 1864-September 12, 1864," Donald F. Danker,
       ed. Nebraska History, v. 38, pp. 81-125, June, 1957.

1549. SHELDON, Charles LeRoy (1840-1925)
       October 3, 1864-June 22, 1865
       Military diary; with the 1st Michigan Cavalry and the 23rd
Army Corps; drumming in the occupied South; camp life; return to
Detroit; well done.
       • "The Diary of a Drummer," John L. Melton, ed. Michigan
       History, v. 43, pp. 315-48, September, 1959.

1550. SMALL, Abner R. (1836-1910)
       August 19, 1864-February 24, 1865
       Prison diary; captured at Petersburg, Virginia; in Libby
Prison; much on food and money matters in prison.
       • The Road to Richmond: The Civil War Memoirs of Maj. Ab-
       ner R. Small of the 16th Maine Volunteers, with His Diary as
       a Prisoner of War. Harold Adams Small, ed. Berkeley: Uni-
       versity of California Press, 1939.

1551. SMEDLEY, Charles (1836-64)
       May 5-July 5, 1864
       Prison diary; captured at the Battle of the Wilderness; died
in Andersonville.
       • Life in Southern Prisons: From the Diary of Corp. Charles
       Smedley of Co. G, 90th Regiment Pennsylvania Volunteers.
       Lancaster, Pa.: Ladies' and Gentlemens' Fulton Aid Society,
       1865.

1552. SMITH, John Henry (1827-   )
       April 30-November 17, 1864
       Military diary; from Davenport, Iowa; weather, skirmishes;
march to Atlanta; captured south of Atlanta and imprisoned at Charleston; escaped through the swamp to a Union blockade boat.
       • "The Civil War Diary of Colonel John Henry Smith," David
       M. Smith, ed. Iowa Journal of History, v. 47, pp. 140-70,
       April, 1949.

1553. SNOWDEN, George Randolph (-1932)
       April 18-May 16, 1864

Travel diary; from Washington, D.C. to Franklin, Pennsylvania; discharge and adjustment to civilian life.
- Ness, Charles H. "Home to Franklin! Excerpts From the Civil War Diary of George Randolph Snowden," Western Pennsylvania Historical Magazine, v. 54, pp. 158-66, April, 1971.

1554. STANFIELD, Howard Stillwell (1846-1923)
March 22, 1864-May 11, 1865
Travel diary; likeable young man prevented by poor health from joining the army or going to college went west with a neighbor; by wagon and stage from Virginia City to Salt Lake City.
- Diary of Howard Stillwell Stanfield: Overland Trip from Indiana to California 1864, Via Virginia City Montana Territory and Sea Voyage from San Francisco to New York, Via Panama. Jack J. Detzler, ed. Bloomington: Indiana University Press, 1969.

1555. STARR, Darius (1842-64)
January 1-August 22, 1864
Military diary; going into battle with the 2nd Regiment U.S. Sharpshooters; capture; sickness and death in prison.
- "From Spotsylvania Courthouse to Andersonville: A Diary of Darius Starr," E. Merton Coulter, ed. Georgia Historical Quarterly, v. 41, pp. 176-90, 1957.

1556. STEPHEN, Asbery C. (1839-1929)
June 5, 1864-May 3, 1865
Military diary; life on the march with the 116th Ohio Volunteer Infantry; wounded in Piedmont battle.
- The Civil War Diary of Asbery C. Stephen. Oscar F. Curtis, ed. Bloomington: Monroe County, Indiana Historical Society, 1973.

1557. STORTZ, John (1842-)
Military diary; member of the 16th U.S. Infantry; his capture and escape.
- "Experiences of a Prisoner During the Civil War In and Out of the Hands of the Rebels July 23, 1864-December 27, 1864," Annals of Iowa, v. 37, pp. 167-94, Winter, 1964.

1558. THOMAS, Anna Hasell
December 26, 1864-May 31, 1865
Travel diary; journey from Federal lines to South Carolina with a dying sister; encounters with troops.
- "The Diary of Anna Hasell Thomas," Charles E. Thomas, ed. South Carolina Historical Magazine, v. 74, pp. 128-43, July, 1973.

1559. THOMPSON, Henry Allen (1846-1939)
January 1, 1864-1932
Personal diary; excerpts and connecting narrative; terse Vermonter; prices, weather, family visits and work.

- "The Life of a Vermont Farmer and Lumberman: The Diaries of Henry Allen Thompson of Grafton and Saxtons River," Stuart F. Heinritz, ed. Vermont History, v. 42, p. 89-139, Spring, 1974.

1560. TURNER, Rev. Henry M. (-1915)
December 8, 1864-January 18, 1865
Military diary; black chaplain to the 1st Regiment, U.S.
Colored Troops; from Bermuda Hundred, Virginia, on a headquarters boat; mess with white officers; failure of Christmas Day assault on Fort Fisher; its subsequent fall to General Alfred Terry (q.v.).
- "Rocked in the Cradle of Consternation," Edwin S. Redkey, ed. American Heritage, v. 31, pp. 70-79, October/November, 1980.

1561. VAN DUSER, John
November 15, 1864
Military diary; chief telegrapher and federal; route through Milledgeville and Savannah.
- "The John Van Duser Diary of Sherman's March From Atlanta to Hilton Head," Georgia Historical Quarterly, v. 53, pp. 220-40, June, 1969.

1562. WASHINGTON, Ella (-1898)
May 27-June 13, 1864
Personal diary; in Hanover County, Virginia; visits from assorted Yankees and General George Armstrong Custer.
- "'An Army of Devils': The Diary of Ella Washington," James O. Hall, ed. Civil War Times Illustrated, v. 16, pp. 18-25, February, 1978.

1563. WATSON, Robert
December 22, 1864-April 25, 1865
Sea diary; Confederate Navy seaman on the CSS Savannah; ship was destroyed to prevent its falling into Sherman's hands; at Fort Buchanan; in Washington for Lincoln's funeral.
- "'Yankees Were Landing Below Us'", William N. Still, Jr., ed. Civil War Times Illustrated, v. 15, pp. 12-21, April, 1976.

1564. WEIMER, John (1836-)
September 9, 1864-October 19, 1865
Sea diary; Ohioan from a family of riverboatmen served on the USS Nymph, an armored patrol boat; Federal blockade of the Mississippi; life in the engine room; straightforward.
- The Diary of a Union Soldier, 1864-1865. Walter Rankins, ed. Frankfort, Ky.: Roberts Printing Co., 1952; 100 copies.

1565. WILEY, Harvey W. (1844-1930)
May 30-September 17, 1864
Military diary; son of an abolitionist; with the 137th Indiana

Infantry at Tullahoma, Tennessee; good descriptions.
- Fox, William L. "Corporal Harvey W. Wiley's Civil War Diary," Indiana Magazine of History, v. 51, pp. 139-62, June, 1955.

1865

1565a. ANONYMOUS [Samuel Howard Gray? (1846-85)]
Military diary; signalman's diary; to Appomattox; news of Lincoln's assassination.
- "A Confederate Diary of the Retreat From Petersburg, April 3-20, 1865," Richard B. Harwell, ed. Atlanta: The Library, Emory University, 1953.

1566. BOOTH, John Wilkes (1838-65)
April 13-21, 1865
Personal diary; Lincoln's assassin made two diary entries during his escape attempt.
- Hanchett, William "Booth's Diary," Illinois State Historical Society Journal, v. 72, pp. 39-56, February, 1979.

1567. BOWEN, Clarissa Adger
May 1-November 24, 1865
Personal diary; plantation mistress in the first days of Reconstruction; visit by Yankees looking for Confederate government gold; stillbirth of a son; visits to and from family; uncertainties of life under Yankee rule.
- The Diary of Clarissa Adger Bowen, Ashtabula Plantation, 1865. Mary Steenson, comp. Pendleton, S. Car.: Research and Publication Foundation for Historic Restoration in Pendleton Area, 1973.

1568. BURTSELL, Richard L. (1840-1912)
January 31, 1865-February 14, 1868
Personal diary; American Catholic priest, trained in Rome, was pastor of a New York City parish; church duties and finances; social life with priests who were fellow students in Rome; concern for newly freed blacks and European Catholic immigrants.
- The Diary of Richard L. Burtsell, Priest of New York: The Early Years, 1865-1868. Nelson J. Callahan, ed. New York: Arno Press, 1978.
   REVIEW: Catholic Historical Review, v. 66, pp. 255, April, 1980.

1569. CARY, Wilson Miles (1835-1914)
April 2-3, 1865
Military diary; Confederate quartermaster in the area of Petersburg, Virginia.
- "From the Diary of Wilson Miles Cary," Francis Burton Harrison, ed. Tyler's Quarterly, v. 24, pp. 106-09, 1942-43.

1570. CLEMENT, Abram Wilson
       February 4-March 3, 1865
       Military diary; associated with Captain Joseph J. Wescoat,
(q.v.).
       • "Diary of Abram W. Clement, 1865," Slann L. C. Simmons,
       ed. South Carolina Historical Magazine, v. 59, pp. 78-83,
       1958.

1571. COOKE, Jay (1821-1905)
       June 15, 1865-July 18, 1906; gap 1874-79
       Public diary; Gibraltar is an island in Lake Erie; owned by
financier Cooke in the period covered; entries made by himself,
friends and family while on vacation; weather, recreation.
       • The Journal of Jay Cooke: or The Gibraltar Records, 1865-
       1905. Columbus: Ohio State University Press, 1935.

1572. COX, Abner R.
       April 11-27, 1865
       Personal diary; member of the Palmetto Sharpshooters of the
Army of Northern Virginia; surrender and making his way home to
Belton.
       • "South from Appomattox: The Diary of Abner R. Cox,"
       Royce Gordon Shingleton, ed. South Carolina Historical Mag-
       azine, v. 75, pp. 238-44, 1974.

1573. EATON, Amasa M. (1841-1914)
       October 7-17, 1865
       Travel diary; oil dealer of Providence, Rhode Island, traveled
from New York City to Titusville, Pennsylvania; much detail on prices
and drilling.
       • "A Visit to the Oil Regions of Pennsylvania in 1865," West-
       ern Pennsylvania Historical Magazine, v. 18, pp. 189-208,
       September, 1935.

1574. FLEMING, Robert H. (1846-)
       March 28-May 15, 1865
       Military diary; midshipman of the Confederate Naval Academy
was detailed to escort archives and bullion to a safe location; discharge and arrival home.
       • "The Confederate Naval Cadets and the Confederate Treas-
       ure: The Diary of Midshipman Robert H. Fleming," G. Melvin
       Herndon, ed. Georgia Historical Quarterly, v. 50, pp. 207-
       16, June 1966.

1575. GALLAHER, William Houston (1840-74)
       March 29-October 19, 1865
       Travel diary; by steamboat to Fort Benton; by wagon to Gal-
latin, Montana Territory; good descriptions.
       • "Up the Missouri in 1856: The Journal of William H. Gal-
       laher," James E. Moss, ed. Missouri Historical Review, v. 57,
       pp. 156-83, January, 1963; pp. 261-84, April, 1963.

1576. GILPIN, E. N.
       March 11-14, 1865
       Military diary; clerk of the 3rd Iowa Cavalry at General Up-
ton's headquarters; well-done, lengthy entries.
       • The Last Campaign: A Cavalryman's Journal. Leavenworth,
       Kan.: Press of Ketcheson Printing Co., 1908; reprint of
       Journal of the U.S. Cavalry Association, v. 18, no. 68, April,
       1908.

1577. HAMILTON, Edward John (1834-1918)
       March-July 7, 1865
       Military diary; Presbyterian minister; with the Army of the
Potomac; service in Virginia.
       • "A Union Chaplain's Diary," Chase C. Mooney, ed. New
       Jersey Historical Society Proceedings, v. 75, pp. 1-17, Jan-
       uary, 1957.

1578. HOBSON, William (1820-91)
       March 17, 1865-June 22, 1891
       Missionary diary; entries here relate to his work in California,
Oregon and Washington.
       • "William Hobson, Quaker Missionary," Oregon Historical
       Quarterly, v. 34, pp. 134-43, March, 1933.

1579. HORTON, Dexter (1837?-)
       January 20-May 3, 1865
       Military diary; Michigan volunteer and commissary department
captain under Sherman; sharing food with Southern civilians.
       • "Diary of an Officer in Sherman's Army Marching Through
       the Carolinas," Clement Eaton, ed. Journal of Southern His-
       tory, v. 9, pp. 238-54, 1943.

1580. HULTERT, Eri Baker
       February 28-April 2, 1865
       Personal diary; extracts; visits to Philadelphia, Baltimore and
Washington.
       • "The Civil War Diary of a Christian Minister," Leo P. Kibby,
       ed. Journal of the West, v. 3, pp. 221-32, April, 1964.

1581. INGALLS, William Bowers Bourn (1853-1922)
       October 2, 1865-
       Travel diary; voyages to California and return; life and school-
ing in San Francisco.
       • "A Boy's Voyage to San Francisco, 1865-66," F. Bourn
       Hayne, ed. California Historical Society Quarterly, v. 36,
       pp. 205-12, September, 1957; pp. 293-306, December, 1957.

1582. JERVEY, Susan Ravenel
       February 16-May 12, 1865
       Personal diary; suffering depredations of black and white
Yankee troops.

• "Extracts from Journal Kept by Miss Susan R. Jervey at Northampton Plantation," in: Two Diaries From Middle St. John's, Berkeley, South Carolina. Charleston, S. Car.: St. John's Hunting Club, 1921; pp. 3-26.

1583. KIMBALL, Gorham Gates (1838-1904)
June 6-August 16, 1865
Trail diary; sheep drive from Red Bluff, California, to Boise City, Idaho Territory; kept at the behest of his mother.
• "Trailing Sheep From California to Idaho in 1865: The Journal of Gorham Gates Kimball," Agricultural History, v. 28, pp. 49-83, April, 1954.

1584. LEASK, Thomas Smith (1839-)
June 12, 1865-November 8, 1870
Personal diary; Orkney Islander immigrated to Port Natal; trips to Matabeleland and the Zambezi; partly business, partly horse trading; native life; wide range of subjects from natives as servants to the beauty of Victoria Falls.
• The Southern African Diaries of Thomas Leask, 1865-1870. J. P. R. Wallis, ed. London: Chatto and Windus, 1954.

1585. LOVELL, Captain Samuel C.
March 27-April 13, 1865
Military journal; with the 4th Massachusetts Cavalry before and after the battle.
• "With Lee After Appomattox," Stuart H. Buck, ed. Civil War Times Illustrated, v. 17, pp. 38-43, November, 1978.

1586. McCORMICK, Henry (1835?-)
June 21-November 4, 1865
Travel diary; Civil War veteran went with two friends to the West Coast to study mining methods; one friend died at Denver; on to Salt Lake City; comments on terrain, especially its mining potential; to Portland and San Francisco; southern California; terse but informative entries.
• Across the Continent in 1865, as Told in the Diary of the Late Colonel Henry McCormick. Harrisburg, Pa.: Prv. ptd., 1937.

1587. MATHEWS, G. H. ("Porte")
June 23-October 19, 1865
Travel diary; aboard the steamer Lafayette to Europe; dramatic rescue of victims of a sunken Dutch ship; visits to major European cities; tour of Waterloo; in England and Scotland; ornate style; later additions to some entries.
• Diary of a Summer in Europe, 1865. New York: Marsh's Print, 1866.

1588. MINOR, John Barbee
February 28-March 7, 1865

Personal diary; law professor at the University of Virginia
notes the approach and departure of Yankees.
- "John Barbee Minor's Civil War Diary," Anne Freudenberg
  and John Casteen, eds. Magazine of Albemarle Country History, v. 22, pp. 45-56, 1963-64.

1589. OURY, Mrs. Granville H.
June 20-November 11, 1865
Travel diary; Confederate family immigrated to Mexico after
the Civil War; roundabout route to Guaymas, Mexico, from San Antonio, Texas; on to Tucson where they settled; travel conditions;
state of former Confederates.
- "An Old Diary Found in Mexico," Col. C. C. Smith, ed.
  Arizona Historical Review, v. 4, pp. 50-63, 1931-32; pp. 46-
  57, January, 1932; v. 5, pp. 62-70, April, 1932; pp. 146-56,
  July, 1932; pp. 234-41, October, 1932; pp. 333-40, January,
  1933; v. 6, pp. 45-64, January, 1935.

1590. PENDLETON, William Frederic (1845-   )
January 11-April 22, 1865
Military diary; life on the march and at home in Georgia.
- Confederate Diary: Capt. W. F. Pendleton, January to
  April, 1865. Bryn Athyn, Pa.: Prv. ptd., 1957.

1591. PENNOCK, Jake
May 1-September 25, 1865
Military diary; with the 11th Kansas Cavalry from an unnamed
starting point to the Wind River; trailing an Indian war or hunting
party; several skirmishes and hard-won battles with larger forces;
well done.
- "Diary of Jake Pennock," Annals of Wyoming, v. 23, pp.
  4-29, July, 1951.

1592. RAVENEL, Charlotte St. John
February-April 22, 1865
Personal diary; last days of the war; hiding silver, etc. from
Yankees; "today's news is very cheering; it is that Lincoln ... as-
sassinated."
- "Journal Letter Kept by Miss Charlotte St. John Ravenel
  of Pooshee Plantation for Miss Meta Heywards," in: Two Di-
  aries From Middle St. John's, Berkeley, South Carolina.
  Charleston, S. Car.: St. John's Hunting Club, 1921; pp.
  27-45.

1593. ROCKAFELLOW, B. F. (1835-   )
Military diary; march from Fort Leavenworth, Kansas, to establish Fort Connor in Wyoming.
- "Diary of Capt. B. F. Rockafellow Sixth Michigan Cavalry,"
  in: LeRoy R. and Ann W. Hafen, eds. Powder River Campaigns and Sawyers Expedition of 1865. Glendale, Cal.: Arthur H. Clark, 1961; pp. 153-203.

1594. SEMMES, Raphael (1809-77)
    1. February 19-May 27, 1865; Travel diary; former captain
of the Confederate ship Alabama; trip from Greensboro, North Carolina, to Mobile, Alabama.
    • "Admiral on Horseback: The Diary of Brigadier General
    Raphael Semmes, February-May, 1865," W. Stanley Hoole, ed.
    Alabama Review, v. 28, pp. 129-50, April, 1975.

    2. December 15, 1865-March 5, 1866; Prison diary; arrested
on charges stemming from the Kearsarge engagement.
    • "The Prison Diry of Raphael Semmes," Elizabeth Bethel, ed.
    Journal of Southern History, v. 22, pp. 498-509, November,
    1956.

1595. STRICKLER, Sarah Ann G. (1845-   )
    March 2-10, 1865
    Personal diary; General Sheridan's approach to Charlottesville,
Virginia; behavior of the inhabitants.
    • Freudenberg, Ann. "Sheridan's Raid: An Account by
    Sarah A. G. Strickler," Albemarle Country History Magazine,
    v. 22, pp. 57-65, 1963-64.

1596. THOMAS, Martha Carey (1857-1935)
    January 2, 1865-March 30, 1879; many gaps
    Personal diary; Quakeress and second president of Bryn Mawr
College; school days; visits with relatives; preparing for college; decision not to marry; difficulties with Greek at Johns Hopkins; interesting picture of a 19th century woman trying to be independent of
her family.
    • The Making of a Feminist: Early Journals and Letters of
    M. Carey Thomas. Marjorie Housepain Dobkin, ed. Kent,
    O.: Kent State University Press, 1979.
        REVIEW: Maryland Historical Magazine, v. 75, pp. 255-56,
        Fall, 1980.

1597. TOWNSEND, Harry C.
    January 1-May 8, 1865
    Military diary; with the 1st Company of Richmond Howitzers;
defeat and homecoming.
    • "Townsend's Diary--January-May, 1865. From Petersburg
    to Appomattox, Thence to North Carolina to Join Johnston's
    Army," Southern Historical Society Papers, v. 34, pp. 99-127,
    1906.

1598. WAGNER, Richard (1813-83)
    August 10, 1865-March 4, 1882; many gaps
    Personal diary; German composer; lover and later husband of
Franz Liszt's daughter Cosima (q.v.); brown calf book given to him
by Cosima when it appeared they would never be able to marry; entries include sketches, essays, poems and projected works.
    • The Diary of Richard Wagner 1865-1883: The Brown Book.

George Bird, trans. Joachim Bergfeld, annot. New York:
Cambridge University Press, 1980.
   REVIEWS: Book Review Index 1980, p. 529; 1981, p. 576.
   Book Review Digest 1981, p. 1480.

1599. WOODRUFF, Mathew (1843?-82)
      June 29-December 31, 1865
      Military diary; with Yankees occupying Alabama.
      • A Union Soldier in the Land of the Vanquished: The Diary
      of Sergeant Mathew Woodruff, June-December, 1865. F. N.
      Boney, ed. University, Ala.: University of Alabama Press,
      1969.

1600. YOUNG, Will H. (1845?-)
      April 22-December 15, 1865
      Personal diary; cursory notes of a store clerk at Fort Laramie;
consuming interest in food.
      • "Journals of Travel of Will H. Young, 1865," Annals of Wy-
      oming, v. 7, pp. 378-82, October, 1930.

1601. YOUNG, William H.
      May 10-18, 1865
      Travel diary; lengthy descriptions by one of a small party.
      • Journal of an Excursion, From Troy, New York to General
      Carr's Headquarters at Wilson's Landing [Fort Pocahontas] on
      the James River, Virginia, During the Month of May, 1865.
      Troy, N.Y.: Priv. ptd., 1871.

                                1866

1602. ADAMS, George Russell (1845-1938)
      December 25, 1866-July 30, 1867
      Survey diary; purpose of the expedition was to establish a
telegraph line through Canada to Siberia; work, food, harsh weather.
      • "Journal of George Russell Adams: Member, Exploring Ex-
      pedition in Russian America, 1865-67," California Historical
      Society Quarterly, v. 35, pp. 291-308, December, 1956.

1603. ALEXANDER, Eveline (1843-)
      April 30, 1866-January 20, 1867
      Personal diary; New York to Fort Smith, Arkansas; Colorado
and New Mexico; scenery; social life; interesting.
      • Cavalry Wife: The Diary of Eveline Alexander, 1866-67,
      Being a Record of Her Journey from New York to Fort Smith
      to Join Her Cavalry-officer Husband. Sandra L. Myres, ed.
      College Station: Texas A & M Press, 1977.

1604. ARNDT, Harriet Amelia (1834-)
      January 1-December 31, 1866
      Personal diary; woman living in Lancaster County, Pennsylvania;
being courted by a local doctor.

• "'In This Place'--Manheim, 1866," Pennsylvania Folklife, v. 29, pp. 56-71, Winter, 1979-80.

1605. BLUMENTHAL, Leonhard, Graf von (1810-1900)
May 4-August 29, 1866; July 21, 1870-March 16, 1871
Military diary; Seven Weeks' War with the Austrians; Franco-Prussian War and the siege of Paris.
• Journals of Field-Marshal Count von Blumenthal for 1866 and 1870-71. Count Albrecht von Blumenthal, ed. A. D. Gillespie-Addison, trans. London: Edward Arnold, 1903; reprinted New York: AMS Press, 1971.

1606. BURGESS, Perry A.
March 29-September 6, 1866; July 7-28, 1868
Travel diary; Indian raid; bad weather.
• "From Illinois to Montana in 1866: The Diary of Perry A. Burgess," Pacific Northwest Quarterly, v. 41, pp. 43-65; 1950.

1607. CONANT, Roger (1833-1915)
January 16-April 24, 1866
Travel diary; batchelor reporter accompanied a party of widows and single women by ship from New York via Cape Horn to San Francisco; party was sponsored by Asa Mercer in his effort to remedy the shortage of females in the Oregon Territory; entertaining.
• Mercer's Belles: The Journal of a Reporter. Lenna A. Deutsch, ed. Seattle: University of Washington Press, 1960.

1608. CRANBROOK, Gathorne Gathorne-Hardy, Earl of (1814-1906)
[B243]
January 9, 1866-August 19, 1892
Political diary; British cabinet minister for 16 of the years covered here; popular speaker adept at parliamentary debate; hot-tempered and opposed by Disraeli; never reached the heights of power he thought he deserved; entries evolve from a short recital of events to longer essays addressed to his inner self; valuable for reports of cabinet meetings; colorful notes on atmosphere; comments on a wide variety of non-political figures and events from Queen Victoria to his valet; very important diary.
• The Diary of Gathorne Hardy, Later Lord Cranbrook, 1866-1892: Political selections. Nancy E. Johnson, ed. Oxford: Clarendon Press, 1981.
    REVIEWS: English Historical Review, v. 98, p. 161, January, 1983. Times Literary Supplement, p. 100, September 4, 1981.

1609. CREIGH, Thomas Alfred (1840-1909)
May 17-October 4, 1866
Travel diary; Civil War veteran managed a wagon train taking machinery to the Virginia City, Montana, mines.
• "From Nebraska City to Montana, 1866: The Diary of Thomas Alfred Creigh," Nebraska History Magazine, v. 29, pp. 208-37, September, 1948.

1610. CROMMELIN, Claude August
        June 9-20, 1866
        Travel diary; jaunt to see the railroads in operation in the
U.S. with an eye for further investment.
        • "A Dutch Investor in Minnesota, 1866: The Diary of Claude
        August Crommelin," Minnesota History, v. 37, pp. 152-60, De-
        cember, 1960.

1611. DOANE, Didama Kelley
        May 19, 1866-September 28, 1868
        Sea diary; extracts; around the Horn in a clipper ship.
        • The Cap'n's Wife, The Diary of Didama Kelley Doane of
        West Harwich, Mass. Wife of Cap'n Uriel Doane, on a Two
        Year Voyage with Her Husband Aboard the Ship Rival, 1866-
        1868. Syracuse, N.Y.: Syracuse University Press, 1946.

1612. DRIVER, William (1837-)
        May 3-September 25, 1866
        Travel diary; Mormon convert went with his family by ship,
train and wagon.
        • "London to Salt Lake City in 1867: The Diary of William
        Driver," Frank Driver Reeve, ed. New Mexico Historical Re-
        view, v. 17, pp. 37-63, January, 1942.

1613. DUFFIELD, George Crawford
        1. February 17-November 7, 1866; Trail diary; trip from Iowa
to Texas to buy cattle; driving them north; map.
        • "Driving Cattle From Texas to Iowa 1866," Annals of Iowa,
        v. 14, pp. 242-62, 1923-25.

        2. "Diary Excerpts," in: Philip Dunaway and Mel Evans, eds.
A Treasury of the World's Great Diaries. New York: Doubleday,
1975; pp. 72-76.

1614. FOX, George W. (1838-)
        January 1-September 6, 1866
        Trail diary; cattle drive through Wyoming; matter of fact with
notes on weather and terrain; "Our cook John flew the ranks; nothing
lost."
        • "George W. Fox Diary; Annals of Wyoming, v. 8, pp. 580-
        601, January, 1932.

1615. GILCHRIST, Leonard W. (1831-1919)
        May 12-June 28, 1866
        Travel diary; journey from Nebraska City by steamboat to
Fort Benton, Missouri; good descriptions of passing scenery; buffalo
hunt; map.
        • "The Missouri River Journal of Leonard W. Gilchrist, 1866,"
        James E. Potter, ed. Nebraska History, v. 58, pp. 267-300,
        Fall, 1977.

1616. HARLAN, Wilson Barber (1848-)
       June 16-September 29, 1866
       Travel diary; walked 1035 miles from St. Cloud, Minnesota to
Helena, Montana; gold prospecting.
       • "A Walk with a Wagon Train: A 'teen-age Civil War Veteran
       Strolls into the West," Gilbert Drake Harlan, ed. Journal of
       the West, v. 3, pp. 141-62, April, 1964; pp. 291-312, July,
       1964.

1617. HERSHEY, Benjamin Hostetter (1847-)
       January 1-December 31, 1866
       Personal diary; Mennonite in Lancaster County; farm work.
       • "'In This Place'--Manheim, 1866," John D. Kendig, ed.
       Pennsylvania Folklife, v. 29, pp. 56-71, Winter, 1978-80.

1618. JACKSON, W. H.
       June 22-August 6, 1866
       Travel diary; driving a six-yoke freight wagon; lengthy, de-
tailed entries.
       • "The Most Important Nebraska Highway: Nebraska City--
       Fort Kearny--Denver Trail, or "Steam Wagon Road," Nebraska
       History Magazine, v. 13, pp. 137-59, July, 1932.

1619. JACKSON, William Henry (1843-1942)
       1. 1866-67; 1873; 1874; Travel diaries; from New York City
to California and return; with the Hayden geology survey to Yellowstone and the Central Rockies; photographing the cliff dwellings at
what is now Mesa Verde National Park; several original photos included in the illustrations.
       • The Diaries of William Henry Jackson, Frontier Photographer.
       LeRoy R. and Ann W. Hafen, eds. Glendale, Cal.: Arthur H.
       Clark, 1959.

       2. August 16-24, 1874; Travel diary; with the Hayden Survey
in Colorado; very full account with many details of Indians.
       • "A Visit to the Los Pinos Indian Agency in 1874: Extract
       from the Diary of W. H. Jackson, with an Introduction and
       Notes by the Original Diarist," Colorado Magazine, v. 15, pp.
       201-09, November, 1938.

1620. JONSSON, Peter Johan (1835-1914)
       May 8-August 3, 1866
       Sea diary; immigrating from Sweden to America; voyage plagued
by sickness and death.
       • "'Some Cried and Some Sang...': The Emigrant Journal of
       Peter Johan Jonsson, 1866," Alan Swanson, ed. and trans.
       Swedish Pioneer Historical Quarterly, v. 26, pp. 157-84, July,
       1975.

1621. KEAYS, Elizabeth Parke (1830-1922)
       April 21-June 9, 1866

Travel diary; widow with ten-year old son went from Bloomington, Illinois, to Fort Collins, Colorado; by rail and wagon; uneventful trip.
- The Saga of "Auntie" Stone and Her Cabin ... With the
Overland Diary of Elizabeth Parke Keays. Boulder, Col.:
Johnson Publishing, 1964; 500 copies; pp. 51-93; reprinted
from Colorado Magazine, v. 10, pp. 71-78, March, 1933.

1622. LATHAM, Henry (1828/29-71)
December 12, 1866-March 20, 1867
Travel diary; from Liverpool to New York, Washington and
other East Coast cities with a jaunt to Cuba; much comment on post
war conditions and stories told to him about the war; quotes prices;
well done.
- Black and White: A Journal of Three Months' Tour in the
US. London: Macmillan, 1867; New York: Negro Universities
Press, 1969.

1623. LESTER, Gurdon P.
May 31-October 5, 1866
Travel diary; by stage and steamboat; from Lodomillo, Iowa,
to Helena and return; via Missouri River and Platte River Trails.
- "A Round Trip to the Montana Mines: The 1866 Travel
Journal of Gurdon P. Lester," Nebraska History, v. 46, pp.
273-313, December, 1965.

1624. McKAY, William C. (-1893)
November 1, 1866-November 29, 1867
Military diary; commander of the U.S. Indian Scouts was of
Scots and Indian background; in General Crook's campaign against
Snake and Piute tribes; raids, skirmishes.
- Clark, Keith and Donna. "William McKay's Journal: 1866-
67: Indian Scouts," Oregon Historical Quarterly, v. 79, pp.
121-71, Summer, 1978; pp. 269-333, Fall, 1978.

1625. MUZZALL, Thomas Abram (1834-1915)
June 8-October 19, 1866
Personal diary; Civil War veteran and former Pony Express
rider; with the 3rd U.S. Cavalry and a wagon train from Fort Smith,
Arkansas, to Fort Union, new Mexico on foot; mileage, sights; laconic
entries.
- "Across the Plains in 1866," New Mexico Historical Review,
v. 32, pp. 246-58, July, 1957; Shirk, George H. "The Lost
Colonel," Chronicles of Oklahoma, v. 35, pp. 180-93, Summer,
1957.

1626. POWDERLY, Terence V. (1849-1924)
1866-1878
Personal diary; article based on manuscript diaries now in the
archives of Catholic University.
- Walker, S. "Terence V. Powderly, Machinist: 1866-1877,"
Labor History, v. 19, pp. 165-84, Spring, 1978.

1627.   REAGLES, Dr. James, Jr.
        November 7, 1866-December 10, 1867
        Personal diary; with the 10th Cavalry in Indian Territory;
army life; details on Comanches and other tribes.
        • "A View from Oklahoma, 1866-1868: The Diary and Letters
        of Dr. James Reagles, Jr., Assistant Surgeon, U.S. Army,"
        Jere W. Roberson, ed. Red River Valley Historical Review,
        v. 3, pp. 19-46, Fall, 1978.

1628.   SMITH, Charles Edward (1838-79)
        March 22, 1866-March 17, 1867
        Sea diary; on a whaling voyage from Hull, England, to the
Davis Strait, Baffin and Frobisher Bays and return; encountered
heavy ice in August; the captain deliberately rammed the ship into
an icepack so that it would be carried out to the Atlantic; unneeded
wood was used as fuel; birds shot for food; scurvy; the captain's
death; final release from the pack ice; riveting.
        • From the Deep of the Sea: The Diary of Charles Edward
        Smith, Surgeon of the Whale-ship Diana. Charles E. S. Harris,
        ed. Annapolis: Naval Institute Press, 1977.

1629.   STUART, Granville (1834-1918) [A340]
        January 6-June 8, 1866
        Travel diary; pioneer Montana cattleman and civic leader; from
Chicago to Salt Lake City via Denver; return from Fort Benton down
the Missouri River.
        • Diary and Sketchbook of a Journey to America in 1866, and
        Return Trip up the Missouri River to Fort Benton, Montana.
        Carl Schaefer Dentzel, intro. Los Angeles: Dawson's Book
        Shop, 1963; reprinted from the Virginia City, Montana Post,
        January, 1867.

1630.   WAGNER, George (1841-1906)
        May 26, 1866-December 20, 1868
        Personal diary; life in Atlanta and the surrounding area;
weather; fragmentary notes on his work.
        • "A Freedmen's Bureau Diary by George Wagner," William A.
        Campbell, ed. Georgia Historical Quarterly, v. 48, pp. 196-
        214, June, 1964; pp. 333-60, September, 1964.

1631.   WESTON, Daniel H. (1835-1908)
        April-June 29, 1866
        Travel diary; excerpts; by steamboat up the Missouri River
from Sioux City, Iowa, to Fort Benton, Montana Territory; detailed.
        • "'Up the Great River': Daniel Weston's Missouri Steamboat
        Diary," Lee Silliman, ed. Montana, v. 30, pp. 31-42, July, 1980.

                                    1867

1632.   BARNETT, Samuel Augustus (1844-   )
        1867

Personal diary; extracts; British clergyman visited the South; his own attitudes and his comments on post-war conditions.
- Abel, Emily K. "Victorian Views Reconstruction: The American Diary of Samuel Augustus Barnett," Civil War History, v. 20, pp. 135-56, June, 1974.

1633. BARNITZ, Albert (1835-1912), and Jennie BARNITZ (-1927)
January 15, 1867-January 11, 1869
Personal diaries and letters; communications between a couple stationed at Forts Riley and Leavenworth; social life; military matters; trivia.
- Life in Custer's Cavalry: Diaries and Letters of Albert and Jennie Barnitz, 1867-1868. Robert M. Utley, ed. New Haven: Yale University Press, 1977.
  REVIEW: Montana, v. 28, p. 65, Spring, 1978.

1634. DERBY, Emma C.
Travel diary; to European capitals with historian H. H. Bancroft, his wife and niece; engaging.
- "Diary of Emma C. Derby: Bancroft's Guest Keeps Record of European Tour March 25-August 6, 1867," California Historical Society Quarterly, v. 31, pp. 219-28, September, 1952; pp. 355-74, December, 1952; v. 32, pp. 65-80, March, 1953.

1635. DEVOL, Bitha Marshall (1838-96), and William Dudley DEVOL (1834-1906)
December 27, 1867-February 19, 1873
Letter-diary; prosperous farmer sold his produce; interesting sidelights on practices and problems of flatboaters.
- "Flatboating Down the Ohio and Mississippi, 1867-1873: Correspondence and Diaries of the William D. Devol Family of Marietta, Ohio," Robert Leslie Jones, ed. Ohio State Archaeological and Historical Quarterly, v. 59, pp. 287-309, July, 1950; pp. 385-418, October, 1950.

1636. DOSTOEVSKY, Anna (1846-1918)
1. May 2-August 12, 1867; Travel diary; Russian novelist and his wife fled to Germany to escape their creditors; life in Switzerland; beset by money troubles.
- The Diary of Dostoyevsky's Wife. René Fülöp-Miller and Dr. F. Eckstein, eds. Madge Pemberton, trans. New York: Macmillan, 1928.

2. "Diary Excerpts," in: Mary Jane Moffat and Charlotte Painter, eds. Revelations: Diaries of Women. New York: Random House, 1974; pp. 131-37.

1637. HASKELL, Rachel Mitchell (1829-   )
March 3-April 3, 1867
Personal diary; domestic life in Aurora, Nevada.
- "A Literate Woman in the Mines: The Diary of Rachel Haskell," Mississippi Valley Historical Review, v. 36, pp. 81-98, 1944-45.

1638. LUEG, Henry (1830-1906)
       1867
       Travel diary; German immigrant in a party of 77; from Minne-
sota to the Montana mines; on to Walla Walla; interesting extracts.
       • "The Northern Overland Route in 1867: Journal of Henry
       Lueg," Pacific Northwest Quarterly, v. 41, pp. 234-53, 1950.

1639. SCHLIEMANN, Heinrich (1822-90)
       November 13-17, 1867
       Travel diary; hard-headed businessman and archaeologist who
later uncovered Homer's Troy; extracts; visited the stockyards, a
school and a waterworks.
       • Zochert, Donald. "Heinrich Schliemann's Chicago Journal,"
       Chicago History, v. 2, pp. 173-81, Spring-Summer, 1973.

1640. TROBRIAND, Philippe Régis Denis de Keredern, Comte de
       (1816-97)
       August 4, 1867-April 25, 1869
       Personal diary; French-born Civil War veteran; commander at
Fort Stevenson, Dakota Territory; life on a remote post; relations
with Indians; pays tribute to the military wives for their guts and
ability to laugh at hardships and endure.
       • Military Life in Dakota: The Journal of Philippe Régis de
       Trobriand. Lucile M. Kane, trans. and ed. St. Paul: Al-
       vord Memorial Commission, 1951.

                                1868

1641. BARD, Isaac Newton (1842-)
       August 12-December 7, 1868
       Personal diary; New Yorker worked near Leadville for a daily
wage with a short stint at the diggings.
       • "Isaac Newton Bard Dug Potatoes, Not Gold--1868," Colorado
       Magazine, v. 33, pp. 161-76, July, 1956.

1642. BETTERMAN, Dr. Amos
       January 1, 1878-1910; extracts from the years listed in the
       title.
       Personal diary; notes on his practice, treatments and medica-
tions for various illnesses; social and family life; comments on national politics; a storyteller; rambling but interesting account of a
small town general practioner.
       • Dr. Betterman's Diary for the Years 1868, 1873, 1893, 1909,
       1910. Charles E. Blanchard, ed. Youngstown, O.: Medical
       Success Press, 1934.

1643. CHISHOLM, James (1838-1903)
       September 8-18, 1868
       Travel diary; Chicago Tribune reporter was sent to Wyoming
to write about the gold rush; several long entries of description.

• South Pass, 1868, James Chisholm's Journal of the Wyoming Gold Rush. Lola M. Homsher, ed. Lincoln: University of Nebraska Press, 1960.

1644. COOK, Joseph Witherspoon (1836-1902)
    1. January 14, 1868-May 9, 1869; Letter diary; beginnings of the church in Wyoming; parish work; notes on vigilantes.
    • Diary and Letters of the Rev. Joseph W. Cook, Missionary to Cheyenne. reprinted from Wyoming Churchman, 1917-18; Laramie, Wyo.: Laramie Republican Co., 1919.

    2. Article with extracts.
    • Young, Gertrude S. "The Journal of a Missionary to the Yankton Sioux: 1875-1902," South Dakota Department of History Report and Historical Collections, v. 29, pp. 63-86, 1958.

1645. CORMIER, Moise (1849-1915)
    February 12, 1868-March 25, 1870
    Military diary; French Canadian enlisted in a unit raised by the Pope to defend the Papal States; from Montreal to Italy; very short entries listing sights.
    • The Journal of Moise Cormier, Zouaves Pontificaux 1868-1870. Winnipeg: Manitoba Museum of Man and Nature, 1975.

1646. DAVIS, Mark S. (-1893)
    May 12-June 21, 1868
    Travel diary; from Wabash, Indiana, to southwestern Missouri; good description of countryside.
    • "By Spring-wagon to Missouri and Kansas," Indiana Magazine of History, v. 29, pp. 48-65, 1933.

1647. GALPIN, Charles
    June 3-22, 1868
    Travel diary; member of the Indian Peace Commission of 1868 with Father P.-J. de Smet; from Fort Rice on the Missouri River to the Powder River in the Montana Territory.
    • "The Galpin Journal: Dramatic Record of an Odyssey of Peace," Rev. Louis Pfaller, OSB, ed. Montana: The Magazine of Western History, v. 18, pp. 2-23, April, 1968.

1648. HARVEY, Winfield Scott (1848-1931)
    September 1, 1868-March 6, 1869
    Personal diary; Civil War veteran; present at the Battle of the Washita.
    • "Campaigning with Sheridan, A Farrier's Diary," George H. Shirk, ed. Chronicles of Oklahoma, v. 37, pp. 68-105, Spring, 1959.

1649. HOWELL, Saul Sylvester (1841-79)
    January 1-June 23, 1868
    Personal diary; Union veteran; professor of Greek and Latin at the State University of Iowa; weather and prices; churchgoing.

• "Diary of S. S. Howell, 1868," Frederick I. Kuhns, ed.
Iowa Journal of History and Politics, v. 49, pp. 143-67, April,
1951.

1650. MUIR, John (1838-1914)
    1. December, 1868-1913; some undated; gaps; Nature diary;
Scottish-born American naturalist; foreign journals are omitted; forays
to Yosemite, Alaska, Mt. Rainer and the southern states.
    • John of the Mountains: The Unpublished Journals of John
    Muir. Linnie Marsh Wolfe, ed. Boston: Houghton Mifflin,
    1938; Madison: University of Wisconsin Press, 1979.

    2. August-November 12, 1875; Nature diary; record of ex-
ploration of the redwood belt between the White and Yosemite Rivers;
reprint of a chapter from John of the Mountains.
    • "An Unpublished Journal of John Muir," Linnie Marsh Wolfe,
    ed. North American Review, v. 245, pp. 24-51, 1938.

1651. RICHMOND, Rebecca (1840-1925)
    January 1-April 24, 1868; February 19-March 24, 1870
    Personal diary; first cousin to Libbie Custer, wife of George;
social life with the Custers at Fort Leavenworth on two visits; interesting account of fort life by an outside observer.
    • "Rebecca Visits Kansas and the Custers: The Diary of
    Rebecca Richmond," Minnie Dubbs Millbrook, ed. Kansas His-
    torical Quarterly, v. 42, pp. 366-402, Winter, 1976.

1652. ROLLIN, Frances Anne (1848?-   )
    Personal diary; educated black woman lived in Boston while
working on a biography of Major Martin R. Delany of the Freedmen's
Bureau; heard Charles Dickens lecture; received criticism on the manuscript from Wendell Phillips.
    • "Diary January 1-July 8, 1868," in: Dorothy Sterling, ed.
    We Are Your Sisters: Black Women in the Nineteenth Century.
    New York: Norton, 1984; pp. 453-61.

1653. SMITH, Sallie D. (1849?-71)
    June 3-October 18, 1868
    Travel journal; from Howard County, Missouri, to Kentucky;
via St. Louis and up the Ohio River; visits to relatives; amusements.
    • "The Journal of Sallie D. Smith," Mrs. Dana O. Jensen, ed.
    Missouri Historical Society Bulletin, v. 20, pp. 124-45, January,
    1964.

1654. SPEAR, Laura Jernegan
    December 1, 1868-March 1, 1871; gaps
    Sea diary; from New Bedford around Cape Horn on her father's
ship Roman with her mother and two-year old brother; a stop in Honolulu.
    • "A Child's Diary on a Whaling Voyage," Marcus Wilson Jer-
    negan, ed. New England Quarterly, v. 2, pp. 125-39, Jan-
    uary, 1929.

1655. VOGDES, Ada A. (-1919)
       November 5, 1868-February 24, 1871
       Personal diary; excerpts from the journal of a "delicately-
bred" army wife at Forts Laramie and Fetterman; much about the
Sioux, especially Red Cloud; found Indians "too disgusting to be let
live another day."
       • "The Journal of Ada A. Vogdes, 1868-71," Donald K. Ad-
       ams, ed. Montana: The Magazine of Western History. v. 13,
       pp. 2-18, July, 1963.

                                1869

1656. BEGG, Alexander (1839-97) [C12]
       November 16, 1869-July 23, 1870
       Personal diary; Canadian pioneer; this journal was the basis
of his book The Creation of Manitoba; metis of the Northwest Territory objected to the annexation of their land to the Dominion of Canada; details of American, French, and British factions; political ma-
nuevering; Louis Riel (q.v.) and Dr. John C. Schultz mentioned;
social and family notes; important document in Canadian history.
       • Alexander Begg's Red River Journal and Other Papers Rela-
       tive to the Red River Resistance of 1869-1870. Toronto:
       Champlain Society, 1956.

1657. BRADLEY, George Young (1836-85)
       Travel diary; Massachusetts native and Civil War veteran joined
John Wesley Powell's (q.v.) expedition as chief boatman and geological assistant; arduous work and near starvation.
       • "George Y. Bradley's Journal May 24-August 30, 1869,"
       Utah Historical Quarterly, v. 15, pp. 31-72, January, 1947.

1658. BUNYARD, Harriet (1850-1900)
       April 25-October 28, 1869
       Travel diary; from Collin County, Texas, via the Butterfield
Overland stage route to California; wagon train captained by her
uncle; chatty style noting mileage, weather and terrain.
       • "Diary of a Young Girl," in: Sandra L. Myres, ed. Ho
       for California! San Marino, Cal.: Huntington Library, 1980;
       pp. 199-252.

1659. CAMPBELL, John A. (1835-)
       April 3, 1869-February 24, 1875
       Personal diary; first governor of the Wyoming Territory; cryp-
tic notes; line-a-day entries; weather, personal life.
       • "Diary, John A. Campbell," Annals of Wyoming, v. 10,
       pp. 5-11, January, 1938; pp. 59-78, April, 1938; pp. 120-43,
       July, 1938; pp. 155-85, October, 1938.

1660. GARDINER, Joseph Phelps
       November 2-December 4, 1869

Personal diary; short entries on the Canadian conflict.
• Pannekoek, Frits. "Rev. Griffiths Owen Corbett and the
Red River Civil War of 1869-70," Canadian Historical Review,
v. 57, pp. 133-49, June, 1976.

1661. JENKINS, Joseph (1818-98)
March, 1869-December 12, 1894
Personal diary; extracts; Welsh farmer and poet of note,
estranged from his wife spent 25 years in Australia; began keeping
a diary to improve his English; worked at threshing and as a farm
laborer; observations on the aborigines, the people he worked for
and with, the English character; dry humor; interesting.
• Diary of a Welsh Swagman 1869-1894. William Evans, ed.
South Melbourne, Victoria: Macmillan, 1975.
REVIEW: Times Literary Supplement, April 9, 1976, p. 439.

1662. KOCH, Peter (1844-1917)
August 20, 1869-January 24, 1870
Personal diary; Danish emigrant's life in the Montana Territory;
work; trip from Fort Browning to Fort Ellis.
• "Journal of Peter Koch, 1869-1870," Elers Koch, ed. Fron-
tier, v. 9, pp. 148-60, January, 1929.

1663. LARGE, Samuel Pollock (-1912)
January 1-December 31, 1869
Personal diary; boat builder in business in Elizabeth Town-
ship, Pennsylvania; business and family life.
• "Samuel Pollock Large's Diary of 1869," Margaret Pearson
Bothwell, ed. Western Pennsylvania Historical Magazine, v.
47, pp. 111-23, April, 1964.

1664. McQUIG, John
February 24-July 23, 1869
Personal diary; life in Treasure City, Nevada Territory; work
at the Never Sweat Mine; a falling out with his partners.
• "Diary, 1869," Nevada Historical Society Quarterly, v. 6,
pp. 3-27, April/June, 1963.

1665. NEWBERRY, Julia (1853-76)
1. June 6, 1869-October 19, 1871; Personal diary; daughter
of wealthy Chicagoans whose fortune founded the Newberry Library;
begun six months after her father's death; social life in the city;
abroad with her mother and sister; sprightly, humorous, unaffected
comments on beaux, her sister and acquaintances.
• Julia Newberry's Diary. New York: Norton, 1933.

2. Personal diary; social life of a young heiress in Europe
and Chicago.
• "Diary Excerpts," in: Philip Dunaway and Mel Evans, eds.
A Treasury of the World's Great Diaries. New York: Doubleday, 1957; pp. 30-34.

1666. NORTH, Frank Joshua (1840-85)
       January 1-December 23, 1869
       Military diary; commanded the Pawnee scouts who were com-
missioned to protect railroad construction crews; social life in town
contrasts with raids against marauding Indians.
       • "The Journal of an Indian Fighter: The 1869 Diary of Major
       Frank J. North," Donald F. Danker, ed. Nebraska History,
       v. 39, pp. 87-177, June, 1958.

1667. PAXSON, Dr. Joseph Armitage (1842-88)
       July 1, 1869-June 30, 1870
       Personal diary; Quaker doctor with a medical degree from the
University of Pennsylvania; visiting Nebraska Indian villages; vac-
cinating children; well done.
       • "Diary of Dr. Joseph A. Paxson, Physician to the Winne-
       bago Indians, 1869-1870," James L. Sellers, ed. Nebraska
       History, v. 27, pp. 143-204, July, 1946; pp. 244-75, October,
       1946.

1668. POWELL, John Wesley (1834-1902)
       1. May 24-September 1, 1869; Exploration diary; American
geologist traveled from Green River, Wyoming, to the area of modern
Lake Mead; lengthy descriptions of the river and its surroundings
are augmented by modern photos.
       • Down the Colorado: Diary of the First Trip Through the
       Grand Canyon 1869. New York: Dutton, 1969; abridgement
       of the Journal in Part 2 "History of the Exploration of the
       Canons of the Colorado."

       2. Exploration diary; down the Colorado River.
       • "Major Powell's Journal July 2-August 28, 1869," Utah His-
       torical Quarterly, William Culp Darrah, ed. v. 15, pp. 125-
       31, 1947.

1669. PRICE, Captain W. E.
       1. October 9-December 10, 1869
       Travel diary; English member of Parliament; with three friends
visited Niagara Falls, Omaha, Yosemite, New Orleans; weekly entries.
       • "American Journey," in: Morgan Philips Price. American
       After Sixty Years. London: Allen and Unwin, 1936; pp. 15-
       58.

       2. 1878; Travel letter/diary; honeymoon journey; stops in
Chicago, Denver and the West Coast; time spent with General Sherman.
       • "Major and Mrs. Price's American Tour," in: Morgan Phil-
       ips Price. American After Sixty Years. London: Allen and
       Unwin, 1936; pp. 59-81.

1670. SUMNER, John Colton (1840-1907)
       Exploration diary; with John Wesley Powell (q.v.) down the
Colorado River.

• "J. C. Sumner's Journal July 6-August 31, 1869," William
Culp Darrah, ed. Utah Historical Quarterly, v. 15, pp. 113-
24, 1947.

1671. WAGNER, Cosima Liszt (1837-1930)
       January 1, 1869-February 12, 1883
       Personal diary; includes entries by composer Richard Wagner
(q.v.); kept as her justification to her children for her affair and
marriage to Wagner; begun while married to Hans von Bulow; wide
ranging; social, family and musical life; full entries and much quoted
conversation.
       • Cosima Wagner's Diaries. Martin Gregor-Dellin and Dietrich
       Mack, eds. Geoffrey Skelton, trans. 2 vols. New York:
       Harcourt Brace Jovanovich, 1978-80.

1672. WOOLLEY, Edwin G. (1844-1930)
       February 25-March 12, 1869; November 5-18, 1869
       Military diary; in St. George and Kaneb areas.
       • "Journal of Two Campaigns by the Utah Territorial Militia
       Against the Navaho Indians, 1869," C. Gregory Crampton and
       David E. Miller,e ds. Utah Historical Quarterly, v. 29, pp.
       148-76, April, 1961.

                                    1870

1673. ARNY, William Frederick Milton (1813-81)
       May-November 28, 1870
       Travel diary; agent covered 3100 miles taking a census of In-
dians in New Mexico; observations on Indian life.
       • Indian Agent in New Mexico: The Journal of Special Agent
       W. F. M. Arny, 1870. Lawrence R. Murphy, intro. Santa
       Fe: Stagecoach Press, 1967.

1674. BISHOP, Francis Marion (1843-1933)
       Exploration diary; science student of John Wesley Powell
(q.v.) at Illinois Wesleyan University; joined his teacher's second
Colorado River Expedition as a topographer.
       • "Captain Francis Marion Bishop's Journal August 15, 1870-
       June 3, 1872," William Culp Darrah, ed. Utah Historical Quar-
       terly, v. 15, pp. 159-238, 1947.

1675. BRIGHT, Abbie (1848-1926)
       September 2, 1870-December 20, 1871
       Personal diary; spunky Pennsylvanian visited relatives in In-
diana; taught school; journeyed to Wichita alone; made a claim; lively
and interesting.
       • "Roughing It On Her Kansas Claim: The Diary of Abbie
       Bright, 1870-1871," Joseph W. Snell, ed. Kansas Historical
       Quarterly, v. 37, pp. 233-63, Autumn, 1971; pp. 394-428,
       Winter, 1971.

1676. BRYCE, James, Viscount (1838-1922)
       September 1-22, 1870
       Personal diary; British jurist, historian and diplomat; visited
the White Mountains and Boston; comments on American manners.
           • Lefcowitz, A. B. and B. F. Lefcowitz. "James Bryce's
           First Visit to America: The New England Sections of His 1870
           Journal and Related Correspondence," New England Quarterly,
           v. 50, pp. 314-31, June, 1977.

1677. BUSCH, Moritz (1821-99)
       February 23, 1870-May 5, 1893
       Personal diary; German journalist became Bismarck's mouth-
piece in the German press; Franco-Prussian War; press campaign
against the Empress Augusta; domestic politics; relations with England and Queen Victoria.
           • Bismarck, Some Secret Pages of His History: Being a Diary
           Kept by Dr. Moritz Busch During Twenty-five Years Official
           and Private Intercourse with the Great Chancellor. New York:
           Macmillan, 1898; New York: AMS Press, 1970.

1678. DOANE, Gustavus Cheyney
       August 22-September 24, 1870
       Exploration diary; geology; flora.
           • "Lieutenant G. C. Doane: His Yellowstone Exploration
           Journal," O. H. Bonney and L. Bonney, eds. Journal of the
           West, v. 9, pp. 222-39, April, 1970.

1679. EDMONDS, Joseph A. (1837-1913)
       November 30, 1870-November 16, 1871
       Travel diary; from Baxter Springs, Kansas to Sherman, Texas;
through Indian Territory; good description.
           • "Diary of Joseph A. Edmonds," James W. Moffitt, ed.
           Chronicles of Oklahoma, v. 17, pp. 309-14, 1939.

1680. FRIEDRICH III, German Emperor (1831-88)
       July 11, 1870-July 17, 1871
       Diplomatic diary; the Franco-Prussian War from the pen of the
victor; Battles of Weissenburg, Worth and Sedan; seige of Paris;
armistice negotiations; relations with the future kaiser Wilhelm and
Bismarck; holds the Empress Eugenie chiefly to blame for the war.
           • The War Diary of the Emperor Frederick III 1870-1871. A.
           R. Allison, trans. and ed. New York: Stokes, 1926; West-
           port, Conn.: Greenwood Press, 1971.

1681. HECKER, August (-1872)
       September 23, 1870-November 13, 1872
       Personal diary; shipboard bandmaster on voyages from Liver-
pool to Halifax and the West Indies; music played; storms at sea.
           • Withers, Maurine. "The Diary of August Hecker: Band-
           master of HMS Royal Alfred From 1870 to 1872," Dalhousie Re-
           view [Canada] v. 58, pp. 489-510, 1978; pp. 373-52, 1978-79.

1682.   KILVERT, Francis (1840-79) [B279]
        1. Personal diary; rural curate's life in Central Wales at the
height of Victorianism; lengthy entries convey the flavor of the times;
good picture of country life.
        • Kilvert's Diary: Selections: 1 January 1870-13 March 1879.
        William Plomer, ed. new rev. ed. 3 vols. London: Jonathan
        Cape, 1960.
            REVIEW: Book Review Digest 1961, p. 760-61.

        2. "Diary Excerpts," in: Philip Dunaway and Mel Evans,
eds. A Treasury of the World's Great Diaries. New York: Doubleday, 1957; pp. 309-15.

1683.   LANGFORD, Nathaniel Pitt (1832-1911)
        August 17-September 27, 1870
        Exploration diary; very full account; geysers, mud flats and
other natural wonders; breathless style.
        • Diary of the Washburn Expedition to the Yellowstone and
        Firehole Rivers in the Year 1870. St. Paul, Minn.: J. E.
        Haynes, 1905; reprinted Western Americana: An Annotated
        Bibliography to the Microfiche Collection of 1012 Books and
        Documents of the 18th, 19th and Early 20th Century. Ann
        Arbor, Mich.: University Microfilms International, 1976;
        WA16014.

1684.   LABOUCHERE, Henry Du Pre (1831-1912)
        September 18, 1870-February 10, 1871
        Letter diary; foreign correspondent for newspapers in London
and New York; detailed account of the German siege of Paris during
the Franco-Prussian War.
        • Diary of the Besieged Resident in Paris. New York: Har-
        per, 1871.

1685.   MACKAY, John Alexander (1838-1923)
        November 9, 1870-November 9, 1872
        Missionary diary; Anglican pastor on the Churchill River; con-
ducted a school; visiting the sick; with the Cree Indians.
        • "The Journal of the Reverend J. A. Mackay, Stanley Mis-
        sion, 1870-72," Saskatchewan History, v. 16, pp. 95-113, Au-
        tumn, 1963.

1686-   NICHOLSON, William
  87.   October 4-December 28, 1870
        Travel diary; Quaker inspected agencies run by the Society
of Friends to help the Indians; extensive notes on Indian culture;
details of travel.
        • "A Tour of Indian Agencies in Kansas and the Indian Ter-
        ritory in 1870," Kansas Historical Quarterly, v. 3, pp. 289-
        326, August, 1934; pp. 343-84, November, 1934.

        ROSSETTI, William Michael (1829-1919) see No. 867

1688.   SCOTT, P. G. (1841-1930)
        August 17-September 7, 1870
        Travel diary; many details of the terrain and fellow travelers.
        • "Diary of a Freighting Trip From Kit Carson to Trinidad in
        1870," Colorado Magazine, v. 8, pp. 146-54, July, 1931.

1689.   SHRODE, Maria (1826?-)
        May 16-December 25, 1870
        Travel diary; emigrating from Hopkins County, Texas, with
a herd of cattle to Duarte, California; short entries; accounts of
several accidents and the theft of mules.
        • "Journal," in: Sandra L. Myres, ed. Ho for California!
        San Marino, Cal.: Huntington Library, 1980; pp. 255-95.

1690.   VAN OSTRAND, Ferdinand A. (1848-73)
        December 26, 1870-July 17, 1872
        Fur trade diary; fur trader at Fort Berthold, Dakota Terri-
tory; trip home to Marion, New York; dealings with Indians; good
account of life at a trading post.
        • "Diary of Ferdinand A. Van Ostrand," Russell Reid, ed.
        North Dakota Historical Quarterly, v. 9, pp. 219-42, July,
        1942; v. 10, pp. 3-46, January, 1943; pp. 83-124, March,
        1943.

1691.   WOOLDRIDGE, Emily (1840?-1920s)
        February 17-April 3, 1870
        Sea diary; wife of the captain of the brigantine; written on
Staten Island off the coast of Tierra del Fuego; salvaged a longboat
from the wreckage; reached the Falklands.
        • The Wreck of the Maid of Athens: Being the Journal of
        Emily Wooldridge, 1869-1870. Laurence Irving, ed. New York:
        Macmillan, 1952.

                                1871

1692.   ANDERSON, George C.
        Travel diary; with a committee from the Ohio Soldiers Colony
which was looking for land for members; started from St. Louis; a
buffalo hunt and a circus; keen observer.
        • "Touring Kansas and Colorado in 1871: The Journal of
        George C. Anderson--May 16-July 7, 1871," Kansas Historical
        Quarterly, v. 22, pp. 193-219, 1956; pp. 358-84, Winter, 1956.

1693.   AVERY, Samuel P. (1822-1904)
        April 12, 1871-October 15, 1882
        Business diary; New Yorker was a founder of the Metropolitan
Museum of Art and other cultural bastions; began as an engraver and
moved on to collecting; summer art buying trips abroad; pithy recital
of his activities with almost no elaboration.
        • The Diaries of Samuel P. Avery, Art Dealer. Madeleine
        Fidell Beaufort, ed. New York: Arno, 1979.

REVIEWS: Times Literary Supplement, p. 348, March 28, 1980. Book Review Index 1981, p. 34.

1694. BARTRAM, Mordecai (1843-1904)
June 6-29, 1871
Hunting diary; Quaker operated the Great Nemaha Agency store on the Kansas-Nebraska line; detailed and interesting.
• "Notes on a Buffalo Hunt--the Diary of Mordecai Bartram," Nebraska History Magazine, v. 35, pp. 193-222, September, 1954.

1695. COLLINSON, Thomas Henry (1858-   )
October 5, 1871-August 7, 1875
Personal diary; later first organist and choirmaster of St. Mary's Cathedral, Edinburgh; indentured "to be taught the profession of a cathedral Organist Pianist"; studies; life with other apprentices and choiristers, "a rough lot"; delightfully unsophisticated.
• The Diary of an Organist's Apprentice at Durham Cathedral 1871-1875. Francis Collinson, ed. Aberdeen: Aberdeen University Press, 1982.

1696. DEADY, Judge Matthew Paul (1824-93)
January 9, 1871-November 26, 1892
Personal diary; sober member of the bar at Portland, Oregon, confided his private thoughts to his journal; varied social contacts through business and family; vestryman; Chautauqua lecturer; of local interest.
• Pharisee Among Philistines: The Diary of Judge Matthew P. Deady, 1871-1892. Malcolm Clark, Jr., ed. 2 vols. Portland: Oregon Historical Society, 1975.

1697. HART, William Jeremiah (1843-   )
January 1, 1871-September 20, 1873
Personal diary; listing of farm chores.
• "A Virginia Small Farmer's Life After the Civil War: The Journal of William Jeremiah Hart, 1871-1873," Charles W. Turner, ed. Virginia Magazine of History and Biography, v. 63, pp. 286-305, July, 1955.

1698. HASTINGS, John Irving
Personal diary; article with extracts; life in Denver; trips to surrounding settlements.
• Hastings, James K. "A Winter in the High Mountains, 1871-72," Colorado Magazine, v. 27, pp. 225-34, July, 1950.

1699. JAMES, Charles Albert (1841-75)
August 1, 1871-June 24, 1872
Travel diary; trip to Mexico for his health by Virginian and Civil War veteran; visited Saltillo, Monterrey; interesting picture of conditions by a literate observer.
• "Excerpts from the Mexican Diary of Charles Albert James,

1871-72," Fleming H. James, ed. New Mexico Historical Review, v. 30, pp. 44-71, January, 1955.

1700. JONES, Stephen Vandiver (1840-1920)
Exploration diary; assistant topographer on the second Powell expedition; commanded the Emma Dean; hard working, uncomplaining member.
* "Journal of Stephen Vandiver Jones, April 21, 1871-December 14, 1872," Utah Historical Quarterly, v. 16-17, pp. 11-174, 1948-49.

1701. McGREGOR, G. C.
June 19, 1871-[no closing date]
Travel diary; medical doctor's journey from Wesley to Groesbeck.
* "Journal of a Saddle Trip Through Central Texas in 1871," Roger N. Conger, ed. Southwestern Historical Quarterly, v. 55, pp. 262-66, 1951.

1702. MORRIS, William (1834-96)
July 6, 1871-September 7, 1871; July 24-August 19, 1873
Travel diary; English poet went to Iceland to trace the sagas to their home ports; from London Bridge to Scotland; via ship to Iceland; touring the western half of the country.
* Icelandic Journals. James Morris, intro. New York: Praeger, 1969.

1703. POWELL, Walter Clement (1850-83)
Exploration diary; cousin of John Wesley Powell (q.v.); assisted Beaman, the official photographer of the Colorado River Expedition; little of the scientific side but much on the personalities of his companions.
* "Journal of W. C. Powell: April 21, 1871-December 7, 1872," William Culp Darrah, ed. Utah Historical Quarterly, v. 16-17, pp. 253-478, 1948-49.

1704. RICKETSON, Anna Holmes (1841-)
May 17, 1871-October 17, 1874
Whaling diary; captain's wife accompanied him on a voyage to the Indian Ocean; birth and speedy demise of their first child; "gamming" with other whalers; landfalls; untutored writing conveys the meager education of a good sport and a good sailor.
* The Journal of Annie Holmes Ricketson on the Whaleship A. R. Tucker 1871-1874. Philip F. Purrington, ed. New Bedford: Old Dartmouth Historical Society, 1958.

1705. ROSSER, Thomas Lafayette (1836-1910)
September 12-26, 1871
Travel diary; former cavalry officer was the head of a railroad survey party in the Dakota Territory; hunting and a spectacular accident.

• "Rosser's Journal, Northern Pacific Railroad Survey, September, 1871," William D. Hoyt, Jr. North Dakota Historical Quarterly, v. 10, pp. 47-51, January, 1943.

1706. SHIPP, Ellis Reynolds (1847-1939)
       May 3, 1871-March 14, 1878
       Personal diary; 1878 graduate of the Woman's Medical College of Pennsylvania and Mormon; came to Utah from Iowa at the age of five; covers her early marriage and years at medical school; Relief Society work; her husband took another wife; much on her feelings about being a plural wife; earnest, well-meaning woman, striving for self-improvement.
       • The Early Autobiography and Diary of Ellis Reynolds Shipp, M. D. Ellis Shipp Musser, ed. Salt Lake City: Deseret News Press, 1962.

1707. SLAUGHTER, B. F.
       June 1-August 28, 1871
       Personal diary; at Fort Rice on the west Bank of the Missouri River; post life; Indians.
       • "Portions of the Diary of Dr. B. F. Slaughter, Dakota Territory," North Dakota Historical Quarterly, v. 1, pp. 36-40, January, 1927.

1708. STOVIN, Cornelius (1830-1921)
       August 7, 1871-December 19, 1872; September 7, 1874-June 7, 1875
       Personal diary; Lincolnshire tenant farmer and Methodist lay preacher; beset by shrinking profit margin and poor harvests in the period covered; conflicts with his wife over lack of material prosperity; his misunderstanding of her psychological needs; much material on prices, farming practices and the economy of the time; lengthy, thoughtful entries by a well-read man.
       • Journals of a Methodist Farmer 1871-1875. Jean Stovin, ed. London: Croom Helm, 1982.
       REVIEW: Book Review Index 1982, p. 493.

1709. STEWARD, John F. (1841-1915)
       Expedition diary; with Powell (q.v.) on the second Colorado River expedition; substantial entries for each day; much emended at a later date.
       • "Journal of John F. Steward: May 22-November 3, 1871," William Culp Darrah, ed. Utah Historical Quarterly, v. 16-17, pp. 175-251, 1948-49.

1710. THOMPSON, Almon Harris (1839-)
       May 22, 1871-September 1, 1875
       Exploration diary; married to Major John W. Powell's sister; scientific aide to Powell (q.v.) on his preliminary survey; navigation of the Green and Colorado Rivers; mapped Utah and northern Arizona.
       • "Diary of Almon Harris Thompson, Geographer: Explorations

of the Colorado River at the West and Its Tributaries, 1871-
1875," Utah Historical Quarterly, v. 7, pp. 3-138, 1939.

1872

1711. BEALS, Ella Amanda (1857?-)
        August 31-September 19, 1872
        Travel diary; from Douglas County, Oregon, to Marysville,
California; mileage and weather.
        • "Oregon to California by Wagon, 1872," Oregon Historical
        Quarterly, v. 38, pp. 109-14, March, 1937.

1712. DOMETT, Alfred (1811-87)
        February 29, 1872-June 3, 1885
        Personal diary; close associate of British poet Robert Brown-
ing; notes on their friendship; relations with Gustave Doré, Oscar
Wilde and Lord Tennyson; some reworking of the original entries.
        • The Diary of Alfred Domett, 1872-1885. E. A. Horsman,
        ed. London: Oxford University Press, 1953.

1713. FUNK, John F. (1835-1930)
        September 21, 1872-October 2, 1872; June 3-July 26, 1873
        Travel diary; Indiana Mennonite minister's journey through
Minnesota and the eastern Dakotas; helped European Mennonites look
for suitable settlements.
        • "John F. Funk's Land Inspection Trips as Recorded in His
        Diaries, 1872 and 1873," Kempes Schnell, ed. Mennonite Quar-
        terly Review, v. 24, pp. 295-311, October, 1950.

1714. HALVERSON, Knut (1847-1939)
        May 6, 1872-[no closing date]
        Personal diary; article based on the diary of Norwegian emi-
grant to Waupaca County, Wisconsin; farm work; family life.
        • Rosholt, Malcolm. "A Pioneer Diary from Wisconsin," Nor-
        wegian-American Studies, v. 21, pp. 198-211, 1962.

1715. HAMP, Sidford (1855-)
        May 5-November 30, 1872
        Exploration diary; English boy accompanied the Hayden Expe-
dition as a general assistant; voyage to America; stops in New York
and Washington, D.C.; through Yellowstone and the Tetons; lengthy,
well done entries; a different view of the expedition.
        • "Exploring the Yellowstone with Hayden, 1872: Diary of
        Sidford Hamp," Herbert Oliver Brayer, ed. Annals of Wyom-
        ing, v. 14, pp. 253-98, October, 1942.

1716. HANCOCK, Edwin B. (1856?-1916)
        November 22, 1872-April 25, 1873
        Personal diary; schoolboy in Austin, Texas; a spelling bee;
baseball; a picnic.

- "The Diary of Edwin B. Hancock: 1872-1873," Ford Dixon, ed. Texana, v. 3, pp. 297-320, Winter, 1965.

1717. KELLOGG, Miner Kilbourne (1814-89)
        May 18-September 27, 1872
        Travel/exploration diary; minor 19th century American artist accompanied an expedition in search of minerals to north Texas; from Sherman to Kiowa Peak; sketching, weather, illness; travel conditions.
        - M. K. Kellogg's Texas Journal 1872. Llerena Friend, ed. Austin: University of Texas Press, 1967.

1718. McENTEE, Jervis (1828-)
        May 14, 1872-June 1, 1874
        Personal diary; American landscape painter acquainted with many of his peers; difficulties with buyers; accounts of his work; Horace Greeley's funeral; financial woes.
        - "Jervis McEntee's Diary," Archives of American Art Journal, v. 8, pp. 1-29, July/October, 1968.

1719. MONTGOMERY, Mary Virginia (1849?-1902?)
        Personal diary; black woman living near Vicksburg, Mississippi; sheltered by her family, she reflects middleclass white culture.
        - "Diary February 3-December 25, 1872," in: Dorothy Sterling, ed. We Are Your Sisters: Black Women in the Nineteenth Century. New York: Norton, 1984; pp. 462-72.

1720. RAYMOND, Henry Hubert (1848-1936)
        November 11, 1872-
        Personal diary; hunter and buffalo skinner lived in Dodge in its first year; acquainted with Bat Masterson and his brothers; town life; musical interests; target shooting.
        - "Diary of a Dodge City Buffalo Hunter, 1872-1873," Joseph W. Snell, ed. Kansas Historical Quarterly, v. 31, pp. 345-95, Winter, 1965.

1721. SMITH, Elizabeth (1859-1949)
        June 2, 1872-June 22, 1884
        Personal diary; Canadian schoolgirl living in southwest Ontario; family life; became a teacher; "boarding out"; growing determination to become a doctor; failure at medical school entrance exams; later accepted at Queen's Medical School; highminded, earnest young woman leavens her entries with tales of flirtations and humor.
        - "A Woman with a Purpose": The Diaries of Elizabeth Smith, 1872-1884. Veronica Strong-Boag, ed. Toronto: University of Toronto Press, 1980.

1722. SMYTHE, Patrick Murray (1860-1935)
        March 11, 1872-March 5, 1935
        Fishing diary; English parson who never fished on Fridays or during Lent; notes on excursions in Britain; weather; catches; companions; holds allure for armchair fishermen.

• Diary of an All-round Angler: Extracts from the Fishing
Journal Kept for Over 60 Years (1872-1935). Patrick C. Smythe,
ed. London: Faber and Faber, 1956.

1723. THOMSON, James (-1882)
       May 18, 1872-January 3, 1873
       Travel diary; poet, journalist and secretary sent by a British
company to inspect mining property in Colorado; little work; lots of
social life and sightseeing.
       • "James Thomson's Colorado Diary, 1872," K. J. Fielding,
         ed. Colorado Magazine, v. 31, pp. 202-16, 1954.

                              1873

1724. BASHKIRTSEVA, Marie (1860-84)
       1. January, 1873-October 20, 1884; Personal diary; daughter
of wealthy Russian noble family; studied painting in Paris; family life
and travels in and out of Russia; notes on her reading and painting;
much conversation quoted from memory; comments on the work of
other artists; doubts about her talent; early death caused by tuberculosis; one of the outstanding diaries of the nineteenth century.
       • Maria Bashkirtseva, The Journal of a Young Artist, 1860-
         1884. new and rev. ed. Mary J. Serrano, trans. New York:
         E. P. Dutton, 1919.
         REVIEW: Book Review Digest 1919, p. 31.

       2. "Diary Excerpts," in: Mary Jane Moffat and Charlotte
Painter, eds. Revelations: Diaries of Women. New York: Random
House, 1974; pp. 46-55.

       3. "Diary Excerpts," in: Philip Dunaway and Mel Evans,
eds. A Treasury of the World's Great Diaries. New York: Doubleday, 1957; pp. 16-20.

1725. BROWN, Riney L.
       March 24, 1873-August 19, 1877
       Personal diary; West Virginian worked as a baker in Defiance,
Ohio; recipes and cash receipts listed; moved to Texas in 1877 and
tried to begin a sheep ranch.
       • Diary. Boerne, Tx.: Toepperwein Publishing Co., 1949.

1726. HUNTON, John (1838-1928)
       March 26, 1873-July 8, 1882
       Personal diary; Virginian moved to Fort Laramie after Civil
War service; cowman of early Wyoming; information on the cattle trade
and prominent Wyoming pioneers; Indian attacks; prices; laconic entries.
       • Diary. L. G. Flannery, ed. Lingle, Wyo.: Guide-Review,
         1956-63; 1500 copies.

1727. LAGERLOF, Selma (1858-1940)
        1. January 20-May 13, 1873; Personal diary; adolescent diary
of Swedish novelist and poet; recipient of 1909 Nobel Prize for literature; living with relatives in Stockholm; study, sightseeing; yearning
and planning to be a novelist.
        • The Diary of Selma Lagerlof. Velma Swanston Howard,
        trans. New York: Doubleday, Doran, 1936.
        REVIEW: Book Review Digest 1936, pp. 562-63.

        2. "Diary Excerpts," in: Philip Dunaway and Mel Evans,
eds. A Treasury of the World's Great Diaries. New York: Doubleday, 1957; pp. 350-52.

        3. "Diary Excerpts," in: Mary Jane Moffat and Charlotte
Painter, eds. Revelations: Diaries of Women. New York: Random
House, 1974; pp. 314-24.

1728. MAGHEE, Thomas G. (1842-1927)
        May 28, 1873-August 14, 1875
        Personal diary; employed as a contract doctor for the U.S.
Army at forts in Nebraska and Wyoming; with the O. C. Marsh scientific expedition; medical work; wide range of interests and comments.
        • "The Diary of Dr. Thomas G. Maghee," Charles Lindsay,
        ed. Nebraska History Magazine, v. 12, pp. 247-304, 1929.

1729. MILLER, George
        October 8, 1873-May 17, 1874
        Travel diary; Englishman emigrated to New Mexico to become
a rancher.
        • "Ranching in Chicorica Park: A Diary Kept by George
Miller, 1873-74," Colorado Magazine, v. 33, pp. 52-66, January, 1956.

1730. PAGE, Anne Nelson (1855-1936)
        January 4-December 29, 1873
        Personal diary; young girl's life in Annapolis and Albemarle
County, Virginia; visiting, lessons, reading; an inconstant beau;
melodramatic style.
        • "Diary of a Young Girl in Albemarle 1873," Anne Page Bry-
        don, ed. Magazine of Albemarle County History, v. 20, pp.
        5-73, 1961-62.

1731. RICHARDS, W. A.
        May 26-November 18, 1873
        Survey diary; surveying the southern boundary of Wyoming;
camping; trouble with equipment.
        • "Diary Kept by W. A. Richards in Summer of 1873," Annals
of Wyoming, v. 7, pp. 467-82, April, 1931; v. 8, pp. 492-505,
July, 1931.

1732. ROSEBERY, Archibald Philip Primrose, 5th Earl of (1847-1929)
        October 1-December 28, 1873

Travel diary; shy British aristocrat unbent on a tour of Canada and the U.S.; stops in New York, Chicago, Ottawa, Montreal and Quebec; saw Uncle Tom's Cabin acted in Salt Lake City; voyage home.
- Lord Rosebery's North American Journal-1873. A. R. C. Grant with Caroline Combe, eds. London: Sidgwick and Jackson, 1967.

1733. TCHAIKOVSKY, Peter Ilyitch (1840-93)
June 11-July 18, 1873; April 12, 1884-May 29, 1891; gaps
Personal diary; Russian composer; concerts; social life; travel in Russia and abroad; pithy.
- The Diaries of Tchaikovsky. Wladimir Lakond, trans. New York: Norton, 1945.
REVIEW: Book Review Digest 1945, p. 700.

1734. TENNEY, Rollin Q. (1838-1932)
January 1-March 29, 1873
Personal diary; dairyman and farmer of Larimer County, Colorado; social life and work.
- Clark, Jessie L. "R. Q. Tenney, Pioneer of Many Enterprises," Colorado Magazine, v. 29, pp. 210-18, 1952.

1735. WEBB, Beatrice Potter (1858-1943)
1. September 25, 1873- ; Personal diary; British socialist; received a liberal education; travels with her family; marriages of her elder sisters; work in London's East End; marriage to Fabian Society member Sidney Webb; subject to depression and psychosomatic illness.
- The Diary of Beatrice Webb. Norman and Jeanne MacKenzie, eds. 3+ vols. Cambridge: Harvard University Press, 1982-

2. March 29-July 25, 1898; Travel diary; tour of America with husband Sidney Webb to study local government; in New York, Philadelphia, Washington and points west; some entries by her husband; observed the workings of Congress; much description and generalization.
- American Diary, 1898. David A. Shannon, ed. Madison: University of Wisconsin Press, 1963.

3. September 5, 1912-May 17, 1932.
- Diaries, 1924-1932. Margaret I. Cole, ed. Lord Beveridge, intro. 2 vols. London: Longmans, Green, 1952.
REVIEW: Book Review Digest 1952, p. 934.

1736. WYANT, Alexander Helwig (1836-92)
August 16-November 7, 1873
Travel diary; landscape painter joined the Wheeler party for his health; at Canyon de Chelly, Black Mesa and return to Fort Defiance, Arizona.
- "The Wyant Diary: An Artist with the Wheeler Survey in

Arizona, 1873," Doris Ostrander Dawdy, ed. Arizona and the
West, v. 22, pp. 255-78, Fall, 1980.

1874

1737. ADAIR, Cornelia Wadsworth
       Travel diary; voyage to New York; to the Midwest, Denver and
St. Louis by boat and train.
       • My Diary, August 30th to November 5th, 1874. Montagu K.
Brown, intro. Austin: University of Texas Press, 1965.

1738. APPLETON, Thomas Gold (1812-84)
       November 30, 1874-February 16, 1875
       Travel diary; classically educated Bostonian; went down the
Nile on a dahabeah; self-consciously "literary"; through the first and
second cataracts; by camel into the desert; to Karnak.
       • A Nile Journal. Boston: Roberts Bros., 1876.

1739. BIRCH, James Wheeler Woodford (1826-75)
       March 29-April 21, 1874; October 30, 1874-October 24, 1875
       Personal diary; British envoy to the Malay States was assas-
sinated a few days after his last entry setting off the Perak War;
first section tells of a visit; second covers his official term; lengthy
entries with many details of native life; interesting.
       • The Journals of J. W. W. Birch, First British Resident to
Perak, 1874-1875. P. L. Burns, ed. New York: Oxford
University Press, 1976.
          REVIEW: Journal of Asian Studies, v. 36, p. 594, May,
       1977.

1740. BULLENE, Thomas B.
       March 20, 1874-July 5, 1880
       Personal diary; extracts; old settler and leading merchant;
owned a department store; business and social history of Kansas City.
       • Wilson, William H. "The Diary of a Kansas City Merchant
1874-1880," Missouri Historical Society Bulletin, v. 19, pp.
247-59, April, 1963.

1741. CALHOUN, James (1845-76)
       Exploration diary; regular army officer married to Custer's
sister; traveled with a geologist and a photographer to map and examine the Black Hills; notes that two thirds of the army's enlistees
in this era were foreigners; died at the Little Big Horn.
       • With Custer in '74: James Calhoun's Diary of the Black
Hills Expedition. Lawrence A. Frost, ed. Provo, Utah:
Brigham Young University Press, 1979.
          REVIEW: South Dakota History, v. 10, p. 67, Winter,
       1979.

1742. CURTISS, Roswell C. (1840-   )
       August 11-23, 1874

Travel diary; pleasure and business trip with his wife; from Cleveland, Ohio, to Duluth and return.
- "A Trip Up the Lakes in 1874," Inland Seas, v. 29, pp. 163-69, Fall, 1973.

1743. LUDLOW, William (-1901)
July 2-August 23, 1874
Expedition diary; interesting, well-written.
- "Army Engineer's Journal of Custer's Black Hills Expedition, July 2, 1874-August 23, 1874," E. V. McAndrews, ed. Journal of the West, v. 13, pp. 78-85, January, 1974.

1744. McFADDEN, Thompson (fl. 1868-76)
August 6-December 25, 1874
Military diary; civilian scout with the army during the Red River War; removing Indians from the Texas Panhandle to Cheyenne and Arapaho Reservations; life in Fort Dodge, Kansas; full entries by a well-educated, observant writer.
- "Thompson McFadden's Diary of an Indian Campaign, 1874," Robert C. Carriker, ed. Southwestern Historical Quarterly, v. 75, pp. 198-232, October, 1971.

1745. REYNOLDS, Etta Parkerson (1853-89)
Personal diary; four-foot tall, probably hunchbacked woman; kept house for an uncle; courted by a neighbor; classes and friends at Kansas State Agricultural College in Manhattan; well done picture of rural life.
- "Etta's Journal: January 2, 1874-July 25, 1875," Ellen Payne Paullin, ed. Kansas History, v. 3, pp. 201-19, Autumn, 1980; pp. 255-78, Winter, 1980.

1746. SAMS, Joseph (1855-)
September 21-November 16, 1874
Travel diary; British clerk sailed in second class from Gravesend to Melbourne, Australia, via the Cape of Good Hope; caustic, judgmental comments on his fellow passengers and close quarters.
- The Diary of Joseph Sams: An Emigrant in the "Northumberland" 1874. Simon Braydon and Robert Songhurst, eds. London: HMSO, 1982.

1747. SANFORD, Wilmot P.
September 26, 1874-May 23, 1875
Personal diary; with the 6th Infantry; common soldier's routine in a frontier fort; food, work; an "operator."
- "The Fort Buford Diary of Pvt. Sanford," Ben Innis, ed. North Dakota History, v. 33, pp. 335-78, Fall, 1966.

1748. SHAW, Albert (1857-)
March 2-April 24, 1874
Personal diary; diarist's mother joined a temperance movement in Butler County, Ohio; son's view of her "saloonatics."

• "The Whiskey War at Paddy's Run: Excerpts from a Diary of Albert Shaw," Lloyd J. Graybar, ed. Ohio History, v. 75, pp. 48-54, Winter, 1966.

1749. STANLEY, Henry Morton (1841-1904) [B274]
November 12, 1874-August 10, 1877
Exploration diary; American journalist and trader explored Africa; from Zanzibar to Lake Victoria and around it; on to Lake Tanganyika and the Atlantic coast at the mouth of the Congo River; weather, mileage estimates; description of countryside; impatient with the natives and hinderances to his progress.
• The Exploration Diaries of H. M. Stanley Now First Published From the Original Manuscripts. Richard Stanley and Alan Neame, eds. New York: Vanguard, 1961.

1750. SWETTENHAM, Sir Frank Athelsane (1850-1946)
January 12, 1874-February 15, 1876
Diplomatic diary; British Resident in the Malay Peninsula tried to keep the peace and encourage economic stability; lengthy entries; local color, history; laments on the natives' ingratitude.
• Sir Frank Swettenham's Malayan Journals, 1874-1876. P. L. Burns and C. D. Cowan, eds. New York: Oxford University Press, 1975.

1751. WILLIAMS, Espy (1852-1908)
January 12, 1874-February 10, 1875
Personal diary; life in the New Orleans theatrical world; his writing; comments on actors and the work of other playwrights.
• "The Journal of a Young Southern Playwright, Espy Williams of New Orleans, 1874-75," Paul T. Nolan, ed. Louisiana Studies, v. 1, pp. 30-50, Fall, 1962; pp. 33-54, Winter, 1962.

1875

1752. GLOVER, Eli Sheldon (1845-1919)
October 17-December 10, 1875
Travel diary; by horseback, railroad and steamboat from Missoula County, Montana Territory, to the lower Willamette Valley, Oregon; much detail; well done.
• The Diary of Eli Sheldon Glover, October-December, 1875. Portland: Oregon Historical Records Survey Project, 1939.

1753. HAYES, Rutherford Birchard (1822-93) [A290]
March 28, 1875-March 10, 1881; gaps
Personal diary; Ohioan was the 19th U.S. president; "covering the disputed election, the end of Reconstruction, and the beginning of civil service"; problems with the South and Republicans; lively style.
• Hayes: The Diary of a President, 1875-1881. T. Harry Williams, ed. New York: McKay, 1964.
    REVIEW: Book Review Digest 1964, pp. 542-43.

1754. MacLEOD, Norman (1839-1929)
        January 19, 1875-November 24, 1876
        Travel diary; from Natal to Zambezi.
        • "Diary," in: Edward C. Tabler. Trade and Travel in
        Early Barotseland. Berkeley: University of California Press,
        1963; pp. 105-112.

1755. RONEY, Frank
        Personal diary; Irish immigrant and iron molder; coping with
unemployment and poverty which resulted from a nationwide depression; prices.
        • Shumsky, N. L. "Frank Roney's San Francisco--His Diary:
        April, 1875-March, 1876," Labor History, v. 17, pp. 245-64,
        Spring, 1976.

1756. TRUE, Theodore E. (-1925)
        January 28-March 7, 1875
        Personal diary; regular army man sent to Dawson County,
Nebraska, to distribute clothing to victims; dry but with insights
into the plight of the people.
        • "Relief for Nebraska Grasshopper Victims: The Official
        Journal of Lt. Theodore E. True," Gary D. Olson, ed. Ne-
        braska History, v. 48, pp. 119-40, Summer, 1967.

1757. WHITNEY, Clara A. (1861-)
        August 3, 1875-April 17, 1887; gaps
        Personal diary; in Japan with her family; mother's work as a
lay missionary; father operated a business school; marriage to a
Japanese and birth of their five children; her developing maturity;
distaste for, then understanding and adoption of Japanese customs;
lively, entertaining.
        • Clara's Diary: An American Girl in Meiji Japan. M. Wil-
        liam Steele and Tamiko Ichimata, eds. New York: Kodansha
        International, 1979.

1758. WILLIAMS, Howard (1854-1933)
        July 31-August 22, 1875
        Travel diary; son of a successful merchant went with two
brothers and two friends on a tour through the canals of the West
Country; details of the workings of locks; nice slice of social history; illustrated with sketches by participants.
        • The Diary of a Rowing Tour: From Oxford to London Via
        Warwick, Gloucester, Hereford and Bristol, August 1875.
        Gloucester: Sutton, 1982.
        REVIEW: Book Review Index 1982, p. 547.

1759. WOLSELEY, Garnet Joseph, Viscount (1833-1913) [C127]
        1. March 20, 1875-September 10, 1875; Diplomatic diary;
British officer, veteran of the Sepoy Rebellion and the Red River
Uprising; arrival at Table Bay; service as governor of South Africa.
        • The South African Diaries of Sir Garnet Wolseley, 1875.
        Adrian Preston, ed. Cape Town: A. A. Balkema, 1971.

2.   June 8, 1879–May 25, 1880; Military diary; voyage to South
Africa; negotiations with the Zulus; administering the Transvaal; Se-
kukuni campaign; in Pretoria and Natal; relations with the Boers;
"ambitious and controversial" individual; valuable for details of British colonial policy.
> • The South African Journal of Sir Garnet Wolseley, 1879–
> 1880. Adrian Preston, ed. Cape Town: A. A. Balkema,
> 1973.

3.   August 22, 1884–July 13, 1885; Military diary; commander
of the forces sent to rescue General Charles Gordon from the Mahdi's
siege of Khartoum; traveling down the Nile against advice from several
knowledgeable sources he reached his objective two days too late;
blamed his failure on Gladstone (q.v.).
> • In Relief of Gordon: Lord Wolseley's Campaign Journal of
> the Khartoum Relief Expedition 1884–1885. Adrian Preston,
> ed. Rutherford, N.J.: Fairleigh Dickinson University Press,
> 1970.

1876

1760.   BAELZ, Erwin O. E. von (1849–1913)
January 1, 1876–August 29, 1905
Personal diary; German-born medical doctor lived and worked
in Japan for 30 years; family life; record of patients; Russo-Japanese
War.
> • Awakening Japan: The Diary of a German Doctor. Toku
> Baelz, ed. Eden and Cedar Paul, trans. New York: Viking
> Press, 1932; reprinted Bloomington: Indiana University Press,
> 1974.

1761.   BERENSON, Mary Smith (1864–1945)
October 24, 1876–January 27, 1937; gaps
Personal diary; daughter of preaching Philadelphia Quakers
married art critic Bernard Berenson (q.v.) after her first husband's
death; personal life; art work; her relations; quarrels and contretemps of modern art criticism; diary entries are vastly outnumbered
by snippets from letters to BB and a cast of relatives and acquaintances; engaging.
> • Mary Berenson: A Self Portrait From Her Letters and Di-
> aries. Barbara Strachey and Jayne Samuels, eds. New York:
> Norton, 1983.
> REVIEWS: Library Journal v. 109, p. 579, March 15, 1984.
> Publishers Weekly v. 225, pp. 78, 80, March 2, 1984.

1762.   BRODERICK, James Lonsdale (1841–86)
October 29, 1876–
Travel diary; land agent for the 1st Earl of Wharncliffe went
to the Philadelphia Centennial Exposition; on to Iowa to visit people
who immigrated from his native Yorkshire; literate, opinionated man
interested in all aspects of life in Dubuque.

- The Character of the Country: The Iowa Diary of James
L. Broderick, 1876-1877. Iowa City: Iowa State Historical
Department, 1976.
   REVIEWS: Wisconsin Magazine of History, v. 61, p. 71,
   Autumn, 1977. Agricultural History, v. 52, pp. 222-23,
   January, 1978. Journal of the Illinois State Historical So-
   ciety, v. 70, p. 336, November, 1977.

1763. BRYAN, Jerry
        March 13-August 17, 1876
        Travel diary; from Rock Island County to the Black Hills; via
Cheyenne to Rapid City; "I have learned a lesson that will not be
forgotten [sic] soon."
   - An Illinois Gold Hunter in the Black Hills. Clyde C. Walton, intro. Springfield: Illinois State Historical Society, 1960.

1764. COLEMAN, Thomas W. (1849-1921)
        June 18-July, 1876
        Military journal; service with Company B under Captain Mc-
Dougall at the Little Big Horn; pp. 12-25 are the diary; remainder
of the book is commentary on the battle and its participants.
   - I Buried Custer: The Diary of Pvt. Thomas W. Coleman,
   7th U.S. Cavalry. Bruce R. Liddic, ed. John M. Carroll,
   intro. College Station, Tx.: Creative Publishing Co., 1979.
      REVIEW: South Dakota History, v. 10, pp. 66-67, Winter,
      1979.

1765. CUSHMAN, Mary Ames (1864-   )
        August 2, 1876-July 18, 1880
        Travel diary; American girl's trip to Europe with her widowed
mother and siblings; school, social life, sights.
   - She Wrote It All Down. New York: Scribner, 1936.

1766. DeWOLF, James M. (-1876)
        March 10-June 21, 1876
        Letter journal; stationed at Fort Lincoln; killed in the Custer
massacre; details of army life.
   - "The Diary and Letters of Dr. James M. DeWolf, Acting
   Assistant Surgeon, U.S. Army: His Record of the Sioux Expedition of 1876 as Kept Until His Death," Edward S. Luce,
   ed. North Dakota History, v. 25, pp. 33-81, 1958.

1767. FREEMAN, Henry Blanchard (1837-   )
        March 21-October 6, 1876
        Military journal; not with Custer's troops; found the bodies
after the massacre; "The stench from the dead ... was something
terrible."
   - The Freeman Journal: The Infantry in the Sioux Campaign
   of 1876. George A. Schneider, ed. San Rafael, Cal.: Presidio, 1977.
      REVIEW: New Mexico Historical Review, v. 54, pp. 157-58,
      April, 1979.

1768. GODFREY, Edward Settle (1843-1932)
       May 17-September 24, 1876
       Military diary; served with troops near Custer's on the battle-
field but did not learn of the disaster till later; helped bury Custer
and 211 others.
       • The Field Diary of Lt. Edward Settle Godfrey, Commanding
       Co. K, 7th Cavalry Regiment Under Lt. Col. George Armstrong
       Custer in the Sioux Encounter at the Battle of the Little Big
       Horn. Edgar I. Stewart and Jane R. Stewart, eds. Portland,
       Ore.: Champoeg Press, 1957.

1769. HAWKES, Edward (1837-1902)
       January 1, 1876-December 31, 1877
       Personal diary; Jefferson County farmer; short entries; weather,
farm work, prices.
       • "The Diaries of a Nebraska Farmer, 1876-1877," Clarence
       S. Paine, ed. Agricultural History, v. 22, pp. 1-31, 1948.

1770. HUNNIUS, Carl Julius Adolph (1842-   )
       January 20-24, 1876
       Personal diary; German immigrant, draftsman and Civil War
veteran; civilian in the employ of the U.S. Army as a surveyor;
work, food, collecting Indian artifacts.
       • Mothershead, Harmon. "The Journal of Ado Hunnius, In-
       dian Territory, 1876," Chronicles of Oklahoma, v. 51, pp.
       451-72, Winter, 1973-74.

1771. JACKSON, William Emsley (1858-1945)
       June 23-September 17, 1876
       Trail diary; followed the Overland Trail eastward with devia-
tions for grass and water; comments on people and scenery; passed
westward moving emigrants; good.
       • "William Emsley Jackson's Diary of a Cattle Drive from La
       Grande, Oregon to Cheyenne, Wyoming, in 1876," J. Orin
       Oliphant and C. S. Kingston, eds. Agricultural History, v.
       23, pp. 260-73, December, 1949.

1772. KELLOGG, Mark
       May 17-June 9, 1876
       Personal diary; newspaper correspondent for the New York
Herald and the Bismarck Tribune; killed with Custer at the Little
Big Horn; Hixon's article "Custer's 'Mysterious' Mr. Kellogg" (pp.
145-63) in the same issue has much background information.
       • "Mark Kellogg's Diary," John C. Hixon, ed. North Dakota
       History, v. 17, pp. 164-76, July, 1950.

1773. SAUNDERS, Margaret Marshall (1861-1947)
       September 21-December 29, 1876
       Travel diary; prolific Canadian author of novels and juvenile
books; experiences at a finishing school in Scotland; at the head of
her French and German classes; school life, sightseeing and shopping.

• "Margaret Marshall Saunders: Edinburgh Diary, 1876,"
Atlantis [Canada], v. 6, pp. 68-82, 1980.

1774. TERRY, Alfred Howe (1827-90)
May 17-August 23, 1876
Military diary; Civil War veteran; with Custer at the Little
Big Horn; impersonal, cryptic notes.
• The Field Diary of General A. H. Terry: The Yellowstone
Expedition-1876. 2nd ed. Bellevue, Neb.: Old Army Press,
1970.

1877

1775. BISCHOFF, Herman
July 26-September 6, 1877
Travel diary; German immigrant brought merchandise to Dead-
wood and rented a store; sold out and put together a wagon train;
meeting with Mormons; detailed entries.
• "Deadwood to the Big Horns 1877, A Diary Kept in German
by the Late Herman Bischoff," Edna LaMore Waldo, trans.
Annals of Wyoming, v. 9, pp. 19-34, April, 1933.

1776. CANNARY, Martha Jane (Calamity Jane) (1852-1903)
September 25, 1877-April, 1902
Letter diary; addressed to her daughter Janie Hickok; sent
to counteract the stories which were spread about her; moving.
• Calamity Jane, 1852-1903: A History of Her Life and Ad-
ventures in the West. Nolie Mumey, ed. Denver: Range
Press, 1950.

1777. DODGSHUN, Arthur W. (1847-79)
March 29, 1877-April 1, 1879
Travel diary; minister sent out by the London Missionary Society with several other Englishmen; inland from Zanzibar with bul-
locks and wagons; battling tsetse fly and rough terrain; rigors of
travel.
• From Zanzibar to Ujiji: The Journal of Arthur W. Dodgshun, 1877-1879. Norman Robert Bennett, ed. Boston:
Boston University Press, 1969.

1778. HILL, Erastus G.
January 29-February 22, 1877
Personal diary; from Chicago to Florida; in Gainesville and
Jacksonville; beginnings of a homestead.
• "A Florida Settler of 1877: The Diary of Erastus G. Hill,"
Florida Historical Quarterly, v. 28, pp. 271-94, April, 1950.

1779. HUFTALEN, Sarah Gillespie (1865-1952)
January 4-14, 1877
Personal diary; daughter of Emily H. Gillespie (q.v.); extracts;

classes in a one room school with a teacher who expended more effort
on punishment than teaching.
> • Smith, L. Glenn. "The Gillespie/Huftalen Diaries--A Window
> on American Education," Vitae Scholasticae, v. 2, pp. 243-66,
> Spring, 1983.

1780. JAMES, Frank Lowber (1841-1907)
       September 14, 1877-April 16, 1878
       Personal diary; studied chemistry at the University of Munich
and medicine in Paris; practiced in Osceola, Arkansas, on the banks
of the Mississippi; his reading and study; comment on social life and
customs of the town; details of patients' illnesses and their treatment;
interesting.
> • Years of Discontent: Dr. Frank L. James in Arkansas,
> 1877-78. W. David Baird, ed. Memphis: Memphis State Uni-
> versity Press, 1977.
> > REVIEWS: Journal of the History of Medicine and Allied
> > Sciences, v. 35, pp. 126-27, January. 1980. Tennessee
> > Historical Quarterly, v. 37, pp. 112-15, Spring, 1978.

1878

1781. BROWN, William Carey (-1939)
       June 7-October 23, 1878
       Military journal; 2nd lieutenant in the 1st U.S. cavalry under
General Oliver O. Howard; on the march against the Piutes.
> • "Two Cavalrymen's Diaries of the Bannock War, 1878,"
> George F. Brimlow, ed. Oregon Historical Quarterly, v. 68,
> pp. 221-58, September, 1967.

1782. DRINKWATER, Alice Gray (1861-1915) and DRINKWATER,
       Sumner Pierce, 1859-1942
       1879-1908
       Sea diary; excerpts; life aboard ship and ashore.
> • A Seafaring Legacy: The Photographs, Diaries, Letters
> and Memorabilia of a Maine Sea Captain and His Wife, 1859-
> 1908. Julianna Freehand, ed. New York: Random House,
> 1981.

1783. HARDESTY, George Washington (1850-1926)
       June 1, 1878-August 7, 1879; gaps
       Travel diary; over the Santa Fe Trail from Missouri to Colo-
rado; life in New Mexico and the Indian Territory; good descriptions
of scenery and family life; well done.
> • "Diary of George W. Hardesty," Richard H. Louden, ed.
> Colorado Magazine, v. 38, pp. 174-87, July, 1961.

1784. HARROWBY, Dudley Ryder, 3rd Earl of (1831-1900)
       Political diary; served in Disraeli's cabinet; covers events
before and after the Congress of Berlin; very detailed.

- The Cabinet Journal of Dudley Ryder, Viscount Sandon
(11 May-10 August, 1878). Christopher Howard and Peter
Gordon, eds. London: Institute of Historical Research, 1974.

1785. IDE, Lucy A. (1838-1903)
May 1-September 15, 1878
Travel diary; from Buffalo County, Wisconsin, to Dayton,
Washington Territory; not an easy trip but an engaging diary.
- "In a Prairie Schooner, 1878-Mrs. Lucy Ide's Diary," Wash-
ington Historical Quarterly, v. 18, pp. 122-31, 191-98, 277-88,
1927.

1786. LEE, Francis H.
January 2-February 3, 1878
Personal diary; everyday life.
- "Forty Years Ago in Salem: Extracts from the Diary of
Francis H. Lee," Essex Institute Historical Collections, v. 59,
pp. 102-04, April, 1923; pp. 359-60, October, 1923; v. 60,
pp. 75-80, January, 1924; v. 61, pp. 396-400, October, 1925.

1787. McNAUGHT, John S. (1843-1914)
June 10, 1878
Military journal; punitive expedition against Mexican troops;
apparently written from earlier notes.
- "A Border Incident of 1878 From the Journal of Captain
John S. McNaught," George A. Schneider, ed. Southwestern
Historical Quarterly, v. 70, pp. 314-20, October, 1966.

1788. MAYER, Frederick W. (1855-1934)
June 4-October 23, 1878
Military journal; mileage and location of day's camp.
- "Two Cavalrymen's Diaries of the Bannock War, 1878,"
George F. Brimlow, ed. Oregon Historical Quarterly, v. 68,
pp. 293-316, December, 1967.

1789. MORAN, George Henry Roberts (1840-   )
February 13-September 21, 1878
Personal diary; diarist was paid $100 a month plus fuel and
quarters to provide medical aid to soldiers in the territory; marched
with them through "infernal country."
- "Arizona Territory-1878: The Diary of George H. R. Moran
Contract Surgeon, United States Army," E. R. Hagemann, ed.
Arizona and the West, v. 5, pp. 249-67, Autumn, 1963.

1790. MORGAN, William Fellowes (1860-1943)
August 6-21, 1878
Expedition diary; excerpts; member of an expedition to Colo-
rado and New Mexico to study the Pueblo Indians.
- Hollcroft, Temple R. "The Diary of William Fellowes Morgan,"
Scientific Monthly, v. 77, pp. 119-28, September, 1953.

1791. PETROFF, Ivan (1842-   )
       July 11-October 27, 1878
       Expedition diary; Russian-American sent to Alaska to collect
information for the Bancroft Library; many observations on Eskimos.
       • "Journal of a Trip to Alaska in 1878," T. C. Hinckley and
       C. Hinckley, eds. Journal of the West, v. 5, pp. 25-70, Jan-
       uary, 1966.

1792. SUKHOTINA, Tatiana Lvovna Tolstoya (1864-1950)
       1. November 11, 1878-April 6, 1911; many gaps; Personal
       diary; eldest daughter of Russian novelist Leo Tolstoy (q.v.) and
       his wife Sophia (q.v.); introspective girl had a close relationship
to her father; little mention of her mother; affairs of the heart; marriage; several stillbirths; an unhappy life despite an abundance of
material goods.
       • The Tolstoy Home: Diaries of Tatiana Sukhotina-Tolstoy.
       Alec Brown, trans. London: Harville Press, 1951.

       2. May 13-November 17, 1891; Personal diary; taking dicta-
tion from her father; visiting famine-stricken peasants.
       • "At My Father's Side: From the Diary," A. Shifman, ed.
       A. Miller, trans. Soviet Literature, v. 10, pp. 112-27, 1975.

1793. WOOD, Charles Erskine Scott
       June 7, 1878-May 14, 1879
       Personal diary; aide-de-camp to General Oliver O. Howard;
from Portland by steamer; treaty with the Indians; barracks life; interesting descriptions of soldiers' social life; observations on Indian
customs.
       • "Private Journal, 1878," Oregon Historical Quarterly, v. 70,
       pp. 5-38, March, 1969; pp. 139-70, June, 1969.

                                  1879

1794. BROSS, William
       May 27-June 30, 1879
       Travel diary; to Manitoba, Montana and Dakota Territories;
short entry; mileage; weather.
       • "Diary of a Journey into the Valleys of the Red River of
       the North and the Upper Missouri, 1879," Chester McArthur
       Destler, ed. Mississippi Valley Historical Review, v. 33, pp.
       425-42, 1946-47.

1795. DE LONG, George Washington (1844-81)
       July 8, 1879-October 30, 1881
       Sea diary; commanded a Polar expedition financed by newspa-
per mogul James Gordon Bennett; from San Francisco to the Bering
Strait; bear hunting; description of daily routine; polar phenomena;
ship entrapped by ice, damaged and sunk; crew made its way overland in Siberia; separated into three parties; deaths of De Long and
his party from starvation; rescue of survivors.

● The Voyage of the Jeannette, The Ship and Ice Journals
of George W. De Long, Lt-Commander U.S.N., and Commander
of the Polar Expedition of 1879-1881. Emma De Long, ed. 2
vols. Boston: Houghton, Mifflin, 1884.

1796. DUVAL, Burr G.
December 13, 1879-April 10, 1880
Exploration diary; trip to the Rio Grande and south Texas to
ascertain the area's mineral content; prospecting; hunting.
● "The Burr G. Duval Diary," Sam Woolford, ed. Southwest-
tern Historical Quarterly, v. 65, pp. 487-511, April, 1962.

1797. HEWARD, Teancum William (1854-1915)
1879-1881
Personal diary; Utah native proselytizing in northern Georgia.
● Buice, David. "Excerpts From the Diary of Teancum Wil-
liam Heward, Early Mormon Missionary to Georgia," George
Historical Quarterly, v. 64, pp. 317-25, Fall, 1980.

1798. PALMER, Horace L. (1849?-   )
October 25, 1879-March 14, 1880
Sea diary; extracts; whaling voyage from the South Atlantic
to Tristan da Cunha Islands; good observer.
● "A Wisconsin Whaler: The Letters and Diary of Horace L.
Palmer," Virginia A. Palmer, ed. Wisconsin Magazine of His-
tory, v. 54, pp. 87-118, Winter, 1970-71.

1799. PARSONS, George Whitwell (1850-1933)
March 27, 1879-June 27, 1882
Personal diary; bank teller in San Francisco; to Tombstone,
Arizona, for the mining boom; details of mining.
● The Private Journal of George Whitwell Parsons. Phoenix:
Arizona Statewide Archival and Records Project, 1939.
REVIEW: Pacific Historical Reviews, v. 10, pp. 136-37,
1941.

1800. RANOUS, Dora Knowlton Thompson (1859-1916)
September 4, 1879-August 7, 1880
Theatrical diary; ingenue in Augustin Daly's theatrical company;
in New York City and on tour; well-written, lively account of stage
life of the time.
● Diary of a Daly Debutante, Being Passages From the Journal of a Member of Augustin Daly's Famous Company of Players. New York: B. Blom, 1972; reprint of 1910 edition.

1801. TUGGLE, William Orrie (1841-84)
1. August 30-October 6, 1879; January 21-May 21, 1880;
February 1, 1881-December 19, 1882; Personal diary; Georgian and
Civil War veteran; legal agent for the Creek Nation in a suit against
the Federal government; resided in Oklahoma for three years; humorous, curious, intelligent observer of Indian life and Washington
politics.

• Shem, Ham & Japheth: The Papers of W. O. Tuggle, Comprising His Indian Diary, Sketches & Observations, Myths & Washington Journal in the Territory & at the Capital, 1879-1882. Eugene Current-Garcia with Dorothy B. Hatfield, eds. Athens: University of Georgia Press, 1973.

2. Fuller, William E., Jr. "William Orrie Tuggle: Journal of 1880-1882," Master's Thesis, Auburn University, 1964; not seen.

1880

1802. BANDELIER, Adolph Francis (1840-1914)
August 20, 1880-December 31, 1892
Expedition diary; combined with field notebooks; Swiss-born anthropologist/archaeologist working in the southwestern U.S. and northern Mexico; candid observations by a pioneering scholar.
• The Southwestern Journals of Adolph F. Bandelier, 1880-1882. 4 vols. Charles H. Lange and Carroll L. Riley, eds. Albuquerque: University of New Mexico Press, 1966-85.
REVIEWS: Choice, v. 1, pp. 1880-82, December, 1966; v. 2, pp. 1883-84, June, 1971; v. 3, pp. 1885-88, 1975; v. 22, p. 1558, June, 1985.

1803. CONSTANT, Rezin H.
July 13-August 24, 1880
Travel diary; from Ottawa, Kansas, to Denver and surrounding area; much description of people, sights and climate.
• "Colorado as Seen by a Visitor of 1880," Colorado Magazine, v. 12, pp. 103-16, May, 1935.

1804. GODBOLD, John Cooper (1847-1918)
Personal diary; excerpts; practiced in Wilcox County, Alabama; comments on medicines, treatment and patients.
• Partin, Robert. "A Black Belt Doctor's Diary, 1880," Alabama Review, v. 7, pp. 136-51, April, 1954.

1805. HAMILTON, Sir Edward Walter (1847-   )
April 24, 1880-July 1, 1885
Diplomatic diary; principal private secretary in Gladstone's second ministry; some personal items but mostly political; long, full entries; astute observer; valuable for an understanding of Gladstone (q.v.).
• The Diary of Sir Edward Walter Hamilton, 1880-1885. Dudley W. R. Bahlman, ed. Oxford: Clarendon Press, 1972.
REVIEW: Book Review Digest 1973, p. 523.

1806. HARRISON, William Gregory (1855-82)
Personal diary; life on a family farm in Indiana.
• "'Chronicles of Upper Burnet': William Gregory Harrison's Morgan County Journal October 2, 1880-May 23, 1881," Roger

G. Miller, ed. Indiana Magazine of History, v. 74, pp. 316-
63, December, 1978; v. 75, pp. 147-210, June, 1979.

1807. PETERSON, Nels (1832-)
July 28-September 7, 1880
Travel diary; extracts; Danish immigrant's journey with his
family by wagon from Westbourne, Manitoba.
  • Friesen, Victor Carl. "Nels Peterson of Wingard--and His
  Diary," Beaver [Canada] v. 311 pp. 43-48, Summer, 1980.

1808. SITWELL, Florence Alice (1858-1930) [B282]
January 1-April 17, 1880; June 5, 1891-December 31, 1892;
February 24-September 25, 1893
Personal diary; upper class British lady and relative of the
literary family; chatter over the teacups; some mention of politics.
  • "Vestals and Vestries: Extracts From the Journals of F.
  A. Sitwell, 1880-1893," Osbert Sitwell, ed. Life and Letters
  To-day, v. 44, pp. 67-81, February, 1945; pp. 133-46, March,
  1945; v. 45, pp. 4-17, April, 1945; pp. 109-26, May, 1945.

1809. STANTON, Elizabeth Cady (1815-1902)
November 12, 1880-October 17, 1902
Personal diary; American suffragette; opens with the death
of Lucretia Mott; woman's rights; agitation for suffrage in the U.S.
and abroad; spirited defense of women with whomever she meets;
notes on her writing.
  • Elizabeth Cady Stanton: As Revealed in Her Letters, Diary
  and Reminiscences. Theodore Stanton and Harriot Stanton
  Blatch, eds. New York: Harper, 1922; v. 2, pp. 177-369.

1810. STEVENSON, Robert Louis (1850-94)
May 22-June 30, 1880
Personal diary; Scottish essayist, novelist and poet; honey-
moon period with wife Fanny in a California mining camp; much of the
material here was transmuted and used in his The Silverado Squatters.
  • Silverado Journal. John E. Jordon, ed. San Francisco:
  Book Club of California, 1954; 400 copies.

1811. WHITMAN, Walt (1819-92)
June 18-August 29, 1880
Travel diary; leading American poet; sightseeing in Ontario
and Quebec Provinces.
  • Walt Whitman's Diary in Canada with Extracts from Other of
  His Diaries and Literary Note-books. William S. Kennedy, ed.
  Boston: Small, Maynard and Co., 1904.

1812. WISE, Major Lewis Lovatt Ashford
August 29-November 2, 1880
Hunting diary; bagged 23 head; meeting with Moreton Frewen;
lengthy entries; good humored amusement over finding Americans
"very decent fellows."

- "Diary of Major Wise, and Englishman, Recites Details of Hunting Trip in Powder River Country in 1880," Howard B. Lott, ed. Annals of Wyoming, v. 12, pp. 85-118, April, 1940.

1813. WITHERLEE, George H.
       September 17-30, 1880; September 2-29, 1881; September 18-October 15, 1886; September 9-25, 1895; September 15-30, 1898; September 11-19, 1899; September 5-17, 1901
       Personal diary; hiking and camping in the Maine woods.
       - Explorations West and Northwest of Katahdin in the Late 19th Century. Henry R. Buck and Myron H. Avery, eds. 2nd ed. Augusta, Me.: Appalachian Trail Club, 1950.

                                   1881

1814. BACON, Francis H.
       March 29, 1881-October 16, 1883
       Expedition diary; excerpts; accompanied Joseph T. Clarke for three seasons of digging at an archaeological site at Assos, Turkey; exuberant.
       - "Assos Journals of Francis H. Bacon," L. O. K. Congdon, ed. Archaeology, v. 27, pp. 83-95, April, 1974.

1815. BENTON, Virginia Belle (1863-   )
       June 15-October 14, 1881
       Travel diary; from the Republican River to Little Goose Creek, Wyoming; work; reading; camping with settlers along the way; lively account.
       - "Diary-Journey From Kansas to Wyoming-1881," Annals of Wyoming, v. 14, pp. 108-20, April, 1942.

1816. CHASE, Josephine Streeper (1835-94)
       April 19, 1881-July 5, 1894; gaps
       Personal diary; polygamous second wife and overworked Mormon mother; life in a rural Utah community.
       - "The Josephine Diaries: Glimpses of the Life of Josephine Streeper Chase, 1881-94," Fae Decker Dix, ed. Utah Historical Quarterly, v. 46, pp. 167-83, Spring, 1978.

1817. GARFIELD, Lucretia Rudolph (1832-1918)
       Personal diary; wife of President James A. Garfield; inaugural preparations.
       - "Diary: March 1-April 20, 1881," in: Diary of James A. Garfield. Lansing: Michigan State University Press, 1981; v. 4, pp. 625-41.

1818. GOODALE, Ephraim (1806-87)
       November 22, 1881-June 7, 1883; gaps
       Personal diary; life in the fort; weather; short entries.

- "A Civilian at Old Fort Bayard 1881-1883," Roy Goodale,
ed. New Mexico Historical Review, v. 25, pp. 296-304, October, 1950.

1819. GROTH, Charles
        May 12, 1881-1887
        Personal diary; Danish immigrant homesteading in British
Columbia.
        - "Galiano Island Pioneer: Extracts From the Diary ... 1881-
        1887," Marie Elliott, ed. Beaver [Canada], v. 311, pp. 51-54,
        Winter, 1980.

1820. JAMES, Henry (1843-1916) [B285]
        November 25, 1881-November 11, 1882
        Personal diary; American novelist; concentrates on his return
to America from abroad and the death of his mother.
        - "Diary Excerpts," in: Philip Dunaway and Mel Evans, eds.
        A Treasury of the World's Great Diaries. New York: Double-
        day, 1957; pp. 477-80.

1821. McCONNELL, Robert (1828-1914)
        March 16, 1881-
        Travel diary; from Xenia, Illinois, to Moscow, Idaho, with his
wife and son by train; prices; telegraphic style.
        - "Businessman's Search; Pacific Northwest, 1881," John A.
        Brown, ed. Oregon Historical Quarterly, v. 71, pp. 5-25,
        March, 1970.

1822. PEARSON, Clement
        June 25-September 28, 1881
        Travel diary; product of the Gilded Age on a tour of Europe;
England, Scotland, Germany, Italy, Belgium and Switzerland; interest
in mechanical apparatus aboard ship and in the construction of car-
riages he saw and rode in; knowledgeable about the historical sites
he visited; inspected the battlefield of Waterloo; comments on tour-
ists' shopping are still timely.
        - A Diary of Travels in Europe During the Summer of 1881.
        2nd ed. Washington, D.C.: Judd and Detweiler, 1885.

1823. POTTER, Beatrix (1866-1943)
        November 4, 1881-January 31, 1897
        Personal diary; English author of The Tale of Peter Rabbit
and similar juveniles kept this journal in a simple substitution code;
family life; art exhibits; visits; travel throughout Britain; sketches
and studies reproduced; genealogies of the Leech, Potter and Cromp-
ton families.
        - The Journal of Beatrix Potter From 1881 to 1897. Leslie
        Linder, trans. New York: Warne, 1966.
        REVIEW: Book Review Digest 1966, p. 970.

1824. SAUNDERS, Frank M. (1860-)
        January 15-September 6, 1881

Personal diary; work and weather in Gilliam County, Oregon.
● "Rock Creek Shepherd, 1881," Oregon Historical Quarterly,
v. 81, pp. 260-80, Fall, 1980.

1825. SIMMONS, Rachel Emma Woolley (1836-1926)
March 14, 1881-January 1, 1891; gaps
Personal diary; Mormon mother of ten became a midwife after
being widowed; helping lay out the dead; trip to St. George; family
life; hard working, unselfish individual.
● "Journal of Rachel Emma Woolley Simmond," Heart Throbs
of the West, v. 11, pp. 153-208, 1950.

1826. WEBBER, Anna (1860-1948)
May 9-July 27, 1881
Classroom diary; young teacher's first assignment; comments
on her pupils; getting new desks; weather.
● "Diary of Anna Webber: Early Day Teacher of Mitchell
County," Lila Gravatt Scrimsher, ed. Kansas Historical Quar-
terly, v. 38, pp. 320-37, 1972.

<u>1882</u>

1827. BENT, Levancia (1833-1900)
July 11-October 27, 1882
Trail diary; spinster sister-in-law of the drive's organizer;
by wagon, buggy and train; visitors; her efforts at painting; stops
at Laramie, Cheyenne and Salt Lake City.
● "Levancia Bent's Diary of a Sheep Drive, Evanston, Wyoming to Kearney, Nebraska, 1882," George Squires Herrington,
ed. Annals of Wyoming, v. 24, pp. 24-51, January, 1952.

1828. CARPENTER, Julia Gage (-1931)
1. February 9, 1882-June 10, 1901; gaps; Personal diary;
her marriage and life in a claim shack in North Dakota; birth of
children; visits to New York State; good picture of frontier life.
● "Diary," in: Elizabeth Hampsten. To All Inquiring Friends:
Letters, Diaries and Essays in North Dakota. Grand Forks:
University of North Dakota, 1979; pp. 199-252.

2. "Julia's Diary, Bride on a Prairie Claim," Fargo [N.D.]
Forum, June 15, 1975, n.p.

1829. CHISSIN, Chaim (1865-1932)
February 10, 1882-October 14, 1887
Personal diary; Russian Jew joined with other immigrants to
found a settlement in Palestine; struggle to become self-sufficient;
manual labor left no time for study; beset by doubts and the need
to accept charity to keep the colony going; well-written, interesting
diary by someone who appreciates life's little ironies.
● A Palestine Diary: Memoirs of a Bilu Pioneer, 1882-1887.
Frances Miller, trans. New York: Herzl Press, 1976.

1830. COMPTON, Charles (1828-84)
    January 1-December 31, 1882
    Personal diary; British artist turned civil servant in Ordnance
Department of the War Office; family and social life; his work.
    • The Diary of Charles Compton: Artist and Civil Servant.
    Eunice H. Turner, ed. Ilfracombe: Stockwell, 1980.
        REVIEW: Times Literary Supplement, June 19, 1981, p.
        709.

1831. DAVIES, William Gilbert (1842-1910)
    January 27-31, 1882
    Travel diary; New York lawyer, his wife, child and her nurse
went south in search of better health; very detailed.
    • "Leaves From a Travel Diary: A Visit to Augusta and Sa-
    vannah, 1881," Samuel Proctor, ed. Georgia Historical Quar-
    terly, v. 41, pp. 309-15, September, 1957.

1832. DENT, John Harry (1815-   )
    Plantation diary; article based on the diaries now at the Uni-
versity of Alabama; details of plantation life in Alabama and farming
in Georgia.
    • Smith, Warren I. "The Farm Journal of John Harry Dent,
    1882-1884," Georgia Historical Quarterly, v. 42, pp. 44-53,
    March, 1958.

1833. EVANS, Hartman K.
    May 27-September 29, 1882
    Trail diary; drove 23,000 sheep 850 miles; accompanied by 15
men and several sheepdogs.
    • "Sheep Trailing from Oregon to Wyoming by Hartman K.
    Evans," Robert H. Burns, ed. Mississippi Historical Review,
    March, 1942; reprinted Annals of Wyoming, v. 23, pp. 77-96,
    January, 1951.

1834. FORSYTH, William Joseph
    June 16, 1882-February, 1883; August 24-October 16, 1887
    Travel diary; intrepid English botanist in Hawaii, Mexico and
South American collecting specimens; visited British copra and tea
plantations in the Pacific Islands; comments on a wide variety of
topics; interesting.
    • Journal of W. J. Forsyth. L. N. Forsyth, ed. Boston:
    Christopher Publishing House, 1940.

1835. GILBOY, Bernard (1852-   )
    August 18, 1882-April 9, 1883
    Sea diary; first man to voyage alone from San Francisco to
Australia; vessel resembled a Columbia River salmon boat; picked up
in distress by a ship 160 miles short of his goal.
    • A Voyage of Pleasure: The Log of Bernard Gilboy's Trans-
    Pacific Cruise in the Boat Pacific, 1882-1883. John Barr Tomp-
    kins, ed. Cambridge, Md.: Cornell Maritime Press, 1956;

1883 ed. titled Voyage of the Boat Pacific From San Francisco
to Australia.

1836. PRATT, Teancum (1851-1900)
       June 5, 1882-January 19, 1900; gaps
       Personal diary; son of Parley Parker Pratt; Mormon arrested
and imprisoned for polygamy; family notes on two wives and 22 children.
       • "Teancum Pratt, Founder of Helper [Utah]," Edna Romano,
         ed. Utah Historical Quarterly, v. 48, pp. 328-65, Fall, 1980.

1837. PRICE, Dr. George M. (-1942)
       May 3-July 12, 1882
       Travel diary; Russian Jew emigrated to New York; by ship
from Hamburg; very descriptive of conditions in Russia and his journey to dockside.
       • Shpall, Leo. "The Diary of Dr. George M. Price," Ameri-
         can Jewish Historical Society Publications, v. 40, pp. 173-81,
         December, 1950.

                                  1883

1838. BRADFORD, Gamaliel (1863-1932)
       February 13, 1883-January 19, 1932
       Personal diary; descendant of the Mayflower Bradfords and
associate of Boston Brahmins; disciplined man; gifted in languages;
novelist; ill health; "psychography," psychoanalysis of various writers
and others; the "literary struggle."
       • The Journal of Gamaliel Bradford, 1883-1932. Van Wyck
         Brooks, ed. Boston: Houghton Mifflin, 1933.

1839. FEDDE, Elizabeth (1850-)
       April 8, 1883-May, 1888
       Personal diary; Norwegian woman trained as a deaconess; es-
tablished a hospital and relief organization in New York City for her
countrymen.
       • "Elizabeth Fedde's Diary, 1883-88," Beulah Folkedahl, trans.
         and ed. Norwegian-American Studies and Records, v. 20, pp.
         170-96, 1959.

1840. MASTON, George A. (1849-1913)
       January 3, 1883-June 30, 1885
       Personal diary; Methodist Episcopal minister born a slave;
transferred from Missouri to Lincoln to obtain a better education for
his children; preaching; life in the black community; his reading.
       • "The Diaries and Writings of George A. Maston, Black Cit-
         izen of Lincoln, Nebraska 1901-1913," Lila Gravatt Scrimsher,
         ed. Nebraska History, v. 52, pp. 133-68, Summer, 1971.

1841. RUSSELL, Charles Russell, Baron (1832-1900)
       August 14-October 13, 1883

Travel diary; British judge and member of Parliament; by ship from England to America; sightseeing, chiefly on the West Coast; agreeable travelogue.
- Diary of a Visit to the United States of America in the Year 1883. New York: U.S. Catholic Historical Society, 1910.
  REVIEW: Book Review Digest 1910, p. 346.

1842. SPEAR, Willis (1862-1936)
August 2-September 24, 1883
Travel diary; wagon trip from New Chicago, Montana, to the Big Horn Mountains, of Wyoming; 350 miles of monotony, danger and hardship.
- "The Spears of Sheridan County," Annals of Wyoming, v. 14, pp. 98-127, April, 1942.

1843. TRAIL, Florence (1854-)
1. April 26-August 22, 1883; Travel diary; American on a European Grand Tour; sightseeing in London and environs; visiting art treasures in France, Italy and Germany; lists of sculpture and paintings viewed.
- My Journal in Foreign Lands. 2nd ed. New York: Putnam, 1885.

2. September 9-December 30, 1891; Travel diary; an American family sightseeing in France.
- Foreign Family Life in France in 1891. Boston: B. Humphries, 1944.

<u>1884</u>

1844. AH QUIN (1848-1914)
January 2-December 28, 1884
Business diary; Christianized immigrant from Canton; supervising laborers.
- "Rebuilding the California Southern Railroad: The Personal Account of a Chinese Labor Contractor, 1884," Andrew Griego, ed. Journal of San Diego History, v. 25, pp. 324-337, 1979.

1845. GORDON, Charles George (1833-85)
1. September 10-December 14, 1884; Military diary; commander of the besieged British Forces at Khartoum from his arrival to shortly before being overrun by the Mahdi's forces; details of military and diplomatic maneuvering; readable and immediate.
- The Journals of Major-General C. G. Gordon, C. B., at Khartoum. A. Egmont Hake, intro. Boston: Houghton Mifflin, 1885; reprinted New York: Negro Universities Press, 1969.

2. September 10-December 14, 1884; a "slightly abbreviated" edition; introduction provides a good background on Gordon and the disastrous siege with details of events occurring after Gordon's last entry.

• Khartoum Journal. Lord Elton, ed. London: Kimber,
1961.

1846. RIEL, Louis (1844-85)
Spiritual diary; half-breed Canadian rebel hanged for his part
in the Red River Rebellion; left a teaching post at a Montana Indian
school to return to Canada; filled with prayers; has little bearing on
the political situation.
• The Diaries of Louis Riel. Thomas Flanagan, ed. Edmonton: Hurtig, 1976.
REVIEW: Saturday Night, v. 92, p. 76, January, 1977.

1847. ROBERTS, May Bethia (1868-1954?)
May 17, 1884-December 11, 1888; gaps
Personal diary; life on a homestead in North Dakota; farm work;
visiting; classes at the University of North Dakota.
• "Diary of Miss May Bethia Roberts," in: Elizabeth Hampsten. To All Inquiring Friends: Letters, Diaries and Essays
in North Dakota. Grand Forks: University of North Dakota,
1979; pp. 253-62.

1848. STEWART, Helen Wiser (-1926)
June 4, 1884-January 15, 1900
Personal diary; widowed Lincoln County, Nevada, ranchowner's
letter journal was kept in account books; married her children's tutor.
• "Diary," in: Cathy Luchetti and Carol Olwell. Women of
the West. St. George, Utah: Antelope Island Press, 1982;
pp. 151-59.

1849. WALLBROOK, William (1864?-99)
August 24, 1884-January 9, 1899; scattered entries
Spiritual diary; minister praises the Lord for blessings re-
ceived; amounts of church collection plates recorded; striving for
self-improvement; exclamatory style.
• Diary of, and Poems By. College Point, N.Y.: A. K.
Schultz, 1900.

1850. WOODWARD, Mary Dodge (1826?-90)
January 1, 1884-December 31, 1888
Personal diary; widowed Wisconsin native moved with her
grown children to a farm in the Red River Valley of the Dakota Ter-
ritory; wheat growing was supervised by a son; farm life, blizzards;
receiving mail once a week; good description of life on a wheat farm;
weather conditions; pleasant reading.
• The Checkered Years. Mary Boynton Cowdrey, ed. Cald-
well, Ida.: Caxton Printers, 1937.
REVIEW: Mississippi Valley Historical Review, v. 24, p.
567, 1938.
(For comments on Woodward and her diary see: Elizabeth
Hampsten. Read This Only to Yourself. Bloomington:
Indiana University Press, 1982; pp. 227-32.)

1885

1851. ALLAN, Robert K. (1862?-1942)
        March 26-July 13, 1885
        Military diary; with the 90th Battalion, Co. C from Winnipeg;
hunting down rebels; the battle of Batoche.
        • "A Riel Rebellion Diary," Iris Allan, ed. Alberta Historical
        Review, v. 12, pp. 15-25, 1964.

1852. CARLINGFORD, Chichester Samuel Parkinson-Fortescue, Baron
        (1823-98)
        January 1-December 31, 1885
        Political diary; Irish Protestant landlord and member of Glad-
stone's cabinet; the fall of Khartoum, Russia's Central Asian policy
and Egyptian finance are the main topics.
        • Lord Carlingford's Journal: Reflections of a Cabinet Min-
        ister, 1885. A. B. Cooke and J. R. Vincent, eds. Oxford:
        Clarendon Press, 1971.

1853. EDISON, Thomas Alva (1847-1931)
        1. July 12-21, 1885; Personal diary; American inventor; ob-
servations in the form of short essays on movies, music, the inventor's lot, life after death, etc.; entertaining.
        • The Diary and Sundry Observations of Thomas Alva Edison.
        Dagobert D. Runes, ed. New York: Philosophical Library,
        1948.
            REVIEW: Book Review Digest 1948, p. 239.

        2. "Diary Excerpts," in: Philip Dunaway and Mel Evans,
eds. A Treasury of the World's Great Diaries. New York: Doubleday, 1957; pp. 481-83.

1854. HAMILTON, Laura (1864-98?)
        Personal diary; black Ohioan living in Alexandria, Virginia;
she is six months pregnant when the diary opens; birth of her baby,
housework and visiting.
        • "Diary February 26, 1885-February 3, 1886," in: Dorothy
        Sterling, ed. We Are Your Sisters: Black Women in the Nine-
        teenth Century. New York: Norton, 1984; pp. 472-79.

1855. KASSLER, E. S.
        July 7-August 22, 1885
        Travel diary; a hunting trip in the Bear River, Colorado,
area.
        • "A Trip to the Troublesome," Colorado Magazine, v. 33,
        pp. 67-73, January, 1958.

1856. LUCY, Sir Henry William ("M. P. Toby") (1845-1924)
        November 13, 1885-October 31, 1917; 1885-1917; 1890-1910;
        1910-1916
        Personal diary; long, detailed entries; British political and
social life.

• Diary of a Journalist. 3 vols. New York: Dutton, 1920–
23.
REVIEWS: Book Review Digest 1920, pp. 336-7; 1923, p. 314.

1857. ORLOV, Vasilii
December 20, 1885–March 18, 1886
Travel diary; Russian deacon on a mission up the Kuskokwim
River; suggestions for future outposts.
• Shalkop, Antoinette. "The Travel Journal of Vasilii Orlov,"
Pacific Northwest Quarterly, v. 68, pp. 131-40, July, 1977.

1858. TOWNLEY, Sidney Dean (1867-   )
October 1, 1885–June 17, 1890
Personal diary; native of rural Wisconsin received his BS and
MS; studied astronomy; classes; public events; restrained and stilted.
• Diary of a Student of the University of Wisconsin, 1886-1892.
Palo Alto: Stanford University, 1940?

1859. WESTBEECH, George (-1888)
March 20, 1885–April 16, 1888
Travel diary; exploration, trade and travel in what is today
Rhodesia and nearby regions.
• "Diary," in: Edward C. Tabler. Trade and Travel in Early
Barotseland. Berkeley: University of California Press, 1963;
pp. 25-101.

1860. WISTER, Owen (1860-1938)
1. July 2, 1885–July 17, 1895; gaps; Travel diaries; American
novelist wrote The Virginian; summer travel; gathering material for
his writing; relaxing, hunting; in Wyoming mostly but with visits to
Texas, Washington and California.
• Owen Wister Out West: His Journals and Letters. Fanny
Kemble Wister, ed. Chicago: University of Chicago Press,
1958.

2. January 1, 1914-1915; Personal diary; death of his cousin,
Dr. S. Weir Mitchell; writer's block; period of much personal distress;
journey to England.
• "The Diary of Owen Wister, 1914-1915," in: Fanny Kemble
Wister, ed. That I May Tell You: Journals and Letters of
the Owen Wister Family. Wayne, Pa.: Haverford House,
1979; pp. 229-68.

1886

1861. ABER, Martha Wilson McGregor (1861-1932)
June 9–September 4, 1886
Travel diary; journey with her husband and his relatives by
wagon from Aurora, Nebraska, to Wolf Creek Country, Wyoming; fragmentary notes.

● "Our Western Journey: Journal of Martha Wilson McGregor Aber," Clifford P. Westermeier, ed. Annals of Wyoming, v. 20, pp. 90-100, July, 1950.

1862. ASHBROOK, William Albert (1867-   )
December 24, 1886-December 31, 1934
Personal diary; editor and publisher of a Johnsontown, Ohio, newspaper; in the insurance business; family life, socializing; much concerned with his financial standing in comparison to other towns-people; somewhat patronizing big fish in a little pond; of genealogical interest.
● A Line a Day for Forty Odd Years, from the Diary of William A. Ashbrook. 3 vols. Johnstown, Ohio: Johnstown Independent, 1930-32.

1863. BROOKE, Edward Gant (1865-1907)
March 29-April 18, 1886
Travel diary; with a party of 22 adults and five children; from Virginia City, Montana, to the Yellowstone River; return to Bozeman after an Indian attack.
● The Adventure of E. G. Brooke on the Yellowstone in 1886, Virginia Lee Speck, ed. Montana Magazine of History, pp. 49-56, January, 1951.

1864. BROWN, William Harvey
September 21-December 22, 1886
Personal diary; University of Kansas student accompanied William T. Hornaday, taxidermist of the Smithsonian Institution, to Montana to collect buffalo bones and remains; "skinning and skeleton-izing."
● "Buffalo Hunting in Montana in 1886: The Diary of W. H. Brown," John M. Peterson, ed. Montana: Magazine of Western History, v. 31, pp. 2-13, pp. 2-13, October, 1981.

1865. GIBSON, Walter Murray (1822-88)
January 1, 1886-December 31, 1887
Personal diary; American adventurer; elected to the Hawaiian legislature; supporter of planters and businessmen; became premier in 1882; fragmentary notes.
● The Diaries of Walter Murray Gibson, 1886, 1887. Jacob Adler and Gwynn Barrett, eds. Honolulu: University Press of Hawaii, 1973.
REVIEW: Book Review Digest 1974, p. 430.

1866. KELLOGG, David Sherwood (1847-1909)
January 2, 1886-August 16, 1909; gaps
Personal diary; Vermonter practiced in Plattsburg, New York; his rounds; family life with wife and five children and three nieces and nephews they gave a home to; humorous man of wide interests; literature, collecting Indian relics; geology; medic for the Plattsburgh Barracks during the Spanish-American War; acquainted with William

Dean Howells who vacationed in the town; entertaining picture of small town life.

- A Doctor at All Hours: The Private Journal of a Small-town Doctor's Varied Life, 1886-1909. Allan S. Everest, ed. Brattleboro, Vt.: Stephen Greene Press, 1970.

1867. OGDEN, Anna Harder (1867-1960)
December 4, 1886-September 4, 1896; gaps
Personal diary; German immigrant in California worked at a variety of jobs; her reading; learning telegraphy.

- "Diary," in: Cathy Luchetti and Carol Olwell. Women of the West. St. George, Utah: Antelope Island Press, 1982; pp. 193-98.

1868. WELLS, Ida Bell (1862-1929)
January 5-July 16, 1886
Personal diary; black public school teacher in Memphis, Tennessee; writing for black newspapers; courting; visit to San Francisco; a tart pen wielded by a strong character.

- "Diary," in: Dorothy Sterling, ed. We Are Your Sisters: Black Women in the Nineteenth Century. New York: Norton, 1984; pp. 479-95.

1869. WOOD, Leonard (1860-1927)
May 4-September 8, 1886
Military diary; American army officer and later a Rough Rider; expedition to capture the Apaches with Geronimo ranged through Arizona and the Mexican province of Sonora; heat, tarantula bite and killing conditions; ended in Geronimo's surrender.

- Chasing Geronimo: The Journal of Leonard Wood, May-September, 1886. Jack C. Lane, ed. Albuquerque: University of New Mexico Press, 1970.

1887

1870. BEADLE, Charles
March 21-June 18, 1887
Travel diary; well-to-do Briton visited Philadelphia and Baltimore; across the country to San Francisco and stops in Canada; observations on Chinese, Blacks, baseball ("altogether a good game"); detailed observations by a likeable chap.

- A Trip to the United States in 1887. London: Prv. ptd., 1887.

1871. CLIFFORD, Hugh (1867?-   )
Diplomatic diary; Briton in the Straits Civil Service was sent to negotiate a treaty between the ruler of Pahang and the British in Singapore; information on mining concessions, native people; factual, unemotional account by a conscientious civil servant.

- Journal of a Mission to Pahang January 15 to April 22, 1887.

Peter Wicks, intro. Honolulu: University of Hawaii, Southeast
Asian Studies Program, 1978.
REVIEW: Pacific Affairs, v. 51, pp. 720, Winter, 1978-79.

1872. GISSING, George (1857-1903) [B291]
December 27, 1887-November 1, 1902
Personal/literary diary; English novelist; his reading; a record
of his work; negotiating with publishers; writer's block; "a wasted
day"; trips abroad to Rome and Paris; life in lodgings and its vicis-
situdes.
• London and the Life of Literature in Late Victorian England:
The Diary of George Gissing, Novelist. Pierre Coustillas, ed.
Lewisburg, Pa.: Bucknell University Press, 1978.

1873. JEPHSON, Arthur Jermy Mounteney (1858-1908)
January 20, 1887-October 17, 1889
Expedition diary; candid and probably the fullest account of
the expedition; an uncomplimentary portrait of African "expert" Henry
Morton Stanley (q.v.); from the Congo's mouth east to Zanzibar;
Emin Pasha had reservations about being "relieved."
• The Diary of A. J. Mounteney Jephson: Emin Pasha Relief
Expedition 1887-1889. Dorothy Middleton, ed. London: Pub-
lished for the Hakluyt Society by Cambridge University Press,
1969.
REVIEW: Book Review Digest 1969, p. 665.

1874. LESLIE, Hyde (1852-   )
April 5-December 11, 1887
Personal diary; farmhand worked for a neighbor; chores; some
interesting archaic and regional words.
• "The Diary of Hyde Leslie 1887 Plymouth Notch, Vermont,"
in: Blanche Brown Bryant and Gertrude Elaine Baker, eds.
The Diaries of Sally and Pamela Brown 1832-1838. Springfield,
Vt.: William L. Bryant Foundation, 1970; pp. 95-169.

1875. RENARD, Jules (1864-1910)
August, 1887-April, 1910
Literary diary; French playwright and founder of Mercure de
France; some personal notes; his work and relations with other French
writers; short word sketches; aphorisms.
• Journal. Louise Bogan and Elizabeth Roget, eds. New
York: Braziller, 1964.
REVIEW: Book Review Digest 1964, pp. 980-81.

1888

1876. CANNON, George Q. (1827-1901)
September 17-December 12, 1888
Prison diary; in a Utah penitentiary for polygamy; treated
more as a guest than a prisoner; record of visitors.

• "The Prison Diary of a Mormon Apostle," M. Hamlin Cannon, ed. Pacific Historical Review, v. 16, pp. 393-409, 1947.

1877.   CUYLER, Telamon Cruger (1873-1951)
        October 23-31, 1888
        Travel diary; teenage boy journeyed in luxury in a private
railroad car from Chattanooga with a large party; exuberant.
        • "Telamon Cuyler's Diary: To Texas in 1888," John Hammond Moore, ed. Southwestern Historical Quarterly, v. 70, pp. 474-88, January, 1967.

1878.   MOORE, Frank Lincoln (1866-1935)
        September 10, 1888-October 7, 1890; gaps
        Personal diary; Michigander and Congregational minister sent
to Wyoming to establish Sunday schools; interspersed with letters to
his family and fiancee; plagued by poor health; fair picture of early
statehood and missionary efforts.
        • Souls and Saddlebags, The Diaries and Correspondence of
Frank L. Moore, Western Missionary, 1888-1896. Austin L.
Moore, ed. Denver: Big Mountain Press, 1962.

1879.   PARRISH, Helen (1859-1942)
        July 3, 1888-
        Personal diary; philanthropist rented living quarters to blacks;
followed the example of British social reformer Octavia Hill.
        • "Reform and Uplift Among Philadelphia Negroes: The Diary
of Helen Parrish, 1888," Pennsylvania Magazine of History and
Biography, v. 94, pp. 496-517, October, 1970.

1880.   PEABODY, Marian Lawrence (1875-   )
        November 17, 1888-May 8, 1906
        Personal diary; excerpts; daughter of the Episcopal bishop of
Massachusetts; life in Cambridge and summers at Nahant in a large,
loving family; trip to Europe; ends with her marriage to a cousin;
enchanting.
        • To Be Young Was Very Heaven. Boston: Houghton Mifflin,
1967.

1881.   PERKINS, Daniel M. (1844-1904)
        January 4-December 25, 1888
        Personal diary; excerpts; farm life, weather and social visits.
        • Sherman, Rexford B. "One Year on a New Hampshire
Farm," Historical New Hampshire, v. 32, pp. 1-17, 1977.

1882.   WOODMAN, Abby Johnson (1828-   )
        April 5-May 14, 1888
        Travel diary; picturesque tourist notes.
        • Picturesque Alaska: A Journal of a Tour Among the Mountains, Seas and Islands of the Northwest From San Francisco
to Sitka. Boston: Houghton Mifflin, 1889.

1889

1883. BOND, J. H.
August 26-October 8, 1889
Travel diary; family returned to Missouri by wagon after two
years homesteading in the San Luis Valley, Colorado.
  • "Old Trails in Reverse," I. W. Bond, comp. Colorado Mag-
  azine, v. 32, pp. 225-33, July, 1955.

1884. CARROLL, L. F.
April 9-May 6, 1889
Personal diary; terse account of the race for a land claim.
  • "The Diary of an Eighty-niner," Chronicles of Oklahoma,
  v. 15, pp. 66-69, 1937.

1885. FRASER, Mary Crawford (1851-1922)
April, 1889-April, 1894
Personal letter/diary; sister of writer Francis Marion Crawford;
cosmopolitan wife of British legation head to Japan; interesting trave-
logue on life in Japan; an abridgement of the 1899 London edition
titled A Diplomatist's Wife in Japan: Letters From Home to Home.
  • A Diplomat's Wife in Japan: Sketches at the Turn of the
  Century. Hugh Cortazzi, ed. New York: Weatherhill, 1982.

1886. GIDE, Andre Paul Guilaume (1869-1951)
Autumn, 1889-June 10, 1949
Personal and literary diary; early entries are concerned with
himself and his thoughts; later his reading, literary output and interest in others is evident; though financially independent, he was aware
of the plight of those less fortunate; often contradictory; leading figures of a half century of French literary and political life appear;
lively, interesting.
  • The Journals of Andre Gide. Justin O'Brien, trans.   4
  vols. New York: Knopf, 1947-51; abridged edition, New
  York: Vintage Books, 1956.

1887. GRIFFIN, Charles Eldridge (1859-1914)
April 29-
Business diary; family circus traveled by rail through Ohio,
Pennsylvania, New York and New Jersey; hoodlums, weather and the
box office take.
  • "'Bob' Hunting's Great Show": The Diary of a Pennsyl-
  vania Circus," H. Roger Grant, ed. Western Pennsylvania
  Historical Magazine, v. 58, pp. 95-108, January, 1975.

1888. GUNN, Alexander (1837-1901)
November 12, 1889-November 30, 1900
Personal diary; German-born inhabitant of Zoar, Ohio, community; travels to Italy, Egypt and England; introspective; notes on
his mostly male companions; nostalgia for his youth; many musical
evenings with friends.

• The Hermitage-Zoar Note-book and Journal of Travel.
New York: De Vinne Press, 1902.

1889. JAMES, Alice (1848-92) [B292]
        1. May 31, 1889-March 4, 1892; Personal diary; sister of
American novelist Henry James (q.v.); unexpurgated text is here
persented for the first time; wry, spinsterish comments on others'
marital states; babies; biting words on newspaper stories; ends with
her death from breast cancer.
        • The Diary of Alice James. Leon Edel, ed. New York:
        Dodd, Mead, 1964.
        REVIEW: Book Review Digest 1964, pp. 617-18; 1965; pp. 633.

        2. "Diary Excerpts," in: Mary Jane Moffat and Charlotte
Painter, eds. Revelations: Diaries of Women. New York: Random
House, 1974; pp. 192-205.

1890. LECHAPTOIS, Father Adolphe
        May 29, 1889-June 30, 1891
        Missionary diary; White Fathers ministered to the Yao of Mal-
awi; marches throughout the territory; tribal politics.
        • "Mponda Mission Diary, 1889-1891," I. Linden, trans. and
        ed. International Journal of African Historical Studies, v. 7,
        pp. 272-303; 493-515, 688-728, 1974; v. 8, pp. 111-35, 1975.

1891. LOTI, Pierre (1850-1923)
        May 26-May 4, 1889
        Personal diary; French novelist was a member of a diplomatic
mission to Fez, Morocco.
        • "Diary Excerpts," in: Philip Dunaway and Mel Evans, eds.
        A Treasury of the World's Great Diaries. New York: Double-
        day, 1957; pp. 402-08.

1892. LUGARD, Frederick John Dealtry, Baron (1858-1945)
        November 4, 1889-April 17, 1895; March 13-June 6, 1898
        Personal diary; Indian-born British career military man sought
adventure in Africa after a broken love affair; arrival; in Uganda and
Mombasa; wars, negotiations, treaties; lengthy, detailed entries; dealings with slave traders, missionaries and other Europeans.
        • The Diaries of Lord Lugard. Margery Perham and Mary
        Bull, eds. Evanston, Ill.: Northwestern University Press,
        1959-63.
        REVIEW: Book Review Digest 1961, pp. 881-82.

1893. LUKENS, Matilda Barns
        June 16-30, 1889
        Travel diary; by steamer from Tacoma and return; tourist
notes.
        • The Inland Passage, A Journal of a Trip to Alaska. 1889;
        microfiche reprint, Lost Cause Press, 1977.

1890

1894. BERRY, Katherine Fiske (1877-   )
        August 31, 1890-November 13, 1893
        Personal diary; daughter of missionary parents stationed in
Japan; excerpts interleaved with letters to family at home in the U.S.;
an earthquake; school, childhood escapades.
        • Katie-san: From Maine Pastures to Japan Shores. Cam-
        bridge, Mass.: Dresser, Chapman and Grimes, 1962.

1895. CONRAD, Joseph (1857-1924) [B292]
        June 13-August 1, 1890
        Travel diary; Polish-born novelist in Africa; from Matadi to
Kinshasa overland; weather, scenery.
        • Congo Diary and Other Uncollected Pieces. Zdzislaw Najder,
        ed. New York: Doubleday, 1978; pp. 7-16.

1896. GARNETT, Oliver Rayne (1871-1958)
        1890-1906
        Personal diary; extracts; marriage and breakdown of Ford by
a friend.
        • Moser, Thomas C. "From Oliver Garnett's Diary: Impres-
        sions of Ford Madox Ford and His Friends, 1890-1906," Texas
        Studies in Literature and Language, v. 16, p. 511-33, Fall,
        1974.

1897. HEYWOOD, Daniel E.
        October 11-December 31, 1890
        Camp diary; trapping and hunting in the Maine woods; detailed
descriptions of stalking; photographs and their development under
primitive conditions.
        • Diary of Daniel E. Heywood, A Parmachence Guide at Camp
        Cariboo, Parmachence Lake, Oxford County, Maine, Fall of
        1890. Bristol, N. H.: R. W. Musgrove, 1891.

1898. HOGG, Margaret Alice Muir (-1943)
        September 9, 1890-
        Personal diary; life in Manhattan, Kansas; homesick for Eng-
land; a trip to a Texas ranch.
        • "A British Bride in Manhattan, 1890-1891: The Journal of
        Mrs. Stuart James Hogg," Louise Barry, ed. Kansas Histor-
        ical Quarterly, v. 19, pp. 269-86, August, 1951.

1899. JACKSON, Nannie Stillwell (1854-   )
        June 11, 1890-April 15, 1891
        Personal diary; farmwife of Desha County, Arkansas, notes
the tedium and narrowness of her life; struggling against the ele-
ments and falling cotton prices to make a crop; bouts of "fever"; relations with black people of the community; birth of a baby; close
circle of women friends supported her in an unromantic marriage.

• Vinegar Pie and Chicken Bread: A Woman's Diary of Life
in the Rural South, 1890-1891. Margaret Jones Bolsterli, ed.
Fayetteville: University of Arkansas Press, 1982.

1900. STEVENSON, Fanny (1840-1914)
        September 30, 1890-July 27, 1893
        Personal diary; wife of writer Robert Louis Stevenson (q.v.);
settled in Samoa for his health; daily life; an earthquake; RLS worked
on David Balfour; clashes of culture with the Samoans; humorous,
acute observer.
        • Our Samoan Adventure: With a Three-year Diary of Mrs.
        Stevenson. Charles Neider, ed. New York: Harper, 1955.

1901. STURT, George ("George Bourne") (1863-1927) [B292]
        October 21, 1890-January 25, 1927
        Personal/literary diary; minor English writer ran a wheelwright
shop in Surrey; notes on his reading; writing projects; social condition of the people he dealt with, especially the lower classes; manifests a provincial attitude in many passages despite his wide reading;
plagued by ill health; much on English rural life.
        • The Journals of George Sturt, 1890-1927: A Selection. E.
        D. Mackerness, ed. London: Cambridge University Press,
        1967.
            REVIEW: Book Review Digest 1968, p. 1291.

1902. WILSON, Elizabeth Ruffner, 1810-
        1890's
        Personal diary; extracts.
        • Trotter, Margaret G. "A Glimpse of Charleston in the
        1890s From a Contemporary Diary," West Virginia History,
        v. 35, pp. 131-44, January, 1974.

1903. WRIGHT, Louisa Stephens (1871-)
        April 12, 1890-May 29, 1891
        Travel diary; young American girl on a trip around the world
with her family; longing for a sweetheart left behind; by ship to Ireland and England; sightseeing in major European cities; lengthy stay
in Egypt and a romantic interlude; India, China, Japan; good picture
of the activities and attitudes of an upper class family of the gilded
age.
        • Golden Adventure: A Diary of Long Ago. Pasadena, Cal.:
        San Pasqual Books, 1941.

                              1891

1904. CRAWFORD, Florence (-1926)
        June 19, 1891-February 29, 1892
        Personal diaries; engaged couple's entries are interleaved; she
was the daughter of Kansas governor Samuel J. Crawford; he was a

journalist working in New York, Boston and Washington; longing for each other; a trip to Nantucket with her family.
- "The Private Journals of Florence Crawford and Arthur Capper, 1891-1892," Homer E. Socolofsky, ed. Kansas Historical Quarterly, v. 30, pp. 15-61, Spring, 1964; pp. 163-208, Summer, 1964.

1905. HAZELRIGG, Charles (1856-)
July 5, 1891-September 10, 1893
Personal diary; Disciples of Christ preacher journeyed to Oklahoma to look over the country; settled there with his wife and child; preaching and baptizing; good account of social conditions in the area.
- "The Diary of Charles Hazelrigg," Angie Debo, ed. Chronicles of Oklahoma, v. 25, pp. 229-70, 1947.

1906. JACKSON, Sheldon
May 19-October 3, 1891
Personal diary; missionary went to Siberia to buy reindeer from the natives; he transported them to Alaska where they were used by the Eskimos for food; notes on weather, geology and education of Eskimos; anthropology.
- "Exploring for Reindeer in Siberia Being the Journal of the Cruise of the U.S. Revenue Steamer Bear," Charles A. Anderson, ed. Presbyterian Historical Society Journal, v. 31, pp. 1-24, March, 1953; pp. 87-112, June, 1953.

1907. PAGE, Thomas Nelson
April 11-17, 1891
Personal diary; lawyer's visit to Kentucky after many years absence.
- "The Kentucky Journal of Thomas Nelson Page," Harriet R. Holman, ed. Kentucky Historical Society Register, v. 68, pp. 1-16, January, 1970.

1908. PEABODY, Josephine Preston (1874-1922)
May, 1891-December, 1915
Personal/literary diary; American poet, playwright; taught at Harvard; family life; her work; bouts with "lockjaw of the mind"; interesting portrait of a writer who worked in spurts of inspiration.
- Diary and Letters of Josephine Preston Peabody. Christina Hopkinson Baker, ed. New York: Houghton Mifflin, 1925.
    REVIEWS: Book Review Digest 1925, p. 547; 1926, p. 556-57.

1909. PEARY, Josephine Diebitsch (1863-1925)
June 24, 1891-August 20, 1892
Personal diary; wife of the American Polar explorer; accompanied her husband on the North Greenland Expedition; life at McCormick Bay between the Arctic Circle and the North Pole in a community of 350 Eskimos; self-conscious Lady Bountiful attitude;

condescending; refers to her husband as "Mr. Peary" throughout; nevertheless, very descriptive.
- My Arctic Journal: A Year Among the Ice-fields and Es-kimos. With an Account of the Great White Journey Across Greenland by Robert E. Peary. New York: Contemporary Publishing Co., 1893.

1892

1910. BROWN, Josephine Edith (1878-1964)
September 12, 1892-February 16, 1901
Personal diary; school; fashion and dress; college at Iowa State in Ames.
- "Diary of an Iowa Farm Girl: Josephine Edith Brown, 1892-1901," Vivian C. Hopkins, ed. Annals of Iowa, v. 42, pp. 126-46, Fall, 1973.

1911. MODERSOHN-BECKER, Paula (1876-1907)
1. October 21, 1892-July 20, 1906; gaps; Personal diary; North German Expressionist painter; study in Paris after her mar-riage; thoughts on her work and that of other artists; introspective; died of an embolism a few days after the birth of her child; based on the 1920 German edition.
- The Letters and Journals of Paul Modersohn-Becker. J. Diane Radycki, trans. Metuchen, N.J.: Scarecrow, 1980.

2. September 8, 1895-July 20, 1906; Personal diary; journal entries make up a smaller part of the text than the letters; a new translation of the 1979 German edition with some additional material; marriage to widowed painter Otto Modersohn; friend and correspon-dent of Rainer Maria Rilke; trips to Paris; art studies and her work; disintegration of the marriage when she sought greater artistic and personal freedom; reconciliation and pregnancy.
- Paula Modersohn-Becker: The Letters and Journals. Gun-ter Busch and Liselotte von Reinken, eds. Arthur S. Wen-singer and Carole Clew Hoey, trans. New York: Taplinger, 1984.
   REVIEW: Library Journal v. 109, p. 370, February 15, 1984.

1912. MOORE, Ealy (1866-)
April 20, 1892-[no closing date]
Trail diary; trail boss of a cattle drive; from the XIT ranch in Texas to Montana; expenses and weather.
- "A Log of the Montana Trail as Kept by Ealy Moore," J. Evetts Haley, ed. Panhandle Plains Historical Review, v. 5, pp. 44-56, 1932.

1913. SLEMMONS, John W. (1841-1901)
January 2-December, 1892

Personal diary; prosperous Johnson County, Iowa, farmer; farm chores; prices paid; earnings for his crops.
- "'Terrace Mount Farm': The 1892 Diary of John W. Slemmons," H. Roger Grant, ed. Annals of Iowa, v. 45, pp. 620-44, Spring, 1981.

1914. TAYLOR, Annie R.
September 2, 1892-April 15, 1893
Travel diary; intrepid Englishwoman went from northern China through Tibet and return; trouble with guides, brigands and officials; interesting.
- Adventures in Tibet: Including the Diary of Miss Annie R. Taylor's Remarkable Journey From Tau-Chau to Ta-Chien-Lu Through the Heart of the "Forbidden Land." Chicago: Student Missionary Campaign Library, 1901.

1893

1915. BRYUSOV, Valerii (1873-1924)
January 2, 1893-1905; gaps
Personal diary; Russian Symbolist poet, editor and translator; abridged translation of the 1927 Moscow edition.
- The Diary of Valery Bryusov (1893-1905) with Reminiscences by V. F. Khodasevich and Marina Tsvetaeva. Joan Delaney Grossman, ed. and trans. Berkeley: University of California Press, 1980.
    REVIEWS: Library Journal, v. 105, p. 1735, September 1, 1980. World Literature Today, v. 55, p. 495, Summer, 1981.

1916. DAWES, Charles Gates (1865-1951) [B309]
January 1, 1893-October 6, 1912; later entries are fragmentary
Political diary; American financier and diplomat; the Panic of 1893; move to Chicago; work in the McKinley (q.v.) campaign; became Comptroller of the Currency; the Spanish-American War; McKinley's assassination; some family notes.
- A Journal of the McKinley Years. Bascom N. Timmons, ed. Chicago: Lakeside Press, 1950.
    REVIEW: Book Review Digest 1951, p. 226.

1917. LENERU, Marie (1875-1918)
September 5, 1893-August 1, 1918; some years have only two or three entries.
Personal diary; young Parisienne began a diary at age ten at her mother's insistence; early entries to 1893 are excerpted in the introduction; by 1893 she was deafened and partially blind as a result of illness; her first play Les Affranchis won an award from La Vie Heureuse in 1908 but was not produced till 1911 at the Odéon; thought of herself as a peer of Amiel (q.v.) and Maria Bashkirtseff (q.v.) in diary writing; peppered with aphorisms ("suicides are

people in great hurry to arrive"), French puns; despair and humor.

> • Journal of Marie Leneru. William Aspenwall Bradley, trans.
> New York: Macmillan, 1923.
> REVIEW: Book Review Digest 1923, p. 299.

1918. "MORLEY, Helena" (Mme. Alice Dayrell Brant) (1881-   )
January 5, 1893-December 31, 1895
Personal diary; Brazilian girl with an English father lived in
Diamantina, a mining town; unpretentious, straightforward account of
her life from ages 12 to 15; refreshing.

> • The Diary of Helena Morley. Elizabeth Bishop, trans. New
> York: Farrar, Straus, 1957.
> REVIEW: Book Review Digest 1958, pp. 776-77.

1919. SLOANE, Florence Adele (1873-1960)
January 1, 1893-August 12, 1896
Personal diary; wealthy heiress and descendant of Commodore
Vanderbilt married well; courtship, marriage, birth and death of her
first child told against a background of travel, money and privilege;
first hand picture of the Four Hundred; unmarred by snobbishness or
envy.

> • Maverick in Mauve: The Diary of a Romantic Age. New
> York: Doubleday, 1983.

1920. WOOD, Anna S. Prouty (1844-1926)
September 1-November 12, 1893
Travel diary; diarist and her son went to obtain a section of
land; by covered wagon from Denver; well-written, detailed and very
interesting.

> • "The Diary of Mrs. Anna S. Wood: Trip to the Opening
> of the Cherokee Outlet in 1893," H. D. Ragland, ed. Chron-
> icles of Oklahoma, v. 50, pp. 307-25, Autumn, 1972.

1921. WOOD, Erskine
September 19-December 8, 1893
Personal diary; tribal life, hunting, horse racing; his mentor
was the Nez Perce chief; photography with an early camera.

> • "Diary of a Fourteen Year Old Boy's Days with Chief Jo-
> seph," Oregon Historical Quarterly, v. 51, pp. 71-94, June,
> 1950; reprinted as Days with Chief Joseph: Diary, Recollec-
> tions and Photos. Portland: Oregon Historical Society, 1970.

1894

1922. ENGLISH, James Douglass (1858-1929)
June 6-August 24, 1894
Travel diary; with a companion by railroad, bike, carriage and
steam line to the West Coast; on to Hawaii and northern Mexico; very
detailed and well written.

- To the West in 1894: Travel Journal of Dr. James Douglas
English of Worthington, Indiana. (Indiana Historical Society
Publications v. 25, no. 3) Indianapolis: Indiana Historical
Society, 1977.

1923. FOX, Ruth May (1853-1958)
December 29, 1894-November 2, 1895
Personal diary; Mormon wife and mother; prominent joiner
active in politics for the diary period in order to further woman suf-
ferage.
- "'I Care Nothing for Politics': Ruth May Fox, Forgotten
Suffragist," Linda Thatcher, ed. Utah Historical Quarterly,
v. 49, pp. 239-53, Summer, 1981.

1924. HODGKIN, Jonathan Edward (1875-1952)
March 24-April 9, 1894
Travel diary; young Englishman went to South Africa by sea
for his health; tourist notes.
- "Jonathan Edward Hodgkin's Diary, 1894," Africana Notes
and News, v. 19, pp. 102-08, 1970.

1925. LONDON, Jack (1876-1916)
April 6-May 18, 1894
Travel diary; American novelist and correspondent; from Oak-
land, California, by train with Kelly's Industrial Army; to Omaha;
halted at the Missouri River; contemporary photos.
- "Tramping with Kelly Through Iowa: A Jack London Diary,"
Palimpsest, v. 7, pp. 129-58, May, 1926.

1926. PALEOLOGUE, Georges Maurice (1859-1944)
October 12, 1894-September 15, 1899
Personal diary; Frenchman assigned to the ministry of Foreign
Affairs and involved in the Dreyfus case; other political events also
noted.
- An Intimate Journal of the Dreyfus Case. Eric Mosbacher,
trans. New York: Criterion Books, 1957; reprinted Westport,
Conn.: Greenwood Press, 1975.

1927. WILDER, Laura Ingalls (1867-1957)
July 17-August 30, 1894
Travel diary; American author of children's books, Little House
on the Prairie, etc.; by wagon through Nebraska and Kansas to a
farm in Mansfield.
- On the Way Home: The Diary of a Trip from South Dakota
to Mansfield, Missouri in 1894. New York: Harper and Row,
1962.

1895

1928. ANONYMOUS (Japanese woman, 1866-1900)
1895-1900

Personal diary; 29-year-old woman marries a widower by arrangement; birth and death of their child; from a translation by Lafcadio Hearn.
- "Diary Excerpts," Moffat, Mary Jane and Charlotte Painter, eds. Revelations: Diaries of Women. New York: Random House, 1974; pp. 163-77.

1929. BOURKE, John Gregory (1846-   )
June 29, 1895; February 22-23, 1896
Personal diary; a boat trip and a sleigh ride.
- "Two Excursions on Lake Champlain in the 1890's: Excerpts From the Diaries of Captain John G. Bourke," Vermont History, v. 39, pp. 62-71, Winter, 1971.

1930. HERZL, Theodor (1860-1904)
1. May, 1895-May 16, 1904; Personal diary; Viennese Jew and founder of Zionism; feuilletonist and playwright; this edition "contains ... every word Herzl entered"; letters to many different people transcribed; notes for writing projects; laid down principles for the Zionist state in the manner of More's Utopia.
- The Complete Diaries of Theodor Herzl. Raphael Patai, ed. Harry Zohn, trans. 5 vols. New York: Herzl Press and Thomas Yoseloff, 1960.

2. June, 1895-May 13, 1904; Personal diary; promulgated the idea of a separate Jewish state while writing for a Vienna newspaper; work in Paris; publication of The Jewish State; travels; First Zionist Congress; dealings with prominent politicians in Europe and the East; portrait of an idea whose time has come.
- Diaries. Marvin Lowenthal, ed. and trans. New York: Dial, 1956.
  REVIEW: Book Review Digest 1956, p. 434.

1931. JOHN XXIII, Pope (1881-1963) (Angelo Giuseppe Roncalli)
1895-1963
Spiritual diary; seminary life in Rome and Bergmo; ordination; Papal representative in Bulgaria, Turkey and Greece; Cardinal of Venice; his year as pope.
- Journal of a Soul. Dorothy White, trans. New York: McGraw-Hill, 1964; rev. ed. Garden City, N.Y.: Image Books, 1980.
  REVIEW: Book Review Digest 1965, p. 644.

1932. LYTTON, Edith Bulwer-Lytton (1841-1936)
October, 1895-August 27, 1899
Personal diary; lady-in-waiting to Queens Victoria and Alexandra; attended Victoria at Balmoral, Windsor; useful for glimpses of English court life.
- Lady Lytton's Court Diary, 1895-1899. Mary Lutyens, ed. London: Hart-Davis, 1961.

1896

1933. AMERY, Leopold Stennett (1873-1955) [C2]
December 17, 1896-June 5, 1919; gaps in the diary entries are
filled by extracts from his correspondence.
Diplomatic diary; secretary to the War Cabinet, 1917-18; British cabinet minister 1923-29; leading correspondent for the London
Times and member of Parliament for 35 years; Boer War service; active duty 1915-16; in the governments of Bonar Law and Baldwin;
mostly politics with a few family notes; one of the most complete
records by a highly ranked figure for the period.
   • The Leo Amery Diaries. John Barnes and David Nicholson,
   eds. London: Hutchinson, 1979.

1934. BENNETT, Arnold (1867-1931) [B294]
1. May 15, 1896-September 25, 1929; English novelist and
dramatist.
   • The Journals. Frank Swinnerton, ed. London: Penguin
   Books, 1954.

2. Travel diary; notes on sights; his reading; working on
Clayhanger and several articles; news of the death of Edward VII.
   • Florentine Journal, 1st April-25th May 1910. Dorothy Ches-
   ton Bennett, ed. London: Chatto and Windus, 1967.

3. January 1-December 12, 1929; Personal diary; a year's
adventures in Paris, Italy and London; musings on his reading, people he meets, scenes he witnessed or is told of; entertaining.
   • Journal of Things New and Old. New York: Doran, 1930.
   REVIEW: Book Review Digest 1930, p. 77.

4. "Diary Excerpts," in: Philip Dunaway and Mel Evans,
eds. A Treasury of the World's Great Diaries. New York: Doubleday, 1957; pp. 484-99.

1935. CHITTENDEN, Hiram Martin (1858-1917)
December 9, 1896-January 8, 1897; April 29-May 17, 1897;
August 2-September 11, 1897
Personal diary; trip to dams in the West to see irrigation
projects; notes on travel.
   • H. M. Chittenden: A Western Epic. Bruce Le Roy, ed.
   Tacoma: Washington State Historical Society, 1961.

1936. HOPPIN, Benjamin (1851-1923)
July 15-September 26, 1896
Expedition diary; New Haven, Connecticut, resident and min-
erologist; objective was the recovery of a known meteorite; sailed up
the west coast of Greenland and through northern Baffin Bay aboard
SS Hope, a three masted steamer of 350 tons; notes on findings,
weather.
   • A Diary Kept While with the Peary Arctic Expedition of
   1896. New Haven, Conn.: n.p., 1897?

1937. STRINDBERG, August (1849-1912)
       May 31, 1900-July 11, 1908
       Personal diary; Swedish playwright and novelist; pseudosci-
entific jottings in early entries give way to more prosaic notes on
his romance with actress Bosse who became his third wife; the marriage was eventually dissolved; overwrought, hysterical.
       • From an Occult Diary: Marriage with Harriet Bosse. Tor-
       sten Eklund, ed. Mary Sandbach, trans. London: Secker
       and Warburg, 1965.

1938. VAN BUSKIRK, Philip Clayton
       August 9-23, 1896
       Travel diary; retired sailor on a wife hunting expedition to
Alaska; interesting descriptions of Wrangell and Indians.
       • Monroe, Robert D. "An Excursion to Wrangell, 1896,"
       Pacific Northwest Quarterly, v. 50, pp. 48-52, January, 1959.

                              1897

1939. HARRISON, Thomas Skelton (1837-1919)
       October 28, 1897-March 14, 1899
       Diplomatic diary; Philadelphian was Consul-General in Cairo;
active in social life of the international set; received by the Khedive;
visit of the King of Siam; attended an Arab wedding; comments on
food, guests, his work; some interesting passages.
       • The Homely Diary of a Diplomat in the East, 1897-1899.
       Boston: Houghton Mifflin, 1917.

1940. KLEE, Paul (1879-1940)
       1. November 10, 1897-December 16, 1918; Personal diary;
Swiss modernist painter; his studies; poetry, musings, work; in Italy,
Munich and Tunisia; drafted into the German Army.
       • The Diaries of Paul Klee, 1898-1918. Felix Klee, ed.
       Berkeley: University of California Press, 1964.
          REVIEW: Book Review Digest 1965, pp. 697-98.

       2. April 15-19, 1914; Travel diary; journey with August
Macke and Louis Moilliet to Tunis to paint; many sketches and watercolors.
       • "Diary of Trip to Tunisia," in: August Macke. Tunisian
       Watercolors and Drawings. New York: Abrams, 1969; pp.
       25-85.

1941. POSEY, Alexander Lawrence (1873-1908)
       Personal diary; half Creek Indian and poet; employed as super-
intendent of a Creek orphanage; his reading, teaching, and literary
work; social life; well written.
       • "The Journal of Alexander Lawrence Posey: January 1 to
       September 4, 1897," Edward Everett Dale, ed. Chronicles of
       Oklahoma, v. 45, pp. 393-432, Winter, 1967-68.

1942. SLAYDEN, Ellen Maury (1860-1926)
        January, 1897-March 4, 1919; gaps
        Personal diary; kept at the request of her husband, a Con-
gressman for San Antonio, Texas, for 21 years; native of Charlottesville, Virginia; well-read; newspaper contributor; life in Washington;
visits home; poised, elegant, witty woman not above skewering those
she dislikes or distrusts; excellent.
        • Washington Wife, Journal of Ellen Maury Slaydon from 1897-
        1919. Walter Prescott Webb, ed. New York: Harper, 1962.

1943. WELLS, E. Hazard (1860?-1940)
        August 13, 1897-January 24, 1898
        Travel diary; experienced reporter went to Alaska to report
on conditions; articles and diary entries are reprinted together; many
of the columns were polished transcriptions of diary notes; photos
by the diarist.
        • Magnificence and Misery: A Firsthand Account of the 1897
        Klondike Gold Rush. Randall M. Dodd, ed. New York:
        Doubleday, 1984.
                REVIEWS: Wall Street Journal, p. 24, May 21, 1984. Li-
                brary Journal, v. 110, p. 1325, July, 1984.

                              1898

1944. GARLAND, Hamlin (1860-1940)
        1. January 1, 1898-March, 1940; Personal and literary diary;
American regional novelist; the editor has arranged the entries by
subject rather than chronologically; entries were used as the basis
for much of his fiction; family and literary life; disappointed by his
lack of financial success; morose.
        • Hamlin Garland's Diaries. Donald Pizer, ed. San Marino,
        Cal.: Huntington Library, 1968.

        2. An article about the diaries in which Higgins concludes
they offer "little new material of historical significance."
        • Higgins, John E. "A Man From the Middle Border: Hamlin
        Garland's Diaries," Wisconsin Magazine of History, v. 46, pp.
        294-302, Summer, 1963.

1945. JARVIS, Joseph Russell (-1906)
        July 25, 1898-June 9, 1899
        Travel diary; prospecting in Alaska with his father and friends.
        • "The Cape Nome Gold Rush: The Diary, with Photographs
        by Joseph Russell Jarvis," Alan Probert, ed. Journal of the
        West, v. 9, pp. 153-95, April, 1970.

1946. JOHNSON, William R. (1880-1952)
        December 6, 1898-January 16, 1902
        Personal diary; Indiana native fought in the Philippine insur-
rection; garrison duty.

• "Three Years in the Orient: The Diary of William R. Johnson, 1898-1902," Donald F. Carmony and Karen Tannenbaum, eds. Indiana Magazine of History, v. 63, pp. 263-98, December, 1967.

1947. LEAUTAUD, Paul (1872-1956)
September 10, 1898-December 31, 1907
Personal diary; French journalist and drama critic; personal and literary life; literary criticism; life in turn-of-the-century Paris.
• Journal of a Man of Letters, 1898-1907. Geoffrey Sainsbury, trans. London: Chatto and Windus, 1960.

1948. LONGDEN, Charles E.
May 25-December 28, 1898
Personal and official diary; Kentucky pharmacist enlisted in the Spanish-American War; extracts paraphrased; duty as a hospital corpsman; interested in his work; growing cynicism.
• Agnew, James B. "Private Longden and the Medical Corps of 1898," Military Review, v. 59, pp. 11-21, July, 1979.

1949. ROBERTS, William Ransom (1879?-1940s)
June 26-July 14, 1898
Military diary; enlistee in the 34th Michigan; life on shipboard to Cuba; scenes in Cuba; battle of San Juan Hill; life in camp.
• "Under Fire in Cuba: A Volunteer's Eyewitness Account of the War with Spain," American Heritage, v. 29, pp. 78-91, December, 1977.

1950. SMITH, John (1859-1950)
March 15-June 17, 1898
Travel diary; East Anglian immigrant to Canada went to the Klondike on the Stikine River route; from Vancouver to Dawson by train, horse sleigh, steamer and rowboat; returned after deciding the gold hunt would be fruitless because all likely spots were already claimed.
• "Record of a Trip to Dawson, 1898: The Diary of John Smith," Walter N. Sage, ed. British Columbia Historical Quarterly, v. 16, pp. 67-97, 1952.

1899

1951. BEAN, Warren G. (1866-)
Personal diary; Mennonite minister in Skippack Township, Pennsylvania; record of farm work.
• Moyer, Willoughby W. "Abstract of Diary of Warren G. Bean, 1899," Pennsylvania Folklife, v. 28, pp. 32-36, Summer, 1979.

1952. CARSON, Carrie McKinley
July 31-August 23, 1899

Personal diary; wife of the Marengo, Iowa, school superintend-
ent; "a fine vacation."
- "A Summer at Lake Okoboji: Excerpts from a Vacation Diary, 1899," Clifford M. Carson, ed. Palimpsest, v. 57, pp.
86-95, May/June, 1976.

1953. HOLLOWAY, Joseph (1861-1944)
January 5, 1899-October 8, 1926
Personal diary; eccentric Irish bachelor witnessed the high
points of Irish drama; comments on plays, actors, writers, and aud-
ience; excerpts from 25 million word manuscript diary; encounters
with the leading figures in Dublin at rehearsals and performances.
- Joseph Holloway's Abbey Theatre: A Selection from His
Unpublished Journal Impressions of a Dublin Playgoer. Rob-
ert Hogan and Michael J. O'Neill, eds. Carbondale: Southern
Illinois University Press, 1967.

1954. HORNEY, Karen (1885-1952)
June 7, 1899-June 29, 1911
Personal diary; future psychoanalyst's life in a convent school
in Hamburg, Germany; studied at a gymnasium; poetry; thoughts on
love and marriage; wedding and birth of her first child; expresses
her maturity and changes of adolescent years; early clinical training;
interesting.
- The Adolescent Diaries of Karen Horney. New York: Basic
Books, 1980.
REVIEW: Library Journal, v. 105, p. 2196, October 15,
1980.

1955. LACEY, Edwin M.
February 26-May 20, 1899
Personal diary; telephone lineman in the U.S. Signal Corps
worked in Cuba stringing wire; description of countryside and people.
- "The Cuban Diary of Edwin M. Lacey," Donald F. Tingley,
ed. Illinois State Historical Society Journal, v. 56, pp. 20-
35, Spring, 1963.

1956. MOORE, Frank L.
July 12-August 25, 1899
Travel diary; Presbyterian circuit rider accompanied a party
of University of Minnesota geologists; they drew on his knowledge
of the terrain and personal contacts with residents; attended, by
mistake, a Mormon Bible school class.
- "Fossil Hunting in the Big Horn Basin: The Diary of Frank
L. Moore, 1899," Annals of Wyoming, v. 36, pp. 22-33, April,
1964.

1957. PLAATJE, Solomon Tshekisho (1877-1932)
October 29, 1899-March 30, 1900
Personal diary; member of the Barolong boo Ratshidi tribe;
educated in mission schools; presents the African view of the siege.

• The Boer War Diary of Solomon T. Plaatje: An African at Mafeking. John L. Comaroff, ed. London: Macmillan, 1973.

1958. TUCKER, Frederick (1875-   )
October 15, 1899-August 29, 1902
Military diary; son of a lifeboatman served with the 1st Rifle Brigade; voyage via Teneriffe and St. Helena; Battles of Colenso and Spion Kop; burning Boer farms; simply written and sometimes repetitious.
• Private Tucker's Boer War Diary: The Transvaal War of 1899, 1900, 1901 & 1902 with the Natal Field Forces. Pamela Todd and David Fordham, comps. London: Elm Tree Books, 1980.
REVIEW: Library Journal, v. 105, p. 2405, November 15, 1980.

1900

1959. BAINBRIDGE, Mrs. William E.
May 6-August 17, 1900
Personal diary; wife of a secretary of the American Legation in Peking during the Boxer Rebellion; siege and rescue by American Marines.
• "Diary of an Iowan Under Fire in Peking," Henry Borzo, ed. Annals of Iowa, v. 36, pp. 613-40, Spring, 1963.

1960. GOSCHEN, Sir Edward (1847-1924)
July 31, 1900-December 30, 1914
Diplomatic diary; British ambassador to Vienna; at Berlin at the outbreak of World War I; made Bethmann Hollweg's phrase "a scrap of paper" about the London Treaty of 1839 guaranteeing Belgium's independence a byword for German intentions.
• The Diary of Edward Goschen 1900-1914. Christopher R. Howard, ed. London: Royal Historical Society, 1980.
REVIEW: Book Review Index 1981, p. 221.

1961. JESSON, Edward R.
February-March 28, 1900
Travel diary; a thousand-mile trip over hard-packed snow without a tire puncture; well done.
• "From Dawson to Nome on a Bicycle," Ruth Reat, ed. Pacific Northwest Quarterly, v. 47, pp. 65-74, July, 1956.

1962. WILSON, Edward Adrian (1872-1912)
1. July, 1900-September 7, 1904; Exploration diary; accompanied Scott's expedition to map the interior of Antarctica as second surgeon, artist and vertebrate zoologist; voyage from London to New Zealand; Wilson's illustrations reproduced.
• Diary of the Discovery Expedition to the Antarctic Regions 1901-1904. Ann Savours, ed. New York: Humanities Press, 1967.

REVIEWS: Book Review Digest 1967, p. 1411. Book Review Index 1981, p. 600.

2. June 1, 1910-February 27, 1912; Exploration diary; scientific member of Scott's ill-fated Antarctic expedition; preparations in the Shetlands; stops in Australia and New Zealand; setting out for the South Pole.
  • Diary of the Terra Nova Expedition to the Antarctic, 1910-1912. H. G. R. King, ed. New York: Humanities Press, 1972.
  REVIEWS: Book Review Digest 1973, p. 1409.

1901

1963. BEDFORD, Mary Russell, Duchess of (1865-1937)
     July 13, 1901-March 17, 1937
     Personal diary; extracts; archdeacon's daughter married the heir to the Bedford dukedom; poor relations with her husband; equipped and ran a hospital at Woburn during the first World War; became a radiologist; world traveler and bird watcher; obtained a pilot's license; disappeared on a flight from Woburn; sprightly.
       • The Flying Duchess: The Diaries and Letters of Mary, Duchess of Bedford. John, Duke of Bedford, ed. London: Macdonald and Co., 1968.

1964. CHAMBERS, John Whiteclay (1848-)
     May 26, 1901-
     Travel diary; extracts; on the steamship Ruth from San Francisco to Nome; prospecting; return trip.
       • "Under Steam for the Gold Rush," American West, v. 11, pp. 30-39, September, 1974.

1965. LASHLY, William (1867-1940)
     August 17, 1901-December 15, 1903; October 24, 1911-February 19, 1912
     Exploration diary; excerpts; career Navy man and chief petty officer joined Captain Robert Scott on two polar expeditions: 1. to the South Polar lands; 2. the race with Amundsen for the Pole; discovery of the bodies of Scott and his companions.
       • Under Scott's Command: Lashly's Antarctic Diaries. A. R. Ellis, ed. New York: Taplinger, 1969.

1966. MAHONEY, Mary (1874-1964)
     May 6-27, 1901
     Travel diary; by wagon from Alliance, Nebraska, to Colorado looking for better land to farm.
       • "End of an Era: The Travel Journal of Mary Mahoney," Donald Mahoney, ed. Nebraska History, v. 47, pp. 329-38, September, 1966.

1967. PRICE, Harry (1877-1965)
      February 27-November, 1901
      Travel diary; petty officer on board the Ophir; voyage of
the Duke and Duchess of York (later King George V and Queen Mary)
to British possessions; facsimile of the journal with the diarist's illustrations.
        • The Royal Tour, 1901, or, The Cruise of H. M. S. Ophir.
      New York: Morrow, 1980.

1968. TOMLINSON, Ambrose Jessup (1865-1943)
      1901-1943; gaps
      Spiritual diary; Quaker founder of the Church of God; founda-
tion; ministry; church politics; work with the American Bible Society;
split and resurgence.
        • Diary of A. J. Tomlinson. Homer A. Tomlinson, ed.   3
      vols. New York: Church of God, World Headquarters, 1953.

                              1902

1969. DREISER, Theodore (1871-1945)
      October 22, 1902; February 17, 1903; January 26-March 18,
      1916; May 15, 1917-March 4, 1918; June 15, 1919-July 2, 1924;
      December 8, 1925-January 25, 1926
      Literary/personal diary; American novelist; his mental break-
down following the publication of Sister Carrie; vacation in Savannah;
daily life in Greenwich Village and interplay between the women in
his life and his writing; visits to Indiana and the Jersey shore; life
with his second wife; working on movie scripts in California; began
writing An American Tragedy; reflections on his mental state and
literary work; self-questioning, moody.
        • American Diaries, 1902-1926. Thomas P. Riggio, James L.
      West III and Neda M. Westlake, eds. Philadelphia: University
      of Pennsylvania Press, 1982.

1970. SILVER, Henry Dayton (1865-1930)
      March 30, 1902-November 22, 1905
      Personal diary; small business man in Rochester, New York;
prices, family vacations; reading.
        • "Diary of a One-horse Enterpriser: Fifty Years Ago in
      Upstate New York," James W. Silver, ed. New York History,
      v. 33, pp. 164-91, April, 1952.

                              1903

1971. CASEMENT, Roger (1864-1916)
      February 14, 1903-January 8, 1904; January 13, 1910-December
      31, 1910
      Travel diary; consular agent hanged by the British as a trai-
tor; in the Congo investigating the treatment of natives on rubber

plantations; in Peru observing the treatment of Indians; notes of homosexual encounters.

* The Black Diaries: An Account of Roger Casement's Life and Times with a Collection of His Diaries and Public Writings. Peter Singleton Gates and Maurice Girodias, eds. New York: Grove Press, 1959.
   (For a commentary on the use of the diaries in his treason trial see: Campbell, John. "'Give a Dog a Bad Name': The Curious Case of F. E. Smith and the 'Black Diaries' of Sir Roger Casement," History Today, v. 34, pp. 14-19, September, 1984.)

1972. DUNN, Robert
   June 23-September 24, 1903
   Travel diary; veteran of the Klondike gold rush went as a geologist with a party of four others to conquer Mt. McKinley; slogging through wet terrain, harrassed by millions of mosquitoes; laboring under poor leadership.
   * The Shameless Diary of an Explorer. New York: The Outing Publishing Co., 1907.

1973. JOYCE, Stanislaus (1883?-1955)
   September 26, 1903-January, 1905
   Personal diary; younger brother of Irish writer James Joyce; begins shortly after their mother's death; family life; much about his brother; his reading.
   * The Dublin Diary. George Harris Healey, ed. London: Faber and Faber, 1962.

1974. LEITCH, John Strickland (1882-   )
   February 27-June 13, 1903
   Exploration diary; with a party seeking coal deposits; shooting the Peace River Canyon in a raft; good description of the hazards; lively writing.
   * "Coal-Seekers on Peace River, 1903: Diary of My Journey to and Stay in the Peace River District in the Year 1903," British Columbia Historical Quarterly, v. 14, pp. 83-108, 1950.

1974a. MEINERTZHAGEN, Richard (1878-   )
   October 28, 1903-July 25, 1958
   Personal diary; extracts; Briton of Danish ancestry was a political officer in the Middle East; with the Colonial Office and the Palestine Mandate; comments on T. E. Lawrence, politics, people, Allenby; wide-ranging, shrewd assessments of personalities and events.
   * Middle East Diary, 1917-1956. New York: Yoseloff, 1959.

1975. MOSELEY, Sydney Alexander (1888-1961)
   May, 1903-January, 1960
   Personal diary; young Englishman began his working life in a

Dickensian counting house; sojourn in Egypt before World War I; moved on to Fleet Street and the BBC; editor and writer; active in the early days of British tv; stood for Parliment; ebullient; given to exclamatory style; opinionated.
> • The Private Diaries of Sydney Moseley. London: Parrish, 1960.

1976. SNOW, Francis H.
> December 27, 1903–November 14, 1907
> Personal diary; former chancellor of the University of Kansas and director of its Natural History Museum; family life; collecting specimens in the Southwest.
> • "The Diaries of F. H. Snow," John M. Peterson, ed. Kansas History, v. 1, pp. 101–32, Summer, 1978.

1977. WANNER, Louisa (1882–   )
> Personal diary; maid's work; washing and ironing; visits with and thoughts on a sweetheart.
> • "Louisa Wanner's Diary as a Hotel Chamber Maid in Tintah, Minnesota (December 23, 1903–May 21, 1904)," in: Elizabeth Hampsten. To All Inquiring Friends: Letters, Diaries and Essays in North Dakota. Grand Forks, University of North Dakota, 1979; pp. 275–83.

1904

1978. ANONYMOUS
> January 2, 1904–April 15, 1906
> Personal diary; order of French Catholic nuns was dispersed because of political pressure; events leading up to the convent's dissolution; activities of the sisters afterward; founding of a school and reunion; sweetly sentimental.
> • The Diary of an Exiled Nun. 2nd ed.   St. Louis: B. Herder, 1910.

1979. MANSFIELD, Katherine (1888–1923) [B303]
> 1. January 1, 1904–November, 1922; gaps; Personal diary; New Zealander and writer of English fiction; includes passages deliberately omitted from the 1927 edition; decision to become a writer; desire for a child; poems, fragments of stories, musings.
> • Journal of Katherine Mansfield. J. Middleton Murry, ed. definitive ed. London: Constable, 1954.

> 2. Letters and Journals of Katherine Mansfield: A Selection. London: Allen Lane, 1977; journal extracts taken from Middleton Murry's 1954 edition of Mansfield's Journal.

> 3. "Diary Excerpts," in: Philip Dunaway and Mel Evans, eds. A Treasury of the World's Great Diaries. New York: Doubleday, 1957; pp. 419–22.

4. "Diary Excerpts," in: Mary Jane Moffat and Charlotte
Painter, eds. Revelations: Diaries of Women. New York: Random
House, 1974; pp. 325-34.

1905

1980. CULMER, Henry Lavenner Alolphus (1854-   )
April 1-30, 1905
Travel diary; artist with a survey party; bridges were photo-
graphed, measured and described.
*   "The Natural Bridges of White Canyon: A Diary of H. L. A.
Culmer, 1905," Charlie R. Steen, ed. Utah Historical Quar-
terly, v. 40, pp. 55-87, Winter, 1972.

1981. FROST, Lesley (1899-1983)
February 22, 1905-August, 1909
Personal diary; daughter of poet Robert Frost kept a journal
of her activities while living in Derry, New Hampshire; short essays
on various topics ("About My Doll"; "The Rainy Day"); facsimile re-
production in childish but legible handwriting.
*   New Hampshire's Child: The Derry Journals of Lesley
Frost. Albany: State University of New York Press, 1969.

1982. HOWE, Edgar Watson (1853-1937)
October 27, 1905-March 11, 1906
Travel diary; American journalist began his journey aboard a
Santa Fe train in Kansas; by ship to India; extended travel there
and in Egypt and Palestine; observant gossip; humorous with an eye
for interesting detail.
*   Daily Notes of a Trip Around the World. St. Clair Shores,
Mich.: Scholarly Press, 1974; reprint of Minton, Balch ed.
of 1927.

1983. SAGIRASHVILI, David A. (-1962)
1905-1922
Political diaries; Georgian poet and patriot; Stalin's rise to
power; view of the Social Democrats; defeat of Mensheviki by the
Bolsheviks.
*   De Lon, Roy S. "Stalin and Social Democracy: 1905-1922:
The Political Diaries of David A. Sagirashvili," Ph.D., Georgetown University, 1974. (Dissertation Abstracts 35/07-A, p.
4371)

1906

1984. BINGHAM, Hiram (1875-1956)
December 4, 1906-June 5, 1907
Travel diary; American historian and U.S. Senator; in research-
ing a biography of Simon Bolivar undertook to retrace his route;

numerous photos; details of life in the area just after the turn of the century.

> • The Journal of an Expedition Across Venezuela and Colombia, 1906-1907: An Exploration of the Route of Bolivar's Celebrated March of 1819. New Haven: Yale Publishing Association, 1909.
> REVIEW: Book Review Digest 1909, p. 41.

1985. HARDY, Lileen
November, 1906-April 1, 1912
School diary; written by a teacher in a poor section of Edinburgh as a series of letters to friends; revised for publication; sympathetic portrayal of children's limited lives and a slice of social history.

> • Diary of a Free Kindergarten. Kate Douglas Wiggin, intro. New York: Houghton Mifflin, 1913.
> REVIEW: Book Review Digest 1913, p. 233.

1986. KING, Cardenio Flournoy, Jr. (1889-   )
July 5-August 25, 1906
Travel diary; teenager and his brother toured Europe and kept a diary in fulfillment of a promise to his father; aboard White Star liner Arabic; London, Paris and Rome; on the Orient Express; in Greece and Athens; a dandy diary of a bully vacation; photos by the diarist.

> • A Boy's Vacation Abroad: An American Boy's Diary of His First Trip to Europe. Boston: C. M. Clark, 1907.

1907

1987. BRAUN, Otto (1897-1918)
January 13, 1907-September 17, 1914
Personal diary; extracts; German prodigy killed in action in World War I; his schooling; travel with his family; study and reading.

> • The Diary of Otto Braun with Selections from His Letters and Poems. New York: Knopf, 1924.
> REVIEW: Book Review Digest 1924, p. 80.

1988. JACQUIER, Ivy
January 4, 1907-December 23, 1926; gaps
Personal diary; daughter of a French Catholic father and an English Protestant mother was raised in a large family in Lyon; the family did not "fit" well into the social life of the town; family visits to England; school life, crushes, lessons; studied art; many untranslated French passages; marriage and the birth of her daughter; melodramatic posturing.

> • The Diary of Ivy Jacquier, 1907-1926. Sir Francis Meynell, intro. London: Gollancz, 1960.
> REVIEW: Choice, v. 16, p. 1274, December, 1979.

1989. WILSON, Sir Arnold Talbot (1884-   ) [B310]
       March, 1907-September 29, 1914
       Personal diary; dated and undated extracts from a diary and
letters home; oil discovery; travel throughout the country; comments
on Iranians and fellow Britons; good reading.
       • Southwest Persia: A Political Officer's Diary 1907-1914.
       London: Oxford University Press, 1941.

1990. YOUNGER, Maud
       May 6-June 29, 1907
       Personal diary; writer took a job as a waitress; unions; work-
ing conditions.
       • "Diary of an Amateur Waitress: An Industrial Problem
       From the Worker's Point of View," McClure's, v. 28, pp. 543-
       52, 665-77, March/April, 1907.

                                1908

1991. CHARCOT, Jean Baptiste (1867-1936)
       December 16, 1908-June 4, 1910
       Exploration diary; French expedition sponsored by the Prince
of Monaco studied a small portion of Antarctica off Cape Horn; detailed observations; difficulties.
       • The Voyage of the "Why Not?" in the Antarctic: The Jour-
       nal of the 2nd French South Polar Expedition, 1908-1910. Philip
       Walsh, trans. New York: Hodder and Stoughton, 1911.

1992. DZHERZHINSKY, Felix Edmundovich (1877-1926)
       April 30, 1908-August 8, 1909
       Prison diary; Polish disciple of Lenin; in the Warsaw citadel;
communication with other prisoners by tapping on walls; occasional
visits; forthright, unself-pitying account.
       • Prison Diary and Letters of Felix Dzherzhinsky. John Gib-
       bons, trans. Moscow: Foreign Languages Publishing House,
       1959.

1993. HILL, John Ensign (1887-1950)
       November 12, 1908-May 9, 1911
       Personal diary; newlywed Mormon set off from Utah on a mis-
sion to Hungary; learning the language and translating LDS material
into Hungarian; proselytizing; quotes Hungarians on their dislike of
the Emperor; useful Mormon history.
       • Diaries and Biographical Material. Ivy Hooper Blood Hill,
       comp. and ed. Logan, Utah: J. P. Smith, 1962; pp. 19-82.

1994. PERKINS, Edith Forbes (1843-1925)
       1908-May 25, 1925
       Personal diary; wife of the president of the Chicago, Burling-
ton and Quincy Railroad; begun after his death in 1907 and ended
with her own in a California earthquake; little historical interest.

● Letters and Journal of Edith Forbes Perkins, 1908-1925.
Edith Perkins Cunningham, ed. Cambridge, Mass.: Prv.
ptd. 1931.

1995. WOOLF, Leonard Sidney (1880-1969)
August 28, 1908-May 20, 1911
Official diary; British civil servant, writer, founder with his
wife, Virginia Woolf (q.v.) of the Hogarth Press; diary kept while
he was in the Ceylon Civil Service as assistant government agent in
the Hambantota District; daily duties and events; his novel The Village in the Jungle had its basis in these years.
● "Diaries in Ceylon, 1908-1911: Records of the Colonial
Administrator ... Official Diaries ... August, 1908-May, 1911,"
Ceylon Historical Journal, v. 9, nos. 1-4, July, 1959-April,
1960; reprinted London: Hogarth Press, 1963.

1996. YEATS, William Butler (1865-1939)
December, 1908-September 11, 1911; several others to 1930
Literary diary; Irish poet, dramatist and winner of the Nobel
Prize; poems in rough draft; notes for future projects; some mention
of friends.
● Memoirs: Autobiography-First Draft Journal. Denis Dono-
ghue, ed. New York: Macmillan, 1972.

1909

1997. KOLLWITZ, Käthe Schmidt (1867-1945)
1. September 9, 1909-May, 1943; Personal diary; excerpts;
German painter and lithographer; family life; her work; death of a
son in World War I; reading; travel; a very full interior life.
● Diary and Letters. Hans Kollwitz, ed. Richard and Clara
Winston, trans. Chicago: Regnery, 1955.
REVIEW: Book Review Digest 1956, p. 527.

2. "Diary Excerpts," in: Mary Jane Moffat and Charlotte
Painter, eds. Revelations: Diaries of Women. New York: Random
House, 1974; pp. 237-52.

1998. "PALMER, William Scott" (Mary Emily Dowson)
July 7, 1909-July 6, 1910
Spiritual diary; meditations on the feasts of the church year.
● Diary of a Modernist. London: Arnold, 1910.
REVIEW: Book Review Digest 1911, p. 361.

1910

1999. ASHURST, Henry Fountain (1874-   )
June 17, 1910-July 27, 1937
Personal/political diary; one of the first of Arizona's U.S.

senators; life in Washington; trips abroad; written for publication;
"nothing in this diary will cause pain to any living person"; pedestrian.
- A Many-colored Toga. George F. Sparks, ed. Tucson:
University of Arizona Press, 1962.

2000. BALANO, Dorothea Moulton (1881-   )
June 21, 1910-January 6, 1913
Personal diary; Minnesota schoolteacher went as a chaperone
aboard a Maine windjammer and wound up marrying the captain (who
wanted intercourse "every change of watch"); birth of a son; sailing
the Atlantic as a family on several voyages; lively, earthy and good
reading.
- The Log of a Skipper's Wife. James W. Balano, ed. Camden, Me.: Down East Books, 1979.

2001. KAFKA, Franz (1883-1924)
1. May 17, 1910-December 18, 1923; Literary/travel diaries;
Austrian poet and novelist; notes on projected fiction; daily life;
dreams; thoughts on World War I; travel to Switzerland and Weimar.
- The Diaries of Franz Kafka. Max Brod, ed. Martin Green-
berg and Hannah Arendt, trans. 2 vols. New York: Schocken, 1948.

2. "Diary Excerpts," in: Philip Dunaway and Mel Evans,
eds. A Treasury of the World's Great Diaries. New York: Doubleday, 1957; pp. 147-56.

2002. SCOTT, Robert Falcon (1868-1912) [B299-300]
1. October 18, 1910-March, 1912; Exploration diary; English
Antarctic explorer in a race for the South Pole; work at the base;
sledging excursions; perished with his party due to bad weather and
insufficient food; "For God sake look after our people"; facsimile edition is barely legible and very difficult to read.
- The Diaries of Captain Robert Scott: A Record of the Second Antarctic Expedition 1910-1912. 6 vols. High Wycombe,
Bucks.: University Microfilms, 1968.

2. "Diary Excerpts," in: Philip Dunaway and Mel Evans, eds.
A Treasury of the World's Great Diaries. New York: Doubleday,
1957; pp. 431-35.

3. "Diary Excerpts," in: Elizabeth D'Oyley, ed. English
Diaries. London: Edward Arnold, 1930; pp. 225-37.

2003. WILLIAMS, Earl Trumbull (1888-1918)
July 2-September 26, 1910
Travel diary; by ship to Europe; tourist sights with a con-
genial group; return to the U.S. aboard the Lusitania.
- Diary of a Trip Abroad in the Summer of 1910. Brooklyn,
N.Y.: Yale University Press, 1920.

1911

2004. ELMHIRST, Willie (1892-1916)
       October 11, 1911-June 20, 1912
       Personal diary; Oxford undergraduate; lectures, rowing, social
life; letters from home; very full description of activities and some
scrapes.
       • A Freshman's Diary, 1911-1912. Oxford: Blackwell, 1969.

2005. FRANKFURTER, Felix (1882-1965)
       October 20, 1911-March 9, 1948
       Personal diary; excerpts; associate justice of the U.S. Supreme
Court; editor notes that material seems to be written with an eye to
publication; incidents at Harvard; list of his law clerks; tendency to
support judgments as though they were court opinions.
       • Lash, Joseph. From the Diaries of Felix Frankfurter with
       a Biographical Essay and Notes. New York: Norton: 1975.

2006. HALL, Sharlot Mabridth (1870-1943)
       July 23-August 31, 1911
       Travel diary; first woman to hold public office in Arizona;
wagon trip through northwest corner of Arizona and southern Utah;
flora, fauna, geology; some history.
       • Sharlot Hall on the Arizona Strip: A Diary of a Journey
       Through Northern Arizona in 1911. C. Gregory Crampton,
       ed. Flagstaff, Ariz.: Northland Press, 1975.

2007. HOWARD, Lawrence C. (1893?-)
       November 19, 1911-March 11, 1912
       Sea diary; Maine native signed on as an ordinary seaman on
a four-masted bark; from New York to San Francisco; an Atlantic
gale; around the Horn; quotes from the first mate's log.
       • Log of the Edward Sewall, 1911-1912. Salem, Conn.: Prv.
       ptd., 1958.

2008. INGE, William Ralph (1860-1954)
       1. April 18, 1911-October, 1934; gaps; Personal diary; An-
glican prelate and "gloom Dean"; church work; preaching to King
George and Queen Mary; lecturing; family life.
       • Diary of a Dean: St. Paul's, 1911-1934. New York: Mac-
       millan, 1950.

       2. "Diary Excerpts," in: Philip Dunaway and Mel Evans,
eds. A Treasury of the World's Great Diaries. New York: Doubleday, 1957; pp. 500-04.

2009. KENNET, Kathleen Bruce Scott (1881?-1947)
       September 3, 1911-February 25, 1913
       Personal diary; wife of Polar explorer Scott (q.v.) fears for
his life and then learns of his death.
       • "Diary Excerpts," in: Philip Dunaway and Mel Evans, eds.

A Treasury of the World's Great Diaries. New York: Doubleday, 1957; pp. 436-39.

2010. LOWNDES, Marie Adelaide Belloc (1868-1947)
December 1, 1911-August 9, 1946; gaps
Personal diary; British playwright and novelist; sister of
writer Hilaire Belloc; married to a journalist for the London Times;
literary and social life in London; good for ideas and attitudes of
the British upper classes.
• Diaries and Letters 1911-1947. Susan Lowndes, ed. London: Chatto and Windus, 1971.

2011. SCOTT, Charles Prestwich (1846-1932)
February 2, 1911-December 7, 1928
Political diary; former Liberal MP and editor of the Manchester
Guardian; suffragettes; Irish Home Rule; World War I; relations with
Lloyd George (q.v.), Churchill and other political figures.
• The Political Diaries of C. P. Scott, 1911-1928. Trevor
Wilson, ed. Ithaca, N.Y.: Cornell University Press, 1970.

2012. WAUGH, Evelyn (1903-66)
1911-1916; 1919-1921; 1924-1928; 1930-1956; 1960-1965
Personal diary; British novelist and Catholic convert; entries
were edited with an eye to English libel laws; school days at Lancing;
aimlessness of his life in the twenties; tone of the entries changes in
the thirties following his divorce from his first wife; literary success;
service in the Royal Marines; to be read in conjunction with his novels for a portrait of English life of the era.
• The Diaries of Evelyn Waugh. Michael Davie, ed. London:
Weidenfeld and Nicolson, 1976.
REVIEW: Book Review Digest 1978, p. 1371.

2013. WILLIAMS, William H.
Travel diary; with three friends; record of birds shot and
fishing; lighthearted, lengthy entries.
• "Diary of a Taxidermist's Field Trip (June 16-July 16,
1911)," in: Elizabeth Hampsten. To All Inquiring Friends:
Letters, Diaries and Essays in North Dakota. Grand Forks:
University of North Dakota, 1979; pp. 284-92.

1912

2014. BENEDICT, Ruth Fulton (1887-1948)
1. "Diary Excerpts," in: Mary Jane Moffat and Charlotte
Painter, eds. Revelations: Diaries of Women. New York: Random
House, 1974; pp. 148-62.

2. January 1-March 20, 1923; January 1-February 10, 1926;
October, 1912-June 9, 1934; Personal diary; American anthropologist
and student of Margaret Mead; study, work, social; third section is
written in a philosophical vein.

● An Anthropologist at Work: Writings of Ruth Benedict.
Margaret Mead, ed. Boston: Houghton Mifflin, 1959.

2015. BRANHAM, L. B.
December 11, 1912–March 6, 1931
Business diary; extracts; hotel manager in Napponee, Indiana.
● Stauffer, Florence S. "Branham Diary," Indiana History
Bulletin, v. 50, pp. 51–57, May, 1973.

2016. KAMBOURIS, Haralambos K. (-1965)
1912–1915
Personal diary; young Greek's experiences in Oregon; work
on a railroad gang; relations with Americans; courting.
● "Oregon Experiences: Haralambos K. Kambouris," Helen
Papanikolas, ed. C. V. Vasilacopulos, trans. Oregon Historical Quarterly, v. 81, pp. 4–39, Spring, 1981.

2017. MACRAE, Kenneth A. (1883–1964)
April 25, 1912–October 27, 1963
Spiritual diary; Presbyterian minister to congregations at Kil-
muir and Stornoway; distilled from 41 manuscript volumes; emphasis
on passages which demonstrate recurring concerns of the diarist;
early years as a student-preacher; work with parishioners; vigorous
life; visit to Australia.
● Diary of Kenneth A. Macrae: A Record of Fifty Years in
the Christian Ministry. Iain H. Murray, ed. Carlisle, Pa.:
Banner of Truth Trust, 1980.

2018. POWELL, Sydney Walter (1878-)
February 9, 1912–April 27, 1913
Personal diary; British-born South African civil servant; came
to the South Seas by way of Australia; consciously kept to be read
by others; life on a vanilla/copra plantation outside Papeete with a
native woman; plantation work; beset by illness and then death of his
helpmate; unsentimental but affecting.
● A South Sea Diary. New York: Penguin, 1945.

2019. SINTZENICH, Arthur H. C. (Hal; "Snitch")
December 13, 1912–[no closing date]
Personal diary; article with some dated excerpts; motion picture cameraman from 1909 to the late 1960's; production techniques;
work; travels on assignment.
● Barnouw, Erik. "The Sintzenich Diaries," Quarterly Journal of the Library of Congress, v. 37, pp. 310–31, 1980.

1913

2020. BRITTAIN, Vera (1893–1970)
January 1, 1913–May 27, 1917
Personal diary; student at Somerville College, Oxford; desire

to be a novelist; enters nursing after the outbreak of war; feminist and pacifist; death of several men close to her in the fighting; high quality writing.

- Chronicle of Youth: The War Diary 1913-1917. Alan Bishop with Terry Smart, eds. New York: Morrow, 1982.

2021. COPELAND, Estella McNutt (1879-1938)
        May 15-July 24, 1913
        Travel diary; kept by the mother of the family; routed by AAA and burdened with "a few spare parts for the car"--6 inner tubes, 100 feet of 3/4" rope, block and tackle and camping equipment; averaged about one hundred miles a day.
- Overland By Auto in 1913: Diary of a Family Tour From California to Indiana. Indianapolis: Indiana Historical Society, 1981.

1914

2022. BALFOUR, Charles James (-1939)
        August, 1914-April, 1916
        Military journal; transport and machine gun officer in the Scots Guards; retreat from Mons; fighting near Givenchy and Cuinchy; Arras-Ypres offensive.
- Goldsmith, R. F. K. "From Mons to the Aisne: A Subaltern's Diary--August and September, 1914," Army Quarterly and Defence Journal [Great Britain], v. 103, 91-100, 230-37, 369-77, 1972.
- Goldsmith, R. F. K. "Extracts from the Diary of Captain C. J. Balfour, 1st Scots Guards," Army Quarterly and Defence Journal [Great Britain], v. 103, pp. 369-77, 1972.

2023. BALFOUR, Duncan
        September-November, 1914
        Military journal; extracts; brother of Charles James Balfour (q.v.); first battle of Ypres.
- Goldsmith, R. F. K. "Territorial Vanguard: A London Scottish Diary," Army Quarterly and Defence Journal [Great Britain], v. 103, pp. 230-37, 1972.

2024. BORTON, Arthur Close (1851?-1927)
        August 4, 1914-December 31, 1918
        Personal diary; kept by the father of the family; activities of his wife, two sons, a daughter and others; High Tory endures the war and its vicissitudes noting its effects on county life and mores.
- My Warrior Sons: The Borton Family Diary, 1914-1918. Guy Slater, ed. London: P. Davies, 1973.

2025. COOK, Arthur Henry (1888-1956)
        August 4, 1914-November 11, 1918

Military diary; NCO at the battles of Ypres and Arras and in the trenches; somewhat impersonal but with flashes of humor.
- A Soldier's War: Being the Diary of the Late Arthur Henry Cook, During Four Years Service with the 1st Battalion, The Somerset Light Infantry, on the Western Front, France, During the Great War, 1914-18. Lt.-Gen. G. N. Molesworth, ed. Taunton: Goodman and Son, 1958.

2026. CORDAY, Michel (1870-1937)
August, 1914-November 11, 1918
Public/private diary; notes his reading and hearsay reports on the war by a Frenchman; much color but how much truth?
- The Paris Front: An Unpublished Diary: 1914-1918. New York: Dutton, 1934.

2027. DESAGNEAUX, Henri
August 1, 1914-February 11, 1919
Military diary; rose to lieutenant colonel in the Somme; at Verdun; with the occupying forces in Germany; great sense of immediacy.
- A French Soldier's War Diary, 1914-1918. Jean Desagneaux, ed. Godfrey J. Adams, trans. Morley: Elmfield Press, 1975.

2028. FARMBOROUGH, Florence (1877?-)
August, 1914-April, 1918
Personal diary; Briton working in Russia as an English tutor to the daughters of a surgeon; joined a medical staff as a surgical nurse at the outbreak of the war; service in Galicia; excellent description of wartime conditions, lives of civilians and the effects of the Bolshevik overthrow of the Czar; well done.
- Nurse at the Russian Front: A Diary, 1914-18. London: Constable, 1974.

2029. GÁG, Wanda (1893-1946)
December 11, 1914-September, 1915
Personal diary; American painter and illustrator of children's books; study at the Minneapolis School of Art; meeting with Adolf Dehn, "a man with big possibilities."
- "Diary Excerpts," in: Philip Dunaway and Mel Evans, eds. A Treasury of the World's Great Diaries. New York: Doubleday, 1957; pp. 130-38.

2030. GIBSON, High Simons (1883-1954)
July 4-December 31, 1914
Personal diary; American legation secretary sent to a quiet post in Brussels "where nothing ever happens"; spy stories; German invasion; trip to London and return; worked with Herbert Hoover who chaired the American Relief Committee; very full account of conditions under German occupation.
- A Journal From Our Legation in Belgium. New York: Doubleday, Page, 1917; London edition by Hodder and Stoughton entitled A Diplomatic Diary.

REVIEW: Book Review Digest 1917, p. 218.

2031. GLASPELL, Kate Eldridge
January 14-August 27, 1914
Travel diary; tourist notes on a trip through the Mediter-
ranean, Egypt and Europe; ended in London with the outbreak of war;
some humor.
• Diary of a Trip Abroad in 1914 When all the World Was at
Peace and Every Nation Loved the USA. Philadelphia: Dor-
rance Press, 1942.

2032. HAGGARD, Sir Henry Rider (1856-1925)
July 14, 1914-March 26, 1925
Personal diary; British author of 70 books including several
best-selling novels; in Canada to survey natural resources; experiences as a non-combatant in World War I; embodies the point of view
of the landed gentry; efforts against Communism; friend of Kipling
and Teddy Roosevelt; plagiarism suit against a film company; ill
health.
• The Private Diaries of Sir H. R. Haggard 1914-1925. D. S.
Higgins, ed. New York: Stein and Day, 1980.

2033. HAIG, Douglas Haig, 1st Earl (1861-1928) [B288]
Military diary; political aspect of the war; dealings with King
George, the Cabinet, the War Office, journalists and the Allies;
shrewd assessments of other personalities; valuable.
• The Private Papers of Douglas Haig, 1914-1919; Being Se-
lections From the Private Diary and Correspondence of Field-
Marshal the Earl Haig of Bemersyde. Robert Blake, ed. Lon-
don: Eyre and Spottiswoode, 1952.

2034. HANSSEN, Hans Peter (1862-1936)
August 1, 1914-November 14, 1918
Political diary; member of the Danish minority in the German
Empire; war's beginning; submarine warfare; Russian Revolution;
party politics; wartime censorship.
• Diary of a Dying Empire. Oscar Osburn Winther, trans.
Ralph H. Lutz, ed. Bloomington: Indiana University Press,
1955; reprinted Port Washington, N.Y.: Kennikat Press, 1973.
REVIEW: Book Review Digest 1956, pp. 407-08.

2035. HAWKINGS, Frank (1898?-   )
August 10, 1914-September 27, 1918
Military diary; enlisted in Queen Victoria's Rifles; straight-
forward account of the second Battle of Ypres; Cambrai.
• From Ypres to Cambrai: The Diary of an Infantryman,
1914-1919. Arthur Taylor, ed. Morley: Elmfield Press, 1974.

2036. HULME, Thomas Ernest (1883-1917)
December 30, 1914-April 19, 1915
Military diary; philosopher and poet's experiences in France;

reactions to everlasting shelling and lying face down in mud; some
good description.
> - "Diary From the Trenches," in: Sam Hynes, ed. <u>Further</u>
>   <u>Speculations</u>. Minneapolis: University of Minnesota Press,
>   1955; pp. 147-69.

2037.   JACK, James Lochhead (1880-1962)
        July 28, 1914-November 11, 1918
        Military diary; service in France with the Scottish Rifles and
the West Yorkshire Regiment; very stiff upper lip; good picture of
trench warfare.
> - <u>General Jack's Diary, 1914-1918: The Trench Diary of</u>
>   <u>Brigadier-General J. L. Jack, D. S. O.</u> John Terraine, ed.
>   London: Eyre and Spottiswoode, 1964.

2038.   JEFFREYS, George Darell (1878?-1960)
        August 12-December 31, 1914
        Military diary; editor uses the diary of the major's service in
the 1st Grenadier Guards as a base to chronicle their progress from
Mons to Ypres via the Marne and the Aisne; some material was drawn
from the diary of Major Lord Bernard Gordon-Lennox; vivid descriptions.
> - <u>Fifteen Rounds a Minute: The Grenadiers at War, August</u>
>   <u>to December, 1914</u>. J. M. Craster, ed. London: Macmillan,
>   1976.

2039.   JEFFRIES, Jouett
        June 28-November 17, 1914
        Personal diary; American woman in Germany; overdramatized
account which seems to be embellished with descriptions taken from
newspapers.
> - <u>War Diary of an American Woman to the Proclamation of the</u>
>   <u>Holy War, 1914</u>. New York: The Fatherland Corp., 1915.

2040.   KLEIN, Felix
        August 3-December 31, 1914
        Personal diary; chaplain at the American hospital in Meudon;
giving comfort to the dying; frequent visits from relatives; praises
the Americans who funded the hospital; pious, old-maidish quality.
> - <u>Diary of a French Army Chaplain</u>. M. Harriet M. Capes,
>   ed. Chicago: McClurg, 1918.
>   REVIEW: <u>Book Review Digest</u> 1918, p. 254.

2041.   LLOYD GEORGE, Frances Louise Stevenson (1888-)
        September 21, 1914-July 2, 1936
        Political diary; mistress and confidential secretary for many
years before becoming the wife of the British politician in 1943; ef-
ficient worker with suffragist leaning; feminine angle of British politics; more a record of Lloyd George's thoughts and work than her
own.
> - <u>Lloyd George: A Diary</u>. A. J. P. Taylor, ed. New York:
>   Harper and Row, 1971.

2042. MALINOWSKI, Bronislaw (1884-1942)
       September 20, 1914-March 4, 1915; November 10, 1917-July 18,
       1918
       Personal diary; Polish-born founder of modern social anthro-
pology did much to advance methods of field research; work in New
Guinea and Trobriand Islands; observations on the natives and himself; longing for the woman he later married.
       • A Diary in the Strict Sense of the Term. Norman Guterman,
       trans. New York: Harcourt, 1967.
          REVIEW: Book Review Digest 1967, p. 849.

2043. MARITAIN, Raissa (1883-1960)
       November 26, 1914-December 15, 1931; 1931-60 are fragmen-
       tary entries, some dated only by year
       Spiritual journal; wife of French Catholic philosopher Jacques
Maritain; enigmatic entries; "interior affliction."
       • Raissa's Journal: Presented by Jacques Maritain. Albany,
       N.Y.: Magi Books, 1974.

2044. MOORE, Benjamin Burges (1878-1934)
       February 8-May 10, 1914
       Travel diary; by rail across the Volga, to the east of the Aral
Sea; through Tashkent, Samarkand and Isfahan to Bushir on the gulf;
found the scenery monotonous; lengthy entries possibly revised for
publication.
       • From Moscow to the Persian Gulf: Being the Journal of a
       Disenchanted Traveller in Turkestan and Persia. New York:
       Putnam, 1915.

2045. MORRISON, Anna Daly (1884-   )
       February 1-June 4, 1941; gaps
       Personal diary; wife to the half owner of a construction com-
pany; from courtship and early days of marriage to grandchildren;
chronicles early days and growth of the firm which helped build
Boulder Dam; breezy and humorous but of little value as history.
       • Diary. Boise, Ida.: Em-Kayan Press, 1951.

2046. MÜLLER, Georg Alexander von (1854-1940)
       June 28, 1914-November 9, 1918
       Personal diary; outbreak of World War I; German advances;
entry of the U.S. into the war; Kaiser's abdication; interesting
picture of a dedicated, patriotic officer trying to do a job while beset by the stupidities of those around him; unsympathetic portrait of
the Kaiser.
       • The Kaiser and His Court: The Diaries, Note Books and
       Letters of Admiral Georg Alexander von Müller, Chief of the
       Naval Cabinet, 1914-1918. Walter Görlitz, ed. Mervyn Savill,
       trans. London: Macdonald and Co., 1961.

2047. MURRAY, Joseph (1896-   )
       December 5, 1914-April 28, 1917

Military diary; written up from diary scraps made in the field; Scots miner joined early in the war; landing at Gallipoli where "we were beaten by our own High Command"; service in France; Arras offensive; wounded at Gavrelle.

- Call to Arms: From Gallipoli to the Western Front. London: Kimber, 1980.

2048. NIN, Anaïs (1903-77)

1. July 25, 1914-February 18, 1923; Personal diary; one of the leading diarists of the century; by ship from Spain to New York; father a pianist, mother a singer; father's desertion of the family; money problems; study at Columbia University; modeling for magazines; ends with her engagement to Hugo Guiler; life in Paris; torn between being a wife and a writer.

- Linotte: The Early Diary of Anaïs Nin. v. 1, 1914-1920; The Early Diary of Anaïs Nin. v. 2, 1920-1923; New York: Harcourt, Brace, Jovanovich, 1978-83.

2. March 20, 1923-1931; Title for this portion of the diaries was Le journal d'une epouse; covers her marriage to Hugh Guiler; their move to Paris; meeting with her estranged father; struggling to write.

- The Early Diary of Anaïs Nin. v. 3, 1923-27; v. 4, 1927-1931; New York: Harcourt, Brace Jovanovich, 1983-85.

3. Winter, 1931-Summer, 1974; Personal diary; novelist whose friends and acquaintances constitute a cross-section of figures in the literary and artistic life of the century; Laurence Durrell, Henry Miller, Dr. Otto Rank figure in the early volumes; when her early work, novels and a study of D. H. Lawrence did not bring the fame and fortune she expected the diaries became the chief vehicle of her writing.

- The Diary of Anaïs Nin. 7 vols. Gunther Stuhlmann, ed. New York: Swallow and Harcourt, Brace and World, 1966-80. REVIEWS: Book Review Digest 1966, pp. 890-91; 1967, p. 974; 1969, p. 972; 1971, p. 1008; 1974, p. 894; 1976, pp. 883-84; 1980, p. 893.

4. "Diary Excerpts," in: Mary Jane Moffat and Charlotte Painter, eds. Revelations: Diaries of Women. New York: Random House, 1974; pp. 86-97.

2049. RAYMOND, William Lee (1877-)
1914-December 31, 1923
Personal diary; Congregationalist residing in Boston; service in the Police Strike; aphorisms, character portraits of loved ones; essays on politics with a special interest in Russia; general observations on World War I.

- An Occasional Diary by X. Boston: Twentieth Century Publishing, 1924.

2050. STUMPF, Richard (1892-)
August 2, 1914-November 24, 1918
Personal diary; tinsmith, Catholic, trade unionist; enlisted in
the German Navy in 1912; seaman for six years on the Helgoland; self-
educated and well-read; this diary was cited as evidence by the Reich-
stag Investigating Committee examining the reasons for the naval re-
volt of November, 1918; excitement of battles contrasted with the poor
conditions of everyday shipboard life; interesting and very well writ-
ten.
   • War, Mutiny and Revolution in the German Navy. Daniel
   Horn, ed. and trans. London: Frewin, 1969; reprinted from
   The Private War of Seaman Stumpf: The Unique Diaries of a
   Young German in the Great War. New Brunswick: Rutgers
   University Press, 1967.

2051. WADDINGTON, Mary Alsop (-1923)
August 1, 1914-February 28, 1916
Personal diary; British (?) woman with grandchildren resided
in France during World War I; family news; friendly relations with
British upper class, embassy staff and wealthy French and Americans;
spent time in Paris and also rural areas; good account of the effects
of the war on the civilian population.
   • My War Diary. New York: Scribner's, 1918.

2052. WHITLOCK, Brand (1869-1934)
August 1, 1914-December 28, 1921
Personal diary; American journalist and politician was American
minister to Belgium at the outbreak of war; German invasion of Belgium; in the country throughout the war years; execution of Edith
Cavell; the Peace Conference; President Wilson's visit; post-war politics; very full entries with much detail on diplomatic moves; important.
   • The Letters and Journal of Brand Whitlock. Allan Nevins,
   ed. New York: Appleton-Century, 1936.
   REVIEWS: American Historical Review, v. 43, pp. 174-75,
   1936. Journal of Modern History, v. 9, pp. 249-51, 1937.
   Mississippi Valley Historical Review, v. 24, pp. 112-13,
   1937.

2053. YOUNG, Mary Sophie (1872-1919)
August 2-September 15, 1914
Exploration diary; Wellesley graduate was botany instructor at
the University of Texas in Austin; Austin to Marfa; comments on the
countryside and people encountered; interesting; map, photos.
   • "Mary S. Young's Journal of Botanical Explorations in
   Trans-Pecos, Texas, August-September, 1914," B. C. Tharp
   and Chester V. Kielman, eds. Southwestern Historical Quarterly, v. 65, pp. 366-93, January, 1962; pp. 512-38, April,
   1962.

1915

2054. ANONYMOUS
       July 18, 1915-October 6, 1917
       Personal diary; well-born, highly-place Briton moved easily
through Russian court circles and among British embassy personnel
in Petrograd; view of Russian customs through foreign eyes; in Yalta
and Tsarskoe Selo; effect of the Revolution on Russian aristocrats.
       • The Russian Diary of an Englishman, Petrograd, 1915-1917.
       London: Heinemann, 1919.

2055. ALBERT I, King of the Belgians (1875-1934)
       April 14, 1915-March 20, 1918
       Diplomatic diary; relations with his ministers, the British and
French statesmen and military figures; opposition to British demands;
interesting view of World War I from the Belgian angle.
       • The War Diaries of Albert I, King of the Belgians. General
       R. van Overstraeten, ed. Mervyn Savill, trans. London:
       Kimber, 1954.

2056. ASQUITH, Lady Cynthia Mary Evelyn (1887-1960)
       April 15, 1915-September 28, 1918
       Personal diary; daughter of 1st Earl of Wemyss; married the
second son of Prime Minister Asquith in 1910; husband's enlistment
in the army; lived with their two sons; a peripatetic existence due
to the lack of a permanent home; privy to much political gossip;
lively, opinionated.
       • Diaries 1915-1918. E. M. Horsley, ed. New York: Knopf,
       1968.
          REVIEW: Book Review Digest 1969, p. 51.

2057. BRUCKSHAW, Horace (1891-1917)
       January 27, 1915-November 12, 1916
       Personal diary; volunteered at the war's beginning for the
Royal Marines; at Gallipoli, "Turkish shells for breakfast"; cold,
short rations and boredom interrupted by fierce fighting.
       • The Diaries of Private Horace Bruckshaw 1915-1916. Martin
       Middlebrook, ed. Hamden, Conn.: Archon, 1980.
          REVIEWS: Choice, v. 18, p. 575, December, 1980. Ob-
          server, January 27, 1980, p. 38.

2058. COOLIDGE, John Gardner
       January 1, 1915-October 24, 1917
       Personal diary; appointed special agent to the U.S. Embassy
in Paris at the opening of the war; work with refugees; some entries
by his wife Helen.
       • A War Diary in Paris, 1914-1917. Cambridge, Mass.: Riv-
       erside Press, 1931.

2059. CUSHING, Harvey Williams (1869-1939)
       March 18, 1915-November 16, 1918

Personal diary; neurosurgeon served with an American ambulance unit in France in 1915; later with the American Expeditionary Forces in the front lines; long, full entries, excellently portray life in World War I.

- From a Surgeon's Journal, 1915-1918. Boston: Little, Brown, 1936.
  REVIEWS: Canadian Historical Review, v. 18, pp. 79-81, 1937. New England Quarterly, v. 9, pp. 529-30, 1936.

2060. DENHAM, H. M.
January 1, 1915-January 19, 1916
Sea diary; graduate of Osborne Naval College was aboard the Agamemnon in the Dardanelles campaign; minesweeping duty; landing troops at Gallipolli and Suvla Bay; evacuation of Gallipolli; much detail with good descriptions of naval tactics.

- Dardanelles: A Midshipman's Diary 1915-16. London: Murray, 1981.

2061. GLUBB, Sir John Bagot (1897-   )
November 24, 1915-December 30, 1918
Military diary; subaltern who later became "Glubb Pasha"; in Ypres Salient, Somme, Arras and Cambrai; wounded and spent a year in convalescence; lengthy entries give a good picture of a soldier's life.

- Into Battle: A Soldier's Diary of the Great War. London: Cassell, 1978.

2062. LOCKHART, Robert Hamilton Bruce (1887-1970)
February 15, 1915-December 23, 1938
Personal diary; Scots government official, journalist for the Evening Standard and broadcaster; confided to his diary what he couldn't say in print; Edward VIII's abdication; political and social celebrities abound; gossipy and entertaining.

- The Diaries of Sir Robert Bruce Lockhart 1915-1938. Kenneth Young, ed. New York: St. Martin's Press, 1974.
  REVIEW: Book Review Digest 1975, p. 775.

2063. NICOLAS, Rene
February 12-June 25, 1915
Personal diary; life in the trenches; boredom alternating with death.

- Campaign Diary of a French Officer by Sous-Lieutenant Rene Nicolas of the French Infantry. Katharine Babbitt, trans. New York: Houghton Mifflin, 1917.

2064. SASSOON, Siegfried (1886-1967)
November 17, 1915-November 11, 1918
Personal diary; English writer of prose and verse; life in the trenches; writing poetry between times; leave in England; invalided out after being shot by his sergeant who mistook him for a German; introspective with much description of the beauties of nature.

• Siegfried Sassoon Diaries: 1915-1918. Rupert Hart-Davies,
ed. 3+ vols. London: Faber and Faber, 1983-

2065. SPERANZA, Gino Charles (1872-1927)
August 12, 1915-May 9, 1919
Personal diary; American of Italian ancestry; trained as a lawyer;
turned correspondent for the New York Evening Post; interpreted
America to the Italians and Italy to the Americans; long, thoughtful
entries; excellent primary material on Italy in World War I.
• The Diary of Gino Speranza, Italy, 1915-1919. Florence
Colgate Speranza, ed. 2 vols. New York: Columbia Univer-
sity Press, 1941; reprinted New York: AMS Press, 1966.

2066. WOOLF, Virginia Stephen (1882-1941)
1. January 1, 1915-1941; Personal/literary diary; British
novelist and essayist; wife of Leonard Woolf (q.v.); begins shortly
after their marriage; social life; founding the Hogarth Press; book
reviewing and writing fiction; episodes of insanity; gradual easing of
financial worries with literary and publishing success; a parade of
British literary and artistic personalities march through the pages;
brisk, witty and entertaining; one of the best diaries of the century.
• The Diary of Virginia Woolf. Anne Olivier Bell, ed. 5
vols. New York: Harcourt Brace Jovanovich, 1977-84.
REVIEWS: Book Review Digest 1977, pp. 1448-49; 1979,
pp. 1388-89; 1980, pp. 1331-32; 1982, p. 1471.

2. August 4, 1918-March 8, 1941; Personal diary; extracts
chosen to illuminate her as a writer; comments on her reading; effect
of her observations on her writing; practice pieces of writing; "I will
go down with my colours flying."
• A Writer's Diary: Being Extracts From the Diary of Virginia Woolf. Leonard Woolf, ed. New York: Harcourt, Brace,
1954.

3. "Diary Excerpts," in: Philip Dunaway and Mel Evans,
eds. A Treasury of the World's Great Diaries. New York: Doubleday, 1957; pp. 423-30.

4. "Diary Excerpts," in: Mary Jane Moffat and Charlotte
Painter, eds. Revelations: Diaries of Women. New York: Random
House, 1974; pp. 225-36.

1916

2067. BOYLE, Laura
August 5, 1916-August 3, 1917
Personal diary; British wife in Africa in the Ashanti area and
on the Gold Coast; enthusiastic and detailed.
• Diary of a Colonial Officer's Wife. Oxford: Alden Press,
1968.

2068. BULLITT, Ernesta Drinker
       May 14-September 28, 1916
       Personal diary; experiences in Germany, Belgium and Austria
in the company of her newspaper correspondent husband; wartime
rationing, relief work; interesting account by a lively, witty woman.
       • An Uncensored Diary From the Central Empires. New York:
       Doubleday, Page and Co., 1917.

2069. CAROSSA, Hans (1878-1956)
       October 4-December 15, 1916
       Personal diary; German poet in the army stationed in Rumania;
observations on fellow officers and civilians encountered; introspective and "literary."
       • A Roumanian Diary. Agnes Neill Scott, trans. New York:
       Knopf, 1930.

2070. CLARK, Coleman Tileston (1896-1918)
       March, 1916-May 27, 1918
       Personal diary; left his studies at Yale to enlist as an ambu-
lance driver; when his service ended he joined the French Foreign
Legion; with the 28th Field Artillery; wounded in the last German offensive; in Salonika and Serbia; wide-eyed observer of foreign customs.
       • Soldier Letters by Coleman Tileston Clark and Salter Storrs
       Clark, Jr., Their Stories in Extracts From Their Letters and
       Diaries. New York: Prv. ptd., 1919; pp. 1-132.

2071. DODD, William E. (-1940)
       August 24, 1916-December 30, 1920
       Personal diary; visiting professor at the University of Chicago;
visits with President Wilson for a biography of him; lengthy entries;
well-done and interesting.
       • "Professor William E. Dodd's Diary, 1916-1920," W. Alexan-
       der Mabry, ed. John P. Branch Historical Papers of Randolph-
       Macon College, new ser. v. 2, pp. 7-86, March, 1953.

2072. DUNHAM, Frank (1897-)
       April 10, 1916-December 15, 1918
       Military diary; lengthy entries, perhaps augmented at a later
date; nonconformist Norfolkman with many Victorian attitudes; received a good education for his social class which manifests itself in
well-written entries; one of the better non-combatant diaries of World
War I in the trenches.
       • The Long Carry: The Journal of Stretcher Bearer Frank
       Dunham, 1916-18. R. H. Haigh and P. W. Turner, eds. Ox-
       ford: Pergamon, 1970.

2073. JONES, Thomas (1870-1955)
       1. December 7, 1916-October 31, 1930; Political diary; Welsh-
man educated at Glasgow University; "the little Welsh socialist"; cabinet secretary under Lloyd George (q.v.) and the three following
prime ministers.

- Whitehall Diary. Keith Middlemas, ed. 3 vols. London: Oxford University Press, 1971.

2. January 20, 1931-October 18, 1950; Personal diary; begins with his retirement from government and acceptance of a position with the Pilgrim Trust, a charitable foundation; more letters than diary entries; visitor to the Astors and Cliveden; knew George Bernard Shaw; visits to Germany before World War II.
- A Diary with Letters, 1931-1950. London: Oxford University Press, 1954.
REVIEW: Book Review Digest 1955, p. 475.

2074. MARIE, Queen Consort of Ferdinand I of Rumania (1875-1938)
August 30, 1916-November 17, 1918
Personal diary; view of the royal family's activities in the war; evacuation, Russian Revolution and its effects; typhus; war's end; involved in the political situation.
- Ordeal: The Story of My Life. New York: Scribner's, 1935.

2075. MERIWETHER, Lee (1862-)
August 6, 1916-October 17, 1918
Personal diary; as a neutral in the days before U.S. entry into World War I, the diarist was sent to observe the treatment of German prisoners in France; short stay in the U.S. and then abroad again; very well-done; sympathetic to the French and British.
- The War Diary of a Diplomat. New York: Dodd, Mead, 1919.

2076. NEWTON, Joseph Fort (1876-1950)
1. June 20, 1916-November 14, 1919; Personal diary; Iowa minister was asked to preach at City Temple in London; war conditions in the city and countryside; object of prejudice because he was an American.
- Preaching in London: A Diary of Anglo-American Friendship. New York: George H. Doran Co., 1922.

2. November 14, 1919-November 6, 1921; Personal diary; continues his previous diary; return to the U.S. and his ministry in New York; comments on life in the city, open air preachers, his reading, the state of the nation and the world; thoughtful and sometimes humorous.
- Preaching in New York, Diaries and Papers. New York: Doran, 1924.

1917

2077. BARCLAY, Harold (1872-1922)
June 30, 1917-January 2, 1919
Personal diary; preparations to sail to France from New York; to Liverpool; treating patients; life off-duty.

• A Doctor in France, 1917-1919: The Diary of Harold Barclay. New York: Prv. ptd., 1923.

2078. BOWERMAN, Guy Emerson, Jr. (1896-1947)
June 28, 1917-November 10, 1918
Personal diary; Yale freshman too young for the draft signed
up with the U.S. Army Ambulance Service; lively and somewhat
naive.
    • The Compensations of War: The Diary of an Ambulance
    Driver During the Great War. Austin: University of Texas
    Press, 1983.

2079. CARRINGTON, Dora (1893-1932)
January 1, 1917-February 22, 1932
Personal diary; British painter; letters to her live-in companion Lytton Strachey, Maynard Keynes, David Garnett, Virginia
Woolf (q.v.) and others are interspersed chronologically with diary
entries; interpersonal relations, her painting; the death of Strachey;
letters far outweigh diary entries in wordage; sketches and some of
her paintings are reproduced.
    • Carrington: Letters and Extracts from her Diaries. David
    Garnett, intro. London: Cape, 1970.

2080. EHRMANN, Max (1872-1945)
May 12, 1917-December 27, 1936
Personal diary; American poet, playwright, scholar and philosopher; worked as a lawyer and deputy prosecutor; introspective;
thought-provoking; occasionally humorous.
    • Journal. Bertha K. Ehrmann, ed. Boston: Bruce Hum-
    phries, 1952.

2081. FLOREZ, C. de
August 6-September 16, 1917
Military diary; young man's account of his term as a driver.
    • No. 6: A Few Pages From the Diary of an Ambulance
    Driver. New York: Dutton, 1918.
        REVIEWS: New York Times, June 23, 1918, p. 293. Book
        Review Digest 1918, pp. 157-58.

2082. GIBBS, George (1861-1940)
May 29-October 9, 1917
Travel diary; railway expert sent to improve the running of
the Trans-Siberian Railroad; Vancouver to Vladivostok to Petrograd;
interested in conditions but often blind to their implications.
    • "Railways and Politics: The Russian Diary of George Gibbs,
    1917," Joe Michael Feist, ed. Wisconsin Magazine of History,
    v. 62, pp. 179-99, Spring, 1979.

2083. GREELEY, Colonel William B.
August 20, 1917-July, 1919
Military diary; U.S. Forest Service employee was made an en-
gineer in the AEF to help in getting lumber for docks, railroad ties,

etc.; excerpts and connecting narrative; good picture of the kind of work not usually noted in official histories.

- "A Forester at War," George T. Morgan, Jr., ed. Forest History, v. 4, pp. 3-15, Winter, 1961.

2084. GRIDER, John McGavock (1892-1918)
        September 20, 1917-August 27, 1918
        Personal diary; pilot in the AEF from training in the U.S. to aerial combat in Germany; lighthearted flyboy with occasional somber thoughts; wine, women and the daring young men in their flying machines; ends with his death in the air over Germany.

- War Birds: Diary of an Unknown Aviator. Elliott White Springs, ed. New York: Doran, 1926; excerpts reprinted Aerospace Historian, v. 13, pp. 97-104, Autumn, 1966; pp. 141-48, Winter, 1966; v. 14, pp. 37-41, Spring, 1967; pp. 151-58, Autumn, 1967; pp. 219-23, Winter, 1967; v. 15, pp. 34-38, Summer, 1968.

2085. HARBORD, James Guthrie (1866-1947)
        May 29, 1917-November 15, 1918
        Military diary; General Pershing's Chief of Staff in the AEF; chief of Services of Supply; written for his wife; by ship to England and on to France; mostly behind the lines; somewhat stiff.

- Leaves from a War Diary. New York: Dodd, Mead, 1925.

2086. HUGHTELING, James Lawrence (1883-   )
        January 18-April 8, 1917
        Personal diary; optimistic American in Russia on unstated business; reports, hearsay and his own experiences.

- A Diary of the Russian Revolution. New York: Dodd, Mead, 1918.
  REVIEW: Book Review Digest 1918, p. 224.

2087. JOHNSON, Hiram Warren (1866-1945)
        1. April 6, 1917-November 3, 1944; Personal diary; California governor and U.S. senator; not really a diary but long letters to his children; excerpts from his Senate term when Wilson was president; early 1933 entries; fragments from the period of 1936-43.

- "The 'Diary' of Hiram Johnson," American Heritage, v. 20, pp. 64-76, August, 1969.

        2. 1917-1945; photocopied letters; "rich information about California politics, domestic legislation, foreign affairs and ... public figures."

- The Diary Letters of Hiram Johnson, 1917-1945. Robert E. Burke, ed. 7 vols. New York: Garland, 1983.
  REVIEW: Choice, v. 22, p. 611, December, 1984.

2088. JUDY, William Lewis (1891-   )
        August 21, 1917-June 19, 1919
        Military diary; from enlistment to boot camp, fighting in France, discharge; much posturing; author's sketches.

• A Soldier's Diary: A Day-to-day Record in the World War. Chicago: Judy Publishing Co., 1930.

2089. KIMMEL, Martin Luther (1883-1971)
September 3-December 17, 1917; gaps
Personal diary; enlistment in Vancouver, Washington, in the 147th Field Artillery AEF; at Camp Mills, Long Island; ends with his departure for France; introspective.
• "To Be a Soldier: 1917 Diary," Moss K. Brown, ed. Oregon Historical Quarterly, v. 75, pp. 241-69, September, 1974.

2090. LAHM, Frank Purdy (1877-1963)
August 24, 1917-August 10, 1919
Military diary; West Point graduate was the first U.S. military man to fly in an airplane; knew and flew with the Wright brothers; in charge of AEF balloon services in the period covered here; interesting account of a little-known aspect of the war.
• The World War I Diary of Col. Frank P. Lahm Air Service, A. E. F. Albert F. Simpson, ed. Maxwell Air Force Base, Ala.: Historical Research Division Aerospace Studies Institute, 1970.

2091. LILIENTHAL, David E. (1899-   )
May 17, 1917-1981
Personal diary; from his education at De Pauw; lawyer; on the original board of the Tennessee Valley Authority; dealings with President Roosevelt and Congress; first chairman of the Atomic Energy Commission; Congressional hearings, debates; dealings with President Truman; very full record; frank, well done.
• The Journals of David E. Lilienthal. 7 vols. New York: Harper, 1964-83.
    REVIEWS: Book Review Digest 1964, p. 737; 1965, p. 775; 1966, p. 717; 1967, p. 793; 1969, p. 793; 1971, pp. 827-28.

2092. MANNOCK, Edward (1889-   )
April 1-September 5, 1917
Military diary; tactless and abrasive British ace with the RAF in France; blinded in one eye by childhood illness, he refused to let this deter him; flying without parachutes; details of missions; shot down after the diary's end; received posthumous Victoria Cross.
• The Personal Diary of Major E. "Mick" Mannock. Frederick Oughton, intro. London: Spearman, 1966.

2093. MATHER, William D. (189?-197?)
January 31, 1917-February 4, 1919
Military diary; British university student joined the army; posted to the Balkans; cynical, humorous episodes of war in the area; well-written account of little-noticed Eastern Front.
• "Muckydonia," 1917-1919; Being the Adventures of a One-time "Pioneer" in Macedonia and Bulgaria During the First World War. Ilfracombe: Stockwell, 1979.

2094. O'BRIEN, Howard Vincent (1888-)
       November 27, 1917-January 25, 1919
       Military diary; American in the AEF in France worked in Intel-
ligence; censored mail; irritating, superior attitude toward the French
and most of his compatriots and officers; elliptical style.
       • Wine, Women and War: A Diary of Disillusionment. New
       York: J. H. Sears and Co., 1926.

2095. O'SHAUGHNESSY, Edith Louise (1870-1939)
       June 7, 1917-January 7, 1918
       Personal diary; wife of an American diplomat; life behind the
lines in France; excursions to the battlefields; curiously detached
from the tragedy around her.
       • My Lorraine Journal. New York: Harper and Bros., 1918.

2096. ROBIEN, Louis, Comte de (1888-1958)
       March 8, 1917-January 11, 1919
       Personal diary; diplomat with the French embassy in Russia;
opening day of the Revolution; transfer to Archangel under American
protection; political and social life in the capital; some sarcasm from
a superior Frenchman but with an appreciation of Russians' suffering
in the war; well written.
       • The Diary of a Diplomat in Russia, 1917-1918. Camilla
       Sykes, trans. London: Joseph, 1969; New York: Praeger,
       1972.
       REVIEW: Book Review Digest 1972, p. 1096.

2097. ROMEO, Guiseppe L. (1891-)
       October 4, 1917-May 1, 1918
       Military diary; Italian immigrant and U.S. citizen was drafted
in Seattle; service in France reported in laconic entries; "cooties
wouldn't let us sleep at night."
       • Diary of Pvt. Giuseppe L. Romeo Co. E, 361st Inf. 91st
       Division, A. E. F. During the War. Tacoma: T. V. Copeland
       and Son, 1919.

2098. SHINGAREV, Andrei Ivanovich (1869-1918)
       November 27, 1917-January 5, 1918
       Prison diary; law professor and member of the Constituent
Assembly after the Russian Revolution; arrested by Lenin's order;
executed two days after the last entry.
       • The Shingarev Diary: How It Was: The Peter and Paul
       Fortress 27-XI-17--5-I-18. Felicty Ashbee and Irina Tidmarsh,
       trans. Royal Oak, Mich.: Strathcona Publishing Co., 1978.

2099. STRAUB, Elmer Frank
       October 27, 1917-August 7, 1919
       Military diary; Indiana University student joined up; at Chateau
Thierry and the Meuse-Argonne; lengthy, detailed entries.
       • A Sergeant's Diary in the World War: The Diary of an En-
       listed Member of the 150th Field Artillery (Forty-Second [Rain-

bow] Division). Indianapolis: Indiana Historical Commission, 1923.

2100. THOMAS, Edward (-1917)
Military diary; minor English poet; service in the war and death there.
• The Diary of Edward Thomas 1 January-8 April 1917.
Gloucestershire: Whittington Press, 1977.

2101. URUSOV, Princess Vera (1864-)
December 28, 1917-May 26, 1918
Personal diary; wrote entries in place of letters to her husband in the Caucasus; life under the Bolsheviks and then occupation by a German-Austrian force.
• "Ekaterinoslav in Revolution: Excerpts From the Diary of the Princess Urusov," Allen A. Sinel, ed. Mrs. George E. Kirby, trans. Russian Review v. 29, pp. 192-208, 1970.

2102. VAUGHAN, Edwin Campion (1897-1931)
January 4-August 28, 1917
Military diary; Catholic officer in the Royal Warwickshire Regiment on the Western Front; arrival in France; life in the trenches; lengthy, descriptive entries reveal his feelings of inadequacy and concern for his men.
• Some Desperate Glory: The Diary of a Young Officer, 1917.
London: Warne, 1981.

2103. WALDNER, Jakob (1891-)
December 21, 1917-December 31, 1918
Prison diary; Hutterite from Montana was interned at Camp Funston, Kansas; camp life; trials of conscience; U.S. government policy.
• "An Account: Diary of a Conscientious Objector in World War I," Theron Schlabach, ed. Ilse Reist and Elizabeth Bender, trans. Mennonite Quarterly Review, v. 48, pp. 73-111, January, 1974.

2104. WIGHTMAN, Orrin Sage (1873-)
July 26-December 16, 1917
Travel diary; member of the American Red Cross Mission to Russia; from Vladivostok on the Trans-Siberian Railway; visit to Tsarskoye Selo; in Petrograd, Moscow, Odessa and Kiev; visit to Romania and a meeting with the king; numerous photos taken en route; evenhanded, sympathetic account.
• The Diary of an American Physician in the Russian Revolution, 1917. Brooklyn, N.Y.: Brooklyn Daily Eagle, 1928.

1918

2105. ALLEN, Hervey (1889-1949)
July 1-August 14, 1918

Personal diary; American author of the novel <u>Anthony Adverse</u>;
from the Marne to Vste and in the area of Chateau-Thierry; undated;
larger part was written during a hospitalization following the events
related here; remainder in 1919.
- <u>Toward the Flames: A War Diary</u>. New York: Farrar and
  Rinehart, 1934; Pittsburgh: University of Pittsburgh Press,
  1968.

2106. ANDERSON, LeRoy
       October 10-November 25, 1918
       Military diary; Illinois resident in the U.S. Army 33rd Division
at the Argonne Forest; Armistice and afterward with French civilians
vying for the privilege of billeting American soldiers.
- "The Last Days of the War: Memories From a Doughboy's
  Journal," <u>American History Illustrated</u>, v. 16, pp. 38-41, 1981.

2107. "BARBELLION, William Nero Pilate" (Bruce Frederick Cummings)
       (1889-1919) [B297]
       March 25, 1918-June 3, 1919
       Personal diary; British biologist dying of multiple sclerosis
hanging on for dear life.
- "Diary Excerpts," in: Philip Dunaway and Mel Evans, eds.
  <u>A Treasury of the World's Great Diaries</u>. New York: Doubleday, 1957; pp. 342-49.

2108. BECK, James Montgomery (1861-1936)
       Personal diary; by ship to Europe through submarine-infested
waters; in London for the Armistice; much name dropping.
- <u>A Diary of Armistice Days, From October 20, 1918 to December 21, 1918</u>. Philadelphia: Allen, Lane and Scott, 1923.

2109. BOYLSTON, Helen Dore (1895-1984)
       February 8-December 21, 1918
       Personal diary; early nursing career of the American author
of the Sue Barton series of books for teenage girls; hospital work in
France; a bout of diptheria; social life and rest and recreation at
the end of the war; hectic account in lively style.
- <u>Sister: The War Diary of a Nurse</u>. New York: I. Wash-
  burn, 1927.

2110. CAMPBELL, Peyton Randolph (1894-1918)
       April 15-August 28, 1918
       Letter diary; written to his mother; Buffalo, New York native
worked in advertising; lengthy well-written descriptions of life aboard
a vessel to France and in combat; killed in action.
- <u>The Diary-letters of Sergt. Peyton Randolph Campbell</u>.
  Buffalo, N.Y.: Pratt and Lambert, 1919.

2111. CASEY, Robert Joseph (1890-   )
       August 22, 1918-
       Military diary; executive officer of the 3rd Illinois Field

Artillery which used horses to move the guns; much transcribed con-
versation; hard-bitten, ironic style; entertaining.
* The Cannoneers Have Hairy Ears: A Diary of the Front
Lines. New York: J. H. Sears and Co., 1927.

2112. CLARK, Salter Storrs, Jr. (1890-1918)
        February 27-October 18, 1918
        Military diary; Yale graduate rejected by the U.S. Army be-
cause of poor eyesight; joined the French Army; at Signal School;
killed in action.
        * Soldier Letters by Coleman Tileston Clark and Salter Storrs
        Clark, Jr. New York: Prv. ptd., 1919; pp. 134-74.

2113. FURMAN, Emma LeConte (1847-   ) See also #1520
        January 1-August 12, 1918
        Personal diary; Macon, Georgia, resident comments on family
life and World War I; shortages, Red Cross work, suffrage meeting.
        * "A Righteous Aim: Emma LeConte Furman's 1918 Diary,"
        Lester D. Stephens, ed. Georgia Historical Quarterly, v. 62,
        pp. 213-24, Fall, 1978.

2114. GIMPEL, René (1881-1945)
        February 12, 1918-September 3, 1939
        Personal diary; brother-in-law of art connoisseur Joseph Du-
veen; dealings with collectors, artists and other dealers throughout
Europe; social and high life of the period between the wars; master
of the revealing detail; witty, lively.
        * Diary of an Art Dealer. John Rosenberg, ed. New York:
        Farrar, Straus, 1966.
          REVIEWS: Book Review Digest 1966, pp. 438-39; 1967, p.
          496.

2115. GUTTERSEN, Granville (1897-1918)
        January 2-November 25, 1918
        Personal diary; Minnesotan in flight training at Ellington Field,
Houston, Texas; later an instructor; social life.
        * Granville: Tales and Tail Spins From a Flyer's Diary.
        Alma A. Guttersen, ed. New York: Abington Press, 1919.

2116. HOLLERAN, Owen Cobb
        January 1-December 7, 1918
        Military diary; Georgian in the National Guard resigned to join
the British Army; regiment sent to Cork for training; eventually became part of the RAF; the foregoing is recounted in narrative form;
diary is on pp. 106-97; shot down over France and caught by the
Germans; repatriated through Switzerland at war's end; well-done
with a good deal of atmosphere and detail.
        * Holly, His Book: Being a Diary of the Great War. Chicago:
        Rogerson Press, 1924.

2117. JOHNSON, Edith E.
        1918-June 14, 1953

Medical diary; Nebraskan graduated from Cornell Medical
School and opened a practice in Palo Alto, California; indigent Mexicans, Orientals and Anglos were her patients; their names have been
changed for reasons of privacy but their stories make interesting
reading for medical buffs and hypochondriacs.
- *Leaves from a Doctor's Diary*. Palo Alto, Cal.: Pacific
Books, 1954.

2118. KENT, Rockwell (1882-1971)
1. August 28, 1918-March 17, 1919; Travel diary; American
painter spent the winter on Fox Island, Alaska; opens with a listing
of provisions, literary, edible and otherwise; painting, reading; bad
weather.
- *Wilderness: A Journal of Quiet Adventure in Alaska*. New
York: Putnam, 1920.

2. July 13, 1931-September 9, 1932; Personal diary; a year
spent among the natives; entries are essays on their culture; comparisons with Americans; comments on the bureaucracy of the ruling
Danes.
- *Greenland Journal*. New York: Obolensky, 1962.

2119. KESSLER, Harry (1868-1937)
1. November 6, 1918-September 30, 1937; son of a German
banker and an Irishwoman; art patron, collector and writer; involved
in the political and social worlds of the Europe of his time; astute
observer who managed to be at the center of things.
- *In the Twenties: The Diaries of Harry Kessler*. Charles
Kessler, trans. New York: Holt, Rinehart, and Winston,
1971; British edition titled *The Diaries of a Cosmopolitan*.
REVIEW: *Book Review Digest* 1971, p. 740.

2. Davis, Wayne K. "Time's Passenger: The Diaries of
Count Harry Kessler, 1887-1918," Ph.D., University of Missouri,
1977. (Dissertation Abstracts, 39/02A p. 1031-A). (A commentary
on the contents of the diary.)

3. January 28, 1919-March 8, 1933; excerpts from *In the
Twenties*.
- "In the Twenties: Diary of a Vanished Age," *Encounter*,
v. 29, pp. 3-17, July, 1967; pp. 7-17, August, 1967; pp. 17-
28, September, 1967.

2120. McELROY, John Lee
September 16, 1918-February 12, 1919
Military diary; the last months of fighting and the first days
of peace; going home on a troop ship.
- *War Diary of John Lee McElroy, 1st Lieut. 315th Field Ar-
tillery, 155th Brigade*. Camden, N.J.: Haddon Press, 1929.

2121. MANN, Thomas (1875-1955)
September 11, 1918-December 26, 1939; gaps 1922-32

Personal diary; German novelist and playwright received the Nobel Prize for literature in 1929; his work, relations with his wife and family; comments on politics; research for his writing; upheavals caused by Hitler; decision to immigrate; his arrival at Princeton; excellent.

- Diaries 1918-1939. Richard and Clara Winston, trans. New York: Abrams, 1982.

2122. MELLON, Thomas, Jr. (1880-   )
August 8-December 13, 1918
Personal diary; Pittsburgh native worked in Washington, D.C. with YMCA assisting American troops.

- Army "Y" Diary. Pittsburgh: The Crescent Press, 1920.

2123. MEYER, Ernest Louis (1892-1953)
July 26-December 9, 1918
Personal diary; introspective student at the University of Wisconsin refused to fight after being drafted; time in prison; return to civilian life.

- 'Hey! Yellowbacks!' The War Diary of a Conscientious Objector. New York: John Day, 1930; reprinted New York: J. S. Ozer, 1972.

2124. MILLARD, Shirley
March 16-November 10, 1918
Military diary; American woman with a command of the language went to France to nurse wounded in a requisitioned chateau; notes are appended with entries which fill in some of the gaps; visits from her fiancé and her fears for his safety.

- I Saw Them Die: Diary and Recollections of Shirley Millard. Adele Comandini, ed. New York: Harcourt, Brace, 1936.

2125. NIJINSKY, Vaslav (1890-1950)
1918-February 27, 1919
Personal diary; Russian danced with the Ballet Russe; reminiscences as madness closed in.

- "Diary Excerpts," in: Philip Dunaway and Mel Evans, eds. A Treasury of the World's Great Diaries. New York: Doubleday, 1957; pp. 353-57.

2126. PETERSON, Ira Lee (1896-   )
February 18, 1918-April 4, 1919
Military diary; at Chateau Thierry; gassed at the second Battle of the Marne; keen observer.

- "Journal of a War Veteran," Wisconsin Magazine of History, v. 8, pp. 199-220, December, 1924; pp. 328-48, March, 1925.

2127. PRATT, Joseph Hyde
May 18-November 11, 1918
Military diary; left Greensboro, North Carolina; from Montreal by ship to Dover, England; full entries for the fighting in France.

• "Diary of Colonel Joseph Hyde Pratt, Commanding 105th Engineers, A. E. F.," <u>North Carolina Historical Review</u>, v. 1, pp. 35-70, January, 1924; pp. 210-236, April, 1924; pp. 344-80, July, 1924; pp. 475-540, October, 1924; v. 2, pp. 117-44, January, 1925; pp. 269-99, April, 1925.

2128.   PTASHKINA, Nelly L'vovna (1903-20)
        1.   January 13, 1918-October 21, 1919; Personal diary; daughter of a Russian middle class insurance executive; play going; friends, family life; daily life affected by the Russian Revolution; flight from Moscow to Kiev and on to Paris; died by accidentally stepping over a precipice at Chamonix; dreamy, introspective; focusing on the future she would not have.
        • <u>The Diary of Nelly Ptashkina</u>.   Pauline de Chary, trans. Boston: Small, Maynard and Co., 1923?

        2.   "Diary Excerpts," in: Mary Jane Moffat and Charlotte Painter, eds.   <u>Revelations: Diaries of Women</u>.   New York: Random House, 1974; pp. 56-66.

2129.   SERGEANT, Elizabeth Shepley (1881-1965)
        October 20, 1918-May 15, 1919
        Personal diary; American woman in the American Hospital in Paris; her convalescence and thoughts on the war; Armistice; President Wilson's visit; self-indulgent.
        • <u>Shadow-shapes: The Journal of a Wounded Woman, October 1918-May 1919</u>.   Boston: Houghton, Mifflin, 1920.

2130.   SHERWOOD, Elmer W.
        July 13-November 1, 1918
        Military diary; lengthy entries; identifies other divisions and notes their actions, i.e. 167th Alabama Rainbows attacked <u>boches</u> with bowie knives when they ran out of ammunition; saw a plane shot down with a rifle bullet; simply written with snatches of song verses and quoted poetry.
        • <u>Diary of a Rainbow Veteran, Written at the Front</u>.   Terre Haute, Ind.:   Moore-Langen, 1929.

2131.   WHITE, Viola Chittenden (1890-1977)
        February 10, 1918-December 13, 1941
        Personal diary; American poet and librarian put down "a record of ideas"; time at the MacDowell Colony; getting a doctorate at the University of North Carolina; years of work at Middlebury College; reflections on current events interspersed with notes on her personal life; interesting.
        • <u>Partridge in a Swamp: The Journals of Viola C. White, 1918-1941</u>.   W. Storrs Lee, ed.   Taftsville, Vt.:   Countryman Press, 1979.
            REVIEW: <u>Vermont History</u>, v. 48, pp. 248-51, Fall, 1980.

<u>1919</u>

2132. ALLEN, Henry Tureman (1859-1930)
       June 27, 1919-February 19, 1923
       Personal diary; general in command of the American occupation
forces in Germany after World War I; Pétain, Foch, Ludendorff, British royalty, Henry Morgenthau, Lord Curzon and Lloyd George (q.v.)
make appearances; interplay of French, German, British and American
desires and demands are dealt with; German inflation, the occupation
of the Ruhr and the final withdrawal of American forces; social, political and military matters covered; interesting picture by a forthright, humane man.
       • <u>My Rhineland Journal</u>. Boston: Houghton Mifflin, 1923.

2133. BANDHOLTZ, Harry Hill (1864-1925)
       August 7, 1919-February 6, 1920
       Personal diary; appointed with the generals of the British,
French and Italian armies to the mission to carry out Armistice
terms; dry, sometimes humorous style; very detailed.
       • <u>An Undiplomatic Diary, By the American Member of the In-
       terallied Military Mission to Hungary, 1919-1920</u>. Fritz-Konrad
       Krüger, ed. New York: Columbia University Press, 1933;
       reprinted New York: AMS Press, 1966.
             REVIEWS: <u>American Historical Review</u>, v. 39, pp. 172-73,
             1933. <u>American Journal of International Law</u>, pp. 580-83,
             1933. <u>Political Science Quarterly</u>, v. 49, pp. 308-09, 1934.

2134. GHIKA, Princess Marie Chassaigne ("Liane de Pougy") (1869-
       1950)
       July 1, 1919-January, 1941
       Personal diary; a lesser light in the Parisian demimonde; mis-
tress to a French noble; wife of a Russian prince; philanthropist and
Dominican lay nun in her last years; intimate of Cocteau (q.v.),
Proust, Natalie Barney; mistress to d'Annunzio; exclamatory style;
high-flown sentiments intermingle with mundane needs to raise money
to pay her taxes; flashes of delicious spite, "for a little girl she has
very big arms, bottom and bust."
       • <u>My Blue Notebooks</u>. Diana Athill, trans. London: Deutsch,
       1979.

2135. SHAW, Llewellyn Dorrington (1904-   )
       April 13-May 19, 1919
       Personal diary; kept for a school project; hunting, a fight;
to the movies to see <u>Tarzan of the Apes</u>; delightful.
       • "Dorry's Diary: Enderlin, North Dakota, in 1919," Alpha
       B. Shaw, ed. <u>North Dakota History</u>, v. 42, pp. 18-25, Sum-
       mer, 1975.

<u>1920</u>

2136. BIDDLE, George (1885-1973)

May 4, 1920-September 19, 1922; some excerpts from 1917-20
journal
Personal diary; American painter sought to develop his art by
isolating himself in Tahiti; his reading; comments on artistic projects;
interesting for its non-judgmental comments on native life and customs.
• Tahitian Journal. Minneapolis: University of Minnesota
Press, 1968.

2137. BRECHT, Bertolt (1898-1956)
June 15, 1920-February 16, 1922
Personal diary; German poet and playwright; at a turning
point in his life; before his big successes; relations with women; his
work; illusions to later poems; not a likeable person.
• Diaries 1920-1922. Herta Ramthun, ed. John Willett, trans.
New York: St. Martin's, 1979.
REVIEW: New York Review of Books, v. 27, p. 13, May
15, 1980.

2138. GUNNISON, Esther
November 28, 1920-July 17, 1922
Personal diary; graduate of Greeley State Teachers' College;
one of 24 "ladies" accepted into the first Oxford class to admit women
to work on the same basis as men; sightseeing.
• "Esther Gunnison: A Nebraskan at Oxford, 1920-1921,"
Dolores Gunnerson, ed. Nebraska History, v. 59, pp. 1-30,
Spring, 1978.

2139. "MARTIN, Martha"
Exact days unrecorded
Personal diary; wife of a gold prospector in southeast Alaska
delivered her own child while cut off from help by a snowstorm.
• "Diary Excerpts," in: Mary Jane Moffat and Charlotte
Painter, eds. Revelations: Diaries of Women. New York:
Random House, 1974; pp. 301-13.

1921

2140. BASON, Frederick Thomas (1907-73)
1. 1921-1950; Personal diary; Cockney author ran a book shop;
details of his life and work; acquainted with prominent people in the
theatre and publishing; opinions on books and plays; good account
of British cultural life for the period; entertaining.
• Fred Bason's Diary. Nicolas Bentley, ed. London: Wingate, 1951.

2. 1922-July 2, 1952; Personal diary; most entries dated only
by year.
• Fred Bason's 2nd Diary. L. A. G. Strong, ed. London:
Wingate, 1952.

3. 1922-January, 1955; Personal diary.
• <u>Fred Bason's 3rd Diary</u>. Michael Sadleir, ed. London: Deutsch, 1955.

4. August 25, 1922-March 1, 1960; Personal diary.
• <u>The Last Bassoon: From the Diaries of Fred Bason</u>. Noel Coward, ed. London: Parish, 1960.

2141. KOLB, Ellsworth L.
September 3-October 13, 1921
Travel diary; by boat through Cataract Canyon of the Colorado River.
• "River Running 1921: The Diary of E. L. Kolb," W. L. Rusho, ed. <u>Utah Historical Quarterly</u>, v. 37, pp. 269-83, Spring, 1969.

2142. LEWIS, Warren Hamilton (1895-1973)
January 9, 1921-July 12, 1972
Personal diary; brother of writer C. S. Lewis; the editors here distill 140,000 words from the one and a quarter million in the diarist's 23 volumes; Sandhurst cadet's education was accelerated by World War I; family matters, walking tours, literary work of diarist and his brother; supportive of each other despite Warren's bouts with alcoholism; sharing "made all the difference."
• <u>Brothers and Friends: The Diaries of Major Warren Hamilton Lewis</u>. Clyde S. Kilby and Marjorie Lamp Mead, eds. New York: Harper and Row, 1982.
   REVIEW: <u>Library Journal</u>, v. 107, p. 1091, June 1, 1982.

2143. McGILL, Vernon
October 9-29, 1921
Travel diary; diarist drove with his wife and twelve-year old daughter in a seven-passenger 1919 Wyllis Knight averaging 21 miles per hour; gas cost from 19 to 50 cents per gallon; two oil changes and one flat tire; tourist notes.
• <u>Diary of a Motor Journey from Chicago to Los Angeles</u>. Los Angeles: Grafton Publishing, 1922.

2144. SHERIDAN, Clare Consuelo Frewen (1885-1970)
February 2, 1921-January 9, 1922
Travel diary; English sculptor and writer; on a lecture tour of the U.S. recounting her stay in Russia after the Revolution; wide acquaintance of publishing people in New York; breezy travelog with many comments on American mores.
• <u>My American Diary</u>. New York: Boni and Liveright, 1922.

<u>1922</u>

2145. BEATON, Cecil (1904-80)
1. October 4, 1922-September, 1939; Personal diary; British

photographer and writer; undergraduate life at Cambridge; Venice; to America and North Africa; with the Duke of Windsor and Mrs. Simpson; Alice B. Toklas and Gertrude Stein; Anita Loos and Aimee Semple MacPherson.
- The Wandering Years: Diaries, 1922-1939. Boston: Little, Brown, 1961.

2. September, 1939-August 23, 1944; Military diary; army duty in North Africa, China, India; visits to Britain; very full entries.
- The Years Between: Diaries, 1939-44. London: Weidenfeld and Nicolson, 1965.

3. December 11, 1963-March 13, 1974; Personal diary; photographing and sightseeing in Britain and abroad; encounters with painters Picasso and David Hockney; Mae West and Garbo; when his camera is not in hand he takes pictures with his pen; entertaining shots of the famous.
- The Parting Years: Diaries, 1963-74. London: Weidenfeld and Nicolson, 1978.

4. December 7, 1926-March 13, 1974; Personal diary; reprint of sections of previously published diaries; ceased keeping a diary when he lost the use of his right hand.
- Self Portrait with Friends: The Selected Diaries of Cecil Beaton, 1926-1974. Richard Buckle, ed. New York: Times Books, 1979.

2146. CARROLL, Gladys Hasty (1904-)
August 14, 1922-June 30, 1923
Personal diary; American novelist; sophomore year at Bates College in Maine; studies, thoughts, social life; death of a grandfather.
- To Remember Forever: The Journal of a College Girl, 1922-1923. Boston: Little, Brown, 1963.

2147. LINDBERGH, Anne Morrow (1906-)
1. September 17, 1922-October 8, 1928; Personal diary; daughter of Dwight Morrow, U.S. ambassador to Mexico; entries written "to savor" her experiences are interspersed with letters to family and friends; meeting with aviation pioneer Charles A. Lindbergh (q.v.); series is a portrait of a woman from adolescence to maturity; weathering great personal difficulties; inspirational without being sentimental.
- Bring Me a Unicorn: Diaries and Letters of Anne Morrow Lindbergh, 1922-1928. New York: Harcourt, Brace, Jovanovich, 1972.

2. May 16, 1929-December 28, 1932; Personal diary; marriage to Lindbergh; learning to fly; kidnapping of their son and the attendant publicity was one of the sensations of the Depression years; life in the public eye; birth of a second son; trip to the Far East.

- Hour of Gold, Hour of Lead: Diaries and Letters of Anne Morrow Lindbergh 1929-1932. New York: Harcourt Brace Jovanovich, 1973.

3. January 1, 1933-December 31, 1935; Personal diary; more air travel; lengthy trips, the kidnap trial; periods of personal depression worked through by "plugging along ... stubbornly"; death of her sister Elisabeth.
- Locked Rooms and Open Doors: Diaries and Letters of Anne Morrow Lindbergh, 1933-1935. New York: Harcourt Brace Jovanovich, 1974.

4. January 10, 1936-April 20, 1939; Personal diary; expatriate life in England where they fled to escape the kidnapping publicity; experiences in pre-war Europe.
- The Flower and the Nettle: Diaries and Letters of Anne Morrow Lindbergh, 1936-1939. New York: Harcourt Brace Jovanovich, 1976.

5. April 28, 1939-October 27, 1944; Personal diary; the couple's return to America; embracing isolationism and abandoning it after the country's entry into the war; life in a Detroit suburb while her husband worked at the Ford plant building planes; "I wanted to show the unwritten side of his wartime journals."
- War Within and Without. New York: Harcourt Brace Jovanovich, 1980.

2148. SEYMOUR, Helen Wells (-1937)
March 14, 1922-February 27, 1926
Personal diary; American on the art faculty of Doshisha Women's College in Kyoto; by ship from the East Coast via Panama and Honolulu; energetic, humorous artist was very involved in the life of her students; refugee work with victims of the Yokohama-Tokyo earthquake; visits to India and China; return via Suez Canal; entertaining.
- A Japanese Diary. New Haven: Yale University Press, 1952.

2149. WIDTSOE, John A.
September 4-19, 1922
Travel diary; survey of water resources; geology, scenery.
- "Diary of John A. Widtsoe: Colorado River Party, September 3-19, 1922, Preliminary to the Santa Fe Conference Which Framed the Colorado River Compact," A. R. Mortensen, ed. Utah Historical Quarterly, v. 23, pp. 196-231, July, 1955.

1924

2150. LEOPOLD, Aldo
June 11-25, 1924; August 8-16, 1925; 1926; 1927; 1929; 1937-38

Personal diary; notes of a naturalist on camping trips in Canada, Wisconsin and Illinois; some essays included here are reprinted from A Sand County Almanac; leisurely, thoughtful entries on flora and fauna observed.
* Round River, From the Journals of Aldo Leopold. Luna B. Leopold, ed. New York: Oxford University Press, 1953.

2151. MILLER, H. Earl (-1978)
October 15, 1924-July 10, 1925
Personal diary; student at St. Louis seminary went to Canada with a classmate to assist with church work.
* "Edmonton Diary: 1924-1925," Concordia Historical Institute Quarterly, v. 54, pp. 74-81, Summer, 1981.

2152. RITCHIE, Charles (1906-)
1. September 19, 1924-February 2, 1927; Personal diary; begun in his freshman year at King's University, Halifax; continued study at Oxford; university life in Canada and England; very well done.
* An Appetite for Life: The Education of a Young Diarist. Toronto: Macmillan, 1977.

2. July 1, 1937-September 23, 1945; Personal diary; officer in the Canadian Foreign Service; private secretary in the Washington legation; duty in wartime London: "Living in London is like being an inmate of a reformatory school."; passing love affairs; ironies of war; social life with prominent Britons; enjoyable.
* The Siren Years: Undiplomatic Diaries, 1937-1945. London: Macmillan, 1974.

3. August 21, 1946-April 27, 1962; Personal diary; posted to Paris, Delhi, Bonn, London and New York; leaves out official business and acts as a detached observer; reflections on politics and personalities; pungent phrases and vivid word pictures.
* Diplomatic Passport: More Undiplomatic Diaries, 1946-1962. Toronto: Macmillan, 1981.

2153. ROERICH, Nicholas (1874-1947)
1924-1928
Travel diary; Russian painter traveled from India through Sikhim, Mongolia and Tibet recording his impressions in words and paintings; uncooperative officials, caravans, peoples, beliefs and customs; interesting.
* Altai-Himalaya: A Travel Diary. New York: Frederick A. Stokes, 1929.

2154. TAGORE, Sir Rabindranath (1861-1941)
September 24, 1924-February 15, 1925
Spiritual diary; Hindu poet and winner of the Nobel Prize for Literature; interior monologues on a variety of subjects.
* The Diary of a Westward Voyage. Indu Dutt, trans. London: Asia Publishing House, 1962.

1925

2155. BARRYMORE, John (1882-1942)
December 27, 1925-January 19, 1926
Travel diary; American actor and screen idol on vacation in Mexico.
* "Diary Excerpts," in: Philip Dunaway and Mel Evans, eds. A Treasury of the World's Great Diaries. New York: Doubleday, 1957; 165-71.

2156. CLAYTON, Sir Gilbert Falkingham (1875-1929)
September 24, 1925-March 20, 1926
Personal diary; British diplomat in the Sudan Service during negotiations with Ibn Saud to fix the borders of Saudi Arabia, Trans-Jordan and Iraq; life in Cairo, Delhi and the desert while talks proceeded.
* An Arabian Diary. Robert O. Collins, ed. Berkeley: University of California Press, 1969.

2157. GOEBBELS, Joseph Paul (1897-1945)
1. August 12, 1925-October 30, 1926; Personal diary; German opportunist and early Nazi rose to post of Hitler's minister for propaganda; work with the Nazi party; speaking engagements; love life; reading; self-congratulatory, exclamatory style.
* The Early Goebbels Diaries, 1925-1926. Helmut Heiber, ed. Oliver Watson, trans. New York: Praeger, 1962.

2. January 1, 1939-July 8, 1941; Personal diary; persecutions of the Jews; Kristallnacht; the German invasion of Poland; stormy relations with his wife, Magda.
* The Goebbels Diaries, 1939-1941. Fred Taylor, trans, and ed. New York: Putnam, 1983.

3. January 21, 1942-December 9, 1943; gaps; Personal diary; he becomes a workaholic in his lust for power.
* The Goebbels Diaries. Louis P. Lochner, ed. and trans. New York: Doubleday, 1948.

4. February 27-April 9, 1945; Personal diary; the last days of the war; sinking German morale; food shortages; Allied advances; persists in drawing conclusions favorable to the Reich in the face of contradictory evidence.
* Final Entries, 1945: The Diaries of Joseph Goebbels. Hugh Trevor-Roper, ed. Richard Barry, trans. New York: Putnam, 1978; British edition titled The Goebbels Diary: The Last Days.

2158. HEFFERNAN, Leo G. (1889-1956)
September 28, 1925-January 23, 1927
Military diary; life at the Air Service Tactical School, Langley Field, Va.; courses in cavalry, balloons and flying.

• "The Adventures of a Junior Military Aviator," R. K. Mc-
Master, ed. Aerospace Historian, v. 25, pp. 92-102, 1978.

2159. OLSEN, Nils Andreas (1886-1940)
       May 11, 1925-April 15, 1935; gaps
       Personal diary; assistant chief of the Bureau of Agricultural
Economics which was supposed to serve farmers and consumers through
production, marketing and general service; often at odds with President Hoover's policies; much infighting and jockeying for position.
       • Journal of a Tamed Bureaucrat: Nils A. Olsen and the
       BAE, 1925-1935. Richard Lowitt, ed. Ames: Iowa State
       University Press, 1980.
              REVIEW: Journal of American History, v. 67, p. 728, De-
              cember, 1980.

2160. SHERMAN, Jane (1908-)
       August 1, 1925-January 7, 1927
       Personal diary; with Ruth St. Denis and her company on a
dance tour to Japan, China and India; sightseeing; much hard work
and dancing under poor conditions; lively and exuberant.
       • Soaring: The Diary and Letters of a Denishawn Dancer in
       the Far East, 1925-1926. Middletown, Conn.: Wesleyan Uni-
       versity Press, 1976.

                                   1926

2161. CHRISTIAN, Edgar Vernon (1908-27) [C24]
       October 14, 1926-June 1, 1927
       Exploration diary; Welshman and last survivor of a expedition
which set out to explore a route from the Great Slave Lake in northern Canada to Chesterfield Inlet on Hudson Bay; the party took little
food with them because their route lay across a game reserve; settled
in an old cabin; hunting and fishing were bad and all eventually
starved to death; harrowing.
       • Unflinching, A Diary of Tragic Adventure. New York:
       Funk & Wagnalls, 1938.

2162. MOTLEY, Willard (1909-69)
       January 1, 1926-June 1, 1943
       Personal diary; black American novelist; high school days and
life in an integrated Chicago neighborhood; by bike to New Jersey;
traveling about the U.S.; looking for work in the Depression; writing;
ends with his finishing his first novel (not published until 1948)
Knock on Any Door; lively, likeable person.
       • The Diaries of Willard Motley. Jerome Klinkowitz, ed.
       Ames: Iowa State University Press, 1979.
              REVIEWS: Book Review Index 1979, p. 327. Journal of
              American Studies, v. 14, p. 303, August, 1980.

2163. ROSENBERG, James Naumburg (1874-1970)

April 30-May 26, 1926
Travel diary; American went to study the agricultural settlements of Jews in Russia; interesting picture of a people trying to
make accommodations to the government; comments on prices, shortages, anti-Semitism; hopeful skeptic.
  • On the Steppes: A Russian Diary. New York: Knopf,
    1927.

1927

2164. GOLDFELD, Abraham
       June 1, 1927-December 26, 1930
       Personal diary; manager of a low-rent housing project on the
Lower East side of New York City; began by interviewing applicants
before the building was completed; daily entries are distinguished
from comments interpolated in later years; compassionate, sensible
man dealing with a variety of problems from retaining janitors to a
child molestation and the effects of the deepening Depression.
  • The Diary of a Housing Manager. Chicago: National Asso-
    ciation of Housing Officials, 1938.
       REVIEW: Annals of the American Academy, v. 198, p. 210,
       July, 1938.

2165. MEDRICK, George (1893-)
       March 24-November 14, 1927
       Personal diary; immigrant who started working in the mines
at age eleven; United Mine Workers' organizer on the picket lines;
collecting money and goods for strikers and observing scabs.
  • Filippelli, Ronald L. "Diary of a Strike: George Medrick
    and the Coal Strike of 1927 in Western Pennsylvania," Penn-
    sylvania History, v. 43, pp. 253-66, July, 1976.

2166. MICHAUX, Henri (1899-)
       1. December 25, 1927-January 15, 1928; Travel/literary diary;
Belgian writer; from Amsterdam by ship through the Panama Canal to
Ecuador; Brazil; return to France; poetry; essays on the sights.
  • Ecuador: A Travel Journal. Robin Magowan, trans. new
    ed., rev. and corrected. Seattle: University of Washington
    Press, 1970.

       2. January 6-December 15, 1928; Travel journal; poetry inter-
spersed with entries and essays.
  • "Ecuador," Robin Magowan, ed. and trans. Chicago Re-
    view, v. 20, pp. 5-25; pp. 60-75, 1968.

2167. MORAY, Alastair
       September 1, 1927-August 20, 1928
       Sea diary; Scot went as a supercargo on a four-masted schooner
running liquor to Prohibition America; lengthy entries, transcribed
conversation; several varieties of humor; good account of smuggling
practices by an articulate participant.

• Diary of a Rum-runner. Boston: Houghton Mifflin, 1929.
REVIEW: Book Review Digest 1929, p. 666.

1928

2168.   "Darbinian, Reuben" (Artasches Tchillingarian) (1883-   )
September 30, 1928-October 17, 1929
Personal diary; Armenian educated at the universities of Mos-
cow and Munich; emigrated to the U.S. after the Russian Revolution
and became editor of Armenian publications; wrote to practice his
English; social life, work, reading.
• "Two Newly-discovered English-language Journals or Work-
books, of Reuben Darbinian, Late Editor-in-chief, Hairenik
Publications," James H. Tashjian, ed. Armenian Review, v.
33, pp. 246-68, 1980; v. 34, pp. 147-73, 1981.

2169.   GREEN, Julien (1900-   )
1.   September 17, 1928-February 5, 1939; Personal diary;
novelist of American descent living in France and writing in French;
meetings with Gide (q.v.) and Malraux; his work; comments and
assessments of his reading; social life; interesting and well done.
• Personal Record, 1928-1939. Jocelyn Godefroi, trans. New
York: Harper, 1939.

2.   September 17, 1928-December 16, 1957; Personal diary;
army service; his work, reading and travel; acquainted with the
major French writers of the era; "I was sent into this world to write";
thoughts on Catholicism; easily dipped into with profit.
• Diary, 1928-1957. Selected by Kurt Wolff. Anne Green,
trans. New York: Harcourt, Brace and World, 1964; reprinted
New York: Carroll and Graf, 1985.
REVIEWS: Book Review Digest 1964, p. 495; 1965, p. 503.

2170.   LOW, Ann Marie (1912-   )
April 30, 1928-June 4, 1937
Personal diary; daughter of a stockfarmer in southeastern
North Dakota; typeface distinguishes diary entries from later additions; failure of the town bank; graduation and entrance into James-
town College; much on falling prices paid for farm produce; dust
storms; Civilian Conservation Corps project; teaching school; illuminating look at life in the Dust Bowl and one family's efforts to sur-
vive.
• Dust Bowl Diary. Lincoln: University of Nebraska Press,
1984.
REVIEWS: Library Journal, v. 109, pp. 2272, December,
1984. Choice, v. 22, pp. 1218, April, 1985.

2171.   PETERSEN, William J.
July 13-26, 1928; May 4-9, 1976
River diary; former editor of the State Historical Society of

Iowa Journal took his first towboat voyage while working on a doctorate in history; entries here cover 28 trips over six decades; well
written and filled with information on the industry and its changing
character; many photos.
* Towboating on the Mississippi. South Brunswick, N.J.:
Yoseloff, 1979.

2172. ROBERTS, Daniel A.
March 6, 1928-December 31, 1929
Political diary; lawyer active in ward politics and on the park
board.
* "A Chicago Political Diary, 1928-1929," Daniel J. Roberts,
ed. Illinois State Historical Society Journal, v. 71, pp. 30-56,
January, 1978.

2173. STANTON, Madeline Earle
June 2, 1928-1941
Medical diary; medical librarian kept notes on American neurosurgeon Dr. Harvey Cushing and his activities; extracts.
* Thomson, Elizabeth H. "Madeline Earle Stanton, Disciple:
the Years 1920 to 1941," Journal of the History of Medicine
and Allied Sciences, v. 36, pp. 151-67, 1981.

1929

2174. BLANTON, Smiley (1882-1966)
September 1, 1929; 1930, 1935; 1937, 1938
Psychoanalytic diary; highlights of his analysis made with the
knowledge and approval of Freud; discussions of his dreams; inter-
esting portrait of Freud.
* Diary of My Analysis with Sigmund Freud. Iago Galdston,
intro. New York: Hawthorn Books, 1972.
REVIEW: Book Review Digest 1972, p. 121.

2175. KIBBEY, William Beckford
Personal diary; American rancher in Sonora, Mexico; his ex-
periences in the "railroad and banking revolution" after the assas-
sination of President Alvaro Obregón.
* "El Alamo Prepares for a Siege: The Diary of W. Beckford
Kibbey April 15-May 4, 1929," Juliet Kibbey England, ed.
Journal of Arizona History, v. 20, pp. 121-38, Spring, 1979.

2176. REIMER, John B.
1929
Séance diary; record of psychic and spiritualist phenomena;
"actuated by the desire to personally convince myself of the survival
of human consciousness, my wife having died some time previously";
photos.
* The Diary of a Spiritualist. New York: The Author, 1930.

2177. STORRS, Monica (1888-1967)
       September 27, 1929-October 10, 1931
       Personal diary; Englishwoman went to the Peace River area of
Canada to carry out a lay apostolate for the Church of England; dealing with the vastness of Canada, its differences from England and
life as she knew it; "food ... depend[s] upon circumstances"; humorous, interesting writing by a sensible, dedicated woman.
       • God's Galloping Girl: The Peace River Diaries of Monica
       Storrs, 1929-1931. W. L. Morton, ed. Vancouver: University
       of British Columbia, 1979.
              BOOK REVIEWS: Alberta History, v. 28, pp. 38-39, Winter,
              1980. BC Studies, v. 45, pp. 137-41, Spring, 1980.

                              1930

2178. CARR, Emily (1871-1945) [C21]
       November 23, 1930-March 7, 1941
       Personal diary; Canadian painter began an introspective diary
in her 58th year; thoughts on art and her way of painting; the lone-
liness of marching to a different drummer.
       • "Diary Excerpts," in: Mary Jane Moffat and Charlotte
       Painter, eds. Revelations: Diaries of Women. New York:
       Random House, 1974; pp. 372-91.

2179. DAVIS, Lavinia Riker ("Wendell S. Farmer") (1909-61)
       January, 1930-January 9, 1955; gaps
       Personal diary; writer of children's book and adult mysteries;
introspective observations on her writing and family; "I ... concen-
trate on these journals in order to clarify what I think...."
       • Journals. New York: Prv. ptd., 1964.

2180. HARROLD, Ernest William (1889-1945)
       December 13, 1930-October 19, 1945
       Public diary; published in the Ottawa Citizen from 1923-45;
a royal visit; newspaper work; war news; some seventeenth-century
orthography; bits of his personal life; pleasing but not revealing.
       • Diary of Our Own Pepys: Record of Canadian Life. I.
       Norman Smith, ed. Toronto: Ryerson Press, 1947.

2181. KAHN, Edgar A. (1900-   )
       February 15-December 7, 1930
       Medical diary; period in his early practice while at the Univer-
sity of Michigan hospital; details and comments of cases seen; for
medical historians and the curious.
       • Journal of a Neurosurgeon. Springfield, Ill.: Thomas,
       1972; pp. 40-60.

2182. NICHOLSON, Sir Harold George (1886-1968)
       1. January 1, 1930-June 2, 1962; Personal diary; British dip-
lomat, biographer and critic; began entries upon his leaving the

British Foreign Office and taking up journalism; Depression years; involved with the Lindberghs (q.v.) after the kidnapping of their son; visits to the U.S.; European political situation: World War II; service in Parliament; knighted by Queen Elizabeth II; knew, visited and wrote about the leading figures, especially British, of political and cultural life of the 32 years covered in the diary; letters are those to his wife, Vita Sackville-West, with some of her replies; entries cease with her death; excellent.

● Diaries and Letters 1930-39. The War Years 1939-45. The Later Years 1945-1962. Nigel Nicholson, ed. New York: Atheneum, 1966-68.

REVIEWS: Book Review Digest 1966, pp. 887-88; 1967, p. 971; 1968, p. 995.

2. January 1, 1930-July 7, 1963; Material abridged from the three volume edition; asterisks mark passages not found there.

● Diaries and Letters, 1930-1964. Stanley Olson, ed. rev. ed. New York: Atheneum, 1980.

REVIEWS: Choice, v. 18, p. 1328, May, 1981. Times Literary Supplement, p. 1279, November 14, 1980.

2183. SIMPSON, George Gaylord (1902-   )
October 11, 1930-April 24, 1931
Expedition diary; armed with a doctorate in archaeology from Yale, he accompanied the Scarritt Expedition to Argentina to look for mammal fossils; comments on his work, the incessant wind, manners of the people, food; humorous, observant, tolerant; excellent reading for armchair archaeologists.

● Attending Marvels: A Patagonian Journal. New York: Macmillan, 1934; Chicago: University of Chicago Press, 1982.

2184. SOUTAR, William (1898-1943)
May 21, 1930-October 14, 1943
Personal diary; Scottish poet, bedridden by complications from arthritis, continued versifying; introspective; wide range of topics; poems interspersed; "... uncertain and unreasonable life which is mine is my choice, tho' it may seem to have been put upon me."

● Diaries of a Dying Man. Alexander Scott, ed. London: Chambers, 1954.

2185. WILSON, Edmund (1895-1972)
1. April 4, 1930-June 18, 1940; Personal/literary diary; American literary critic; marriage to his second wife; touring the South to see the effects of the Depression; conceives To the Finland Station and travels to Russia on a Guggenheim Fellowship for research; marriage to novelist Mary McCarthy after being widowed; American literary life of the 1930's and comments on its leading figures; thoughts on Marxism and American politics.

● The Thirties; From Notebooks and Diaries of the Period. Leon Edel, ed. New York: Farrar, Straus and Giroux, 1980.

2. March 23, 1940-December 15, 1949; Personal/literary diary;
deaths of F. Scott Fitzgerald and John Peale Bishop; mid-life crisis;
divorces Mary McCarthy and remarries; travels in Europe and the
U.S.; meeting with Edna St. Vincent Millay after a long separation.
 • The Forties: From Notebooks and Diaries of the Period.
Leon Edel, ed. New York: Farrar, Straus and Giroux, 1983.

3. 1950-59; Personal/literary diary; life with his fourth wife
and family; tracking the Dead Sea Scrolls through Israel; reworking
his earlier nonfiction; researching material for Patriotic Gore; meetings with Faulkner, Morley Callaghan, Robert Lowell and Cyril Connolly; stays at Princeton and Harvard universities.
 • The Fifties: From Notebooks and Diaries of the Period.
Leon Edel, ed. New York: Farrar, Straus and Giroux, 1986.

1931

2186. CARAWAY, Hattie (1878-1950)
December 14, 1931-March 28, 1934; gap from June 10, 1932-
January 3, 1934
Political diary; first woman elected to the U.S. Senate; filled
out her dead husband's unexpired term and then ran on her own;
New Deal supporter; fragmentary.
 • Silent Hattie Speaks: The Personal Journal of Senator Hattie Caraway. Diane D. Kincaid, ed. Westport, Conn.: Greenwood Press, 1979.
   REVIEWS: Arkansas Historical Quarterly, v. 38, pp. 369-
   70, Winter, 1979. American Political Science Review, v. 74,
   p. 1088, December, 1980. Journal of Southern History, v.
   46, pp. 617-18, November, 1980.

2187. POWERS, Elmer G. (1886-1942)
1. April 3, 1931-December 31, 1936; Personal diary; begun at
the request of a rural newspaper editor; his formal education stopped
short of graduation but he read widely and critically; Iowa farmlife
during the Depression.
 • Years of Struggle: The Farm Diary of Elmer G. Powers,
1931-36. H. Roger Grant and L. Edward Purcell, eds. Ames:
Iowa State University Press, 1976.
   REVIEWS: Agricultural History, v. 51, pp. 462-63, April,
   1977. Annals of Iowa, v. 43, pp. 643-44, Spring, 1977.
   Arizona and the West, v. 19, pp. 173-75, Summer, 1977.
   Minnesota History, v. 45, pp. 159-60, Winter, 1976. North
   Dakota History, v. 44, pp. 33-34, Spring, 1977.

2. January 19-September 9, 1936; Personal diary; Boone
County, Iowa, farmer beset by severe weather, both hot and cold;
the Depression.
 • "A Year of Struggle: Excerpts From a Farmer's Diary,

1936," H. Roger Grant and L. Edward Purcell, eds. Palimpsest, v. 57, pp. 14-29, January/February, 1976.

2188. SYLVESTER, Albert James (1889-)
       January 1, 1931-February 21, 1945
       Political/personal diary; principal private secretary to former
British prime minister Lloyd George (q.v.); political life in and out
of office; Lloyd George's private life and much about Frances Stevenson (q.v.), his second wife; dealings with Hitler, Chamberlain and
Churchill.
       • Life with Lloyd George: The Diary of A. J. Sylvester,
       1931-45. Colin Cross, ed. London: Macmillan, 1975.

                                1932

2189. ANONYMOUS
       Political diary; purportedly by a German War Office general;
Dr. Bruning and Chancellor von Papen dismissed; General von Sch-
leicher's chancellorship; accession of Hitler; the diarist resorts to
subterfuge and welcomes the aid of any willing collaborator in free-
ing Germany from the Allies' yoke; reader may try to sift truth from
possible fiction.
       • Klotz, Helmut, ed. The Berlin Diaries, May 30, 1932-
       January 30, 1933. Foreword by Edgar Ansel Mowrer. New
       York: Morrow, 1934; reprinted New York: AMS Press, 1972.

2190. HATCH, Olivia Stokes
       July 15-December 19, 1932
       Travel diary; daughter of Canon Anson Stokes of Washington
Cathedral accompanied her parents and acted as her father's secretary; he was to report to the Carnegie Corporation on native missions and schools and race relations; 14,000 miles by boat, car and
train; tourist notes with a few insights into British and Dutch differences in the Union of South Africa before apartheid became en-
trenched.
       • Olivia's African Diary: Cape Town to Cairo 1932. Wash-
       ington, D.C.: Smithsonian Institution Press, 1980.

2191. HURD, Peter (1904-84)
       October 24, 1932-March 12, 1935; May 25, 1942-March 19, 1944
       Personal diary; West Pointer from New Mexico became a leading
landscape painter of the twentieth century; married the painter daughter of artist N. C. Wyeth; 1930's entries concern his budding career;
1940's entries cover two assignments from Life magazine to do watercolors of American servicemen fighting in Europe and Africa; more
letters than diary material.
       • My Land is the Southwest: Peter Hurd Letters and Jour-
       nals. Robert Metzger, ed. Paul Horgan, intro. College Sta-
       tion: Texas A & M University Press, 1983.
           REVIEW: Publisher's Weekly, v. 224, p. 47, October 14,
       1983.

2192. LAMONT, Corliss (1902-   ) and Margaret LAMONT
       July 1-September 23, 1932
       Travel diary; American couple toured Russia; Leningrad, Mos-
cow; down the Volga to Georgia and Yalta; fair-minded observations
on customs, scenery.
       • Russia Day by Day: A Travel Diary. New York: Covici,
       Friede, 1933.

2193. MUGGERIDGE, Malcolm (1903-   )
       September 16, 1932-June 6, 1962; gaps
       Personal diary; British journalist went to Moscow as Manches-
ter Guardian contributor; to India on the Calcutta Statesman; military
service in North Africa and Europe; editing Punch; American lecture
tour; very readable.
       • Like It Was: The Diaries of Malcolm Muggeridge. John
       Bright-Holmes, ed. New York: Morrow, 1982.

2194. NOCK, Albert Jay (1873-1945)
       1. June 10, 1932-December 31, 1933; Personal diary; Ameri-
can critic ranges over a sea of subjects; Walter Lippmann, the Republican Party; Roosevelt; Judas; Bank Holiday; travel abroad; entries
are interesting essays on news events of the Depression era.
       • A Journal of These Days, June 1932-December 1933. New
       York: Morrow, 1934.
       REVIEW: Book Review Digest 1934, pp. 691-92.

       2. May 5, 1934-October 27, 1935; Personal diary; a trip to
Florida; Mrs. Roosevelt and American politics; Hitler; books read and
plays attended; sex appeal; a vacation in Europe; German cooks; gin;
another enjoyable compilation.
       • Journal of Forgotten Days, May 1934-October, 1935. Hins-
       dale, Ill.: Henry Regnery, 1948.
       REVIEW: Book Review Digest 1949, pp. 685-86.

2195. RUMBOLD, Richard William (1913-61)
       July 4, 1932-September 21, 1960
       Personal diary; minor British writer who suffered lifelong
chronic tuberculosis also had psychological problems; his life at Oxford; in the RAF in World War II; resided in Ceylon for a time; befriended by Sir Harold Nicolson (q.v.) and Paul Bowles; "my diary
is the debating chamber of my mind"; part-time postulant in a Japanese Zen monastery; revealing look at a troubled personality.
       • A Message in Code: The Diary of Richard Rumbold, 1932-
       60. William Plomer, ed. London: Weidenfeld and Nicolson,
       1964.

                                   1933

2196. CLARK, Edith K. O. (-1936)
       August 8, 1933-September 5, 1934

Personal diary; homesteading in Wyoming; active in education
in the state as a teacher and in legislative capacity; two summers
spent building a cabin.
* "The Diary of Edith K. O. Clark: The Summer of 1933,"
Annals of Wyoming, v. 39, pp. 217-44, October, 1967.

2197. ICKES, Harold LeClair (1874-1952)
1. March 5, 1933-December 14, 1941; Political diary; Republican lawyer turned Democrat; as Secretary of the Interior under
President Roosevelt he was instrumental in many Depression era public works projects; much on FDR and other high in his administration; "packing" the U.S. Supreme Court; TVA; approach of war in
Europe; FDR's reelection; very full, frank record; interesting for
its personal insight and revelations of character of the diarist and
the people around him.
* The Secret Diary of Harold Ickes. 3 vols. New York:
Simon and Schuster, 1953-54.

2. "Diary Excerpts," in: Philip Dunaway and Mel Evans,
eds. A Treasury of the World's Great Diaries. New York: Doubleday, 1957; pp. 394-401.

2198. LORANT, Stefan (1901-   )
March 14-September 27, 1933
Prison diary; incarcerated as a political offender; never had
a hearing; extracts from his wife's diary; she was imprisoned when
she tried to gain his release.
* I Was Hitler's Prisoner: Leaves from a Prison Diary.
James Cleugh, trans. New York: Putnam, 1935.

2199. OWEN, Ruth Bryan (1885-1954)
July 28-September 14, 1933
Travel diary; daughter of William Jennings Bryan was U.S.
Minister to Denmark; by ship from Copenhagen; daily life in Green-
land; description of inhabitants and customs; interesting.
* Leaves from a Greenland Diary. New York: Dodd, Mead,
1935.

2200. POWNALL, Sir Henry (1887-1961)
1933-1944
Military diary; professional British soldier and staff officer;
military consultant on Churchill's The Second World War; army politics; growing threat from Hitler; used this diary to vent his frustrations; often proved right by hindsight; dry humor; especially
good for the years before the war began.
* Diaries. Brian Bond, ed. 2 vols. Hamden, Conn.: Archon Books, 1973.

1934

2201. ARCHER, Laird (1892-   )

June, 1934-July 28, 1941
Personal diary; head of the Athens office of the Near East
Foundation; Greece and the surrounding area in the years leading
up to World War II by an individual only peripherally involved in
politics but knowledgeable.
   • Balkan Journal: An Unofficial Observer in Greece. New
York: Norton, 1944.

2202. CHANNON, Sir Henry (1897-1958)
February 12, 1934-November 18, 1958
Personal diary; American-born Briton spared by inheritance
from having to work for a living; member of Parliament; social and
political life; master of the amusing detail; closely involved with Ed-
ward VIII and Mrs. Simpson; excellent.
   • "Chips": The Diaries of Sir Henry Channon. Robert
Rhodes James, ed. London: Weidenfeld and Nicolson, 1967.

2203. KILLEARN, Sir Miles Lampson, Baron (1880-1964)
January 7, 1934-March 9, 1946
Personal and diplomatic diary; dealings with Churchill, King
Farouk and the Foreign Office; life of several different classes of
people outside diplomatic circles also; full entries of historical inter-
est.
   • The Killearn Diaries, 1934-1946: The Diplomatic and Per-
sonal Record of Lord Killearn, High Commissioner and Ambas-
sador, Egypt. Trefor E. Evans, ed. London: Sidgwick and
Jackson, 1972.

2204. LIGHT, Richard Upjohn (1902-   )
Travel diary; Yale senior and a friend (Robert French Wilson)
left New Haven headed east; radio transmissions are included; maps
help chart the trip in sections; extended entries on landing spots,
Greenland, Stockholm; good account of a lighthearted journey.
   • Journal of a Seaplane Cruise Around the World August 20,
1934 to January 24, 1935. Crawfordsville, Ind.: n. p., 1937.

2205. MITCHISON, Naomi Haldane (1897-1964)
February 23-April 10, 1934
Political diary; British writer; politics in Austria; visit to the
Social Democrats.
   • Naomi Mitchison's Vienna Diary. New York: H. Smith and
R. Haas, 1934.

2206. SENESH, Hannah (Szenes) (1921-44)
   1. September 7, 1934-January 11, 1944; Personal diary; Hungarian Jew emigrated to Palestine and with 32 others was parachuted
into Yugoslavia to try to rescue Allied pilots and organize resistance;
executed by the Nazis; school days; belief in Zionism; life in Palestine; training for her mission.
   • Hannah Senesh: Her Life and Diary. Marta Cohn, trans.
London: Vallentine, Mitchell, 1971; New York: Schocken, 1972.

2. "Diary Excerpts," in: Mary Jane Moffat and Charlotte Painter, eds. Revelations: Diaries of Women. New York: Random House, 1974; pp. 67-74.

2207. "SENKEVICH, Tatyana"
October 11, 1934-November 13, 1942
Personal diary; extracts; schooldays as a Young Pioneer; teachers and parents of her friends are denounced as "enemies of the people"; approach of the German army; occupation; conscripted by the Germans to work in Salzburg, Austria; bewilderment and fear of events she cannot control.
• "A Soviet Girl's Diary," in: Louis Fischer, ed. Thirteen Who Fled. New York: Harper and Bros., 1949; pp. 111-130.

2208. SHIRER, William Lawrence (1904-   )
1. January 11, 1934-December 13, 1940; Personal diary; author of the authoritative wrapup on Nazi Germany, The Rise and Fall of the Third Reich (Simon and Schuster, 1960); "written for pleasure and peace of mind" but also because the writer knew his job as a journalist gave him opportunities to be where the action was; some parts reconstructed from notes, scripts and memory; written primarily in Berlin with jaunts to other European capitals; family life, work; portrait of a continent headed toward war; excellent.
• Berlin Diary: The Journal of a Foreign Correspondent: 1934-1941. New York: Knopf, 1941.
(For a backward glance at these years see The Nightmare Years [Little, Brown, 1984], which contain excerpts from the diaries and the tale of how they were smuggled out of Germany.)

2. July 20, 1944-December 9, 1945; Personal diary; early days in the U.S. and the remainder in Germany; lengthy quotes from Nazi writings, Hitler's speeches; thoughts and actions of Berliners after the end of the war.
• End of a Berlin Diary. New York: Knopf, 1947.

WILSON, Robert F. see LIGHT, Richard U.

1935

2209. DAWSON, Percy Millard (1873-   )
July 3, 1935-May 30, 1936
Travel diary; lengthy, detailed notes by a Johns Hopkins-trained doctor; uses simplified spelling; good for medical and scientific theories and experiments he witnessed.
• Soviet Samples: Diary of an American Physiologist. Ann Arbor, Mich.: Edwards Bros., Inc., 1938.

2210. EISENHOWER, Dwight David (1890-1969)
December 27, 1935-1937; January 1, 1942-March 14, 1967; sporadic entries in the 1942-67 section

Personal diary; West Pointer and 34th U.S. president; service
in the Philippines under General Douglas MacArthur with notes on
their incompatability; in the War Department in Washington in early
1942; in Britain, North Africa and Italy; chief of staff after the Allied victory; presidency of Columbia University; NATO; two presidential terms; retirement; frank, sometime humorous and rueful.
- The Eisenhower Diaries. Robert H. Ferrell, ed. New York:
Norton, 1981.

2211. MacVEAGH, Lincoln (1890-1972)
April 24, 1935-April 28, 1945; gaps
Personal and political diary; founder of the Dial Press, clas-
sicist and U.S. envoy to Greece; "the Greeks are my passion in life";
from the fall of the republic to the implementation of the Marshall
Plan.
- Ambassador MacVeagh Reports: Greece, 1933-1947. John
O. Iatrides, ed. Princeton: Princeton University Press, 1980.

2212. PAVESE, Cesare (1908-50)
1. December, 1935-August 18, 1950; Literary diary; Italian
novelist and translator; anti-Fascist; many thoughts on suicide after
two friends take their own lives; quotes and notes on his reading.
- The Burning Brand: Diaries 1935-1950. A. E. Murch,
trans. Frances Keene, intro. New York: Walker and Co.,
1961.

2. Literary diary; the translator believes Pavese has been
shortchanged by previous English language renderings of his work
and seeks to remedy the situation. He compares this diary to those
of Gide and Kafka.
- Koffler, Richard M. "The Job of Living (Diary 1935-1950):
An Annotated Translation of Cesare Pavese's Diary 'Il mestiere
di vivere'," Ph.D., Rutgers University, 1973. (Dissertation
Abstracts, 34/10-A, p. 6646)

2213. TROTSKY, Leon (1877-1940)
February 7-September 8, 1935
Personal diary; Russian Communist leader who lost a power
struggle with Stalin after Lenin's death; expelled for antiparty activities; philosophical; comments on his reading and past life; worry
about his family; lived in France and Norway; much on his intellec-
tual life.
- Diary in Exile, 1935. Elena Zarudnaya, trans. Cambridge:
Harvard University Press, 1958.
REVIEWS: Book Review Digest 1958, p. 1062; 1959, p.
996-97.

2214. "WOODLEY, Winifred" (Worth Tuttle Hedden) (1896-)
1935; 1937; 1939; 1955
Personal diary; American novelist and educator; family life;
writing; domestic comedy; fiction?

• <u>Two and Three Make One</u>. New York: Crown, 1956.

<u>1936</u>

2215. DUGDALE, Blanche Elizabeth Campbell Balfour (1880-1948)
January 1, 1936-August 3, 1947
Personal and political diary; granddaughter of the 8th Duke
of Argyll and fervent Zionist; intimate of Chaim Weizmann and privy
to many British cabinet decisions and policies; peopled with British
Establishment figures; interesting portrait of behind-the-scenes ma-
neuvers.
• <u>Baffy: The Diaries of Blanche Dugdale, 1936-1947</u>. N. A.
Rose, ed. London: Valentine and Mitchell, 1973.

2216. FITZGERALD, F. Scott (1896-1940)
Personal diary; leading American fiction writer of the Jazz Age;
excerpts; living cheaply in Hendersonville, North Carolina.
• "Diary Excerpts," in: Philip Dunaway and Mel Evans, eds.
<u>A Treasury of the World's Great Diaries</u>. New York: Double-
day, 1957; pp. 340-41.

2217. GASCOYNE, David (1916-   )
1. September 9, 1936-June 8, 1937; Personal diary; British
poet; charter member of the "Mass-Observation" movement; author of
one of the first books in English on surrealism; trip to Spain; visit
with Picasso; notes on his work, social life and reading.
• <u>Journal, 1936-37</u>. London: Enitharmon Press, 1980; pp.
23-105.
REVIEWS: <u>Observer</u>, p. 47, January 11, 1981. <u>Times Educational Supplement</u>, p. 16, December 26, 1980. <u>Times
Literary Supplement</u>, p. 132, February 6, 1981.

2. June 19, 1937-October 10, 1939; Personal diary; living in
Paris and trying to write after a year's sabbatical due to depression;
money troubles; in analysis; introspective; beset by life's mundane
realities.
• <u>Paris Journal 1937-1939</u>. London: Enitharmon Press, 1978.

2218. "HURNSCOT, Loran" (Gay Stuart Taylor) (-1970)
May 26, 1936-October 4, 1941
Personal diary; Englishwoman was a partner in a publishing
house; followed and then rejected the teachings of Russian psychol-
ogist P. D. Ouspensky.
• "Diary Excerpts," in: Mary Jane Moffat and Charlotte
Painter, eds. <u>Revelations: Diaries of Women</u>. New York:
Random House, 1974; pp. 335-46.

2219. KELLER, Helen Adams (1880-1968)
November 4, 1936-April 14, 1937
Personal diary; deaf and blind American who worked on behalf

of the handicapped; begun shortly after the death of her teacher
Annie Sullivan Macy; accompanied by a companion on a voyage to
Scotland; lengthy visit and meetings with many prominent figures;
home to Forest Hills, New York; preparation for a voyage to Japan
via Honolulu; determination to "be as independent as I may under
the circumstances."
- Helen Keller's Journal 1936-1937. New York: Doubleday,
  1938.

2220. KOSTERINA, Nina Alekseevna (1921-41)
Personal diary; daughter of Russian Communist party members
and a Young Pioneer; school life; becoming aware of boys; friends,
relatives and her father arrested as "enemies of the people"; her
reading; killed shortly after joining a partisan unit.
- The Diary of Nina Kosterina. Mirra Ginsburg, trans.
  New York: Crown, 1968.
  REVIEW: Book Review Digest 1969, p. 729.

2221. LOCHNER, Louis P. (1886?-)
May 6-14, 1936
Travel diary; American was the Berlin bureau chief of the
Associated Press; Berlin to Lakehurst, New Jersey and return; de-
tails of life aboard the dirigible, accommodations, etc.
- "Aboard the Airship Hindenburg: Louis P. Lochner's Diary
  of Its Maiden Flight to the United States," Wisconsin Magazine
  of History, v. 49, pp. 101-21, Winter, 1965-66.

2222. RECK-MALLECZEWEN, Fritz (Friedrich) Percyval (1884-1945)
May, 1936-October, 1944
Personal diary; son of a Junker family was appalled by Nazism
and the rise of Hitler, whom he terms a "senile ... coffeehouse ora-
tor"; arrested for not reporting for duty in the Home Guard and shot
at Dachau; literate, compelling.
- Diary of a Man in Despair. Paul Rubens, trans. New
  York: Macmillan, 1970.
  REVIEW: Book Review Digest 1970, p. 1165.

2223. TILLICH, Paul (1886-1965)
April 11-September 19, 1936
Spiritual diary; German Protestant theologian and philosopher;
his first trip back to Europe since leaving Germany in 1933; notes
kept for his wife while attending an Oxford Conference; reveals his
theological thinking; love of nature and man-made beauty; one foot
in America and one in Europe.
- My Travel Diary: 1936; Between Two Worlds. Jerald C.
  Brauer, ed. Maria Pelikan, trans. New York: Harper &
  Row, 1970.

1937

2224. CIANO, Galeazzo (1903-44)

1. August 23, 1937-December 31, 1938; Political diary; Mussolini's son-in-law; begins as Foreign Minister; Anglo-Italian relations; Italy's part in the Spanish Civil War; Anschluss; the Anti-Comintern Pact; the Czech crisis; Munich; portrays himself as the protagonist and others as supporting players.
- Hidden Diary, 1937-1938. Andreas Mayor, trans. New York: Dutton, 1953.
   REVIEW: Book Review Digest 1953, p. 181.

2. January 1, 1939-December 23, 1943; Political diary; text was smuggled out of Italy by his wife; became a Fascist while in the Italian diplomatic service; was helpless to stop Mussolini's headlong dash to disaster; of historical interest.
- The Ciano Diaries, 1939-1943: The Complete Unabridged Diaries of Count Galeazzo Ciano. Hugh Gibson, ed. New York: Doubleday, 1946.
   REVIEW: Book Review Digest 1946, pp. 150-51.

2225. DORIAN, Emil (1891-1956)
December 30, 1937-September 13, 1944
Personal diary; Rumanian-Jewish doctor and poet; notes on family and political situation; Jewish persecution; anti-Semitism from the Rumanians and occupying Nazis; bitter humor, "Dear God ... choose another [people] now!"; compassionate, sensitive man.
- The Quality of Witness: A Romanian Diary 1937-1944. Marguerite Dorian, ed. Mara Soceanu Vamos, trans. Philadelphia: Jewish Publication Society of America, 1982.
   REVIEWS: Library Journal, v. 107, p. 2167, November 15, 1982. Publishers Weekly, v. 222, p. 63, November 5, 1982.

2226. HARVEY, Oliver, Baron Tasburgh (1893-1968)
1. February 23, 1937-June 24, 1940; Diplomatic diary; private secretary to Anthony Eden and Lord Halifax; opposed Chamberlain's appeasement policy; witnessed the Fall of France; written down "hot"; pleasing, breathless flavor.
- The Diplomatic Diaries of Oliver Harvey, 1937-1940. John Harvey, ed. New York: St. Martin's, 1970.

2. June 25, 1940-August 7, 1945; Political diary; at the center of things throughout the war; the raising of a Jewish Army; a drunken dinner with Stalin in the Kremlin; sheer physical exhaustion of Eden, Churchill and others by the end of the war; valuable for its insights into British policies; succinct.
- The War Diaries of Oliver Harvey. John Harvey, ed. London: Collins, 1978.

2227. IRONSIDE, Sir Edmund (1880-1959)
May 13, 1937-August 18, 1940
Personal diary; career military man and commanding officer of the UK Home Forces; meeting with Hitler, Churchill; German negotiations; invasions; Dunkirk collapse and evacuation; thoughtful; of historical importance.

• Time Unguarded: The Ironsides Diaries, 1937-1940. Rod-
erick Macleod and Denis Kelly, eds. New York: David McKay,
1962.

2228. PAPANIN, Ivan Dmitrievich (1894-1986)
       May 21, 1937-February 19, 1938
       Exploration diary; Russian Arctic specialist lived on an ice
floe with three other Soviet scientists while it drifted from the North
Pole down the east coast of Greenland; interesting, detailed account
of a man excited about his work while not minimizing its hardships.
       • Life on an Ice Floe: Diary of Ivan Papanin. Fanny Smit-
       ham, trans. London: Hutchinson and Co., 1947.

2229. SANDERSON, ---
       August 5-9, 1937
       Personal diary; American delegate to a British convention on
current Russian developments; cryptic.
       • "The Sanderson Family and International Relations," Stud-
       ies in Soviet Thought [Dutch], v. 21, no. 1, p. 31-38, 1980.

                              1938

2230. BRADLEY, Sir Kenneth (1904-)
       May 4-December 15, 1938
       Personal diary; duties of a British colonial official in Northern
Rhodesia (now Zambia); native life, travel throughout the district;
well done.
       • The Diary of a District Officer. 4th ed. London: Macmil-
       lan, 1966.

2231. CADOGAN, Sir Alexander (1884-1968)
       January 1, 1938-August 16, 1945
       Personal diary; wealthy, titled Permanent Under-Secretary in
the British Foreign Office; Munich; war declaration; collapse of
France; Operation Overlord; the only diary kept in this period by
someone in his position.
       • The Diaries of Sir Alexander Cadogan, O. M., 1938-1945.
       David Dilks, ed. London: Cassell, 1971.
            REVIEW: Book Review Digest 1972, pp. 194-95.

2232. De GEER, Vilhelm
       January 1-December 31, 1938
       Personal diary; some entries rewritten and rearranged from
the original; Dane comments on English life, mores and character;
Americanisms in the language, visit to Sweden; interesting portrait
by a man who expected the war to break out.
       • Diary of an Alien. London: Oliver and Boyd, 1959.

2233. De ROUSSY DE SALES, Raoul Jean J. F. (1896-1942)
       September 30, 1938-November 30, 1942

Personal diary; Frenchman who was an American correspondent for Paris Soir; thoughtful entries by a keen observer; Dorothy Thompson, Henry Luce and other American journalists appear.
- The Making of Yesterday, The Diaries of Raoul de Roussy de Sales. Walter Millis, intro. New York: Reynal and Hitchcock, 1947.

2234. KURTZ, Wilbur G. (1882-   )
January 26, 1938-March 20, 1939
Personal diary; artist and history buff was employed to insure the accuracy of the film version of Margaret Mitchell's novel; entertaining.
- "Technical Adviser: The Making of Gone with the Wind: The Hollywood Journals of Wilbur G. Kurtz," Richard Barksdale Harwell, ed. Atlanta History, v. 22, pp. 8-131, Summer, 1978.

2235. LINDBERGH, Charles Augustus (1902-74)
March 11, 1938-June 15, 1945
Personal diary; American aviation pioneer and husband of Anne Morrow Lindbergh (q.v.); moved to Europe after the kidnapping of his son; felt war was imminent and began keeping a diary; visits to Paris, Berlin, Moscow; worked with Henry Ford on plane construction; flew combat missions; several trips to the U.S.; war in the Pacific; well done, long entries; good picture of the war years and his work for the U.S. government.
- The Wartime Journals of Charles A. Lindbergh. New York: Harcourt Brace Jovanovich, 1970; excerpts in American Heritage, v. 21, pp. 32-37, 114-15, October, 1970.

2236. PAQUIN, Grete
October 22, 1938-April 10, 1945
Personal diary; widowed German mother of four adult children worked for the University of Gottingen; lived in a cabin outside of town; believed Nazis did some good things for children but was generally against their excesses; hid her diaries better than her opinion and was questioned by the Gestapo; sympathetic account of an ordinary woman in difficult times.
- Two Women and a War. Anna Pettit Broomell, ed. Philadelphia: Muhlenberg Press, 1953.

2237. VON HASSELL, Ulrich (1881-1944)
September 17, 1938-July 13, 1944
Personal diary; German career diplomat and ambassador to Italy; ousted by Hitler in late 1937; joined a group interested in European economic conditions which he used as a cover for his part in a conspiracy against Hitler; arrested and executed in the aftermath of the July 20, 1944 assassination attempt against Hitler; well done.
- The von Hassell Diaries, 1938-1944: The Story of the Forces Against Hitler Inside Germany. New York: Doubleday, 1947.

2238. WOLFE, Thomas (1900-38)
        Travel diary; American novelist; account of a trip made with
two newspapermen shortly before his death; Portland, Oregon to
Yosemite, Sequoia, the Grand Canyon and Yellowstone.
        • A Western Journal: A Daily Log of the Great Parks Trip,
        June 20-July 2, 1938. Pittsburgh: University of Pittsburgh
        Press, 1951.

                                    1939

2239. BARLONE, D.
        Military diary; captain in the 2nd North African Division; mo-
bilization; the collapse of France; enlistment in de Gaulle's Free
French Forces; interesting diary of a thoughtful career military man
with great love of his country and concern for his men.
        • A French Officer's Diary (23 August, 1939-1 October 1940).
        L. V. Cass, trans. Cambridge: The University Press, 1942.

2240. BERG, Mary (1924-   )
        October 10, 1939-March 5, 1944
        Personal diary; teenage daughter of an American citizen; in
Lodz at the opening of the war, she was interned in the Warsaw
ghetto; school attendance; murder and starvation; transfer to Vittel,
France; news of the Warsaw uprising; repatriation to the U.S.; grip-
ping.
        • Warsaw Ghetto, A Diary. S. L. Shneiderman, ed. New
        York: L. B. Fischer, 1945.

2241. CZERNIAKOW, Adam (1880-1942)
        September 6, 1939-July 23, 1942; gap from December 14, 1940-
        April 22, 1941
        Personal diary; active in Polish political and social life before
the war; during the siege of Warsaw he became head of the Jewish
Council; when the Germans moved in he remained; straightforward
account of events within the Warsaw ghetto reveals much material not
available in any other source; very good introduction.
        • The Warsaw Diary of Adam Czerniakow: Prelude to Doom.
        Raul Hilberg, Stanislaw Staron and Joseph Kermisz, eds. S.
        Staron and the Staff of Yad Vashem, trans. New York: Stein
        and Day, 1978.

2242. DUNCAN, Ronald Frederick Henry (1914-   )
        June, 1939-October 8, 1942
        Personal diary; British poet and city person went to the West
Country to farm; 40 acres of weeds and too many jobs to do; joined
by fellow pacifists with no farming experience; harvest of wry observations.
        • Journal of a Husbandman. London: Faber and Faber, 1944.

2243. ETZDORF, Rüdiger von
        September, 1939-1942

Military diary; extracts; German opposed to Hitler became a British agent.
- "Diary of a British Agent," Royal United Service Institute Journal, v. 114, pp. 49-55, 1969.

2244. HAECKER, Theodor (1889-1945)
November, 1939-February 9, 1945
Philosophical journal; mini-essays on a variety of topics.
- Journal in the Night. Alexandr Dru, trans. New York: Pantheon, 1950.
REVIEW: Book Review Digest 1950, p. 391.

2245. HALDER, Franz (1884-1972)
August 14, 1939-September 24, 1942
Military diary; chief of the General Staff under Hitler; Polish campaign to mid-war; mostly cryptic field notes, reports, orders; some fuller entries in the later days.
- The Halder Diaries: The Private War Journals of Col. Gen. Franz Halder. Arnold Lissance, ed. Boulder, Col.: Westview Press, 1976.

2246. KAPLAN, Chaim Aron (1880-1942/43)
September 1, 1939-August 4, 1942
Personal diary; principal of a Hebrew elementary school in Warsaw; German invasion of Poland; dealings with Adam Czerniakow (q.v.); last entries deal with his attempts to elude the Nazis; died with his wife at Treblinka; diary entries were made several times a day to record the changing conditions.
- Scroll of Agony: The Warsaw Diary of Chaim A. Kaplan. Abraham I. Katsh, trans. and ed. New York: Macmillan, 1965; 1973 edition titled The Warsaw Diary of Chaim A. Kaplan.

2247. LONG, Breckinridge (1881-1958)
September 2, 1939-December 4, 1944; gaps in later years
Political diary; former ambassador to Italy was assistant Secretary of State under President Roosevelt for the years covered here; much about Cordell Hull; valuable, full record.
- The War Diary of Breckinridge Long: Selections from the Years 1939-1944. Fred L. Israel, ed. Lincoln: University of Nebraska Press, 1966.

2248. MALAQUAIS, Jean (1908-   )
August 28, 1939-July 13, 1940
Military diary; Frenchman fighting the Germans early in the war; lengthy entries, possibly augmented with later comments; gritty, dailiness of duty, frustrations and nostalgia for better times.
- Jean Malaquais' War Diary. Peter Grant, trans. New York: Doubleday, Doran, 1944.

2249. MERTON, Thomas (1915-68)
1. October 1, 1939-November 27, 1941; Personal/spiritual

diary; American Catholic convert and Trappist monk; life at Columbia
University as a graduate student and teaching at St. Bonaventure
University; trip to Cuba; musings on his reading; vibrant with youth.
   • A Secular Journal. New York: Farrar, Straus and Cud-
   ahy, 1959.

   2. October 15-December 8, 1968; Travel diary; to Bangkok
for a conference on Asian monasticism; meetings with Buddhists and
the Dalai Lama; stops in India; poetry; last entry two days before
his death by electrocution caused by faulty wiring of a fan.
   • The Asian Journal of Thomas Merton. Naomi Burton et al.
   New York: New Directions, 1973.

   3. "Diary Excerpts," in: Philip Dunaway and Mel Evans,
eds. A Treasury of the World's Great Diaries. New York: Doubleday, 1957; pp. 209-17.
   (For information on his journals for the years 1956-68,
   which will be released in 1993, see Richard N. Ostling, "Merton's Mountainous Legacy," Time, v. 124, p. 65, December
   31, 1984.)

2250. MILBURN, Clara (1883-1961)
   August, 1939-May 12, 1945
   Personal diary; ntoes on the war and family life by a no-
nonsense resident of Coventry; rationing, gardening and anxieties
about her son who was a German prisoner for most of the war; interesting.
   • Mrs. Milburn's Diaries: An Englishwoman's Day-to-day
   Reflections 1939-45. Peter Donnelly, ed. New York: Schocken, 1979.
      REVIEW: Library Journal, v. 105, p. 2404, November 15,
      1980.

2251. MILLIN, Sarah Gertrude Liebson (1889-1968)
   September 1, 1939-October 14, 1946
   Public diary; impersonal, journalistic accounts of war news.
   • World Blackout. The Reeling Earth. The Pit of the Abyss.
   The Sound of the Trumpet. Fire out of Heaven. The Seven
   Thunders. London: Faber and Faber, 1944-58.

2252. PHILLIPS, Janine (1929-   )
   May 16, 1939-May 20, 1940
   Personal diary; irrepressible ten-year-old in a small Polish
village close enough to the German invasion to see the sky reddened
by flames; the orphaned maid pregnant out of wedlock; the dogs
chewed on grandpa's false teeth; the homemade beer blew its top;
death of Grandma and the coming of war.
   • My Secret Diary. London: Shepheard Walwyn, 1982.

2253. PRÜLLER, Wilhelm (1916-   )
   August 30, 1939-April, 1945

Military diary; Austrian belonged to Hitler Youth and the SS; ardent Nazi; the invasion of Poland; believed uncritically in Nazi propaganda; in the Balkans and Russia; wounded; fascinating and well written.

* Diary of a German Soldier. H. C. Robbins Landon and Sebastian Leitner, eds. H. C. Robbins Landon, trans. New York: Coward-McCann, 1963.
    REVIEW: Book Review Digest 1963, p. 821.

2254. STOVER, Elisha Terrill (1920-44)
    August 25, 1939-June 4, 1943
    Military diary; native Texan became an aviation cadet in the Naval Reserve; training in Pensacola, Florida; aboard USS Saratoga and Yorktown; on Guadalcanal; well-done account of life on an aircraft carrier in the Pacific war.

* The Saga of Smokey Stover. Clark G. Reynolds, ed. Charleston, S. C.: Tradd Street Press, 1978.
    REVIEW: Technology and Culture, v. 20, pp. 825-26, October, 1979.

2255. TURNBULL, Agnes Sligh (1888-1982)
    September 8, 1939-March 25, 1941
    Personal diary; American novelist and writer for children; after twenty years of fiction writing "... speaking for somebody else ... crawl[ing] into the skins of heaven knows how many heroines ... I'm tired of it"; at a time when she was under contract for yet another novel she began this diary; life with her husband, twelve-year-old daughter Faith and a cocker spaniel; lecture tours, writing; of interest to her fans and budding fiction writers.

* Dear Me, Leaves From the Diary of Agnes Sligh Turnbull. New York: Macmillan, 1941.

2256. VAUGHAN, Keith (1912-)
    August 25, 1939-August 17, 1965; many lengthy gaps
    Personal journal; English painter and photographer; introspective; conscientious objector; prison and then labor service during the war; postwar visits to Mexico and Italy.

* Journal and Drawings, 1939-1965. London: A. Ross, 1966.

1940

2257. BILAINKIN, George (1903-)
    January 1-December 31, 1940
    Diplomatic diary; correspondent for the Allied Newspaper Group in Britain; stationed in London; observations on the world situation.

* Diary of a Diplomatic Correspondent. London: George Allen and Unwin, 1942.

2258. BRUSSELMANS, Anne
    May 9, 1940-September 9, 1944

Personal diary; Belgian woman whose mother was English
worked with the Resistance to help downed Allied flyers escape the
Gestapo; many narrow escapes; exciting.
- Rendez-vous 127: The Diary of Mme. Brusselmans, M. B.
  E., September 1940-September 1944. London: Benn, 1954.

2259. CITRINE, Walter, Baron (1887-   )
January 21-February 8, 1940
Diplomatic diary; activist in the trade union movement went
with two other Britons to Finland at the request of Clement Atlee;
toured the country after the Russian invasion.
- My Finnish Diary. New York: Penguin, 1940.

2260. GROULT, Benoîte (1922-   ) and Flora GROULT (1926-   )
May 6, 1940-January 18, 1945
Personal diary; two Parisian sisters; the elder was at the Sorbonne; visits to grandparents in the country; rationing and German
occupation; mercurial; allusions to French literature; generally lighthearted despite fears for the safety of those they loved.
- Diary in Duo. Humphrey Hare, trans. New York: Appleton-Century, 1965.
  REVIEW: Book Review Digest 1965, p. 516.

2261. GUEST, John
May 16, 1940-October 11, 1945
Letter diary; written to his friend poet Christopher Hassall
detailing service in the 11th Light Anti-Aircraft Regiment; training in
Scotland; in North African and Italian campaigns; well-done, lengthy
entries describing the changing scene and people.
- Broken Images: A Journal. London: Longmans, 1949;
  reprinted London: Leo Cooper, 1970.

2262. "HEIDE, Dirk van der"
May 7-September 28, 1940
Personal diary; reconstructed entries by a veterinarian's son;
mother killed in a bombing raid; evacuated to America; matter-of-fact
style.
- My Sister and I: The Diary of a Dutch Boy Refugee.
  Mrs. Antoon Deventer, trans. New York: Harcourt, Brace,
  1941.

2263. HIGGS, Dorothy Pickard
July 2, 1940-May 10, 1945
Personal diary; life on the island throughout the Nazi occupation; the "visitors" took supplies for transport to Germany; wireless
sets were confiscated; food always scarce; good picture of the priva-
tions endured.
- Guernsey Dairy, 1940-1945. London: Linden, Lewis, 1947;
  reprinted Life in Guernsey Under the Nazis, 1940-45. St.
  Peter Port: Toucan Press, 1979.

2264. HODGSON, Vere
June 25, 1940-May 8, 1945
Personal diary; social worker and former teacher employed at
a shelter for homeless women in London; very detailed; excellent
for reports on a large circle of friends and how they coped.
* Few Eggs and No Oranges: A Diary Showing How Unim-
portant People in London and Birmingham Lived Through the
War Years, 1940-1945. London: Dobson, 1976.

2265. IONESCO, Eugene (1912-)
1940, 1967
Literary diary; excerpts; French playwright; political musings.
* "Journal," Encounter, v. 31, pp. 13-20, September, 1968.

2266. KING, Cecil Harmsworth (1901-)
1. January 3, 1940-September 2, 1945; Personal diary; director of the London Daily Mirror and Pictorial; modernized both publications; war seen from a newspaper publisher's viewpoint; censorship
troubles; assessments of major British personalities; interesting.
* With Malice Toward None: A War Diary. William Armstrong,
ed. London: Sidgwick and Jackson, 1970.

2. July 12, 1965-June 20, 1970; Political diary; chairman of
a corporation which published London newspapers; full entries on
politicians, international relations.
* The Cecil King Diary, 1965-1970. London: Cape, 1972.

3. June 21, 1970-December 12, 1974; more in the same vein.
* The Cecil King Diary, 1970-1974. London: Cape, 1975.

2267. LAWRENCE, David (1888-1973)
May 10, 1940-May 30, 1942
Political diary; record by an American journalist of the U.S.
involvement in World War II; supports Roosevelt's policies; Pearl
Harbor and its aftermath.
* Diary of a Washington Correspondent. New York: Kinsey,
1942.
REVIEW: Book Review Digest 1942, pp. 455-56.

2268. LEE, Raymond Eliot (1886-1958)
June 3, 1940-November 29, 1941
Personal diary; American Army general and head of U.S. in-
telligence in London; Anglophile with a sense of history and a gift
for seeing the telling detail; life in London at all levels during the
early days of the war; excellent.
* The London Journal of General Raymond E. Lee, 1940-1941.
James Leutze, ed. Boston: Little, Brown, 1971; reprint
titled The London Observer: The Journal of General Raymond
E. Lee, 1940-1941. London: Hutchinson, 1972.

2269. LOOMIS, Charles P.

May 1-7, 1940
Personal diary; a sociologist studying the Amish took a job
as a farmhand near Lancaster, Pennsylvania; farm chores.
  • "A Farmhand's Diary," Mennonite Quarterly Review, v. 53,
  pp. 235-56, July, 1979.

2270. MANSEL, John (1909-74)
       May 21, 1940-May 6, 1945
       Personal diary; with the Queen's (West Surrey) Regiment; cap-
tured at Abbeville, France; camp life; under the guise of art work
he produced forged passes and identity cards for escapees throughout the war rather than trying to escape himself; well done.
  • The Mansel Diaries: The Diaries of Captain John Mansel,
  Prisoner-of-war and Camp Forger, in Germany, 1940-45. E.
  G. C. Beckwith, ed. Oxfordshire: Burgess and Son, 1977.

2271. MAYR, Richard (1924-43)
       December 9, 1940-April 30, 1941
       Personal diary; Viennese Catholic schoolboy active in the Youth
Movement; strong spiritual bent; harrassment from Nazis and passive
resistance.
  • Diary and Letters. Lilian Stevenson, trans. and ed. London: Lutterworth, 1948.

2272. MORAN, Sir Charles Wilson, Lord (1882-1977)
       May 24, 1940-March 28, 1960
       Personal diary; designated Churchill's personal physician early
in the war and became a close friend; traveling together during the
war; narrative written later is added and clearly distinguished from
the diary proper.
  • Churchill: Taken From the Diaries of Lord Moran: The
  Struggle for Survival 1940-1965. Boston: Houghton Mifflin,
  1966.

2273. MOUCHOTTE, René (-1943)
       June 17, 1940-July 9, 1943
       Military diary; opens with the fall of France of which the di-
arist hears while in Oran, Algeria; escaped to join the Free French;
missions from RAF bases in England; killed in action; lengthy entries,
well-phrased, with much atmospheric detail.
  • The Mouchotte Diaries, 1940-1943. Andre Dezarrois, ed.
  Philip John Stead, trans. London: Staples Press, 1956.

2274. OFFENBERG, Jean Henri Marie (1916-42)
       May 10, 1940-January 21, 1942
       Military diary; Belgian in an RAF squadron with some of his
countrymen; received a Distinguished Flying Cross; long, descriptive
entries with much transcribed conversation; recaptures the flavor of
events with novelistic style.
  • Lonely Warrior: The Journal of a Battle of Britain Fighter
  Pilot. Victor Houart, ed. Mervyn Savill, trans. London:
  Souvenir Press, 1956; reprinted St. Albans: Mayflower, 1974.

2275.   PERRY, Colin A. (1922?-)
        June 17-November 5, 1940
        Personal diary; English teen living with his family in London;
his first job; letters to and from a sweetheart in Australia; wide range
of topics all hinging on war news and the Blitz, seen with a fresh eye.
        • Boy in the Blitz. London: Leo Cooper, 1972.

2276.   PLATT, J. Ellison, M. B. E. (-1973)
        October 26, 1940-April 13, 1945; most entries for 1943 omitted
        Prison diary; Methodist chaplain captured at Dunkirk was one
of the earliest British arrivals at Colditz, the German POW camp which
contained officers adept at escape; a good account which supports
other extant Colditz literature.
        • Padre in Colditz: The Diary of J. Ellison Platt. Margaret
        Duggan, ed. London: Hodder and Stoughton, 1978.

2277.   REYNOLDS, Quentin James (1902-65)
        October 1-December 1, 1940
        Personal diary; American war correspondent kept a diary for
his family "with no serious stuff" because he believed the unimportant
would eventually have great meaning; witness to the Battle of Britain
and nightly bombing raids; conveys a novelistic sense of immediacy.
        • A London Diary. New York: Random House, 1941.

2278.   RINGELBLUM, Emmanual (1900-44)
        January 1, 1940-December 14, 1942
        Personal diary; Labor Zionist and professional historian was
in the ghetto from the first and refused to be smuggled out; gathered
material for a history of the ghetto until his execution; contains little
of his personal life but is a running account of conditions; appalling.
        • Notes from the Warsaw Ghetto: A Journal of Emmanuel
        Ringelblum. Jacob Sloan, ed. and trans. New York: McGraw-
        Hill, 1958; reprinted New York: Schocken, 1974.

2279.   RUBINOWICZ, Dawid (1927-42)
        March 21, 1940-June 1, 1941
        Personal diary; Jewish boy living on a rural Polish dairy farm
with his family; father imprisoned; family robbed; probably died at
Treblinka; horrifying.
        • The Diary of Dawid Rubinowicz. Derek Bowman, trans.
        Edinburgh: Blackwood, 1981.

2280.   SINEL, Leslie Philip
        June 19, 1940-June 7, 1945
        Occupation diary; editor of the island's newspaper; the Island
of Jersey was declared a demilitarized zone by the British Government and promptly occupied by the Germans; news items; rationing;
proclamations by German authorities; impersonal tone gives details of
attempted escapes, confiscations and punishments.
        • The German Occupation of Jersey: A Diary of Events from
        June 1940 to June 1945. rev. ed. London: Howard Baker,
        1969.

2281. SOMERHAUSEN, Anne S. (1903-   )
       May 10, 1940-May 12, 1945
       Personal diary; life in Brussels as lived by a woman and her
three sons; husband imprisoned early in the war; work in the Resistance; food shortages; literate.
       • Written in Darkness, A Belgian Woman's Record of the Oc-
       cupation, 1940-1945. New York: Knopf, 1946.

2282. STEINBECK, John (1902-68)
       March 12-April 11, 1940
       Sea diary; American novelist on a voyage in the Sea of Cortez
off California to collect marine specimens; dashes of science, fishing
and fun.
       • "Diary Excerpts," in: Philip Dunaway and Mel Evans, eds.
       A Treasury of the World's Great Diaries. New York: Double-
       day, 1957; pp. 317-23.

2283. WOLFF-MONCKEBERG, Mathilde (1879-1958)
       October 10, 1940-1945
       Journal letters; German mother wrote to her grown children
who were on the side of the Allies; life in Hamburg; heavy Allied
bombing of 1943; news of rationing; semblance of normal life; interesting.
       • On the Other Side: To My Children: From Germany 1940-
       1945. Ruth Evans, trans. and ed. New York: Mayflower
       Books, 1979.

                              1941

2284. ABRIKOSSOW, Dmitri (1876-1951)
       Personal diary; undated excerpts; Russian living in Japan
throughout World War II.
       • "White Russians in Wartime Japan: Leaves From the Diary
       of Dmitri Abrikossow," George Alexander Lensen, ed. Rus-
       sian Review, v. 25, pp. 268-84, July, 1966.

2285. ASHTON-WARNER, Sylvia (1908-   )
       February, 1941-March 22, 1942
       Personal diary; New Zealander, author of Teacher; taught
Maori children; close relationship with her husband; thoughts on
teaching.
       • "Diary Excerpts," in: Mary Jane Moffat and Charlotte
       Painter, eds. Revelations: Diaries of Women. New York:
       Random House, 1974; pp. 206-17.

2285a. BARTON, Cornelius W. (1910-   )
       May 5-December 19, 1941
       Military diary; duty in a medical battalion in the U.S. and
Ireland.
       • "Diary," in: Donald Vining, ed. American Diaries of
       World War II. New York: Pepys Press, 1982; pp. 3-27.

2286. BIRNN, Roland R. (-1942)
       November 1, 1941-July 2, 1942
       Military diary; by ship to the Philippines; outbreak of war;
service in Australia; flying missions in poorly maintained planes;
killed on a test flight.
       • "A War Diary," Air Power Historian, v. 3, pp. 195-202,
       October, 1956; v. 4, pp. 40-45, January, 1957; pp. 98-103,
       April, 1957.

2287. BOND, Charles R., Jr. (1915-)
       September 24, 1941-August 7, 1942
       Military diary; Texan joined the American Volunteer Group led
by Claire Chennault to defend China against the Japanese before
America entered the war; training as a fighter pilot in Burma; air
battle for Rangoon; internal politics; eventual disbanding of the
group; of primary importance for its picture of the Flying Tigers
and their mission; modest man with an unassuming style.
       • A Flying Tiger's Diary. College Station: Texas A & M
       University Press, 1984.

2288. BRERETON, Lewis Hyde (1890-1967)
       October 3, 1941-May 8, 1945
       Military diary; commander of the Far East Air Forces under
General MacArthur; service in the Philippines, China, India, the
Mediterranean and England; troop deployments, air strength, etc.;
little personal comment.
       • The Brereton Diaries: The War in the Air in the Pacific,
       Middle East and Europe. New York: Morrow, 1946; reprinted
       New York: Da Capo Press, 1976.

2289. CATES, Tressa R.
       December 8, 1941-June 24, 1945
       Prison diary; American nurse imprisoned with her fiancé by
the Japanese after the fall of Manila; life in camp; occasional help
from friends outside; increasing illness due to poor diet; an affecting
tale undermined by an exclamatory style.
       • The Drainpipe Diary. New York: Vantage, 1957.

2290. COWARD, Noel (1899-1973)
       1. April 19, 1941-December 31, 1969; Personal diary; English
playwright, actor and composer; his professional and private lives;
staging plays and revues; triumphs and low blows; some cutting remarks on people and criticism of acting performances and shows; entertaining, witty, blithe spirit.
       • The Noel Coward Diaries. Graham Payn and Sheridan Mor-
       ley, eds. Boston: Little, Brown, 1982.
         REVIEWS: Library Journal, v. 107, p. 1765, September
         15, 1982. Publishers Weekly, v. 222, p. 61, August 20,
         1982.

       2. July-October 9, 1943; Travel diary; entertaining the troops
and wounded in Egypt and vicinity.

● <u>Middle East Diary</u>. London: Heinemann, 1944.

2291. CRIMP, Reginald Lewis
       July 23, 1941-May 12, 1943
       Military diary; Briton in a light infantry division saw service
in North Africa; lengthy descriptions of conditions; fair.
       ● <u>The Diary of a Desert Rat</u>. Alex Bowlby, ed. London:
Cooper, 1971.

2292. CROUTER, Natalie (1898-)
       1. November 28, 1941-July 27, 1945; Prison diary; American
woman spent the war years in Camp Holmes, Luzon, the Philippines;
trying to maintain sanity and family life amidst prison conditions;
very human observations and reactions; excellent.
       ● <u>Forbidden Diary: A Record of Wartime Internment, 1941-
1945</u>. Lynn Z. Bloom, ed. New York: Burt Franklin, 1980.

       2. "Courage Is 'Grace Under Pressure': A Woman's Diary of
Captivity," <u>New America: A Review</u>, pp. 60-68, Fall, 1975-Spring,
1976.

       3. December 27, 1941-February 5, 1945; Prison diary; ex-
cerpts; with drawings by a fellow prisoner.
       ● "Forbidden Diary," <u>American Heritage</u>, v. 30, pp. 78-95,
April/May, 1979.

       4. Bloom, Lynn Z. "The Diary as Popular History," <u>Journal
of Popular Culture</u>, v. 9, pp. 794-807, Spring, 1976. Most of the
article focuses Crouter's diary.

2293. EHLERS, Reginald Gordon Morris (1886-)
       August 20-November 22, 1941
       Sea diary; medical man with saltwater in his veins sailed from
San Francisco to Penang and return with a load of tin and rubber;
talk of Japanese intentions; two typhoons; ashore in Manila, Shanghai and Singapore; treating the crew for accidents and venereal dis-
ease; interesting comments and good picture of life aboard a freighter.
       ● <u>Diary of the Ship's Surgeon: Being the Diary of a Ship's
Surgeon on a Voyage to the Orient Just Before Pearl Harbor</u>.
Boston: Meador, 1944.

2294. GEREN, Paul Francis (1913/17-)
       December, 1941-July 30, 1942
       Personal diary; "more a diary of the spirit than of actual
events"; harrowing journey from Rangoon to Assam, India.
       ● <u>Burma Diary</u>. New York: Harper, 1943.

2295. GREENE, Graham (1904-)
       December 9, 1941-January 3, 1942; January 31, 1959-March
       8, 1959
       Personal/literary diary; English novelist; first, on a convoy

to West Africa, from Liverpool to Freetown; second, research in the
Belgian Congo for The Heart of the Matter.
- In Search of a Character: Two African Journals. London:
Bodley Head, 1961.

2296. HILLESUM, Etty (1914-43)
      March 9, 1941-August 24, 1943
      Personal diary; Dutch Jew was a student and lover of Julius
Spier, "psychochirologist"; worked on the Dutch Jewish Council under
the Nazis; in Westerbork camp; transported to Auschwitz; introspective entries in which she "turn[s] inwards"; achievement of inner
peace despite the end she knows is coming.
- An Interrupted Life: The Diaries of Etty Hillesum 1941-
1943. Arno Pomerans, trans. New York: Pantheon, 1983.
      REVIEWS: Choice, v. 21, p. 1662, July/August, 1984.
      Publishers Weekly, v. 224, p. 77, December 2, 1983.

2297. INBER, Vera Mikhailovna (1893-1972)
      August 22, 1941-June 7, 1944
      Personal diary; Russian poet's account of the German siege of
Leningrad; crossing frozen Lake Ladoga for supplies.
- Leningrad Diary. Serge M. Wolff and Rachel Grieve, trans.
New York: St. Martin's, 1971.

2298. KIKUCHI, Charles
      December 7, 1941-August 31, 1942
      Personal diary; Nisei child of Japanese immigrants was incar-
cerated with his family at the outbreak of World War II; camplife; the
writer places psychological distance between himself and other people
and events.
- The Kikuchi Diary: Chronicle from an American Concentration Camp: The Tanforan Journals of Charles Kikuchi. John
Modell, ed. Urbana: University of Illinois Press, 1973.

2299. KOGAN, David S. (1929-51)
      July 29, 1941-March 7, 1951
      Personal diary; Jewish boy in Westchester, New York; school
and family life; Dodger rooter; his Bar Mitzvah; college at Cornell
and preparation for law school; died of an undisclosed illness.
- The Diary of David S. Kogan. Meyer Levin, ed. New
York: Beechhurst Press, 1955.

2300. MALTHE-BRUUN, Kim (1923-45)
      May 18, 1941-April 4, 1945
      Personal diary; Canadian-born Dane wrote letters and a diary
to a sweetheart and his mother; life as a seaman; Resistance work;
imprisoned and executed by the Germans; intense spirituality with a
light-heartedness that makes for affecting reading.
- Heroic Heart: The Diary and Letters of Kim Malthe-Bruun,
1941-1945. Vibeke Malthe-Bruun, ed. Gerry Bothmer, trans.
New York: Random House, 1955; reprinted New York: Sea-
bury Press, 1966.

2301. MORELL, Theodor Gilbert (1886-1948)
       August 7, 1941-April 23, 1945
       Medical diary; fashionable doctor came to be Hitler's personal
physician after successfully treating his photographer; used Hitler as
a guinea pig for his drugs; interesting.
       • The Secret Diaries of Hitler's Doctor. David Irving, ed.
New York: Macmillan, 1983.

2302. STEIN, Leo (1872-1947)
       September 9, 1941-June 12, 1945; a few lengthy entries
       Personal diary; brother of American novelist and expatriate
Gertrude Stein; introspective and caught up in the writings of others.
       • Journey into the Self, Being the Letters, Papers and Jour-
nals of Leo Stein. Edmund Fuller, ed. New York: Crown,
1950.

2303. STILWELL, Joseph Warren (1883-1946)
       December 7, 1941-October 27, 1944
       Military diary; West Pointer; student of the Chinese language
in China in the 1920's; amalgam of military journal, reflections and
letters to his wife; opening days of U.S. particiaption in the war;
Burmese and Chinese theaters; relations with Chiang K'ai-shek; dislike of Mountbatten and British behavior; portrait of a decent soldier
battling corrup politicians and incompetent allies.
       • The Stilwell Papers. Theodore H. White, ed. New York:
W. Sloane Associates, 1948.

2304. THISTLE, Lt. R.
       December 7, 1941-June 21, 1942
       Military diary; intelligence officer in a Canadian Scottish Regi-
ment; privy to classified information; fears of a Japanese invasion of
Canada after Pearl Harbor; evacuation of Japanese-Canadians; terse
but informative.
       • "The Defence of Prince Rupert: An Eyewitness Account,"
Dr. R. H. Roy, ed. BC Studies [Canada], no. 31, pp. 60-
77, 1976.

2305. WALKER, Fred L. (1887-)
       September 12, 1941-July 17, 1944
       Military diary; major general of the 36th Division and DSM re-
cipient; at the Salerno, Italy, landing; Rapido River Fiasco; army
politics; sarcastic messages from the Germans via carrier pigeon; occasionally humorous.
       • From Texas to Rome: A General's Journal. Dallas: Taylor
Publishing Co., 1969.

                                    1942

2305a. BIELIK, Casimir
       August 25, 1942-October 14, 1944

Sea diary; seaman had a variety of duties; ashore in Spain, Brazil, Venezuela and Italy.
- "Diary," in: Donald Vining, ed. American Diaries of World War II. New York: Pepys Press, 1982; pp. 180-95.

2306. BLOOM, Freddy
March 4, 1942-August 21, 1945
Prison diary; American newspaperwoman married nine days to a British doctor was interned in the civilian section of Changi after the fall of Singapore; camp life, friendships, Japanese atrocities.
- Dear Philip: A Diary of Captivity, Changi 1942-45. London: Bodley Head, 1980.

2306a. BRUMMER, Francis H.
January 21, 1942-November 11, 1945
Sea diary; signalman on the USS Ironclad on a voyage to Murmansk from Ireland; other runs to Russia; a victim of German bombing and torpedo runs.
- "Diary," in: Donald Vining, ed. American Diaries of World War II. New York: Pepys Press, 1982; pp. 133-43.

2307. FAHEY, James J.
1. October 3, 1942-November 8, 1945; Sea diary; seaman 1st class on the cruiser USS Montpelier; enlistment; at Great Lakes Naval Training Station; from Philadelphia through the Panama Canal; service in the Solomons, Marianas, Philippines, China and Japan; simply written but interesting.
- Pacific War Diary, 1942-1945. Boston: Houghton Mifflin, 1963.

2. January 29, 1943-January 21, 1944; Excerpts.
- "Diary," in Donald Vining, ed. American Diaries of World War II. New York: Pepys Press, 1982; pp. 196-215.

2308. FRANK, Anne (1929-45)
1. June 14, 1942-August 1, 1944; Personal diary; probably the most famous diary of World War II; with her parents, sister and four other Jews, she hid from the Nazis in the Secret Annex in wartime Amsterdam; has been dramatized as a play and a movie and translated into many languages; life in the cramped hideout; her growing feeling for teenaged Peter; troubles with her mother and sister; overriding all, the constant terror of discovery; the last entry was made three days before the Gestapo sent them all to concentration camps; funny, sad, horrifying.
- Anne Frank: The Diary of a Young Girl. B. M. Mooyaart, trans. New York: Doubleday, 1952.
     REVIEW: Book Review Digest 1952, pp. 320-21.

2. "Diary Excerpts," in: Philip Dunaway and Mel Evans, eds. A Treasury of the World's Great Diaries. New York: Doubleday, 1957; pp. 1-15.

3. "Diary Excerpts," in: Mary Jane Moffat and Charlotte
Painter, eds. <u>Revelations: Diaries of Women</u>. New York: Random
House, 1974; pp. 34-45.

4. <u>Anne Frank's Tales from the Secret Annex</u>. Ralph Mann-
heim and Michel Mok, trans. New York: Doubleday, 1984. Sketches,
stories and vignettes are dated and could be paired with her diary
entries.

2309. GABLE, Edgar (-1945)
        August 22, 1942-
        Prison diary; American mining company employee caught in the
Philippines during the Japanese invasion; at Cabanatuan; work details, food; maltreatment of prisoners by the Japanese.
        • "Edgar Gable's Prison Camp Diary," Roybert Ryal Miller,
        ed. <u>South Dakota Report and Historical Collections</u>. v. 30,
        pp. 317-48, 1960.

2310. GUSTAFSON, Walter
        October 2, 1942-February 8, 1946
        Military diary; entries interspersed with letters to his wife;
at Jefferson Barracks, St. Louis; in Kansas and Texas; in Europe.
        • <u>My Time in the Army: The Diary of a World War II Soldier</u>.
        Chicago: Adams Press, 1968.

2311. HAYS, Marion Prather
        July 29, 1942-April 27, 1944
        Personal diary; wife of a U.S. congressman from Arkansas'
5th District; "A person in her own right"; exuberant account of life
in Washington.
        • "From the Political Diary of an Unpolitical Person," <u>Arkansas
        Historical Quarterly</u>, v. 36, pp. 158-91, Summer, 1977.

2312. HODGE, Grover C., Jr.
        October 15, 1942-February 3, 1943
        Personal diary; pilot and 1st lieutenant of a B-26 Martin Ma-
rauder guiding a formation of fighters to England ditched in Labrador;
survival tactics; the whole crew was found dead by Eskimoes a month
after the last entry.
        • "A Diary Found in the Snow," <u>Air Power Historian</u>, v. 6,
        pp. 262-78, October, 1959.

2313. KARDORFF, Ursula von (1911-   )
        October 28, 1942-October 7, 1945
        Personal diary; journalist at a prominent daily newspaper; her
father was a portrait painter and two brothers were in the service;
involved in hiding people from the Gestapo; "everyday life in Berlin";
good.
        • <u>Diary of a Nightmare: Berlin, 1942-1945</u>. Ewan Butler,
        trans. New York: John Day, 1965.
        REVIEW: <u>Book Review Digest</u> 1966, p. 627.

2314. KIMBALL, Clyde E. (1908-44)
       August 20, 1942-
       Personal diary; dedicated Army chaplain and recipient of the
Silver Star; died of wounds received while rescuing members of his
unit; duty in Iceland, England and Belgium; conducted services and
consoled men far from home while longing for his own wife and sons;
excellent.
       • Diary of My Work Overseas. Nashua, N. H.: The Author,
       1947.

2315. McCALLUM, Neil
       July, 1942-July 17, 1943
       Personal diary; journal with a literary style and presentation;
transported from Norwich to Suez; service in North Africa, Malta and
Sicily; many literary allusions.
       • Journey with a Pistol: A Diary of War. London: Gollancz,
       1959.

2316. McCORMICK, Vincent A. (1886-1963)
       July 14, 1942-September 12, 1943
       Personal diary; extracts; enemy alien in the Vatican bureau-
cracy; very American spirit while sympathetic to individual Italians.
       • Hennesey, James. "American Jesuit in Wartime Rome: The
       Diary of Vincent A. McCormick, S. J., 1942-1945," Mid-America,
       v. 56, pp. 32-55, January, 1974.

2316a. McNamara, Joseph (1911-   )
       October 28, 1942-November 15, 1945
       Sea diary; machinist's mate on a destroyer in the Pacific.
       • "Diary," in: Donald Vining, ed. American Diaries of
       World War II. New York: Pepys Press, 1982; pp. 144-79.

2317. NORQUIST, Ernest O.
       June 26, 1942-1945
       Prison diary; excerpts; a survivor of the Bataan siege; at
Cabanatuan, the Philippines and in Japan; interesting.
       • "Three Years in Paradise: A GI's Prisoner-of-war Diary,
       1942-1945," Wisconsin Magazine of History, v. 63, pp. 2-35,
       Autumn, 1979.

2317a. QUINN, Michael A. (1895-   )
       Prison diary; American POW kept the notebooks in which these
entries were made in a water canteen; life at two camps in the Philippines and on Formosa; in Manchuria; poor diet and many deaths are
offset by reminiscences of good times with Mike, his wife.
       • Love Letters to Mike: 40 Months as a Japanese Prisoner
       of War, April 9, 1942 to September 17, 1945: The Diary of
       Col. Michael A. Quinn. New York: Vantage, 1977.

2317b. SCHLOSS, Harry
       August 4, 1942-November 18, 1944

Military diary; waistgunner in the 17th Bomb Group; training; flew over 60 missions in Italy; records the fates of other crew members.
- "Diary," in: Donald Vining, ed. American Diaries of World War II. New York: Pepys Press, 1982; pp. 269-85.

2318. SULLIVAN, Joseph P.
December 22-28, 1942
Military diary; extracts; with General Mark Clark and the Fifth Army in Algiers preparing for the Italian campaign.
- "Diary Notes of an Army Quartermaster," Quartermaster Review, v. 28, pp. 38-40, 104-06, July-August, 1948.

2319. TOMITA, Saku
May 5-August 17, 1942
Personal diary; Issei woman interned before relocation to Idaho; makeshift accommodations, boredom and uncertainty.
- "Portland Assembly Center: Diary of Saku Tomita," Zuigaku Kodachi and Jan Heikkala, trans. Janet Cormack, ed. Oregon Historical Quarterly, v. 81, pp. 149-71, Summer, 1980.

2320. TREGASKIS, Richard William (1916-)
1. July 26-September 26, 1942; Personal diary; American correspondent on Guadalcanal with troops bent on defeating the Japanese; very full entries expanded from notes; well done.
- Guadalcanal Diary. New York: Random House, 1943.

2. July 9, 1943-January 8, 1944; Personal diary; with American troops thorugh Italy; wounded and partially paralyzed for a short period.
- Invasion Diary. New York: Random House, 1944.

3. October 9, 1962-March 9, 1963; Personal diary; journalistic style.
- Vietnam Diary. New York: Holt, 1963.

2321. VLADIMIROV, Petr Parfenovich (1905-53)
May 10, 1942-September 4, 1945
Personal diary; Soviet advisor and Tass correspondent; dealings with and observations of prominent Chinese Communists; conduct of the war around the world but especially as it affected Russia; colloquial, interesting.
- The Vladimirov Diaries: Yenan, China, 1942-1945. New York: Doubleday, 1975.

2322- WELCH, Denton (1915-48)
23. July 10, 1942-August 31, 1948
Personal diary; minor British writer who became an invalid at 20; did his best to get about, overcoming physical difficulties; introspective; his writing, hopes for the future; regrets over some of the past; generally buoyant.

  • The Denton Welch Journals. Jocelyn Brooke, ed. London:
Hamish Hamilton, 1952.

2324. WILKINSON, Gerald Hugh
        1942-43
        Personal diary; excerpts; British businessman pressed into
service as an observer of the Japanese; Churchill's link to MacArthur.
        • Thorne, Christopher. "MacArthur, Australia and the Brit-
        ish, 1942-1943: The Secret Journal of MacArthur's British
        Liaison Officer," Australian Outlook [Australia], v. 29, pp.
        53-67, 197-210, 1975.

2325. WYCOTT, Sara Jean Clark (1924-60)
        January 24, 1942-November 28, 1946; gaps
        Spiritual diary; extracts; written while she studied at Agnes
Scott College in Decatur, Georgia.
        • Everywhere God: A Spiritual Autobiography. Odessa Grist
        Clark, ed. New York: Greenwich Book Publishers, 1961.

2326. YOUNG, James Webb (1886-   )
        Personal diary; Chicago advertising pro sees the war years
and FDR in terms of what is selling and why; full of stories about
leading advertisers.
        • Diary of an Ad Man: The War Years June 1, 1942-December
        1943. Chicago: Advertising Publications, 1944.

                                1943

2327. ANONYMOUS
        May 1-December 8, 1943
        Prison diary; German noncommissioned officer of the 15th
Panzer Division was captured in North Africa and sent to a POW
camp in Mississippi; by ship to the U.S.; life in camp; ironic title
taken from the entries.
        • And Still We Conquer! The Diary of a Nazi Unteroffizier
        in the German Afrika Corps Who Was Captured by the U.S.
        Army, May 9, 1943 and Imprisoned at Camp Shelby, Mississippi.
        W. Stanley Hoole, ed. Irving Shater, trans. University, Ala.:
        Confederate Publishing Co., 1968.

2328. ARDIZZONE, Edward (1900-79)
        July 10, 1943-May 18, 1945
        Personal diary; An official "war artist" attached to the British
Army; service in North Africa and Europe; troop movements; many
of his sketches reproduced.
        • Diary of a War Artist. London: Bodley Head, 1974.

2328a. BOOKE, Kenneth E. (1918-73)
        December 10, 1943-August 25, 1944
        Military diary; piloted a B-17 bomber in the 8th Air Force; a
record of his 30 missions.

● "Diary," in: Donald Vining, ed. American Diaries of World War II. New York: Pepys Press, 1982; pp. 286-307.

2929. COZZENS, James Gould (1903-78)
October 27, 1943-October 20, 1945
Personal diary; American novelist based his book Guard of Honor on the raw material presented here; began as a writer of training manuals; later a speechwriter; preparing film scripts; word portraits of many career army men, General Curtis LeMay and Lauris Norstad; notes the contrasts between his own literary persona and those of the single-minded, unread men he dealt with; for military buffs and his fans.
● A Time of War: Air Force Diaries and Pentagon Memos, 1943-45. Matthew J. Bruccoli, ed. Columbia, S. Car.: Bruccoli Clark, 1984.

2330. DORMER, Hugh (1919-44)
April 8, 1943-May 25, 1944
Military diary; commissioned in the Irish Guards early in the war, he left to carry on sabotage behind the German lines and aid the Resistance; riveting.
● Diaries. Westminster, Md.: Newman Press, 1948.

2331. DRURY, Allen (1918-   )
November 21, 1943-July 28, 1945
Political diary; American journalist and political novelist; reported for United Press on the actions of the U.S. Senate; soldier-vote fight, OPA; FDR's death and Truman's early days in the White House; chamber doings and cloakroom deals; biographical notes on prominent senators; well-done assessment of a turbulent period.
● A Senate Journal 1943-1945. New York: McGraw-Hill, 1963.

2332. GANNON, Robert I.
March 7-May 21, 1943
Personal diary; good will mission to England to report on conditions.
● "A Wartime Diary, 1943," Thought, v. 44, pp. 247-67, 1969.

2333. GERKEN, Mable R.
January 8, 1943-August 17, 1945
Personal diary; sprightly, forty-ish female war worker in a bomber factory; interesting.
● Ladies in Pants: A Home Front Diary. New York: Exposition Press, 1949.

2334. GUARESCHI, Giovanni (1908-68)
September 20, 1943-September 16, 1945
Personal/literary diary; Italian author of the fictional Don Camillo series; military internee of the Germans in Poland; camp life.
● My Secret Diary, 1943-1945. Frances Frenaye, trans. New York: Farrar, Straus and Cudahy, 1958.

2335. LOCHEMES, Mary Frederick, Sister (1904-   )
       March 10, 1943-March 20, 1944
       Travel diary; touring South America in order to develop class-
room material; travel by train, plane and bus; visits to many schools,
educational institutions and factories; tourist notes with little real insight.
       • We Saw South America: A Diary of Two Franciscan Nuns.
       Milwaukee: Bruce, 1946.

2336. LORD, Caroline M.
       June 19, 1943-December 31, 1960
       Personal diary; record by the librarian of a small New Hamp-
shire town; thoughts on books and borrowers; delightful and good
social history.
       • Diary of a Village Library. Somersworth: New Hampshire
       Publishing Co., 1971.

2336a. LOVELL, Frank
       March 16-May 3, 1943
       Military diary; with the 9th Infantry, First Army in North
Africa as a warrant officer.
       • "Diary," in: Donald Vining, ed. American Diaries of World
       War II. New York: Pepys Press, 1982; pp. 49-62.

2336b. McCAUGHEY, Anne (1915-   )
       December 15, 1943-June 15, 1945
       Personal diary; American Red Cross aide at the U.S. Army
50th General Hospital; to London and at a field hospital in France;
descriptive and well done.
       • "Diary," in: Donald Vining, ed. American Diaries of World
       War II. New York: Pepys Press, 1982; pp. 82-106.

2337. MACMILLAN, Harold (1894-   )
       January 7, 1943-May 26, 1945
       Diplomatic/personal diaries; British Minister Resident in North
Africa; sent to deal with an Algerian matter, he ended by running a
large office which controlled a good bit of the Mediterranean; entries
here were later used for his book on the era The Blast of War; relations with Churchill and Roosevelt; Duff Cooper, De Gaulle, Eisenhower; Casablance Conference; King George VI's visit to Malta; Cairo
Conference; important details of agreements with Tito, Archbishop
Damaskinos and others which had repercussions in peacetime.
       • War Diaries: Politics and War in the Mediterranean January
       1943-May 1945. New York: St. Martin's Press, 1984.

2337a. MESECHER, Thearl (1914-   )
       Prison diary; machine gunner captured in North Africa; by
plane and rail to Germany; forced labor six miles south of the Baltic
with civilians and military prisoners of several nations; befriended
by a German farm family; good.
       • "Diary," in: Donald Vining, ed. American Diaries of World
       War II. New York: Pepys Press, 1982; pp. 343-73.

2338. NALKOWSKA, Zofia (1885-1954)
          April 28, 1943-February 10, 1945
          Personal diary; Polish novelist and playwright; life in the
Warsaw ghetto and escape to Adamowizna; mentions other prominent
Polish authors.
          • "A Wartime Journal," Edward Rothert, trans. Polish Per-
          spectives [Poland] v. 14, pp. 32-44, March, 1971.

2339. ORIGO, Iris Cutting, Marchesa (1902-   )
          January 30, 1943-July 5, 1944
          Personal diary; Englishwoman married to an Italian; family life
on an estate in Southern Tuscany; Germans quartered about them;
took in Italian children who were evacuated from their homes; dealing with bullying Germans and wounded partisans; very good.
          • War in Val D'Orcia: A Diary. London: Cape, 1947.

2340. PARKIN, Ray
          January 4, 1943-March, 1945
          Prison diary; Aussie who survived the sinking of his cruiser
in the Sunda Straits worked at forced labor building a railway; at
Changi camp and on Hintok Road; appalling conditions; 304 men died
for each mile built; moving.
          • Into the Smother: A Journal of the Burma Siam Railway.
          London: Hogarth Press, 1963.

2340a. PETR, Otto V. (1915-   )
          March 13-April 17, 1943
          Military diary; Illinoisan on Guadalcanal as a private doing
garrison duty with the 132nd Infantry; enduring Japanese bombing.
          • "Diary," in: Donald Vining, ed. American Diaries of World
          War II. New York: Pepys Press, 1982; pp. 75-81.

2340b. SIEGEL, Max (1913-   )
          March 4, 1943-[no closing date]
          Military diary; rifleman with the 18th Infantry in Italy.
          • "Diary," in: Donald Vining, ed. American Diaries of World
          War II. New York: Pepys Press, 1982; pp. 63-74.

2341. SNYDER, Robert Strong (1919-44)
          August 31, 1943-March 10, 1944
          Military diary; Washington state native at boot camp in Arkan-
sas; trained as a Browning Automatic rifleman; by troopship to Malta;
with the Fifth Army in Italy and North Africa; low-key with a religious bent.
          • And When My Task on Earth is Done. Kansas City, Mo.:
          Graphic Laboratory, 1950.

2342. STETTINIUS, Edward Reilley (1900-49)
          September 24, 1943-June 4, 1946
          Political diary; American industrialist; undersecretary, then
Secretary of State under FDR; U.S. representative to the UN;

"Calendar notes" are summaries of the day's activities; transcripts of phone conversations.
- The Diaries of Edward R. Stettinius, Jr., 1943-46. Thomas M. Campbell and George C. Herring, eds. New York: New Viewpoints, 1975.
  REVIEW: Book Review Digest 1975, p. 1220.

2343. STUDNITZ, Hans-Georg von (1907-   )
February 1, 1943-April 4, 1945
Personal diary; portrait of wartime Germany by one unsympathetic to the Nazis yet holding a position in the German Foreign Ministry; candid; excellent.
- While Berlin Burns: The Diary of Hans-Georg von Studnitz, 1943-1945. R. H. Stevens, trans. Englewood Cliffs, N.J.: Prentice-Hall, 1964.

2344. SULZBERGER, Cyrus Leo (1912-   )
1. June 7, 1943-September 8, 1954; Journalistic diary; kept by New York Times writer for future use; "kind of a verbal diarrhea"; believes luck rather than talent makes a great newspaperman; material on the Balkans, John Foster Dulles, Eisenhower; a humorous, fair-minded reporter; comments on the foibles and policies of world leaders and the lessons he learned.
- A Long Row of Candles: Memoirs and Diaries [1934-1954]. New York: Macmillan, 1969.

2. September 27, 1954-December 12, 1963; Political diary; Churchill and de Gaulle are the giants striding through the diary; claims the confidences entrusted to him were the product of following his first editor's advice, "Keep your ears open and your mouth shut"; telling comments on and quotes from political leaders of the era.
- The Last of the Giants. New York: Macmillan, 1970.

3. December 13, 1963-December 31, 1971; Political diary; opens with a pessimistic commentary "The Mediocre Shall Inherit the Earth" chastizing statesmen and journalists; aftermath of the Kennedy assassination; first American journalist to interview Nixon after he became president; much material on de Gaulle and French politics, Lyndon Johnson and Nixon; incisive, humorous and sometimes earthy.
- An Age of Mediocrity: Memoirs and Diaries 1963-1972. New York: Macmillan, 1973.

1944

2345. BAKER, Richard Brown
May 19-December 22, 1944
Personal diary; American who had attended Oxford; in a highly placed military capacity; survived the German bombings unharmed.
- The Year of the Buzz Bomb: A Journal of London, 1944. New York: Exposition, 1952.

2346. BEATTIE, Edward William (1909-   )
       September 12, 1944-May 4, 1945
       Prison diary; American war correspondent captured by the
Germans in France; imprisoned in Berlin and Luckenwalde; fluent
in German and well able to converse with his guards; long entries
with details of treatment; excellent for the short time covered.
       • Diary of a Kriegie. New York: Crowell, 1946.
          REVIEW: Book Review Digest 1946, p. 48.

2347. BOGUSLAWSKA, Anna
       August 2-September 21, 1944
       Personal diary; woman who lived in Warsaw took part in the
insurrection of the Polish Home Army against the Germans; defeat
and escape into the countryside.
       • Food for the Children. Ewa Barker, trans. London:
       Cooper, 1975.

2347a. CHRISTENSEN, Keith (1921-   )
       Military diary; testing Army rations at Camp Carson, Colorado;
staccato style.
       • "Diary," in: Donald Vining, ed. American Diaries of World
       War II. New York: Pepys Press, 1982; pp. 28-48.

2348. COLVILLE, Alexander (1920-   )
       July 22, 1944-May 3, 1945
       Military diary; Canadian artist was sent to record the war in
pictures and sketches; his art is reproduced, adding eloquence to
the straightforward daily entries.
       • Alexander Colville: Diary of a War Artist. Graham Metson
       and Cheryl Lean, comps. Halifax, N.S.: Nimbus, 1981.

2348a. EDWARDS, Ralph G. (1920-   )
       January 10-May 27, 1944
       Military diary; tail gunner flying bombing missions from a
base in Italy.
       • "Diary," in: Donald Vining, ed. American Diaries of World
       War II. New York: Pepys Press, 1982; pp. 308-18.

2349. GILES, Henry E.
       May 7, 1944-
       Personal diary; son of American novelist Janice Holt Giles;
service with the 291st Engineer Combat Battalion; invasion preparations in Gloucester; crossing France; Battle of the Bulge, Remagen;
interleaved with accounts from other company members written for
this publication.
       • The G. I. Journal of Sergeant Giles. Janice Holt Giles, ed.
       and comp. Boston: Houghton Mifflin, 1965.

2349a. GOLDMAN, Paul (1910-   )
       March 3-July 21, 1944
       Military diary; chemist served as a pharmacist's mate on ship-

board to Europe; D-Day landings; treating German casualties and Allied troops.
- "Diary," in: Donald Vining, ed. <u>American Diaries of World War II</u>. New York: Pepys Press, 1982; pp. 216-41.

2349b. HARKOVICH, Mike (1920-)
December 4, 1944-May 13, 1945
Prison diary; staff sergeant with the 8th Air Force in a POW camp in Germany; lengthy entries with many details of food and treatment.
- "Diary," in: Donald Vining, ed. <u>American Diaries of World War II</u>. New York: Pepys Press, 1982; pp. 381-415.

2349c. LEWIS, Carroll A., Jr.
November 10, 1944-January 21, 1945
Military diary; Houstonian; co-pilot and tail gunner in the 379th Bomber Group (Heavy); record of 18 missions.
- "Diary," in: Donald Vining, ed. <u>American Diaries of World War II</u>. New York: Pepys Press, 1982; pp. 319-28.

2350. LINDSAY, Sir Martin (1905-)
July 12, 1944-April 26, 1945
Military diary; Sandhurst graduate; service in France, Holland, Belgium and Germany; details of the British effort after D-Day; slightly wounded; considerate of his subordinates who often had few resources; nice touches of irony.
- <u>So Few Got Through: The Journal of Lieutenant-Colonel Sir Martin Lindsay Who Served with the Gordon Highlanders in the 51st Highland Division</u>. London: Collins, 1946.

2351. MAURIAC, Claude (1910-)
August 16, 1944-May 9, 1954
Personal diary; son of French writer Francois Mauriac; last days of the war; life in postwar France; politics; very full entries for early years, growing shorter as time goes on; de Gaulle's Boswell.
- <u>The Other de Gaulle: Diaries 1944-1954</u>. Moura Budberg and Gordon Latta, trans. New York: John Day, 1973.

2351a. MAZZA, Michael
August 6, 1944-April 14, 1945
Prison diary; rifleman doing farm labor in Germany.
- "Diary," in: Donald Vining, ed. <u>American Diaries of World War II</u>. New York: Pepys Press, 1982; pp. 374-80.

2352. MENON, Kumara P. S. (1898-)
August 16-December 12, 1944
Travel diary; by pony, auto and air from Srinagar, India, to Chungking, China; view of a part of the world not engulfed in World War II; good descriptions of scenery and people; comparisons with other, earlier travelers' accounts of the areas.

• Delhi-Chungking, A Travel Diary. New York: Oxford University Press, 1947.

2353. MOEN, Petter (1901-44)
February 10-September 4, 1944
Prison diary; Norwegian underground journalist arrested by the Gestapo for publishing; diary was pricked with a pin into sheets of toilet paper; interrogation; in solitary.
• Diary. Bjorn Koefoed, trans. New York: Creative Age Press, 1951.

2354. NANSEN, Odd (1901-)
January 13, 1944-April 28, 1945
Prison diary; Norwegian in a Nazi concentration camp.
• "Diary Excerpts," in: Philip Dunaway and Mel Evans, eds. A Treasury of the World's Great Diaries. New York: Doubleday, 1957; pp. 561-70.

2355. PEARCE, Donald R. (1917-)
June 26, 1944-June 11, 1945
Military diary; infantry platoon commander with the First Canadian Army in the Netherlands-Belgium campaign; by convoy through U-boat Alley from New York; good descriptions and telling observations, e.g. "London is a childless city"; impersonal tone; hardly a word about comrades or subordinates.
• Journal of a War; North-west Europe, 1944-1945. Toronto: Macmillan of Canada, 1965.

2355a. RHINEHART, Walter L. (1909-)
January 21, 1944-June 13, 1945
Military diary; officer on an LSD destroyer; service in the Pacific; melancholy reminiscences.
• "Diary," in: Donald Vining, ed. American Diaries of World War II. New York: Pepys Press, 1982; pp. 242-50.

2355b. SAIS, Desiderio J.
February 2, 1944-June 2, 1945
• "Diary," in: Donald Vining, ed. American Diaries of World War II. New York: Pepys Press, 1982; pp. 107-21.

2355c. SULLIVAN, William J. (1917-)
April 10-June 15, 1944
Military diary; gunner on a B-17 flying missions from a Belgian airfield; rescued after ditching in the water.
• "Diary," in: Donald Vining, ed. American Diaries of World War II. New York: Pepys Press, 1982; pp. 329-39.

2356. TOBIN, Richard Lardner
April-August 9, 1944
Military diary; New York Herald Tribune correspondent; by ship to England; in France; very full entries; written up later?

- Invasion Journal. New York: Dutton, 1944.

2357. TREVELYAN, Raleigh (1924?-)
March 17-July 5, 1944
Military diary; British subaltern, untried in battle, was sent
to command a unit at the beachhead; detailed account of tactics with
drawings of troop positions; vivid character sketches of his trench-
mates; revised for publication?
- The Fortress: A Diary of Anzio and After. London: Collins, 1956.

2358. VÖRÖS, Julius (1891-)
April 18-October 15, 1944
Military diary; dealings with his staff, the Regent, Nicholas
Horthy and the Germans.
- "Document: The War Diary of the Chief of the Hungarian
General Staff in 1944," East European Quarterly, v. 2, pp. 315-
31, 1968.

1945

2358a. ASKIN, William D. (1924-)
January 1-March 21, 1945
Military diary; on office duty in the Philippines; listening to
Tokyo Rose broadcast; notes on his reading and movies seen.
- "Diary," in: Donald Vining, ed. American Diaries of World
War II. New York: Pepys Press, 1982; pp. 251-65.

2359. COCTEAU, Jean (1889-1963)
August 26, 1945-June 1, 1946
Film diary; "La belle et la Bete"; work, weather, difficulties;
interesting to film buffs.
- Diary of a Film. Ronald Duncan, trans. London: Dennis
Dobson, 1950?
REVIEW: Book Review Digest 1950, pp. 185-86.

2360. ELATH, Eliahu (1903-)
April 30-July 2, 1945
Diplomatic diary; adviser to the delegation seeking recognition
for Israel at the postwar conference in San Francisco; political ma-
neuvering.
- Zionism at the UN: A Diary of the First Days. Michael
Ben-Yitzhak, trans. Philadelphia: Jewish Publication So-
ciety of America, 1976.

2360a. ELLIS, Edward Robb (1911-)
August 5-September 24, 1945
Military diary; newspaperman and diarist noted in the Guin-
ness Book of Records for the world's longest diary; service in Oki-
nawa; lengthy entries in journalistic style.

• "Diary," in: Donald Vining, ed. American Diaries of World War II. New York: Pepys Press, 1982; pp. 122-29.

2360b. EPSTEIN, Bernard
January 9-April 31, 1945
Prison diary; lieutenant with the 99th Infantry imprisoned in Brunswick, Germany; Allies approaching from the West; details of his liberation.
• "Diary," in: Donald Vining, ed. American Diaries of World War II. New York: Pepys Press, 1982; pp. 416-23.

2361. GAITSKELL, Hugh (1906-63)
August 6, 1945-October 9, 1956; gaps
Political diary; Labour Party MP progressed from back bencher to minister to a member of the Shadow Cabinet; Leader of the Opposition; party infighting; relations with the U.S. and Communists; Suez crisis; important for British postwar history.
• The Diary of Hugh Gaitskell 1945-1956. Philip M. Williams, ed. London: Jonathan Cape, 1983.

2362. GAYN, Mark J. (1909-   )
December 5, 1945-December 21, 1946
Personal diary; American reporter living in Japan during the Occupation; in cities and the countryside; tales and observations on the behavior of Japanese and Americans; very readable.
• Japan Diary. New York: W. Sloane Associates, 1948.

2363. GILBERT, G. M.
October 23, 1945-July 27, 1946
Personal diary; German-speaking military intelligence officer and psychologist in daily contact with Nuremberg war criminals; interviewed Goering, von Ribbentrop, Hess, Speer, von Papen, Doenitz, Jodl and Keitel; chilling.
• Nuremberg Diary. New York: Farrar, Straus and Giroux, 1961.

2364. HACHIYA, Michihiko
1. Personal diary; doctor injured in the bomb blast by flying glass; discusses radiation sickness in himself and others; gives the Japanese reaction to the country's surrender and their surprise at the way American soldiers treated them afterward; very interesting.
• Hiroshima Diary: The Journal of a Japanese Physician August 6-September 30, 1945. Warner Well, M.D., trans. and ed. Chapel Hill: Unviersity of North Carolina Press, 1955.

2. "Diary Excerpts," in: Philip Dunaway and Mel Evans, eds. A Treasury of the World's Great Diaries. New York: Doubleday, 1957; pp. 582-86.

2365. HELLER, Paul
January 17-February 7, 1945

Prison diary; Jewish Auschwitz inmate was marched by the Germans from Eastern Silesia to the Breslau area ahead of the advancing Russians; cruelty and hardship.
- "A Concentration Camp Diary," Midstream, v. 26, pp. 29-36, April, 1980.

2366. Johnston, Russell R.
May 3, 1945-September 12, 1946
Personal diary; Red Cross field director for Civilian Relief spent time in Russia and Poland; encounters with Russian bureaucracy and their mismanagement of Red Cross aid; trying to steer clear of political pitfalls; some interesting moments.
- Poland 1945: A Red Cross Diary. Philadelphia: Dorrance, 1973.

2367. LEHNDORFF, Hans, Graf von
January 13, 1945-May, 1947
Personal diary; "partly from notes in a rescued diary and partly from memories"; member of the group involved in the July 20, 1944, assassination attempt on Hitler: Konigsberg before and after the Russian takeover; in Poland under Russian domination; practicing physician throughout; distances himself from events he describes to appear "literary."
- Token of a Covenant: Diary of an East Prussian Surgeon, 1945-47. Elizabeth Mayer, ed. Chicago: Henry Regnery, 1964.

2368. LIEBOW, Averill A.
September 18, 1945-January 25, 1946
Medical diary; pathologist on Saipan was sent to Hiroshima after the A-bomb was dropped to study casualties; close work with Japanese counterparts; pictures of blast victims' injuries and destruction; harrowing.
- Encounter with Disaster: A Medical Diary of Hiroshima, 1945. New York: Norton, 1970.

2369. SPEIER, Hans
October 4, 1945-October 8, 1955
Personal diary; German-born academic who spent the war years in the U.S. returned for nine visits to Germany and Austria in the period covered here; thoughtful.
- From the Ashes of Disgrace: A Journal from Germany, 1945-1955. Amherst: University of Massachusetts Press, 1981.

2370. TRUMAN, Harry S (1884-1972)
1. April 12, 1945-January 10, 1951; Personal diary; fragmentary extracts; politics and family matters; very down-to-earth.
- Mr. President: Personal Diaries, Private Letters, Papers and Revealing Interviews of Harry S Truman, 32nd President of the USA. William Hillman, ed. New York: Farrar, Straus and Young, 1952.

2. July 7-August 5, 1945; Personal diary; on board the Augusta; conditions in Germany; tells Stalin of the A Bomb; later re-
alized he had been fooled by Stalin; "And I liked the little son of a
bitch."
   • "Truman at Potsdam," Robert H. Ferrell, ed. American
Heritage, v. 31, pp. 36-47, June/July, 1980.

3. July 16-30, 1945; Personal diary; record of conversations
with Churchill and Stalin; pessimistic tone.
   • Mark, Eduard. "'Today Has Been a Historical One': Harry
S Truman's Diary of the Potsdam Conference," Diplomatic History, v. 4, pp. 317-26, Summer, 1980.

1946

2371. LEES-MILNE, James (1908-)
        January 1, 1946-December 31, 1947
        Personal diary; civil servant with the British National Trust
toured and inspected possible sites for trust designation; familiar
with upper class society; caustic; reveals some of the monetary arrangements made with owners and tenants.
   • Caves of Ice. London: Chatto and Windus, 1983.

2372. MAUROIS, André (1885-1967)
        1. January 1, 1946-January 1, 1947; Travel and personal
diary; French novelist and critic; in the U.S. and France; contrasts
between the two countries; his work; teaching in Kansas; interesting.
   • From My Journal. Joan Charles, trans. New York: Harper,
1948; London edition entitled My American Journal.

        2. August 7-October 1, 1952(?); Travel diary; on a lecture
tour to Brazil and Argentina.
   • My Latin-American Diary. Frank Jackson, trans. London:
Falcon, 1953.

2373. SPEER, Albert (1905-81)
        Prison diary; Hitler's Minister for Armament and War Produc-
tion; imprisoned for Nazi war crimes; much reminiscing, reading,
sketching, gardening; realtions with other political prisoners; very
interesting picture of a man who only came to an understanding of
Hitler and his policies long after World War II.
   • Spandau: The Secret Diaries. Richard and Clara Winston,
trans. New York: Macmillan, 1976.

1947

2374. BERENSON, Bernhard (1865-1959)
        January 1, 1947-April 15, 1958
        Personal diary; American art critic at home in his last years

at I Tatti in Tuscany; musings on life and old age, visitors, the state
of the world; to be read and savored.
  • Sunset and Twilight: From the Diaries of 1947-1958. Nicky
  Mariano, ed. New York: Harcourt, Brace and World, 1963.

2375. MALINA, Judith
        June 4, 1947-August, 1957
        Personal dairy; actress associated with New York's Living
Theatre; its inception and development; professional and personal
life; much editing and rewriting; evidence that others were reading
the diary as it was written; for drama enthusiasts.
  • The Diaries of Judith Malina, 1947-1957. New York: Grove
  Press, 1984.
        REVIEWS: Library Journal, v. 109, p. 893, May 1, 1984.
        Booklist, p. 1428, June 15, 1984. Publishers Weekly, pp. 59-
        60, March 23, 1984. Book Review Index 1984, p. 465.

2376. O'BRIEN, Margaret (1937-)
        January 15, 1947-December 31, 1947
        Personal diary; American child movie star; begun on her tenth
birthday; life in Hollywood; lunch with the Trumans at the White
House; making a movie; delightfully unaffected.
  • My Diary with Drawings by the Author. Lionel Barrymore,
  foreword. Philadelphia: J. B. Lippincott, 1948.

2377. SCHLOSSER, Frank G.
        June 12-November 4, 1947
        Political diary; delegate to the New Jersey Constitutional Con-
vention helped write the document which passed by a large margin;
detailed account of behind-the-scenes work by a conscientious citizen;
regrets the haste with which the body acted on some matters.
  • Dry Revolution: Diary of a Constitutional Convention.
  Newton, N.J.: Onnabrite Press, 1960.

                                1948

2378. BODDE, Derk (1909-)
        August 29, 1948-October 10, 1949
        Personal diary; first Fulbright Fellow to go to China; siege
of Peking by the Communists and its occupation; Shanghai; interesting.
  • Peking Diary, A Year of Revolution. New York: Schuman,
  1950.

2379. CRAFT, Robert (1923-)
        March 31, 1948-November 17, 1962; gaps
        Personal diary; notes from Craft's diary on Igor Stravinsky.
  • Dialogues and a Diary. New York: Doubleday, 1958.

2380. ELLIOT, James (1927-56)
        January 17, 1948-December 31, 1955

Spiritual/personal diary; member of the Plymouth Brethren;
Wheaton College (Illinois) graduate who was martyred with four other
missionaries by Indians in Ecuador; introspective.
- The Journals of Jim Elliot. Elisabeth Elliot, ed. Old Tappan, N.J.: F. H. Revell, 1979.
  REVIEW: West Coast Review of Books, v. 4, p. 43, September, 1978.

2381. LEVIN, Harry
March 25-July, 1948
Personal diary; British correspondent reporting on the Israeli
war for independence.
- "Diary Excerpts," in: Philip Dunaway and Mel Evans, eds.
  A Treasury of the World's Great Diaries. New York: Double-
  day, 1957; pp. 571-79.

2382. MARSTON, Otis
May 13-25, 1948
Travel diary; voyage by one of the first people to take a canoe
through the Grand Canyon; a rapid excursion.
- "Running the Dolores River, 1948," Colorado Magazine, v.
  26, pp. 258-70, October, 1949.

2383. MOSS, Anne Stanley (1925-   )
October 26, 1948-April 7, 1949
Travel diary; log of a woman who worked as a crew member
on a grain-carrying sailing barque from Bristol, England, to Aus-
tralia.
- "Journal Kept ... During the Last Passage to Australia of
  the Passat 1948-9," in: Basil Greenhill. Women Under Sail.
  Newton Abbott: David and Charles, 1970; pp. 151-208.

1949

2384. BARTON, Betsey Alice
June, 1949-November, 1955
Personal diary; paralyzed after an auto accident in her teens;
closeness to her parents; excerpts are concerned with her reaction
to her mother's bout with cancer and death; deeply-felt, spiritual
quality.
- As Love Is Deep. New York: Duell, Sloan and Pierce,
  1957.

2385. COLLIS, Maurice (1889-1973)
January 13, 1949-December 31, 1968
Personal diary; Irish writer and essayist; formerly in the Indian civil service; life in London; visits to Cliveden and the Astors;
knew leading writers and artists; uninhibited opinions; good reading.
- Diaries 1949-1969. Louise Collis, ed. London: Heinemann,
  1977.

Review: <u>Book Review Digest</u> 1977, p. 98.

2386. DRAKE, Gladys E. (1889-)
      January 1, 1949-May 1, 1950
      Personal diary; American widow active in the Chinese relief
efforts during World War II; professor of English at Yunnan University; entries are essays on Chinese culture and customs; civil war;
visits to surrounding area; escaped as the Communists won.
      • <u>Chinese Diary</u>. Denver: A. B. Hirschfeld Co., 1968.

2387. "MacLIAMMOIR, Micheál" (Alfred Willmore) (1899-1978)
      January 27, 1949-March 7, 1950
      Film diary; Irish playwright; played Iago to Orson Welles'
<u>Othello</u>; filmed in Venice; money problems; much ado about almost
nothing; for film buffs.
      • <u>Put Money in Thy Purse: The Diary of the Film of "Othello."</u>
Orson Welles, preface. rev. ed. London: Methuen, 1976.

2388. MAIS, Gillian
      December 18, 1949-January 7, 1950
      Travel diary; English family in search of warmth; shopping,
touring and sampling the madeira.
      • <u>Madeira Holiday</u>. London: Redman, 1951.

2389. MAIS, Stuart Peter Brodie
      April 4-May 1, 1951
      Travel diary; tourist notes; obsession with prices.
      • <u>Austrian Holiday</u>. London: Redman, 1952; pp. 9-184.

2390. PEARSON, Drew (1897-1969)
      January 1, 1949-December 5, 1959
      Personal diary; nationally syndicated newspaper columnist;
politics; national life; good picture of 1950's America; very readable.
      • <u>Drew Pearson: Diaries 1949-1959</u>. Tyler Abell, ed. New
York: Holt, 1974.
      REVIEW: <u>Book Review Digest</u> 1974, pp. 943-44.

2391. SALISBURY, Harrison E. (1908-)
      March 1, 1949-October 4, 1953
      Personal diary; <u>New York Times</u> correspondent to Moscow; last
years of Stalin; extracts from the diary, letters and dispatches to
the <u>Times</u>; Korean War; "Doctor's Plot" against Stalin and his death;
rise of Khrushchev; well done.
      • <u>Moscow Journal: The End of Stalin</u>. Chicago: University
of Chicago Press, 1961.

                              1950

2392. BODKIN, Amy Maud (1875-1967)
      1950-56

Literary diary; British critic; her reading and an account of its influence on her critical theory.

• Zagorski, Irene H. "'Images of Encounter': Maud Bodkin's Journal of Her Psychology of Literary Response," Ph.D., Syracuse University, 1978. (Dissertation Abstracts 40/01A, p. 273).

2393. PLATH, Sylvia (1932-63)
July, 1950-May 16, 1962; gaps during and after breakdowns
Personal diary; American poet who committed suicide; begun the summer before she entered Smith College; written on different levels with accounts of everyday events and also her fantasies; some sections appeared in The Bell Jar; Fulbright scholarship; marriage to British poet Ted Hughes; birth of two children; ends before her separation from Hughes.

• The Journal of Sylvia Plath. Frances McCullough, ed. New York: Dial Press, 1982.

2394. POTTER, Ursula Barnett
December 7, 1950-January 25, 1951; October 16-December 3, 1951
Travel diary; diarist and her husband, a BBC radio commentator made two trips with their children in a private plane; up and down the coasts of Africa; around the Belgian Congo; spends much ink on delays and red tape; all surface and no penetrating insights.

• I'll Fly No More: An Airwoman's Diary. London: Allen and Unwin, 1951.

1951

2395. CROSSMAN, Richard Howard (1907-74)
1. October 30, 1951-December 19, 1963; Political diary; Oxford don, journalist and Labour MP; an "independent personality"; German rearmament, British defence, inflation and the Suez Crisis are major topics; dictated weekly to a secretary and latterly taped; list of cabinet members 1951-63.

• The Backbench Diaries of Richard Crossman. Janet Morgan, ed. London: Hamish Hamilton, 1980.

2. October, 1964-June, 1970; Political diary; as minister of housing and local government; Lord President and Leader of the House of Commons; Secretary of State at the Department of Health and Social Security; events leading up to General Election in June, 1970.

• The Diaries of a Cabinet Minister. 3 vols. New York: Holt, 1975-78.
REVIEWS: Book Review Digest 1977, p. 291; 1978, pp. 291-92.

3. October 22, 1964-June 19, 1970; Political diary; a condensation of the three volume edition.

• The Crossman Diaries: Selections From the Diaries of a
Cabinet Minister, 1964-70. Anthony Howard, ed. London:
Hamish Hamilton, 1979.

2396. DUNFORD, Katherine (1920-)
January, 1951-September, 1953
Spiritual diary; Connecticut housewife and mother of two;
"pilgrimage ... between the desk and the kitchen sink"; a search
for God and meaning in her life; thoughts on her reading which
ranged from the New Testament to Winnie the Pooh.
• Journal of an Ordinary Pilgrim. Philadelphia: Westminster
Press, 1954.

2397. GRIFFITH, Margaret D.
September 15, 1951-September 16, 1952
Travel diary; American family of a Fulbright professor to Ox-
ford drove 24,000 miles thorugh Europe, managing nicely on $5 per
day per person; picture of Europe still coping with the aftermath of
World War II through rationing.
• Unconventional Europe: A Diary of a Family. Washington,
D.C.: Peabody Press, 1956.

2398. JOY, Charles Turner (1895-1956)
July 1, 1951-May 22, 1952
Political diary; head of the United Nations delegation to the
Korean Armistice Conference; believed the strategy he was ordered
to follow lengthened the war; three main issues caused the deadlock:
Chinese troops' presence, 38th parallel and repatriation of POWs;
wrote details of the day's work to clarify matters in his own mind.
• Negotiating While Fighting: The Diary of Admiral C. Turner
Joy at the Korean Armistice Conference. Allan E. Goodman,
ed. Stanford, Cal.: Hoover Institution Press, 1978.

1952

2399. DALI, Salvador (1904-)
May 1, 1952-September 3, 1962; gaps
Personal diary; Spanish Surrealist painter; daily life, work,
reminiscences; filmmaking; sometimes amusing; posturing and quite
pleased with himself.
• Diary of a Genius. Richard Howard, trans. New York:
Doubleday, 1964.
REVIEW: Book Review Digest 1965, p. 298.

2400. GINSBERG, Allen (1926-)
March 12, 1952-February 11, 1962
Personal/literary diary; intermittent entries; poetry, dreams;
travel to Mexico and Europe; fragmentary.
• Journals: Early Fifties, Early Sixties. Gordon Ball, ed.
New York: Grove Press, 1977.

REVIEWS: <u>Book Review Digest</u> 1977, p. 494; 1978, p. 498.
<u>Book Review Index</u> 1977, p. 164.

2401. RUSS, Martin
        August 20, 1952-September 10, 1953
        Military diary; from basic training at Camp Pendleton to Hill
229 in Korea; very readable.
        • <u>The Last Parallel: A Marine's War Journal</u>. New York:
        Rinehart, 1957.

2402. TEALE, Edwin Way (1899-1980)
        October 15-16, 1952
        Nature diary; American naturalist and writer observed the
birds returning to Milburn Swamp.
        • "Diary Excerpts," in: Philip Dunaway and Mel Evans, eds.
        <u>A Treasury of the World's Great Diaries</u>. New York: Double-
        day, 1957; pp. 324-26.

                                  <u>1953</u>

2403. POLLITT, Harry (1890-1960)
        December 12, 1953-January 7, 1954
        Travel diary; British Communist visited India for the Third
National Party Congress; triumphant; looking forward to the time
when "this pack of parasites [the British] will be driven out of India."
        • <u>Indian Diary</u>. London: Communist Party, 1954.

2404. SCOTT, Winfield T.
        June 14-25, 1953
        Nature diary; written on Cape Cod and dedicated to Beston,
author of <u>The Outermost House</u>; ruminations on Beston's books, Thoreau's <u>Walden</u>; a visit to Beston's house.
        • "A Journal for Henry Beston," in: <u>Exiles and Fabrications</u>.
        New York: Doubleday, 1961; pp. 170-82.

2405. STAATS, Henry Philip (1900-)
        November 15, 1953-February 15, 1954
        Travel diary; picture safari on the Serengeti Plain and Ngoron-
goro Crater area; Murchison Falls; travelogue.
        • <u>African Journal: 1953-1954</u>. New Haven: Prv. ptd., 1954.

                                  <u>1954</u>

2406. HAGERTY, James C. (1909-81)
        January 1, 1954-December 14, 1955
        Political diary; press secretary to President Eisenhower (q.v.);
first to use tv to a president's advantage; Churchill's visit; Senator
Joseph Mc Carthy's antics; had a father-son realtionship with the
president; very full entries.

• The Diary of James C. Hagerty: Eisenhower in Mid-course,
1954-1955. Robert H. Ferrell, ed. Bloomington: Indiana
University Press, 1983.
        REVIEWS: Library Journal, v. 108, p. 494, March 1, 1983.
        Publishers Weekly, v. 223, p. 56, March 18, 1983.

2407. MARKOPOULOS, Gregory J.
        October 19, 1954-September 12, 1963
        Personal diary; cryptic entries by a filmmaker on making a
movie entitled Serenity in Greece with unknown actors; for film buffs.
        • Quest for Serenity: Journal of a Film-maker. New York:
        Film-Makers' Cinematheque, 1965; 1000 copies.

2408. MURRAY, Michele (Judith Michele Freedman) (1933-74)
        December 31, 1954-March 9, 1974
        Personal diary; excerpts; writer, mother of four and cancer
victim at 41; disappointments and joys; poignant.
        • "Creating Oneself From Scratch," Thomazine Shanahan,
        ed. in: Janet Sternburg, ed. The Writer on Her Work.
        New York: Norton, 1980; pp. 71-93.

                              1955

2409. GARDNER, Dorothy Williams (1904-   )
        January 29-April 30, 1955
        Travel diary; writer and her husband spent a monetary wind-
fall on a trip to the Orient; breezy tourist notes with a sense of humor.
        • Fun on a Freighter. New York: Vantage, 1957.

2410. JESUS, Carolina Maria de (1913-   )
        1. July 15, 1955-January 1, 1960; Personal diary; Brazilian
woman's life in a São Paulo slum; constant battle to subsist and provide for her children; social and cultural life; turns at the communal
water spigot; rising cost of living; gathering rags and bottles for
resale.
        • Child of the Dark: The Diary of Carolina Maria de Jesus.
        David St. Clair, trans. New York: Dutton, 1962.

        2. "Diary Excerpts," in: Mary Jane Moffat and Charlotte
Painter, eds. Revelations: Diaries of Women. New York: Random
House, 1974; pp. 288-300.

2411. MORROW, Everett Frederic
        July 12, 1955-November 10, 1960
        Political diary; former CBS public affairs staff member; de-
plores the administration's treatment of blacks; good account of his
own treatment.
        • Black Man in the White House: A Diary of the Eisenhower
        Years by the Administrative Officer for Special Projects, The
        White House, 1955-1961. New York: Coward-McCann, 1963.

1956

2412. "BEKE, Laszlo" (1932-   )
Personal diary; artist and charter member of the Free Students'
Council; Hungarian Uprising and the Russian occupation; written from
notes after his escape to Canada.
   • A Student's Diary: Budapest, October 16-November 1,
   1956. Leon Kossar and Ralph M. Zoltan, eds. and trans.
   New York: Viking Press, 1957.

2413. DAYAN, Moshe (1915-81)
September 1-November 6, 1956
Military diary; Israeli army officer and politician; military and
political aspects of the campaign; supplemented with additional ma-
terial.
   • Diary of the Sinai Campaign. New York: Harper, 1966.
   REVIEW: Book Review Digest 1966, p. 288.

2414. GOMBROWICZ, Witold (1904-69)
1956
Literary diary; Polish novelist and playwright.
   • "Journal Excerpts," June Guicharnaud, trans. Yale French
   Studies, no. 39, pp. 200-09, 1967.
   (For critical material, especially the use of parody, see:
Alex Kurczaba. Gombrowicz and Frisch: Aspects of the Literary
Diary. Bonn: Bouvier Verlag, 1980.)

2415. MIČUNOVIĆ, Veljko (1916-   )
March 7, 1956-October 12, 1958
Diplomatic diary; life-long Communist and Tito's ambassador
to the Soviet Union; Khrushchev's speech denouncing Stalin; Polish
and Hungarian uprisings; Suez Crisis; his relations with Khrushchev
are a recurring theme; trenchant comments on the Russians; one of
the more interesting diaries of a political bent for the general reader.
   • Moscow Diary. David Floyd, trans. New York: Doubleday, 1980.

2416. RODMAN, Selden (1909-   )
October 21, 1956-April 6, 1957
Travel diary; American author of children's books; trip to
verify research for a study of Mexico; examines the animosity between
Americans and Mexicans; visits with leading Mexicans including artist
Rufino Tamayo and writer Carlos Fuentes; sympathetic to Mexico.
   • Mexican Journal: The Conquerors Conquered. Carbondale:
   Southern Illinois University Press, 1958.

1957

2417. FREDERIKSEN, Thomas (1939-   )
March 7, 1957-October 25, 1963

Personal diary; Greenlander recorded daily life in sporadic entries; English and Eskimo texts are presented in facing pages with watercolors depicting appropriate scenes; simple but beautiful rendering of Inuit life.

- Eskimo Diary. Jack Jensen and Val Clery, trans. London: Pelham, 1980.

1958

2418. ERNST, Morris Leopold (1888-1976)
1. August 23, 1958-August 22, 1959; Personal diary; partner in a New York law firm and ardent civil libertarian; book lover; ranges from politics to socializing with prominent people; conveys the flavor of the fifties.

- Touch Wood, A Year's Diary. New York: Atheneum, 1960.

2. December 31, 1959-December 21, 1960; Personal diary; activist lawyer served Roosevelt and Truman; musings on law and politics; irreverent and irrepressible.

- Untitled: The Diary of My 72nd Year. New York: R. B. Luce, 1962.

2419. HARNWELL, Gaylord Probasco (1903-)
June 26-July 11, 1958
Travel diary; junket by the president of the University of Pennsylvania with his wife and other university presidents to the Soviet Union to visit schools of higher education.

- Russian Diary. Philadelphia: University of Pennsylvania Press, 1960.

1959

2420. BECK, Frances
February 2, 1959-March 10, 1962
Personal diary; diarist's husband died at age 35 leaving her with three small children; facing the loss of his love and support; coping with life's mundane aspects; coming to terms with her grief; meeting and marrying another man.

- The Diary of a Widow. Boston: Beacon Press, 1965.

2421. GAJDUSEK, Daniel Carleton (1923-)
1. Travel diary; doctor involved in several types of research; observations of fellow travelers, his own problems, his reading; medical, social and linguistic notes about the people visited.

- New Guinea Journal, June 10, 1959 to August 15, 1960. Bethesda, Md.: National Institute of Neurological Diseases and Blindness, 1963.

2. Journal of a Trip to the Shepherd, Bank and Torres Islands

and to Espiritu Santo, and Efate in the New Hebrides, November 15, 1963 to December 24, 1963. Bethesda, Md.: National Institute of Neurological Diseases and Blindness, 1965.

3. Journal of Expeditions to the Soviet Union, Africa, the Islands of Madagascar ... June 1, 1969 to March 3, 1970. Bethesda, Md.: National Institute of Neurological Diseases and Stroke, 1971.

2422. MASLOW, Abraham Harold (1908-70)
      March 2, 1959-May 7, 1970
      Personal diary; American psychologist; wide-ranging; a variety of topics relating to his theories and study of psychology; academic infighting; Eleanor Roosevelt's personality, politics, new topics for research, the generation gap; lively, opinionated.
      • The Journals of A. H. Maslow. Richard J. Lowry, ed.
      Monterey, Cal.: Brooks/Cole, 1979; abridged edition by Jonathan Freedman. Lexington, Mass.: Lewis, 1982.

1960

2423. BEVINGTON, Helen Smith (1906-   )
      January, 1960-December, 1969
      Personal/literary diary; American poet; entries are dated by month; verging on a commonplace book; poetry; musings of a sprightly mind.
      • Along Came the Witch: A Journal in the 1960's. New York: Harcourt Brace Jovanovich, 1976.

2424. EVANS, Harold (1911-   )
      January 5, 1960-October 27, 1963
      Political diary; British journalist and former Colonial Office civil servant; press secretary to Prime Minister Harold Macmillan; overseas tours; talks with Kennedy and de Gaulle ("old Ramrod"); the Profumo scandal; enlightening look at the upper reaches of government with entertaining asides.
      • Downing Street Diary: The Macmillan Years 1957-1963.
      London: Hodder and Stoughton, 1981.

2425. GALBRAITH, John Kenneth (1908-   )
      December 7, 1960-November 26, 1963
      Personal diary; Harvard professor; ambassador to India under President Kennedy; worldwide travels; 1962 Sino-Indian border war; hosted Jacqueline Kennedy's visit; Vietnam problems; includes letters he wrote to President Kennedy about ambassadorial life; wry, lively; presents most Indians sympathetically and occasionally skewers American agencies.
      • Ambassador's Journal: A Personal Account of the Kennedy Years. Boston: Houghton Mifflin, 1969.

2426. SJÖMAN, Vilgot
      1. December, 1960-May 9, 1963; Film diary; film director

Ingmar Bergman was the diarist's mentor; L136 is the project number
given Bergman's film Winter Light; record of seemingly endless re-
takes to get the effect right; some scenes filmed for this project were
used in Bergman's later works; for film buffs.
* L136 Diary with Ingmar Bergman. Alan Blair, trans. John
Simon, intro. Ann Arbor, Mich.: Karoma Publications, 1978.

2. October 31, 1965-July 30, 1967; Film diary; Swede direct-
ing I Am Curious--Yellow; excerpts from the diary of the female lead
Lena Nyman are interspersed; inception through final cut and screen-
ing.
* I Was Curious: Diary of the Making of a Film. Alan Blair,
trans. New York: Grove Press, 1968.

2427. SPARROW, Jane
March 21-August 26, 1960
Personal diary; Briton serving the last part of an internship
in a rural English county; her case load, committee meetings, plans
for foster-home placements; bureaucracy balanced with common sense;
informative portrait of a social worker's tasks.
* Diary of a Student Social Worker. Boston: Routledge and
Kegan Paul, 1978.
REVIEW: Social Work, v. 25, p. 72, January, 1980.

1961

2428. PROUDFOOT, Merrill
June 9-July 24, 1961
Personal diary; white professor at Knoxville College took part
in an effort to integrate Rich's Department Store lunch counter; well-
done.
* Diary of a Sit-in. Chapel Hill: University of North Caro-
lina Press, 1962.
REVIEW: Book Review Digest 1962, p. 978.

2429. SOYER, Raphael (1899-   )
May 15, 1961-May 24, 1977; gaps
Personal diary; American artist; part memoir; rambling, intro-
spective notes on his work, trips abroad, visits with his contempor-
aries.
* Diary of an Artist. New York: Simon and Schuster, 1977.
REVIEWS: Book Review Digest 1978, p. 1239. Book Review
Index 1977, p. 412.

1962

2430. GIESE, Vincent J.
November 28, 1962-December 30, 1965
Personal/spiritual diary; decision at age 37 to study for the

Roman Catholic priesthood; at Beda Seminary in Rome; struggle to learn Latin; unpreachy and very human.

> • <u>Journal of a Late Vocation</u>. Notre Dame, Ind.: Fides, 1966.

2431.   MORRIS, Walter Ripton (1907-)
        December 2, 1962-June 30, 1963
        Personal diary; white collar employee fired after 18 years with the company; a year afterward he still hasn't found work; joined the Forty Plus Club, composed of unemployed male executives; keeps his sense of humor throughout; no happy endings but some major decisions.

> • <u>The Journal of a Discarded Man</u>. Englewood, N.J.: Knabe-North, 1965.

2432.   STERN, Richard
        July 3, 1962-August 23, 1973
        Personal diary; random extracts; visits to Ezra Pound in Italy and Robert Lowell in Chicago.

> • "Extracts from a Journal," <u>Triquarterly</u>, no. 50, pp. 261-73, Winter, 1981.

1963

2433.   JOHNSON, Claudia Alta Taylor (Lady Bird) (1912-)
        November 22, 1963-January 20, 1969
        Personal diary; wife of President Lyndon B. Johnson; edited from tapes; assassination and funeral of President John F. Kennedy; "onstage for a part I never rehearsed"; often a recital of appointments and people met; best when she speaks of her family.

> • <u>A White House Diary</u>. New York: Holt, Rinehart and Winston, 1970.

2434.   WHITE, Terence Hanbury (1906-64)
        September 17-December 16, 1963
        Travel diary; British author of the Arthurian retelling <u>The Once and Future King</u>; on a lecture tour and on the wagon; "The good part is seeing America, the bad part is being seen"; to New York on the <u>Queen Elizabeth II</u>; across the country, speaking at schools and colleges; delightful.

> • <u>America at Last: The American Journal of T. H. White</u>. David Garnett, intro.   New York: Putnam, 1965.

1964

2435.   "MITCHELL, Suzanne"
        July 3, 1964-December 19, 1970
        Psychological diary; woman began seeing a psychiatrist with her husband about their teenage daughter; eventually saw the doctor

on her own; breakup of the marriage; romantic involvement with the
therapist; change of doctors and a working through of her problems;
gets her life in order and becomes a therapist; jargon-free account
of a little-girl wife progressing to emotional and psychological maturity.

* My Own Woman: The Diary of an Analysis. New York:
Horizon Press, 1973.

2436. NAPEAR, Peggy
July 23, 1964-August 10, 1972
Medical/personal diary; mother of a spastic, cerebral-palsied,
mentally deficient child; followed a regimen laid down by the Institute
for the Achievement of Human Potential; battles with hostile medical people; trying to be a normal family with two other children and a husband;
excellent.

* Brain Child: A Mother's Diary. New York: Harper & Row,
1974.
REVIEW: Book Review Digest 1974, p. 878.

2437. SANTAMARIA, Frances Karlen
1. March 21, 1964-February 16, 1965; Personal diary; excerpts; American accompanied her husband to Greece while pregnant
with Joshua; entries center on the pregnancy, birth and early months;
reactions of the Greeks to leaving the baby unswaddled, breastfeed-
ing, etc.; naivete and wonder.
* Joshua Firstborn. New York: Dial Press, 1970.

2. "Diary Excerpts," in: Mary Jane Moffat and Charlotte
Painter, eds. Revelations: Diaries of Women. New York: Random
House, 1974; pp. 109-15.

1965

2438. PARKS, David (1944-   )
1. November 21, 1965-September 12, 1967; Personal diary;
son of the black photographer Gordon Parks; original entries expanded
with description and background material; Army induction, boot camp,
tour in Viet Nam; encounters with discrimination from officers and
men of his company; ends with orders for home; good portrayal of
atmosphere; includes his own photos.
* GI Diary. New York: Harper and Row, 1968.

2. "Vietnam Diary: Excerpts from GI Diary," Look, v. 32,
pp. 28-42, 45, March 19, 1968.

2439. SZULC, Tad (1926-   )
April 24-May 27, 1965
Political diary; New York Times correspondent covered the
U.S. intervention in the Dominican civil war.
* Dominican Diary. New York: Delacorte, 1965.

<u>1966</u>

2440. "BRAULIO" (no surname)
       October 25, 1966-August 9, 1967
       Personal diary; some entries rewritten at a later date; Cuban
guerrilla and veteran of an earlier Congo expedition; fragmentary.
           • "Braulio's Diary," in: Che Guevara. <u>The Complete Boliv-</u>
           <u>ian Diaries of Che Guevara and Other Captured Documents</u>.
           London: Allen and Unwin, 1968; pp. 315-22.

2441. GUEVARA, Ernesto "Che" (1928-67)
       1. November 7, 1966-October 7, 1967; Military diary; Argentine-
born physician and Cuban guerrilla; leader of a group aiming at drawing U.S. forces into "another Vietnam" in Bolivia; this transcription
includes material omitted from the official Cuban text; literate, sometimes humorous and unsparingly honest.
           • <u>The Complete Bolivian Diaries of the Che Guevara and</u>
           <u>Other Captured Documents</u>. Daniel James, ed. London: Al-
           len and Unwin, 1968.

       2. Military diary; ends with the survivors taken prisoner by
the Bolivian army.
           • <u>The Diary of Che In Bolivia, November 7, 1966-October 7,</u>
           <u>1967</u>. Robert Scheer, ed. New York: Bantam Books, 1968.
           (The Diaries were to be sold at auction by Sotheby's in
London in July, 1984. The Bolivian government won a temporary in-
junction halting the sale in June, 1984.)

       3. November 7, 1966-October 7, 1967; in addition to the daily
entries there is a summation at the end of each month which analyzes
events; "This book is a translation of the official Cuban version published in Havana on June 26th, 1968."
           • <u>Bolivian Diary of Ernesto Che Guevara</u>. Fidel Castro, intro.
           Carlos P. Hansen and Andrew Sinclair, trans. London: Lor-
           rimer, 1968.

2442. "POMBO" (no surname)
       July 14, 1966-May 29, 1967
       Military diary; a Cuban black with little education but shrewd
insight; a realist and a survivor in the psychological sense; describes
the political and personality conflicts inside the group.
           • "Pombo's Diary," in: Che Guevara. <u>The Complete Bolivian</u>
           <u>Diaries of Che Guevara and Other Captured Documents</u>. Lon-
           don: Allen and Unwin, 1968; pp. 253-314.

2443. "ROLANDO" (no surname)
       August 11, 1966-April 20, 1967
       Military diary; Che's intended commander of a second front
died before reaching his objective; details of camp life and skirmishes.
           • "Rolando's Diary," in: Che Guevara. <u>The Complete Boliv-</u>
           <u>ian Diaries of Che Guevara and Other Captured Documents</u>.
           London: Allen and Unwin, 1968; pp. 225-51.

2444. RUSSELL, Stephen
       March 10, 1966-April 13, 1967
       Personal diary; Young Catholic priest living in a parish rec-
tory was a hospital chaplain; constantly on the run; physical and
mental fatigue; doubts about his faith; trying to interpret Vatican II
to his congregation; many amusing comments on the portrayal of
clergymen in literature.
       • A Man in the Middle: The Journal of a Young Priest in
       Conflict with Himself. Dayton, Ohio: Pflaum Press, 1969.

2445. SALISBURY, Charlotte Y.
       1. May 16-July 30, 1966; Travel diary; wife of New York
Times associate editor, Harrison Salisbury (q.v.); excursion to Hong
Kong, Cambodia, Thailand, India, Sikkim and Japan.
       • Asian Diary. New York: Scribner, 1967.

       2. May 27-July 3, 1972; Travel diary; jaunt through China
shortly after it was reopened to Americans; chiefly concerned with
the life of the common people.
       • China Diary. New York: Walker and Co., 1973.

       3. August 21-September 10, 1977; Travel diary; through
China by train and plane; Canton, Shanghai, Peking, and Harbin;
many contrasts with visit her five years previously.
       • China Diary: After Mao. New York: Walker, 1979.

       4. July 20-August 28, 1980; Travel diary; archaeological dig
at Xi'an, Buddhist caves in Xinjiang Province; effects of the Chinese
invasion of Tibet during the Cultural Revolution.
       • Tibetan Diary and Travels Along the Old Silk Route. New
       York: Walker, 1981.

2446. TAYLOR, Kathrine Kressmann
       November 6, 1966-March 4, 1967
       Personal diary; American writer living in Florence describes
the effects of torrential autumn rains which damaged priceless art
work and destroyed the homes and workplaces of the inhabitants;
sympathetic portrait of Florentines and how they coped.
       • Diary of Florence in Flood. New York: Simon and Schus-
       ter, 1967; English edition titled Florence: Ordeal by Water.
       REVIEW: Book Review Digest 1967, p. 1293.

2447. WEISS, Joseph J.
       September-October, 1966
       Medical diary; undated diary with comments on conditions in
Camau where he volunteered in a civilian hospital.
       • "Vietnam--A Doctor's Journal," Commentary, v. 43, pp. 52-
       59, May, 1967.

1967

2448. BRISCOE, Edward Gans (1937-)
       November 16, 1966-May 6, 1967
       Military diary; surgeon in Vietnam writes on the unending
parade of casualties, mistakes and medical infighting; M*A*S*H*
without humor.
         • Diary of a Short-timer in Vietnam. New York: Vantage,
         1970.

2449. GLUECK, Nelson (1900-)
       June 15-August 27, 1967
       Travel diary; archaeologist arrived shortly after the end of
the Six Day War; survey of sites in newly conquered territory; cloak
and dagger escape with a Dead Sea scroll; bird's-eye view of a unique
situation.
         • Dateline: Jerusalem; A Diary. Cincinnati: Hebrew Union
         College Press, 1968.

2450. HASKINS, James
       September 29, 1967-June 28, 1968
       Classroom diary; former Wall Street Broker taught in an ele-
mentary school in the Ocean Hill-Brownsville area; teachers politicking;
very little education.
         • Diary of a Harlem Schoolteacher. New York: Grove Press,
         1970.
              REVIEWS: New York Times Book Review, p. 37, January
              20, 1980. Book Review Digest 1970, p. 621.

2451. ROOK, Alan
       January, 1967-August 23, 1969
       Personal diary; wine merchant bought a house and land in
Lincolnshire and turned the kitchen garden into the northernmost
vineyard in the world; record of the problems, weather and three
harvests; the pleasure of succeeding in a venture which many "ex-
perts" said would fail.
         • The Diary of an English Vineyard. London: Wine & Spirit
         Publications, 1972.

2452. SEXTON, Anne Harvey (1928-74)
       June 16-October 31, 1967
       Personal diary; American poet; teaching a class for the
Teachers and Writers Collaborative.
         • "Journal of a Living Experiment," in: Phillip Lopate, ed.
         Journal of a Living Experiment. New York: Teachers and
         Writers, 1979.
              REVIEW: Book Review Index 1980, p. 316.

2453. SPOERRI, Daniel (1930-)
       April 27-June 3, 1967
       Culinary diary; Romanian who escaped the Nazis was a ballet

dancer and director of avant-garde theatre; on the island of Symi;
recipes interspersed with notes on his companions and native life.
- Mythology and Meatballs: A Greek Island Diary/Cookbook.
Berkeley, Cal.: Aris, 1982.

2454. SWISHER, Peter Nash (1944-)
November 20, 1967-May 5, 1971; gaps
Military diary; episodic, reflective diary by an Officer Candi-
date School graduate; service at Cam Canh Bay.
- A Vietnam Diary. Richmond: Hesperia Publications, 1975.

2455. THEODORAKIS, Mikis (1925-)
April 21, 1967-April 13, 1969
Prison diary; Greek composer; incarcerated for his resistance
to the Greek coup; his music was banned; in and out of prison;
hunger strike; doubtful this is a true diary; most likely written after
his escape to France.
- Journal of Resistance. Graham Webb, trans. New York:
Coward, McCann and Geoghegan, 1973.
REVIEW: Book Review Digest 1973, p. 1282.

1968

2456. BERRIGAN, Philip (1923-)
July 22-September 24, 1968; November 9-28, 1968
Prison diary; Catholic priest imprisoned and tried with the
Catonsville Nine for napalming draft files in protest against the
Vietnam war; his reading; comments on other inmates and the prison
system; his anti-war beliefs.
- Prison Journals of a Priest Revolutionary. New York: Holt,
Rinehart and Winston, 1967.

2457. GREEN, Jerry
April 9-October 10, 1968
Sports diary; Detroit News sportswriter chronicles the year
the Tigers won the pennant; Denny McLain, Al Kaline, Mickey Lo-
lich and Willie Horton are the featured players; most likely written
up from earlier notes; photos.
- Year of the Tiger: Diary of Detroit's World Champions.
New York: Coward-McCann, 1969.

2458. KOHOUT, Pavel (1928-)
January 7, 1968-January 25, 1969
Personal diary; Czech poet and playwright; "Prague Spring"
and the Soviet takeover of his country.
- From the Diary of a Counterrevolutionary. George Theiner,
trans. New York: McGraw-Hill, 1972.

2459. SHUB, Anatole
January 16-April 5, 1968

Political diary; Moscow correspondent for the Washington Post; trial of Ludmilla Ginsburg and others for magazine publishing; travel to Eastern European capitals.

- "One Hundred Days From Moscow to the Moldau: A Reporter's Notebook," Encounter, v. 31, pp. 75-93, July, 1968.

2460. TILLMAN, Seth P.
December 5, 1968–January 2, 1969
Travel diary; consultant to the Committee went to Japan to soothe relations between program participants; stops in India and Thailand; thoughtful, balanced view of U.S. aid abroad.

- Diary of a Trip to Asia: The Peace Corps and the Fulbright Program. Washington, D.C.: U.S. Government Printing Office, 1969. (91st Congress, 1st Session. Committee Print)

2461. YEZZO, Dominick
August 14, 1968–August 16, 1969
Military diary; drafted into the 1st Air Cavalry Division; arrival at Cam Ranh Bay; fighting in various locations; a self-conscious quality.

- A G.I.'s Vietnam Diary, 1968-1969. New York: Franklin Watts, 1974.

1969

2462. DAVIDOW, Mike
March 12, 1969–December 12, 1974
Personal diary; Russian-born American citizen and his family went to Moscow to seek medical aid for an autistic child; sympathetic to the Russian people and their government; interesting for its viewpoint; comments on black Americans who live better in the USSR than in the U.S.

- Moscow Diary. Moscow: Progress, 1980.

1970

2463. BERGER, William (1928-)
October 15, 1970–March 29, 1971
Prison diary; sometime actor and his wife, a member of the Living Theater (see Judith MALINA), were arrested by Italian police for drug possession; she died after a mysterious operation in prison; this is his attempt to come to terms with her death.

- House of Angels: Love Notes From the Asylum. Timothy Wilson, ed. New York: Viking, 1973; pp. 143-295.

2464. CULBERTSON, Manie
January 2–May 30, 1970
Personal diary; white teacher in Louisiana was transferred to

an all black school to comply with a federal court order; her initial
qualms were overcome; fair, balanced view of a situation which was
difficult for both the teacher and her students.
- **May I Speak? Diary of a Crossover Teacher**. Sue Eakin,
  ed. Gretna, La.: Pelican Publishing Co., 1972.

2465. FENN, Charles
March 13-August, 1970?
Sea diary; voyage in a small boat from Ceylon with another
man; shipwrecked just south of the equator; died?
- **Journal of a Voyage to Nowhere**. New York: Norton, 1972.
  REVIEW: Book Review Digest 1972, p. 407.

2466. KUZNETSOV, Edward (1939-   )
October 27, 1970-November 28, 1971
Prison diary; imprisoned for his part in an aborted airplane
hijacking; introspective; musings on Soviet life, thought and politics.
- **Prison Diaries**. Howard Spier, trans. New York: Stein
  and Day, 1975.

2467. WAUGH, Harry (1904-   )
February 2-December, 1970; March 30-August 26, 1971
Wine diary; British oenophile toured French and American vineyards; discussion of vintages, history and management of vineyards,
prices and tastings.
- **Diary of a Winetaster: Recent Tastings of French and California Wines**. New York: Quandrangle Books, 1972.

2468. WILLWERTH, James
April 3, 1970-May 22, 1971
Personal diary; reporter for CBS in Vietnam and Cambodia;
talks with GIs and Vietnamese; hearing about the Kent State killings;
impressionistic pastiche.
- **Eye in the Last Storm: A Reporter's Journal of One Year
  in Southeast Asia**. New York: Grossman, 1972.

2469. WITKIN, Irving
March 20-October 27, 1970
Official diary; overcrowded school in upper Manhattan was
disrupted by factions seeking control.
- **Diary of a Teacher: The Crisis at George Washington High
  School**. New York: Untied Federation of Teachers, 1970?

1971

2470. ABZUG, Bella (1920-   )
January 18-December 28, 1971
Political diary; Congresswoman for a diversified New York City
district; her first year's work in the 92nd Congress; personal life;
relations with her staff, family and political opponents and allies; out-
spoken.

• <u>Bella! Ms. Abzug Goes to Washington</u>. Mel Ziegler, ed.
New York: Saturday Review Press, 1972.

2471.   CARR, Jess
June 23, 1971–January 25, 1972
Personal diary; kept while working on a biography of regional interest; it was turned down by the author's previous publisher and privately printed.
• <u>Birth of a Book: A Diary of the Day-to-day Writing of the Saint of the Wilderness</u>.   Radford, Va.:   Commonwealth Press, 1974.

2472.   SMITH, Fredrick W.
May 19–June 6, 1971
Spiritual diary; a "spiritual and physical adventure ... to see more deeply into myself"; an extended meditation.
• <u>Journal of a Fast</u>.   New York: Schocken Books, 1972.

2473.   WESKER, Arnold (1932–   )
November 8, 1971–May 4, 1972
Personal diary; British playwright and poet; working on the play <u>The Journalists</u>; diary was kept with the idea of its being the basis of a series of lectures.
• "Journal of <u>The Journalists</u>," <u>Theatre Quarterly</u>, v. 7, pp. 3–10, 12–17, Summer, 1977.

<u>1972</u>

2474.   AIKEN, George David (1892–1984)
Political diary; senior U.S. Senator from Vermont in his sixth term; an independent wearing a Republican label; known for his maxim on the Vietnam War "Just say we won and get out!"; first hand look at political maneuvering in getting bills passed or dropped; ranking member on Agriculture and Atomic Energy Committees in these years; of historical importance.
• <u>Aiken: Senate Diary January 1972–January 1975</u>.   Brattleboro, Vt.:   Stephen Green Press, 1976.

2475.   BALLIETT, Whitney
January 4, 1972–November 4, 1975
Music diary; jazz critic for the <u>New Yorker</u>; events in the jazz world; criticism; comments on Jerry Mulligan, Earl Hines, etc.; obituaries of jazz figures; written up from earlier notes?
• <u>New York Notes: A Journal of Jazz 1972–1975</u>.   Boston: Houghton Mifflin, 1976.

2476.   BREMER, Arthur H. (1950–   )
April 4–May 13, 1972
Personal diary; attempted the assassination of Governor George Wallace at a Maryland campaign rally; six weeks' odyssey in Milwaukee

and Canada trying to assassinate Richard Nixon; pathetic and illiterate.
- An Assassin's Diary. New York: Harper's Magazine Press, 1973.

2477. CUOMO, Mario Matthew (1932-   )
    1. May 17-October 27, 1972; Political diary; lawyer and Queens Borough resident mediated a dispute between the New York City Housing Authority and the residents of Forest Hills, site of a proposed low-income housing project; emotional political controversy seen through the eyes of someone trying to be fair to both sides.
- Forest Hills Diary: The Crisis of Low-income Housing. New York: Vintage, 1974.

    2. November 5, 1980-January 8, 1983; Political diary; son of Italian immigrants running for governor of New York; lieutenant-governor under Hugh Carey; victory in the Democratic primary; campaign against Lewis Lehrman who far outspent him; shrinkage of an early lead and an election-night cliffhanger; victory; strong character and firm principles.
- Diaries of Mario M. Cuomo: The Campaign for Governor. New York: Random House, 1984.

2478. HALL, Sir Peter (1930-   )
    March 27, 1972-January 29, 1980
    Personal diary; British stage and film director; succeeded Sir Laurence Olivier at the National Theatre; because of government subsidies he was immersed in politics and management of the enterprise as well as play production; producing Amadeus, Hamlet, Tamburlaine the Great, and The Tempest; appearances by Albert Finney, Harold Pinter, Peter Brook, Dame Peggy Ashcroft and walkouts by various unions.
- Peter Hall's Diaries: The Story of a Dramatic Battle. John Goodwin, ed. New York: Harper and Row, 1984.

2479. KAMATA, Satoshi (1938-   )
    September 12, 1972-May 5, 1973
    Personal diary; freelance Japanese journalist took an assembly line job in a Toyota factory; as a "seasonal worker" he lived in a dormitory and ate at a company canteen; though the work was not difficult the monotony and fast pace took a heavy toll.
- Japan in the Passing Lane: An Insider's Account of Life in a Japanese Auto Factory. Tatsuru Akimoto, trans. and ed. New York: Pantheon Books, 1983.
    REVIEWS: Time v. 121, p. 62, February 14, 1983. Library Journal, v. 107, p. 2160, November 15, 1982.

2480. WHITLAM, Margaret
    December 15-November 3, 1972
    Personal diary; wife of the prime minister of Australia; official entertaining; visits to London, India and Japan; hosted a tour by

Queen Elizabeth II; comments are well mannered rather than candid.
- My Day. London: Collins, 1974.

<hr/>

1973

2481. COLEMAN, John Royston (1921-   )
        1. February 16-April 15, 1973; Personal diary; 51-year-old
academic who had not applied for a job in 30 years; spent eight weeks
digging ditches in Atlanta and making salads in Boston; interweaves
biographical notes with observations on money, work and interpersonal
relations; absorbing.
- Blue-collar Journal: A College President's Sabbatical.
Philadelphia: Lippincott, 1974.

        2. Excerpts; "Blue Collar Journal," in: Organizational Re-
ality: Reports from the Firing Line. 2nd ed. Glenview, Ill.: Scott,
Foresman, 1982; pp. 137-49.

2482. DJERASSI, Norma Lundholm
        May 22-June 15, 1973
        Travel diary; teacher and poet traveled with her husband to
China at the invitation of the Chinese Academy of Sciences; Peking,
Nanking, Shanghai; contrasts with life in America.
- Glimpses of China From a Galloping Horse (A Woman's Jour-
nal). New York: Pergamon Press, 1974.

2483. DREW, Elizabeth Brenner (1935-   )
        May 1-31, 1973
        Political diary; American correspondent; mostly Watergate do-
ings but with flashbacks to earlier relevant events and comments on
unrelated happenings; bombing of Cambodia and the state of the
stock market.
- "A Watergate Diary: Notes of a Washington Correspondent
During the Month of May, 1973," Atlantic, v. 232, pp. 60-70,
August, 1973.

<hr/>

1974

2484. CASSERLY, John J. (1927-   )
        November 14, 1974-January 23, 1976
        Personal diary; nonpartisan reporter hired as a speechwriter
for President Gerald Ford; left because he felt Ford had no coherent
policy; much behind the scenes gossip and jockeying; lively, political
scoop.
- The Ford White House: The Diary of a Speechwriter.
Boulder, Col.: Associated Universities Press, 1977.

2485. CASTLE, Barbara Anne (Betts) (1911-   )
        January 1, 1974-April 13, 1976

Political diary; in Harold Wilson's Labour Party cabinet; from election to stepping down.
- The Castle Diaries, 1974-76. New York: Holmes and Meier, 1981.
  REVIEW: Economist, p. 27, September, 1980. American Political Science Review, v. 75, p. 1081, December, 1981.

2486. HOEKINGA, Dr. Mark T.
April 13-May 26, 1974
Personal diary; medical work at a provincial hospital in the Mekong Delta; recreation; bull sessions on the pros and cons of being in Vietnam.
- "'It Almost Makes Me Cry'--What a Doctor Sees in Vietnam: Excerpts from Diary," U.S. News and World Report, v. 61, pp. 74-6, 78, September 19, 1976.

2487. HUXLEY, Elspeth (1907-   )
April 2, 1974-March 28, 1975
Personal diary; examination of the village of Oaksey and its people over the course of a year; talking to old-timers to chart changes in village life; well done.
- Gallipot Eyes: A Wiltshire Diary. London: Weidenfeld and Nicolson, 1976.

2488. KLEIN, Henry (1951-   )
September 10, 1974-September, 1976
Personal diary; West Virginian began his stint at the time of the overthrow of Haile Selassie; teaching students with a poor command of English, the official language of instruction; they were "nowhere as good at cheating as American kids"; disillusioned early on by political chaos, intertribal rivalries and general anarchy; unvarnished picture by a misplaced volunteer.
- Through Ferrengi Eyes: The Diary of a Peace Corps Volunteer in Ethiopia, 1974-1976. Hicksville, N.Y.: Exposition Press, 1979.

2489. RAJ, Kakkadan Nandanath (1924-   )
November 6-13, 1974
Travel diary; Indian visited Hanoi; detailed impressions; talks with ranking officials.
- Hanoi Diary. Bombay: Oxford University Press, 1975.

2490. ROREM, Ned (1923-   )
June 20-September 20, 1974
Personal diary; American writer on music; Nantucket vacation; comment on Cosima Wagner's diaries (q.v.), pp. 135-37.
- Setting the Tone: Essays and a Diary. New York: Coward, McCann, 1983.
  REVIEW: Library Journal, v. 108, p. 587, March 15, 1983.

2491. SARTON, May (1912-   )
1. November 13, 1974-August 17, 1976; Personal diary;

American poet and novelist moved to the Maine seacoast for a change
of scene; personal life and literary work; deaths of elderly friends;
relaxing.
> • The House by the Sea: A Journal. New York: Norton,
> 1977.

2. May 3, 1982–May 2, 1983; Personal diary; entries begin
on her 70th birthday; poetry readings given; comments on President
Reagan, the Falklands War, gardening; believes "English is the best
language for poetry"; much reminiscing; to be read and savored.
> • At Seventy: A Journal. New York: Norton, 1984.
>   REVIEWS: Library Journal, v. 109, p. 484, March 1, 1984.
>   Publishers Weekly, v. 225, p. 78, February 17, 1984.

2492. TRUITT, Anne (1921–)
June 6, 1974–June 4, 1975; June, 1978–September, 1980
Personal diary; single mother of three kept his diary in an
attempt to confront the artist in herself and integrate it with the
other parts of her life and "impose my own order on matter"; visits
to friends; a stay at Yaddo Colony; reminiscences and introspection
thoughtfully combined; excellent picture of a creative individual.
> • Daybook: The Journal of an Artist. New York: Pantheon,
> 1982.
>   REVIEW: Library Journal, v. 107, pp. 1748–49, September
>   15, 1982.

1975

2493. HORNER, Joyce Mary (1903–80)
March 11, 1975–July 27, 1977
Personal diary; Oxford graduate, poet, novelist and professor
at Mount Holyoke; semi-invalid from complications of a fall; her ups
and downs; comments on other inmates and the staff; witty asides on
popular song lyrics and a Red Sox loss; a woman of true grit.
> • That Time of Year: A Chronicle of Life in a Nursing Home.
> Amherst: University of Massachusetts Press, 1982.

2494. "MATTHEWS, Ellen"
August 21, 1975–May, 1976
Personal diary; diarist and her husband sponsored a Vietnamese refugee couple and two relatives; clash of differing expectations;
thoughtful, provocative appraisal of government and private charity
programs.
> • Culture Clash. Chicago: Intercultural Press, 1982.
>   REVIEW: Wall Street Journal, p. 24, January 31, 1983.

2495. NARAYAN, Jayaprakash (1902–79)
July 21–November 4, 1975
Prison diary; founder of the Indian Congress Socialist party
and opponent of Indira Gandhi; imprisoned without trial; much time
in solitary confinement.

- <u>Prison Diary</u>. A. B. Shah, ed. Seattle: University of Washington Press, 1978.

1976

2496. MATTHEW, Christopher (1939-)
September 2, 1976-June 2, 1977
Personal diary; entertaining account of a Londoner's love life and foibles; fiction?
- <u>Diary of a Somebody</u>. London: Hutchinson, 1978.
REVIEW: <u>Book Review Index</u> 1979, p. 308.

2497. RADJI, Parviz C. (1936-)
June 16, 1976-January 26, 1979
Diplomatic diary; upper class Iranian and Cambridge graduate in his country's Foreign Service; friendly with the Shah's sister, Princess Ashraf; trying to counter Amnesty International's charges of torture by the Savak; relations with the British government and royals; ends with the overthrow of the shah.
- <u>In the Service of the Peacock Throne: The Diaries of the Shah's Last Ambassador to London</u>. London: Hamish Hamilton, 1983.
REVIEW: <u>Choice</u>, v. 22, pp. 332-33, October, 1984.

1978

2498. BRANDYS, Kazimierz (1916-)
October, 1978-November, 1981
Personal diary; Polish novelist and former Communist Party member was blacklisted by the government; suffering from writer's block and bad health; upheavals caused by Solidarity; musings on Polish history with many present-day comparisons and contrasts; spiritual, psychological and mundane trials of Polish life.
- <u>A Warsaw Dairy: 1978-1981</u>. Richard Lourie, trans. New York: Random House, 1984.
REVIEW: <u>Publishers Weekly</u>, v. 224, p. 55, November 4, 1983.

2499. McMENEMY, Lawrie (1936-)
July 18, 1978-May 14, 1979
Sports diary; a season convering 100,000 miles, 150 games with three vacation days; relations with press, players and fans; more wins than losses.
- <u>The Diary of a Season: His Account of the 1978-9 Season as Manager of Southampton Football Club</u>. Brian Scovell, ed. London: Barker, 1979.

2500. PRICE, Eugenia (1916-)
September 13, 1978-September 6, 1979

Literary diary; American novelist; researching and writing of
Margaret's Story; notes on her personal life; one novelist's working
method.
- Diary of a Novel. New York: Lippincott & Crowell, 1980.
  REVIEWS: Kirkus, v. 48, p. 1343, October 1, 1980. Pub-
  lishers Weekly, v. 218, p. 110, September 26, 1980.

2501. WILLIS, Bob
      April 22-September 8, 1978
      Sports diary; member of the Warwickshire County Cricket Club;
breezy account for Anglophiles and cricketeers.
      - Diary of a Cricket Season. London: Pelham Books, 1979.
        REVIEWS: Guardian Weekly, v. 121, p. 23, August 26,
        1979. New Statesman, v. 98, p. 30, July 6, 1979.

1979

2502. KLINE, Peter
      February 3-May 6, 1979
      Classroom diary; high school drama teacher and his class put
on Romeo and Juliet; photos; he draws several lessons from the experience, for life as well as theatre.
      - Diary of a Play Production. New York: Richards Rosen
        Press, 1980.

2503. MARSHALL, Bob
      October 29, 1979-October 11, 1980
      Sports diary; long-time hater of the New York Yankees be-
cause "they win too much"; a record of the 1980 season; comments
on games and the tv and newspaper coverage; for diehard baseball
fans.
      - Diary of a Yankee-hater. New York: Franklin Watts,
        1981.
          REVIEWS: Book Review Index 1981, p. 371. Book Review
          Digest 1981, pp. 938-39.

2504. WHITNEY, Cornelius Vanderbilt (1899-)
      January 1-June 29, 1979
      Personal diary; Yale graduate, polo player and horsebreeder;
business and social entertaining; 21st wedding anniversary; uninten-
tionally humorous.
      - "Live Six Months with a Millionaire," in Harper's, v. 264,
        pp. 37-45, May, 1982; Live a Year with a Millionaire. New
        York: Prv. ptd., 1981.

1980

2505. CASSON, Sir Hugh (1910-)
      January 6-December 30, 1980
      Personal diary; kept at the behest of the publisher; his year

as president of the Royal Academy; RA business and socializing; committee work; energetic.
- Diary. London: Macmillan, 1981.
  REVIEWS: Book Review Index 1981, p. 101. Apollo, v.
  117, p. 151, February, 1983.

2506. SICKMANN, Rocky (1957-)
       Prison diary; Marine security guard at the U.S. Embassy in
Teheran; taken hostage 28 days after his arrival in the city; diary
begins on Day 92 of his captivity and ends on Day 437; sorting truth
from the news their captors give them; boredom, fear and longing
for home.
- Iranian Hostage: A Personal Diary of 444 Days in Captivity. Erin L. Antrim, ed. Topeka, Kans.: Crawford Press,
  1982.

1981

2507. LONGFORD, Frank Pakenham, Earl of (1905-)
       January 1-December 31, 1981
       Personal diary; kept at the request of the publisher; father
of the biographer and mystery novelist Antonia Fraser and husband of
of the writer Elizabeth Longford with whom he celebrated a golden
wedding anniversary during this year; wide range of activities and
observations; politics, publishing and the Royal Family; excellent
reading for Anglophiles.
- Diary of a Year. London: Weidenfeld and Nicolson, 1982.
  REVIEW: Listener, v. 108, p. 37, December 23, 1982.

1982

2508. YERMIYA, Dov (1914-)
       Military diary; lieutenant-colonel in the Israeli Defence Forces
dealt with civilian relief after the 1982 invasion of Lebanon; mistreat-
ment of Arabs and Lebanese by the Israeli Army; his efforts to get
food and water for the refugees; the Israeli publication of this diary
resulted in his expulsion from the IDF.
- My War Diary: Lebanon, June 5-July 1, 1982. Hillel
  Schenker, trans. Boston: South End Press, 1984.

1983

2509. GREENE, Bob (1946?-)
       June 11, 1983-June 11, 1984
       Personal diary; syndicated columnist for the Chicago Tribune;
an account of his daughter's first year and the changes she caused
in the lives of her parents; colic, her first words, jealousy and her

partiality for a beeper and hinges; daily vignettes on the life of a growing girl.

    • <u>Good Morning, Merry Sunshine: A Father's Journal of his Child's First Year</u>. New York: Atheneum, 1984.

INDEX OF DIARISTS

Names enclosed in quotes are pseudonyms.
Numbers refer to entries.

Sylvester, Albert J. 2188
Symes, Michael 370
Szenes, Hannah see Senesh, Hannah
Szulc, Tad 2439

Tagore, Sir Rabindranath 2154
Talbot, Joseph C. 1458
Tallman, Augusta 1141
Tappan, Henry 873
Tarbuck, Edward L. 777
Tas, Adam 104
Tasburgh, Baron see Harvey, Oliver
Tasman, Abel J. 64
Tate, James A. 874
Tayler, William 642
Tayloe, Edward T. 516
Taylor, Annie 1914
Taylor, Calvin 919
Taylor, Gay S. see "Hurnscot, Loran"
Taylor, Isaac L. 1376
Taylor, James W. 717
Taylor, Kathrine K. 2446
Taylor, Robert B. 1377
Taylor, Thomas J. 1378
Taylor, William E. 778
Tchaikovsky, Peter 1733
Tchillingarian, Artasches see "Darbinian, Reuben"
Teal, John W. 1254
Teale, Edwin W. 2402
Teas, Thomas S. 484
Temple, Edmund 517
Tennery, Thomas D. 779
Tenney, Luman H. 1255
Tenney, Rollin Q. 1734
Tennyson, Emily S., Baroness 920
Teonge, Henry 86
Terry, Alfred H. 1774
Thacher, Peter 92
Theodorakis, Mikis 2455
Thistle, Lt. R. 2304
Thomas, Aaron 336
Thomas, Anna H. 1558
Thomas, Edward 2100
Thomas, Martha C. 1596
Thomas, Mary H. 630
Thomason, Jackson 874a
Thompson, Almon H. 1710
Thompson, David 352
Thompson, Henry A. 1559
Thompson, Henry Y. 1459
Thompson, Joseph D. 1379

Thompson, Philo E. 631
Thomson, James 1723
Thoreau, Henry D. 643
Tillich, Paul 2223
Tillman, Seth P. 2460
Tinker, Charles 875
Tobin, Richard L. 2356
"Toby, M. P." see Lucy, Sir Henry W.
Todd, John B. S. 1023
Todd, Matthew 423
Toketa 485
Tolstoy, Count Leo N. 780
Tolstoy, Countess Sophia 1142
Tolstoy, Tatiana L. see Sukhotina, Tatiana L. T.
Tomita, Saku 2319
Tomlinson, Ambrose J. 1968
Tomlinson, Ruffin W. 707
Tonge, Israel 89
Torbert, James M. 821
Torre, Tomás de la 38
Torrence, Leonidas 1256
Torrey, Rodney W. 1380
Torrington, Viscount see Byng, John
Toulmin, Harry 325
Tourgée, Albion 1460
Tourtillott, Jane H. G. see Gould, Jane H.
Towne, Laura M. 1381
Townley, Sidney D. 1858
Townsend, Edward D. 934
Townsend, Harry C. 1597
Tracy, Albert 1080
Trail, Florence 1843
Trask, Sarah E. 876
Travis, William B. 581
Tregaskis, Richard W. 2320
Trevelyan, Raleigh 2357
Trimble, Isaac R. 1382
Triplett, J. F. 1383
Trobriand, Philippe R. D. de K. 1640
Tromp, Martin H. 59
Trotsky, Leon 2213
Trowbridge, Charles C. 466
Trowbridge, William P. 985
True, Theodore E. 1756
Truitt, Anne 2492
Truman, Harry S 2370
Trumbull, Benjamin 160
Tucker, Frederick 1958
Tucker, John S. 1384
Tucker, St. George 255
Tuggle, William O. 1801
Tully, William 394

INDEX TO MATTHEWS' BIBLIOGRAPHIES

Numbers refer to pages.

a = American
b = British
c = Canadian

Allan, A. A. (Scotty) c2
Allan, Fletcher c2
Allan, George T. a289, c2
Allan, Dr. James Watson, -1925
b293
Allan, Col. John, 1746-1805 a136
Allan, William, -1939 c2
Allen, Daniel, 1744-77 a123
Allen, Hannah S., 1813-80 b231
Allen, Gen. Ira, 1751-1814 a157
Allen, James, 1742-78 a97
Allen, Capt. James, 1806-46 a296
Allen, John b30
Allen, John, 1737-1808 b114
Allen, Samuel a190
Allen, Rev. Thomas, 1743-1810
a136
Allen, William b30
Allen, William, 1770-1843 b128
Allen, Rev. William Y., 1805-85
a283
Allies, Rev. Thomas William b250
Allin, Sir Thomas, 1612-85 b28
Alline, Rev. Henry, 1748-84 a109
Alling, Jeremiah, 1763-1830 a167
Alling, Prudden, 1809-79 a273
Allingham, William, 1820-89 b252
Allis, Rev. Samuel a270
Allwyn, John b164
Allyn, Henry a336
Almy, Mary a143
Alnutt, Mrs.--- b222
Amberley, John Russell, Viscount,
1792-1878 b262
Amberley, Kate Stanley Russell,
Lady, -1874 b269
Amery, Leopold c2
Ames, Dr. Nathaniel, 1741-1822
a72
Amherst, Major-General Jeffery,
1717-97 a72, c2
Amherst, Lt. Gen. William, 1732-
81 a72, c2
Amory, Katherine, 1731-77 b109
Amoss, H. E. c3
Anahareo c3
Anderson, Andrew c3
Anderson, Lt. Aeneas, fl. 1802
b151
Anderson, Dr. Alexander, 1775-
1870 a188
Anderson, Rev. Alexander, 1822-55
b257
Anderson, Rev. Christopher, 1782-
1852 b155
Anderson, Rev. David, 1814-85
a332, c3

Anderson, Lt. Isaac, 1758-1839 a157
Anderson, James a341, c3
Anderson, John b192
Anderson, Rev. John, 1823- c3
Anderson, Maj. M. H., 1873-1915
b300
Anderson, Lt. Thomas a154
Anderson, Capt. Thomas Gummersall,
1779-1875 a225, c3
Anderson, W. b126
Anderson, W. K. c3
Anderson, William, 1756?- b183
Anderson, William Marshall, 1807-
81 a270
André, Major John, 1751-80 a136
Andrews, John, 1743-1822? a100
Angell, Col. Israel, 1740-1832 a143
Angell, Samuel, -1802 b116
Anglesey, Arthur Annesley, 1st
Earl of, 1614-86 b32
Anthony, Joseph, 1797- a245
Anthony, Susanna, 1726-91 a50
Anthony, Webster D., 1838- a351
Apperley, Captain Newton Wynn,
1846-1925 b275
Arbuthnot, Mrs. --- b198
Arbuthnot, Rev. Alexander b189
Archer, Sir John, 1598-1682 b27
Argall, Phyllis, 1909- c129
Armitage, Whaley b133
Armstrong, Andrew b130
Armstrong, Benjamin John b257
Armstrong, Edmund John, 1841-65
b270
Armstrong, Captain John a176
Armstrong, Nevill A. D. c8
Arnett, Thomas, 1791-1877 a251
Arnold, Gen. Benedict, 1741-1801
a109
Arnold, Seth Shaler, 1788-1871
a215
Arnold, Dr. Thomas, 1795-1842
b209
Arredondo, Don Antonio de a38
Asbury, Rev. Francis, 1746-1816
a99
Ash, Captain Thomas b44
Ashburton, Alexander Baring, 1st
Baron, 1776-1848 b164
Ashe, Lt. Edward David, R. N.
a352, c8
Ashe, Thomas, 1770-1835 a211
Ashley, Dr. Elihu, 1750-1817 a105
Ashley, William Henry, 1778-1838
a247
Ashmole, Elias, 1617-92 b14
Ashton, Philip, 1703-46 a25

Ashwell, Lena, 1871-   c8
Ashworth, Cornelius   b121
Ashworth, John, 1813-74   b276
Askin, Captain Charles, 1780-
   a218, c8
Askin, John, 1765?-1820   a218, c8
Assheton, Nicholas, 1590-1625   b9
Assheton, Susannah, 1767-   a199
Aston, John, 1601-50?   b16
Aston, Sir Willoughby, 1640-1702
   b40
Astry, Diana, 1671-1716   b54
Atherton, Frederick   b289
Athlone, Godert de Ginkel, 1st
   Earl of, 1630-1703   b48
Atkins, Josiah,   -1781   a158
Atkins, Quintius F., 1782-1859
   a211
Atkins, T.   c8
Atkinson, Rev. George Henry,
   1819-89   a306
Atkinson, Hon. Theodore, 1697-
   1779   a28
Atlee, Col. Samuel John   a123
Attmore, William,   -1800   a171
Aubrey, Francis Xavier, 1824-54
   a336
Auckland, William Eden, 1st Baron,
   1744-1814   b128
Audrain, Peter   a190
Audubon, John James, 1785-1851
   a238
Audubon, John Woodhouse, 1812-61
   a313
Auld, James,   -1780   a91
Aupamut, Captain Hendrick   a178
Austen, Kate   c8
Austin, Herbert Henry, 1794-1881
   b172
Austin, Col. Jonathan Loring, 1748-
   1826   a136
Austin, Moses, 1761-1821   a190
Austin, Stephen Fuller, 1793-1836
   a219
Auzias-Turenne, Raymond, 1861-
   c9
Avery, Rev. Daniel, 1746-1818
   a109
Avery, Rev. Joseph, 1743-   a195
Awdry, Cecile   b277
Awdry, Miss S. V.   b276
Ayer, Sarah Connell, 1791-1835
   a208
Ayers, Elisah   a306
Aylmer, L. A.   c9
Ayshcombe, William   b8

B., J., Esq.   a252
B., J. C., French soldier   c9
B., R.   b73
Babington, Charles Cardale, 1808-
   95   b209
Babington, Rev. Mathew Drake,
   1788-1851   b253
Baby, William Lewis   c9
Back, Sir George, 1796-1878   a267,
   c9
Backhouse, Anna, 1820-48   b235
Backhouse, Hannah Chapman, 1787-
   1850   a259, b160
Backhouse, James, 1721-98   b81
Backus, Captain Electus, 1804-62
   a278
Backus, Elijah, 1759-   a136
Backus, Rev. Isaac, 1734-1806   a78
Backus, James, 1764-1816   a172
Bacon, Major D'Arcy   b205
Bacon, Jane M.   b236
Bacon, Mary Ann, 1787-1815   a201
Bacon, Rev. Samuel, 1781-1820
   a233
Bacon, Captain William, 1716-61
   a65
Badcock, Rev. Josiah, 1752-1831
   a165
Badcock, Lt. Col. Lovell   b224
Badeaux, Jean Baptiste, 1741?-96
   c9
Baden-Powell, Robert Stephenson
   Smyth, Lord   c9
Badger, Rev. Joseph, 1757-1846
   a199
Bagley, Lowell, 1784-1860   a236
Bagot, Mary   b198
Bagshaw, Rev. Edward   b67
Bagshaw, William   b138
Bagshaw, William, 1628-1702   b50
Bagshawe, Catherine, 1760-1818
   b135
Bailey, Hinton Richard   b186
Bailey, Rev. Jacob, 1731-1808   a56,
   c9
Bailey, John Cann, 1864-1931   b289
Bailey, Joseph Whitman, 1865-   c9
Bailey, Laurestine d'Avray, 1841-
   c9
Bailey, Loring Woart, 1830-1925   c10
Bailey, Thomas   a307
Baillargeon, Pierre   c10
Baillie, Col. John, 1772-1833   a254
Baillie, Matthew, 1761-1823   b129
Baillie, Robert, 1599-1662   b15
Baillie-Grohman, William Adolph,
   1851-1921   c10

Blore, Thomas b136
Blount, William, 1749-1800 a176
Blumenfeld, Ralph David, 1864-
  b290
Blundell, Captain William 1620-98
  b28
Blunt, Wilfrid Scawen, 1840-1922
  b279
Boardman, Rev. Benjamin, 1731-
  1802 a111
Boardman, John, 1824-83 a292
Boardman, Oliver, 1758-1826 a136
Boardman, Timothy, 1754-1838
  a144
Boddy, A. A. c15
Bodfish, Mercy Goodwin, 1752-
  1803 a22
Bogle, George, 1746-81 b92
Bohun, Edmund, 1645-97 b37
Bois, John, 1561-1644 b12
Bolduc, Mgr. J. B. Zacharie c15
Bolling, Col. William, 1777- a252
Bolton, Charles E., 1840?- a349
Bol[t]zius, Rev. John Martin, 1703-
  65 a32
Bompas, Charlotte Selina Cox, 1830-
  1917 c15
Bonar, Rev. Andrew Alexander,
  1810-92 b215
Bond, Ens. J. Harman a352, c15
Bone, Peter Turner, 1859-1947?
  c15
Bonhereau, Dr. Elie, -1719 b51
Bonnefoy, Antoine a37
Bonner, Captain James a222
Bonnivert, Gideon b46
Boone, Captain Nathan, 1782-1857
  a293
Boone, Susanna, 1731-89 b106
Booth, George, 1635-1719 b58
Booth, Captain Joseph, 1736-1810
  a82
Booth, Lt. William, -1827? c15
Boothby, Captain Charles, 1786-
  1846 b161
Borden, Sir Robert Laird, 1854-
  1937 c15
Borland, Rev. Francis, 1633-
  b29
Borradaile, John, 1815- b239
Borron, E. B. c15
Borrow, George Henry, 1803-81
  b264
Bosanquet, Charles B. P. b281
Bosanquet, Rev. R. W. b198
Boscawen, Hon. Frances Evelyn,
  1719-1805 b82

Boswell, James, 1740-95 b95
Bosworth, N. c15
Boteler, Captain Nathaniel b16
Botfield, Beriah, 1807-63 b218
Botsford, Jabez Kent a267
Boucher, Georges Alphonse, 1865-
  c15
Boucher de Boucherville, R. T. V.
  c16
Bouchette, Robert Shore Milne, 1805-
  40 c16
Boudinot, Col. Elias, 1740-1821 a111
Bougainville, --- c16
Boultbee, Rosamond c16
Boulton, Alexander Claude Forster,
  1862- c16
Boulton, Major Charles Arkell, 1841-
  c16
Bouquet, Col. Henry, 1719-65 a90
Bourget, Mgr. c16
Bourget, Clermont, 1884- c16
Bourgoyne, Dr. ---- b4
"Bourne, George" see Sturt,
  George
Bourne, Rev. Hugh, 1772-1854
  b158
Boutflower, Charles, 1782-1844 b169
Boutwell, Rev. William T. a264
Bowen, Ashley, 1727-1813 a78
Bowen, Edward, 1755- a148
Bowen, Silas, 1722-90 a48
Bowen Family b283
Bower, Anna Catherina, 1768-
  b127
Bower, Fred, 1871- c16
Bowlby, Sir Anthony Alfred, 1855-
  1929 b301
Bowles, George, 1802- b92
Bowman, E. I. a313
Bowman, Major Joseph, 1752-82
  b148
Bowne, John, 1628-95 a4
Boyden, Seth, 1788-1870 b313
Boyer, Lt. John a185
Boyle, John, 1746-1819 a79
Boyle see also Cork
Boynton, Lucien C., 1811-86 a273
Boys, Jeffrey b33
Brackenridge, Henry Marie, 1786-
  1871 a217
Brackenridge, William Dunlop, 1810-
  93 a289
Bradburn, Samuel, 1751-1814 b107
Bradbury, John a215
Bradbury, Lt. John, 1736-1821 a82
Bradley, Arthur Granville, 1850-
  1943 c16

Henshaw, Col. William, 1735-1820
a80
Henson, Rt. Rev. Herbert Hensley,
1863- b277
Henson, Rev. Josiah c57
Herbert, Hon. Aubrey Nigel, 1880-
1923 b302
Herbert, Charles, 1757-1808 a139,
b114
Herbert, Sir Henry, 1595-1673 b10
Herbert, Henry see Pembroke
Herford, Edward, 1815- b226
Herklots, Rev. H. G. G. c130
Heron, Robert, 1764-1807 b131
Herr, Benjamin a261
Herrick, Captain Israel, 1721-82
a69
Herring, Frances Elizabeth Clarke,
1851- c57
Herrman, Augustine a4
Hertford, Francis, Countess of,
1699- b77
Hervey, Augustus see Bristol
Hervey, Rev. James, 1714-56 b71
Hervey, John see Bristol
Hervey, Rev. Romaine b143
Hervey, Hon. William, 1732-1815
a62, b87, c57
Hesdin, Raoul b141
Heslep, Dr. Augustus M., 1806-
a318
Hess, John W., 1824- a248
Heth, Lt. William, 1750-1807 a127
Heugh, Rev. Hugh, 1782-1846
b161
Heward, Hugh, -1803 a177
Hewins, Amasa, 1795-1855 a261
Hewins, W. A. S. b298
Hewitson, Rev. William Hepburn,
1812-50 b248
Hewitt, Henry Leeds a325
Hewlett, Maurice, 1861-1923 b293
Hexham, Captain Henry, 1585?-
1650? b13
Heywood, George, 1788?- b178
Heywood, Rev. Oliver, 1630-1702
b31
Heywood, Captain Peter, 1773-1831
b139
Heywood, Robert a271
Heywood, Col. William, 1728-1803
a47
Hickman, Richard Owen, 1831-95
a333
Hicks, Rev. Elias, 1748-1830 a223
Hicks, Elijah a298
Hicks, P. Thomas b193

Higbee, Lucy Ann a280
Higbee, William F. a229
Higginson, Rev. Francis, 1588-1630
a1
Higginson, Henry Lee, 1834-1919
a333
Higginson, Louisa S. a253
Higginson, Thomas Wentworth, 1823-
1911 a318
Higinbotham, John David, 1864-
c57
Hildreth, Lt. Micah, 1749-1826 a128
Hildt, George H., 1855-1913 a346
Hill, Alexander Staveley c57
Hill, Allan Massie, 1876-1943 c57
Hill, H. b223
Hill, Isaac a77
Hill, James, 1735-1811 a63
Hill, Lydia b118
Hill, Matthew Davenport, 1792-1872
b190
Hill, Rev. Rowland, 1744-1833 b106
Hill, Sir Rowland, 1795-1879 b188
Hill, Captain Samuel, 1777- a227
Hill, Thomas, -1828 a196
Hillard, Harriet, 1809-77 a258
Hilton, Major Winthrop, 1671-1710
a17
Hilts, Joseph Henry, 1819-1903 c57
Hiltzheimer, Jacob, 1729-98 a92
Hincks, Sir Francis, 1807-85 c57
Hinchman, Dr. Joseph a69
Hinds, E. M. c57
Hines, Celinda E. a337
Hines, John, 1850- c57
Hinrichs, Captain Johann a151
Hinsdale, Rev. Theodore, 1738-1818
a189
Hitchcock, Dr. Enos, 1744-1803
a139
Hitchcock, Major General Ethan
Allen, 1798-1870 a235
Hitchcock, Captain Francis Clere
b304
Hoare, Richard b76
Hoare, Sir Richard Colt, 1758-1838
b139
Hobart, David, 1651?-1717 a9
Hobart, Rev. Peter, 1604-79 a2
Hobbes, Robert b153
Hobbie, Hannah, 1806-31 a253
Hobhouse see Broughton
Hobson, John, -1735 b68
Hoby, Lady Margaret, 1570-1633 b7
Hodges, Mr. --- b53
Hodges, Captain Thomas Law b149
Hodgkinson, Mary b178

Pond, Peter, 1740-1807 a67
Ponsonby, Col. Arthur, 1837-68
    b256
Poole, Caroline B., 1802-44 a275
Poole, Fitch, 1803-73 a321
Poole, Francis c97
Poole, Rev. Sir Henry,   -1821
    b136
Poole, John b109
Poor, Mary, 1747-1834 a261
Pope, Amos, 1772-1837 a187
Pope, Col. John, 1770-1845 a177
Pope, William, 1811-1902 c97
Popp, Stephen, 1755?-   a141
Porrett see Monkswell
Porter, General Andrew, 1743-1813
    a169
Porter, Charles Henry, 1811-41
    a266
Porter, Captain David, 1780-1843
    a220
Porter, Deborah H., 1809-47 a281
Porter, Col. Elisha, 1742-96 a131
Porter, Rev. John Paul, 1759-1832
    b155
Porter, Moses, 1794-1858 a249
Porterfield, Charles, 1750-80 a131
Post, Charles C., 1831-1906 a351
Post, Christian Frederick, 1710-85
    a75
Post, Frederic James, 1819-35 b221
Pote, William, 1718-55 a45
Potter, Captain Cuthbert,   -1691
    a12
Potter, Richard, 1778-1842 b139
Pouchot, Captain --- a81, c97
Poutré, Felix, 1817?-85 c97
Powell, Ann, 1769- a175
Powell, Cuthbert, 1779- a192
Powell, Lt. David, 1771-1848 b134
Powell, H. M. T. a321
Powell, Lewis b237
Powell, T. P. c97
Powell, Walter, 1581-1656 b7
Powell, William Dummer, 1726-1805
    a98
Powell, William Dummer, 1755-1834
    c97
Powers, Captain Peter, 1707-57
    a59
Powis, Littleton b132
Pownall, Thomas, 1722-1805 a59
Powys, Caroline Girle, 1737-1808
    b89
Powys, Eleanor b208
Powys, Llewellyn, 1884- b299
Pratt, Orson, 1811-81 a266

Pratt, Parley Parker, 1807-57 a331
Pratt, Elder William, 1659-1713 a13
Preble, Commodore Edward, 1761-
    1807 a196
Preble, Admiral George Henry, 1816-
    85 a292
Preble, General Jedidiah, 1707-84
    a119
Prentice, Charles, 1774-1820 c98
Prentiss, Elizabeth, 1818-78 a277
Preston, John, 1717-71 a40
Preston, Samuel a172
Preston, T. R. c98
Preston, Mrs. William a272
Preston, William Thomas Rochester
    c98
Prévost, Major General Augustine,
    1752-86 a153
Price, Edward b213
Price, Ezekiel, 1728-1802 a119
Price, John b288
Price, John, 1734-1813 b92
Price, John J. b270
Price, Joseph, 1753- a173
Pridgeon, John b22
Prieur, Francois-Xavier, 1814-91
    c98
Prince, Elizabeth W., 1805- b221
Prince, Hezekiah, 1771-1840 a184
Prince, Dr. Jonathan, 1734-59 a57
Prince, Rev. Thomas, 1687-1758
    a34
Prindle, Rev. Alexander c98
Pringle, Robert, 1702-76 a47
Pringle, Virgil K. a304
Pringle, Walter, 1625-67 b30
Prior, Francis,   -1788 b100
Prisiart, Shon William, 1749-1829
    b147
Pritchard, Dr. Edward William, 1825-
    65 b276
Pritchard, Captain J. A. a321
Pritchard, J. F., 1857- c98
Pritchard, Rev. John Lamb, 1811-
    62 a290
Procter, Captain Jonathan, 1739-
    1821 a81
Proctor, Col. Thomas, 1739-1806
    a180
Proudfoot, Rev. William, 1787-1851
    a266, c98
Proulx dit Clément, Jean Baptiste,
    1846-1904 c98
Prowse, D. W. c99
Puget, Lt. Peter, 1764?-1822 a182,
    c99
Pugsley, Lt. William H. c99

Punshon, William Morley, 1824-81
 b266
Purcell, John Baptist, 1800-83
 b269
Purefoy, Henry b68
Pursh, Frederick, 1774-1820
 a213
Putnam, Archelaus, 1787-1818
 a210
Putnam, General Israel, 1718-90
 a102
Putnam, Israel, 1766-1824 a188
Putnam, John Harold, 1866-   c99
Putnam, General Rufus, 1738-1824
 a70
Pyke, Magnus c99
Pynchon, Major John,   -1705
 a10
Pynchon, William, 1723-89 a131
Pyne, Rev. Alexander c99

Quillinan, Dorothy Wordsworth,
 1804-47 b251
Quincy, Eliza Susan a250
Quincy, Josiah, 1744-75 a92, b109
Quincy, Josiah, 1772-1864 a200
Quincy, Samuel, 1735-87 a132,
 b113
Quitman, Major General John An-
 thony, 1798-1858 a305

R., Alexander b45
R., C. b176
Rack, Edward, 1735?-87 b117
Radisson, Pierre Esprit, 1620?-
 1710 c99
Rae, Herbert c99
Rae, John, 1813-93 c99
Raffles, Rev. Thomas, 1788-1863
 b166
Raikes, Thomas, 1777-1848 b227
Rainsford, Col. Charles a132
Ramage, Lance-Corporal George
 b304
Ramsay, Lt. Col. Balcarres Dalrym-
 ple Wardlaw, 1822-85 b268
Ramsay, Margaret b211
Ramsay, Martha Laurens, 1759-
 1811 a180
Ramsden, Diana b296
Ramsey, Archibald a150
Ramsour, David (Ramsauer),
 -1785 a55
Rand, S. T. c99
Randell, Jack, 1879-   c99

Randle, William a334
Randolph, Edward, 1632-1703 a7
Ranken, Major George, 1828-56
 b260, c100
Rankin, Charles, 1797-1886 a281,
 c100
Ransom, Mercy, 1728-1811 b157
Raper, Elizabeth,   -1778 b89
Raper, Fred c100
Rastrick, John Urpeth,1780-1856
 b165
Ratcliff, Mildred, 1773-1847 a210
Rathbone, Hannah Mary, 1761-1839
 b124
Rathborne, Kate F. P. b221
Raven, Rev. John James, 1850-1906
 a257
Ravenel, Henry, 1729-85 a55
Ravenel, Dr. Henry, 1790-   a244
Ravenel, René, 1762-1822 a169
Ravenscroft, John Stark, 1772-1830
 a246
Rawdon-Hastings see Hastings
Rawle, Anna a160
Rawle, William c100
Rawlinson of Trent, Henry Seymour,
 Lord, 1864-1925 b296
Raymond, Gérard, 1912-32 c100
Raymond, Henry Jarvis, 1820-69
 a312
Rea, Dr. Caleb, 1727-60 a76
Read, Dr. George Willis, 1819-80
 a327
Reader, Samuel James, 1836-1914
 a344
Reading, John a22
Reading, Pierson Barton, 1816-69
 a294
Reath, B. B. a288
Redgrave, Richard, 1804-88 b253
Reed, Rev. Isaac a250
Reed, James Frazier a309
Reed, Rev. Solomon, 1719-85 a40
Reeder, Andrew H., 1807-64 a344
Rees, David Rice b231
Rees, Rev. Thomas b273
Rees, William b235
Rees ap Rees b59
Reeve, Dr. Henry, 1780-1814 b163
Reeve, Henry, 1813-95 b191
Reeves, Charles,   -1847 b244
Reichel, Rev. Gotthold Benjamin,
 1785-1833 a228
Reichel, Johann Friedrich a156
Reid, John a182
Reid, John C., 1824-   a347
Reid, William, 1880-   c100

Simcoe, John Graves, 1752-1806
c109
Sime, Jessie Georgina, 1880-
c109
Simitière, Pierre Eugène du,
-1784 a96
Simmonds, James, 1847-1915 a335,
c109
Simmons, Major George, 1786-
b171
Simmons, Mervic C. c109
Simmons, Nicholas a27
Simmons, Dr. W. H. a246
Simond, Louis, 1767-1831 b174
Simpson, George, 1792-1860 a240,
c110
Simpson, Lt. James Hervey, 1813-83
83 a321
Simpson, Mrs. L. M., 1839-
b285
Simpson, Mrs. M., 1787-1829
b163
Simpson, Thomas, 1808-40 c110
Sinclair, Mr. --- c110
Sinclair, Alexander, 1828-97 c110
Sinclair, Gordon c110
Sing, Josiah Gershom, 1857-1921
c110
Singer, F. B. c110
Sinton, Robert, 1854- c110
Sippi, Charles Augustus, 1844-
c111
Sitgreaves, Captain Lorenzo, 1811-
88 c321
Sitwell, Florence Alice, 1858-1930
b282
Sitwell, George b34
Skead, Captain Francis c111
Skene, James, 1775-1864 b157
Skinner, Rev. John, 1772-1839
b130
Skinner, Richard, 1666?-1727 a27
Slade, General Jeremiah a238
Slade, William, 1753-1826 a133
Slaney, Robert Aglionby, 1792-
1862 c111
Slater, James c111
Sleigh, Burrows Willcocks Arthur,
1821-69 c111
Slingsby, E. H. b273
Slingsby, Sir Henry, 1601-58 b16
Smades, Elijah c111
Small, Rev. T. J. c111
Smart, Sir George, 1776-1867
b157
Smeaton, John, 1724-92 b87
Smethurst, Gamaliel, 1738-1826 a86

Smith, Col. --- b191
Smith, Abigail Tenney, 1809-85
a266
Smith, Albert Richard, 1816-60
b256
Smith, Benjamin, -1852 c111
Smith, Rev. Charles Lesingham,
1806-78 b233
Smith, Charles W. a327
Smith, Damaris Isabella, 1831-1931
c111
Smith, General Daniel, 1748-1818
a153
Smith, E. Willard, 1814- a287
Smith, Ebenezer, 1785- b156
Smith, Elizabeth Dixon a310
Smith, Elizabeth Murray, 1726-86
a97, b102
Smith, Captain Ephraim Kirby, 1807-
45 a310
Smith, Frederick Culling b214
Smith, G. Watt c112
Smith, Goldwin, 1823-1910 c112
Smith, Lt. Col. Henry Robert
c112
Smith, Rev. Hezekiah, 1737-1805
a88
Smith, Jacob, 1756-1844 a141
Smith, Rev. James, 1757-1800 a164
Smith, Rev. James Frazer, 1858-
c112
Smith, Jedediah, 1798-1831 a254
Smith, Major John a68
Smith, Sergt. John a133
Smith, John, 1722-71 a38
Smith, Joseph, 1735-1816 a76
Smith, Joseph E. c112
Smith, Joshua Toulmin, 1816-69
a281
Smith, Josiah, 1731-1826 a156
Smith, Larratt William, 1820-1905
c112
Smith, Lowell, 1802-91 a266
Smith, Lydia a210, b163
Smith, Captain Nicholas c112
Smith, Richard, 1735-1803 a97
Smith, Richard, 1784-1824 a233,
b191
Smith, Rev. Dr. Thomas, 1638-1710
b32
Smith, Thomas, 1673-1723 b66
Smith, Rev. Thomas, 1702-95 a25
Smith, Thomas B. c112
Smith, W. C. S. a322
Smith, Rev. William, 1702-83 a35
Smith, Major William, -1810 b166
Smith, William Edward, 1864- c112

Williamson, Samuel, 1792-1840 b195
Williamson, Hon. William, D., 1779-
1846 a243
Willing, Dr. George M. a351
Willis, Benjamin, 1686-1767 a55
Willis, R. L. b135
Willison, Sir John Stephen, 1856-
1927 c126
Williston, Josiah a214
Williston, Rev. Dr. Seth, 1770-
1851 a192
Wills, Rev. William Henry, 1809-89
a283
Willson, Henry Beckles, 1869-1942
c126
Wilmore, Louisa E.,   -1839 b224
Wilmot, Catherine, 1773?-1824
b156
Wilmot, Martha, 1775-1825 b159
Wilson, Alexander, 1766-1813
b133
Wilson, Sir Arnold Talbot, 1884-
b310
Wilson, Sir Charles Rivers, 1831-
1916 b126
Wilson, Edward F. c126
Wilson, Elizabeth, 1792-   b200
Wilson, Sir Henry Hughes, 1864-
1922 b294
Wilson, James, 1777-1851? c126
Wilson, James, 1805-60 b259
Wilson, Robert, 1772-1837 b204
Wilson, Sir Robert Thomas, 1777-
1849 b154
Wilton, David, 1633-78 a7
Wimbledon, Edward Cecil, Viscount,
1572-1638 b11
Windebank, Sir Thomas,   -1607 b8
Windham, Sir Charles Ash, 1810-70
b264
Windham, Rt. Hon. William, 1750-
1810 b102
Wing, Captain Vincent b264
Winslow, Anna Green, 1759-79
a100
Winslow, Harriett Lathrop, 1796-
1833 a225
Winslow, Col. John, 1703-74 a60
Winslow, John Whitmore, 1835-56
b256
Winslow, Joshua, 1727-1801 a53,
c126
Winstanley, James Winckworth,
1816-91 b234
Winter, William H., 1819-79 a294
Winthrop, Adam,   -1623 b6
Winthrop, Major General Fitzjohn,

1639-1707 a12
Winthrop, John, 1588-1649 a1
Winthrop, John, 1606-76 a3
Winthrop, John, 1714-79 a86
Winthrop, Theodore, 1828-61 a339
Wire, John b112
Wire, William b245
Wister, Sally, 1761-1804 a143
Wiswall, Rev. John, 1731-1821 a89
Wither, Charles b66
Witherspoon, John a71, c126
Wix, Rev. Edward c127
Wodrow, Rev. Robert, 1679-1734
b55
Wolcott, Roger, 1679-1767 a46
Wolf, Captain Lambert Boman, 1834-
1918 a345
Wolfe, Major-General James, 1727-
59 c127
Wolseley, Garner Joseph, 1st Vis-
count, 1833-1913 c127
Wood, Anthony à, 1632-95 b27
Wood, Elizabeth a331
Wood, Rev. J., 1797-1869 b200
Wood, J. C. a347
Wood, Col. J. H. c127
Wood, James c127
Wood, John, 1825-96 a328
Wood, Lemuel, 1741-1819 a82
Wood, Solomon, 1722-66 a94
Wood, Thomas Peploe, 1817-45
b241
Wood, William, 1809-94 a299
Wood, William Page see Hatherley
Woodberry, Lt. G., 1792-   b182
Woodbridge, Dr. Dudley, 1705-90
a30
Woodcock, Thomas Swann, 1805-63
a278
Woodforde, Rev. James, 1740-1803
b91
Woodforde, Julia, 1789-1873 b195
Woodforde, Mary b41
Woodforde, Nancy, 1757-   b137
Woodforde, Robert, 1606-54 b15
Woodforde, Samuel, 1763-1817 b126
Woodington, Henry c127
Woodruff, Samuel a254
Woods, Daniel B. a323
Woods, Rev. James, 1815-86 a341
Woods, John, 1735-1816 a82
Woods, John,   -1829 a241
Woods, Margaret, 1748-1821 b105
Woodsworth, Rev. James,   -1917
c127
Woodward, Thomas, 1806-78 a329
Woolman, John, 1720-72 a24, b105

GENERAL INDEX

(Authors, Editors, Book Titles, Subjects)

Numbers refer to entries.

1793-1804, 1806, 1809, 1811, 1813-18, 1820-22, 1824-28, 1831-33, 1835-
36, 1839, 1842-43, 1847-50, 1853-55, 1858, 1860-66, 1868-69, 1874, 1876-
84, 1887-89, 1893-94, 1897, 1899, 1902-10, 1912-13, 1916, 1919-23, 1925,
1927, 1929, 1935-36, 1939, 1941-46, 1948-49, 1951-52, 1955-56, 1959,
1961, 1964, 1966, 1968-70, 1972, 1976-77, 1980-82, 1984, 1986, 1990,
1993-94, 1999-2000, 2003, 2005-07, 2013-15, 2019, 2021, 2029-31, 2039,
2044-45, 2048-49, 2052-53, 2058-59, 2065, 2068, 2070-71, 2075-78, 2080-
91, 2094-95, 2097, 2099, 2103-06, 2108-13, 2115-18, 2120, 2122-24, 2126-
27, 2129-33, 2135-36, 2138-39, 2141, 2143, 2145-51, 2155, 2158-60, 2162-
65, 2169-76, 2179, 2181, 2183, 2185-87, 2190-92, 2194, 2196, 2199, 2201,
2204, 2208-11, 2214, 2216, 2219, 2221, 2229, 2234-35, 2238, 2240, 2247,
2249, 2254-55, 2257, 2267-69, 2277, 2282, 2285a, 2286-89, 2292-94,
2298-99, 2302-03, 2305-06a, 2307, 2309-12, 2314, 2316-20, 2325-26,
2328a, 2329, 2331-33, 2335-36b, 2337a, 2340a-42, 2344-45, 2347a,
2348a-49c, 2351a, 2355a-56, 2358a, 2360a-b, 2362-63, 2366, 2368,
2370, 2374-80, 2382, 2384, 2386, 2390-91, 2393, 2396-98, 2400-02,
2404-06, 2408-09, 2411, 2416, 1418-23, 2425, 2428-33, 2435-39, 2444-
50, 2452, 2454, 2456-57, 2459-65, 2468-72, 2474-77, 2481-84, 2486,
2488, 2490-94, 2500, 2502-04, 2506, 2509

American Diaries 595
American Diaries, 1902-1926 1969
American Diaries of World War II 2285a, 2305a, 2306a, 2307, 2316a, 2317b,
     2328a, 2336a-b, 2337a, 2340a-b, 2347a, 2348a, 2349a-c, 2351a, 2355a-c,
     2358a, 2360a-b
American Diary 1735
An American Diary, 1857-8 1043
American Diary Literature 1620-1799 13
An American Diplomat in Hawaii 1853-1858 969
American Expeditionary Force 2059, 2083-85, 2089-90, 2094, 2097, 2127
An American Family 527
American Fur Company 574
An American in Maximilian's Mexico: 1865-1866 582
American Indian Mission Association 714
American Navy 702-03, 726, 730, 743, 756, 758, 955, 976-77, 980, 1005,
     1151, 1211, 1281, 2305a, 2306a, 2307, 2316a
American Philosophical Society 178
American Red Cross 2104, 2336b, 2366
American Revolution 139, 153, 158, 175, 201, 210, 213, 216, 220-23, 226-31,
     233-34, 236-38, 240-46, 249-67, 270-73, 275-78, 280-85, 287, 314, 456
American Tract Society 745
An American Tragedy 1969
American Volunteer Group 2287
American Women's Diaries: New England Women 298, 309, 355, 357, 363,
     637, 698, 878
Amish 2269
Amundsen, Roald 1965
And Still We Conquer 2327
And When My Task on Earth Is Done 2341
Andersen, Gerda M. 608
Andersen, Mary A. 1189
Anderson, Carl M. 177
Anderson, Charles A. 1906
Anderson, Charles R. 709
Anderson, Frederick 1024
Anderson, Isabel 989
Anderson, John Q. 1252
Anderson, Lars 989

British Army (cont.)
   1st Grenadier Guards 2038
   Irish Guards 2330
   <u>jager</u> company 240
   King's German Legion 411
   11th Light Anti-Aircraft Regiment 2261
   15th Light Dragoons 409
   Queen Victoria's Rifles 2035
   Queen's (West Surrey) Regiment 2270
   22nd Regiment 176
   53rd Regiment 253
   1st Rifle Brigade 1958
   Royal Artillery 258
   Royal Engineers 1086
   Royal Marines 2057
   Royal Warwickshire Regiment 2102
   Scots Brigade 209
   Scots Guards 2022
   Scottish Rifles 2037
   Somerset Light Infantry 2025
   West Yorkshire Regiment 2037
British Boundary Commission 1086
<u>British Diarists</u> 20
British National Trust 2371
British Navy 74, 144, 153, 336
Broadbridge, S. R. 185
Brockbank, W. 134
Brod, Max 2001
Broderick, John C. 643
<u>Broken Images</u> 2261
<u>Brokenburn</u> 22, 1252
Brooke, Jocelyn 2322
Brooks, Charles V. W. 782
Brooks, Clinton E. 828
Brooks, George R. 574
Brooks, Juanita 736, 766, 903, 990, 1096
Brooks, Richard A. E. 576
Brooks, Van Wyck 782, 1838
Broomell, Anne P. 2236
<u>Brothers and Friends</u> 2142
Brougham, Lord 551
Brown, Alan K. 219
Brown, Alec 1792
Brown, Harry J. 809
Brown, Ida C. 17
Brown, John A. 1821
Brown, Lloyd A. 227
Brown, Montagu K. 1737
Brown, Moss K. 2089
Brown, Norman D. 1308
Brown, R. A. 220
Brown, Ralph H. 466
<u>The Brown Book</u> 1598
Brown University 571
Browne, Lina F. 710
Browning, Robert 554, 1712
Brownson, Orestes A. 615

Mead, Marjorie L.   2142
Meade, General George G.   1426
Mears, W. G. A.   628
Medical diaries   105, 107, 116, 134, 305, 394, 536, 1148, 1281, 1303, 1450,
    1462, 1780, 1804, 2117, 2173, 2181, 2301, 2368, 2436, 2447
Mediterranean Sea   72
Medlicott, Alexander G., Jr.   232
Melton, John L.   1549
Melville, Herman   587, 709
Melvin, Patrick   88
Memoirs: Autobiography--First Draft Journal   1996
Memoirs of a Volunteer   1153
Mennonites   1361, 1617, 1713, 1951
Menominee River   1001
Mensheviks   1983
Mercenary   75
Mercer, Asa   1607
Mercer's Belles   1607
A Merchant Family in Early Natal   890-91
Merchants   307, 312, 332, 361, 874a, 890, 895, 1061, 1740, 1775
Mercure de France   1875
Merrens, H. Roy   252
Merrie Wakefield   556
Merwin, M. M.   314
Mesa Verde National Park   1619
Meskill, John   31
A Message in Code   2195
Metcalf, Eleanor M.   858
Meteorological diaries   389
Methodists   135, 138, 576, 932, 1708
Metson, Graham   2348
Metzger, Robert   2191
Mexican diaries   316, 616, 1089
Mexican Gold Trail   839
Mexican Journal   2416
Mexican War   699, 719, 726, 734, 756-57, 760, 762, 764, 768, 776, 781, 786,
    792-95, 797-98, 801
The Mexican War Diary of Thomas D. Tennery   779
Mexico   38, 384, 516, 582, 611, 667, 719, 757, 768, 807, 859, 1270, 1589,
    1699, 1802, 1834, 1922, 2155, 2256, 2400, 2416
    Campeche   38
    Mazatlan   743, 792
    Mexico City   786, 797, 801
    Monterrey   1699
    Saltillo   1699
    Sonora   1869, 2175
Mexico, 1825-1828   516
Meyer, Richard E.   896
Meynell, Sir Francis   1988
Miami Indians   378
Michigan   17, 466, 684, 693
    Beaver Island   562
    Calhoun County   1387
    Detroit   265
Michigan Men in the Civil War   17
Middle East   815, 2044
Middle East Diary   2290